The Invention of Race in the European Middle Ages

In *The Invention of Race in the European Middle Ages*, Geraldine Heng questions the common assumption that race and racisms only began in the modern era. Examining Europe's encounters with Jews, Muslims, Africans, Native Americans, Mongols, and the Romani ("Gypsies") from the twelfth through fifteenth centuries, she shows how racial thinking, racial law, racial practices, and racial phenomena existed in medieval Europe before a recognizable vocabulary of race emerged in the West. Analyzing sources in a variety of media, including stories, maps, statuary, illustrations, architectural features, history, saints' lives, religious commentary, laws, political and social institutions, and literature, she argues that religion – so much in play again today – enabled the positing of fundamental differences among humans that created strategic essentialisms to mark off human groups and populations for racialized treatment. Her groundbreaking study also shows how race figured in the emergence of *homo europaeus* and the identity of Western Europe in this time.

Geraldine Heng is Perceval Fellow and Associate Professor of English and Comparative Literature, Middle Eastern Studies, and Women's Studies at the University of Texas, Austin. She is the author of *Empire of Magic: Medieval Romance and the Politics of Cultural Fantasy* (2003, 2004, 2012) and *England and the Jews: How Religion and Violence Created the First Racial State in the West* (Cambridge University Press 2018).

Originally from Singapore, Heng has held the Winton Chair (for "paradigm-shifting scholarship") at the University of Minnesota, Twin Cities. She has received a number of fellowships and grants, and currently holds an ACLS fellowship to begin a new book, *Early Globalities: The Interconnected World, 500–1500 CE*. Heng is also the founder and director of the Global Middle Ages Project: www.globalmiddleages.org.

THE INVENTION OF RACE IN THE EUROPEAN MIDDLE AGES

GERALDINE HENG

CAMBRIDGE
UNIVERSITY PRESS

CAMBRIDGE
UNIVERSITY PRESS

University Printing House, Cambridge CB2 8BS, United Kingdom

One Liberty Plaza, 20th Floor, New York, NY 10006, USA

477 Williamstown Road, Port Melbourne, VIC 3207, Australia

314–321, 3rd Floor, Plot 3, Splendor Forum, Jasola District Centre, New Delhi – 110025, India

79 Anson Road, #06–04/06, Singapore 079906

Cambridge University Press is part of the University of Cambridge.

It furthers the University's mission by disseminating knowledge in the pursuit of education, learning, and research at the highest international levels of excellence.

www.cambridge.org
Information on this title: www.cambridge.org/9781108422789
DOI: 10.1017/9781108381710

First published 2018
Reprinted 2018

Printed in the United States of America by Sheridan Books, Inc.

A catalogue record for this publication is available from the British Library.

ISBN 978-1-108-42278-9 Hardback

To Leah Marcus, David Theo Goldberg, and Susan Noakes
compagnons de route

Contents

List of Illustrations

Acknowledgments

T HE DEBTS for *The Invention of Race*, twelve years in the making, are more numerous than for my first large book, *Empire of Magic*, and I can only hope to make a small dent here with my deep thanks. Long before I read a medieval manuscript or any race theory, when I was an eighteen-year-old freshman, Koh Tai Ann taught me how to read, taking me through William Empson's "Missing Dates" word by word, line by line. Across my undergraduate years, she inculcated practices of close attention and analysis that have made possible my academic career. Concomitantly, Edwin Thumboo stretched youthful horizons and made available crucial opportunities. Since *The Invention of Race* begins with a vignette from Singapore, it seems apposite to recognize here these two earliest influences in my academic life.

Later, Gene Vance, Pete Wetherbee, Jane Chance, and Gayatri Chakravorty Spivak generously stepped into the breach and wrote for me after the passing of my magister, Bob Kaske, thus ensuring that I would have a career.

Leah Marcus, David Theo Goldberg, and Susan Noakes – to whom this book is dedicated – patiently listened to early arguments that what we call race is already seen in premodernity, and provided critical support over the years. Hannah Wojciehowski, Matt Cohen, and Leah Marcus read early versions of chapters. Regenia Gagnier made the decision in 2011 to publish in *Literature Compass* my two-part article introducing premodern race, thus helping to win over the unconvinced on what was (and still may be?) considered by some a controversial subject. The article has since garnered some 25,000 document views on Academia.edu. Ellen Rooney and Elizabeth Weed ensured that an article on the Assassins and religious race (adapted from a section of Chapter 3) was published in *differences*, and Steve Nichols ensured the publication of an article on Jewish boy murder stories and race in England (adapted from a section of Chapter 2) in *MLN*. Cathy Davidson never failed to offer staunch support in creative ways.

Two residential workshops at the University of California Humanities Research Institute – "Theorizing Pre- and Early Modern Race," convened by Margo Hendricks and Karen Bassi, and "Holy Wars Redux," convened by the unfailingly generous and illustrious John Ganim – offered stimulating environments in which to develop hypotheses and draft chapters on early race. The Friedrich Solmsen Fellowship at the University of Wisconsin's Institute for Research in the Humanities, two semester-long competitive leaves granted by the University of Texas, and the Winton Chair at the University of Minnesota also afforded important time to think and write among supportive colleagues.

Visiting lectures, keynote addresses, and conference plenaries created audiences for testing hypotheses and arguments. My warmest thanks to all who participated, especially the many wonderful graduate students I've met, and also to (in chronological order): Carla Freccero and Sharon Kinoshita (UC Santa Cruz), Marc Schachter (Duke), Heather Love

(Penn), Dan Donoghue and James Simpson (Harvard), Lawrence Wheeler (Portland State), Philomena Essed (UC Irvine), Leah Marcus (Vanderbilt), Kathy Lavezzo (Iowa), Julie Couch (Texas Tech), Tom Hahn, Alan Lupack, and Russell Peck (Rochester), Thomas Hanks (Baylor), Richard Firth Green and Ethan Knapp (Ohio State), Susan Noakes and Andy Scheil (Minnesota), Jonathan Boyarin (Kansas), Kathy Biddick (Temple), Jane Chance and Joe Campana (Rice), Suzanne Yeager and Nicholas Paul (Fordham), John Ganim (UC Riverside), Zrinka Stahuljak (UCLA), Bonnie Wheeler (SMU), Iain Higgins (Victoria), Donnalee Dox (TAMU), Neferti Tadiar and Chris Baswell (Barnard), Andrew Arnold and Andy Galloway (Cornell), Vincent Lloyd (Syracuse), Andrew Klein (Notre Dame), Elizabeth Voss (Virginia), Diane Wolfthal (Rice), Laura Doyle (Massachusetts), Sahar Amer and Hélène Sirantoine (Sydney), Chris Chism and Ali Behdad (UCLA), Nico Wey-Gomez (Caltech), Seth Lerer (English Institute), Gaurav Desai and Cathy Sanok (Michigan), and Christine Marie Pruden and Jillian Standish Patch (Medieval Institute).

Audience responses to my talks have shaped book chapters. Answering Barbara Fuchs's question, What differences were there in race-making *before* and *after* Jews were expelled from England? required transhistorical comparison of a cluster of Hugh of Lincoln's boy-murder stories across more than a century – from an Anglo-Norman ballad to Chaucer's *Prioress's Tale* and the Vernon manuscript – to see how the story differed before and after Jewish Expulsion, and why. An astute graduate student at Penn (who did not offer her name) put her finger on why it was imperative to name certain acts and institutions in the Middle Ages for what they were, i.e., *racial*: not to do so, she averred, would be to destigmatize them, allow them to be seen as less heinous. Jonathan Boyarin pointed to the Fourth Lateran Council as an instantiation of modernity in the West, and Judith Ferster suggested that, were one to track the expulsions of Jews country-by-country across medieval Europe, one would likely be able to establish how early or late a country underwent nation formation, thus gathering a map of comparative medieval nationalisms.

A faculty member in one audience even disclosed her understanding of the disciplinary stakes that underpinned discussions of race: If you are correct, she said, that race was invented in premodernity and not the modern era, then the modern era will become less important, the Middle Ages will become more important, and everyone would be forced to learn about the Middle Ages. Though I may disagree with her prognostications, I admire the unvarnished earnestness of her vision of the academic interests at stake.

Two keen-eyed anonymous manuscript readers, likely a literary scholar and a historian, submitted very helpful reviews (twelve single-spaced pages) with indispensable advice for the book. My wise editor at Cambridge, the remarkable Beatrice Rehl, went the extra mile by reading a hefty portion of the manuscript while on vacation, and added her own indispensable advice to ensure "a better reader experience." Kristy Barker has been an invaluable and tactful copyeditor, and Kaye Tengco Barbaro and Shaheer Anwarali have been exemplary production managers. The consistently high level of courtesy, kindness, and professionalism I've encountered at Cambridge speaks volumes for this outstanding university press.

The Invention of Race also owes a signal debt to those who commissioned, first an anthology, then a short book, on medieval race, though these formats ultimately proved unfeasible: Rick Emmerson, David Staines, and the MART board of the Medieval Academy of America. Medievalist colleagues have been especially generous in sharing their work. Bob Stacey shared his archive on Jews in England; Ian Hancock, Peter Biller, Kathy Biddick, Paul Kaplan, Debra Strickland, John Tolan, Tomaz Mastnak, Tim Pauketat, Ellie Pruitt, and Miri Krummel, among others, sent articles; Chris Atwood, Dede Ruggles, Reuven Amitai, Chap Kusimba, Valerie Hansen, Michael Puett, Gabriela Currie, Geoff Wade, Renata Holod, Susan McIntosh, Astrid Ogilvie, Wim Phillips, Susan Whitfield, Cyndy Talbot, Maggie Ragnow, Evelyn Edson, Michael Lower, Ramzi Rouighi, Anjelica Afanadol-Pujol, and others answered questions; and David Johnson and Geert Claassens shared their very important translation-in-progress of the Middle Dutch *Roman van Moriaen*.

A talented group of graduate students over the years has helped to lighten the labor of producing *The Invention of Race*: Rebecca Wilcox, April Jehan Morris, Ishan Chakrabarti, Pax Gutierrez-Neal, Elizabeth Florea, and Nick Holterman all rendered invaluable assistance, tackling onerous tasks. Rachel Roepke created the index of this book, and James Hammond lent his formidable powers of attention to the proofreading process.

Part of Chapter 1 was first published as "The Invention of Race in the European Middle Ages 1: Race Studies, Modernity, and the Middle Ages" and "The Invention of Race in the European Middle Ages 2: Locations of Medieval Race," *Literature Compass* 8(5) (2011). A section of Chapter 2 appeared in "England's Dead Boys: Telling Tales of Christian-Jewish Relations before and after the First European Expulsion of the Jews," *MLN* 127(5) Supplement (2012). Parts of Chapters 1 and 2 have also been reframed, recontextualized, and redacted as *England and the Jews: How Religion and Violence Created the First Racial State in the West* (Cambridge *Elements* digital series on religion and violence, 2018). A section of Chapter 3 was adapted as "Sex, Lies, and Paradise: The Assassins, Prester John, and the Fabulation of Civilizational Identities," *differences* 23(1) (2012), and an abridged section of Chapter 4 appeared as "An African Saint in Medieval Europe: The Black Saint Maurice and the Enigma of Racial Sanctity" in Vincent Lloyd and Molly Bassett's *Sainthood and Race: Marked Flesh, Holy Flesh* (New York: Routledge, 2015).

The Office of the Vice President for Research at the University of Texas contributed a subvention for this book, and the Department of English and College of Liberal Arts contributed funding for indexing and graduate assistance: I am grateful to James Garrison, Elizabeth Cullingford, Martin Kevorkian, Richard Lariviere, Esther Raizen, and Cecilia Smith-Morris.

Finally, no book is written without an intimate community of people who offer unwavering support when vicissitudes strike, and who celebrate your breakthroughs. The steadfastness of my family – Janadas Devan, Shaan Heng-Devan, Cindy Ji, George Heng, and Karen Er – and my friends, in particular Suporn Arriwong, Hannah Wojciehowski, Eric Chapelle, Amy Wong Mok and Al Mok, Jake Henson and Odessa Fleming, and Leticia Jaimes, makes me appreciate my sheer good luck.

Beginnings

Racial Worlds, Medieval Worlds: Why This Book, and How to Read a Book on Medieval Race

G ROWING UP in a Singapore that was undergoing a process of decolonization from the British Empire, one of my earliest memories of race came as a result of having to earn a badge in the Girl Guides – which was at that time the tepid equivalent, for girls, of the Boy Scout corps created by Lord Baden-Powell and spread across the British imperial world of the twentieth century. As I was born female and Chinese (the majority racial group in Singapore), sexism and misogyny were not unfamiliar recognitions in childhood (for instance, the old immigrant woman from China who lived downstairs in our apartment block still had tiny, crippled, bound feet, or "lotus buds," as the classic pillow book *The Golden Lotus* called them), but race is not as easily recognizable for those who inhabit a majority race. Malay neighbors, Indian classmates, Eurasian friends, and the intertwining, multicultural, multireligious life-worlds in Singapore did not foreground racial apartness or a palpable racial hierarchy for a child who belonged to the majority race.

To earn my Laundress badge in the Girl Guides, however, I had to travel to the home of an Englishwoman in a tony part of town, and show her that I knew how to launder, iron, and care for clothing of various kinds. I had to show her that I knew how to wash woolen sweaters by hand, for instance, and dry them not on a line or a bamboo pole – as most Singaporeans dried their clothing before the widespread advent of washing machines and dryers – but laid flat and spread out on a towel, to soak in the moisture, so that the knit would not lose its shape.

I had never before been to this opulent part of town, where mostly the English lived in large, mansion-like houses nestled in green groves of manicured lawns tended by local servants, in what were called, appropriately, *residential estates* where people did not live cheek-by-jowl in government-built public apartment blocks. I remember the hushed, spacious interiors of the Englishwoman's enormous house, the servants moving invisibly, soundlessly, unobtrusively – the sheer quiet. I washed a woolen sweater to perfection, and dried it on a towel. I passed my laundress test and got my Laundress badge.

I also left the Girl Guides soon after. Not only did it seem wrong that there was a badge to be earned for laundry, only by girls, but the *type* of clothing that one was expected to know how to launder in this equatorial city-state in maritime Southeast Asia struck me as ludicrous. Why, in an equatorial country located 1 degree 20 minutes north of the equator, where days and nights were blazingly, steamingly hot year-round (this was before the advent of air conditioning) and the humidity close to unbearable, would one need specialized knowledge of how to launder woolens made in England? And how come white people got to live in enclaves of grand mansions on manicured grounds, tended by a servant population of Asians?

This small encounter with colonial race – a "click" moment in an unsuspecting childhood – even as decolonization was in the process of transforming the country brought a recognition that race, like the structure of power exercised by even would-be benign forms of colonial privilege, can only be made visible when the conditions of privilege inhabited by those who wield power are not invisible, natural, and the norm. Decades later, teaching and publishing as a gendered, raced, postcolonial subject in one of the most conservative fields in the Western academy – medieval studies – I would unsuspectingly encounter another "click" moment.

A white, male English medievalist from London, at a metropolitan university in the heart of the old British Empire, decided that my literary practice of reading, which he labeled "postcolonial," was inadequate and inadequately "postcolonial," unlike the practice of many of my colleagues, because I had not sufficiently promoted the paramount importance of medieval French – the lingua franca of the European Middle Ages – in my first book, *Empire of Magic: Medieval Romance and the Politics of Cultural Fantasy.*

The irony was remarkable: When the importance of French – an imperial language – is not sufficiently thematized and its literature sufficiently held up for attention, female nonwhite postcolonial subjects do not adequately practice "postcolonial" critical readings of medieval texts. A white Englishman at the metropolitan heart of the old British Empire had pronounced this *ex cathedra.*

Who gets to speak for us? an old friend and renowned doyenne of postcolonial theory used to ask. Who gets to decide how we should conduct ourselves? The answer, from these small memories bookending several decades, had to be relearnt again and again: Those in command of racial, gender, class, and colonial privilege, then and now – in decolonizing Singapore and in the Western academy today. Racial-colonial privilege, with its institutional power, becomes visible only when occasions of privilege are looked at more closely.[1]

Remarkably, questions of power and privilege were also on the minds of other medievalists. In 2004, David Staines and Richard Emmerson, representing the Medieval Academy of America, requested that I edit an anthology of essays for a volume to be entitled *Medieval Ethnicities* or *Medieval Race* and published in the Academy's MART series. After I had gathered a selection of essays, however, and after various committee meetings by the MART board had taken place, in 2008 this request instead became a commission from the Medieval Academy and its publisher, Toronto University Press, to write a short book on medieval race, intended as the inaugural volume for a new series of volumes being planned by the Academy and Toronto Press.

As I undertook the commission, however, it became clear that it would not be possible to write a *short* book on race in the European Middle Ages. The subject was enormous and immensely complex, and I wanted to treat a variety of populations – not just Jews and Muslims and the portrayal of blackness in literature, which was the focus of a few medievalists who were tentatively working on the subject of ethnorace at the time.

Moreover, the Academy was, in many ways, ahead of its time, as were Rick Emmerson, the-then executive director; David Staines, chair of the MART board; and the enthusiastic members of the board itself, which included Bob Stacey and Pamela Sheingorn. In 2008, medievalists in general were not convinced the concept of race had any purchase for the medieval period. Race theorists also deemed the project presentist, convinced that race was a *modern* phenomenon and that they could safely ignore the Middle Ages, which they saw as a prepolitical era with scant relevance for the cultures of modernity that followed, and thus a period of little interest to them.[2]

It became clear that race needed to be understood differently from its definition by canonical twentieth-century race theories, and in ways apposite to the medieval past, for medievalists and race theorists to be willing to look at the past anew. After testing the waters for a few years with talks delivered across the country in different venues to different types of audiences, in 2011 I published a two-part article, "The Invention of Race in the European Middle Ages 1: Race Studies, Modernity, and the Middle Ages" and "The Invention of Race in the European Middle Ages 2: Locations of Medieval Race." Race theorists, and medievalists, began to change their minds. As of September 2017, this two-part article has garnered more than 25,000 document views on Academia.edu. One of the scholars to whom this book is dedicated is a renowned race theorist who eventually became convinced that the European Middle Ages, after all, was a time that was part of the long history of race.

The working minimum hypothesis of race that I devised, a hypothesis that animates this present volume, is found in Chapter 1:

> *"Race" is one of the primary names we have – a name we retain for the strategic, epistemological, and political commitments it recognizes – that is attached to a repeating tendency, of the gravest import, to demarcate human beings through differences among humans that are selectively essentialized as absolute and fundamental, in order to distribute positions and powers differentially to human groups. Race-making thus operates as specific historical occasions in which strategic essentialisms are posited and assigned through a variety of practices and pressures, so as to construct a hierarchy of peoples for differential treatment. My understanding, thus, is that race is a structural relationship for the articulation and management of human differences, rather than a substantive content.[3]*

Given the variety of scholarship that critical race studies had amassed over the decades, my working hypothesis was hardly controversial. It stood to reason that the differences selected for essentialism would vary in the *longue durée* – perhaps battening on bodies, physiognomy, and somatic attributes such as skin color in one location; perhaps on social practices, religion, and culture in another; and with perhaps a multiplicity of interlocking discourses elsewhere.

Moreover, in addressing the nested discourses formative of race in the European Middle Ages, it was particularly important to note that *religion* – the paramount source of authority in the medieval period – could function both socioculturally and biopolitically: subjecting peoples of a detested faith, for instance, to a political theology that could biologize, define, and essentialize an entire community as fundamentally and absolutely different in an interknotted cluster of ways. Nature/biology and the sociocultural should not thus be seen as bifurcated spheres in medieval race-formation: They often crisscrossed in the practices, institutions, fictions, and laws of a political – and a *bio*political – theology operationalized on the bodies and lives of individuals and groups.

This was not to claim, of course – absurdly – that race-making throughout the medieval period was in any way uniform, homogenous, constant, stable, or free of contradictions or local differences across the countries of Latin Christendom in all localities, regions, and contexts through some three or four centuries of historical time. Neither would it be to concede, in reverse, that local differences – variation in local practices and contexts – must always render it impossible to think translocally in the medieval period. The effort to think across the translocal does not require any supposition of the universal, static, unitary, or unvarying character of medieval race.

The chapters of this volume thus point to particular *moments* and *instances* of how race is made, to indicate the exemplary, dynamic, and resourceful character of race-making under conditions of possibility, not to extract repetitions without difference. They point to racializing momentum that manifests unevenly, and nonidentically, in different places and at different times – to sketch the dynamic field of forces within which miscellaneous instances of race-making can occur under varied local conditions.

But, more fundamental than arriving at a reformulation of what race is, why in the first place would we need a long history of race that recognizes and acknowledges racial practices and racial forms in the medieval period? Like other sociopolitical endeavors that have engaged with the past – feminism comes readily to mind as a predecessor moment; queer studies is another – the project of revising our understanding by inserting premodernity into conversations on race is closely dogged by accusations of presentism, anachronism, reification, and the like. Why call something *race* when many old terms – "ethnocentrism," "xenophobia," "premodern discriminations," "prejudice," "chauvinism," even "fear of otherness and difference" – have been used comfortably for so long to characterize the massacres, brutalizations, executions, and mass expulsions of the medieval period?

The short answer is that the use of the term *race* continues to bear witness to important strategic, epistemological, and political commitments not adequately served by the invocation of categories of greater generality (such as *otherness* or *difference*) or greater benignity in our understanding of human culture and society. *Not* to use the term *race* would be to sustain the reproduction of a certain kind of past, while keeping the door shut to tools, analyses, and resources that can name the past differently. Studies of "otherness" and "difference" in the Middle Ages – now increasingly frequent – must then continue to dance around words they dare not use; concepts, tools, and resources that are closed off; and meanings that only exist as lacunae.

Or, to put it another way: The refusal of race destigmatizes the impacts and consequences of certain laws, acts, practices, and institutions in the medieval period, so that we cannot name them for what they are, and makes it impossible to bear adequate witness to the full meaning of the manifestations and phenomena they installed. The unavailability of race thus often colludes in relegating such manifestations to an epiphenomenal status, enabling omissions that have, among other things, facilitated the entrenchment and reproduction of a certain kind of foundational historiography in the academy and beyond.

To cite just one example, explored in Chapter 2: How often do standard ("mainstream") histories of England discuss as constitutive to the formation of English identity, or to the nation of England, the mass expulsion of Jews in 1290, the marking of the Jewish population with badges for three-quarters of a century, decimations of Jewish communities by mob violence, statutory laws ruling over where Jews were allowed to live, monitory apparatuses such as the Jewish Exchequer and the network of registries created by England to track the behavior and lives of Jews, or popular lies and rumors like stories of ritual murder, which facilitated the legal execution of Jews by the state?

That the lives of English Jews were *constitutive*, not incidental, to the formation of England's history and collective identity – that the built landscape of England itself, with its cathedrals, abbeys, fortifications, homes, and cities, was dependent on English Jews – is not a story often heard in foundational historiography. Scholars who are invested in the archeology of a past in which alternative voices, lives, and histories are heard, beyond those canonically established as central by foundationalist studies, are thus not well served by evading the category of race and its trenchant vocabularies and tools of analysis.

For race theorists, the study of racial emergence in the longer *durée* is also one means to understand if the configurations of power productive of race in modernity are, in fact, genuinely novel. Key propensities in history can be identified by examining premodernity: the modes of apparent necessity, configurations of power, and conditions of crisis that witness the harnessing of powerful dominant discourses – such as science *or* religion – to make fundamental distinctions among humans in processes to which we give the name of race.

A reissuing of the medieval past in ways that admit the ongoing interplay of that past with the present can therefore only recalibrate the urgencies of the present with greater precision.[4] An important consideration in investigating the invention of race in medieval Europe (an invention that is always a *re*invention) is also to grasp the ways in which *homo europaeus* – the European subject – emerges in part through racial grids produced from the twelfth through fifteenth centuries, and the significance of that emergence for understanding the unstable entity we call "the West" and its self-authorizing missions.[5]

How to Read This Book on Medieval Race

The aim of this book is to sketch paradigms and models for thinking critically about medieval race, not to produce a thin description of all the territories of racial Europe from west to east, north to south. The book is organized around case studies and the identification of modular instants, exemplars, iconic events and symbols, and key artifacts of culture or history that call attention to tendencies and patterns, inventions and strategies in race-making and identify crucibles and dynamics that conduce to the production of racial form and raced behavior. A number of territories, however – England, the Mediterranean, parts of Western and Eastern Europe, Eurasia and China, the American continent and the North Atlantic – do weave in and out of individual chapter discussions.

Necessarily, the book investigates the materialization of race and racisms through different kinds of critical attention. You will find a variety of formal approaches and styles in the pages below because of the variety of subjects the book treats.[6] This means that, unlike *Empire of Magic*, *The Invention of Race* is not a volume of readings of literature as such, with comprehensive bibliographies of literary scholarship (apologies, therefore, to those in search of literary criticism and literary bibliographies per se).[7] The book tries not to privilege literature over all other disciplines (especially as literature is my home discipline), and only analyzes literary texts when these are the documents most trenchantly apposite to the discussion of race – when they are the fittest and most revealing exemplars of racial terrain.[8]

As often as not, with guidance from the scholarship of economic historians and art historians, historical sociology and anthropology, and religious studies, *The Invention of Race* works to retrieve the economic and social relations between ethnoracial groups; grasp the politics of international war, colonizing expeditions, and commercial trade; unravel the meaning of iconic artifacts or phenomena – such as the baffling statue of a black African St. Maurice in Germany or Marco Polo's mercantile gaze on the races of the world – or calibrate from eyewitness and other accounts the West's understanding of global ethnoracial relations in macrohistorical time.

This book is marked by its early beginnings, and continues to honor stipulations made in the original arrangements to produce the book. In commissioning the short volume, the Medieval Academy envisaged multiple audiences, with the book aimed at the widest possible readership and not directed solely to professional medievalists or to academic faculty. To reach as many readers as possible, I was asked to use translations in English, or supply translations with every use of a non-English or nonmodern language.

In its present long form, *The Invention of Race* hews closely to those original commitments. I have assiduously sought out translations in English for ease of reading whenever available (but often point to the original languages in sources for those wishing to undertake professional research). I also avoid the use of distracting diacritical marks for non-European languages – tutored by the example of scholars such as David Nirenberg, who pointedly remind us that diacritics are superfluous for those who already have familiarity with a language and alienating for those who do not.

Most importantly, this book stands on the shoulders of scholarship in several disciplines, and features, foregrounds, and highlights the accomplishments of many distinguished scholars on whose work it depends, and without which it could not have been written. No one person in a lifetime can amass the range of knowledges and specializations needed in the many disciplines that must be put into play for the discussion of medieval race. The book is thus guided by and depends on the work of the disciplinary specialists it cites, without which it would not have been possible to build a discussion of medieval race.

These scholars furnish important points of entry into a field, a subject, or a focus, and have bibliographies that support investigations farther afield. The volume also owes much to the generosity of colleagues who have shared their work in progress, and their understanding of their subject or field; they are thanked and acknowledged in the Acknowledgements and in the pages that follow.

What This Book Contains

Chapter 1, "Race Studies, Modernity, and the Middle Ages," begins by outlining a critical vocabulary and apparatus useful for the discussion of the ethnoracial in the European Middle Ages, surveys how canonical race studies has treated the premodern past, and suggests possible new trajectories that can acknowledge a long history of racial relations. The chapter summarizes how premodernists themselves have treated the subject of race, and sketches some of the locations of medieval race – in the treatment of Jews, in medieval cartography, in the conquest and colonization of fellow-Christian neighboring countries, and in the treatment of skin color, blackness, and Africans.[9] Religious race, colonial race, cartographic race, and epidermal race are critically surveyed.

Chapter 2, "A Case Study of the Racial State: Jews as Internal Minority in England," delineates the conditions – economic, legal, theological, sociocultural, biopolitical – that enabled manipulations of English Jews, and that resulted in the emergence of the first racial state in the history of the West. The chapter is a sustained case study of an internal minority in a country of the Latin West that Robert Stacey has called "archetypical" of Europe, and considers the following: English laws and statutes ruling on Jewish domicile, livelihood, conduct, dress, and relations with Christians; state institutions and bureaucracies that administered race, such as the Exchequer of the Jews and the *Domus Conversorum*; the vexed economic relations between Christians and Jews; collusions between state and church; the power of *story* (like ritual murder and blood libels) to congeal communities of consent to violence; the success or failure of religious conversion as a *techne* to effect racial transformation or racial passing; the instrumentality of *sensory race* – racial understanding that is absorbed through the senses – and the imagining of an English national community after the expulsion of England's Jews in 1290, in the first ever forcible mass expulsion initiated by a country in the West.

The chapter's final section, "England's Dead Boys," offers a finer-grained, longer-range view of ritual boy murder by analyzing a cluster of four texts in the thirteenth and fourteenth centuries, written before and after the Expulsion: a pre-Expulsion Anglo-Norman ballad and two post-Expulsion Middle English texts (including Chaucer's *Prioress's Tale*) that group themselves around the story of young Hugh of Lincoln's putative slaughter by Jews, with a fourth text as a coda that turns on its head the formula of Jewish child murder altogether. A comparative view of thematically grouped stories fanning out across time allows us to see – up close, through the prism of a popular tale of child murder – how the cultural treatment of Jews before and after the Expulsion changes, and how the changes install a new vision for England.

Chapter 3, "Race Figures in the International Contest: the Islamic 'Saracen'," zooms out from the analysis of a single country in Europe to survey the panorama of the international contest between Latin Christendom and Islamdom. The chapter's first two sections discuss how Islam and its Prophet were understood, the killing fields of war as a crucible of race-making, and political theology as a racializing system of knowledge: as blood-races are theorized; as the enemy is dehumanized into an abstraction, or evil incarnate, or comestibles; and as *gens Christiana* emerges as the name of Latin Christian racial form in the First Crusade.

The section entitled "Sex, Lies, and Paradise" details how a cultural fiction about "Saracens" (a name ingeniously characterizing the enemy as liars, through the narration of a lie about them) enables a heretical, outcast Islamic group abominated by Sunni and Shiite Islam alike to be transformed into an icon of Islam, in order that an icon of Christianity, the equally fictitious Prester John, might defeat them and establish the civilizational identities of Christendom and Islamdom as absolutely and fundamentally unalike and opposite.

The chapter's penultimate section explores the ironies of racial mixing and miscegenation, and the creation of de facto new races: in the Iberian peninsula, where the Caliphs of Córdoba were blond-haired, mostly blue-eyed men (with one exception, who was red-haired) because of their Caucasian slave mothers; and in Egypt, where European, especially Italian (and especially Genoese) slavers supplied the Mamluk dynasties with boys from elsewhere, including, prominently, the Caucasus. For 300 years, the racial resupply of Islamic Egypt, issuing from the greed of European slavers, ensured the replenishment of the finest professional army in Dar al-Islam, and sustained a military race of Mamluks who vanquished crusaders, recaptured territory from Europeans, and defeated Christendom in its holy wars. The blond-haired caliphs of Islamic Spain and the Caucasian sultans of Islamic Egypt bookend the panorama of racial ironies produced by war and mercantile capitalism.

Chapter 3 thus concludes by studying the impact of the profit motive on race relations. Do the imperatives of European, especially Italian, mercantilism — business at any cost, all the time, even during the long centuries of holy war — trump enmity, elide ethnoracial/religious differences, and undermine allegiance to homeland and Christianity? What do the racial economies of greed look like?

Chapter 4, "Epidermal Race, Fantasmatic Race: Blackness and Africa in the Racial Sensorium," turns its attention to the politics of color in the European Middle Ages. Most studies of medieval race fix attention on *blackness* as their ground of racial identification in literary, historical, and artistic representations of the European Middle Ages. By contrast, returning to a question that is raised in Chapter 1 – when does *whiteness* ascend to centrality as a marker of Latin Christian European identity? – Chapter 4 begins by exploring how *whiteness* became normative, integral, and central to Christian European identity in the thirteenth century.

Guided by the work of art historians such as Madeline Caviness and Paul Kaplan, this chapter investigates *both* epidermal whiteness and epidermal blackness as touchstones of raced identity by evaluating the meaning of a series of cultural creations: Wolfram von Eschenbach's brilliant early thirteenth-century Middle High German romance, *Parzival*; the remarkable mid- to later-thirteenth-century Middle Dutch *Moriaen*; the late medieval Middle English *King of Tars* and *Sultan of Babylon*; and the extraordinary sandstone statue of the Black St. Maurice of Magdeburg Cathedral in east Germany, issuing from the first third of the thirteenth century.

Three sections address the meaning of gender, color, and religion as they intersect in the charged depictions of a symbolic, putatively Christian Arthurian white knight, a symbolic Christian black African knight, a symbolic black African heathen queen, and offspring of color miscegenation who range from newborns to adults. The final section, "The Racial Saint," suggests how Africa is mobilized to serve Latin Christian Europe's needs beyond the simple equivalence of blackness with sin and/or the demonic. Chapter 4 also studies the power of blackness, paradoxically, to confer reassurance to sinners and enact promises of salvation, and contemplates the charged erotics of female-gendered black skin.

The final three chapters of *The Invention of Race* extend the book's attention beyond the Abrahamic religions to see how the West made intelligible for itself the strange races encountered that did not fit into the triangulated grid of religious race supplied by Judaism–Christianity–Islam. More than the others, two of these last chapters depend on a number of literary-textual accounts – the only surviving evidence from the medieval period that describes indigenes in the North American continent and Mongols in Eurasia and China. Chapter 7 relies on decades of Romani studies scholarship to understand the plight of the peoples who traveled westward out of India and into the countries of Europe after traversing the Islamic Near East and Byzantium.

Chapter 5, "A Global Race in the European Imaginary: Native Americans in the North Atlantic," examines the depiction of Native North Americans in the Old Norse Vinland Sagas – narrative accounts of expeditionary voyaging and colonization in the North American continent by Greenlanders and Icelanders in the first years of the eleventh

century. Cultural memories encapsuled in the saga narrations are read against the archeological record accrued from excavations at L'anse aux Meadows in Newfoundland and
studies on the paleo-ancestors of Native American and First Nation populations compiled
by historical anthropologists. Trade, war, food, technology, animals, children, climate
and environmental conditions, relations between women, and relations between women
and men form the thematic clusters of discussion in this section.

Chapter 6, "The Mongol Empire: Global Race as Absolute Power," traces the dramatic
history of how the Latin West received the arrival of Mongol armies at its doorstep, and
witnessed with horror the rise and consolidation of the Mongol empire. Beginning with
early denunciations of this alien, catastrophic, and relentless enemy race, missionary
accounts and travel narratives track the stage-by-stage transformation of the Mongol
peoples for the Latin West, recording changing perspectives as the initially demonized
race is reevaluated when the greatest civilization in the world – Yuan China – is folded into
the Mongol imperium.

To plot the evolution of Western response, the first two sections compare early eyewitness accounts by two Franciscan friars written soon after the Mongol onslaught on Europe.
Within a single decade of the thirteenth century, 1246–55, we have the terse formal report of
John of Plano Carpini, who was sent by Pope Innocent IV and was the first official envoy
from Europe to reach the Mongol court, and who directed his report to everyone in the
Latin West; and the expansive account of William of Rubruck eight years later, who
undertook a preaching mission to Eurasia with the blessing of King Louis IX of France,
but was not Louis's ambassador and corresponded only with one addressee in view, the
French king.

In the course of these early missionary encounters, we see how Mongols gradually
became familiar aliens in less than a decade, transmuting from the inhuman barbarians
without civilized practices, mores, and customs described by the Pope's alarmed
ambassador into the possessors of rudimentary culture and ceremony pictured by
William of Rubruck, who lived with Mongols at close range as a camp follower of
the Great Khan Mongke. Concomitantly, we see how, as the inhumanness of Mongols
begins to recede for William, Nestorian Christians come to supply the face of the alien
instead, and are fingered as agonists to be reckoned with in the competition for
Christian dominion.

William's report instructively demonstrates how, under the umbra of the thirteenth-
century Latin Christian church, differences of faith, liturgy, and practice in other Christianities could harden into absolute and fundamental differences – predisposing *heretics*,
so called, who practiced other forms of Christianity into a virtual race. These sections also
address the letters written by Franciscan missionaries later in fourteenth-century China,
when enmity with Nestorian Christians escalated and ramified in the contest of Christianities once the Great Khans countenanced the presence of Latin Christian missions
in China.

The third section on Mongols examines the vision proffered in Marco Polo's/Rustichello
da Pisa's hybrid narrative, *Le Devisement du Monde* (The Description of the World), as this
seminal text surveys the magnificence of Mongol China's cities, ports, and hinterlands and
details a vision of modernity, security, efficiency, welfare, success, and unimaginable
prosperity and power the like of which is found nowhere else in the world. From the
gigantic tax receipts of its ports to the glories of imperial gardens and architecture; from

exorbitant feasts to massive granaries; from the exquisite abstraction of paper money as symbolic currency to the high-speed postal relay gridding the empire; from welfare and disaster relief to a panoptic surveillance system; from military might to statesmanlike innovations in governance – Mongol China's incarnation of an economic, aesthetic, technological, and ethical sublime for Polo/Rustichello transmutes the Mongol race and empire into an object of fascination and desire under the Western gaze.

Extraordinary, iconic Mongols – not only the Great Khan Kublai, so beloved of Marco, but also the indomitable warrior princess Aiyurug-Khutulun, both of whom were well-attested historical personages – are held up for attention or admiration, as Mongols transmogrify, in this third phase of their depiction by Western authors, into a kind of racial sublime. Moreover, the inventory of the world's diverse races, religions, and resources furnished by this narrative text in the course of tallying up the world's commodities, manufacturers and exporters, markets, and forces of supply and demand raises an urgent question with which this section engages: Do race and religion become irrelevant and of scant import when the world is viewed as a network of goods and trading relations, webbed by the dynamics of mercantile capitalism and driven by the profit motive?

The fourth and last section, on Mongols, examines the politics immanent in a purported travel account of even greater influence and dispersion than Polo's/Rustichello's, and which exercised an authoritative impact on how the world and its peoples should be viewed for two and a half centuries: *Mandeville's Travels*, or the *Book of John Mandeville*. Cited as an authority on the world and its peoples in a variety of contexts – even making an appearance on world maps and the first globe ever fashioned – this fictitious blockbuster survives in twice as many manuscripts as Polo's/Rustichello's account, was translated into all the major European languages, and was carried as a truthful guide by explorers such as Columbus and Frobisher as they journeyed into terra incognita.

Mandeville's Travels adds little on the subject of the Mongol race that is new or not already found in Polo/Rustichello. However, this resourceful creation affords the West a threshold onto the fabulous Mongol empire by producing an emperor and an empire that are equally – indeed, more – desirable by virtue of their Christian faith: Prester John and his wondrous kingdom. Resurrecting the old legend of a priest-king located somewhere in the East, this ingenious text fructifies the old legend by making it a window that opens onto a panorama of early global Christianity, and adds the promise that Christianity will one day be global again, if certain simple conditions are met by Latin Christians and crusaders.

The seductive promise of a triumphal pan-Christianity winds its way through a number of scenarios and depictions of non-Christian religions such as Islam, Hinduism, animism, and the like: At one point, the promise is even vouched for by the supreme representative of an enemy faith, the Sultan of Egypt. The text is thus a wonderful exemplar of the work – the kind of service – that culture, always resilient, can perform to improve on intractable historical circumstances.

In narrating non-Christian religions, the Mandeville author is generous to a fault – bending over backward even to ameliorate censure of human sacrifice that is committed before a gigantic idol on the Indian coast, by reverting to the default position that religious piety and devotional intensity should be admired and valued. The *Travels* insists, moreover, that peoples everywhere, however different, have some understanding – intuitively or consciously – of the tenets of Latin Christianity, and harbor some knowledge – by virtue of nature or culture – of the Christian God. Unlike other texts examined in this chapter, *Mandeville's Travels* does not inveigh against multifarious Christianities or condemn them as heresies. This text doesn't sweat the small stuff, and never fails to keep its eye on the prize: the paramount importance that the Christian faith *must* become global (again).

This part of the chapter is also an appropriate place to discuss the journey made by a pious Far Eastern Christian monk of Uighur or Ongut descent, Rabban Sauma, who was born in Beijing and journeyed to the West as the Nestorian ambassador of the Ilkhan Arghun near the end of the thirteenth century. Sauma's report of his visit to the holy places and shrines of the West to revere relics, his saying mass at the behest of Edward I of England, and his diplomatic disputations with the Roman Curia on differences of creed takes the measure of tolerance evinced by churchmen and monarchs in the late thirteenth-century West, and indicates what might successfully bridge cleavages within the Christian faith that otherwise seemed insuperable.

Just as it would seem, however, that we are finally at the point of history where a literary-textual informant can be found in the West that looks past religious race as the identifier of human difference, *Mandeville's Travels* damns the Jews. A series of anti-Semitic narrations culminates in a horrific vision of eschatology, in which a multitude of Jews imprisoned behind Alexander's gate of mountains, and guarded by the Queen of the Amazons (gender versus race is one of the text's talented formulations), will break loose to war upon Christendom in the last days, joined by their eager coreligionists in the countries of the West. This sanguinary vision of primal, and also terminal, hatred is the threat faced by Europe, and it looms over the prospect of an incandescent future in which Christianity can be global again. We are back at the Jews, and enmity made manifest in the endless religious-racial war of Abrahamic faiths.

Chapter 7, "'Gypsies': A Global Race in Diaspora, a Slave Race for the Centuries," ends this book by calling attention to a people thus far mostly neglected in investigations of medieval race: the Romani. Tracing their trajectory out of Northwestern India, Chapter 7 engages with the Romani peoples' struggles, adaptations, and strategies as they journeyed through Western and Eastern Europe in the late medieval period. Initially received with curiosity, even kindness, in the West, these sojourners are subsequently resisted with increasing hostility in country after country, particularly in the Rhineland, and, as the diaspora of their communities advanced, persecutions unfolded and intensified. In South-eastern Europe the Romani were enslaved, and remained in slavery for centuries into the modern era, so that their very name became synonymous with enslavement and "Gypsy" was the name of a slave race.

Most importantly, the determination of the Romani to retain their ethnoracial identity – through all the long history of their enslavement and persecution, and after gaining the status of free peoples – testifies to the tenacity of racial identity, even for a diasporic community as heterogeneous and internally differentiated as the Romani. The Romani offer an example of the desire *for* racial identification, in a paradigm of racialism issuing from the minority community itself. Persistent Romani allegiance to a collective ethnor-acialization across all the cultural, national, and religious multifariousness of their far-flung communities attests the intransigence of race as an element of human identity that is embraced as integral, both for those who are raced by others and for those who declare their own racial identifications.

The story of race thus does not come to an end.

What This Book Does Not Contain

That this book addresses race in the European Middle Ages does not mean, of course, the book assumes there was no race, and there were no racisms, outside medieval Europe. Others have found analogues for the instantiations and phenomena discussed in the pages to come. For instance: The badge or *signum* that medieval Jews were forced to wear in Christian lands is analogous to the belt or *zunnar* that the Peoples of the Book or *Dhimmi*, including Christians and Jews, had to wear in Islamic lands, and that is attested in the Pact of Umar. Bernard Lewis has volumes (*Race and Color in Islam, Race and Slavery in the Middle East*) on Islamic civilizations' negative responses to black skin and Africans (despite, apparently, al-Jahiz' laudatory *Treatise on the Pride of the Black Race*).

Geoff Wade discusses fourteenth- and fifteenth-century Chinese imperialism, a strain of which is spectacularly manifest in the shock-and-awe "treasure-ships" of the Ming imperial fleet commanded by the eunuch admiral Zheng He in the fifteenth century. Though Zheng He's naval expeditions are popularly assumed to be voyages of "exploration," Wade points to the Chinese fleet's colonial behavior in maritime Southeast Asia, where the fleet forcibly deposed local rulers, installed surrogates, and intervened in a muscular fashion to shape local and regional politics in the South China Sea and Indian Ocean.

It is thus worth reiterating that it's not the particular intention of this book to seek to "blame the West, not the rest." Here and there, the book takes a moment to notice homologies or resemblances between cultural responses that a reader may find salient. A note in Chapter 2 observes that while medieval Christians viewed Jews as the killers of Christ, and thus *God-killers*, several *suras* of the Quran refer to Jews as the killers of *prophets* – and prophets, including Muhammad and Jesus, are the most esteemed personages in Islam (e.g., suras 2:61, 2:87, 2:91, 3:181, 3:183, 4:155, 5:70 passim).

A note in Chapter 4 recalls that, like some medieval Christian authors, the highly admired sociologist-historiographer Ibn Khaldun, subscribing to theories of climate as determinative of racial physiognomy and character, discusses black Africans pejoratively in his fourteenth-century *Muqadimmah*, where African character traits are presented in racially essentialist terms and black peoples are even called stupid (63).

But obviously, *The Invention of Race in the European Middle Ages* is not a study of how the entire premodern world conceptualized and instantiated race. Because we work within the fields of our training (however broadly conceived), where we can hope to have some competence, it is up to others – Indologists, Japanologists, Sinologists, Asianists, Africanists, Islamicists, Eurasianists, Mesoamericanists, and others – to extend the work on premodern race as they see fit or not, in their own fields of training and competence.

How China or Japan has treated its minority communities; what relations religion might have predisposed between the Hindu and Muslim populations of South Asia, or whether the caste system is a racial system; and what racialization might look like in sub-Saharan or Sudanic Africa or in Native America and Mesoamerica, is beyond the scope of this (already long) book, and will perhaps require more volumes on premodern race.

Because *The Invention of Race* concentrates on how larger populations, especially populations of wide dispersal, are racialized in the European Middle Ages, it does not focus on individual minority groups in Europe that are unique and singular and constitute a special, localized phenomenon, such as the *Cagots* who lived on either side of the western Pyrenees – a group whose name, provenance, and characteristics are still not well understood. The contradictory descriptions of *Cagots* in the historical record – a group that may or may not have originated in local leper colonies, that may or may not once have been Muslims or Christian heretics or the "poor of Christ" (*pauperes Christi*), and that was or was not possible to distinguish phenotypically from non-*Cagots* – have produced a scholarship that is still in flux and divergent.[10]

The radical othering of *heretics*, too, is so large a subject that it deserves a separate volume of its own. Whether or not individual heretical groups in the territories of the Latin West are transmogrified into virtual races, depending on locale, period, and historical circumstances, is for others to decide. Nestorians are the only "heretical" peoples discussed in this book, as they transformed into de facto racial others for thirteenth-century Franciscans such as William of Rubruck in his sojourn in Eurasia, and became the enemies and competitors of Franciscan missionaries in fourteenth-century China.

This book is thus, in a crucial sense, unfinished. Just as it builds upon the work of others in order to begin the task of discussing medieval race, so too it asks for others to continue that task and keep building the discussion. Like *Empire of Magic*, *The Invention of Race in the European Middle Ages* offers no conclusion at the end of its seven chapters. In large part, this is because there is no easy summation to be had, issuing out of the long, multifaceted conversations in the preceding pages, no neat and tidy closure to the discussion of medieval race.

This book can only say, with T. S. Eliot, *In my end is my beginning*. The conversation on premodern race needs to re-begin, again and again, and continue.

Notes

1 Recently, at the 2017 conference of the International Medieval Congress at Leeds, non-Caucasian medievalists were outraged that despite the conference theme – "Otherness" – every plenary speaker pronouncing on "otherness" was a white male European, who seemed, like the Englishman at the University of London, oblivious of any irony in their speaking position. One plenary lecturer even made a racial joke trivializing skin color, again outraging the nonwhite scholars in the audience at this conference of 2,400 people from fifty-six countries. After the cultural trauma inflicted by the conference, fraught conversations on "the whiteness of medieval studies" ignited on both sides of the Atlantic, and made their way into the *Chronicle of Higher Education* (see Chan): www.chronicle.com/article/Medievalists-Recoiling-From/240666. Who gets to speak for scholarship on the Middle Ages, and for medievalists – and not just on otherness, postcoloniality, or race – is now a heated question to be taken up at panels planned for several conferences in 2018.

2 For an argument on the repeated efflorescence of modernities within premodern time, and alternate views of temporality that are afforded by a global perspective of the thousand years conventionally assigned as the time of the Middle Ages, see my "Early Globalities."

3 Definitions and formulations here in this introduction can also be found in the various chapters that follow.

4 The understanding that *religion* – not just science, the principal authorizing discourse of the high modern racism that characterized the eighteenth through mid-twentieth centuries – can predispose racial practices and racial phenomena has turned out to be apposite, not only for the European Middle Ages, but also for today's twenty-first century: a time when religion is once

again on the rise as a prime factor in differentiating among human groups, and assigning selective essentialisms.

5 The *invention* of race, a key term for this book, is not the same thing as the *origin* of race. An *origin* is the coming into being of what has never before existed, whereas an invention is often a *re*invention, as fields of force within society and culture shift, alter, and reconstitute at particular historical junctures. Invention, unlike origin, can thus be a re-patterning, or re-beginning, that occurs at various historical moments, and becomes productive of exemplars.

6 Where appropriate, I have chosen not to eschew what in the Western academy is usually called "theory": This is in part to avoid the condescending assumption that most readers outside literary studies would find "theory" too difficult to follow, and in part to acknowledge that all writing embeds theoretical positions of some kind, whether these are explicit or not – there is no "outside" where one can stand, which is devoid of theoretical subscription. That being said, I attempt to avoid opaque, jargon-filled terminology, and strive for plainness.

7 My apologies, also, to literary scholars who may not find their work cited in this volume. For economy, I cite only work most directly pertinent to how I discuss race in each literary text, and regrettably eschew the full apparatus of citations I would ordinarily undertake in a volume of literary readings.

8 Though I consciously attempt not to over-privilege the scholarship of my home discipline, literature, I concede that some unconscious attention of this kind may be unavoidable. Like *Empire of Magic*, which identified and analyzed a number of literary texts that were little known and little discussed at the time, and that now receive significant attention from medievalists and graduate students, *The Invention of Race* also identifies cultural creations, issues, and phenomena deserving of future work and that are likely to prove productive, including, I may hope, for literary scholars.

9 Since Chapter 1's primary aim is to introduce a critical vocabulary and apparatus and supply some background to how medieval race has been discussed, this chapter does not traverse the full panoply of subjects treated in the rest of the volume. Muslims, Native North Americans, Mongols, and the Romani are not discussed in Chapter 1, but are treated in subsequent chapters.

10 For a point of entry on the *Cagots* – or *capots, cassots, gésitains, crestiaa, gahets, agots,* among the various names this group that is found in Béarn, Aquitaine, Navarre, and the Toulousain has been called – see Daniel Hawkins' revised Master's thesis on Academia.edu (www.academia.edu/15057536/Chimeras_that_degrade_humanity_the_cagots_and_discrimination) which surveys theories on the *Cagots* and furnishes a bibliography. Hawkins makes a strong argument for the *Cagots* as impoverished, subaltern peoples who at some point likely decided to band together in hamlets, then possibly became conflated with lepers (whether or not they actually had Hansen's disease), and who may have been further ostracized and abjected because of the occupations in which they worked.

1

Inventions/Reinventions

Race Studies, Modernity, and the Middle Ages

[T]he extent to which contemporary discourses, consciously or not, are affected by
pre-modern paradigms is, at times, surprising.

Khaled Abou El Fadl, *And God Knows the Soldiers* (18)

I N 1218, Jews in England were forced by law to wear badges on their chests, to set them
apart from the rest of the English population. This is the earliest historical example of
a country's execution of the medieval Church's demand, in Canon 68 of the Fourth
Lateran Council of 1215, that Jews and Muslims be set apart from Christians by a
difference in dress. In 1222, 1253, and 1275, English rulings elaborated on this badge for
the Jewish minority – who had to wear it (men and women at first, then children over the
age of seven) – its size, its color, and how it was to be displayed on the chest in an
adequately prominent fashion. In 1290, after a century of laws that eroded the economic,
religious, occupational, social, and personal status of English Jews, Jewish communities
were finally driven out of England *en masse*, marking the first permanent expulsion
in Europe.[1]

Periodic extermination of Jews was also a repeating phenomenon in medieval Europe. In
the so-called Popular and First Crusades, Jewish communities were massacred in the
Rhineland, in Mainz, Cologne, Speyer, Worms, Regensburg, and several other cities.
The Second Crusade saw more Jew-killing, and the so-called Shepherds' Crusade of 1320
witnessed the genocidal decimation of Jewish communities in France. In England, a trail of
blood followed the coronation of the famed hero of the Third Crusade, Richard Lionheart,
in 1189, when Jews were slaughtered at Westminster, London, Lynn, Norwich, Stamford,
Bury St. Edmunds, and York, as English chronicles attest.[2]

Scientific, medical, and theological treatises also argued that the bodies of Jews differed
in nature from the bodies of Western Europeans who were Christian: Jewish bodies gave
off a special fetid stench (the infamous *foetor judaicus*), and Jewish men bled uncontrollably
from their nether parts, either annually, during Holy Week, or monthly, like menstruating
women. Some authors held that Jewish bodies also came with horns and a tail, and for
centuries popular belief circulated through the countries of the Latin West that Jews

constitutionally needed to imbibe the blood of Christians, especially children, whom they periodically mutilated and tortured to death, especially little boys.[3]

Cultural practices across a range of registers also disclose historical thinking that pronounces decisively on the ethical, ontological, and moral value of black and white. The thirteenth-century encyclopedia of Bartholomeus Anglicus, *De Proprietatibus Rerum* (On the Properties of Things), offers a theory of climate in which cold lands produce white folk and hot lands produce black: white is, we are told, a visual marker of inner courage, while the men of Africa, possessing black faces, short bodies, and crisp hair, are "cowards of heart" and "guileful."[4]

A carved tympanum on the north portal of the west façade of the Cathedral of Notre Dame in Rouen (*c.* 1260) depicts the malevolent executioner of the sainted John the Baptist as an African phenotype (*Figure 1*), while an illustration in six scenes of Cantiga 186 of *Las Cantigas de Santa Maria*, commissioned by Alfonso X of Spain between 1252 and 1284, performs juridical vengeance on a black-faced Moor who is found in bed with his mistress; both are condemned to the flames, but the fair lady is miraculously saved by the Virgin Mary herself (*Figure 2*). Black is damned, white is saved. Black, of course, is the color of devils and demons, a color that sometimes extends to bodies demonically possessed, as demonstrated by an illustration from a Canterbury psalter, *c.* 1200 (*Figure 3*). In literature, malevolent black devilish Saracen enemies – sometimes of gigantic size – abound, especially in the *chanson de geste* and romance, genres that tap directly into the political imaginary, as some have argued.[5]

White is also the color of superior class and noble bloodlines. In the fourteenth-century *Cursor Mundi*, when four Saracens who are "blac and bla als led" ("black and blue-black as lead") meet King David and are given three rods blessed by Moses to kiss, they transform from black to white upon kissing the rods, thus taking on, we are told, the hue of those of noble blood: "Als milk thair hide bicom sa quite/And o fre blode thai had the hew" ("Their skin became as white as milk/And they had the hue of noble blood" [Morris ll. 8072, 8120–1]). Elite human beings of the fourteenth century have a hue, and it is white. The few examples I cite here from medieval England, Germany, France, and Spain – examples from state and canon law, chronicles and historical documents, illuminations, encyclopedias, architecture, devotional texts, rumor and hearsay, and recreational literature – form only a miniscule cross-section of the cultural evidence across the countries of Western Europe.

Yet, in spite of all this – state experiments in tagging and herding people, and ruling on their bodies with the violence of law; exterminations of humans under repeating conditions, and disparagement of their bodies as repugnant, disabled, or monstrous; in spite of a system of knowledge and value that turns on a visual regime harvesting its truths from polarities of skin color, and moralizing on the superiority and inferiority of color and somatic difference – canonical race theory has found it difficult to see the European Middle Ages as the time of race, as racial time. Conditions such as these typically constitute race theory's standard identifiers of race and racism, so it's logical to ask: How is such obliviousness possible?

Canonical race theory understands "racial formation" (Omi and Winant 55) to occur only in *modern* time. Racial formation has been twinned with conditions of labor and capital in modernity such as plantation slavery and the slave trade, the rise of capitalism or bourgeois hegemony, or modern political formations such as the state and its apparatuses (we think of

Figure 1. African executioner of John the Baptist, Cathedral of Notre Dame, Rouen: tympanum, north portal, west façade, *c.* 1260.
Reproduced with permission from the Menil Foundation, Houston; Hickey and Robertson, Houston; and Harvard University's Image of the Black Project.

David Theo Goldberg's magisterial *The Racial State*), nations and nationalisms (Étienne Balibar's chapters in *Race, Nation, Class*), liberal politics (Uday Mehta), new discourses of class and social war (Foucault of the 1975–6 Collège de France lectures), colonialism and imperialism (the work of many of us in postcolonial studies), and globalism and trans-national networks (Thomas Holt on race in the global economy).[6]

Figure 2. Illustration from Cantiga 186, *Las Cantigas de Santa Maria*, commissioned by Alfonso X of Spain. Escorial, Real Monasterio, Biblioteca, second half of the thirteenth century.
Reproduced with permission from the Menil Foundation, Houston; Hickey and Robertson, Houston; and Harvard University's Image of the Black Project.

In the descriptions of modernity as racial time, a privileged status has been accorded to the Enlightenment and its spawn of racial technologies describing body and nature through pseudoscientific discourses pivoting on biology as the ground of essence, reference, and

Figure 3. Healing of the Gadarene demoniacs. Psalter, folio 3v (detail), from Canterbury, *c.* 1200. Reproduced with permission from the Bibliothèque Nationale de France.

definition.[7] So tenacious has been scientific racism's account of race, with its entrenchment of high modernist racism as the template of *all* racisms, that it is still routinely understood, in everyday life and much of scholarship, that *properly* racial logic and behavior *must* invoke biology and the body as their referent, even if the immediate recourse is, say, to theories of climate or environment as the ground by which human difference is specified and evaluated.

In principle, race theory – whose brilliant practitioners are among the academy's most formative and influential thinkers – understands, of course, that race *has* no singular or stable referent: that *race is a structural relationship for the articulation and management of human differences, rather than a substantive content.* Ann Stoler, a particularly incisive scholar of race, voices the common understanding of all when she affirms that "the concept of race is an 'empty vacuum' – an image both conveying [the] 'chameleonic' quality [of race] and [its] ability to ingest other ways of distinguishing social categories" ("Racial Histories" 191).

In principle, then, race studies after the mid-twentieth century, and particularly in the past three and a half decades, encourages a view of race as a blank that is contingently filled under an infinitely flexible range of historical pressures and occasions. The motility of race, as Stoler puts it, means that racial discourses are always both "new and renewed" through historical time (we think of the Jewish badge in premodernity *and* modernity), always "well-worn" *and* "innovative" (such as the type and scale of "final solutions" like expulsion and genocide), and "draw on the past" as they "harness themselves to new visions and projects."[8]

The ability of racial logic to stalk and merge with other hierarchical systems – such as class, gender, or sexuality – also means that race can function as class (so that whiteness is the color of medieval nobility), as "ethnicity" and religion (Tutsis and Hutus in Rwanda, "ethnic cleansing" in Bosnia), or as sexuality (seen in the suggestion raised at the height of AIDS hysteria in the 1980s that gay people should be rounded up and cordoned off, in the style of Japanese American internment camps in World War II). Indeed, the "transformational grammar" of race through time means that the current masks of race are now overwhelmingly cultural, as witnessed since September 11, 2001.[9] Definitions of race in practice today at airport security checkpoints, in the news media, and in public political discourse flaunt ethnoracial categories decided on the basis of religious identity ("Muslims" being grouped as a de facto race), national or geopolitical origin ("Middle Easterners"), or membership in a linguistic community (Arabic-speakers standing in for Arabs).

But if our current moment of flexible definitions – a moment in which cultural race and racisms, and *religious* race, jostle alongside race-understood-as-somatic/biological determinations – uncannily renews key medieval instrumentalizations in the ordering of human relations, race theory's examination of the past nonetheless stops at the door of modern time. A blind spot inhabits the otherwise extraordinary panorama of critical descriptions of race: a cognitive lag that makes theory unable to step back any further than the Renaissance, that makes it *natural* to consider the Middle Ages as somehow outside real time.

Like many a theoretical discourse, race theory is predicated on an unexamined narrative of temporality in the West: a *grand récit* that reifies modernity as *telos* and origin, and that, once installed, entrenches the delivery of a paradigmatic chronology of racial time through mechanisms of intellectual replication pervasive in the Western academy, and circulated globally. This global circulation project is not without its detractors, but the replication of its paradigmatic chronology is extraordinarily persistent, for reasons I outline below.

Race Theory and Its Fictions: Modernity as the Time of Race, an Old Story of *Telos* and Origin

In the *grand récit* of Western temporality, modernity is positioned simultaneously as a spectacular conclusion and a beginning: a teleological culmination that emerges from the ooze of a murkily long chronology by means of a temporal rupture – a big bang, if we like – that issues in a new historical instant. The material reality and expressive vocabulary of rupture is vouched for by symbolic phenomena of a highly dramatic kind – a Scientific Revolution, discoveries of race, the formation of nations, etc. – which signal the arrival of modern time. Medieval time, on the wrong side of rupture, is thus shunted aside as the detritus of a pre-Symbolic era falling outside the signifying systems issued by modernity, and reduced to the role of a historical trace undergirding the recitation of modernity's arrival.

Thus fictionalized as a politically unintelligible time, because it lacks the signifying apparatus expressive of, and witnessing, modernity, medieval time is then absolved of the errors and atrocities of the modern, while its own errors and atrocities are shunted aside as essentially nonsignificative, without *modern* meaning, because occurring outside the conditions structuring intelligible discourse on, and participation in, modernity and its cultures. The replication of this template of temporality – one of the most durably stable intellectual replications in the West – is the basis for the replication of race theory's exclusions.

For the West, modernity is an account of self-origin – how the West became the unique, vigorous, self-identical, and exceptional entity that it is, bearing a legacy – and burden – of superiority. Modernity is *arrival*: the Scientific Revolution, represented by a procession of founding fathers of conceptual and experimental science (Galileo, Descartes, Bacon, Locke, Newton) and the triumph of technology – the printing press ushering in mass culture, heavy artillery ushering in modern warfare.

Or arrival is attested by the Industrial Revolution, witnessing extraordinary per capita and total output economic growth of the Schumpeterian, over the Smithian, kind. Since origin is haunted in the post-Biblical West by the story of a fall from grace, modernity is also necessarily the time when new troubles arrive, the most enduring of which are race and racisms, colonization, and the rise of imperial powers. Regrettable as such phenomena are, their exclusive arrival in modern time (variously located) nonetheless sets off modern time as unique, special: confirming modernity as a time apart, newly minted, in human history.

The dominance of a linear model of temporality deeply invested in marking rupture and radical discontinuity thus eschews alternate views: a view of history, for instance, as a field of dynamic oscillations between ruptures and reinscriptions, or historical time as a matrix in which overlapping repetitions-with-change can occur, or an understanding that historical events may result from the action of multiple temporalities that are enfolded and coextant within a particular historical moment. The dominant model of a simple, linear temporality has geospatial and macrohistorical consequences. Since the prime movers and markers of modernity are exclusively or overwhelmingly discovered in the West, the non-West has long been saddled with the tag of being *pre*modern: inserted within a developmental narrative whose trajectory positions the rest of the world as always catching up.

Some sociological historians and historians of science, working against the grain, have attempted to disrupt the narrative of scientific, economic, and demographic transformation separating modern from premodern time in the West, and the West from the rest.[10] Revisiting the old repertoire of questions, they have argued for the legitimacy of complex, nonlinear temporalities: temporalities in which multiple modernities have recurred in different vectors of the world moving at different rates of speed within macrohistorical time. One position is articulated by Jack Goldstone's thick description of human history as punctuated by scientific and technological "efflorescences" that, coupled with labor specialization and intensive market orientation, have driven *both* Schumpeterian *and* Smithian growth and change in various societies and various eras, thus muddying the monomythic simplicity of a radical break favoring the West in modernity's singular arrival.

Against the putative uniqueness of the Industrial Revolution, we have Robert Hartwell's data showing that the tonnage of coal burnt annually for iron production in eleventh-century northern China was already "roughly equivalent to 70% of the total amount of coal annually used by all metal workers in Great Britain at the beginning of the eighteenth century" ("Cycle" 122). Demographic patterns deemed characteristic of modernity have also appeared in premodernity. Goldstone observes that urban populations in twelfth- and thirteenth-century Europe – a period of extraordinary growth – amounted to 10 percent of the total population, a ratio not exceeded until the nineteenth century (347).

The work of Eric Jones and Robert Hartwell on the extensively developed water power, iron and steel industries, and shipping of Song China; that of Billy So on China's mass-market industrial production of export ceramics; and that of Richard Britnell and Bruce Campbell, Joel Mokyr, D. S. L. Cardwell, Lynn White, and Goldstone himself on the economic and demographic growth, technology, urbanization, and commercialization of twelfth- and thirteenth-century Europe (Goldstone 380–9) furnish material for counter-narratives contesting the fiction of sudden, unique arrival, and the discourse of Western exceptionalism.[11] Some historians of science and sociology accordingly prefer to speak of scientific *revolutions* across time, rather than *the* Scientific Revolution – a single, unique instance, in a single unique modernity (Hart, *Civilizations* chapter 2; "Explanandum") – and of industrial *revolutions*, rather than *the* Industrial Revolution.

Even were we to ignore the demographic, economic, and industrial materialities pains-takingly tracked by these historians, the representation of medieval time as wholly foreign to, and unmarked by, modernity intuitively runs counter to the modes of understanding in contemporary theory undergirding the study of culture today. Studies of culture, literature, history, and art that have been open to late twentieth- and twenty-first-century develop-ments in academic theory across the disciplines will not find unfamiliar the notion that the past is never completely past, but inhabits the present and haunts modernity and contem-porary time in ways that estrange our present from itself.

Modernity and the present can thus be grasped as the habitat of multiple temporalities that braid together a complex and plural "now" that is internally self-divided and contamin-ated by premodern time. In public life, the evocation of Crusades and jihad by Jihadi and Salafi ideologues and by the Western political right after 9/11 is one example of the past in the present, marking an internal cleavage in modern time through which premodern time speaks itself as an active presence.[12]

Dipesh Chakrabarty's meditation on how an earlier time reinscribes itself in later periods (always with difference, never in exactly the same way) is useful here:

> humans from any other period . . . are always in some sense our contemporaries: that would have to be the condition under which we can even begin to treat them as intelligible to us . . . the writing of medieval history for Europe depends on this assumed contemporaneity of the medieval [with our present], or . . . the non-contemporaneity of the present with itself.
>
> (109)

If we grant that the present can be nonidentical to itself in this way, we should also grant the corollary: that *the past* can *also* be nonidentical to itself, inhabited too by that which was out of *its* time – marked by modernities that estrange medieval time in ways that render medieval practices legible in modern terms.

If we allow our field of vision to hatch open these moments in premodernity that seem to signal the activity of varied modernities in deep time (Goldstone's "efflorescences"), our expanded vision will yield windows on the past that allow for a reconfigured understanding of earlier time. Indeed, hatching open such moments in premodernity is what feminists and queer studies scholars have, in a sense, been doing for decades in staking out *their* European Middle Ages – identifying the instances in which a different consciousness and practice erupt and effloresce – even as their earliest archeologies suffered slings and arrows hurled in the name of anachronism and presentism. The "contemporaneity of the medieval" with our time, and the nonidentity of medieval time with itself, thus grants a pivot from which the recloning of old narratives can be resisted.

Nonetheless, at present the discussion of premodern race continues to be handicapped by the invocation of axioms that reproduce a familiar story in which mature forms of race and racisms, arriving in modern political time, are heralded by a shadowplay of inauthentic rehearsals characterizing the prepolitical, premodern past. For discussions of race, the terms and conditions set by this narrative of bifurcated polarities vested in modernity-as-origin have meant that the tenacity, duration, and malleability of race, racial practices, and racial institutions have failed to be adequately understood or recognized. With centuries elided, the long history of race-ing has been foreshortened, truncated to an abridged narrative.

But why would we want a long history of race? Like other theoretical-political endeavors that have addressed the past – feminism comes readily to mind as a predecessor moment; queer studies is another – the project of revising our understanding by inserting premodernity into conversations on race is closely dogged by accusations of presentism, anachronism, reification, and the like.[13] Why call something *race*, when many old terms – "ethnocentrism," "xenophobia," "premodern discriminations," "prejudice," "chauvinism," even "fear of otherness and difference" – have been used comfortably for so long to characterize the genocides, brutalizations, executions, and mass expulsions of the medieval period?

The short answer is that the use of the term *race* continues to bear witness to important strategic, epistemological, and political commitments not adequately served by the invocation of categories of greater generality (such as *otherness* or *difference*) or greater benignity in our understanding of human culture and society. *Not* to use the term *race* would be to sustain the reproduction of a certain kind of past, while keeping the door shut to tools, analyses, and resources that can name the past differently. Studies of "otherness" and "difference" in the Middle Ages – which are now increasingly frequent – must then continue to dance around words they dare not use; concepts, tools, and resources that are closed off; and meanings that only exist as lacunae.

Or, to put it another way: the refusal of race destigmatizes the impacts and consequences of certain laws, acts, practices, and institutions in the medieval period, so that we cannot name them for what they are, and makes it impossible to bear adequate witness to the full meaning of the manifestations and phenomena they install. The unavailability of race thus often colludes in relegating such manifestations to an epiphenomenal status, enabling omissions that have, among other things, facilitated the entrenchment and reproduction of a certain kind of foundational historiography in the academy and beyond.

To cite one example: How often do standard ("mainstream") histories of England discuss as constitutive to the formation of English identity, or to the nation of England, the mass expulsion of Jews in 1290; the marking of the Jewish population with badges for three quarters of a century; decimations of Jewish communities by mob violence; statutory laws ruling over where Jews were allowed to live; monitory apparatuses like the Jewish Exchequer and the network of registries created by England to track the behavior and lives of Jews; or popular lies and rumors like the cultural fiction of ritual murder, which facilitated the legal execution of Jews by the state? That the lives of English Jews were *constitutive*, not incidental, to the formation of England's history and collective identity – that the built landscape of England itself, with its cathedrals, abbeys, fortifications, homes, and cities, was dependent on English Jews – is not a story often heard in foundational historiography.[14] Scholars who are invested in the archeology of a past in which alternate voices, lives, and histories are heard, beyond those canonically established as central by foundationalist studies, are thus not well served by evading the category of race and its trenchant vocabularies and tools of analysis.[15]

For race theorists, the study of racial emergence in the *longue durée* is also one means to understand if the configurations of power productive of race in modernity are, in fact, genuinely novel. Key propensities in history can be identified by examining premodernity: the modes of apparent necessity, configurations of power, and conditions of crisis that witness the harnessing of powerful dominant discourses – such as science *or* religion – to make fundamental distinctions among humans in processes to which we give the name of race.

A reissuing of the medieval past in ways that admit the ongoing interplay of that past with the present can therefore only recalibrate the urgencies of the present with greater precision. An important consideration in investigating the invention of race in medieval Europe (an invention that is always a *re*invention) is also to grasp the ways in which *homo europaeus* – the European subject – emerges in part through racial grids produced from the twelfth through fifteenth centuries, and the significance of that emergence for understanding the unstable entity we call "the West" and its self-authorizing missions.[16]

Premodernists Write Back: Historicizing Alternate Pasts, Rethinking Race in Deep Time

Scholars who have considered race in premodernity have by and large understood race as arguments over nature – how human groups are identified through biological or somatic features deemed to be their durable or intrinsic characteristics, features which are then selectively moralized and interpreted to extrapolate continuities between the bodies, behaviors, and mentalities of the members of the group thus collectively identified. Premodernists subscribing to a view of race as contentions over nature have accordingly focused primary attention on *bodies* in examining the record of images, artifacts, and texts: investigating the meanings of skin color, phenotypes, blood purity and bloodlines, genealogy, physiognomy, heritability, and the impact of environment (including, in the medieval period, macrobian zones, astrology, and humoral theory) in shaping human bodies and human natures, with differential values being attached to groups thus differentially identified.

For antiquity, major studies by Frank Snowden, Benjamin Isaac, and David Goldenberg are among those that consider body-centered phenomena as indicators of race – and in particular, for Snowden and Goldenberg, blackness as a paramount marker of race.[17] Among medievalists, noted studies by Robert Bartlett, Peter Biller, Steven Epstein, David Nirenberg, and contributors to a 2001 issue of the *Journal of Medieval and Early Modern Studies* edited by Thomas Hahn also suggest that medievalists too have understood race as a body-centered phenomenon: defined by skin color, physiognomy, blood, genealogy, inheritance, etc.

Not all medievalists who have considered race believe the concept has purchase for the medieval period. Bartlett, for whom race pivots on biology, not culture, offers this caveat in his volume of 1993: "while the language of race – *gens, natio,* 'blood,' 'stock,' etc. – is *biological,* its medieval reality was almost entirely *cultural*" (*Making of Europe* 197). Bartlett's subscription to the preeminence of biology in race matters wavers, however, when he grants that medieval practices which assume Jewish religious identity to be coterminous with ontological and essential nature *can* be considered racial (at least by other medievalists):

> Many scholars see in the later Middle Ages a tendency for racial discrimination to become sharper and racial boundaries to be more shrilly asserted. The hardening of anti-Jewish feeling between the eleventh and the fifteenth centuries is recognized by all who work on the subject and they disagree only on their dating of the crucial change for the worse.
>
> (*Making of Europe* 236)

Bartlett's later work (in 2001) continues his emphasis on biology, and attends to blood and descent groups in deciding race. For instance, because "environmental influence" is behind the thinking of Bartholomeus Anglicus and Albertus Magnus in their sorting of human kinds based on climatological determinism, Bartlett believes that their linking of skin color, physiognomy, and phenotype to dispositions of group character is not a racial dispensation, but an environmental one ("Medieval and Modern Concepts of Race and Ethnicity" 46–7). In his most recent work of 2009, "Illustrating Ethnicity in the Middle Ages," Bartlett eschews race altogether in favor of "ethnicity."

Peter Biller's studies – among the most impressive and arresting work on medieval race today – focus on the evidence of medieval scientific texts, and on intellectual-pedagogical discourses circulating in medieval universities, in entrenching and diffusing theories of race. Steven Epstein, for whom "race/color" is a compound term (*Purity Lost* 9), scrutinizes the mixing of kinds in the eastern Mediterranean, and concludes that "back in the Middle Ages, color prejudice existed, at times even with few or no people of color to deprecate" (*Purity Lost* 13). In fact, the "literal valuing of people crossed beyond simple color symbolism or even prejudice into a way of thinking that closely resembled modern forms of racism, in a vocabulary suited to the times" (*Purity Lost* 201).

David Nirenberg's interest in body-centered medieval race, based on evidence in Spain, has shifted in recent years: from earlier attention (in 2002) to Spanish historical events at the close of the Middle Ages that feature an obsession with blood purity, genealogical descent, and body-centered essential natures ("Mass Conversion and Genealogical Mentalities," "Conversion, Sex, and Segregation") to his more recent (2009) agnostic stance on medieval race, whether named explicitly as race or not ("Race and the Middle Ages," "Was There Race Before Modernity?").

Observing that "All racisms are attempts to ground discriminations, whether social, economic, or religious, in biology and reproduction. All claim a congruence of 'cultural' categories with 'natural' ones" ("Race" 74; "Before Modernity?" 235), Nirenberg concludes, "I am not making ... claim[s] that race did exist in the Middle Ages, or that medieval people were racist. Such statements would be reductive and misleading, obscuring more than they reveal" ("Race" 74), and adds: "Nor do I aspire to anything so provincial as a proof that late medieval discriminations were racial" ("Before Modernity?" 239).

Nirenberg's ambivalence (he simultaneously resists the notion that modernity is the sole context of race and inveighs against modernists who claim that race and racism are exclusively modern phenomena) may owe something to his conviction that "any history of race will be at best provocative and limited; at worst a reproduction of racial logic itself, in the form of a genealogy of ideas" ("Before Modernity?" 262).

Most contributors to Hahn's issue – in particular Verkerk, J. J. Cohen, Lomperis, and Hahn himself (Kinoshita prefers "alterity" as her category of choice) – perform supple readings of literature and visual images within paradigms of body-centered race, focusing primarily on blackness and color as well as the exotic-foreign. In the same issue, William Jordan's response ("Why Race?") expresses a number of reservations, recommends attention to Jews rather than to color in medieval race, and offers the view that race paradigms may not be useful for the medieval period, especially when imaginative literature is mined for examples (much of the issue consists of literary readings).

Some premodernists have insisted that there must be prior linguistic evidence of the word "race" in European vocabularies before racial phenomena and racializing practices can exist, advocating priority for whether medieval peoples *themselves* saw themselves as belonging to races and practicing racisms. Insistence of this kind may underpin classicist Denise Buell's scrupulous attentiveness to the meaning of the word *genos* in the early centuries of the Common Era, when strategies of Christian universalism rhetorically posit Christians as a new people, a kind of race (*Why This New Race*, "Early Christian Universalism").[18] As a reminder that a gap can exist between a practice and the linguistic utterance that names it, Steven Epstein's discovery of "a way of thinking that closely resembled modern forms of racism, in a vocabulary suited to the times" (*Purity Lost* 201) suggests that "unfamiliar vocabularies and languages" (*Purity Lost* 13) do not in themselves indicate the absence of a phenomenon.

A few premodernists, following examples in critical race theory, have chosen to emphasize cultural and social determinants in racing – including a political hermeneutics of religion – while not eschewing overlapping multiple discourses in racial formation. Unlike many who stress nature-based determinants in racing, and race as body-centered phenomena, premodernists emphasizing sociocultural determinants do not assume that race or racism require human distinctions to be posited as permanent, stable, innate, fixed, or immutable.[19]

Critical race theory itself, of course, has for decades attentively scrutinized culturalist forms of racing – in which culture functions, we might say, as a kind of superstructure that is relatively disarticulated from its base, nature – without assuming that racial distinctions must be grasped as permanent or stable for racial categorizations to occur. Ann Stoler's 1997 study of the colonial Dutch East Indies is a salient and oft-quoted example:

> Race could never be a matter of physiology alone. Cultural competency in Dutch customs, a sense of 'belonging' in a Dutch cultural milieu ... disaffiliation with things Javanese ... domestic arrangements, parenting styles, and moral environment ... were crucial to defining ... who was to be considered European.
>
> ("Racial Histories" 197)

With the appearance of studies (like Gauri Viswanathan's influential *Outside the Fold*) which point suggestively to how racial and religious identities might form interlocking and mutually constitutive categories,[20] the examination of religion-based race has gained increased legitimacy among premodernists (see, especially, Buell; Heng [*Empire of Magic*, chapters 2 and 4; "Invention ... 1" and "Invention ... 2"; "Reinventing Race"]; Lampert, "Race"; Ziegler 198).

In the attempt to suggest how we might rethink the past, I should therefore begin with a modest, stripped-down working hypothesis: that *"race" is one of the primary names we have – a name we retain for the strategic, epistemological, and political commitments it recognizes – attached to a repeating tendency, of the gravest import, to demarcate human beings through differences among humans that are selectively essentialized as absolute and fundamental, in order to distribute positions and powers differentially to human groups.* Race-making thus operates as specific historical occasions in which strategic essentialisms are posited and assigned through a variety of practices and pressures, so as to construct a hierarchy of peoples for differential treatment. My understanding, thus, is that *race is a structural relationship for the articulation and management of human differences, rather than a substantive content.*

Since the differences selected for essentialism will vary in the *longue durée* – perhaps battening on bodies, physiognomy, and somatic attributes in one location; perhaps on social practices, religion, and culture in another; and perhaps on a multiplicity of interlocking discourses elsewhere – I will devote the rest of this introductory chapter to outlining architectures that support the instantiation of race in the medieval period, and to specifying key particularities – distinctive features – of medieval race, working where possible through actual examples. The use of concrete, particularized examples – a small spectrum which is not intended to be exhaustive, nor to duplicate the chapters that follow – will help to indicate how we might identify the varied locations and concretions of race in the Middle Ages, and sketch ways to consider medieval race without recourse to totalizing suppositions.

In addressing the nested discourses formative of race, it is important to note that *religion* – the paramount source of authority in the Middle Ages – can function both socioculturally *and* biopolitically: subjecting peoples of a detested faith, for instance, to a political theology that can biologize, define, and essentialize an entire community as fundamentally and absolutely different in an interknotted cluster of ways. Nature and the sociocultural should not thus be seen as bifurcated spheres in medieval race-formation: they often crisscross in the practices, institutions, fictions, and laws of a political – and a *bio*political – theology operationalized on the bodies and lives of individuals and groups.

Religious Race, Medieval Race: Jews as a Benchmark Example

Medievalists who study Jews will be familiar with my first example of how race emerges as an outcome of clustered forces and technologies. The infamous occasion described in this section issues from thirteenth-century England and is recorded and discussed in three contemporaneous Latin chronicles and an Anglo-Norman ballad, and has a tenacious afterlife for six-and-a-half centuries afterward. It is cited, elaborated, and transformed in drama and ballads, statuary and shrines, preaching and pilgrimage, books of private devotional prayer, miracle tales, etc., until the twentieth century, when a tourist pamphlet of 1911 invites (paid) viewing of the site at which the original atrocity allegedly occurred. The most influential historical account is by the thirteenth-century chronicler of St. Alban's, Matthew Paris, and the finest aesthetic treatment in the Middle Ages is afforded by Chaucer, in the *Prioress's Tale* of *The Canterbury Tales*.[21]

On July 31, 1255, in the city of Lincoln, an eight-year-old boy named Hugh, the son of a widow, Beatrice, fell into a cesspool attached to the house of a member of the Jewish community. There, "the body putrefied for some twenty-six days and rose to the surface to dismay Jews who had assembled from all over England to celebrate a marriage in an important family. They surreptitiously dropped the body in a well away from their houses where it was discovered on 29 August" (Langmuir, "Knight's Tale" 461).[22]

The panicked behavior of the Jews who were gathered in Lincoln for the marriage of Belaset, daughter of Benedict fil' Moses, poignantly expresses the sense of danger and fragility that characterized the quotidian existence of a minority community used to periodic violence from the majority population among which the minority community lived, and by which it was surrounded. Here, Jewish panic also issued from a frightened recognition of threat from a medieval technology of power against Jews, a *techne* that scholarship today calls the "ritual murder libel."

In the standard plot of the libel, Jews were said to seize Christian boys of tender years, on the cusp of childhood, in order to torture, mutilate, and slaughter them in deliberate reenactments of the killing of Christ, for whose deicide Jews were held responsible. By 1255, ritual murder stories were well sedimented in English culture as a popular fantasy of Christian child martyrdom, a fantasy which had proliferating material results, since they installed a series of shrines for the Christian martyred that became public devotional sites around which feelings of Christian community could gather, pool, and intensify, bringing fame and pilgrims to the towns and cities in which the shrines were located.[23]

First invoked at Norwich in 1144, then Gloucester in 1168; Bury St. Edmunds in 1181; Bristol in 1183 or 1260; Winchester in 1192, 1225, 1232, and 1244; London in the 1260s and 1276; and Northampton in 1279, ritual murder libel – to be distinguished from its near-relative in anti-Semitic fiction, the blood libel, and its first cousin, host desecration libel – was the technology of power exercised against the hapless Jews of Lincoln in 1255.[24] Consequently, on October 4, 1255, by order of Henry III of England, ninety-one Jews were imprisoned and one person executed for the "martyrdom" of Hugh. On November 22, eighteen more Jews were executed, "drawn through the streets of London before daybreak and hung on specially constructed gallows" (Langmuir, "Knight's Tale" 477–8).[25] Nineteen Jews were officially executed – murdered – by the state through acts of juridical rationality wielding a discourse of power compiled by communal consent over the generations against a minority target.

When state executions of group victims – unfortunates who were condemned by community fictions allowed to exercise juridical violence through law – occurred in the modern period, such official practices have been understood by race studies to constitute de facto acts of race: institutional crimes of a sanctioned, legal kind committed by the state against members of an internal population identified by their recognized member-ship within a targeted group. In the twentieth century, the phenomenon of legalized state violence occurred most notoriously, of course, under the regime of apartheid in South Africa. Today, Turkey's systematic targeting of its minority Kurdish population for persecution and abuse offers an example of twenty-first-century-style apartheid and state racism.

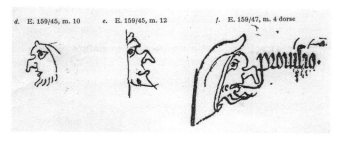

Figure 4. The "Jewish face." The King's Remembrancer Memoranda Rolls, E.159, membranes 10, 12, 4 dorse. Public Record Office, thirteenth century.
Reproduced with permission from the National Archives, UK.

In the United States, an example of state violence against a minority race might be Franklin Roosevelt's Executive Order 9066, an order that created ten internment camps across seven states on the North American continent for the incarceration of 111,000 Japanese Americans during World War II, on the presumption that Japanese Americans constituted a community of internal aliens who would betray their country, the United States of America, to the enemy nation of Japan in wartime by virtue of their race.[26]

Were we to consider thirteenth-century enforcements of state power, which recognized Jews as an undifferentiated population collectively personifying difference and threat, alongside other state enforcements of homologous kinds that occurred in modern time, our aggregated perspective would likely yield an understanding that the legal murder of nineteen Jews in 1255 in England, on the basis of a *community belief* in Jewish guilt and malignity, constituted a racial act committed by the state against an internal minority population that had, over time, become racialized in the European West.

Jews were pivotal to England's commercializing economy of the twelfth and thirteenth centuries, and constituted an immigrant community identifiable by virtue of religious and sociocultural practices, language, dress, and, occasionally, physical appearance (caricatures of Jewish phenotypes and biomarkers survive in English manuscript marginalia and visual art: see, for example, *Figure 4*).

Monitored by the state through an array of administrative apparatuses, and ruled upon by statutes, ordinances, and decrees, they were required to document their economic activity at special registries that tracked Jewish assets across a network of cities. No business could be lawfully transacted except at these registries, which came to determine where Jews could live and practice a livelihood. Jews needed official permission and licenses to establish or to change residence, and by 1275, the *Statutum de Judeismo* (Statute of Jewry) dictated that they could not live in any city without a registry by which they could be scrutinized, and they could not have Christians living in their midst – a thirteenth-century experiment in de facto segregation.

Subjected to a range of fiscal extortions and special, extraordinary taxations (tallages) which milked them to the edge of penury, Jews were barred from marriage with Christians, from holding public office, from eating with Christians or lingering in Christian homes, and even from praying too loudly in synagogues. They were required to wear large, identifying badges on their outer garments (*Figure 5*) and denied the

Figure 5. English Jew wearing the Jewish badge on his chest in the form of the tablets of the Old Testament. BL Cotton MS Nero, D2, fol.180, thirteenth century.
Reproduced with permission from the British Library, UK.

freedoms of walking publicly in city streets during Holy Week and of emigration, as a community, without permission.

A special subset of government known as the Exchequer of the Jews was created to monitor and regulate their lives, residences, activities, and livelihoods. The constraints on their lives are too numerous to list; some would resonate eerily with the treatment of minority populations in other countries, and other eras, linking into relationship moments of medieval and modern time.

Robert Stacey observes that England's example was "archetypical" of how Jews were treated throughout the countries of medieval Western Europe ("Twelfth Century" 340), differing mainly by virtue of the earliness, inventiveness, and intensity of English actions (Skinner 2).[27] But the vast scholarship on Jews in medieval Europe specifies in excruciating detail more than state actions. Across a miscellany of archives, scholarship has tracked how Jews were systematically defined and set apart via biomarkers such as the possession of horns, a male menstrual flux or the generationally inherited New Testament curse of visceral-hemorrhoidal bleeding, an identifying stink (the infamous *foetor judaicus*), facial and somatic phenotypes (the *facies judaica,* "Jewish face"), and charges of bestiality, blasphemy, diabolism, deicide, vampirism, and cannibalism laid at their door through a hermeneutics of theology exercised by religious and laity alike across a wide range of learned and popular contexts.[28]

Instructive as legal, formal instruments of state control are as examples of ethnoracial practices, it is the *extra*legal and *in*formal rehearsals of power that grant special traction and insight into medieval modalities of racial formation. For instance: The popular enthusiasm for community fictions of Jewish violence – stories of ritual murder and host desecration, blood libels; fictions that are designed to authorize and arrange *for* community violence *to* Jews – guides us to an important understanding that, for medieval Jews, it is equally the *ritualized iteration of group practices* that triumphantly enacts racial formation in the medieval period. *Community fictions and community consent, periodically refreshed, augur performances that are ritually productive of race.*

In England, then, the Jewish badge, expulsion order, legislative enforcements, surveillance and segregation, ritualized iterations of homicidal fables, and the legal execution of Jews are constitutive acts in the consolidation of a community of Christian English – otherwise internally fragmented and ranged along numerous divides – against a minority population *that has, on these historical occasions and through these institutions and practices, entered into race.*

Architectures of Racial Formation: Church and State, Law, Learning, Governmentality, Thirteenth to Fifteenth Centuries

I argued in my earlier book, *Empire of Magic*, that the medieval period of the long thirteenth century witnessed a motility in which seemingly opposed forces – universalizing measures set in motion by the Latin Church, in tandem with a partitioning, fractionalizing drive that powered nascent territorial nationalisms – furnished an array of instrumentalities for intensified collective identity-formation (68–73). In the drive for universality, the Church expanded modes of governmentality through exponential elaborations of canon law, circulating new orders of mendicant friars and inquisitions to root out heterodoxy, and systemically sought unity across internal divisions in the Latin West through uniform practices, institutions, sacraments, codes, rituals, and doctrines.[29]

Concomitantly, the West's romance with empire that, from the end of the eleventh century, had seen overseas colonies ("Outremer") established in the Near East for 200 years through the mass military incursions known as the Crusades, saw extraterritorial ambitions ramify from military expansionism to para- and extramilitary endeavors.[30] Long before the territorial loss of the last crusader colony, Acre, in 1291, Dominicans and Franciscans had begun to diffuse worldwide a "soft power" vision of Latin Christianity from Maghrebi Africa to Mongol Eurasia, India to China, insinuating Christendom's reach through missions, conversionary preaching, chapter houses, churches, and foreign-language schools for proselytes.[31]

Universalist ambitions are articulated in letters and embassies from popes and monarchs, ethnographic accounts and field reports, reconnaissance and diplomatic missions, offers of military and political alliances, and conversionary enterprises, the surviving evidence of which has become the miscellaneous records of Europe's presence in the world.[32] One (extreme) strain of universalist ambition is given voice by the English historian Matthew Paris, who conveys a high-ranking English churchman's vision for Christian world domination when he vivaciously reports the Bishop of Winchester as saying, on the question of Mongols and Muslims, that England should leave the dogs to devour one another, so that they may all be consumed and perish; when Christians proceed against those who remain, they will slay the enemies of Christ and cleanse the face of the earth, so that the entire world will be subject to one Catholic church (Luard, *Mathaei Parisiensis* III: 489).

Scholars also point to congruent ambitions in this time such as the reordering of knowledge/power, as universities and scholasticism systematized learning and the reproduction of knowledge, encyclopedias retaxonomized the world, and compilations of *summae* sought to aggregate and systematize the totality of human understanding. More recently, scholars such as Peter Biller and Joseph Ziegler have emphasized how Greek and Arabic texts of science, medicine, and natural history – interpreted, modified, and circulated through university lectures and curricula after the energetic translation movements of the twelfth century – assembled a crucible of knowledge through which scientific, environmental, humoral, and physiognomic theories of race were delivered from antiquity to the Middle Ages.[33]

The Church's bid for overarching authority and uniformity importantly furnished medieval societies with an array of models on how to consolidate unity, power, and collective identity across internal differences. A church with universalist ambitions in effect sought to function like a state, a state without borders: exercising control through a spectrum of supervisory apparatuses, laws, institutions, and symbols; homogenizing belief and coalescing communities of affect around uniform ritual practices; deploying mobile agents-at-large to police conformity within the Latin West and to gather information, extend diplomacy, and propagate doctrine without; and calling forth crusading armies from the countries of Europe at intervals for deployment in the ongoing competition with Islam for territorial, political, and cultural supremacy in the international arena.[34]

Functioning like a state without borders, a Church with universalist ambitions paradoxically also saw a swirl of contrapuntal forces in motion in the historical moment: a concomitant fractionalizing of collective identity in the form of emergent medieval-style nations characterized by intensive state formation and imagined local unities, as territorial nationalisms coalesced within Christendom.[35]

Nascent nationalisms *also* harnessed, and were powered by, expanded formal mechanisms such as law and informal mechanisms such as rituals, symbols, rumors, pilgrimage shrines, and affective communities mobilized by telling and retelling key stories of cultural power. In their mutual resort to overlapping resources, we can see how the interests of church and nation interlocked in logical relationship. Canon laws established by the Church to extend governmentality *across* territorial boundaries, such as Fourth Lateran's Canon 68 requiring Jews to be publicly marked, also enabled the legal manipulation of Jewish populations *within* territorial boundaries: so that, in England, a distinctively *English* communal character was able to emerge through its posited difference from, and opposition to, the Jewish minority within England's borders.[36]

Canon 68 thus in effect instantiates racial regime, and racial governance, in the Latin West through the force of law. It also bears witness to the rise of a political Christianity in the West that installs what Balibar calls "an interior frontier" within national borders, reinforced by affective cultures of fear and hate mobilized through stories of race like the ritual murder lie ("Racism and Nationalism" 42). The coalescence of England's identity as a national body united across disparate (but always Christian and European) peoples thus pivoted on the politico-legal emergence of a visible and undifferentiated Jewish minority *into race*, under forms of racial governance supported by political Christianity, and sustained through the mobilization of affective communities enlisted by stories of race.

This is not to claim, of course – absurdly – that race-making throughout the medieval period is in any way uniform, homogenous, constant, stable, or free of contradiction or local differences across the countries of Europe in all localities, regions, and contexts through some three or four centuries of historical time. Neither is it to concede, in reverse, that local differences – variation in local practices and contexts – must always render it impossible to think translocally in the medieval period. The effort to think across the translocal does not require any supposition of the universal, static, unitary, or unvarying character of medieval race.

Indeed, in *Invention of Race* I point to *particular* moments and instances of how race is made, to indicate the exemplary, dynamic, and resourceful character of race-making under conditions of possibility, not to extract repetitions without difference. In this chapter, I point to homogenizing drives that universalize Christendom, and to fractionalizing drives that fragment Christendom into territorial nationalisms – such drives always manifesting themselves nonidentically and unevenly, in different places and at different times – to sketch the dynamic field of forces within which miscellaneous *particularized* instances of race-making can occur under varied local conditions. The remaining chapters of this book then take up skeins in the warp and weave of this matrix to outline some possibilities for further scholarly investigation.

The field of forces within which race-making occurs is also one of the operative grids through which *homo europeaus* cumulatively emerges over time.[37] A modular feature disclosed by medieval elaborations is that *race is a response to ambiguity*, especially the ambiguity of identity: for among the "new visions and projects" to which the utility of race answers in this time are the specification of an authorized range of meanings for Latin Christian, European identity; the careful disarticulation of that identity-in-flux from its founding genealogies such as Judaism; and the securing of new moorings – including imperial moorings, launched by crusade and war, diplomacy, missions, and propagandizing – that answer to the ambitions and exigencies of the historical moment.

Cartographic Race: The Freakish, Deformed, and Disabled, or a Racial Map of the World in the Middle Ages

In the project of European identity, one of the most spectacular cultural creations of the medieval period – the *mappamundi,* or world map – hits its stride in the thirteenth century and after as a medium that visually unfolds an imagined universe of space-time which pictures the world in extraordinary ways that reflect on, and concretize, locations of race. A thirteenth-century *mappamundi* such as the richly detailed Hereford map, with its more than 500 pictures, 420 towns, 15 Biblical events, 5 scenes from classical mythology, 33 plants and animals, and 32 peoples of the earth puts on display the "cosmological, ethnographic, geographical, historical, theological and zoological state of the world" (Westrem, *Hereford Map* xv; Edson 142) by marking differences of place through the insertion of distinctive objects, narratives, and peoples that it locates *into* place as stakeholders for the meaning of a site.

For the territories of Europe, place is visualized on the Hereford by architectural features such as fortifications and cathedrals – the built environment of civilized urban centers – and

Figure 6. Western Europe with its cathedrals and fortifications, Hereford world map, Hereford Cathedral, thirteenth century.
Reproduced with permission from the Dean and Chapter of Hereford and the Hereford Mappa Mundi Trust, UK.

bordered by natural features such as rivers (*Figure 6*). Outside Europe, however, geography is often dissected as ethnography, with places being identified as the habitat of human groups made distinct by the attribution of traits to them that are notable by virtue of their difference from normativity in the Latin West. Race is what the rest of the world has: Made visible and projected on a map through a human landscape, it indexes each vector of the world according to its relative distance from Europe in human, as well as spatial, terms. Rendered cartographically, the project of European identity, in surveying the world, sees Europe as the civilized territory of urban life – a web of cities – while global races swarm in other vectors of the world.

In its most grotesque and spectacular forms, cartographic race equates with the monstrous races of semihumans located by the Hereford and other *mappaemundi* in Asia and Africa, and especially the coastline of southern Africa, which in the Hereford arrestingly teems with human monsters of many kinds (*Figure 7*).[38] The depiction of pygmies, giants, hermaphrodites, troglodytes, cynocephali, sciapods, and other part-human, misshapen, deformed, and disabled peoples inherited from classical tradition harnesses the inheritance of the past to a medieval survey and anatomization of the world that reflects on the meaning and borders of European self-identity and civilization.

Scholars such as Scott Westrem ("Against Gog and Magog") and Andrew Gow have found a close association between one particular monstrous race in *mappaemundi* – the unclean race of cannibals that was supposedly enclosed by Alexander the Great behind a barrier of mountains – and medieval Jews, also defined as unclean and monstrous by virtue of the blood libel. The eschatological tradition that the enclosed unclean descendants of Cain would break forth in the last days of the world to war on Christendom – supported by the tangible presence of those enclosed creatures visibly marked on *mappaemundi* – is thus doubly overwritten as a racial script that congeals the same external and internal racial target of accusation and fear.

Therefore, though much has been written about a uniquely different, *medieval* – which is to say, authentically unmodern – sense of the marvelous that celebrated "wondrous diversity" through prolific depictions of freaks and monsters in literature, art, and cartography, the insistence that medieval absorption with freakery and monstrosity is exuberantly different from modern absorption should *not* suggest to us that medieval pleasure should be seen as pleasure of a simply and wholly innocent kind.

Cartographic and imaginary race issued a grid through which European culture perceived and understood the global races and alien nations of the world. The "Monstrous Races tradition," as Debra Strickland puts it, "provided the ideological infrastructure" for ruminating on and understanding "other types of 'monsters,' namely Ethiopians, Jews, Muslims, and Mongols" (42).

Gregory Guzman details how a race of Mongols, issuing from Central Asia, was understood by authors in the Latin West, including Matthew Paris, through a conceptual grid of the monstrous cannibal races of the world and their geographic locations. Equated with cannibalistic monsters cartographically found in northwest Asia are in fact a variety of historical races: Jews (in *Mandeville's Travels*), Mongols (in the *Chronica Majora* of Matthew Paris), and Turks (in the Hereford *mappamundi* [Westrem, *Hereford Map 137*, Map section 4).

Finally, if there is a symbolic evocation on the Hereford of the relationship between race and chaos, it would be located in the largest single edifice on the map: an imposing Tower of Babel, key image in the Biblical narrative of the fabulous origin of proliferating human diversity, and a menacing reminder of incommensurate and unassimilable human difference – an edifice in the East that looms in immensity above the castles and cathedrals of Western Europe.

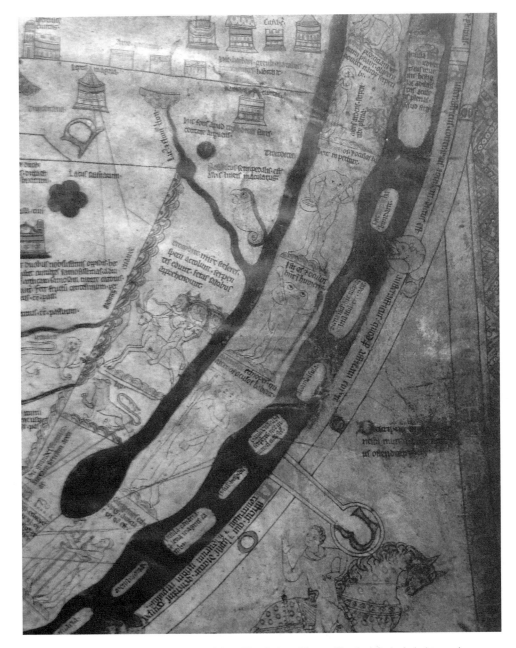

Figure 7. Human monstrosities in southern Africa. Hereford world map, Hereford Cathedral, thirteenth century. Reproduced with permission from the Dean and Chapter of Hereford and the Hereford Mappa Mundi Trust, UK.

Politics of the Neighbor: Race, Conquest, and Colonization within Europe

B ut what of humans *within* Europe who share the most fundamental basis of identity in the Latin West: the European peoples of the Latin rite who are *not* monstrous aliens, nor Jews, Muslims, Mongols, Africans, pagans, heretics, schismatics, nor Greek or Eastern Christians, but neighbors living in proximity and bound by a common Latin Christian faith?

Studies of conquest and colonization in the countries of the "Celtic fringe" – a term ironized by medievalists, and which witnesses the unequal periphery-center relations that bound Wales, Scotland, and Ireland to the metropolitan hub of England – have pointed to English depictions of Celtic barbarity and subhumanness that were standard ideological tropes in England's self-justification for its enterprise of occupying its neighbors.

Reflecting on Wales, Jeffrey Jerome Cohen sums up England's colonial strategy: "An indigenous people are represented as primitive, subhuman, incomprehensible in order to render the taking of their lands unproblematic" ("Hybrids" 87). Though scholars differ on the legacy and intentions of English conquest, few disagree, given the documentary record, that the indigenous colonized were indeed portrayed by England as primitive and even subhuman.

Do such portrayals constitute race-making? A microhistorical example offered by Michael Goodich suggests that in the context of lived relations on the ground, a shared faith can sometimes bridge large enmities. Goodich shows how, in 1290, "when Wales was experiencing the baleful effects of forced colonization and Anglicization" by neighboring England, the attempted execution of a Welsh rebel named William Cragh, who miraculously survived death by hanging – a miracle he and others attributed to St. Thomas of Hereford (d. 1282) – resulted in conciliation between Welsh colonized and English colonizers. Pilgrimage to the English saint's shrine by the subsequently pardoned Welsh ex-rebel, in the company of the local English lord and the lord's wife and household, sealed "public recognition of a shared religious faith which could overcome political differences" (21).

"The religious cult," Goodich concludes, "transcended ... ethnic loyalties" (12), evincing "the power of the faith ... to bring warring groups together .... Despite the destruction inflicted on Swansea and South Wales shortly before" by the English (21). Such Christian amity did not extend to those who were not coreligionists: St. Thomas himself, while bishop of Hereford, had supported the expulsion of Jews from England and confiscation of Jewish property "because they are 'enemies of God and rebels against the faith'" (Goodich 21).[39]

If microhistory suggests that enmity between colonized and colonizers can sometimes be disengaged by a common religion and a shared religious ritual such as pilgrimage, micro-literary example also attests to divisions *not* bridged by a common profession of the Latin Rite. Studies point to how Blind Hary's nationalistic work of the 1470s, *The Wallace*, ferociously insists that *essential differences of blood* fundamentally separate English colonizers from native Scots resisters despite commonality of faith. R. James Goldstein stresses *The Wallace*'s use of "blood as an indicator of both class and race" (237), while Richard J. Moll shows how blood functions less as a genetic or genealogical category in *The Wallace* than as the binding glue of "true Scots" – defined as those who are loyal to the nationalist cause of Scotland's independence, whatever their socioeconomic, personal, or group status (whether highlanders or lowlanders, etc.).[40]

Among neighbors in Latin Christendom, Ireland presents a resonant example of how even commonalities of faith can be adroitly manipulated to subserve colonial interests. English invasion and occupation of Ireland required a theological hermeneutic that insinuated difference of a fundamental kind between the Christianity of the colonized (rendered as inferior, defective, and deviant) and the Christianity of their Anglo-Norman colonizers (assumed as superior and normative).

No less than the magisterial Bernard of Clairvaux in his *Vita Sancti Malachiae* declared the Irish to be "uncivilized in their ways, godless in religion, barbarous in their law, obstinate as regards instruction, foul in their lives: *Christians in name, pagans in fact*" (qtd. in Bartlett, *Gerald of Wales* 169, emphasis added). Given that the Irish members of Latin Christendom were pagans *in fact,* Pope Adrian IV, writing to Henry II of England in 1155, could authorize the English monarch to occupy Ireland – a land that had converted to Christianity a century and a half before England itself – "with a view to enlarging the boundaries of the church ... and for the increase of the Christian religion" (Muldoon, *Identity* 73).[41]

Exposition of a fundamental Irish difference in Christianity is accompanied by the elaboration of Irish socioeconomic difference and Irish cultural differences: Layer upon layer of negative judgments are nested in such a way as to discover a vast civilizational gulf between Ireland and England on a vertical axis of evolutionary development.

Ireland's economic practices of transhumance signified backwardness, evidence that the Irish "have not progressed at all from the primitive habits of pastoral living," as Gerald of Wales, the gifted chronicler and ethnographer who accompanied his Anglo-Norman masters from England to Ireland derisively put it in his *Topographia Hiberniae* (O'Meara 101; Brewer 5: 151).[42] Labor in Ireland is transformed into a condition of lack – moralized as willful laziness and self-indulgence – and assigned to the character of an entire people: "[T]he soil of Ireland would be fertile if it did not lack the industry of the dedicated farmer; but the country has an uncivilized and barbarous people ... lacking in laws and discipline, lazy in agriculture" (William of Newburgh, qtd. by R. R. Davies 124).[43]

> The Irish people are ... a people getting their living from animals alone and living like animals; a people who have not abandoned the first mode of living – the pastoral life. For when the order of mankind progressed from the woods to the fields and from the fields to towns and gatherings of citizens, this people spurned the labors of farming.
>
> (Gerald of Wales, qtd. by Bartlett [*Gerald*] 176)[44]

Even in the Middle Ages, we notice, *modernity* – symbolized by England as a poster child of agricultural cultivation; trade and commerce; urbanization; enlightened laws, usage, and custom; centralized state authority; and even the circulation of coin – is posited against a *premodernity* located in Ireland and rendered as a prior moment of human development that England had long since left behind.

Caricatured as a primitive land – an undeveloped global south lying to the west of England – Ireland was accordingly positioned as a project in need of evolutionary improvement and instruction, in order to force the "savage Irish" ("*irrois savages*" [Lydon, *Lordship* 283]) to emerge one day from their barbaric cocoon into a state of enlightened civilization – an agenda, Robert Bartlett observes, that "would not be out of place in nineteenth-century anthropological thought" (*Gerald* 176).[45]

The logic of evolutionary progress by which colonizers justify their extraterritoriality and craft their right to colonial rule – so much in evidence in later centuries in Africa, India, Southeast Asia, the West and East Indies, the Americas, and elsewhere – is pronouncedly a racial logic, and exercises "the language of colonial racism" (Bhabha 86). Racial logic of the evolutionary kind seems to promise (or even mandate) progress, yet racial logic's ostensible goal of a subject population's achievement of a civilizational maturity which will guarantee their equality with their colonial masters is never attained, but merely floats as a vaunted possibility on an ever-receding horizon.

The not-yet of racial evolutionary logic then becomes perpetual deferment, a "not yet forever" (Ghosh and Chakrabarty 148, 152). Thus we find four centuries later that England's authors – Spenser's *A View of the Present State of Ireland* is especially eloquent – are *still* derisively lamenting the premodern, backward, savage, uncivilized Irish.[46]

"So," R. R. Davies wonders, "what was it . . . about the Irish which persuaded Edmund Spenser that they would never be able to reach that happy state [of English civility]?" (128). The clustering of virulent discourses on the Irish brings into focus processes of racialization that have little to do with skin color, physiognomy, phenotype, genealogy, blood lineage, macrobian zones, or climatology, but point instead to how flexible and resourceful strategies of race-making could be.

The Irish, after all, were Europeans and had converted to Latin Christianity much earlier than their colonizers, and Irish monasticism had famously helped to preserve the cultural record of the Latin West after the dissolution of the Western Roman Empire. Yet "[t]o be *merus Hibernicus* ('pure Irish') meant that one could never be the equal of an Englishman, whether one born in England or in Ireland" (Lydon, *Lordship* 288). Indeed, the Remonstrance of the Irish Princes, written in 1317 and addressed to Pope John XXII, describes how English laity and clergy alike "assert . . . that it is no more sin to kill an Irishman than a dog or any other brute" (qtd. by Lydon, *Lordship* 289, "Nation and Race" 109).[47]

The absence of physiognomic distinction that could enable Christian European groups to be visually distinguished from one another dictated a reliance on other regimes of visual inspection. Pointing to cultural cues to supply visual proofs of deep differences between Irish and English, Gerald of Wales, for one, makes much of the "flowing hair and beards" of the Irish, whose clothing is "made up in a barbarous fashion," and whose warriors "go naked and unarmed into battle" (O'Meara 102, 101; Brewer 5: 153, 5: 151).

But the treacherous slipperiness of cultural markers, which can easily go astray and cue incorrectly, must be arrested, finally, by the force of law. Prohibitions of the infamous 1366 Statutes of Kilkenny – focusing on *both* Irish *and* English populations resident in Ireland – specially target those who, in their outward appearance, their manners, and their mores, enact the uneasy mixing of kinds: Anglo-Irish colonial settlers who have gone native and resemble the native population of Ireland.

Miscegenation – cultural, linguistic, sexual, and marital – is explicitly named in the opening statement of the 1366 legislation as the urgent animating imperative for issuing the Statutes. Enumerating the kinds of mixing that must not occur, the Statutes exhibit a particular distress at nativizing colonials who personify the unnerving difficulty of telling apart colonizers from colonized. The Statutes demand that every Anglo-Irish colonial settler "use the *English* custom, fashion, mode of riding and apparel" (Berry 434–5, emphasis added) because "many English . . . forsaking the English language, fashion, mode of riding, laws and usages, live and govern themselves according to the manners, fashion, and language of the Irish enemies; and also have made divers marriages and alliances between themselves and the Irish enemies" (Berry 430–1).

The Statutes of Kilkenny are rightly identified by scholars as *racial law* – legislating "a racial moment," as Kathy Biddick puts it ("Cut" 453), in "the language of racism," as James

Lydon puts it ("Nation and Race" 106). Yet, issuing centuries after initial colonization, this edict merely ratifies rather than enacts race-making *ab origo*: "[t]he famously discriminatory 1366 Statutes of Kilkenny . . . merely codify a policy long pursued" (Hoffman 7).

Equally haunting is a story told by Gerald of Wales in his *Topographia Hibernia*, an anecdote that drives home both the horrors of miscegenation and the fate of the benighted Irish. Couched as a vignette about an old couple, a man and a woman of Ossory who are outwardly wolves but inwardly human, the story catches the eye of many because of its capacity for poignancy and shock, and for its evocation of the touching devotion of the aged couple and the pathos of their plight. An abbot's curse has caused a human pair to live seven years as wolves; if they survive, the couple is released and replaced by another pair of humans who assume the burden of the curse for the next seven years, and so on, pair by pair, forever.

Narrated in detail and at far greater length than Gerald's cursory accounts of Irish women copulating with goats or Irish men inseminating cows, this allegory of species miscegenation unfolds vividly in our mind's eye as the old male wolf pleads with a priest to bless the female wolf – who is very ill and near death – with last rites and the Host. When the priest performs the rites but withholds communion, the old wolf, to prove that she is human and thus deserving of the Host, uses his paw to peel off the top half of her wolf form, from head down to the navel, shockingly disclosing an old woman beneath.[48]

A woman's body thus proves the humanity of the wolf-couple – sexual difference emerging in the instant of confirming humanity, and issuing as the very ground of confirmation. The human voice alone, emerging from the jaws of a male wolf, has not been adequate to confirm humanness. A woman's face, breasts, and navel are necessary – her navel also presenting proof of human predecessors before her. After she has "devoutly received the sacrament," the skin is folded back again over the woman's humanness, and the two wolves, sharing the priest's fire all night long, depart in the morning, merely the latest pair to endure an unendurable destiny (O'Meara 75, 74, 70–2; Brewer 5: 101–3).

Like the people of Ireland who must bear the burden of imposed subhumanity in perpetuity while striving for admission to full humanity and civilization, the Irish were-wolves of Gerald's story are subhuman in perpetuity and live on the margins of the civilized world, as they ask for the most fundamental gifts of Christian humanity: sacraments and rites. Even if this individual pair survive their seven years of submergence into animalkind, these humans-who-are-wolves continue to be collectively cursed, doomed to subhumanity and outcast status forever. The story's haunting ambience is delivered with wonderful little touches, like the lively presentation of the priest's terrified incredulity, the human speech that startlingly emanates from the male wolf's maw, and the old wolf's desperation as he makes his plea for the dying female.

Finally, though the narrative concludes that "the wolf showed himself . . . to be a man rather than a beast" (72), we are left not with an image of the reassuringly human, nor one of the palpably animal, but with an impression of a profoundly tragic intermixture, and a relentless continuity without end. Through this strange presentation of a story that appeals at the level of affect and intuition, we absorb an allegory of colonial logic rendered as the fearful intermixing of kinds.

Irish appear like savage beasts on the outside, but may really be human under the skin. Their humanity, however, cannot be extricated from their animal nature, and even if some appear Christian, as witnessed by a touching faith in the highest of sacramental rites, the taking of the Host (a faith that confirms the power of those rites over all creation, universally), the Irish – as represented by these unfortunates of Ossory – are in the end tragic beings, mixing dual natures, at best doomed to pity, and forever denied access to full human and civilized status.[49]

The compassion elicited from us by this story and the poignancy that hovers over its narrative arc suggest alternative ways to read even colonial documents, if we attend to the queer residues that exceed the requirements of plot and trajectory. Like the Irish were-wolves, Gerald's text also appears at times to possess dual natures – evincing glimpses, here and there, of a tentative sympathy or wonder that abuts queerly against the more usual vitriol which the text aims at the Irish.

This story of tragic wolf-humans is not the only moment when the empire seems to write back in the interstices of the text or from the textual unconscious. In the annals of colonial documents where anticolonial discourse, oddly secreted in fissures, unexpectedly speaks, Gerald's pithy report of the brief exchange between himself and the Irish Archbishop of Cashel ("a learned and discreet man," says the text) can scarcely be bettered. To Gerald the narrator's complacently superior remark deprecating Irish Christianity for lacking martyrs, given that "no one had ever in that kingdom won the crown of martyrdom in defence of the church of God" before, the Archbishop wryly responds:

> "It is true" he said, "that although our people are very barbarous, uncivilized, and savage, nevertheless they have always paid great honor and reverence to churchmen, and they have never put out their hands against the saints of God. But now a people has come to the kingdom which knows how, and is accustomed, to make martyrs. From now on Ireland will have its martyrs, just as other countries."
>
> (O'Meara 115–16; Brewer 5: 178–9)

The sly civility of this Irish ecclesiastic – adverting to English atrocity to come, and a brave response by Irish resisters, all in the dulcet tones of the colonized but slippery and undefeated subject – belies the very barbarity the Archbishop so readily concedes as the identifying characteristic of his people. Gerald the narrator and Anglo-Norman enthusiast – so often described by scholars as obtuse, humorless, and tone-deaf – deadpans: "the archbishop gave a reply which cleverly got home – although it did not rebut my point" (O'Meara 115; Brewer 5: 178).[50]

In recent years, scholars have increasingly argued that "the experience of the English in Ireland . . . shaped the initial response of the English to the inhabitants of North America" (Muldoon, *Identity* 92):

> justifications contained in the charters that English monarchs granted to colonizers [in North America], echoed the language of the papal documents associated with Henry II's entry into Ireland . . . to the eyes of English colonizers, the Indians with their long flowing hair, deerskin robes, and seminomadic way of life appeared to be living at the same stage of development as the Irish.
>
> (92–3)[51]

Beyond America, Robert Bartlett muses, "the prejudices the English acquired in the course of their colonial experience in Ireland were exported by them and brought to bear on their colonial experience throughout the world" – one result of which, he adds, has been the crafting of "an ideological weapon that has not yet lost its cutting edge" (*Gerald* 177).

Colonial racism of the medieval kind, it would seem, found rich afterlives in the colonial racisms of the postmedieval centuries, as subsequent English empires spread their umbra across the world.

Politics of the Epidermis: Color Differences in the Medieval Sensorium of Race

I have postponed the discussion of color as an index of race to nearly the end of this chapter, partly because color as the paramount signifier of race – the privileged site of race – is too commonly invoked as the deciding factor adjudicating whether racial attitudes and phenomena existed in premodernity, and my preference has been to emphasize multiple, rather than singular, locations of race. But the desire to redistribute attention away from the-epidermal-as-race is also prompted by a recognition that color has a specific resilience in the Middle Ages that overdetermines its coding in some contexts of medieval thinking about difference in which color is called into service.

This is *not at all to cast doubt* that a hierarchical politics of color, centering with precision on the polarity of black and white, existed and is in evidence across the multitude of texts and artifacts, sacred and secular, that descends to us. It is rather to suggest that color is exercised over a range of genres – sermons, letters, romances, chronicles, sculpture, painting, encyclopedias, maps – as a special resource with the ability, *under specific hermeneutic conditions*, to switch between alternate valencies afforded by religious epistemology, in order that it might answer satisfactorily to variable demands.

For instance: Color as a marker of difference answers with precise responsiveness to the demands of the central conceptual paradoxes on which medieval theological Christianity thrives, and on which it is constituted. Color can be deployed conventionally in Christian texts to signal the polar difference between sacred and demonic – as I duly noted at the beginning of this chapter. But color can also be flexibly deployed to underscore the recuperability and pivotal centrality of sin, sinfulness, and the sinner in the salvational narrative of redemption that is the cornerstone of Christian thinking.

Indeed, the importance of sin – whose color is black – in salvational theology often leads, in medieval modes of religious expression, to what David Wallace wittily calls "competitive abjection" between sinners self-proclaimed. Since the condition of being more-sinful-than-thou, and thus more-abject-than-thou, signals the potentiating likelihood of being more-saved-than-thou, and ascending to greater heights of ultimate grace – so much does God love the worst sinners, who are the most abject of all – possessing blackness, *at least in theory and in imagination*, is not always a bad thing. Thus it is possible for the great Bernard of Clairvaux, in his Sermon 25 on the Song of Songs, only half-playfully to refer to Jesus, who among humans has the greatest access to the highest grace (his self-sacrifice being the ultimate abjection), as "obviously black" and "black but beautiful" (Walsh 56).[52]

Should this signal to us that color discourse in the twelfth century of St. Bernard is so unstable that the value of a color such as black can be made to tip over readily into its opposite? Or should we find ourselves cued, instead, to understand that paradoxical play with color is only possible when a signifying field has stabilized to the point that enables such play, and to the degree that allows paradox to be performed? If the contemplation of color polarities affords intellectual pleasures of wit and paradox for the great theological

Figure 8. Statue of the Black St. Maurice of Magdeburg. Magdeburg Cathedral, Germany, 1220–1250. Reproduced with permission from the Menil Foundation, Houston; Hickey and Robertson, Houston; and Harvard University's Image of the Black Project.

minds of the Middle Ages, similar and different kinds of pleasure, consolation, and reassurance are discernible in other modalities of contemplation.

For instance, statuary in thirteenth-century Magdeburg in Germany and regions under the influence of Magdeburg depicting a black African St. Maurice, martyr of the Theban legions under a persecutory Rome (*Figure 8*), has long elicited the interest of art historians, who have reached for explanations as to why a black African saint should be venerated in certain sites of the German empire despite a virulent discourse on blackness and the ubiquity of a white St. Maurice elsewhere in Europe, especially in England and France.

These explanations have variously invoked the politics of the German empire under Frederick II, the machinations of archbishops responsible for commissioning architecture in which the Black St. Maurice appears, and the freedom of thirteenth-century German artisans to invent and fantasize as they wished, while such artistic freedoms were denied to craftsmen in places such as France because of the rapid entrenchment of rigid artistic models and traditions.[53]

By and large, however, considerations of German exceptionalism in the politics of color have not yet engaged with the circuits of pleasure – the consolation, identification, play, and reassurance – that can be apotropaically tapped with the acceptance and welcome, publicly and in contexts of privacy and intimacy, of imaginative representations like that of Maurice: beautiful and comforting renditions of what might otherwise be deemed frightening or malign in other historical contexts.[54]

Private, intimate acceptance and welcome of an otherness signaled by color may be easier to imagine sympathetically when a discourse on color intersects with fantasies of sexuality and gender, even if such acceptance and welcome appear more opaque in religious devotion.

In one of his letters to his wife Heloise, Peter Abelard comments on the blackness of the Ethiopian bride of Canticles in a fairly conventional exposition of the meaning of color (with black standing for disfigurement, shame, and adversity), but suddenly swerves off on a provocative tangent to contemplate the *pleasures* afforded by color in sexed and bodied form, especially when enjoyed and relished in privacy: "it often happens that the flesh of black women is all the softer to touch . . . and for this reason the pleasure they give is greater and more suitable for private than for public enjoyment, and their husbands take them into a bedroom to enjoy them rather than parade them before the world" (Radice 140).[55]

Here, there are fewer obstacles to understanding why black is beautiful under the circumstances, even in a historical context of color virulence. Nothing in the trajectory of forbidden desire outlined by Peter Abelard is novel to any who have read postmedieval literatures of empire or slavery, or have followed the modern-day saga of Strom Thurmond or the historical saga of Thomas Jefferson with any attentiveness.

Vacillations in the field of color would thus suggest the availability of medieval color discourse to strategies of meaningful play, especially in the rarefied symbolic realms of religious subtlety and religious theology, and in the sphere of the fantasmatic: play that otherwise leaves undisturbed hierarchical alignments of color and race. Having said that, I have also argued that a critical shift in our attention to color is timely, to make visible what has been invisible in the field of the specular: the ascension of *whiteness* to supremacy as a category of identity in the definition of the Christian European subject.[56]

For it would be true to say that race makes an appearance in the Middle Ages not only through fantasmatic blackness, Jews, Saracens, Mongols, Africans, Indians, Chinese, tribal islanders, "Gypsies," indigenes in the Americas, and the collections of freakish and deformed humans pressing upon the edges of the civilized world, but is also to be found at the center of things, in the creation of that strange creature who is nowhere yet everywhere in cultural discourse: the white Christian European in medieval time. Seven hundred years after the Hereford, Duchy of Cornwall, and Psalter maps of the world had located monstrous races in southern Africa, there would indeed be a race of human monsters practicing monstrosity in the name of apartheid in South Africa, and the color of that monstrous race, as it turns out, was *not* black.

Notes

1 For the text of Canon 68, see Schroeder 584. For summaries of English rulings, see Roth (*History*) 95–6. On the badge in Europe, see Grayzel 68–9. The literature on medieval English Jews is vast. Adler, Richardson, Roth (*History*), and Mundill provide standard points of entry. England was the first to expel its Jewish population; in 1496, Portugal was the last (France expelled and readmitted Jews several times in the Middle Ages, and only permanently in 1394).

2 For massacres in Germany, see Eidelberg. Chroniclers documenting Jewish slaughter at Richard I's coronation include Richard of Devizes 3–4; Roger of Howden 3: 33–34, Roger of Wendover 1: 176–7, and William of Newburgh 1: 308–10, 564–71.

3 Trachtenberg surveys several traditions, including Jewish possession of horns, a tail (44–52), and a goat's beard (46). Biller examines how a male menses or hemorrhoidal flow is established in thirteenth-century University of Paris theological quodlibets ("Christian or 'Scientific'?" and "A 'Scientific' View"); Ziegler (187) tracks the flux in texts of physiognomy; see Marcus on the relationship of the "bloody flux" to Passion Friday ("Images" 250). Johnson offers the fullest account of how Christian political theology accrues in stages the fiction of the bloody flow. Biller ("Proto-Racial Thought" 177) offers Caesarius of Heisterbach and Berthold of Regensburg ("*ein stinkender Jude*") on the smell of Jews, and Matthew Paris on the Jewish face ("*facies Judaica*"); see also Marcus on Caesarius' depiction of the "evil odour" ("Images" 255). For Jewish phenotypes and somatic features in medieval art, see Mellinkoff I: 127–9 and Strickland 95–155. Blood libels insist that Jews need Christian blood, especially for Passover rites, which is one reason for the ritual murder of Christian children (the flux efficiently overdetermines this: Blood is also needed because Jewish men are supposed to bleed congenitally). See note 28 for fuller documentation.

4 See Seymour et al. 2: 752–3, 763. Ranulph Higden's *Polychronicon* has a similar formulation (Babbington and Lumby 1: 50–3); ethnographic polarities based on phenotype, biomarkers, and color are also posited by texts on physiognomy. Biller ("Proto-Racial Thought") surveys the more influential medieval encyclopedias and medical texts describing how color and biomarkers reveal the moral, psychological, and intellectual character of human groups.

5 See Devisse 72–9 for conventions depicting the Baptist's executioner and Christ's torturers as black Africans. *Figure 1* is from Devisse 74; *Figure 2* from 92; *Figure 3* from 71. On romance, see, e.g., Heng, *Empire of Magic*; Metlitzki, chapter 6. On *chansons de geste*, see, e.g., Daniel, *Heroes and Saracens*; de Weever.

6 My discussion of why race has been located exclusively in modernity merely points to a blind spot in academic culture. Needless to say, it does not detract from the value of, and my admiration for, the work of these and other authors on modern race. I also apologize for naming representative exemplars here: The scholarship on race is vast, and rather than devote this chapter to summarizing more than half a century's work in race theory and critical race studies, I offer exemplars whose studies include extensive bibliographies that can be consulted as starting points.

7 Kwame Anthony Appiah's 1990 "Race," opposing *biology*, in high modernist racism, to *theology* in preracial premodernity, is still widely cited in (especially undergraduate) courses on race. A keynote by Balibar ("Election/Selection") for a 2003 University of California Humanities Research Institute conference, "tRaces: Race, Deconstruction, Critical Theory," shows how little has changed in race theory, despite deconstruction, when it maintains that "the biological" is to racism what "the theological" is to "pre-Modern discriminations," thus continuing race studies' habit of separate and cordoned-off polar oppositions (Balibar, "Election/Selection" 2).

8 I owe the impetus for the following arguments on temporalities, premodernity, and modernity to Stoler's marvelous reading of origins in her "Racial Histories." Quotations are from p. 191.

9 Stoler, *Race and the Education of Desire* 73; Goldberg, *Racist Culture*, "masks," p. 61ff.; see also Goldberg's important formulations on cultural race, "ethnorace," and the "ethnoracial" (70–8).

10 For a trenchant critique of Western exceptionalism and grand narratives of scientific transformation, see Hart ("Explanandum," *Civilizations*, *Algebra*). See especially Biagioli, Terrall, Galison, and Stump on the Scientific Revolution and Goldstone on the Industrial Revolution and multiple economic and demographic modernities. Also useful is the symposium on "Eurocentrism, Sinocentrism and World History" in *Science and History*. In the past three or four decades, euromedievalists have also critiqued the modern/premodern divide, most recently under the rubric of "periodization." For an influential early example, see Jauss. Haskin's 1927 volume on the "renaissance" of the twelfth century may perhaps also be seen as a precursor moment. Among other important issues, euromedievalist critiques have focused attention on literary history (Summit and Wallace), "neo-medievalism" in political writing (Lampert[-Weissig], "Race, Periodicity, and the (Neo-) Middle Ages"; Holsinger), stories of reading and queer relationalities (Dinshaw), epistemologies of feudalism and sovereignty (Kathleen Davis), and the politics of knowledge and disciplinary formations (Biddick, *Typological*).

11 For other comparisons between eleventh-century Song China and eighteenth-century Europe, see Hartwell's "Revolution" 155. Much scholarly work decentering the West has, of course, been inspired by Joseph Needham's magisterial studies on the history of science, and in particular on Chinese science and technology. Rondo Cameron, Eric Jones, and Jan de Vries dismiss an Industrial Revolution in the West or qualitative distinctions between modern and premodern growth (Goldstone 327). For David Levine and Alexander Woodside (Goldstone 331), Michael Mann and Alan McFarlane (Goldstone 347), "modern" growth began in the early or high Middle Ages. Janet Abu-Lughod's *Before European Hegemony* also remains invaluable.

12 I elaborate the politics of temporality more fully in "Holy War Redux." For the strategic value of studying the deep past in postcolonial and global studies in the academy today, see my "Reinventing Race."

13 Medievalists, however, have long been interested in questions of race. Earlier scholarship conjured with "the Celtic races," "Germanic stock," "Indo-Europeans," "the Anglo-Saxon race," *inter alia*, as more than contingently heuristic categories, and discussed relationships between ethnicity, lineage, tribe, *natio*, *gens*, blood, linguistic affiliations, ties to territory, etc. For an example of more recent thinking on Anglo-Saxons, race, and ethnogenesis, see Harris. Twenty-first-century scholarship on medieval race has tended increasingly to focus on non-Christians or non-Europeans such as Muslims, on blackness and fantasmatic Africans in literature and art, and on Jews. For examples of recent euromedievalist work, see Hahn's special issue of the *Journal of Medieval and Early Modern Studies* on race and ethnicity (discussed presently), Lynn Ramey (*Black Legacies*), and Cord Whitaker's special issue of *postmedieval* entitled "Making Race Matter in the Middle Ages." Studies of "otherness" and "difference" are also on the rise, and may or may not invoke race/ ethnicity in discussing "internal foreigners" such as Hungarians (e.g., Hoffman, Sager), "the Celtic fringe" (e.g., Lydon ["Nation and Race," *Lordship*], Lilley, Knight, Moll, Muldoon [*Irish Frontier*]), or preconversion pagan eastern Europe, or Spain (e.g., Mariscal, Kagay, Hoffman, Nirenberg). Importantly, medievalists have shown that studying the Middle Ages reconfigures our understanding of key contemporary concepts such as gender, sexuality, national formations, and even literacy. Race should prove little exception.

14 Foundational historiography's exclusions make Colin Richmond wonder why the Oxford don H. E. Salter's *Medieval Oxford* "ignored [the Jews]"; why "less than three pages" mention Jews in Michael Prestwich's magisterial 567-page volume on Edward I, a volume that amply considers Edward's treatment of the Welsh and Scots; and why James Holt's *Magna Carta* dismisses "the anti-Jewish *clauses 10* and *11* as 'superficial'" (222). Concluding that "non-Jewish historians ignored

the Jews" (214), Richmond wonders if medieval Jews upset the myth of an English England: "The history of the Jews in England enables us to see that [an English England] is myth ... Is this not why the Jewish history of England is not taught in schools – because it is a type of anti-history as perceived by those who finally determine national curricula?" (221). Kathy Lavezzo's *Accommodated Jew* discusses the debt of England's architecture to medieval English Jewry. English historiography, of course, is by no means unique: Menocal astutely remarks, e.g., of medieval Spain: "*Spaniard* is implicitly defined in racial and religious terms. The Cid is a Spaniard, but Ibn Hazm and Maimonides are not; they are an Arab and Jew respectively" (284 n.17).

15 In contrast to foundational historiography, there exists a large and rapidly growing body of scholarship on medieval English Jews that furnishes ample material for counternarratives and alternative histories of England. Studies range from Anglo-Saxon England's conceptual understanding of Jews and Judaism before the eleventh-century post-Conquest arrival of Jews (e.g., Scheil, and Zacher's edited volume) to careful analysis of records of taxation and tallages, registries of debt and financial transactions, trials and imprisonment records, civic and municipal documents, laws and statutes (e.g., Stacey, "Parliamentary Negotiation"; Rokéah; Roth, *Oxford*; Dobson, *York*; Lipman; Hillaby, "Testimony from the Margin"), the political implications of manuscript and codicological artifacts (Bale, *The Jew in the Medieval Book*), and the economic and political bases of expulsion (e.g., Mundill; Abrahams; Menache, "Faith, Myth, and Politics"), among many kinds of archival scrutiny. Literary interpretation of how Jews are portrayed in medieval literature – an endeavor not irrelevant to historiography – is also a large, riveting, and expanding field, and can be bibliographically rendered by subject, genre, author, and *topoi*.

16 Though the focus of this book is the medieval West, this focus in no way suggests that the rest of the world – in premodernity or after – is free of fault in race matters, or innocent in its treatment of minorities and others. This clarification seems necessary to repeat, and is made in response to those who have expressed concern with projects that appear to "blame the West, and not the rest."

17 Snowden, for example, has argued at length that antiquity is a time "before color prejudice." The work of the few named here constitutes examples of studies on antiquity that have appeared in recent years, and that with growing frequency conjure with categories of ethnicity and race. Also important is the work of Martin Bernal's *Black Athena*, despite controversies of scholarship (see Lefkowitz and Rogers; Bernal, *Black Athena Writes Back*) and Jonathan Hall (though Hall's category of choice is "ethnicity"). The wonderful term "deep time" is Dimock's (3).

18 The Introduction in Eliav-Feldon et al. discusses examples of those who believe that the key determinant to whether we can discuss race and racisms in the Middle Ages is what medieval peoples thought about their own identity and behavior. The insistence that the word "race" must first exist in European languages prior to racial phenomena and practices has also led to disagreements over where the term first appears. De Miramon, arguing against common belief that Iberia is where the word "race" first issues, finds late-fifteenth-century French poems to be the earliest provenance. He also finds that the sorting of kinds performed by the word closely relates race to nobility and noble blood.

19 See e.g., Buell; Heng (*Empire of Magic*, chapters 2 and 4; "Invention of Race ... 1" and "Invention of Race ... 2"; "Reinventing Race"); Lampert "Race"; Ziegler.

20 See also Chakrabarty, in Ghosh and Chakrabarty 165, on "homologies between racism and [religious] communalism." Fredrickson wavers on whether premodern race exists and whether religion can constitute racial discourses. He outlines conditions through which anti-Judaism becomes anti-Semitism and anti-Semitism becomes racism (19), which seems to allow for the possibility of premodern race, given the fulfillment of his conditions. But Fredrickson also confusingly concludes that only "the racial antisemitism of the modern era" (23) constitutes racism in "full flower" (47) since the "supernaturalist racism" (46) of the "late medieval and early modern periods" was "primarily religious rather than naturalistic or scientific" (46) and "racism had to be emancipated from Christian universalism" first (47).

21 The three contemporaneous Latin chronicles recording the incident are: Matthew Paris's *Chronica Majora* (Luard, *Mathaei Parisiensis* 5: 516–19, 546, 552); the annals of Burton-on-Trent (Luard, *Annales monastici* 1: 340–8); and Waverley annals (Luard, *Annales monastici* 2: 346–8). For the Anglo-Norman ballad, see Michel 1–16 and Dahood, "Anglo-Norman 'Hugo de Lincolnia'." Hillaby, "Ritual-Child-Murder" (107 n.90) lists sources for the 1911 pamphlet. Chapter 2 closely examines the Anglo-Norman ballad and Chaucer's *Prioress's Tale*.

22 See David Carpenter's two-part study for the reconstruction of events. The records vary in incidental details, as is common with medieval texts – e.g., Matthew Paris puts the child at eight ("*octo annos*," [Luard, *Mathaei Parisiensis* 5: 516]), while the Burton annals call him "a tiny boy of nine years" ("*puerum parvulum ix. annorum*" [Luard, *Annales monastici* 1: 340]) – but not in their narrative trajectory or plot purposefulness.

23 Invented in England, the accusation spread to France, then Germany, Spain, and Italy (Hillaby, "Ritual-Child-Murder" 98–102). Seven English shrines were raised to boy martyrs murdered by Jews, three of which – at Norwich, Bury, and Lincoln – survived to the Reformation. Four had already appeared by the middle of the thirteenth century (Langmuir, "Knight's Tale" 463). Hugh's "was the most popular of all the English pilgrimage sites . . . after that of [Thomas] Becket at Canterbury" (Hillaby, "Ritual-Child-Murder" 96), drawing "extraordinary nationwide interest" (Hillaby, "Ritual-Child-Murder" 7).

24 *Encyclopaedia Judaica* 4: 1122, 6: 748; Langmuir, "Knight's Tale" 462–3; Stacey, "From Ritual Crucifixion to Host Desecration" 23; Adler 185–6; and Hillaby ("Ritual-Child-Murder"). Hillaby ("Ritual-Child-Murder") discusses the boy martyrs William of Norwich, Harold of Gloucester, Robert of Bury, Stephen of Winchester, and Hugh of Lincoln. Stacey ("Ritual Crucifixion") treats Adam of Bristol, and Langmuir ("Thomas of Monmouth") William of Norwich. See also McCulloh on the early years of the accusation.

25 Executions also occurred in Northampton in 1279: "The chronicle of Bury St. Edmunds describes how 'a boy was crucified by the Jews on the Day of the Adoration of the Holy Cross (Good Friday), but was not quite killed. Notwithstanding, numbers of the Jews were torn to pieces by horses in London and hung, immediately after Easter, under this pretext'" (Hillaby, "Ritual-Child-Murder" 94). See Chapter 2 for a comparative examination of four tales, written before and after the Expulsion, grouped around the theme of Hugh of Lincoln and/or Jewish child murder.

26 Away from the mainland, the state of Hawaii had its own internment camps at Sand Island and Honouliuli. As we have noted, AIDS hysteria in 1980s America saw suggestions that gay communities should also be rounded up and cordoned off from the population, in an updated version of internment-quarantine. In addition to tagging and herding Jews, a suggestion was also mooted in medieval England to intern Jews on an island. In 2016, the presidential candidate Donald Trump's proposal of a database for surveillance of all 3.3 million Muslims in the United States astonishingly recalled medieval England's surveillance of Jews through the bureaucratic database created by the special branch of government known as the Jewish Exchequer. Racial homologies across deep time thus seem to accrue around internments and surveillance, actual and anticipated, and perhaps offer ways of "seeing [the medieval] as contemporary with the present," a perspective in which the medieval continues to exist as "an ever-present possibility that haunts the practices of the modern" (Chakrabarty 110).

27 Spain's persecutions of Jews, because of their scale and lateness, are better known to modernists and race theorists than England's, though Stacey and others note that Spain's unique history – of a polyglot, hybridized social matrix, intermingling Arabs, Berbers, Jews, Visigoths, Basques, and a slew of other communities in mixed languages and cultures, leavened by occupation and warfare from the eighth to the fifteenth centuries – means that Spain is less paradigmatic of the rest of Europe. Stacey enumerates several ways in which England's Jews paralleled Jewish populations elsewhere in Ashkenazi Europe ("Twelfth-Century" 340–2). Edwards sums up the views of many: "it is not possible to separate England from the mainland of Western Europe in the period

1066–1290" (94). Skinner suggests that "the really exceptional feature of the Jews in England . . . is how intensively they were recorded by the state" (2).

28 The scholarship is enormous; the few studies listed here offer some points of entry. Trachtenberg, as noted above, surveys several traditions, including the tarring of Jews with infernal diabolism (11–31), bestiality (187), and sorcery (57–87). See also Bonfil's broad survey on Jews and the devil. Note 3 surveys the literature on a male menses or hemorrhoidal flow, the smell of Jews, the Jewish face, and Jewish phenotypes and somatic features in medieval art.

On Jewish carnality, see Anna Sapir Abulafia ("Bodies," "Carnality"). Blood libels insist that Jews need Christian blood (see note 3 above), and cannibalism may join Jewish vampirism (Langmuir *Antisemitism* 263–81): In 1235, thirty-four Jews at Fulda were killed for the deaths of boys for blood-use (264), while in 1247 German Jews were accused of eating "the heart of a murdered child while solemnizing Passover" (265). The plot of host desecration says Jews steal consecrated hosts to re-perform their deicide of Christ (see Rubin, "Desecration," "Eucharist," and *Gentile Tales*), who may materialize as a beautiful child in the host itself (Sinanoglou).

Frey traces how Jews turn into servants of the Antichrist in Christian eschatology, and Gow draws out the implications of this for the envisaged ultimate destruction of Christendom. On the role of Jews in the political hermeneutics of medieval theology, see especially Jeremy Cohen ("High Medieval Theology"), Chazan, Dahan (*"Juifs et judaisme"*), Anna Sapir Abulafia ("Theology and the Jews"), and Lotter, in Jeremy Cohen (*Witness*). Figural manipulations of Jews and Jewish presence/absence are also analyzed in a growing body of studies: For a (non-exhaustive) selection, see Tomasch (on the "virtual" Jew), Kruger ([*Jew*] on the "spectral" Jew), Jeremy Cohen (*Living Letters* [on the "hermeneutical" Jew], and "Synagoga" [on the "eschatological" Jew]), Dahan (*Les intellectuels chrétiens* [on the "theological" Jew, *"le juif théologique"*]), Despres ("[Jew]" on the "protean" Jew), and Biddick ([*Typological*] on "paper Jews").

29 My quick sketch of an overarching architecture cannot, of course, do justice to the complexities and shifting dynamics of what I've called the long thirteenth century, and serves merely to isolate some factors that figure in race-formation. Since history has jagged edges, some have detected an epistemic shift that begins earlier: Moore's study of intolerance – the development of "a persecuting society" – *ends* with the thirteenth century as the culminating point (*Formation*). In the thirteenth century's intensification of surveillance and persecution, especially of Jews, Jeremy Cohen (*Friars*) assigns a primary role to the mendicant orders. On Innocent III's Jewish policies, see Tolan, "Of Milk and Blood." For the narrowing of attitudes and changes in law with vicious consequences for alternative sexualities see Boswell; Mark Jordan tracks the invention of sodomy in this time. The Fourth Lateran Council's massive expansion of canon law in 1215 – more than thrice the decrees of Lateran I, and more than double those of any council of the previous century – meant that canon law, as one scholar put it, "cover[ed] most areas of life" (Tentler 117), strengthened church dominance, and "entailed a level of power which insinuated itself into the heart of secular life" (Tambling 38).

Muldoon's survey of Vatican registers (*Popes, Lawyers, and Infidels*) discerns marked shifts of several kinds. In the late eleventh century, in 1076, two decades before the crusades, a letter from Pope Gregory VII to a Muslim ruler in North Africa expatiates with apparent generosity on shared commonalities between Muslim and Christian monotheisms: "we who believe in and profess the one God, although we do so in different ways, daily praise and worship Him Who is the creator and ruler of this world" (Muldoon, *Popes* 39). By the late thirteenth century, however, the "blurring of distinctions between various non-Christians seems part of a general process of reducing the world to two classes of people, those within the Church and those outside of it" (Muldoon, *Popes* 52).

30 "In the thirteenth century 'the overall strategy of Christendom underwent modification': the battle now was not only military but doctrinal'" (Burns 1387). Muldoon (*Popes*) traces the efforts of some sixteen popes in the thirteenth century and half a dozen in the fourteenth to extend the purview of

the papacy and Latin Christianity to North Africa, Eurasia, eastern Europe, India, and China through a range of initiatives, from conversionist preaching to papal fiefs, from papal treaties to economic threat. This is not to say, of course, that the hope of expanding Christendom's borders and purview through crusade and military adventure ended: Crusading history shows how, even after the last major gathering of international forces foundered at Nicopolis in 1396, the practice and ideology of crusading did not die (Atiya, *Nicopolis*). On late-medieval crusading, see Atiya, *Later Middle Ages.*

31 "As early as 1235 the master-general [of the Dominican friars], writing from Milan to all the order, called for men 'prepared to learn Arabic, Hebrew, Greek, or some other outlandish language'" for programs of conversion (Burns 1402). An early fourteenth-century polemical tract by Pierre Dubois envisages training *women* in foreign languages, theology, and medicine for missionary work: "Pierre Dubois accorded girls an equal place with boys in the schools which he proposed should be founded for the education of a generation which should convert the East ... Like the boys the girls were to be highly educated in the languages which they would need ... trained in medical skills ... especially in those skills needed to deal with women's ills, so that they might then proceed to their conversion ... the girls were also to be trained in theology, since they would need to be able to instruct the women in the tenets of the Christian faith" (Purcell 61). See also David Abulafia ("Monarchs and Minorities" 236).

　　Abulafia finds that whereas in 1293 the Dominican Raymond Llull "had been trying to persuade Pope Celestine V to encourage missions to the Muslims, Mongols, and other nations beyond the Latin frontiers," after 1293 Llull took to organizing conversionist preaching in mosques and synagogues *within* Christendom instead ("Monarchs and Minorities" 242). Abulafia examines the argument that the destruction of Muslim communities inside Europe – Lucera in southern Italy in 1300 and Spanish Minorca in 1287 – and the 1289 expulsion of Jews from Anjou and Maine meant that where mass conversions were impracticable, deportation or enslavement were resorted to instead.

32 "In the 1260s Roger Bacon hungrily eyed the multitudes of Muslims, Mongols, Buddhists, and pagans ripe for conversion ... Thirteenth-century crusading popes like Honorius III, Gregory IX, and Innocent IV encouraged conversion of Muslims by persuasion [and] from time to time the program tended to focus on a promising princely candidate" (Burns 1391). Innocent IV (1243–54), canonist initiator of embassies to the Mongols, developed the theoretical basis for papal interventions worldwide: "the pope's responsibility for the souls of all men, Christian and non-Christian alike, justified papal intervention in the functioning of infidel societies" (Muldoon, *Popes* 9) and "authorized him to send missionaries into their lands to instruct the nonbelievers in the proper way of worshiping God. Should an infidel ruler block the entry of peaceful Christian missionaries, the pope could order him to admit them or face an invasion by Christian armies" (Muldoon, *Popes* 11). Innocent's carefully argued conceptual frame for international relations did not, however, allow for reciprocity and "the right of infidels to send peaceful missionaries into Christian lands" because "The Muslim faith could not be treated as the equal of the Christian faith, and so its missionaries could not be treated as Christian missionaries ought to be, 'because they are in error and we are on the righteous path'" (Muldoon, *Popes* 14). The pope could also judge infidels who violated natural law (the worship of idols constituted one such violation).

　　In Europe itself, Innocent IV and his predecessor Gregory IX (1227–41) ordered the public burning of the Talmud. Nicholas IV (1288–92) renewed ties with Christians living in North Africa and Ethiopia; Boniface VIII (1294–303) granted two islands off Tunis to Roger Doria, the Sicilian admiral who captured them, as a papal fief in 1295 (Muldoon, *Popes* 54–5). Though papal vassals had held papal fiefs for centuries, "In accepting and legitimizing Doria's African conquests, Boniface was extending beyond Europe the traditional papal policy with regard to newly conquered or converted regions" (Muldoon, *Popes* 55). Extensive studies exist on the international relations, embassies, ethnographic accounts, field reports, papal and missionary letters, diplomatic missions, and explorations of this period. For a selection, see Dawson; de Rachewiltz (*Papal Envoys*); Fernández-Armesto; Moule; Muldoon (*Popes*); Setton.

33 Biller ("Christian or 'Scientific',?" "A 'Scientific' View of Jews," "Black Women," "Proto-Racial Thought") emphasizes the power of medieval scientific discourses in shaping medieval racisms; Ziegler, who also considers scientific texts, finds religion and theology to be larger forces in race-formation (198).

34 The status of Muslims in medieval race – Muslims being the primary contestants of Western interests in the international arena in commercial, military, and political spheres, as well as formidable religious opponents on whom the Latin West depended for critical translations and interpretations of knowledge and culture – deserves more attention than can be encompassed here. I treat Muslims in Chapter 3 and in the sections of Chapter 6 devoted to Marco Polo and *Mandeville's Travels*.

35 On medieval-style nations (*not* eighteenth-century nation-*states*), see, e.g., Forde, Johnson, and Murray; Bjørn, Grant, and Stringer; Turville-Petre; Heng, *Empire of Magic* chapters 2 and 4; and Lavezzo, *Imagining*. Judith Ferster made the astute remark, in one audience discussion of my argument here, that if one were to track the expulsions of Jews country-by-country across medieval Europe, one would likely be able to establish how early or how late a country underwent nation formation, and thus gather a map of comparative medieval nationalisms. Stacey ("Medieval English State") relates the treatment of Jews to the growth of the English state. Or, as Dobson asks, "is it altogether a coincidence ... that the Jews were expelled *en masse* from England at the very point of time which witnessed ... *le genèse de l'état moderne?*" ("Jewish Women" 167).

36 Dress is instrumental to both universalizing and partitioning drives in this period. Within Europe, Canon 68 facilitates a partitioning drive by instructing religious and lay rulers to mark off their internal Jewish and Muslim minorities from the Christian majority by a difference of dress. Outside Europe, converts to Christianity were instructed *not* to alter their dress, so that a Christian minority living within a non-Christian majority would not be visibly marked off. Thus Pope Nicholas IV (1288–92) instructed the newly converted Nicholas, Mongol son of the Ilkhan Arghun and a convert to whom the Pope had given his own name, "to refrain from insisting that ... converts make significant changes in the external style of their lives, and pointed especially to changes in dress as something to avoid ... The pope's suggestion was to emphasize that one could be both a Christian and a Tartar" (Muldoon, *Popes* 67).

37 Though the formulation here may seem novel, it builds on the insights of others. Moore, for instance, argues that "the persecution of Jews, and the growth not only of anti-Judaism but of anti-Semitism, were quite central to the developments which taken together I choose to describe, without the faintest tincture of originality, as the birth of Europe" ("Anti-Semitism" 53). On the role played by Muslims and Islam in the creation of "Europe" and *homo europaeus*, see, e.g., Mastnak.

38 For *Figure 6*, see Westrem, *Hereford Map*, Map section 10. Section 1 has northeast Asia's monstrous humans; section 5 the one-legged Monoculi of India; section 6 the web-footed Tigolopes of West Asia; sections 8 and 11 (*Figure 7*) the bestial and deformed races of southern Africa (also seen in Harvey 48). The Duchy of Cornwall map fragment also shows human monsters in Africa; even the tiny Psalter map – nine centimeters across – expends precious space depicting monstrous humans on the south African coast: see Delano-Smith and Kain 39, and Edson's Plates II and VI.

39 However, Goodich reports that "there is also evidence that during his lifetime Thomas of Hereford did not always act as an impartial figure" toward the Welsh. Thomas "didn't speak Welsh," and after Thomas' death, canonization records show that "most of those wounded soldiers aided through invocation of the saint were Englishmen fighting against the Welsh" (20–1). Goodich's microhistory may perhaps be most usefully seen in its immediate context as an important parallel, among warring Christians, to interreligious hostilities wherein an individual

churchman, castellan, pope, or German emperor prevents the massacre of Jews or the looting of Jewish property, though such rescues may not have been aggregated with sufficient frequency and dispersion to form a pattern of widespread incidence over the centuries.

40 *The Wallace* may perhaps be seen as offering an example of medieval *"racialism,"* a species of race-making by the victimized that enables the victimized to define and racialize themselves positively against powerful oppressors wielding negative racial discourses against them (i.e., "racism" in the familiar sense). See Chapter 7 on the Romani, another example. Critical race studies distinguishes between such racial self-descriptions by the marginalized or oppressed and othering descriptions exercised by powerful and metropolitan forces (see, e.g., Goldberg, *Racist Culture* 72; Appiah, "Racisms" 5).

Richard Hoffman also argues at length that the Scots in the late Middle Ages and early Renaissance theorized fundamental divisions among *their own peoples* – divisions that amount to de facto race-making – between highlanders and lowlanders. Hoffman cites John of Fordun in 1387 and John Major in 1521 as examples: "Late fourteenth and early fifteenth century Lowland literature pictured the Highlander as an outlandish character, at once a figure of fun and of menace . . . Highlanders hated and persecuted English-speaking Lowlanders no less than they did the real English" (8). Hoffman analyzes these internal divisions as de facto constructions of race and class. His description of internal race-making in Scotland thus seems to resonate with Foucault's description of the genesis of race in Europe in class war (located, for Foucault, in modernity – not in the medieval period).

41 Irish variation in liturgical practice, degrees of consanguinity in marriage, calendrical marking of the liturgical year, etc., became grist for the mill of theorizing the Irish as "pagans in fact," even if, as Muldoon observes, "the existence of a distinctive Irish liturgy and of various adapt[at]ions to the local culture was not unique in the early Middle Ages . . . until the twelfth century there was wide variation in liturgical practice within the Christian Church" (*Identity* 70).

42 Translations of Gerald of Wales's *Topographia Hiberniae* (Topography of Ireland) are by O'Meara; the original Latin is from J. S. Brewer's edition of Gerald's works (*Giraldi Cambrensis Opera*).

43 The Bretons were similarly moralized: "in William of Poitiers' words, 'they do not engage in the cultivation of fields or of good morals,' as if corn-growing and clean living went together" (Davies 125). "In Wales," remarks David Walker, "conquest introduced a note of racial hatred which has marked historical writing on both sides of the border" (65). In Ireland, "[o]fficial records consistently employed the phrase 'wild Irish,' using the adjective 'wild' to mean uncivilised, and sometimes using 'savage' in the same way . . . Even in the fifteenth century the term 'wild' was still applied to Gaelic Irish . . . the Commons in the English parliament of 1422 petitioned the king that all *wilde Irisshmen* should be excluded from the realm" (Lydon, *Lordship* 284). Beyond the work of historians, literary scholars such as Patricia Ingham and Michelle Warren have also scrutinized England's relations with its neighbors in detailed analysis of literary texts and founding myths.

44 "Gerald's work, especially on Ireland, was profoundly important . . . because it became an almost canonical text of English views of the Irish for the better part of five centuries" (Davies 116).

45 "Ultimately, as almost all observers agreed, the disqualification *par excellence* . . . was . . . fundamentally of economic attitude. [The Irish] simply lack the spirit of economic enterprise and wealth creation and accumulation" (Davies 126). Gerald of Wales snorts, "they think . . . the greatest wealth is to enjoy liberty" (qtd. by Davies 126–7). Davies notes that while "ease-loving, economically unambitious societies" such as Ireland and Scotland "had their virtues – notably a fierce love of liberty, an independence of spirit, a self-denying frugality, and a remarkable etiquette of hospitality," the fact that "there was no well-calibrated set of social distinctions and no recognized hierarchy of landed competence" and thus no "emergence of a truly economically differentiated ruling class," and "capital accumulation [was] ignored and even despised," indicated to the English a lack of civilized values (127–8).

46 Writing in 1577 on Irish inability to move beyond "barbaric rudeness" and stasis, "Sir William Gerrard held that the Irish of his day 'lived as the Irish lived in all respects before the conquest,' some 400 years earlier" (Davies 136). Conveniently, by Spenser's time, the steadfast Latin Christianity of the Irish could now serve as a damnable religious difference: As "Papistes," the Irish were now "*Atheists* or infidels" (*Works* 10: 136). In contrast to the insistence that Ireland was incapable of change, historians today point to material transformation in the colonized "Celtic fringe": "By the end of the twelfth century [there were] forty new burghs ... in Scotland; by 1300 ... some 225 towns in Ireland and some 85 in Wales. The same pattern applies broadly to mints and monetization ... By the thirteenth century coins were minted in sixteen centres in Scotland ... and ... up to six centres in Ireland" (Davies 137–8). Davies finds that "Ireland in the century or so after 1170 underwent 'a radical social and economic revolution'" (139). As importantly, Lilley points out that the very idea "that the Welsh and Irish lacked urban life before the Anglo-Normans imposed their statutes upon them and 'perseveringly civilized' them is, of course, a nonsense. It is now well known that both Ireland and Wales were urbanized before the arrival of the Anglo-Normans ... [yet] despite the presence and existence of important 'Hiberno-Norse' towns in Ireland (such as Dublin and Waterford), many of which were thriving in the mid-twelfth century, William of Malmesbury nevertheless talked of 'rustic Irishmen' in contrast with 'the English and French'" (25).

47 The Remonstrance also points out that far from helping to civilize the Irish, the English "have striven with all their might ... to wipe our nation out entirely and utterly to extirpate it" (qtd. in Muldoon, *Identity* 41).

48 Catherine Karkov importantly reminds us that in early Irish literature, the sovereignty of Ireland is often personified as an old woman: "the old, dying female werewolf can also be understood as a personification of Ireland and her passing from the old to the new order" (99).

49 Karkov, who shows how the wolf is an apposite symbol of Ireland, reads Gerald's story as a colonial narrative that is later answered by an Irish "postcolonial" text, the *Dialogue [or Tales] of the Ancients*. Like Caroline Bynum before her, Karkov (98) reads the wolf-human métissage as a species of *disguise* (Bynum opposes such "disguise" to twelfth-century writing in which *metamorphosis* or *metempsychosis* genuinely appears); unlike Bynum, however, who "ignores the political content of the episode" (95), Karkov is interested in how Gerald's text documents the Irish for English colonial purposes: "no matter how inhuman they might appear, the Irish had to be redeemable, because redemption was part of the justification for the Conquest. The Irish had to be made to seem simultaneously attractive and repulsive, a duality ... that the werewolf is particularly suited to convey, because it is simultaneously human and monster" (98).

50 Bartlett, for example, characterizes Gerald as vain, boastful, "prone to pomposity and, like most vain people, humourless. He took himself very seriously, and had no sense of proportion" (*Gerald* 211).

51 "The charters that Queen Elizabeth I and King James I (1603–25) issued to prospective colonizers employed language clearly drawn from the papal legal tradition developed in a series of documents beginning with Adrian IV's *Laudabiliter* and extending to Alexander VI's *Inter caetera* in 1493. These charters required the colonizers to be responsible for the Christianization and civilizing of the inhabitants of North America, just as *Laudabiliter* had obligated the English to reform the condition of the church in Ireland and to bring the Irish to the civilized way of life" (Muldoon, *Identity* 93). Lilley, who argues against "medieval historians" asserting that "'the colonialism of the Middle Ages is quite different' from that of 'modern' colonialism," emphasizes that "Anglo-Norman 'othering' of subject populations ... was little different from the European othering of peoples in Africa, Asia and the Americas in later centuries" ("Imagined Geographies" 23). For an argument of how Christendom's experience with Jews and Muslims shaped Europe's response to indigenous peoples in the Americas, see Jonathan Boyarin.

52 For nuanced readings on St. Bernard's postulate of Christ as a black man, see Hahn 20 and Epstein, *Purity Lost* 19–21.

53 Jean Devisse (149–205) suggests imperial and ecclesiastical politics to explain Magdeburg's black St. Maurice (*Figure 8* is on p. 163); Gude Suckale-Redlefsen offers the explanation of artistic models and artistic freedoms. See Chapter 4 for Paul Kaplan's arguments ("Black Africans," "Introduction").

54 I consider Africans, blackness, and color – exemplary black knights such as the Dutch Moriaen, virtuous black African queens, black Saracen giants and babies, and the Black St. Maurice of Magdeburg, *inter alia* – in Chapter 4.

55 Biller ("Black Women") thoughtfully surveys the long trail of scientific texts from antiquity – translated, annotated, interpreted, modified, and taught in university lectures and curricula – though which black women arrive in the Middle Ages as sexually superior objects of desire. The *Quaestiones super De animalibus*, "ventilated in 1258" by Albertus Magnus, sums it up thus: "For black women are hotter [a reference to humoral theory], and most of all dusky women, who are the sweetest to have sex with, so lechers say, and because the mouth of their vulva is temperate and gently embraces the penis... '*quia nigrae sunt calidiores, et maxime fuscae, quae sunt dulcissimae ad supponendum, ut dicunt leccatores, et quia temperatum habent os vulvae, quod suaviter amplectitur virgam*'" (486). For a survey of fourteenth through mid-sixteenth century portrayals of sex with black women, see Groebner.

56 The ascension of whiteness is intriguingly complexified by medieval slavery, as well as by gender and sexuality. Constable (275) and Epstein (*Speaking of Slavery* 185–90) both find, for instance, higher prices paid for white slaves in Mediterranean Europe in the thirteenth century and after, and that the majority of slaves were female. I discuss medieval slavery in Chapter 3, and the ascension of whiteness to supremacy as a category of European identity in Chapter 4.

2

State/Nation

A Case Study of the Racial State: Jews as Internal Minority in England

[England] is ... where the new anti-Semitic myths of Jewish greed, filth, and diabolism found some of their earliest and most elaborate iconographic representations, on the west front of Lincoln Cathedral, for example, and in the famous Cloisters Cross. England was also the first European country to stigmatize its entire Jewish population as coin-clippers and hence criminals ... England saw the earliest royally sponsored attempts to convert Jews in numbers to Christianity; and in 1290, it witnessed the first permanent expulsion of an entire Jewish community from any European kingdom.

Robert Stacey, "Anti-Semitism and the Medieval English State" (165)

[I]s it altogether a coincidence ... that the Jews were expelled *en masse* from England at the very point of time which witnessed ... *le genèse de l'état moderne*?

Barrie Dobson, "The Role of Jewish Women in Medieval England" (167)

RACIAL FORM in the medieval period is neither singular nor free of contradiction, as I began to say in Chapter 1, and accrues through variegated and shifting means. In some historical contexts, Jews and Muslims might be treated as proximately alike: so that crusaders setting out to exterminate the infidel occupying the Holy Land, for instance, found it logical first to exterminate the infidel resident in Europe – analogizing readily from one racial-religious enemy to the other – with the result that they wreaked devastation on European Jewish communities en route.[1] In some literary contexts, a slippage between thinking about Muslims and thinking about Jews also leads to conflations of one people with the other: In his celebrated romance, *Parzival*, for instance, Wolfram von Eschenbach refers to the Caliph of Baghdad as "the *Baruch*" of Baghdad, as if the leaders of infidel Abrahamic communities were interchangeably alike.[2]

But there is one way in which the racialization of Jews and that of Muslims was not alike. In the medieval period, Jews functioned as the benchmark by which racial others were defined, measured, scaled, and assessed. Modalities of racial form thus worked with a near monomaniacal attention to congeal Jews as figures of absolute difference. By contrast, the racing of the Islamic Saracen – discussed in Chapters 3 and 6 – did not always require the production of difference as *absolutely* incommensurable.

For instance: Under particular, narrowly defined conditions, Saracens can be allowed to resemble – and are praised for resembling – Christian Europeans, into whose company they might be imagined as inducted. Such is the theoretical universality of elite chivalric culture as a caste/class system, for one, that Saracen "knights" in European literature may be depicted as akin to European chivalry in nobility, gallantry, and prowess. Literary Saracen "knights" like these are perhaps cultural simulacra of historical personages like Saladin – the Kurdish emir Salah ad-Din Yusuf, who expanded and consolidated the work of his predecessors Nuraldin and Zengi in unifying the forces of Islam in countercrusade – a formidable military foe whose reputation for magnanimity nonetheless resounded familiarly, and reassuringly, within the chivalric ethos of the Latin West.[3]

In medieval romance, noble, virtuous Saracens of extravagant military prowess are enthusiastically embraced when they convert to Christianity (and the plot always has them convert). Some, like Ferumbras and Willehalm, even famously end up as sainted, holy figures revered in Christendom. Alternatively, esteemed Saracens may be depicted as secretly European under the skin: The Old French *La Fille du Comte de Ponthieu* (The Daughter of the Count of Ponthieu) and its continuation *Le Roman de Saladin* (The Romance of Saladin) design a French foremother for Saladin, thus claiming the great emir as a son of Europe *dans le sang*, and folding his achievements genealogically back within Europe's embrace.

Jacqueline de Weever's reading of Old French literature amply demonstrates how Saracen *princesses and queens* – the lovely Muslim foes who are female, sexualized versions of the virtuous Saracen knight – have *their* ethnoracial identity discreetly erased at the epidermal level by being presented as fair, light-skinned beauties, in aesthetic erasures of difference that enlist royal Islamic women as objects of desire congenial to Western Europeans.[4]

Chivalry as a structure of unity has the ability to articulate commonalities among foes not only in literature, but also under military field conditions, as the cautious respect that invests military, diplomatic, and political relations between the crusader king of England, Richard I, and the Kurdish sultan of the Islamic empire, Saladin, evinces: a striking demonstration of how theaters of war can unite, even as they divide, warring antagonists.

Living Figures of Absolute Difference: The Racing of Jews, Pre-Expulsion

For medieval Jews, however, chivalry as a structure of rapprochement and convergence between populations – in literature, or in the field – is not available. Jews did not constitute a host encountered by Christian Europe as an external, alien antagonist in the field of war. The threat signaled by Jewish difference, unlike Islamic difference, is the threat of the *intimate alien*, active and embedded in multiple communities and countries in the heartlands of the Christian *domus*.[5] Muslims, with the limited exception of contact zones in the Mediterranean such as Spain, southern Italy, Sicily, and scattered islands, were not residing cheek-by-jowl with Christians in the countries of the Latin West.[6]

By virtue of the character of their labor, Jews were ensconced where population density was greatest: in the urban centers and towns of Western Europe, the hubs of economic and cultural life. Intermingling with Christians in neighborhoods, markets, fairs, towns, and cities, medieval Jews formed concentrations of domestic aliens on whose religion and activity the intellectual and theological traditions, and the economic life, of Christian Europe were deeply and inextricably dependent.

Christian identity itself, issuing from a religion that was a younger branch in the triad of Abrahamic faiths anchored by the Hebrew Bible/Old Testament, was constructed not only in opposition to Judaism, through the typological binary structured by the New Testament's posited supersession of the Old Testament, but also *in terms of* Judaism, and in the terms supplied by Judaism: a tension that can be seen to reverberate even at the micrological level in recreational literature, when Chaucer's famous Prioress in *The Canterbury Tales* hails the mourning mother of a Christian child putatively murdered by Jews as a "newe Rachel" (*Prioress's Tale* l. 627), in the highest form of praise that can be mustered for her – even as the "Hebrayk peple" themselves (l. 560) are vilified, in the same breath, as Satan's people, a "cursed folk of Herodes al newe" (l. 574).[7]

Cordoning off Jews under the sign of an absolute difference, then, efficaciously denied a relationship of dependence and intimacy between Latin Christian Europeans and Jews. Usefully, it established a scale by which other alienness could be calibrated, quantified, and rendered intelligible, thus furnishing a benchmark for evaluating the deeds and character of other vilified peoples. When the thirteenth-century chronicler Robert de Clari reports the attempt by the bishops of Soisson, Troyes, and Halberstadt and the Abbot of Loos to justify the unjustifiable – the invasion and occupation of Greek Christian Constantinople by Latin Christians in the horrendous Fourth Crusade – he explains the churchmen's vindication of the crusaders' actions as being supported by the fact that the Greeks were "worse than Jews" ("*pieur que Juis*" [72]).[8]

To a medieval audience habituated to Jews as personifying absolute difference, historical actions otherwise heinous and incomprehensible – crusaders warring on fellow Christians, not the Islamic foe; the evisceration of a fabled, majestic city that had been the bulwark of Christianity in the East for a millennium; and how to explain the unthinkable – become intelligible when the Greek Christian targets of historical atrocity are knotted into comparative relationship with Jews, and their measure accordingly given.

The scholarship on medieval European Jews is vast. Rather than offer here what can only be a cursory attempt to survey all of Christian–Jewish relations in the European Middle Ages, this chapter and Chapter 1 point to a range of distinguished and able scholars who focus on diverse aspects of Christian–Jewish relations in detail. I urge that this varied, careful, and magnificent scholarship be consulted on any and all topics, from anti-Jewish libels to the symbology of Church and Synagogue (*Ecclesia/Synagoga*); from historical documentation of persecution and demonization to political theology positioning Jews in a supersessionary argument in which Christians became the new inheritors of Biblical traditions; from the politics of eschatology to the politics of pedagogy and disseminations of knowledge and learning.

In Chapter 1, I alluded to a panoply of biopolitical, hermeneutic, legal, canonic, theological, popular, ritual, and state conditions by means of which Jews were marked off as racial subjects, focusing, in particular, on an example of the ritual murder libel to discuss iterative practices that intersect in race-making. What this current chapter offers by way of elaboration is *a case study of medieval race* that concentrates on one country, and its manipulations of its Jewish minority, actual and virtual, over 400 years. I sift through a disparate aggregate of materials on Jews in England to see what among these contribute to the delivery of Jews as a race. The chapter ends by taking up anew the ritual murder accusation, this time in order to see if the Expulsion of 1290 is a watershed moment for cultural manifestations that conjured with ideas of race in the first racial state known to Europe.

England's treatment of Jews has been described by Robert Stacey as "archetypical" of the countries of western Europe, with England's Jewish minority having many parallels in Jewish communities elsewhere ("Twelfth Century" 340). The English example is thus at once situation-specific *and* resonant; and an analysis of English particularities may yield insights for those who would extend case-by-case studies of medieval race to other countries of Europe, carefully accounting for local differences and variations. The history of England's Jews, as scholars have shown, is exceptional principally by virtue of the earliness, speed, and intensity of the racializing processes exhibited on English shores, and remarkable mainly for the inventiveness and energy that was dedicated to the panoply of race-making mechanisms delivered.

The format of a case study – a kind of historical ethnography – facilitates close scrutiny of microparticulars that demonstrate what happens when a state bureaucracy creates institutions specifically for overseeing the governance of a minority population's activities and lives. Attentiveness to local context is also conducive for considering how *conversion* – a process that seems to allow an individual to exit one racial-religious formation and enter another – functions in race-making in a particular society.

This helps to disclose how agents such as children and women – figures who serve as symbolic bearers of sociocultural identity for a community – articulate the seams of race in a single country before and after the expulsion of the country's Jews. The chapter thus ends with an analysis of four literary narratives written in Anglo-French and Middle English on the shared theme of boy-murder, but which are distributed on either side of the 1290 divide of Jewish expulsion. Though some of these narratives have been examined before by others as singular literary texts, their close consideration here *as a grouped cluster* makes it possible to see shifts in racial thinking after 1290, and discloses change in racial emphasis over time.

Economies of the Racial State: Jews as Figures of Capital and Economic Modernity

The ideological edifice manufacturing Jewish essentialism and difference rests on an important cornerstone: the widespread identification of Jews with economic difference, and the hydra-headed personality of capital, and capital accumulation. Stacey suggests that William of Normandy may have solicited the migration of Jews to England from the continent after the Conquest of 1066 *specifically* to avail himself of Jewish competence as economic agents ("Jewish Lending" 78–82).[9] Jewish communities drove the engine of economic modernity in Europe. In England, they dominated credit markets – the basis of economic life, trade, business, construction, war, agriculture, and all activity requiring financing – and were vital to the development of a commercializing land market in the twelfth and thirteenth centuries (101).

Jewish economic success and capital accumulation – on a per capita basis, the community of English Jews has been identified as the wealthiest among all the countries of northern Europe (Stacey, "Jewish Lending," 95) – brought a perilous identification with the vicissitudes of capital, in symbolic as well as material ways. Until they were subjected to systematic impoverishment in the second half of the thirteenth century, capital accumulation by Jews persistently drew the acquisitive gaze of a state and crown bent on extracting financing for its projects, and the resentment of a populace for whom Jews came to signify the materiality of Christian debt and indebtedness. Thus the abstractions of capital – the allure, presumptive power, dangers, and threat of money, dogged uneasily by Christian culture's proscriptions and ambivalence – found personification in the Jewish community, with grave consequences.

One irony besetting largely landless English Jews in a feudal system was their complex association *both* with money, the medium and sign of economic modernity, *and* with land, the medium and basis of feudal premodernity. Intermediaries in an economic machine in which their transactions served as lubricant and motor, Jews aided in the mobility, simultaneously, of money and of land. Historians have noted how land transfer through Jewish financial transactions (land acting as security passing through different hands as loans were purchased, sold, and reassigned) capitalized the market in land to such an extent as to threaten and undermine feudal obligations and relationships, destabilizing the basis of land-based feudalism (Pollock and Maitland 475; Mundill 37; Roth, *History* 64; Richardson 94).[10] Maitland sounds the alarm: "Many an ancient tie between men – the tie of kinship, the tie of homage – is being dissolved or transmuted by the touch of Jewish gold; land is being brought to market and feudal rights are being capitalized" (Pollock and Maitland 475). To put it another way: Jews in England were historically associated with the social cost of unbridled capital.

The individuals and groups in the transactional networks through which land changed hands varied widely: In the twelfth and thirteenth centuries, Cistercian and Augustinian houses (among them Meaux Abbey, Malton Priory, Fountains Abbey, Waltham Abbey, Kirkstead, Biddlesden, Holy Trinity, Aldgate, and Healaugh Park), Premonstratensians, Gilbertines, Cluniacs, and Benedictines all acquired mortgaged properties through Jewish financiers (Richardson 90–103), in a system encompassing "so wide a geographical range and so many religious orders" (99) that it acted as a "solvent which broke down the apparent rigidity of the structure of feudal land tenure and facilitated the transfer of estates to a new capitalist class, the religious communities, or to new men who were making their fortune" (94).[11]

By the reign of Henry III, land transfer through Jewish intermediaries had produced such consequences that the Provisions of Jewry enacted by Henry III in 1269 declared that "no debts whatsoever might be contracted in future on the security of lands held in fee" and "all obligations of the sort already registered were cancelled" (Roth, *History* 65); "the right to make loans on the security of real estate was from this period progressively restricted" (108).[12] Jewish economic practices thus had the startling effect of producing an unsettling fluidity – driving a "commercializing economy," to use Stacey's term – in advance of the institutions of their time.

In an era where theology and religion focused the aspirations of the populace on reward in the afterlife and the soul's salvation – and where *ascesis*, whether perfectly attainable or not, formed the highest of spiritual ideals and practices – an uneasy ambivalence existed toward the demonstration of economic rationality and success. It is difficult to find outright praise of money or the celebration of successful economic agents in the medieval cultural record. Instead, the historical record is rife with the dangers of wealth: Among notorious examples, the massive financial resources of the Order of the Temple were a chief factor in attracting the covetous attentions of Philip the Fair of France, and helped to initiate the events that brought the extirpation and ruin of the Order in the fourteenth century (see, for example, Barber; Demurger).

The cultural record also presents striking instances of resentment toward, and censure of, lower-born but successful economic agents who attempted to better their lot and secure the upward mobility of their families in the socioeconomic class hierarchy, by, say, the seeking of entrance into knighthood: Literature – the cultural product of an elite stratum – weighs in against upstart ambitions of this kind.[13] When immense financial success is conjoined to influence and foreign identity, literature is decisive in identifying unnaturalness and monstrosity: One infamously successful Italian entrepreneur and capitalist is figured as a monstrous cannibalistic giant whose loathsome appetites include the rape of aristocratic women and the hideous devouring of Christian children.[14] How economic monstrosity is figured in the cultural imagination is a subject to which I will return.

Unsurprisingly, those most visibly associated with the active circulation of money – who handle money, benefit from transacting with the medium, and make of its circulation the principal means of their livelihood – are especially vulnerable to the taint of negative ascriptions. From a pragmatic standpoint, Zefira Entin Rokéah points out, charges involving coinage offenses tended to dog constituencies who routinely handled money – Jews, Cahorsins, and Flemings, among others ("Money . . . Part I" 84). Since coinage in precious metals lost its value over time through weight erosion in the course of handling, the deliberate reduction of coin weight through practices such as coin clipping was an accusation that might readily be laid at the door of constituencies through whose hands metal money regularly passed.[15]

That Jews were overwhelmingly singled out and tagged as a population of counterfeiters and coin clippers in medieval England – Jewish men and women were sentenced to the gallows on charges of coin clipping in exponentially greater numbers than their Christian counterparts engaged in the handling of money – is far in excess, however, of naturalizing explanations of the pragmatic dangers of handling money. Matthew Paris, for one, in a revealing instance of strategic essentialism, opined that *Jews in fact could not be made poor – despite fiscal extortions regularly enforced against them by the state – because they were counterfeiters* (Rokéah, "Money . . . Part I" 84).

Medieval chronicles report that as many as 279, 280, or 293 Jews were executed in London alone in 1278 for coin clipping: Men were drawn and hanged, and women burnt (Rokéah, "Money . . . Part I" 86, 96, 108 n.71); women were hanged and men burnt (Richardson 219). Rokéah's meticulous study of pipe rolls for the 1278–9 coinage trials confirms the chronicles' accounts: 269 Jews but only 29 Christians, she concludes, were executed in one incident in London (Rokéah, "Money . . . Part I" 98).

These numbers are staggering: They suggest that *10–15 percent of the Jewish population in England at the time were put to death for coinage offenses in a single incident* (Rokéah, "Money . . . Part I" 86, 97).[16] *More than 600 men and women – constituting approximately 20–30 percent of the Jewish population at the time – were imprisoned for coinage offences.*[17] Concluding that the trials and convictions of the accused turned on "inadequate and perjured evidence" (219), Richardson observes that after the widespread arrests of 1278–9, the homes of the imprisoned were "broken into and plundered" (218).

Clearly, a minority community personifying money and its vicissitudes for the larger population possessed a different, riskier status from its Christian counterparts engaged in similar work. Money is a dangerous sign system in the Middle Ages, and a community with a metonymic association with money endures risks accruing from money's symbolic as well as pragmatic functions.

Underpinning presumptions of Jewish guilt and iniquity was the typing of Jews as a population of *usurers*, practitioners of a livelihood deemed illegitimate in Christian theology and canon law, and condemned.[18] No less than Peter the Venerable, the formidable twelfth-century abbot of Cluny who commissioned the first Latin translation of the Quran, pronounced Jewish earnings through money lending to be theft, and urged that Jewish property accordingly be confiscated and applied to finance the crusade: an economical line of reasoning that seamlessly linked the disciplining of the infidel within Europe to the disciplining of the infidel without.[19]

Since usury was theft, the thirteenth-century English churchman Robert of Flamborough consigned Jews to being numbered among thieves and robbers, in his *Liber poenitentialis* (Watt 164). Despite Church probibitions, Latin Christians also undertook financial transactions in loans and credit – canon law repeatedly inveighed against Christian "usurers" active throughout the medieval period[20] – but limited avenues of labor available to Europe's Jews, combined with spectacular success in networks of credit and finance and, in England, the gradual constriction of Jewish commercial activity as a result of shifting economic conditions, meant a concentration of Jewish specialization in loans.[21]

The identification of Jews with "usury" meant that Christian debt was yoked to Jewish livelihood in a volatile, triangulated relationship with money. Periodic attacks on Jewish communities effecting the slaughter of Jews and the plunder of Jewish property – attacks that, in their immediate contexts, had a variety of triggers – thus became communal performances at which, for Christians, economic advantage and fiscal self-interest could neatly converge with anti-Jewish ideological fervor.

In the waves of massacres that spread through several cities in 1189–90, *when 10 percent of English Jews were slaughtered* – a statistic exceeding the percentage of Jews killed in the better known massacres of late-medieval Spain, as Stacey points out ("Crusades" 233)[22] – medieval chronicles accordingly underscore, among scenes of carnage, plunder, and forcible conversion, the targeted destruction of records of debt to Jews (Roger of Howden 3: 33–34; Roger of Wendover 1: 176–77) and the economic motives of the attackers (William of Newburgh 1: 313–14).[23]

Jews constituted targets with the ability to draw the resentment of virtually all groups in society needing financing of any kind: peasants and townsfolk, knights of the shire, monastic houses, and great magnates.[24] Systemic dependence on Jews at every level of English society, in tandem with the distinctiveness of Jews as a minority population, bred fertile ground for generating racialized modes of group redress against Jews. Redress took a variety of forms. Popular correctives included periodic slaughter in organized or spontaneous mob attacks. State-engineered correctives included sweeping anti-Jewish legislation such as the *Statutum de Judeismo* passed in 1275 by Edward I, which criminalized and rendered illegal all Jewish lending in England henceforward.[25]

The expulsion order of 1290 – painstakingly negotiated, Stacey demonstrates ("Parliamentary Negotiation"), between the Commons of Parliament and Edward I in exchange for Parliament's approval of a widespread tax desired by Edward – constitutes, then, *racialized redress in its logical extremity*. Stacey's careful study detailing the economic background *to* the expulsion insists, with acuity, that economic rationality alone – given the immense fiscal cost borne by laity and clergy alike in what amounted to "the largest single tax of the Middle Ages" awarded by them to the king in order to expel a community that was, by this time, an impoverished and demographically shrinking group of English Jews – cannot be adequate as an explanation *"for* the expulsion." The "willingness of the Christian taxpayers of England in 1290 to pay the king a tax of £116,000 to secure the expulsion of fewer than 2,000 Jews from England cannot," Stacey concludes, "be explained on strictly economic grounds" ("Jewish Lending" 100).[26]

In the extraordinary decision to expel the Jews of England *en masse* from the country, popularly sponsored and state-engineered initiatives converged to generate a final solution, after two centuries, to the intolerable Gordian knot of Jewish economic superiority and theological-social subordination.[27] The expulsion of Jews did not, of course, put an end to Christian debt in England afterward: It merely ensured, by means of a historical maneuver issued as a group decision made by the representatives of government, that the cost of Christian debt was symbolically and materially borne, and expiated, on the backs of what was by then an impoverished community of English Jews.[28]

The economic superiority of Jews, as successful bankers and agents of capital, jostled uneasily against their subordinate status as social and ideological subjects. The logic of capital in a commercializing economy such as England's in the twelfth and thirteenth centuries might suggest the advantages of capital accumulation, whose accrued social, material, and other benefits in such an economy should be manifold.[29] But when economic rationality collides with ideological constrictions that define the minority population managing capital as inferior, morally suspect, and theologically condemned, identification with capital renders the association with wealth, under such circumstances, monstrous and troubling.

For those who must act out rampant contradictions in society – an assigned role of inferiority in religious cosmology, theology, and social life, superscripted over a dynamic role as fiscally successful actors in a moneyed economy where capital accumulation is at once desirable and suspect – being positioned at the site of critical societal tensions brings inordinate danger. Manifestly, in such circumstances, the allure and threat of capital can be transformed into a politics of race that finds its target in the personification of capital: Jews.

It is tempting to suppose that perhaps massacres of English Jews did not derive from a politics of race, but from a simple economics of class: a *mise-en-scène* where an impoverished population of indebted Christians repeatedly rose up, as a class stratum, in popular rebellions against their wealthy Jewish oppressors. But anatomies of the attacks on English Jews reveal significant class heterogeneity among the anti-Jewish assailants – who were not, in fact, a downtrodden stratum of the oppressed Christian poor.

At York in 1190, for instance, the assault upon the Jewish community was not enacted by the urban poor but "organized and led by several of the leading members of the Yorkshire gentry" with familial and tenurial links to "some of the most powerful men in England, including the king's brother, Prince John, and Hugh de Puiset, Bishop of Durham and co-justiciar of England" (Stacey, "Crusades" 248). Indeed, William of Newburgh fingers the leaders of the York massacres as aristocrats, as well as crusaders preparing for their pious military pilgrimage to Jerusalem with the theft of Jewish property (Stacey, "Crusades" 249).[30]

Nor did medieval Jews comprise a homogenously wealthy class of peoples lording it over the Christian poor: That poverty existed among Jews themselves, and that the wealth of the

Jewish community was disproportionately represented by a remarkable handful of immensely successful Jewish financiers in the twelfth and thirteenth centuries, is a point that has been made repeatedly by historians. Richardson's study of the pipe rolls of debts owed to Aaron of Lincoln, "the wealthiest Jew of his time" (115), finds that in addition to Christian debtors, Aaron revealingly made "a good many loans to Jews: whether these bore interest or not does not appear, but they seem to have been made largely to people in poor circumstances, who certainly, in many cases, were unable to repay what they had borrowed" (116).

Just as the economic status of the anti-Jewish assailants cut across class distinctions, so also were the economic circumstances of the Jewish victims accordingly varied. Though unquestionably an important factor in the violence and destruction visited upon Jews, economic motives should not be assumed to offer adequate explanation, nor should they be assumed to be unconditioned by a politics of race.

It is a politics of race that transforms a few individuals who are visible and conspicuous into symbolic icons that represent, and stand for, an entire abominated population – a population which is then read, under such politics, as homogenously alike. The wealthy Jewish financiers, Benedict and Joceus of York, are precisely such icons selected for notice by William of Newburgh's chronicle.

Rendered as unnatural socioeconomic upstarts, they are tellingly likened by the chronicle to "princes" living in abundance and luxury in large houses comparable to royal palaces, and are condemned as "tyrants" who oppress Christians by the "cruel tyranny" of usury (*usurpation*, we note, is the chronicle's metaphor of choice to signal an evil that overturns the rightful order of things, and affects all estates). The chronicle relishes how Christian attackers undo the improper status of these iconic representatives, by plundering and razing the two men's homes, slaying Benedict's family and household, and forcibly transforming him into a Christian, in the mob violence of 1190 (1: 312–13).[31]

Since Benedict and Joceus are evocations of an undifferentiated communal whole whose members are predicated as identical, their condemnation by the chronicle fluidly expands into a condemnation of the *entire* populace of Jews, whose ideological role as the killers of Christ is strategically reintroduced and upheld, closing off the mixed signals and uneasy contradictions – the unresolved conundrum – of England's commercializing economy and its beneficiaries. The extolling of Jewish perfidy, rehearsed anew by the chronicle, vindicates the York massacres, and is ringingly capped by the endorsement of the doctrinal recommendation that Jews be made to live in servitude (William of Newburgh 1: 313).

Following seamlessly from the punishment meted out to two rich men, *all* Jews can be reduced to their proper place in cosmology and society once again, after the redress accomplished by violence successfully visited on two representatives: a violence that appears, under these circumstances, as redemptive. We see thus how a theory of the religious difference embodied by Jews as a community hardens into a theory of ethnoracial difference accompanied by violence as the predicated form of appropriate redress, with the assistance of a political theology of race.

It matters little that resources were not, in fact, evenly or uniformly distributed among individual Jews and the Jewish communities of medieval England. As undifferentiated figures representing economic difference for the majority population, homogeneity is assumed to be a characteristic of the entire minority population. What matters is that on a per capita basis, calculated by an aggregate unevenly compiled, the Jews of medieval England were statistically "the wealthiest Jewish community in Europe" (Stacey, "Parliamentary Negotiation" 93, "Jews and Christians" 342), evincing an economic competence that had to be continually revised by the state through taxations and laws, just as it was also revised at the popular level by massacres and looting of the kind recorded and extolled by medieval chroniclers.

Based on an estimated Jewish population of 4,000–5,000 in 1240,[32] the tiny size and vulnerability of this minority community is dramatically realized when we grasp that it is living in the midst of a national population of perhaps five million people in England at the time (Stacey, "Jews and Christians" 341). The fiscal assets of the Jewish populace, "excluding all interest and penalties owing to them, amounted in 1240 to around 200,000 marks, a sum equivalent to one-third of the total circulating coinage in the kingdom": an accumulation, Stacey reiterates, that was disproportionately accounted for by a handful of very prominent, very successful Jewish financiers (Stacey, "Parliamentary Negotiation" 93).

Such capital accumulation did not, however, remain long in Jewish hands. The unique status of Jews as a minority peoples under the theoretical protection of the crown and, simultaneously, a people subject to being periodically milked by the crown through special tallages and other fiscal extortions – protection and exploitation being twinned aspects of a two-faced state – meant that "by 1258, *more than half* of the total Jewish capital in 1241 had been transferred directly into the king's coffers through taxation alone" (Stacey, "Parliamentary Negotiation" 93; emphasis added). "Between 1240 and 1255 Henry III collected more than £70,000 from the English Jews, at a time when the king's total annual cash revenues rarely exceeded £25,000" (Stacey, "Conversion" 270). In 1274 – a year before the 1275 Statute of Jewry made it illegal for Jews to practice their livelihood – another tax, of 25,000 marks, was levied on the Jewish population, imposing

> enormous financial pressure on the English Jews and through them on their Christian debtors. Hundreds of writs of distraint were issued against Christians owing money to Jews; if the principal debtors could not pay, the debts they owed would be assigned to their sureties and tenants, who would in turn be distrained to pay them. The pressure was relentless. Jews who could not pay their tallage obligations were imprisoned; their property was sold, and their bonds confiscated by the Exchequer, which either collected the debts itself or assigned them to the queen. Either way, the full weight of the king's administration would land on the unfortunate Christian debtor, his heirs and assigns [and, of course, on Jews themselves].
>
> (Stacey, "Parliamentary Negotiation" 96)[33]

In its economic aspect, popular hatred of Jews thus had a spoor that led back to the systematic, exploitative squeezing of Jews by the state. State interference in the collection of debts owed to Jews – using "all of the coercive force of the exchequer" to prosecute the collection of such debts for state coffers – began as a large-scale enterprise in 1186, when the government confiscated the estate of the wealthy financier Aaron of Lincoln at his death, and collected, for the benefit of the crown, on debts owed to him (Stacey, "Jews and Christians" 347; Lipman 67).[34] This profitable and instructive experience led the state shortly after to invent a special branch of government to monitor and rule over the economic lives of Jews in all the ways that were useful to the maximization of state profit: the infamous Exchequer of the Jews.

Arriving in Anglo-Norman England in the wake of the Conqueror, the first French-speaking Jewish migrants from the continent likely represented, to Anglo-Saxons and others who were accommodating themselves to their new Norman masters, figures of the outside associated with the invaders by virtue of a shared linguistic difference from the local population, and perhaps – if Stacey is correct – royal sponsorship. But whether or not Jewish immigration was invited by the Conqueror in the eleventh century, the avid, intensifying interest of the crown in profiting directly from Jewish money lending brought English Jews, over time, a dangerously close identification with the crown that led William of Newburgh, by 1189, to heckle the Jews of England as "the king's usurers" (1: 322–3).

The perilous identification of Jews with crown interests meant that baronial and popular opposition to the crown could come to take racial modes of expression: Resistance to the policies of crown and state could also be visited on Jews as ethnoracist practices. Stacey, who points out that "in the resistance to King John that culminated in the Magna Carta rebellion" there were "associated attacks on Jews and Jewish communities," and that "tensions between the Norman rulers and their English subjects played some role in the emergence of the ritual crucifixion charge at Norwich in 1144" ("Anti-Semitism" 172), suggests that, in the devastating attacks at York which led to the "massacre and mass-suicide of the Jewish community" ("Crusades" 248), "regional animosities between the northerners and the crown" played a significant role ("Crusades" 249; see also Gross 43–4).[35]

A Medieval Panopticon: The State and the Administration of Race

The vexed relationship of English Jews to the crown witnesses how the state, in premodern society, was able to exercise power over a minority group for maximal advantage through the selective exploitation of contradictions implicit in structures of dependence and protection which bound medieval Jews to the umbra of monarchic attention. The compiler of the Laws of Edward the Confessor (*Leges Edwardi Confessoris*), the earliest document touching on the legal status of Jews in England, writing perhaps around the second quarter of the twelfth century, understood English Jews and all their possessions to belong to the king, who, together with his lieges, was required to protect them – a principle sometimes thought to have been later ratified by a charter of Henry II which has not survived, but that is indeed ratified in the charters issued by Henry's sons, Richard I in 1190 and John in 1201 (Pollock and Maitland 468; Richardson 109; Roth, *History*, 96; Mundill 56–7).

In 1275, Edward I's Statute of Jewry (*Statutum de Judeismo, Estatuts de la Jeurie*), issued in Anglo-Norman, confirmed the understanding that a possessive, direct relationship bound the Jewish community to the crown, a relationship lying outside feudatory relations that applied to the rest of the populace and unmediated by hierarchies of subinfeudation.[36] Paragraphs 5, 7, and 8 of the Statute formally refer to Jews as the king's "serfs," and attach rights and protections for Jews devolving from their condition of royal servitude, as well as the burden of capitation and other taxes owed directly and exclusively to the crown, along with other impositions (*Statutes of the Realm* I: 221a).[37]

In its specification of rights and protections on the one hand, and of curtailments, exactions, and impositions on the other, the relationship of Jews to the crown – as the Statute demonstrates – is a two-headed beast. Crown benefits from possession, and crown obligations to protection, are ineluctably twinned aspects of the state's supervision of English Jews.

Jews thus formed a distinct and special category of subjects in medieval England and Europe.[38] The anomaly of their status has little equivalence in medieval time or after – not even in the minority Muslim communities who inhabit, yet seem set apart from, the populations of western European countries today – and is one of the factors, historically, that separates the medieval from the modern.[39] And yet, just as the queer status of medieval Jews attests to the variety of ethnoracial constituencies in history, state practices visited on the lives and bodies of medieval Jews that *produced* them *as* an ethnoracial constituency – such as badges on clothing, mandated locations of residence, segregated social interactions, legalized executions fueled by community fictions – also materialized a seam, as we shall see, at which medieval and modern practices of race meet and touch.[40]

Modern historians, in scrutinizing the queer status of medieval Jewry, have articulated a range of responses scaling from qualified optimism to outright dismay. Following Maitland, the noted authority on thirteenth-century English law who observed that Jewish servility was a "relative" servility since "in relation to all men, save the king, the Jew is free" (Pollock and Maitland 468), Richardson argues that "although ... a Jew, or at least his property, might belong to the king, yet the Jew was a free man and ... against all other men, *except the king*, he was protected" (110, emphasis added). We see that the Jewish community too, when it needed to appeal to the king, sometimes found it strategic and useful to invoke their special relationship to the crown, and the intimacy of a direct, possessive link between crown and community, with the reminder to the king that "We are thy Jews" ("*Nos iudei tui sumus*" [Jessop and James 1896]).[41]

Nonetheless, the legal theory that the crown was "the universal heir to all Jewish property" echoed ominously in various contexts, including an explanation by the author of the thirteenth-century treatise of common law, *De legibus et consuetudinibus Angliae* (On the Laws and Customs of England, traditionally attributed to Henry of Bracton), that "the Jew truly can have nothing that is his own, because whatever he acquires he acquires not for himself but for the king" (Twiss 6: 50).[42] The fundamental unfreedom of Jewish subjects, and their liability to dispossession under the law, is thus underscored. Viewed as a limit case, the juridical concept of royal possession denoted that "the Jew was Crown property" (Mundill 54), "like the forests – a kind of plaything of the crown" (Powicke 111), and "the king ... may at any moment treat [Jewish] possessions as his own" (Jenkinson 25).

Article 11 of the royal charters of Richard I (issued in 1190) and of King John (issued in 1201) explicitly denoted Jews as the property of the king (Rymer et al. I: 51, Hardy 93). Underwriting their juridical status as a species of human chattel is the fact that the king sometimes *leased* his Jews to others: Henry III leased the English Jewry to his brother Richard, earl of Cornwall, for 5,000 marks in 1255, and later to his heir, Edward, for 3,000 marks a year (Edward in turn transferred the Jewry to Cahorsin merchants as *his* security for loans he incurred from the Cahorsins). Henry also made a gift of one special Jew – Aaron son of Vives, a prominent member of the London Jewry – to his other son, Edmund (Matthew Paris 5: 488; Rigg, *Select Pleas* 62–3; Tovey 135, 157–9; Roth, *History* 47–8, 97).

But if the de jure theory of royal possession appeared on the surface of things to be impossibly draconian, and liable to nullify economic initiative on the part of the Jewish community – since all that is gained through Jewish labor would accrue, in theory, to the king – in practice, a system of royal licenses, estate duties, tallages, capitation taxes, fees, fines, and other fiscal exactions (including seizure of the estates of individuals, should they be executed by the state, or convert to Christianity, or if other circumstances might be found to deny inheritance by heirs) de facto allowed for the state to profit by Jewish economic endeavors without extirpating the economic initiative of the community as a whole that laid the golden egg.[43]

Royal protection, to which the community of Jews was entitled by virtue of customary and legal status, was also a chimerical beast. While entitled to sue and be sued in royal courts, and to protection by royal castellans such as sheriffs, town authorities, and other officials from harassment and mob violence, the practice on the ground – since power "was easy to abuse" – meant that "sheriffs and constables, their sergeants and bailiffs ... took advantage of their opportunities; and their gains, which were, in their eyes, legitimate and by no means illicit, set down without concealment in their accounts, were scarcely inferior to those drawn from the Jewry by the king" (Richardson 159–60).[44]

The lure of gains that could be derived from Jews also goaded the bureaucratization, in stages, of techniques of extraction that were incrementally refined to deliver improved efficiency in amassing profit for the state from Jewish economic activity. At the crudest and simplest level, English monarchs, from Henry II onward, ceased to borrow from individual Jewish financiers (loans, after all, required repayment) and instead substituted straightforward tallages – extraordinary taxations – levied at regular and irregular intervals on the Jewish population as a whole.[45] In addition to the large, dramatic hauls harvested by these punctuated extortions, quotidian micropowers emerged in the twelfth and thirteenth centuries to render Jewish lives and livelihoods incrementally transparent and malleable for purposes of fiscal extraction and social control by the state.

At the center of the multipart administrative panopticon that developed, by degrees, to secure the state's gaze on Jews was the collection of key kinds of information for strategic accountability, intervention, and management of this minority population. In 1194, after the anti-Jewish riots of 1189–90 saw Christian destruction of documents of debt to Jews, a network of chirograph chests or *archae* was installed by the state in all the main centers of Jewish settlement in England to ensure that record keeping would not in future be disrupted.

This network of chests – an *economic panopticon* – functioned as the multilocational depository of official written records that registered the assets of individual Jews, and all transactions of loans and credit entered into by Jews: records that were at first administered in duplicate, then later administered in triplicate by official chirographers (Roger of Howden 3: 266; Brand 73; Richardson 118; Roth, *History*, 28–9; Lipman 67; Gottheil and Jacobs, "Archa"; Gross 15–16, 18).[46] Most importantly, the assemblage of chests, or registries, constituted bureaucratic surveillance indispensable to governmental knowledge of Jewish resources in the state's calculation of tallages, taxations, fines, and estate duties to be borne by Jews.[47]

The assembled records of "chirographs" or manuscript bonds also furnished documentary evidence for Jewish litigants in legal actions and prosecutions against recalcitrant debtors, and thus functioned, like the relations between crown and Jewish community, as a double-edged instrument: able to afford some protection at law, while conducing to the state's exploitation of community and individual.[48] From time to time, scrutiny (literally, "*scrutinium*") of an *archa* was ordered, and its contents, or transcripts of contents, were sent to Westminster to be examined by the Treasurer – a preparatory move, especially, that anticipated new state actions and extortions.

Government orders to close the *archae*, to prevent the withdrawal of chirographs preparatory to the levying of new tallages on the Jewish community, became ritualized as an action preceding the harvesting of profit by the state.[49] After the extraordinary government bureau known as the Exchequer of the Jews had been created in the 1190s, with responsibility for "the oversight and control" of England's Jewish community (Brand 73) – the creation of the Jewish Exchequer very likely devolving from the state's profitable realization of the bonds from Aaron of Lincoln's confiscated estate in 1186 – supervision of the *archae* became one of the chief duties of the Jewish Exchequer.[50]

The state system of chirograph chests was a bureaucratic response that answered precisely to how the sprawling, diffuse, and formless aggregate of Jewish economic activity might be given scrutable form, and imparted a degree of documentary durability. By transfixing Jewish activity at key nodal points where that activity could be registered and monitored, the *archae* constituted an important means by which the state successfully exerted force over, and rechanneled, the free circulation of economic flows – the dynamic chaos – set in motion by Jewish initiative.

Since it was only at *archa* towns "that any business could be legally transacted with Jews," financiers who wished to remain within the law and secure future access to legal redress had to confine their economic activity to the nodal centers at which the chirograph chests, and their chirographers and scribes, were situated (Gottheil and Jacobs, "Archa").[51] The network of chests, then – imposing a grid where the free flow of economic interplay could be contingently arrested and scrutinized at key focal points – located one of the state's quotidian instruments of micropower.

As control over the mobility of Jewish economic behavior incrementally came under the ambit of the state, control over the mobility of Jews themselves also increased. Adducively stringent measures were passed to specify and allocate sites of legitimate Jewish habitation. In an uncanny parallel with its regulation of Jewish money, the state disclosed a preference for sedentary human subjects confined to a network of fixed and specified sites over the dynamically free movement of this ethnoracial minority. In 1190, before installation of the web of chests and the Exchequer of the Jews, article 11 of Richard I's royal charter in fact stipulated that Jews, with all their possessions, were allowed to go wherever they wished (Rymer et al. I: 51). In 1201, article 11 of King John's charter confirmed the right of free movement in almost the same words (Hardy 93).

Yet in 1239, legislation restricted mobility by ordering Jews "to remain for a year in their existing place of residence, from which they were not to remove without the king's licence" (Richardson 177). In 1253, Henry III's ordinance to the heads of the Jewish Exchequer, the "Justices and Keepers of the Jews" (*Mandatum Regis Justiciariis ad Custodiam Judeorum*), mandated that Jews were not to be received into any town without special license from the king, with the exception of those towns where they had already been wont to dwell (Rigg, *Select Pleas* xlvii). "By the mid-1260s ... the Exchequer of the Jews ... administered the system controlling where members of the Jewish community could live. No Jew could change his or her residence without official permission" (Brand 74). To establish or change residence, Jews were required to apply for a special license, and "unlicensed residence in a town could lead to an order for the seizure of the body and movable possessions of the Jew concerned, and might lead to the forfeiture of the latter" (Brand 74).

The efficacy of the *archae* as monitory devices also meant that the *archae*'s technology of registration came to dominate the lives of Jews in other ways, further constricting the space allowed to English Jews. Repeated attempts had been made to compel Jews to live in towns with chirograph chests, and in 1275, the Statute of Jewry laid down orders for Jews to live only in *archa* towns. Paragraph 5 of the 1275 Statute mandated that "all Jews shall dwell in the King's own cities and boroughs, where the Chests of Chirographs of Jewry are wont to be" ("*tus les Geus seient menauns en les citez e en les burgs propres les Rey, ou les Whuches Cirograffes de Geurie soleient estre*" [*Statutes of the Realm* I: 221a]). Again, in 1284, "new legislation confining Jewish residence to the *archa* towns was issued" (Mundill 23). The Jewish Exchequer was to ensure that the proscription against living in towns without chests was enforced (Brand 74), with orders from 1277 onward "to arrest Jews not residing in *archa* towns" (Mundill 23; Roth, *History*, 72).

England's demonstration of how the administration of race is accomplished in premodernity thus foregrounds a logic of escalation in monitoring and control. We see how a process of compiling information on the economic behavior and assets of a targeted group congeals, through an evolving logic of bureaucratic management, fiscal exploitation, and social control, into an ethnoracial practice of *herding*, in which people become assigned to designated towns where residence is allowed, or, should they resist their allocations, become subject to arrest.

Mechanisms initially organized to make Jews visible and pliable to the state as an economic entity congruently became the basis to compel Jews as a corporate entity to bend other, fundamental, aspects of their existence to the will and desired ends of the state. The state's improvised responses to Jewish activity – coalescing in a network of chests, chirographers, the Jewish Exchequer – materialized quotidian institutional powers that delivered the state's relations of force and its infrastructure of compulsion.

Although the mode of racial governance practiced by the state's administration of Jews can be seen to assume the profit motive as its point of reference and self-explanatory logic in the first instance, it is important to recognize that the ethnoracial practices of herding devised by the state ostensibly for harvesting profit progressively come to disclose an arc of power severed from mere fiscal necessity. A state exercise of economic rationality is incrementally extended through quotidian micropowers to "domains which are not exclusively or primarily economic," in adducively biopolitical elaborations (Foucault, *Birth* 323).

The Statute of Jewry's confinement of Jews to *archa* towns *begins* by being firmly lodged within the logic of the state's profit motive. As registries of Jewish property, assets, and economic endeavors, the *archae* support forms of fiscal extraction *even after* the Statute's prohibition of loans has superannuated the chests' original function as depositories of debt records. Paragraph 8 of the Statute, which instructs Jews to turn now to new economic endeavors and gain a living by "lawful trade and by their labor" instead of by lending money (*Statutes* I: 221a), "clearly expected them to use the existing *archa* system for their [new] business" (Mundill 147). To carry out this new business of "lawful trade in selling and in buying" ("*leument marchaunder en vendaunt e en echataunt*"), paragraph 8 grants Jews permission to interact lawfully with Christians in work of this new kind.

However, at the same instant that paragraph 8 gives Jews permission to interact with Christians for the purposes of trade, it *also bars Christians from living among Jews, whether for trade or for any other cause*: "*nul Crestien ne seit cochaunt ne levaunt entre eus*" (*Statutes*

I: 221a). Of what use is such a prohibition to the state treasury? A second arc of desire in the exercise of state power has materialized in this legislative demand: Not only have Jews to be weeded out of the rest of England and confined exclusively to *archa* towns (the demand in paragraph 5), but Jewish residential space *within* such towns must be sifted through to empty out Christians (the demand in paragraph 8).

The decision to evacuate Christians exceeds the simple profit motive exercised by *archa* surveillance: It reveals, instead, a desire to cull and organize urban space to prevent contact between human groups at precisely those spaces where life is most intimately and intently lived. Fear of intimacy is palpable even in the idiom of the legal command – "no Christian shall go to bed nor rise up among them" – literally evoking the simple daily gesture of lying down to sleep and waking up as a *topos* for people living together in intimate and creaturely proximity. In voiding Jewish residential quarters of Christian neighbors, the Statute articulates the state's interest in producing a human and urban geography that carves up and designates separate living spaces for Christians and Jews in English cities. What is this, if not a segregation order?[52]

Not coincidentally, the 1275 Statute of Jewry is also the legislation that materializes the largest, most conspicuous, and most visually ostentatious badge that the English state required its Jews to wear on their outer garments: The size (6 by 3 inches), color (yellow), and material of this badge (felt), and the command that Jewish *children* aged seven and above must now display it on their bodies along with adult Jews, directly announce the state's intent – spelled out in paragraph 5's detailed description of badge and wearers (*Statutes* I: 221a) – to draw the eye of the viewer to the certain and unmistakable knowledge of how to tell apart a Jew and a Christian at a glance.

It is not an accident thus that paragraph 8 should deliver a *second* mechanism of sorting and distinction among populations. Just as an ostentatious Jewish badge functions to separate out the two populations in England through a regime of visual inspection, residential segregation devised by organizing the use of space in urban geography to hold apart Christians and Jews accomplishes *spatially* within a city's vectors what the badge accomplishes by sight.[53] The 1275 Statute of Jewry thus issues two related and interlocking segregation orders for medieval English cities.

And what of the Exchequer of the Jews, the administrative panopticon that is one of the few ethnoracial apparatuses unique to England among the countries of Europe, inaugurated in the 1190s to enforce state decisions in Jewish lives, and under which, it has been said, "the whole framework of [Jewish] society passed" in annual review (Gross 38)?

The multifariousness of this specialized agency's functions has been increasingly appreciated by scholars. The Jewish Exchequer acted as a court for civil and criminal litigation involving Jewish litigants; prosecuted debts for the crown when debts passed into royal hands (an event that recurred "on a considerable scale"); took charge of property that escheated to the crown; conducted inquisitions into, and enforced, estate duties; supervised the chirograph chests; controlled the system of permissions, licenses, and enforcements that decided where Jews could live; and punished breaches of all the laws and statutes relating to Jews (Brand 74–6, Gross 37).[54]

In short, the agency's quotidian powers of oversight and intervention intersected at four of the principal powers of governmentality: collection, enforcement, administration, and adjudication. Initially headed by one Jewish and three Christian "Justices" or "Keepers of the Jews" ("*Justitiarii Judeorum*," "*Custodes Judeorum*"), this well-exercised arm of government very quickly (from 1199 on) only had Christian Keepers, assisted by Jewish subordinates (Roth, *History*, 29–30; Lipman 68; Jenkinson 52; Gross 8–11).[55]

The heterogeneity of the Jewish Exchequer's tasks speaks to the kind of racial form and governance that accrues even when race in premodernity emerges, at one of its points of instantiation, from an economic–fiscal nexus. Though this specialized branch of government was the specific "department of State" responsible for ensuring, as its core administrative mission, that the money of Jews would "flow from [Jewish] pockets into the royal coffers" (Gross 25; Lipman 74, 76), the ramification of this agency's purview and powers in multiple spheres of surveillance witnesses the extension of racial governance beyond what can be accounted for and contained by economic factors, and underwrites the irreducibility of racial control.

One example of how far afield the work of the agency had ramified is witnessed in Henry III's 1253 ordinance addressed to the chief officers of the Jewish Exchequer, those "Justices assigned to the custody of the Jews" (*Justitiarii ad custodiam Judeorum assignatis*). This ordinance only touches once or twice on the topic of what is fiscally due from Jews and why.

Moving rapidly from an opening focus reiterating the mandatory service of Jews to the crown, the ordinance requires the Jewish Exchequer to root out, prevent, control, and punish behavior across a diverse range of curtailments and prohibitions: concerning the establishment of synagogues, the appropriate auditory volume of Jewish worship, dues payable to parishes, Christian wet-nurses of male Jewish infants, other Christian servants of Jews, Christians eating and tarrying in the homes of Jews, secret intercourse of an intimate nature between Christians and Jews, Jewish purchase and consumption of meat in Lent, display of the Jewish badge on the chest, hindrances to Jewish conversion to Christianity, Jewish debate or criticism of Christianity, conditions under which Jews are allowed to enter churches, not receiving Jews into various towns, and so forth (Rigg, *Select Pleas* xlviii).

In specifying the ethnoracial panopticon of the Jewish Exchequer's biopolitical powers across a range of surveillance and intervention, the irreducibility of racial treatment and racializing practices to merely fiscal-economic intentions could not be more explicitly announced or delivered.

However, despite the irreducibility of race to economic factors, racial and economic imperatives can occasionally be seen to collude in perverse and ingenious equations in the work of the Jewish Exchequer. The poll tax levied on all Jews aged twelve and above (detailed in paragraph 5 of the Statute of Jewry) and collected by the Jewish Exchequer traces a notation of racial form that is worthy of attention. Once collected, the proceeds of this capitation tax were distributed – in an arc of irony delivering impeccable ethnoracial logic – to the *Domus Conversorum*: the national institutional home of converts from Judaism to Christianity established by Henry III in 1232.

Jews who converted to Christianity, in ceasing to be Jews, were dispossessed of their belongings. Since their assets were amassed through labors deemed sinful ("usurious") under the theological hermeneutic imposed by their conversion, it was deemed unfit for these new Christians to retain their sinfully gained property, and government confiscation ensued. Stripped of their assets, the impoverished new Christians, now forbidden their former livelihood of "usury," needed stipendiary aid and shelter for daily subsistence.

Thus the Exchequer of the Jews and the House of Converts – institutional partners colluding in the state's machinery of racial governance – saw to it that faithful, observant

Jews were made to pay for, and support, once-Jews who had turned their backs on the faith and the community.[56] In its understanding of how to invest the politics and economics of race with a sublimely punitive irony, England's behavior as a racial state in premodernity urges that its bureaucracy was liable to flights of poetic inspiration.

Church and State Partners: Political Theology, Ideological State Apparatuses, Racial Praxis

The church's theological position on Jewish "usury," along with its other theopolitical positions on Jews, might suggest to us that medieval Christianity aggregated theories of Jewish difference that drove a panoply of ethnoracist practices acted out on Jews by the Christian populace and by the state. One might think that the medieval Church furnished society with theories of difference that became, on the ground, practices of race: The Church supplied the theory, and the state and populace supplied the praxis.

But this would not do justice in understanding theory's relations with practice in the production of Jews as ethnoracial subjects. Church *behavior* suggests the extent to which the Church itself trafficked in ethnoracial praxis that surpassed the jurisdiction of political theology's conception of Jews as constituting a differential category of religious subjects, the purpose of whose existence was to bear witness to, and to subserve Christian truth. The medieval Church ascribed to Jews the qualities of animals and of the devil; theology and doctrinal hermeneutics assigned genetic stigmata to mark Jews off as a separate species, like the monthly or annual bleeding supposedly experienced by Jewish men; church theologians taught that Jews were a lower order of creature manifesting bestiality, carnality, diabolism, vampirism, and uncontrollable effluxes of the body. Forces of the Church trafficked in biopolitical theories *and* praxis.

Nor did the state confine its purview to racial praxis alone. Henry III's ordinance of 1253, which bars Jews from eating or buying meat during Lent, hindering the conversion of fellow Jews to Christianity, disputing the tenets of the Christian faith, or "dishonoring" Christ by tarrying in churches, also discloses an avid interest in religious-ideological theory and political theology, whose tenets and values the ordinance endorses, as if an ordinance of state could also be a branch of church writing (Rigg, *Select Pleas* xlviii).

Both the medieval church and the medieval state practiced nascent and developing theories of race, and theorized the racial practices they instituted. This is not surprising perhaps in an era that saw the rise of a new class of churchmen in state government responsible for what has been called "the bureaucratic revolution" of the twelfth and thirteenth centuries (Moore, "Anti-Semitism" 56): churchmen responsible for an expanding administrative culture of record-keeping and documentation that, as we saw, spawned in England the impressive network of registries monitoring Jewish assets and the multifarious activities of the Jewish Exchequer. The growth in bureaucracy and documentary culture staffed by a cohort of clerics also improved communications between the papacy and the secular heads of Europe, so that "papal guidelines for Jewish-Christian relations, dating from both before and after the Fourth Lateran Council in 1215, were increasingly brought to the attention of rulers" (John Edwards 89).[57]

When churchmen, bureaucrats, and administrators overlapped in offices and roles, coordination between church and state in practices of racial governance was one legacy, especially at the higher echelons of government, where "abbots, bishops, and even arch-bishops were conspicuous among the barons and higher functionaries of the Great Exchequer of England" (Gross 14). At the time that English Jews were the first in Europe to be ordered to wear the "badge of shame," on March 30, 1218, during the minority of Henry III, the papal legate Guala happened to be the eleven-year-old king's guardian and "effective ruler of the church in England . . . all-powerful in the king's council" (Richardson 182). After Guala's departure, his successor, the papal legate Pandulf became "as influential in the king's council as he was in the English church" (Richardson 184).[58]

Coincidence in the goals of church and crown in the matter of anti-Jewish directives such as the badge was paralleled by how church scrutiny of Jews – even lacking such state apparatuses as *archae* and exchequers – was also characterized, like state scrutiny, by a peculiar intensity and insistence. Between 1208 and 1290, John Edwards notes, almost a third, or "eleven of the thirty-six sets of canons enacted by councils of the English church touched on Jewish matters":

> English Jews had already been affected by the measures passed by the Third Lateran Council, in 1179 . . . the Bishop of Worcester had already issued statutes forbidding Jews to hold liturgical books, vestments and ornaments as pledges for loans . . . He had also forbidden Christian wetnurses to look after Jewish children, and instructed female Christian servants not to sleep in the house of their Jewish employers. These latter provisions, which were to be enacted throughout Catholic Europe, more than appeared to make a link between religion and genetic origin . . . The 1222 provisions went further.
>
> (John Edwards 91)

In 1222 the archbishop of Canterbury, Stephen Langton, convened the Council of Oxford, which refined the stipulations demanded of Jews and reinforced the requirement that the Jewish badge be worn by "each and every Jew, whether male or female" (Canon 40; Grayzel 314), reiterating the order pronounced four years earlier.[59] In personal life, Jews "were not to make excessive noise while worshipping, and they were not to employ Christian women as servants. Jews were not to buy, or even eat, meat during the Christian penitential season of Lent" (John Edwards 91); they could not build new synagogues or enter churches, but must pay tithes "out of their usury" to the parishes in which they lived (Grayzel 315).

The Oxford provisions were followed by "a series of more locally applicable enactments and reissues between then and the Expulsion," and in 1253 the Oxford provisions were incorporated into secular law through a series of statutes issued by Henry III, as we have already seen (John Edwards 91; Richardson 191). This convergence of statutory and ecclesiastical law merged the power of diocesan authority with the power of the state; and from January 1253, Jewish submission or forfeiture of property was the legal consequence (Richardson 191).[60]

Collusion between canon and secular law – and resistance to law, on the part of the minority population being ruled over – can be micrologically tracked across the documentary record through the obsession with how to mark Jews visibly, on the outside of their bodies, so that they could be told apart, at a glance, from Christians.

In 1215, Canon 68 of the Fourth Lateran Council demanded a difference of *clothing* (*habitus*) for Jews and Muslims living within Christian territory. On March 30, 1218, in England, "where the bishops and the papal legates, Guala and Pandulph, occupied a particularly prominent place in English government," Jews were ordered by the minority council of Henry III to wear "a pair of white rectangular patches (*tabulas*) of cloth or parchment on the front of their upper garment, presumably in imitation of the two stone tablets (*tabulas* in the Vulgate translation) on which Moses had received the law" (Vincent 210; Roth, *History* 95; Richardson 182–4).

A *badge* (*signum*) had crystallized from the general conciliar demand, three years earlier, for a difference of dress (*habitus*).[61] In 1221, a letter from Pope Honorius III to Stephen Langton urged the archbishop "to enforce the distinction in Jewish dress within his own diocese of Canterbury" (Vincent 209); in 1222, the badge was written into Canon 40 of the Council of Oxford convened by Langton (Grayzel 315); in 1253, it was written by Henry III into statutory law. The trajectories of church and state were not parallel or asymptotic, but convergent.

Despite the intensifying pressure of canon and state law in the thirteenth century, defiance by English Jews glimmers through the documentary record: As Nicholas Vincent points out, "it is the very fact that Jews resisted the new dress code, that provides us with much of our information about the code's implementation" (214). In 1229, a second papal letter to Canterbury, this time from Pope Gregory IX to archbishop Richard – on the heels of the complaint by the bishop of Worcester that the Jews of Canterbury were not, in fact, wearing their badges, and continued to have Christian servants – commanded the archbishop of Canterbury to enforce the badge and the prohibition (Vincent 209).[62]

In the documentary record, Jewish refusal of self-marking is visible in the profit the state accrued from Jewish defiance: "from at least 1221, the receipt rolls of the Jewish exchequer record a stream of fines paid by Jews to be released from wearing the *tabula*" (Vincent 215). "[T]he highest payment recorded is that by Moses, the son of Abraham (apparently of Norwich), who had to find £4," while some Jews refused the badge, did not pay for permission, and were punished "for their temerity" (Richardson 179–80). Vincent wryly observes: "in England the implementation of the Lateran decrees was hampered by resistance from Jews and . . . Jews' reluctance to adopt restrictive codes of dress" (215).

For thirty years after England's imposition of the badge, "the series of fines on the Jewish receipt rolls" testifies to how "Jews themselves did their utmost" to refuse the badge, with the exception, presumably, of those too poor to be able to buy themselves freedom from this harassment (Vincent 219, 220).[63] Refusal by Jews to mark themselves unmistakably to all around them may have stemmed from necessities of survival: In Lent and Holy Week, and when preparations for crusades were in process, murderous attacks against Jews escalated, so that even Innocent III, who presided over the canon law that birthed the badge, was conscious that "the imposition of distinctive dress on Jews might make them more liable to attack" (Vincent 215).

We can read the fines imposed on Jews for their repeated refusals to wear the badge, the exemptions purchased by Jews in resistance, and the fines paid by Jews who refused to be herded into towns where their livelihoods and lives could be monitored (Mundill 23 n.39) as some of the ways in which English Jews spoke back to the law and the state: as strenuous attempts to communicate, that have been left to us in the historical record.

We might suspect, also, that the nineteen Jews accused of child slaughter and murdered by the state in 1255 for the putative killing of young Hugh of Lincoln did not go quietly to their death without protesting their innocence. Indeed, we have no incentive to suppose that they obligingly submitted themselves to being dragged through city streets before daybreak, and presented their necks to the noose without a murmur. Neither should we reason that the 269 Jews put to death during the 1278–9 coinage trials of London went docilely and mutely to the hangman, uttering no protest or defiance at their trials.

The historical record is silent because though English Jews might have spoken, they were not heard. What *are* heard are the accusations against them: What speaks more loudly than the documentary marks in pipe rolls is the popular communal lie of child murder that predetermined the fate of Lincoln's Jews and foreordained their death. In their inability *to speak and be heard* – in their silencing by church, state, and populace – we see the subalternizing of England's Jews, the racial subalterns of the medieval West. Their subalternity conferred by their inability to be heard, again and again, over the lies told about them, these racial subalterns are spoken for, and spoken about, by the structures of power ranged against them. The creation of England's Jews as raced subjects, *and* as racial subalterns, are mutually constitutive moments.

But resistance of any kind, over time – even when it feeds state coffers – breeds renewals of disciplinary action, so that in 1253 the series of statutes on Jews issued by Henry III reiterated the demand that all Jews wear "a visible tabula (*manifestem tabulam*) on their breast" (Vincent 219). As we have seen, in 1275, in the notorious *Statutum de Judeismo*, Henry's son Edward I increased the girth of the badge by one and a half times, and extended the order of self-marking to include children over the age of seven (Roth, *History*, 96).

Visible in the myriad details of the panopticonic administration of Jews in medieval England is thus the agile machinery of a peculiarly persistent, energetic, inventive, and invasive species of state racism at work, and the hallmark of its signature on the lives and bodies of Jews.[64] The Jewish Exchequer, the *Domus Conversorum*, the aggregate of laws and decrees ruling on Jewish lives, and the network of *archae* organized state racism's most visible public institutions and infrastructure. These constituted the economic and political machinery of state racism at work.

The tagging of people with a Jewish badge – whose features are prescribed, respecified, enlarged, recolored, moved around into ever more prominent positions on the human body and apparel, and extended to the bodies of little children – and the herding of individuals and families into *archa* towns, the only places they are allowed to reside, in urban spaces segregated from Christians, are part and parcel of state racism's signifying apparatus – the way state racism signs itself materially on the bodies and lives of Jews.[65]

Despite the panoply of effects in the vista afforded by the example of medieval England, however, race was not a matter of centralized, consciously coordinated creation by the administrative state, nor even of the state in collusion with church authority. Race, instead, was the product and consequence of a succession of local, contingent operations – improvisations of law, institutions, apparatuses, and micropowers responsive to opportunity or exigency – that aggregatively interlocked upon the lives, bodies, and livelihoods of their subalternized Jewish subjects.

Conversion as Racial Passing and Strategic Essentialism: Miscegenation, Biopower, Sensory Race

In 1232, Henry III materialized a new state institution in England, the *Domus Conversorum* or "House of Converts," a home where Jews who had converted to Christianity could find shelter, sustenance, a stipendiary income (10*d.* a week for men,

8*d*. for women), as well as instruction and mentoring in the Christian faith (and thus, it was thought, cement their conversion and ward off relapse to Judaism). Records indicate that hundreds of men, women, and children lived in the *Domus* during the three centuries of its existence.[66] Though it was not the first "house of converts" created in England, this was a national institution and the only one founded by a king, and it has been read as a highly visible outcome of the thirteenth century's virulent and invasive public culture of conversionary efforts aimed at Jews. Organized like a monastery, with communal meals, prayer, and mass, and under the supervision of two chaplains, the *Domus* has been seen by some as an interstitial space in thirteenth-century England – simultaneously a peaceful haven and an insecure ground – evanesced between an increasingly aggressive Christian national community and a shrinking demographic of scattered Jewries eking out an ever more regulated and precarious existence.[67]

This odd interzonal space – a doorway through which passed people who had exited one population group to enter another – eventually became the site of Rolls House and the Public Record Office, where Chancery business was conducted and the records of the nation were kept, in an ironic, efficient symbolism that memorialized the purifying of national space by keeping the records of the Christian nation's business sited where the nation's minority community of Jews were made to disappear (Heng, *Empire of Magic* 90).

But did a Jew in fact disappear as a Jew – leaving his/her race behind and transubstantiating into a Christian at conversion? Historians point to sticky residues that uneasily remained. Sometimes the residues took the form of a permanent marking by name, in which a person would be stuck with his/her erstwhile state of Jewishness. "Martin the Convert," "Saer the Convert," "Claricia the Convert," "Leticia the Convert," and "Eleanor the Convert," who lived at the *Domus* in the thirteenth century, all bore the weight of perpetual recall in their naming (Adler 351). "Roger the Convert," who served Henry III and Edward I for twenty years in the royal household, and Roger's son "John the Convert," also in royal service, are permanently once-Jews.

"William the Convert" of Oxford, cruelly deployed as a collector of the capitation tax levied on Jews – the detested *chevage*, a tax channeled to support the *Domus* – was assaulted by Oxford Jews for more, no doubt, than the burden of his name (Stacey, "Conversion" 280; Adler 301). A conversion might also be questioned: The year after the *Domus* opened its doors, an inquiry was created to ascertain if the conversion of Hugh of Norwich, a *Domus* resident, had been sincere (Adler 283).

Decades after a conversion, and even when the convert was a prominent personage – showered with protective privileges by the king, and decorated with the belt of knighthood – a residue of Jewishness would cling tenaciously, to trouble a convert's Christian identity and stir up doubts about him. Historians are struck by the example of Henry of Winchester, converted to Christianity by Henry III himself, and on whom the king generously bestowed his own personal name, at a baptism over which the king presided.[68] This "favorite of the king worked as the king's notary in the Jewish Exchequer," yet when Henry of Winchester was assigned to act as judge in the coin-clipping trials under Edward I (trials in which Christians as well as Jews were implicated, as we saw), his assignment was challenged by Bishop Thomas Cantilupe, a member of the king's council (Elukin, "From Jew to Christian?" 175).

In the fourteenth-century dossier of Thomas Cantilupe's canonization, Ralph de Hengham, later chief justice of the Court of Common Pleas, recorded that the bishop was scandalized that "a certain knight who was a Jew and called Henry of Winchester, the Convert, should have *testimonium et recordum* over Christians who clipped or forged the king's money" because "it was not proper that this convert and Jew should have such power over Christians," given "Jewish perfidy and the ancient hatred of the Jewish people for Christians" (Elukin, "From Jew" 175; Stacey, "Conversion" 277–8; Fogle, "Between" 112).

If decades are insufficient to erase residues of Jewish nature, even after a conversion presided over by the monarch, might the passing of *generational* time minimize or remove such tainting traces of Jewishness? The renowned case of "the Jewish Pope," Anacletus II – rival of Innocent II in the schism of 1130 – guards against optimism. The papal candidacy of Anacletus, whose great-grandfather had been a Jew, was opposed by a shining cohort of twelfth-century notables – the most redoubtable and magisterial churchmen, theologians, intellects, and statesmen of the day, including Peter the Venerable, Suger of St-Denis, Arnulf of Lisieux, Walter of Ravenna, Bernard of Clairvaux – on the grounds that, in the words of St. Bernard in a letter of 1134, "it is an insult to Christ that the offspring of a Jew has occupied the chair of Peter" (Stroll 166).

Four generations after a conversion, the descendant of a once-Jew was still tagged as a Jew. "When St. Bernard insinuated that Jewish character could remain unaffected by conversion, he no doubt was reflecting the common opinion," Mary Stroll soberly concludes (167).[69]

"[W]hat drove Christians like Bernard to reify Jewishness into a physical attribute transmitted by descent and impervious to the effects of baptism?" asks Jonathan Elukin ("From Jews" 183). Stacey's response to the English example of Henry of Winchester is local, but resonant:

> Integration had its limits, even for a man who had been knighted by the king himself. By the middle of the thirteenth century in England, there was clearly an irreducible element to Jewish identity in the eyes of many Christians, which no amount of baptismal water could entirely eradicate ... Through baptism, converts from Judaism became Christians, but this did not mean that they had entirely ceased to be Jews in the eyes of their brothers and sisters in Christ.
>
> ("Conversion" 278)

True conversion by a Jew – *successful* conversion – is, in fact, a kind of *race death*: the end of the converted Jewish subject's life, name, identity, and interior consciousness, *qua* Jew. But the cultural record's wavering and uncertainty over new converts, and even old converts, from Judaism – centuries before the *conversi* of Spain encountered like interrogation, on a grander scale – suggests that such converts created a *category crisis* for Christianity.

Not Jews any more, but unable to disappear into the mass of Christian subjects either, these new Christians troubled the category of "Jew" and that of "Christian" by embodying an indeterminacy of status and identity that had the potential to put the categories *Christian* and *Jew* into crisis. Unsurprisingly, the potential for crisis peaks exponentially when power is recognized to be at stake: when a convert is authorized to sit in judgment over Christians and levy sentences involving the life and limb of Christians, or when a generational descendent of a convert might occupy the throne of St. Peter and exercise panoptic power as the supreme head of all Latin Christendom. At such moments, the horror of category crisis peaks spectacularly, and the resultant drama lodges itself in the cultural record of ideological writing.

At such moments, Christianity's most authoritative voices and personages move to shatter the undecidability of the new-old Christians – of "this new identity somewhere between Christianity and Judaism" (Fogle, "Between" 114). Ecclesiastic authorities choose determinate closure that secures the greatest advantage, by positing a *strategic essentialism*: The converts, and even their descendants, were really Jews all along, because having once been Jews, or having descended from people who had once been Jews, carried an essence that tainted a person forever, and relegated them back to membership in their (great-grandfather's) category of origin. Assigning converts back to Judaism – this imposition is the ironic dark twin of ecclesiastical fears of relapse and recidivism by converts – temporarily ends category crisis until the conundrum of conversion rears its head again.

Despite its vicissitudes, however, Christianity's trafficking in conversion is, in a fundamental sense, unavoidable. Conversion is the cornerstone of Christianity, the *sine qua non* at its beginning, middle, and end. Christendom is founded *ab origo* on conversion: The apostolic mission, Saul's epiphany on the road to Damascus, the first converts and witnesses who form the earliest Christian community, are the foundation that builds the edifice of Christian society and its *grand récit*.

Conversion of Jews is also indispensably part of Christianity's story *ab origo*: Jews are there in the life, death, identity, and community of the Savior, and are the first converts. Equally fundamental, the end of Christianity's story also requires the conversion of Jews – an indispensable feature of medieval theological eschatology based on Paul's epistle to the Romans (Rom. 11: 25–7), that forms the basis of the Augustinian doctrine of relative tolerance affording Jews partial (and at least theoretical) protection in the Middle Ages:

> Throughout the Middle Ages the expectation of eventual Jewish conversion lay at the center of traditional Christian justifications for protecting the Jewish populations which lived within their midst. St. Augustine and later Pope Gregory the Great enunciated a rationale for Christian protection of Jews, based loosely on Romans 11.25–29, that stressed the historical importance of the Jews as living witnesses to the Old Testament prophecies that confirmed Jesus' messiahship and that foresaw the Jews' eventual conversion to Christianity as a harbinger of the end of days.
>
> (Stacey, "Conversion" 263)

Yet the thirteenth century's preoccupation with conversion – both at home and internationally, as witnessed by mendicant missionary activity worldwide among the heathen – floated on volatile waters.

For the public, the phenomenality of conversion rested on ritualized iterations: Beginning with baptism, and extending to other sacramental and institutional practices, the life of the convert would repeat a rhythm of liturgical and calendrical rites to the end of its days, in formal attestation of the material reality, the phenomenality, of successful conversion. Privately, however, conversion was "a long formative process, rather than a sudden, cataclysmic change," the "obscurity and incommunicability" of which meant the impossibility, for those external to the convert, of ascertaining the truth, authenticity, and durability of any conversion by an individual subject (Morrison 23, 2).

Conversion thus vexingly shares some of the character of racial *passing*, a phenomenon in which questions of inscrutability, volatility, and uncertainty also rule. The hybrid character of the religious convert, in whose interior being a Jew and a Christian are conjoined in a relationship of temporal priority that may prove to be unstable, parallels the hybrid character of the person of mixed race, in whom is conjoined two races – say, an Asian and a Caucasian lineage – by virtue of parentage. In a trajectory that Asian American studies tells us is not uncommon, that person of mixed race might pass as Caucasian for much of her life, but later "come out" as Asian when life conditions change or consciousness alters (the reverse might also occur, of course).

Yet a hybrid racial identity means the ontological priority of any identity is insecure: Has the subject *always* really been Asian (which her ritual of "coming out" supposes and announces), but had passed for Caucasian before; or does the subject's earlier identity as Caucasian have priority, as she had earlier professed, and does her current ritual of coming out mean that she is *now* passing as Asian?[70]

The religious version of this conundrum is no less of a Gordian knot, as the responses to new (and old) converts intimate: Which of the subject's two religious identities linked by temporal conjuncture *is* the real identity? Is the subject currently passing? What is the ontological ground on which to decide the priority of each religious identity she has professed, beyond the personal claims of the convert herself, or the public rituals she performs?

Put in the language of our contemporary sexual politics, conversion can thus be seen to initiate a process in which identity is queered, where a destabilization of the relationship between categories of religious identity produces a fluid indeterminacy. The queering process that is conversion points to the very queerness of conversion itself and to the queerness of the new, fledgling religious identity being proclaimed.

If epistemological certainty is elusive, ontological certainty also is elusive, thanks to the inscrutability and interiority of the conversion process. Morrison's fine insight that conversion is, in fact, really a *process*, not a sudden cataclysmic change, in theory holds out hope for converts from Judaism: In due course, the progressivist logic of conversionary momentum should allow for the completion of that process, at the end of a perhaps arduous trajectory, so that the convert arrives, in the fullness of time, at a culminating identity acceptable to all. Religious race as a project of improvement would thus be capped, at the end, by the successful entry of the convert into a new racial-religious formation.

However, the not-yet of progressivist logic – as we saw in Chapter 1, in the progressivist logic of colonial racism that is applied to the Irish and local populations of other English colonies in the "Celtic fringe" – can also become perpetual deferment, a "not yet forever" (Ghosh and Chakrabarty 148, 152). Like the savage Irish who never accomplish civilized status even after four centuries of effort and process, the descendants of Jews, after four generations of effort and process, do not arrive at Christian status either.

To say thus that the identity of the new-old convert from Judaism is in many ways a queer identity is not to minimize the ethnoracial predicament of the convert. Caught between population groups, and embodying the dilemma that conversion, seen from the outside, is never secure and cannot be secured, the convert suffers a symbolic responsibility that configures him as the ground of a perpetual tussle between rival religious power.

A way out of this Gordian knot, Elukin suggests, might be the warranty that is issued when a *miracle* produces a conversion: "[in] post-twelfth-century culture, the most secure conversions were those accompanied by a miracle. Divine signals testified to the changes in the interior identity of the Jews. They confirmed that the journey to God ... had divine guidance" ("Discovery of the Self" 69).

Adducing accounts from the third or fourth, ninth, tenth, and twelfth centuries in which Jewish conversions to Christianity were formally attested by the powerful support of a miracle, Elukin concludes that miracles are crucial proof for medieval Christians who "needed some external confirmation of the change in a Jew's identity" ("Discovery" 65).

Recreational and pious literature is eloquent in confirming that logic: Miraculous conversion – of Jews, Saracens, heathens of every ilk – is not only a commonplace and comforting narrative *topos*, but can also offer a delectable spectacle that is memorably sensational. In the romance known as the *King of Tars*, a sultan's skin color miraculously transforms from a loathsome black to a pure white without taint, and the offspring of his union with a lily-white Christian princess miraculously transforms from a featureless lump of flesh, without face, bone, or body, into the conventional fairest child who ever lived, at the baptism of the heathen and the lump (Heng, *Empire of Magic* 227–36).[71] As a warrant for securing a new *us* against an old *them*, a miracle can guarantee, celebrate, and induce racial emergence, as my analysis in the next section of this chapter will show.

The intangibility and nebulousness of a conversion *sans* miracle abuts peculiarly against the tangible, sensory qualities that seem often to characterize the *agents* and *occasions* of conversion. The cultural record seems rife with the description of tangible, sensual inducements to convert – sometimes in the wrong direction, as the famed thirteenth-century case of the English deacon who converted to Judaism for the love of a Jewess (studied by Maitland across several historical sources) alarmingly notates.

Exempla like those of Caesarius of Heisterbach, which recount how "young Jewish women or girls [are] attracted to Christianity or to young Christian clerics or to both," instantiate a popular narrative arc that can durably produce conversion as an outcome across *la longue durée*, as Shakespeare's *Merchant of Venice* and Scott's *Ivanhoe* demonstrate centuries later (Marcus, "Jews" 218). Ominously, fear of interracial sexual relations is precisely the pressure behind Fourth Lateran's biopolitical Canon 68, which requires a difference of dress for Jews and Saracens in order, the canon says, to prevent inadvertent sexual miscegenation between individuals not differentiable by sight into racial-religious kinds (Grayzel 308).

Intimacies that lead to Christian loss are not limited to the biopolitics of sex, moreover: Canon and secular law also fixate hysterically on wet nurses and the infants they nourish, servants in close domestic proximity with employers of the wrong religion, Jews and Christians eating and "tarrying" together at home, and the like.[72] I will return to the nexus of gender, intermixing, and miraculous conversion in the section that concludes this chapter.

The obsessions articulated in the exercise of church and state biopower point to a broad preoccupation with the sensory character of race in the medieval period. Medieval race is *sensual*: the "continuous caterwauling" of Jews in prayer in their synagogues, Jewish bodies that waft a fetid stench (*foetor judaicus*), or the distorted hypervisibility of the Jewish face (*facies judaica*), so vividly caricatured in medieval manuscript doodles.[73]

The success of strategic essentialism, it would seem, required Jewishness to be vulnerable to sensory detection, so that Jewish bodies were always giving themselves away – as cacophony or noise, as smell, as menstrual effluvia or a bloody flux, as the tactile and visual cut of circumcision.[74] (The irony, of course, if Jewish bodies are always giving themselves away, is how they do not, in fact, get to speak for themselves and be heard, but are silenced by popular lies and the regulative pyschobiographical narratives assigned to them as a collective group.)

Racializing the senses in this way – hearing, seeing, and smelling Jews – helps to bypass rational thought in favor of *feeling and sensing race* through channels more direct, intuitive, and primitive. Sound that hits the ear, smell that assails the nose, bodily cuts that offend the eye: All are ways of sensing and authenticating race through the evocation of a bioscape in which "race-feeling" instead of "race-thinking" predominates. Think less; *feel* more. In this racial bioscape, Jewish bodies just seem to overflow their boundaries, impinging on the Christian bodies around them, imposing on Christian spaces, and dangerously ending, in the process, the appropriate distance between bodies.

A racial bioscape even has fantasmatic machinery for embodying conversion as a state in-between, or imbricating, the races. Elukin points out that in his Manual for the Inquisitor, Bernard Gui, notorious inquisitor of the thirteenth century, bizarrely insists that when "Jews circumcise Christian children," they "cut the foreskin of the penis *only halfway* around the organ. For Jewish children, they circumcise by cutting the skin *all the way* around" ("Conversion" 183, emphasis added). As a sensorium of bodily parts supplying proof of the halfway state of conversion, what could be more poignant than this avid tactility of visual optics visited on a child's body by the luridity of Christian imagination? It seems Christians, rather than Jews accused of child slaughter, were the ones obsessively fixated on the signifying potential of the bodies of young boys, after all.

England's Dead Boys: A New Race, and Its Home, Post-Expulsion

To see if race-thinking and race-feeling are configured in new ways after the expulsion of Jews from England, I turn now to three cultural artifacts that feature Christian boys cut by Jews – a vibrant theme of enduring fascination in England, as we saw in Chapter 1 – the plotting of which can be made to bear emphases that demonstrate how the manipulation of Jews actual and virtual crucially served the national community of England in different historical periods. The first of these is a literary account of the famous death of young Hugh of Lincoln, written in Anglo-French between 1255 and 1272 and amplifying the shorter, more skeletal accounts lodged in contemporaneous chronicles describing Hugh's death, such as Matthew Paris's (written before 1259) and the Waverley Annals (written in 1255, the year of the boy's demise, as noted in Chapter 1 [Brown 89]).

Counterpointing this pre-Expulsion Anglo-Norman ballad are two admired post-Expulsion narratives of Christian-boy-murder by Jews: Chaucer's famed *Prioress's Tale*, in his *Canterbury Tales*, a retelling that deliberately yokes itself to Hugh of Lincoln by its explicit evocation of Hugh's death as an antecedent which occurred "but a litel while ago" (l. 1876), and the Marian miracle story of "The Christian Child Slain by Jews" in the remarkable Vernon compilation – dated, like *The Prioress's Tale*, to the 1390s, a century after the 1290 Expulsion.[75]

I end by analyzing a tale that is a kind of mirror inversion of the three, in which a *Jewish* boy, not a Christian child, is the vulnerable homicidal target, and where, moreover, *the boy does not die*. That last story, "The Jewish Boy," also a Marian miracle tale, enables us to see what is gained or lost when a boy-murder story is turned inside out, to become an Alice-through-the-looking-glass version of the customary Christian-boy-murder accusation.

This English offspring of a traditional tale of long duration and wide dispersion in Europe is also entered in the Vernon codex.[76]

My interest here is to develop a finer-grained understanding of what changed in racialization processes *before* and *after* the expulsion of England's Jews. The four specimens in this cluster of literary tales replay plots that refused to die, but remained a cultural inheritance that generation after medieval generation continued to invest with importance. Tracing cultural patterning in these accounts means following the spoor of characters, plots, and emphases that enthralled their audiences, authors, transmissional communities, and historical contexts – to see why these stories were important for the community on the page, in the mind, and in historical time.

Written shortly after the 1255 death of Hugh, the Anglo-French ballad named for Hugh of Lincoln is the fullest thirteenth-century narration of the boy's martyrdom that descends to us. The freshness and urgency of the historical event that occasions the ballad is palpable in how the narrative is plotted. The ballad presents the Jews of Lincoln in its very first verse, rapidly sketching the entire cruel and treacherous plot of slaughter economically, in just four lines (v. 1, Michel 1; Dahood "Anglo-Norman" 8). The final verse (v. 92) ends with the violent execution of those same Jews, whose bodies, after having been duly dragged though the city behind powerful horses, are now swinging from the gallows – which is how the historical Jews in the events surrounding the unfortunate Hugh were also treated. The last line of the ballad (l. 368) then closes by memorializing Jewish guilt (Michel 16; Dahood, "Anglo-Norman" 21).

Of the ninety-two verses that make up the body of the ballad, fifty-eight verses – 63 percent of content – feature Jews as active agents or speakers, or refer directly to Jews. Indeed, the ballad eyeballs Jews so insistently that its narrative arc steadily loops back to keep Jews pinned in its critical aperture. Not only are the Jews of Lincoln the focal point of interest, but the ballad remembers to convocate the richest Jews from *all over England* (v. 18, ll. 69–70) (Jews did indeed convocate in Lincoln in 1255 from all over, but only to celebrate the wedding of Belaset, daughter of Benedict fil' Moses) to share collectively in the blood guilt of the boy's torture and killing: There was "not a Jew" in all England who wasn't there, or didn't give his counsel for the deed (v. 81).

Invoked as a populace, Jews are also summoned individually by name. They thus circulate menacingly both as a universalized community and as active, gesturing, named, speaking agents: *Jopin li Ju* (l. 80, v. 21; l. 308, v. 78; l. 344, v. 87; l. 351, v. 88; l. 353, v. 89; l. 362, v. 91) *Agon li Ju* (l. 84, v. 22), who also appears as *Agim le Ju* (l. 94, v. 24; l. 121, v. 31; l. 124, v. 32; l. 324, v. 82), *Partenin le Ju* (l. 312, v. 79), and *Falsim* (l. 291, v. 73).[77] Collectively and individually, Jews are never far from the crosshairs of narrative. Given the context – the last decades of the thirteenth century, just before the Expulsion, with the popularity of ritual murder libels and boy martyrs' shrines, and Hugh's story and shrine in particular still luridly alive and well – narrative attention is unsurprisingly focused on racializing Jews as a unified population defined by malignant, homicidal virulence toward Christians.

This race seeks out as a target the most vulnerable member of Christian society, in order to torture and execute him in reperforming the deicide of Christ.[78] With the guilt of the heinous deed being shared by all, English Jews are thus collectively marked as a population that destroys Christian children. Concentrating squarely on Jews, the narrative delineates their collective identity in the most negative terms available in thirteenth-century discourse.

By contrast, Christian society in the ballad takes the form of scattered representatives who lack the coordination, effectiveness, and laser-like intent of the Jewish community. The boy's mother, for instance, who agonizingly searches for her child and pleads with King Henry for justice, is admonished by the king that if she is slandering the Jews, judgment will fall on *her* instead (v. 15–16). Even after the corpse is recovered, processed to the mother church, and entombed, Hugh's mother, with a sorrowful face, does not get to see the body of her beloved son – an unsatisfying turn of plot that frustrates affective closure for this figure of Christian maternity: "*le cors ne poeit vere/ De son cher fiz que ele ont chère*" ("she could not see the body/of her dear son whom she loved" [ll. 282–3, v. 71).

Because Hugh's body has been thrust into the dung hole of a latrine and is covered with ordure when found, Christian response to the disclosure of his sainted body is also unprepossessingly lukewarm. A woman who discovers it in a well (the body must be disposed of thrice, because the earth will not retain the victim) scarcely dares touch it with her hand ("*a pain/L'osa tocher de sa main*" [ll. 190–1, v. 48]) because it is so despoiled with filth (ll. 192–3, v. 49). If Christian laity is daunted, Christian clergy show no greater courage or enthusiasm either, as a priest also proves disappointingly unable to make himself go near it several verses later (ll. 230–1, v. 58).

Such lack of admirable response has to be rectified by a *convert* who pragmatically suggests that the body be washed first with hot water (ll. 256–7, v. 65). Conversion, we note, features in this pre-Expulsion narrative not as the gratifying *dénouement* of the plot, the way post-Expulsion narratives will later like it, but as an offstage *fait accompli*. At a historical moment when there were, in fact, many converts residing at the *Domus Conversorum* and impinging on societal consciousness, a convert here acts with reassuring helpfulness, and his behavior is a corrective to the weak responses of the other Christians, including weak priestly response: No false, insecure, inscrutable, or incommunicable conversion *here*.

As a pre-Expulsion artifact, *Hughes de Lincoln* – written not (yet) in Middle English, but still in the French of Anglo-Norman England – thus notably concerns itself with all the anxieties and obsessions of pre-Expulsion England. A convert from Judaism to Christianity thankfully behaves like a convert should.

The Christian former nurse of a Jew, who secretly conveys the mutilated body away from Lincoln to aid the Jews in evading detection (v. 44–7), also positions eloquent proof, alas, that the prohibition of Third Lateran in 1179 and Henry III's ordinance of 1253, specifying that no Christian nurse should "suckle or nourish the male child of any Jew" – "*lactet aut nutriat puerum alicujus Judei*" (Rigg, *Select Pleas* xlviii) – was a wise, anticipatory precaution, the flouting of which, as amply shown here, breeds treachery to Christian society. As canon and state law repeatedly warned, bodily intimacy between the races, even when not a sexual mixing of kinds, is proven to induce other kinds of dangerous seductions.

If Christian consciousness appears diffuse and scattered, lacking a center – a pallid foil to the supercoordinated malignity of the Jews – where it does crystallize dramatically, in the prolonged suffering of the child under torture, the focus is pinned on the effectivity of *Jewish* actions, and beadily, grimly congeals Jews as child- and God-killers. Despite the conventionality of the ritual murder *topoi* and plot by this time, the boy's suffering as depicted in the ballad is fresh and excruciating. Think less, the ballad urges its Christian audience, and *feel* more.

Always an *enfant* except when he is an *innocent*, Hugh is bound with a cord and stripped naked like Christ was by the Jews (ll. 73–5, v. 19), his nakedness a visual delight for the Jews who taunt him, ritually haggle over him, and condemn him to abuse and death (v. 20–4). He trembles piteously at the sight of the cross that is presented for his execution, though uttering not a sound (v. 26). We see his dread as they unbind him and hang him on the cross (v. 27–8). Moment by moment, one verse at a time, the Jews spread his arms and nail his hands and his feet with sharp nails, crucifying him fully alive on the cross ("*tut vif sur la croiz crucifiez*") as we are invited to imagine the child's terror and agony, and his great suffering (v. 29–31, l. 120). With the boy still alive, "Agim the Jew" then pierces the side of this innocent, thrusts his knife into the child's heart and cuts his heart in two while the evil onlookers smile, and the child at last pathetically cries out for his mother, calling her to pray to Jesus Christ for him, as his soul leaves his body (v. 32–3).

It takes seventeen verses to kill the child, many more to dispose of his body. Even after his death and bodily disposal, the beady eye of consciousness that anneals Jewish evil as definitive does not concede its place at the center of attention. In a *second* narration that holds the torture and slaughter right before our eyes again, *Jopin le Ju* later makes a prolonged public confession that re-dramatizes, in detail, every single step of the excruciating torture and slaughter of the child and the body's disposal (v. 78–86). If the death of a child is a wounding for society – a trauma that registers how significance coalesces upon key symbolic bodies which perform representational labor for human civilization, so that a vulnerable child's death brings home the instant recognition that family, lineage, and futurity have been cut short – Hugh's is a wounding and death that feels interminable.

The narrative ensures this by singling out and dilating the focal point of the child's suffering, teases the suffering out in stages, and restages it again afterward via a Jew's self-incriminating testimony. Narrative attention circles around the gloating, evil, vile Jews, whose unconscionable acts materialize as the emotional centerpiece of the story. Desecration of the child's Christ-like body with dung, as the corpse is flung into a latrine – a desacralization underscored, as we have seen, by the repeatedly queasy responses of various Christians to the body's filth-covered repulsiveness – works to multiply the victimage and outrage that affixes attention squarely on Jews. This French ballad's prolonged focus on the filth and stench of the boy's ordure-covered corpse far surpasses any comparable description of the body in post-Expulsion texts, as we will see.

Beyond his role as innocent victim, Hugh the child is otherwise not distinctive in this early version of the story. The liveliest cast members are the lurking, gesticulating, threatening, ranting Jews prancing about in the narrative, who inhabit the extended apparatus of race-making right to the very last line of narration, where their name is still summoned and haunts the poem to the end. Pre-Expulsion obsessions mean that the story of Hugh is invariably the story of how Jews are transformed into a race in thirteenth-century England.

A century after the 1290 expulsion of Jews from England, Chaucer's celebrated *Prioress's Tale* evokes Hugh of Lincoln's memory, tomb, and anti-Semitic lesson in a purposeful and deliberate foregrounding (ll. 1874–6, ll. 871–2) – yet substitutes a simple, quick slitting of the victim's throat for the elaborate rituals of Jewish child torture and murder, eschewing thus any milking of the emotions that could be had by drawing out the child-killing. The story's plot, moreover, is patterned into the shape of a Marian miracle tale.[79] This recitation ends not with an invocation to remember Jewish malignity, but with an invocation and prayer that says Mary's name ("Marie") in the last line of the poem – indeed, as the tale's very last word before "Amen" (l. 1880). Mary, it seems, has displaced the Jews. But why?

The Blessed Virgin, who has been construed by some scholars as the implacable enemy of Jews – Denise Despres' meticulous scholarship comes to mind – helps to structure and organize this story: A web of invocations, strategically placed, coalesces her presence as a reticulated network that is cast over the entirety of narrated content.[80]

From the get-go, the child's mother has taught him to reverence the Virgin (l. 1699), and each time he sees the Virgin's image, the child (who is a "litel clergeon," a baby clerk [l. 1693]) kneels down and says his *Ave Marie* (l. 1698). He hears, and learns to sing, the Virgin's hymn of praise, *Alma redemptoris mater* ("Kindly Mother of the Redeemer," ll. 1708–12), the repeated joyful singing of which is made the animating trigger that earns him the attention and hatred of Satan and the Jews, hence producing his assassination (ll. 1747–54). Despite his throat being cut, however, Mary's agency enables the dead child to sing *Alma redemptoris mater* again (ll. 1802–3), at exactly the point that the singing enables his body to be detected – leading to the subsequent execution of the Jews, proof of Mary's miraculous patronage, and the triumphal celebration of the Virgin's agency and the boy's martyrdom.

This quick overview should intimate that attention in this post-Expulsion text is not, in fact, primarily vested in the Jews – who are, of course, still the *deus ex machina* responsible for child slaughter – but fans out, widening the horizons of interest. Indeed, structural patterning of the tale as a Marian miracle materializes *Christians* as a protected and watched-over population, despite the sacrifice of one young member: a sacrifice necessary, as we shall see, to enable that privileged, watched-over community of Christians to be called forth as a people, and characterized. The remarkable contribution of the Prioress's narrative to the racialization of England (since this is a post-Expulsion text, "Asia" is the putative locale, just as Shakespeare's Shylock is in "Venice" [l. 1678]) lies in how that narrative brilliantly summons forth *two* races, names each as a population, and defines both indelibly in our mind.

First, the narrative interpellates "Cristen folk" (l. 1685) and their children as a people *who are descended from Christian blood*: "ycomen of Cristen blood" (l. 1687). Christians – who are thus presumably old Christians, not converts – *inherit* Christian-ness through blood descent. This understanding of a religious identity as the inheritance of birth and lineage – staking a genealogical claim that Christians are *born* as Christian – is an understanding that transmogrifies religion into genetic race. The identification of a population yoked by blood occurs early (in the second verse), so that the theme of a blood tie can be invoked again later: It is Christian *blood*, we are told, that cries out against the Jews' deed (l. 1768).

If Christians are a blood race, Jews are an infernal people. Satan himself ("the serpent Sathanas"), the "first foe" of Christians, whose living home is his "wasps' nest in the heart of Jews" (ll. 1748–9), rises up as an incarnated voice, and in a thundering apostrophe summons forth all Jews in the vocative, as a single population: "O Hebrayk peple" (l. 750). In the same instant that he interpellates Jews as a people, Satan declares a primordial clash of religious races, stating an incommensurable enmity between Jewish law and Christian praxis and instigating his Jews against the child who sings the Virgin's hymn.[81]

Editorial commentary in the Riverside edition of the *Canterbury Tales* notes that in several manuscripts of the *Tale*, the devil binds himself with the Jews by referring to Jewish law not as "*youre* lawes" but as "*oure* laws," a reading that Boyd's variorum edition of the

Tale accepts as correct (l. 754; Benson et al. 915 n. 564; Boyd, *Prioress's Tale* 142–3, n.1754, emphasis added). Jews are not a People of the Book, but a people of Satan's laws, and in a *second* thundering apostrophe, the narrative damns them as "new Herods" who shed the blood of Christian offspring in a modern, post-Biblical bloodletting (l. 764). This second apostrophe picks up the theme of Christians bonded through blood inheritance: Christian blood, it charges, is what cries out at the Jews' accursed deed ("The blood out crieth on youre cursed dede" [l. 1768]). Christians are bound by their inheritance of Christian blood; Jews are bound by shedding that Christian blood.

The two populations – one a blood race, the other an infernal race – are *embodied* races. For Jews, the embodiment is spectral, evoked as the liminal space they occupy: The Jewry that is *a street open at both ends* ("open at eyther ende" [l. 1684]) is an alimentary canal transposed onto the city, through which the city's transactions and evil profit pass ("foule usury and lucre of vileynye" [l. 681]). In the recesses of this Jewry, the collective body as a spatialized entity has "an alley with a private place" ("a privee place" [l. 1758]) – the nether region, we might say, of an internal passageway – where the singing child, passing through the murky interiors of this dangerous and defiling Jewish spatial body, can be snatched in an instant, slit open, and flung into a privy, the other "private place" of the body.

For Christians, the singing child's flesh embodies Christian community: The boy's throat is like a street through which Christian song passes delectably twice a day, as naturally as breathing or eating ("Twies a day it passed thurgh his throte" [l. 1738]). Christian sound, we notice, sings in our ears: A hymn to Mary sung sweetly by a seven-year-old has shunted aside distressing earlier noise in the form of Jewish caterwauling in synagogues when Jews once lived in England, noise which no longer impinges here on Christian space, or assails Christian ears. Instead, it is a Christian who transgresses Jewish space, making noise: The boy passes through the Jewry ("thurghout the Juerie" [l. 1741]) to and from school ("as he cam to and fro" [l. 1742]), jubilantly belting out with gusto his antiphon of Marian celebration "everemo" (l. 1744).

Racial embodiment is thus shrewdly unequal. Jews are kept to a shadowy presence, embodied by a street open at both ends, penetrated daily by a Christian who belts out praise of the Virgin ("Ful murily" [l. 1743]) in repeated invasions of Jewish space. Because the Jewish body is externalized and spatialized as a street, racial embodiment renders it liable to entry and penetration.[82] Racial embodiment of Christians takes the reverse route: Christian space is internalized and embodied as the boy's throat, a microlocal passageway through which sacred song passes twice daily, suffusing his throat as sacred space, even as throat and body together penetrate and process through the Jewish-street-as-body twice daily.

These twice-daily passings-through – the one happening internally, the other happening externally – articulate an asymmetry that registers which racial group gets to exercise successful infringement.[83] One reason why child murder in *The Prioress's Tale* does not take the form of a ritual crucifixion is thus the powerful symbolism of the boy's throat as a passageway rendered sacred by song. Christian space daily pushes through Jewish space, which, in effect, it defiles from within, thus instigating the narrative logic that the child's murder must take the form of a throat-slitting that attempts to end the invasion of one body by another. Crucifixion, thus, is not the proper method of murder in *this* tale of child slaughter.

The Prioress's Tale's skillful resignification of older patterns it inherits does not stop here. The boy's mourning mother, forming a dyad with him to represent a Christian family of the first instance recalling Virgin-and-infant-Jesus, is craftily apostrophized as a *new* Rachel ("This newe Rachel" [l. 1817]), offering a Christian resignification of the old Rachel that allows the newly mourning mother to displace the memory of the original Old Testament woman in the very moment of honorific recall. If we suspect, in this tactic of resignification, yet another claim that *Ecclesia* triumphs over *Synagoga* – craftily expressed in an intimate, domestic way – that suspicion is abetted by other resignifications.

Kathy Lavezzo ("Minster") reminds us that the boy singer's throat is not cut all the way through – in a decapitation that would render the boy headless – but just to the neckbone, as the child himself says ("My throte is kut unto my nekke boon" [l. 1839]). We recollect that partway cutting is supposedly a custom of Jews, who, when they circumcise Christian boys, seem not to cut all the way through, but only halfway – the action of cutting, of course, being this time displaced from phallus to the boy's head, the locus on the opposite end, with circumcision and beheading being often symbolically twinned in the imagination.

Despite any mnemonic that may recall Jewish intent or typicality, however, the bioscape in this text is by no means identical to earlier racial bioscapes. Scholars have remarked, for instance, on how *this* child – for all the effort to imbue him with pathos and sentimentality – appears a discomfiting, uncanny figure whose performance as the singing undead is creepy and disturbing, both to the audience in the text and the audience outside. A child made over into a transmissional medium for the Virgin – whose song takes priority, *literally* passing through the boy's throat (l. 1738) – this singing automaton, unnervingly, can be switched on and off.

The grain the Virgin places on the corpse's tongue switches on the singing after death, just in time for the body to be found (ll. 1852–5). Acting as a crank that works the machinery of sound issuing from the dead child's body, this grain also keeps the corpse animated, if not actually alive. When the grain is snatched away by the abbot (l. 1861) – some scholars see this as inducing relief for the audience within and outside the text – it is as if marionette strings are suddenly cut, so that the undead can finally be dead. In this construction of the body as a body-machine, a kind of technological modernity might perhaps be seen to be at work.[84]

Modernity also surfaces in Chaucer's subtle understanding of psychosocial processes, ensuring that his narrative selectively redraws the Christian child's role. The boy's singing is not simply presented as a given, but is shown to be the outcome of a slow process of learning acquisition, as the boy first hears *Alma redemptoris* being sung, attends to the words and tune, absorbs the first verse, pesters a fellow schoolboy for the meaning of the Latin and significance of the song, asks a question from the information he gleans, is taught the song by his friend till he knows it by heart, and then practices the song daily when he walks to school and homeward (ll. 1708–40).

Chaucer's inspired narration of how Christian meaning, ritual, significance, and indeed piety is acquired – through instruction by better-informed guides, and also through autodidactic diligence – registers the crucial lesson that though Christians are *born*, "ycomen of Cristen blood," Christian praxis and piety are *learnt*: a project of intensive pedagogy.[85]

The attention apportioned to Christians and Christianity by the narrative, with a corollary diminution of attention to Jews (who only appear in nine out of twenty-nine verses, about 31 percent of the content) means that Jews, despite Satan's best efforts, are more a shadowy presence in this text than a forceful or imposing one. Jewish evil at times seems to have an oddly executive character, appearing almost a *pro forma* evil (evil is their inherited job). The Jews in this tale are also curiously lacking in initiative.

Not only must Satan summon them and push them toward the project of child-killing, but the Jews do not even commit the homicide themselves, relegating this task to a professional lackey they hire for the job ("An homycyde therto han they hyred" [l. 1757]). Unlike the Jews of the Anglo-French ballad, these lackluster villains do not approach the child themselves, threaten or torture, gesture, prance around, or even speak. They are absent during the performance of the murder, and do not even bother to view the corpse after the deed, let alone gloat over it.

The professional killer (a Jew, of course) rapidly and efficiently slits the boy's throat and thrusts the corpse in the requisite latrine (a Jewish latrine, of course), where presumably it is also requisitely covered with ordure (ll. 1760–3). Yet the body's discovery later and the events of the second half of the poem bring no mention of dung or bodily desecration. Instead, metaphors are crafted for the dead boy that place before our eyes visions of refulgence and radiance: He is a "gem of chastity," an "emerald," a "ruby bright" ("This gemme of chastite, this emeraude ... ruby bright," ll. 1799–800).

Positive, not negative, associations are thus cultivated for the child's signifying body, and highlighted. Narrative attention continues to pivot on the Christian players: the abbot and monks who cast holy water on the corpse, the sanctified recipient lying on the "chief altar" during the mass, the dead boy's voicing of the Virgin's agency, the abbot's removal of the grain from the corpse's tongue, and the final commemoration of the child, the Virgin, and Hugh of Lincoln (ll. 636–84).[86]

To sew this story firmly to Hugh of Lincoln's, the boy is repeatedly called a "martyr" (ll. 1769, 1870) and his death "martyrdom" (l. 1800), and Jews are drawn by horses ("with wilde hors") and hung in juridical acts of law ("by the law" [ll. 1823–4]), repeating the specific form of their execution in Hugh's story. Roger Dahood ("English Historical Narratives") observes that this latest martyr is also conspicuously placed in a tomb of pure bright marble, like Hugh's tomb ("in a tombe of marbul stones cleere" [l. 1871]). Finally, in case we are still able to miss the point after all the embedded reminders, the Prioress ends by conjuring up Hugh himself in a clarion call ("O yonge Hugh of Lyncoln") – Hugh who died, we are told, not centuries back "but a litel while ago" (l. 1876).

The Prioress's little martyr stands on the shoulders of Hugh in yet another way. Roger Dahood ("English Historical Narratives") and David Stocker separately draw our attention to how Hugh's shrine in Lincoln – which appears to have been blazoned with the royal arms of England – is architecturally linked to memorials associated with the expulsion of Jews. By invoking the story of Hugh, but shifting the interest toward Christians and away from Jews, *The Prioress's Tale* slyly reminds us that England – unlike "Asie" – has been purified of Jews. Dahood astutely suggests that the *Tale* offers itself as a midpoint between old ritual murder tales and new stories of Jews and Christians that are alighting on updated interests. Playing with the old plot, *The Prioress's Tale* now conjures England as a new kind of space where Christians are a population "ycomen of Cristen blood" – a de facto race whose time had come, in a post-Expulsion land.

Like *The Prioress's Tale*, "The Christian Boy Slain by Jews," one of nine surviving Marian miracle tales out of forty-one originally collected in the Vernon codex, invokes the Virgin as protector of Christians and evokes the theme of Jewish child murder, though the ritual nature of that murder is increasingly attenuated, as we saw also with Chaucer. Invocation of the Virgin at beginning and end helps to frame the plot as a Marian tale, and the Virgin's lily, inscribed with the gilded words *"Alma Redemptoris Mater"* (l. 123), replaces the Chaucerian "grain" producing the dead child's song. Here, the child's singing halts when the lily is removed from his throat, but resumes at the Introit of his requiem mass, when the corpse sings *"salve sancta parens"* ("hail, holy mother"), another Marian *hommâge*.

The Virgin is thus invoked four or five times, stamping this tale as Marian. Narrative interest, however, is less focused on Mary than on the child and his song, as Julie Couch points out in her fine reading of the unusual attention afforded the child-figure of this tale (205). The boy here is not just mawkishly a widow's son (*Prioress's Tale* l. 1699), or a symbolic sacrificial lamb (*Hughes de Lincoln*), but a hardworking child of the Christian poor, whose beautiful voice and singing skills gain him a living, a means to support his parents and bring food home daily. The narrative repeatedly emphasizes the dignity of the boy's work, though he's technically a beggar (ll. 8–9, 12) – his skillfulness at singing, the sheer delight of his song and the pleasure it brings to listeners, the glory of his voice, and his family's dependence on him as breadwinner (ll. 13–19, 27–9, 35–6, 50–4, 57–8, 64, 78–9, 98–100, 118, 127). This is a hardworking boy singing the Virgin's song as a street busker, and this singing is a form of courageous, dedicated child labor, the plucky child's "craft" (l. 13).

The boy's song fills the narrative, sweet and pure ("swete and cler" [l. 15]), high and clear ("heigh and cleer" [l. 54]), and beautiful ("deynteous" [l. 27]), like an angel's voice ("Riht as an angls vois" [l. 99]). His singing voice conjures up the child to our senses, renders his bodily immanence. A one-boy Vienna choir, his singing suffuses the story from line 15 to line 142, in a poem of only 152 lines – so that we are always conscious of a child's voice in sacred song winding its way through the narrative as an aural background before which the drama unfolds. At intervals, the singing surges to command the forefront of attention, as narrative interest condenses on the figure of the boy.

On the sole occasion that the child's singing briefly stops (when the bishop extricates the Virgin's lily), assembled priests and clerks take up the singing instead (l. 133), and all the bells are caused to ring (l. 134) as the boy's body is triumphantly processed to the minster. That is to say, in the one instant the child is silent, in his place we hear the soaring of skilled adult male voices in song, supported by the percussion of bells, in a vast, resounding amplification of Christian sound. Culture, it seems, hates a vacuum of silence.

So much has the historical memory of Jewish cacophony in prayer receded, dwarfed by the massiveness of Christian music, that the entire malignant race of Jews dwindles down, in this text, to just one individual Jew responsible for the child murder. This sole representative of the race does his best to theatricalize Jewish malignity, but behaves like a crochety nonlover of music who overcorrects. Luring the child into his house, he peremptorily slits the boy's throat, and thrusts the body into the proverbial latrine (ll. 38–40, 48–9); but as the narrative perfunctorily recites this act, it interrupts itself twice to specify that never, at any time, does the child stop singing, but in a continuous loop of music restarts his song each time it ends (ll. 41–4, 50–4), to the annoyance of the killer (l. 45). Sacred song *still* fills our ears, even during the singer's murder. If we are struck by how, in these stories, the singing child resembles a fine music box or musical instrument, this narrative specifies the rich *tonal quality* of the sound, the purity of voice, and the wonderful pitch the boy can attain: "hyghe" notes [ll. 52, 54] that soar ever higher ("herre and herre" [l. 79]) to help in his body's detection.

This text is so little interested in Jews that after its one Jew has been judged guilty, *the plot simply forgets him*. There is no execution, and we have no idea what happens to the killer. What follows instead is the evocation of *a united populace in all its civil and ecclesiastic authority*. Unlike stories of boy murder in which righteous authority is vested in a single person (King Henry in *Hughes de Lincoln*) or a set of persons (the magistrate, abbot, and monks of *The Prioress's Tale*), here the population of the entire city is summoned to judge, bear witness, and support the law. When the boy's mother has taken her case to the mayor and bailiffs (l. 82), the mayor instantly summons forth the people of the city (l. 92), instructs them of her testimony, announces that law must prevail, and orders them to accompany him to see the case brought to a just end (ll. 93–6).

Such formal convocation of the city populace by civil authority is a marked contrast to the spontaneous ad hoc gathering of "Crystene folk" in *The Prioress's Tale* who turn up in curiosity to gawk and "wondre upon this thing" (ll. 614–15). The mustered citizenry bears down upon the sole Jew, to demand the boy's body and to adjudicate with their own eyes, led by their mayor. Citizenry, mayor, and bailiffs thus ensure that justice is seen and performed *en groupe* – not handed down from on high, but the judgment of a collective will. Where once the plot of child murder rounded up a totality of Jews to assign racial guilt, the child-murder plot now vanishes its one Jew summarily, to concentrate on gathering a totality of Christians instead. Post-Expulsion, Jews – though still useful and necessary villains – are no longer the point; the race that matters is the Christian race.

That Christian race is rendered as *both* a civic population *and* a religious community. With judgment over, before the populace can disperse ("er the peple passede in sonder" [l. 115]), religious community gathers: The bishop arrives to deliver the lily from the boy's throat, and leads a grand procession of the corpse – that "holy body" ("holi liche" [l. 136]) – with great solemnity ("with gret solempnete") through all the city ("thorw al the cite"), in a dazzling throng of priests and clerks ("prestes and clerkes"), resounding bells ("belles . . . ryngen"), flaming torches ("torches bre(n)nynge"), and sumptuous vestments ("clothus riche"), into the minster to begin requiem mass (ll. 29–139).

At the juncture where secular and ecclesiastic communities converge, Christians as a totalized racial formation enact rituals that swell into sensory synesthesia. Bells are clamorously rung; voices are lifted in song; burning torches flame before our eyes and fill the nostrils; and elaborate, gorgeous vestments entice: Sound, sight, smell, and tactility enact the sensory totality of Christian-ness as sacred embodiment. If racial formation, as I suggested in Chapter 1, emerges through the ritualized iteration of group practices, post-Expulsion literature in this tale shows us that Christian rituals productive of a Christian race are sensuous – race is enacted and experienced sensorily, through tangible performances.

But the most remarkable tale that narrates how race is enacted through the senses and how Christianity is an embodied experience, told through the figure of a child, is not even a proper child-murder story at all. In the extraordinary narrative with which I will end this chapter, the young child does not die, and he is not even a Christian child, but a Jewish one. Like *The Prioress's Tale*, the Vernon story we call "The Jewish Boy" concerns itself with Christian embodied space and Christian identity and, like "The Christian Boy Slain by Jews," with a Christian community characterized by rich sensory rituals. Also like the three preceding texts, the pivotal figure here is also a vulnerable child-victim facing murder by a Jew or Jews.

"The Jewish Boy," however, plots a different trajectory and affect altogether, and my choice of this text to conclude this chapter stems from the tale's canny ability to evoke key details of the boy-slaughter story yet push forward in the direction of optimism, plotting on a scale that feels intimate, while playing advocate to sociocultural ambitions grander than we have seen thus far.

The tale's 186 lines tell a simple story: A Jewish boy who habitually plays with Christian children is attracted at Easter into a cathedral, where he hears mass performed and takes communion. His father, on finding him and hearing his account of what has transpired, is enraged and thrusts the boy into an oven, to which the boy's distressed mother leads the mayor and bailiffs of the city, who rescue the boy. As he comes out of the oven, not only is the child unharmed, thanks to a Marian miracle, but he also relates a story of wonder, in which the flames of the oven had turned into flowers and the oven itself had felt like a cool arbor for his play. At this, the mother, the boy, and all the Jews of the city convert to Christianity, while the boy's father is executed by being himself placed into the oven, in a juridical irony that appositely visits on the Jew the Old Testament justice of an eye for an eye.

This simple delineation of plot, however, does the narrative no justice; nor does it adequately convey the tone of a poem that is bent on eliciting positive, uplifting emotions and affirmation. Though the story needs a villain, narrative patterning is less preoccupied with the boy's father, an unredeemed Jew who is the sole representative of the old law superseded by the new civil authorities judging him – a jury of twelve (l. 175) who consign him to the flames – than it is concerned with the figure of the child who is the focal center, represented later with his mother by his side in the second half of the story. The narrative is, of course, interested in figurations of paternal authority and law, but its primary fascination lies with significations afforded by manipulating the idea of *the family*.

Most insistently, this narrative focuses on *space*. The child throughout inhabits a series of magicalized spaces – spaces that protect and enrapture, enfold him into their midst, and appear as enchanted ground because we always experience them through his eyes. The narrative follows this Jewish boy affectionately, inviting all to trail along, with eyes open and the boy as guide, to see how the child's passage through the lives of others leaves in its wake magicalized transformations.

In a nameless city where we are told Christians and Jews live together (ll. 15–16) – the Christians in one half (ll. 17–18) and the Jews confined to a single street (l. 20), in a familiar constriction of urban geography – there is a special place – a "croft," or small, enclosed patch of ground (l. 21) – where Christian children have made themselves a lovely habitat in which to play (ll. 21–2). The Jewish boy, whose father does not keep an eye on him or take any heed (ll. 25–6), often goes there to play with the children, coming and going as he pleases, and learning their games (ll. 27–30) exactly as if he were one of them ("riht as on of hem he were" [l. 31]).

If we cynically think that his acceptance by Christian children is intended to presage his conversion at the end – he's already a Christian even before he becomes one – the narrative also eagerly tells us that the Jewish boy is admitted and embraced by the children *with love* ("With loue" [l. 32]).

Love – a generous emotion – marks out this children's space as utopian, registering, as Julie Couch astutely observes, a kind of momentary utopian longing that Jewish and Christian children might play together peacefully (210–11).[87] Rarely do we encounter narrative descriptions of Christian love for a Jew (outside noxious recitations of sexual seduction), and it is his unconditional acceptance by the children that leads the Jewish boy spontaneously to follow his Christian playmates into the magnificent cathedral ("munstre") to hear mass at Easter, in an intuitive act that is a natural extension of their childish interaction.

Momentarily utopian, we see that the first space into which the Jewish boy has been received is a circle formed by Christian children, and designed by the narrative to lead to grander, even more all-embracing Christian spaces.

The instant that the cathedral is mentioned – once sacred architecture rears its spires – all of Christianity's official panoply also returns: The formal solemnities of Easter (ll. 33–4), worship at matins and mass (l. 38), and the duties of "Christian law" ("cristene lawe" [l. 39]) are paraded in series. In a move to which our cluster of post-Expulsion texts has familiarized us, the narrative convenes the entire Christian populace in its array – greater and lesser folk ("more and . . . lasse" [l. 40]), every man in his degree ("Eueri mon in his array" [l. 41]), husbands and wives ("Bothe housbonde and wyf also" [l. 42]) – to do what "cristene men" (l. 44) should at Easter: proceed to the minster for sacred ritual. Mass is thus a utopia of inclusiveness – embracing all classes and stations, men and women – with all boundaries transcended in universal worship.

As the collective Christian body proceeds to church, Christian children, we are told, follow their fathers, as they were ever wont to do (ll. 5–46), while the Jewish child – palpably fatherless, since attention is being conspicuously directed to dyads of Christian fathers and children – eagerly and happily also enters the church ("wel fayn was for to go" [l. 48]). The child's apparent fatherlessness, of course, slyly positions him as highly adoptable by the fathers of church and faith: a condition his Jewish father's execution at the end – an act that does render the child fatherless – will consolidate.

Once inside the cathedral, we are presented with the undivided glory of what Christianity is: an all-enveloping suffusion of the senses, sacred space resplendent as the wholeness of sensory experience. It's Easter, so the interior is transcendent with light, sumptuousness, and fragrance; the very air seems to shimmer. The boy, wide-eyed, absorbs the effulgence, the scented, glowing radiance, enraptured by what he sees: lamps and tapers burning bright and wafting their scents (l. 53); altars elaborately decorated (l. 54); exquisitely crafted statues and images (l. 55); gilt reliquaries for the holy bodies of many saints (l. 56); and a beautiful queen, gloriously dressed in gold, seated elegantly on a throne (ll. 57–8) and bearing a blissful babe, royally crowned, on her arm (ll. 59–60) as folk stand before them offering their prayers (ll. 57–63).

The ambient aura saturates the senses with reverent brilliance, and the heightened use of alliteration to depict the scene delicately points up the importance of what is happening and intensifies consciousness of *sound*, so that all the senses are summoned and engaged. This is what it is to be Christian.

The boy is well-nigh ravished with joy, transported ("For joye hi(m) thoughte i-rauessched neih" [l. 68]). Mesmerized, he happily follows the congregation through all the stages of the mass, kneeling (ll. 70, 76), receiving absolution after the Confiteor (ll. 71–2), and following the throng at communion. Though he is jostled and pushed (l. 77), he spared nothing, fearlessly, till he received the host, and was "houseled" among the Christians ("He spared no thing for no drede,/Among the cristene til he were hoselet" [ll. 78–9]). Nobody pays any heed to him; he's a just a little child that folk don't notice ("Of such a child me tok non hede" [l. 80]), but we've just experienced the magic of Easter high mass through that insignificant child's eyes, and the evoked sense of wonder lingers and ripples out.

All that pertains to church and mass, of course, is familiar to the poem's audience – and might thus be experienced as jaded repetition – but because it is offered here through dazzled young eyes, a fresh, transporting, and rapturous experience ensues. Christianity is here presented in the mode of *romance*, conjured though a vision of magical enchantment, a magicalized space and rituals that feel fresh and new to a Jewish boy who beholds what Christianity signifies for the first time. There is no need to *think* about what Christianity *means*; following the boy, we experience directly what Christianity *does*, how it is sensuously absorbed as an all-body experience.

The culmination of that sensuous experience is absorbing the body of God himself, which through the boy's touch and taste becomes part of his own body. Distilled by a child into an intimate encounter that feels as fresh as if it had occurred at the dawn of time, this is Christianity at its most powerful. Priests and ecclesiastic authority, canons and commandments, councils, laws, institutions, codes, badges, doctrines, theology, ordinances, rulings, and proscriptions, have all disappeared. Christianity is an unmediated bodily experience, immediate, rapturous, intimate.

The strategy of this presentation has not gone unremarked:

> The child's mesmerizing experience of mass communicates the poem's overarching desire for a universal Christendom, a potentially utopian vision in which all children could go to mass without fear. Here, a central Christian project, its mission to the unconverted, is centered in the sensitivity of a child.
>
> (Couch 209–10)

The Christian utopian project that Julie Couch detects – limned, as she says, through the sensitivity of a child – does, indeed, resonantly call everyone to the fold. For those who are already Christian, in all the degrees and array of society the poem has specified, the episode will recall the earliest, most enraptured experience of mass and church in their own lives, reminding them of the transcendent rapture that Christianity is.

But the project also has a clear interest in *non*-believers, symbolized here by a sentient, cooperative Jewish boy. Embracing Christianity as a compellingly intuitive, personal experience that feels intimately and directly natural, this episode registers "The Jewish Boy" as a cultural document participating in the historical context from which it issues, and conversant with the largest, grandest, universalizing project of the European Middle Ages: conversion of the unconverted, so that *all* may be drawn into the Christian fold. If the violent, imperial vision of that conversionary project has been articulated by high-ranking church authority in the person of the Bishop of Winchester and duly reported by Matthew Paris pre-Expulsion – as we saw in Chapter 1 – this is the sublime, affirmative vision of that conversionary project, reported post-Expulsion through the experience of a child.[88]

The charmed Christian spaces that receive the boy, first with love, then with enchantment, are finally capped by a third space: the oven intended for his destruction. This third environment is introduced as a fiery inferno: a glowing cavity supplied with live coals (l. 92), with a roof blazing so bright (l. 131) that the entire oven, from roof to ground, glows like liquid glass (l. 132).

The only entrance to this hell is a stone rolled over the front of the oven, walling off the inside completely. More furnace than oven, the third space the boy enters is thus introduced through disenchanted adult eyes. Yet when the boy emerges from the demonic inferno (he is summoned forth like Lazarus, and the stone is rolled back, like the empty tomb) his report of his experience turns the inferno into yet another magical ground.

For the boy, the oven is a cool arbor of delight, furnished with fair flowers strewn under his feet (ll. 154–5), which give off fragrance like special, sweet-smelling spices (l. 156). Of all the fun he has had before in his life, he announces, never had he experienced such merriment, such glee, till he was put into the oven ("Of alle the murthes that I haue had/ In al my lyf yit hider-to,/Ne was I neuere of gleo so glad/As aftur I was in the nouene i-do" [ll. 149–50]).

The furnace thus transforms into a *second* playground, where the child's company this time is Mary herself with the infant Jesus (ll. 157–60), who together shield him from the red-hot coals, brands, and embers, and the burning wood and flames all around (ll. 161–4). Seen through the boy's eyes, the glowing carapace of flame that surrounds him assumes magical dimensions, with coals and embers flowering into flora and spice, and flames that flow so wildly ("flaumes that flowe(n) so wilde" [l. 163]) yet touch him not, enabling him to take in the visual spectacle with delight. Hell has become paradise.

Each enchanted space has led to the next: The playground of the Christian children issues into the ornamented cavern of the cathedral edifice, which in turn leads to the wondrous paradise of the enchanted oven. Entering each space, the boy is shaped and altered by his experience inside, and exits increasingly Christianized, so that the third and final enchanted space becomes for him the matrix of a new, Christian identity: the oven is the womb that births a new Christian.

In an extraordinary narrative gesture that confirms this child as Wordsworthian father to the man, *the boy converts himself,* as well as every one of the Jews ("The child tok hym to cristes lawe/And alle the Jewes euerichon" [ll. 171–2]). No priest or parent, nor church authority, is needed; adults need not apply. The boy's mother also converts instantly, because of the power of her son's words – "The Jewesse thorw hire sones sawe/Was conuertet to crist a-non" [ll. 169–70]).

A marked contrast to the vulnerable children of Chaucer's *Canterbury Tales* and the Anglo-French ballad of Hugh, where adult power is visited on innocent, hapless children so that their victimage invites us to view them as Christ figures, the characterization of the Jewish boy is an invitation to see what transpires when a child is imagined as self-composed, independent, active, and innocent: the innocence of a Jewish otherness arrested at an early, pliable stage, with its potential for transformation yet intact. A child whose self-sufficiency and composure is remarkably attractive (and unusual in medieval literature), this Jewish boy is an active agent whose agency effects his mother's conversion and that of an entire race.

Naturally, families are heavily alluded to in this poem organized around the centrality of a child. We see Christian fathers form domestic dyads with their children in churchgoing, and the Jewish boy's father surrendered as a plot sacrifice that pronounces the old law of the father ineffectual and dead, superseded by new Christian law and protection by mother figures celestial and terrestrial. The sibling-like play of the Christian children who welcome the boy *with love* into their circle enacts earthly family bonds, while the blissful babe on the Virgin's arm becomes the boy's divine sibling-companion in the oven. There are earthly families and divine families to welcome the Jewish boy.

Most revealing, perhaps, is the role of the Jewess, mother of the attractive child-agent of the narrative. This Jewish mother, in her distress over her child, behaves like *all the Christian mothers* of child-murder stories. On learning that her husband has cast their child into his oven ("his houene" [l. 93]), she is stunned ("In a stude" [l. 98]), terrified into a frenzy ("ffreyed in ffrenesye" [l. 99]), and grows mad with grief ("as waxen wood" [l. 100]), tearing at her hair and calling out (l. 101) in every street of the city, in and out everywhere, like a madwoman ("In eueri stret of that citee,/Nou in nou out so eueriwher" [ll. 102–3]).

This poem has forgotten that pre-Expulsion Jews were not allowed to be publicly outdoors in the streets during Holy Week, let alone at Easter – the Jewish boy has played with his Christian friends and gone to mass, oblivious of all pre-Expulsion ordinances, provisions, and statutes forbidding Jewish–Christian intermingling, and now his mother untimely races through the streets with frantic cries.

If the Jewess' love for her child mimics the gestures of Christian mothers in boy-murder stories, her assumption of that protective role which renders her a worthy and estimable target of conversion is not a perfect fit. When the mayor and bailiffs stop the Jewess (they "arrest her," the narrative says [l. 107]) – not because she's breaking the law, as a Jewess outdoors during Holy Week, but because she's making a racket and becoming a public nuisance on a day of great solemnity, Easter (l. 109–12) – she spills out her story and pleads for justice ("just juggement" [l. 119]), but also attempts to bribe them to do their job, offering to put gold into their (gloved) hands ("I schal giue ow gold to gloune" [l. 124]). Like all Jews who historically needed to bribe officials in order to gain justice or help, the boy's mother, as a virtual Christian, still remembers to act like a Jewess in proffering gold (not, we note, the lesser coinage of Biblical silver, since the gold standard has by this time returned to England) to get results.

The Jewess as a doubled figure, a composite of two temporalities – the Christian woman she will become, and the Jewish woman she still is – means that she can perform as a race traitor with no compunction in betraying a husband who acts like a traitor to the Christian race, and as a loyal parent who, unlike the mothers in Christian-child-murder stories who arrive too late, arrives in time to help produce a salutary outcome this time round. Where the boy's male Jewish parent has been inattentive, negligent, and fails, his female soon-to-be-Christian parent is attentive, loudly insistent, and succeeds.

Whether they are celestial and Christian or Jewish and earthly, mothers are successful protectors of children in this literary text.[89] In this tale, mothers rule. The oven, a demonic inferno initially identified with the Jewish father to whom it belongs (it is *his* oven, "his houene" [l. 93]), is resignified by the intervention of the Virgin as female space, a matrix and womb that births Christians.[90] The Jewess' success in preventing her child from being sacrificed as a martyr also means that the privy/latrine, a symbol deployed by other narratives to mark desecrations of Christian identity, can be replaced by the oven, the symbol deployed by this narrative to mark the point of Christian identity's creation.

The replacement of the privy by the oven bears witness to the story's desire for an affirmation that supplants the old affects induced by narratives of child-murder – affects of outrage, hate, and negativity that pool around the narration of a child's death – so that the happy outcome here allows for affective celebration instead. We note that figures who represent civil and secular law are again accompanied by a crowd to see justice done (l. 125), and a jury of twelve representatives, presided over by the mayor acting as judge, deliberates and comes to a verdict as in a real court of law in convicting and sentencing the Jewish father (ll. 175–80).

Christian justice again is collective, not the whim of a single autocrat or set of officials but genuinely the outcome of the people's will. Christians, it seems, do not enact justice alone but unite as a collective body, a *community*, when they dispense justice: The racial state, murderer of England's Jews, has been replaced by a naturalized Christian community acting in concert. The figure of an innocent child limns that Christian community as a vast extended *family*, utopianized as warmly welcoming, not dangerous or aggressive – Christianity not as the imperium visualized by the Bishop of Winchester, or the racial state that had devolved before Jewish expulsion, but as a benign and kindly, just and loving universal family.

By *not* dying, a child is no longer a helpless victim, but can become an agent who converts himself, cause his mother's conversion, and effect the conversion of an entire ethnoracial group of Jews. We know these conversions to be secure, thanks to the presence of Marian miracle, so that all the utopianized Christian spaces the child inhabits in story converge in the mind's eye to form a welcoming home for all the genuine converts that Christianity's radiant power of ritual, and the persuasional force of Christianity's embodied sensuousness, can create.

This home, this *domus* – the home of the new, composite Christian nation, conjured by the figure of a former Jewish child and the fantasmatic siblings, parents, and family he gains in Christianity – is a true *domus conversorum* indeed. In a post-Expulsion England purified of Jews, the story of English Christians as a de facto new race – a story also told by other narratives – turns out, in *this* narrative, to be a romance of England as a *domus conversorum*, a home of converts in which a race of new Christians is lured into the shining future by the long shadow of an enchanting little boy who has transmogrified the horrors of political theology and state violence historically visited upon Jews into visions of love and welcome that receive new and old Christians alike into the enfolding arms of the Christian communal family of England.

Notes

1 Jewish chronicles document exterminations at Mainz, Worms, Speyer, Cologne, Regensburg, and elsewhere during the so-called Popular Crusade; the Second Crusade also occasioned the sacrificing of medieval Jewries in the Rhineland (Eidelberg). Dobson, like others, attributes the 1190 massacre at York, where the documentary record says anything from 150 to 500 Jews were slaughtered (15), to the crusader king Richard I's preparations for the Third Crusade: "there was a direct correlation between crusading propaganda against the external Moslem pagan and active hostility toward the internal Jewish 'infidel'" (18). The 1190 massacre at Norwich, too, is attributed by the chronicler Ralph de Diceto to Richard's crusade preparations: "Many of those who were hastening to go to Jerusalem determined first to rise against the Jews before they invaded the Saracens. Accordingly, in 6 February, all the Jews who were found in their own houses at Norwich were butchered" (Lipman 580). The association of Jews with Muslims in the Christian imaginary began early: "Already in the 630s, the very decade of the Arab invasion, the Byzantine Christians associated Jews with, and considered them agents of, the Muslims" (Cutler and Cutler 90). "There is ... an eleventh-century tradition that the Jews betrayed Toulouse to the Arabs circa 756–788 ... Toulouse never fell to the Arabs; rather, it fell to the Normans in in 848. This tradition that the

Jews betrayed Toulouse may reflect an earlier ninth- or tenth-century charge that the Jews betrayed Marseilles to the Arabs in 848" (Cutler and Cutler 91).

2 For a discussion of *Parzival*, see Chapter 4. *Empire of Magic*, chapter 2, discusses another literary text in which the shadow of Jews haunts the portrayal of Muslims: *Richard Coer de Lyon*.

3 As a "historical personage," this Saladin is also a cultural simulacrum, of course, his image constructed and contested by Sunni and Shiite authors and by authors in the Latin West. Chapter 3 discusses Saladin's legend and variegated reputation.

4 On depictions of the epidermal variety of Muslim and other heathen women, see Chapters 3 and 4.

5 Of Jewish communities in England, Richardson observes that "What was remarkable about a Jewish *commune* was that it existed within, and yet apart from, an urban commune (134). For the conditions under which Jewish communities existed in individual cities, see, e.g., Lipman on Norwich, Roth (*Jews of Medieval Oxford*) on Oxford, and Dobson on York.

6 Muslim *slaves* in Europe, of course, lived alongside Christian Europeans (see Chapter 3). "Jews and Christians lived cheek by jowl with each other" (Stacey, "Conversion" 264). "Jews lived in 'open' rather than 'closed' Jewries. There were no ghettos in England" (Mundill 33). Roth (*Jews of Medieval Oxford*) and Lipman document details of lived intimacy between Jewish and Christian communities in Oxford and Norwich. Lipman tells us: "there is plenty of evidence for Christians living side by side with Jews in what was in fact only a partly Jewish quarter" (114). By 1275, however, statutory law in the form of the *Statutum de Judeismo* began to insist on the separation of Jews and Christians, who were no longer to be allowed to live in intermingled proximity, in effect imposing a segregation order on the two communities in the last fifteen years of Jewish residence in England. See the discussion that follows.

7 Chaucer's Prioress demonstrates that ritual murder libel is also intended to recall Herod's slaughter of the innocents, damning an entire race of Jews from Biblical time onward.

8 This style of critique – deploying Jews as the baseline by which the difference, and the morality, of others can be measured – was hardly unusual: "in a case brought before the court of a small Provençal town in the thirteenth century, the accusation against a Christian usurer stated that there were many Christian usurers in that place who were worse than the Jews" (Little 45). Jews were also the template in contexts where Christian polemicists found it convenient to argue that Muslims, too, were fundamentally different from Christians: The fourteenth-century treatise of Pedro Pascual in Grenada, for instance, transfers to Muslims the "irrationality" and beast-like characteristics traditionally imputed to Jews, and extends to Muslims the arguments against circumcision usually deployed against Jews (Tolan, *Sons of Ishmael* 135–8).

9 Though some believe that there were already Jews in England before the Conquest, "William of Malmesbury's statement that it was the Conqueror himself who introduced Jews to England from Rouen has survived the critical scrutiny of modern scholars" (Dobson 2). Scheil's study on the figuration of Jews and Judaism in Anglo-Saxon England calls pre-Conquest England "a land without Jewish communities" (3), and Stacey, one of the foremost scholars on Jews in medieval England, suggests that Jews might even "have been kept out of Anglo-Saxon England by deliberate royal decision" ("Jewish Lending" 80). On the Conqueror's motives in establishing Jews in England, Stacey speculates that "he might have expected to continue and extend whatever benefits he was already accustomed to derive from Jewish trade" in Rouen ("Jewish Lending" 82). Stacey adds that a second wave of Jewish emigration to England occurred during the reign of Henry II ("Jews and Christians" 342).

10 "Jewish moneylenders who realized the pledge of property as security could take seisin, and receive the fealty of tenants, but because they could not hold land in fee simple, would sell the acquisition after holding it long enough to establish claim of ownership" (Roth, *History* 107). There were rare exceptions in which Jews possessed land in fee simple in England, but the more common practice was to transfer mortgaged land to buyers (Richardson 108).

11 "Before the expulsion of the Jews, repeated attempts were made to curb their dealings in land or to mitigate the consequences" (Richardson 108). Jewish financiers "introduced abbeys, lay magnates and [also] the growing race of stewards and royal clerks to the opportunities of investment in the property of indebted knights," Mundill observes, quoting Alan Harding: "such introductions were widespread over the whole country" (37). Richardson suggests "religious houses figure prominently in the story . . . principally because they have left more records behind them" (103).

12 Unlike Roth, Stacey points out that the issue in the 1269 legislation was fee-rents, not rents on land held in fee. Perpetual fee-rents were annual payments assigned on land and placed a Christian debtor in perpetual monetary subjection to a Jew, which, as Stacey observes, was both an economic burden and a theological offense that put Christians in economic servitude to Jews, when Jews were supposed to be in perpetual servitude to Christians as witnesses of the truth of the Passion of Christ ("1240–60" 144–5). I am indebted to an anonymous reviewer for the distinction between Roth and Stacey.

13 In the brilliant Middle English *Alliterative Morte Arthure*, Sir Clegis, a knight of King Arthur's, has a passionate outburst that avowedly declares the hallowed antiquity of his family's lineage in arms – a declaration that is designed to address what might be called the challenge from below to hereditary status in arms in fourteenth-century England, when "new men" of inferior social status but superior economic prowess jostled the ranks of knights of hereditary degree (*Empire of Magic* 130–3). In the heated disputes over the right to possess coats of arms (such as the Scrope versus Grosvenor trial of 1386), which required stringent adjudication and policing by professional heralds, anxieties over the ascension of economic upstarts can also be glimpsed. Froissart shows us that in chivalric accounts, low birth disfigured fine knights: Sir Robert Salle, "a paragon of chivalric skill, valor, and beauty" who was knighted by Edward III, was "only the son of a mason," and would "never be accepted as a gentleman" (Thrupp 309–10).

14 I argue in chapter 3 of *Empire of Magic* that Gian Galeazzo Visconti, the Duke of Milan – a human slave trader so fabulously wealthy that he offered to pay the massive ransom of the French king, Jean, captured by England's Black Prince early in the Hundred Years War (600,000 gold florins!) in exchange for marriage to the eleven-year-old child princess of France – is transformed in the *Alliterative Morte Arthure* into the giant of Saint Michael's Mount, a monster whose vast wealth, loathsome lust, and gigantic appetite for acts of dehumanization aptly figured the Visconti's appetites, lust, and loathsome but profitable human trafficking (166–8).

15 Rokéah reminds us that "one can find accusations concerning the abuse of coinage at all periods in which metal coinage was current. Violations such as clipping the coinage were implicit in the very nature of metallic money as it was produced in the centuries before modern machinery and techniques were used, for money formed by hand, with dies from blanks, was irregular in both shape and weight . . . such coinage was [also] subject to wear and tear" (Rokéah, "Money . . . Part I" 83–4).

16 The second part of Rokéah's two-part article has an extensive compilation of the names and details of Jews – men and women – accused of coinage violations, and the penalties and outcomes of the charges against them ("Money . . . Part II" 164–218). Rokéah adds: "Queen Eleanor was granted all the concealed goods of condemned Jews that had not yet come to light, or had not yet been dealt with by the justices appointed to deal with money violations" ("Money . . . Part I" 92).

17 Rokéah had initially dismissed the figure of 600 imprisoned Jews because it seemed improbably large, and only changed her mind after finding documentary evidence of their imprisonment ("Money . . . Part I" 96). Abrahams is among those who believe that all the Jews of England were imprisoned for the coinage offenses of 1278 (49). Rokéah argues that most likely only heads of households – men and women – made up the 600 or more prisoners, since "by no stretch of the imagination can one envisage the imprisonment of babes-in-arms for nearly five months along with their siblings" ("Money . . . Part I" 96–7). Mundill calculates that in the late 1270s "a total

Jewish population of only 2,720 (or more, if non-householders are considered) could be expected"
(26). Shortly after these mass arrests, the poll tax accounts for 1280–3 show that between 1,135 and
1,179 Jews paid the tax each year, which was levied on individual Jews aged twelve and above; and
Mundill concludes that about 2,000 Jews remained less than a decade later, around the time of the
Expulsion (26–7).

18 Christian practitioners of usury – a mortal sin – could be denied communion and Christian burial,
according to Canon 25 of the Third Lateran Council in 1179, reiterated by Canon 27 of the Second
Council of Lyons in 1274. Those who did not consider usury a sin would be punished as heretics
and treated accordingly by inquisitors, as Canon 15 of the Council of Vienne specified in 1311–2
(Schroeder 233, 357, 401). "By the late twelfth century," Lester Little observes, "the new needs of
both business and government for a system of credit collided head on with the old moral and legal
prohibitions against usury" (57).

19 "By 1187," Stacey remarks, "Jewish lenders had become critical figures in crusade finance"
and a conviction grew that "Jews had a special responsibility to pay for the costs of crusading"
("Crusades" 241, 242). "In the thirteenth century, the connection Peter drew between Jews,
moneylending, and crusading would become commonplace, so much so, indeed, that rulers
of tender conscience who confiscated Jewish property were regularly advised to donate that
property to the crusade, so as to cleanse it from the taint of its usurious origins" (Stacey,
"Crusades" 241).

20 "Open" usury by Christians was condemned at the Council of Tours in 1163. Langmuir suggests
that "Since Christians did not want to acknowledge their own involvement in moneylending
openly, it served many interests" that Jews were typed "as the archetypal usurer. That intersection
of religious and material interests made Jews seem even more evil" (*Toward a Definition of
Antisemitism* 10). Christians "who, like Jews, lent money at interest" were called "Judaizers" in
the inquiries of Edward I (Stacey, "Parliamentary Negotiations" 97). Bernard of Clairvaux wrote
that "where there are no Jews, Christian moneylenders 'Jew' or 'Judaize' (*judaizare*), worse than the
Jews, if indeed these men may be called Christians, and not rather baptized Jews" (Little 56). "The
money trade, the crucial activity of the Commercial Revolution, was thus … considered to be
exclusively the work of the Jews. Christian moneylenders were really Jews" (Little 56).

21 Stacey suggests it's unlikely that "the Jews of Norman London ever played the economic role the
Conqueror had envisioned for them when he brought them from Rouen, as important conduits for
the flow of silver and luxury goods into the kingdom" ("Jewish Lending" 81, 83). Instead of trade
and mercantilism, Stacey urges, Jewish economic activity in Norman England focused on bullion
dealing, money changing, and money lending, though by 1180 or so there was a shift "toward a
much more exclusive reliance on moneylending" ("Jewish Lending" 88). In time, Jews "gained such
a reputation for expertise in the handling of money that they eventually became identified with
money and moneylending in the Christian consciousness. And since these were the objects of
profound ambivalence on the part of Christians, such an identification carried dangerous risks"
(Little 42).

Richardson (25–7) and Lipman (79–80) list some of the other occupations held by a handful of
English Jews, a few of whom were physicians, teachers, goldsmiths, soldiers, tailors, and vintners;
two were cheesemongers, one was a fishmonger, and perhaps there was even an ironmonger.
However, Lipman suggests that because of religious injunctions, occupations related to the
provision of food, beverage, and services were likely held by Jews who were serving the Jewish
community, rather than Christians (80). After 1275, the Statute of Jewry prohibited moneylending,
and English Jews were suddenly required to live by crafts, agriculture, and business instead.

22 By contrast, 5 percent of the Jewry in Spain was killed at the height of the worst persecutions.
Stacey emphasizes England's leadership in persecution: England was the first country in Europe to
stigmatize Jews as coin clippers and criminals, the first to administer the Jewish badge, the first to

produce state-sponsored efforts to convert Jews to Christianity, the first to invent the ritual murder libel, and of course the first to expel Jews from its national territory ("Anti-Semitism" 164–5).

23 Stacey points out that when Simon de Monfort controlled the government in 1264–5, his partisans too "massacred many Jews and burned the debt records of many more" ("Parliamentary Negotiations" 94).

24 Stacey suggests that "the numerical majority of Jewish loans in England were for small sums advanced to peasants and townsmen," with "large loans" made to "very great men," "baronial families," "great monastic houses," and the "socially eminent" ("Jewish Lending" 94–5).

25 Characterized by Stacey as "by far the most thoroughgoing piece of anti-Jewish legislation pronounced in medieval England prior to the expulsion" ("Parliamentary Negotiations" 97), the statute merely drove Jewish lending underground, since Jews were unable, despite attempts, to break into avenues of labor in competition with Christians, and by 1285–6 Edward was contemplating further regulating, rather than banning and criminalizing, Jewish lending (Stacey, "Parliamentary Negotiations" 98–9). The Expulsion of 1290, however, provided an alternative solution.

26 Edward I drove a hard bargain: "the Commons representatives gave their consent to a fifteenth on the lay movable property of the kingdom ... The English clergy ... followed suit ... granting the king a tenth of their revenues to match the fifteenth he had received from the laity" (Stacey, "Parliamentary Negotiations" 92). For the Expulsion, "Edward was granted the largest single tax of the Middle Ages, amounting to more than £116,000" (93).

27 By this time, English Jews were impoverished, their resources expropriated through taxes and tallages. Stacey says soberly: "by 1258, more than half of total Jewish capital in 1241 had been transferred directly into the king's coffers through taxation alone" (Stacey, "Parliamentary Negotiations" 93). But Edward succeeded in extracting more profit from his impoverished Jews, even as he banished them from England's shores: "from 1268, and perhaps even from 1258, legislation against Jews and Jewish lending was the essential precondition upon which local society in England was prepared to vote voluntary taxation to the monarchy; and ... the king concluded that in 1290 no lesser measure would secure the consent he needed [from Parliament for his tax]. Edward got his tax, and in return the Commons got the expulsion" (Stacey, "Parliamentary Negotiations" 101).

28 This was not England's first experience of expelling Jews: Smaller regional expulsions preceded the expulsion from England's shores, such as those from Leicester in 1231 (Stacey, "Conversion" 268) and from Bury St. Edmunds in 1190 (Stacey, "Jews and Christians" 350). Henry III's queen, Eleanor of Provence, also expelled Jews in 1275 from the towns she held (John Edwards 91). "Jewish expulsions were not a new idea in England," Stacey tartly notes ("Parliamentary Negotiations" 100).

29 Jews were not the only agents of economic rationality in the period, of course, nor the only successful accumulators of capital. As Richardson observes, "If wealthy Jews were capitalists in the twelfth century, so also were wealthy religious communities" (91): though wealthy religious communities were not subjected, of course, to the massacres, plunder, arson, and other violence enforced on Jews.

30 We thus see connective tissue between the theory supplied by Peter the Venerable of how to finance the crusades on the backs of Jews, and the practice supplied here by English crusaders in the form of looting and plunder. Fogle tells us that "in the vicious attack on the London Jewry in 1264 by Simon de Montfort's baronial supporters" in collusion with "a mob of Londoners," possibly as much as "one-half of the London Jewish community was murdered in one night," along with "vast amounts of property looted or destroyed" ("Between" 110).

31 Benedict was forced to convert, reverted back to Judaism, but died shortly afterward from his wounds (see William of Newburgh 1: 312–13). Joceus was able to escape, but his house was

plundered and razed, and the people who were in it perished. Stacey ("Crusades") traces the whole horrific episode from its beginnings in Richard I's prohibition of Jews at his coronation (245–50).

32 Estimates of the size of the Jewish population in England have varied from 3,000 to 15,000; and, of course, the size of the population fluctuated. Stacey's estimate of 4,000–5,000 Jews in England in 1240 ("Parliamentary Negotiation" 93) may have been reduced after the heavy taxations levied between 1240 and 1274; after the *Statutum de Judeismo* of 1275 prohibited the Jewish livelihood of moneylending (William Jordan, *French Monarchy* 153); and after the mass incarcerations and executions of the coinage trials of the late 1270s.

33 Before 1180, English kings borrowed at interest from the Jews of England. In 1180, however, Henry II ingeniously devised "tallages" or special taxes levied on Jews instead, which had the advantage over loans of not having to be repaid. These tallages had benefits for the state beyond the simple revenue they accrued. On each occasion that a tallage was imposed, Jewish lenders would call in revenue from debts owed to them: "the Jews could thus drain off a layer of money from the population at large and pass it on to the royal treasury without the king's having to get approval to levy a tax or his having to pay the costs of collecting a tax. Therefore the Jews, prior to the development of a general and regular system of taxation, had in effect, if unofficially, become royal tax collectors" (Little 46). Such a role, of course, not only brought Jews popular hatred, but also intensified their association with the crown.

34 Although Aaron of Lincoln had two sons, Vives and Elias, and a nephew, Benedict, "all of whom seem to have been associated with him in business ... none of his relatives succeeded, as heir, to Aaron's estate" (Richardson 115), perhaps because the estate tax demanded by the crown would have been unaffordable: The estate of Aaron "was so immense that his heirs could not, or were not allowed to, make terms for succeeding to it" (Lipman 67). "Whatever the circumstances, Aaron's possessions were seized into the king's hand and the [royal] exchequer proceeded to realize upon them" (Richardson 116). It took the crown more than five years to collect on the debts owed to Aaron (Richardson 117); in some instances, the crown even negotiated reduced payments in cash when it needed liquidity: e.g., in 1189, Richard I exonerated nine Cistercian abbeys whose total indebtedness to Aaron amounted to 6,400 marks, in exchange for a cash payment of 1,000 marks "to defray the expenses of his crusades" (Richardson 90).

35 "Those who attacked and massacred the Jews of York ... were men with wide connections in local society and important links to the political opponents of William de Longchamp around the royal court" (Stacey, "Crusades" 249). See also Jeffrey Jerome Cohen's important study on the role of Anglo-Norman politics in the creation of the ritual murder lie in 1144 Norwich.

36 The ambiguity of *servus*, the term used to categorize Jews, which may arguably be translated as "serf," "slave," or "servant" in earlier Latin decrees, creates a degree of scholarly disagreement on where the emphasis should fall in understanding the status of medieval Jews. Widespread agreement exists, however, that "Jews were too valuable a prey to be left by the Crown to indiscriminate appropriation" (Rigg x). A direct, unmediated, possessive relationship between Jews and the crown was thus theorized. Jews were *"servi camarae nostrae* ('serfs of the royal chamber'), *sicut nostrum proprium catallum* ('our effective property'), those who were to be treated *tanquam servi* ('like serfs'), or simply *judaei nostri* ('our Jews')," Stow remarks (*Alienated Minority* 274). J. A. Watt adds the reminder that "The operative word was *servire*: Jews served. They served both Church and State" (172). Pollock and Maitland agree the emphasis falls on serfdom and servitude: "The Jew's relation to the king is very much like the villein's relation to his lord. In strictness of law whatever the Jew has belongs to the king; he 'acquires for the king' as the villain 'acquires for his lord'" (471).

37 Paragraph 5 stipulates the payment of a capitation tax by each Jew over the age of twelve "to the king, whose serfs they are (*"au Rey qui serfs il sunt"* [*Statutes* I: 221a]). Paragraph 7, which grants rights and protections, specifies that Jews cannot be challenged in any court, except "in the court of

the king, whose serfs they are" ("*en la curt le Rey ky serfs yl sunt*" [*Statutes* I: 221a]). Paragraph 8 stipulates that Jews are taxable to the king "as his serfs, and to none other but the king" ("*come ses serfs e a nul autres, for a Rey*" [*Statutes* I: 221a]). By 1275, Watt observes, "Edward I in the *Statutum de Judeismo* . . . spoke of the Jews as *serf* and did so three times in the course of the same text . . . Jews then had come to be thought of as serfs in medieval England . . . in the language of English medieval law" (156). Serfdom also enables the pretext offered for the expulsion of Jews from Bury St. Edmunds: Since Jews are the king's, and cannot be St Edmund's men, they cannot reside in Bury.

38 Jews were "unique, set apart, and living under a law all their own, *ius singulare*" (Stow 274, 275). "The relation between king and Jew was new . . . and it was in many respects unique; the Jew belonged to a despicable race and professed a detestable creed. For all this, the analogy holds good at the most important point: the Jew . . . is the king's serf" (Pollock and Maitland 472). The king can therefore "mortgage or lease his Jewry, his *Iudaismum*, as a whole . . . [and] there is one known case in which an individual Jew was . . . given by the king to his son" (Pollock and Maitland 472).

39 Talal Asad makes the salient point that Muslims who constitute minority communities in Europe today might be in Europe, but are still essentially outsiders: "Bosnian Muslims may be *in* Europe but are not *of* it . . . though . . . they are not racially distinguishable from other whites in Europe . . . they cannot claim a Europeanness" (164–5). Retrograde as the status of Muslims today in Europe is, it does not, however, approximate the status of medieval Jews. Rather, medieval Jewish "serfdom" resembles more the semifree or quasifree status of some of the Romani in the principalities of medieval southeastern Europe who were not enslaved by the monasteries and the boyars but were subject to the prince (see discussion in Chapter 7, on Romani slavery and "serfdom"), and is one of the distinguishing differences between medieval and modern eras.

40 One might say, therefore, extending an argument by Dipesh Chakrabarty, that the repetition-with-difference of these and other medieval racial practices in the *post*medieval period "opens up a hiatus in the continuity of the present by inserting into it something that is medieval-like and yet not quite so" (110). Postmedieval replay of such old practices – always a replay that has something of the modern built into it – suggests that "alongside the present or the modern the medieval must linger as well" (110). I argue in "Holy War Redux" that the "medieval," in this sense, is thus not merely the name of a temporal interval in the West but also the name of a repeating transhistorical pressure that renders later time nonidentical with itself – in ways that facilitate a number of (political and other) uses (424).

41 Historians have emphasized that English Jews were not unfree in the manner of serfs, and indeed some have observed that the status of Jews was closer, in some respects, to that of free men (Richardson 110). Notably, the special relationship of Jews to the crown meant that they were not subject to infeudation and its regulatory impositions. Historians who emphasize the special, exceptional status of Jews also tend to emphasize the aspect of protection implicit in that status (Richardson 110).

42 "*Judaeus vero nihil proprium habere potest, quia quicquid acquirit non sibi acquirit sed regi*" (not in all manuscripts of Bracton, but see Twiss).

43 Pollock and Maitland note that "just as the lord rarely seizes his villein's chattels save for certain reasons, so the king rarely seizes the Jew's chattels save for certain reasons; until the seizure has been made, the villein or the Jew is treated as an owner and can behave as such" (471). But "The major threat Jews faced," Kenneth Stow drily observes, "was royal arbitrariness" (277). The golden egg to be expropriated was, moreover, sizable: "revenues from the Jewry can be broadly classified under four heads. First, there was the equivalent to the feudal relief – a succession duty . . . of a third of the property of the deceased. Secondly, there were escheats, when the property of a Jew was forfeited to the crown on his conviction of a capital offence . . . 'real or imaginary . . . or

otherwise falling into the King's hands by devolution or arbitrary seizure.' Thirdly, there was a multitude of payments for a great variety of licences and concessions: to move from one town to another, to have bail, to have trial by a mixed jury of Jews and Christians, not to wear the Jewish badge. These can broadly be described as fines, in the medieval sense of putting an end to a dispute by making a settlement . . . Fourthly, there were the tallages . . . an arbitrary imposition of taxation by the Crown . . . normally levied in the form of a fixed sum, e.g. of 10,000 marks, or 20,000 marks . . . [or] a percentage levy on capital assets . . . on average perhaps three or four times a decade" (Lipman 65–6). Paul Brand lists the many kinds of licenses, estate duties, fees, appropriations, entitlements, taxes, tallages, etc. recorded in the archives of the government, disclosing the exhaustive extent to which Jews were squeezed by the state.

44 Mundill details the revenue accruing to one such custodianship of local Jews, by the sheriff of Kent, Reginald of Cobham, in 1251–4: "The responsibility of protecting a Jewry was not without substantial benefits. Out of the collections of money and valuable objects, Cobham was able to pay himself and his officials . . . Canterbury Jews paid officials in order to get inquests held or not to attend inquests, to get justice that was due to them or help in getting debts repaid by Christians, to marry their daughters to Jews of other communities, etc." (Mundill 33–4). Among the many reasons for making payments to the sheriff, Mundill sees that when the term of office of the sheriff's under-constable, John of Northwood, expired, the Canterbury Jews paid the sheriff a bribe *not* to have this particular under-constable reappointed (33). Richardson urges that "the medieval official was notoriously venal . . . The threat of arbitrary imprisonment was constantly hanging over the Jews, and their anxieties were the greater because the relations of sheriffs and constables with them were far more intimate than with any other class or community, extending over much of the Jews' daily life" (159).

45 "Why borrow, with the intention of repaying, when it was simpler merely to take, provided that just enough was left to the Jew to enable him to continue in business and produce revenue in the future?" (Lipman 65).

46 Roger of Howden's *Chronica*, under "*Capitula de Judaeis*," details the creation of the system of *archae* in 1194. All the debts, pledges, lands, houses, rents, and possessions of the Jews are to be registered, and Jews must make their loans in "six or seven" appointed places in the presence of four chirographers, "two lawful Christians and two lawful Jews," "two lawful scribes," as well as the clerks of William of the Church of Saint Mary and William de Chimilli. A deed describing the loan is to be drawn up by the scribes in duplicate, with one part remaining in the hands of the Jew and sealed with the seal of the debtor and the other part deposited in the "common chest," on which there are three locks, with the two Christian chirographers holding one key, the two Jewish chirographers another, and the clerks the third. These keepers of keys also keep three seals, and the clerks keep a roll containing transcripts of all the deeds, with any changes in the deeds also being recorded in the roll. The fee for each deed is three pence, paid by the Jewish creditor and the debtor, and received by the scribes and the keeper of the roll. The Christian chirographers, Jewish chirographers, and roll-keeper also hold the three registers in which repayments of debts to Jews are recorded. No loans, repayments, or alteration in the deeds can be made, except in the presence of these officers of the chest, or the majority of them, if all are unable to be present (1: 266).

47 Before the establishment of the *archae*, Jewish deeds of debt and moneys were often stored in churches, monasteries, or royal castles for safekeeping, but in the 1190 massacre at York, ringleaders forced the sacristan at York Cathedral to surrender the bonds kept there by the Jews, and burnt these records of debt "on the floor of the Minster, kindling the flames with the light from the High Altar" (Roth, *History* 23). Historians conclude that "the setting up of local *archae*, in which all debts and their settlement had to be registered, was influenced by the disasters of 1189–90" (Lipman 67). Though the *archae* contributed to the greater survival of

documentary records than predecessor methods of ad hoc safekeeping, rioters nonetheless continued to attempt the destruction of records of their debts, by making off with *archae* during uprisings (Roth, *History*, 30). Gross (with most historians following him in this) lists twenty-six *archae*: at Bedford, Berkhamstead, Bristol, Cambridge, Canterbury, Colchester, Devizes, Exeter, Gloucester, Hereford, Huntingdon, Lincoln, London, Marlborough, Northampton, Nottingham, Norwich, Oxford, Stamford, Sudbury, Wallingford, Warwick, Wilton, Winchester, Worcester, and York (20). Roth remarks an instance of an individual chirograph chest being maintained just for a single wealthy Jew, Aaron fil' Vives, who was given by Henry III, as we have noted, to his son Edmund (*History* 97).

48 Only *archa* records of transactions were admissible as evidence in royal courts. At the inception of chirographs, "two duplicate deeds were originally written upon one membrane, which was afterwards severed into its two component parts along an indented line dividing horizontally the word "CHIROGRAPHUM," or other capital letters chosen at random" (Gross 15). Henry III's 1233 provisions of Jewry required that chirographs be maintained henceforth in triplicate (Richardson 294), and in 1240, the Colchester chest's custodians were ordered to ensure this: "the first part was to be given to the Christian debtor, the second, called the foot of the chirograph ["*pes*"], which used to be placed in the chest, to remain with the Jewish creditor, and the third part, with the wax (i.e., with the debtor's seal) attached, was to be placed in the chest" (Gross 18). Like modern loans issued by banks and brokers, the Jewish chirographs "were extensively bought and sold" (Gross 40).

49 "A regular preliminary to the imposition of a tallage was the closing of the *archae* and their examination to see what Jewish assets were in them. There are various orders for closing, and subsequently reopening, the [Norwich] archa, as well as memoranda recording that this has been done. One roll records four such operations between 11 November 1259 and 4 June 1261" (Lipman 74). Roth finds that "almost simultaneously with the enactment of the *Statutum de Judeismo*, on November 24, 1275, instructions were issued to seal the chirograph-chests, as a preliminary to the exaction of a last tallage" (*History* 73).

50 The "importance of Aaron's bonds is that the method adopted by the [royal] exchequer for dealing with them illustrates a practice that was capable of development and generalization until it covered nearly all the relations between the Jewish community and the crown" (Richardson 117). For a fine recent contribution on the origins of the Jewish Exchequer, see Stacey, "Massacres."

51 In exchange for future legal access, the system "made it relatively easy for the Crown ... to ascertain the nominal wealth of its Jewish subjects" (Lipman 68). The system, of course, "was not infallible: there was undoubtedly evasion of the requirement to register transactions through the *archa* and the face value of the bond did not necessarily represent ... the real amount of the loan ... nevertheless, it made possible a systematic collection of revenue for the Crown ... The existence of the archae ... also provided a network of local agencies through which the central Government could act in its dealings with the local Jewish communities" (Lipman 68).

52 Lest we think this prohibition refers narrowly to a demand that a Christian may not sleep over in the house of a Jewish friend – an old prohibition, already repeated through the years, that Christians should not linger in the homes of Jews and vice versa – paragraph 8 shows itself to be specifically concerned with work and livelihood: Interaction with Christians for the purpose of lawful trade in selling and buying is permitted, paragraph 8 says. Then it adds: But no Christian *for this cause or any other* shall dwell among them (*Statutes* I: 221a). That is to say, both neighborhoods where Jews and Christians might live together, cheek-by-jowl, for the purpose of facilitating trade ("this cause") and private socializations that involve a Christian dwelling in the house of a Jew ("any other" cause) are prohibited. An anonymous reviewer astutely adds that this segregation order is the logical culmination of earlier legislation prohibiting Christians from working as wetnurses and servants in Jewish homes.

53 English Jews resisted their herding into *archa* towns and paid fines in Bottisham, Holme, Basingstoke, and Abergavenny (Mundill 23 n. 39). We cannot, of course, exclude the possibility that the 1275 Statute's prohibition against residence in non-*archa* towns is also couched with an eye to increasing state revenues through fines and special licenses paid for exemptions.

54 Wide-ranging though their functions were, the Jewish Exchequer and its chirographers (some of whom were prominent Jews) were not entrusted with all bureaucratic management of fiscal matters pertaining to Jews. Chancery oversaw the periodic closing of the *archae*, and tallages imposed on English Jewry required specially appointed commissioners delegated to the major tasks of assessment and collection, with the Jewish Exchequer being inducted "to enforce the payment of arrears" (Brand 80). Chancery also issued the licenses that were required, after the 1269 Statute of Jewry, for the sale of debts by Jewish creditors to Christians, and again, after the 1275 Statute of Jewry, for permission to dispose of real property (Brand 80). Crown interference in the business of Jewish lending also meant that Chancery issued pardons of various kinds to individuals for debts owed to Jews, as well as pardons that manipulated or revised conditions of repayment to Jews (Brand 81). Overseeing the Jewish Exchequer was the Exchequer of England, which sometimes reheard cases initially heard by the Jewish Exchequer and summoned the Justices of the Jews, as it saw fit, for retrials or for alleged misconduct (Brand 83, Richardson 151).

55 The one Jewish Keeper ("Custos") was Benedict de Talemunt, who was assisted by a subordinate official, a Presbyter of the Jews ("*Presbiter Judeorum*") called Jacob (Jenkinson 52). "As the 'Scaccarium Judaeorum' was a department of the Great Exchequer, the Justices of the Jews had the status of barons of the Exchequer, and as such were subject to the superior authority of the Treasurer and Chief Justice of the realm" (Gross 9).

56 In an arc of cruelty in the 1280s, converts were actually used to collect this capitation tax; this "rubbed salt in the wound," and at least one tax collector, "William the Convert of Oxford," was assaulted in February 1290 (Stacey, "Conversion" 280). Stacey suggests that the practice of a convert's property being forfeit to the crown likely began in the reign of John ("Conversion" 266). Fogle emphasizes the extracanonical nature of the practice, since papal preference was for converts *not* to be destitute and desperate after conversion ("*Domus*" 3). Converts were also housed by other means: "in the mid-1250s, Henry [III] sent at least 150 needy converts to various religious houses, each one bearing a special royal letter requesting the house to provide the convert with food and lodging for two years" ("Conversion" 269), so that in 1255 more than 150 converts "were living in the houses of seven different religious orders, throughout England" (John Edwards 93). Nor was Henry's *Domus Conversorum* the only house of converts: Houses were also established in Southwark in 1213 and perhaps in Oxford in 1221 (John Edwards 92). In 1280 Edward modified the escheatment, so that converts could keep half their movable goods for seven years, while the other half went to support the *Domus* (Fogle, "Between" 113).

57 The intensification of bureaucratic culture and rise of a new administrative class had profound implications: "the clerks of western Europe, irrespective of whether they were in the service of 'Church' or 'State,' worked out between the beginning of the twelfth and the middle of the thirteenth century both the theory and the practical implementation of what I have called 'the persecuting society'" (Moore, "Anti-Semitism" 54).

58 In November 1218, Jews in England had to register with the Jewish Exchequer, and could not go overseas without special license (Richardson 178). Pandulf's legation formally began on December 3, 1218 (Richardson 183–4).

59 At this time, Richardson tells us, "there is no indication in the receipt roll that the order [to wear the badge] applied to children" (179).

60 "Of the twelve articles, six covered the same ground as the canons of the council of Oxford: these dealt with the construction of new synagogues, the payment of parochial dues ... miscegenation, the *tabula* and the frequentation of churches" (Richardson 191).

61 Vincent argues: "the decree of 1215 had been extremely vague, and ... its application varied significantly between one country and another. In 1215–16, for example, the archbishops and bishops of France had been asked to 'permit the Jews to dress (*talem gestare habitum*) so that they might be conspicuous among Christians, but not to compel them to dress in such a way that they might be put in danger of their lives.' In Christian Spain, where Jews already appear to have dressed in a distinctive fashion ... the pope was actually forced to intervene in 1219 and 1220 to prevent the impositions of badges or signs. These had been so detested that various members of the Jewish community had preferred to seek refuge with the Moors, rather than wear the new badges (*nova signa*) which the bishops were seeking to impose, as the papal letters put it, not out of excessive respect for the Lateran decrees, but in order to extort money from the Jews" (Vincent 210). The eager alacrity with which England transmogrified a general conciliar demand issued in 1215 into a specific badge in 1218 is thus remarkable (Vincent 210).

62 "Among the English bishops there seems to have been considerable diversity in their approach to Jews. Some, most prominently Peter des Roches, bishop of Winchester, were so closely associated with the secular administration that their chief interest appears to have lain in the financial exploitation of Jews, which in turn led to a fair degree of toleration, provided of course that toleration rather than repression ensured a greater income to the royal exchequer. Others, such as William de Blois, bishop of Worcester, adopted a far harsher approach. William's diocesan legislation for Worcester went even further than the Lateran decrees of 1215 in imposing restrictions on Jewish usury, and it was following complaints from William that Pope Gregory wrote" (Vincent 216).

63 Richardson argues that "poorer members of the urban communities were covered by a general licence" and finds group payments made by the Jews of Canterbury, Hereford, Stamford, Oxford, and London for exemptions from the badge. He adds that these payments may well have been installments of larger sums (179).

64 On state racism, see Goldberg's *The Racial State*. As we saw in Chapter 1, the medieval church, too, functioned like a state – a state whose borders encompassed all of Latin Christendom.

65 It is easier to follow the spoor of state power manifest in law, government institutions, and infrastructure, and the segregations sought by badge and restricted residence, than it is to track a pattern of Jewish resistance to the state. Resistance, however, can be seen when Jews successfully evade the panopticon of the *archae*, causing "the king's ministers" to exclaim against "the malice and falsity of the Jews" (Richardson 147). In such moments, and in the fines and exemptions paid for refusing the badge, may be glimpsed the defiance of English Jews.

66 Stacey estimates that in the 1240s and 1250s, Jewish converts "may have numbered as many as 300 in a total Jewish population that did not exceed 5,000 and that may have been as low as 3,000" ("Conversion" 269). "More than 200 are named in the royal records during these two decades" (269 n.38). John Edwards concludes that "the London House of Converts was apparently full by 1250," since in 1255 Henry had to send more than 150 converts to "the houses of seven religious orders throughout England" (93).

67 Stacey thinks the *Domus* may have been a consoling refuge for its inmates, who did not comfortably belong in either Jewish or Christian society ("Conversion" 275). "Living conditions in the Domus were difficult even in the best of circumstances; and when, as frequently happened, the king failed altogether to pay the wages of its residents, serious privation could result. A 1282 petition from the warden to the king spoke of his 'starving, shivering converts,' who were forced to beg their bread from door to door because their wages were so far in arrears. Similar conditions existed in 1272. A plea for support made to the 1290 Michaelmas Parliament received the cold

response: 'The king will think about it when he can find the time.' The apparent attachment of many converts to life in the Domus, despite its hardships, therefore demands some explanation. In part, the reluctance of converts to leave the Domus must reflect the difficulties they faced in trying to integrate themselves into the mainstream of Christian society . . . But it probably also reflects a positive preference on the part of many converts for this small world they themselves had fashioned, which stood, as they did personally, somewhere between Christian and Jewish society. The Domus was, in this sense, a world the converts made. Like monks and nuns, converts were by and large people without family . . . Life in the Domus was full of hardships, but it did have its consolations. Like a monastery, the Domus must often have compensated for the lack of other family and communal ties . . . Despite its poverty, this may well have been a part of its appeal" (Stacey, "Conversion" 274–5). Stacey's perspective is important, given that Fogle reminds us the privations of "a quiet life of poverty" should not be underestimated, especially in the fiscal insecurity of the fourteenth century, "when royal funding was severely delayed, and many converts died as a result" ("Between" 109).

68 "Under Henry [III], baptisms of converted Jews frequently took place before the king himself, who took evident pleasure in naming the new converts after members of his court, after the saint's day on which they were baptized, and especially after his father, King John. His own name he bestowed more rarely, and only to specially favored individuals" (Stacey, "Conversion" 269).

69 Stroll reports that Anacletus' brother had, at the Council of Rheins in 1119, been made "an object of derision. The brother, Gratianus, had been a hostage, and was released to the care of Calixtus II during the Council. The French and others attending the pope noted his dark, but pallid coloring, and said he looked more like a Jew or Saracen than a Christian. They observed that he was dressed beautifully, but that his body was deformed, and they expressed their dislike for his father, who, they claimed, had accumulated his riches through usury" (167).

70 This formulation of resemblance between conversion and racial passing differs somewhat from trenchant earlier formulations such as Steve Kruger's ("Conversion" 162), where *passing* is read as a condition that does not disturb the ontological status of a racial identity assumed as a prior ground before the act of "passing" occurs. Kruger is particularly astute in reading the intersections of religion, sexuality, and gender (see especially "Conversion" 161, 163, 165, and the later elaborations of these ideas in his *Spectral Jew*, especially chapter 3). In a population census today, of course, it is often the subject's *self-identification* with a race that carries the greatest weight. Such freedom is less readily available to the ethnoracial/religious subject of the European Middle Ages.

71 We might note the queer similarity between the unreconstructed lump of flesh prebaptism and the "pound of (Christian) flesh" demanded by Shylock the Jew in Shakespeare's *Merchant of Venice*.

72 On wetnurses in the provisions of the 1222 Council of Oxford see Grayzel (114). The papal bull of 1205 to the king of France complains: "though it was enacted in the [Third] Lateran Council that Jews are not permitted to have Christian servants in their homes either under pretext of rearing their children, nor for domestic service, nor for any other reason whatever . . . yet they do not hesitate to have Christian servants and nurses, with whom, at times, they work such abominations as are more fitting that you should punish than proper that we should specify" (Grayzel 107). The 1275 statute prohibits Christians and Jews from sharing residential space for *any* reason whatsoever.

73 See Biller ("Christian or 'Scientific'?" and "A 'Scientific' View"), Ziegler, Marcus ("Images" and "Jews"), and Johnson on the bloody flux; Biller ("Proto-racial Thought") and Marcus ("Images") on the Jewish odor; Mellinkoff I: 127–9, Strickland 95–155, Biller ("Proto-racial Thought"); and Chapter 1, *Figures 4* and *5* on Jewish facial phenotypes. Fogle and Stacey each relates an account in the 1268–72 Calendar of Close Rolls where the friars of the Sack complained that "the Jews next door were praying too loudly" (Fogle, *Domus* 2). The "continuous caterwauling" of Jews ("continuum ululatum"), Stacey remarks, had been "a distraction to the friars' divine service" ("Conversion" 265). Henry III's 1253 ordinances thus required Jews praying in synagogues to

"subdue their voices in performing their ritual offices, so that Christians may not hear them" (Rigg, *Select Pleas* xlviii).

74 Contrast this with fears repeatedly voiced in canon and secular law that Jews do not give themselves away sufficiently, and must be made to announce their Jewishness through a difference of dress, such as the badge or the peaked hat assigned to Jews: If Jewish bodies were, in fact, so essentially different from Christian bodies, what need would there be for additional self-marking? The logic of strategic essentialism is thus defied, we see, by the logic of canonic and state impositions.

75 I cite both Dahood ("Anglo-Norman") and Michel for *Hughes de Lincoln*; Boyd's variorum edition of *The Prioress's Tale*; and Couch's transcription of "The Child Slain by Jews" (a.k.a. "The Chorister" in some studies) and "The Jewish Boy" (a.k.a. "The Jew of Bourges" in some studies) in the Vernon manuscript, Oxford Bodleian Library Ms. Eng. Poet. A.1. I amend Couch's editorial title slightly, from "The Child Slain by Jews" to "The Christian Boy Slain by Jews."

76 This tale, a.k.a. "The Jew of Bourges" or "The Jewish Boy of Bourges," was recounted as early as the late sixth century by Evagrious Scholasticus and Gregory of Tours, and circulated in England in the earliest *mariales* compiled between 1100 and 1140 (Frank 178; Despres, "Mary" 377). The extended focus on the child's remarkable agency, vivacity, and – most of all – his subjectivity is the Vernon's contribution. For studies on the Vernon, see Pearsall; on English Marian miracle tales, see especially Boyd (*Miracles*), Meale, and Adrienne Boyarin.

77 Dahood ("Anglo-Norman") translates "Falsim" not as a name, but as "treachery"; Michel, following the manuscript, transcribes *Falsim* with a capital initial, as if it were a name. No "Falsim" appears elsewhere in the poem, and scholars have not identified an historical person of that name. According to Jacobs, "Who Falsim, the convert who betrayed the Jews, was, cannot be at present ascertained" (217). Langmuir observes that Falsim may be fictitious ("The Knight's Tale," 466). "It is likely, however, that the word is the common noun for 'treachery, disloyalty, a lie' and refers not to a person but to the act of betrayal" (35 n.63). Readers may thus want to read *Falsim* here as an allegorical name, a personification, rather than an individual.

78 While the medieval Christian accusation that Jews were the killers of Christ, and thus God-killers, was extreme, the Quran also has *suras* where Jews are the killers of *prophets* (who are, of course, held in the highest esteem in Islam, Muhammad and Jesus both being prophets). See, e.g., *suras* 2:61, 2:87, 2:91, 3:181, 3:183, 4:155, 5:70 passim.

79 Chaucerian scholarship is large; studies on the Prioress and her *Tale* are no exception. I list here only a sampling of work most pertinent to my argument, with apologies for omissions. Brown's scholarship on sources, manuscripts, stemma, and analogues (*Study*, "Prioress's Tale") is supplemented by Boyd's variorum edition (*Prioress's Tale*). Frank, Fradenburg ("*Prioress's Tale*"), Despres ("Cultic Anti-Judaism"), Patterson, Calabrese, Lampert (*Gender*, chapter 3), and Lavezzo ("Minster") offer a range of valuable readings on the Jews and/or the Virgin.

80 Surveying a range of devotional texts, Despres argues that "anti-Judaism is integral to the development of a working iconography of late-medieval Marian devotion" ("Mary" 2; see also her important "Cultic Anti-Judaism," "Immaculate Flesh," and "Protean Jew"). Frank calls "anti-Semitic tales . . . a standard, constituent element" in Marian miracles, about "7 1/2 percent of the common stock of miracles, and they are told again and again and again" (179). William Jordan observes that the saints' days of many child martyrs killed by Jews coincide with Marian feast days (*French Monarchy* 18). We should also note, in passing, that Mary is the patron saint of the *Domus*, which had a shrine dedicated to her.

81 Bernard Lewis' (and, later, Samuel Huntington's) "clash of civilizations" begins here, it seems – not between the West and Muslims, but between the Christian West and Jews. For a discussion of the misnomer "Judeo-Christian" and analogies between the West's treatment of Jews and of Muslims, see my "Holy War Redux."

82 On the feminization and sexualization of the Jewish body, see Kruger ("Bodies") and Lampert (*Gender*).

83 We notice that unlike the Christian child's persistent voice, we scarcely hear from his persecutors – Satan speaks only once, and the Jews Satan calls forth never speak at all.

84 Perhaps this signals an interest in automata, albeit of a miraculous kind. For automata associated with other causes than Christian miracles, see Chapter 3's discussion of the Assassin paradise.

85 Biddick warns that pedagogy's aims, especially when directed against Jews, are always disciplinarian (*Typological*).

86 For a canny reading of the relationship between the minster where the boy's body is conveyed and the privy in which his body is found, and what the politics of space and architecture in medieval England owed to its Jewry, see Lavezzo ("Minster").

87 My reading of this tale is inspired by Julie Couch's work on child-figures in medieval literature and her interpretation of this tale.

88 To recapitulate: Asked what the English should do about Mongols and Muslims, the Bishop of Winchester – Matthew Paris vivaciously reports – suggests that England should leave the dogs to devour one another, so that they may all be consumed and perish, and when Christians proceed against those who remain, they will slay the enemies of Christ and cleanse the face of the earth, so that the entire world will be subject to one Catholic church (Paris 3: 489). We might say the Bishop's strain of universalist ambition, conveying a high-ranking English churchman's vision of Christian world domination, is the proverbial mailed fist, whereas the vision articulated here through a child is the soft-power version, or the proverbial velvet glove.

89 On the mother–child dyad as a unit of family that figures the most basic human community in medieval texts and contexts, see Heng, *Empire of Magic*, chapter 4, 201–7.

90 "The notion that Mary's womb was like an oven may seem peculiar to modern audiences, but, given medieval embryology, especially Galen's tradition in which the mother was an oven in which the foetus cooked, there is an odd logic to the image" of the oven as Mary's womb in this tale (Despres, "Mary" 392).

3

War/Empire

Race Figures in the International Contest: The Islamic "Saracen"

The Middle Ages were the Golden Age of the Islamic problem ... Nothing is more striking ... than the extremely slow penetration of Islam as an ... identifiable fact in Western minds, followed after the year 1100 or thereabouts by a ... rapidity of shifting attitudes, in which the Islamic problem constantly took on new forms.

R. W. Southern, *Western Views of Islam in the Middle Ages* (13)

Holy war ... is a war fought for the "goals or ideals of the faith" or for "religious interests." It is a war that needs to be sanctioned by a religious authority whose power to confer the sacred character upon war is accepted ... the "force of arms is regarded as being not merely justifiable and condoned by God, but positively sanctioned by him" ... participation in holy wars is considered a "positive duty" and seen as conferring positive personal "spiritual merit" on those who fight it.

In the conduct of war, holy warriors are not bound by the restraints typical of just war, which imposes codes of right conduct, grants non-combatant immunity, protects crops, and holds victors back from the utter destruction of the adversaries.

Tomaz Mastnak, "The Muslims as Enemy of Faith" (186–7); "Holy War and the Question of Humanity: The Crusades as Political Theology" (8)

Latin Christians, as they encountered alien peoples in the course of their high medieval expansion, adopt[ed] the terms of race and blood to describe their group identity.

Robert Bartlett, *The Making of Europe* (252)

[T]he Islamic religion has always produced an atmosphere favorable to trade.

W. Montgomery Watt, *The Influence of Islam on Medieval Europe* (16)

AT THE heart of the name by which Muslims – of all races and ethnicities – were known to Western Europeans during the Middle Ages, and for several centuries afterward, was a lie.

Though a number of names existed for the international enemy – Ishmaelites or Ismaelites, Agarenes or Hagarenes, Moors, Turks, Arabs, Persians, Ottomans,

Mohammedans, and, in more general fashion, infidels, heathens, pagans, and even heretics – the preeminent name by which the enemy was known in Latin Europe for centuries was *Saracens*. A word of Greco-Roman provenance that in late antiquity referred to pre-Islamic Arabs, from the late eleventh and the twelfth century onward *Saracens* streamlined a panorama of diverse peoples and populations into a single demographic entity defined by their adherence to the Islamic religion.

The streaming of diverse Muslims – whatever their geographic origins, national provenance, ethnoracial/tribal grouping, or linguistic community – into a corporate entity by virtue of religion alone suggests an extraordinary ability on the part of the Latin West to grant an essence-imparting power to Islam, a power to confer a quintessential identity that horizontally flattens out other identity attributes. For the Byzantine empire, the contact zones of Sicily, southern Italy, and Iberia, the enemy's naming might continue in more varied form – Agarenes, Ismaelites, Moors, and Saracens were all names of choice – but in the Latin West *Saracens* remained the preeminent name of the international foe.

Arabs and Near Easterners who were *Christian* were not called Saracens (Daniel, *Arabs* 53), but were flexibly allowed a play of ethnoracial identity. In a rapturous description of crusader colonization in the aftermath of the First Crusade, Fulcher of Chartres – a key eyewitness chronicler, and chaplain to Baldwin of Boulogne (first count of crusader Edessa and first crowned king of crusader Jerusalem) – tells us that crusader settlers had taken wives "not merely of their own people [that is, western Europeans], but Syrians or Armenians, or even Saracens who have received the grace of baptism" (*History* 271–2; *Historia* 748–9).

Fulcher's ability to see ethnoracial variety among the eastern Christian women married to crusader colonists contrasts markedly with his obliviousness, in the same utterance, to the races he clumps together under the name Saracens (but given that these Saracen women had now received the grace of baptism, they could presumably be viewed in time as fanning out again into varied ethnoracial groups).

The oddity of classing a multiplicity of peoples by their religion calls attention to itself when we grasp that the foe, in their turn, did not group all Europeans under a singular collective rubric defined by Christianity. Islamic historiography in Arabic and other languages, it seems, continued to specify territorial, national, and ethnoracial differences when they referred to Europeans as "Romans, Greeks, Franks, Slavs," and so on (Lewis, "The Other" 379).

Naming the enemy Saracens, however, highlights and repeats the story of an ingenious lie. The story that fabricates the name's medieval and postmedieval connotations appears with St. Jerome (347–420 CE), who suggested that Arabs took for themselves the name of Saracens in order to falsely claim a genealogy from Sara, the legitimate wife of Abraham, "'to conceal the opprobrium of their origin' because their true mother, Hagar, was a slave" (Mastnak, *Crusading Peace* 105, citing Jerome's *Commentariorum in Ezechielem prophetam*). The church historian Sozomen (400–450 CE), proximately coterminous with Jerome, arrived at the same conclusion (Fowden 147 n.33).

Arabs – also known as Ishmaelites because they derived their lineage from Ishmael, the son of Sara's Egyptian bondwoman Hagar – were thus imagined to be acutely sensitive to, and aware of, Galatians 4:30 – "Cast out the slave and her son, for the son of the slave shall not be heir with the son of the free woman" – a stigma they tried to circumvent by manufacturing a false genealogy for themselves which cast them as descendants not of the concubine and slave, but of the authentic wife, "because they were ashamed of their ancestor Ishmael's real mother, Hagar" (Fowden 147). Concealed in the name by which Arabs wanted to be known, that is, was a clever lie that hid the inauthentic genealogy and history of the people it was naming.

Islam's arrival in the seventh century and its rapid succession of territorial conquests added a historical dimension to the manufactured etymology. Spreading imperial dominion like wildfire, Muslim Arabs seemed, like their ancestor Ishmael in Genesis 16:12, to raise their hand against all, with the hand of all raised against them, living at odds with their brethren in the desert. Genesis 16:10, prophesying that the descendants of Ishmael would be an uncountable multitude, now seemed to describe not merely Islamic Arab tribes but a growing and dispersed population of all kinds of Muslims whose numbers were, indeed, becoming uncountable. Though the new Islamic empire did not require conversion by subject peoples, conversion to Islam took root and grew apace for a variety of reasons, including socioeconomic and interpersonal motives (Coope, "Religious"; Bulliet; Levtzion; Montgomery Watt, *History*).

Resuming the investigation of Biblical etymology, Isidore of Seville, in the seventh century CE, also did not find it hard to conclude that "*Saraceni*" was a corruption that made it look as if Ismaelites were descended from Sara ("*quasi a Sara*" [*Etymologiae* IX, ii, 6]). The continuation of Frankish Gaul's Chronicle of Fredegar similarly concludes: "Ismaelites ... are called Saracens, by a corruption of the word" (Daniel, *Arabs* 53). But by *whose* corruption of the word did Ismaelite Arabs and Muslims who were not Ismaelite Arabs transform into *Saracens*? The question did not seem to trouble European minds, leaving Norman Daniel to muse over the oddity that no "medieval [European] writer seems ... to have realized that 'Saracen' has no Arabic equivalent form" – that Muslims and Arabs never in fact referred to themselves as Saracens (*Arabs* 53).

Attributing the invention of the name Saracens *to* the enemy, as a sly act of self-naming *by* the enemy, is thus not only a brilliant lie, but one that brilliantly names the enemy as liars in the very act of naming them as enemies. Ideological combat with the Islamic world would turn on other ingenious lies, a number of which would authoritatively configure the enemy as masters of the cunning lie.[1]

Saracen Fever: A World at War, and the Global System of Islam, Eleventh to Fifteenth Centuries

The international contest between medieval Christendom and Islamdom – *Islamdom* being the shorthand I will use for Dar al-Islam in the medieval period, the agglomerate of dispersed Islamicate worlds from Iberia in the west to India and archipelago Southeast Asia in the east, and from Central Asia and the Near East to Maghrebi and sub-Saharan Africa – to determine military, spiritual, epistemological, territorial, political, and commercial supremacy, took place across multiple, overlapping battlefields. Epistemological and spiritual combat snaked its way through disseminational media such as writing, preaching, debate, visual and plastic arts, and missionary proselytization. Competition for geopolitical power took military form in the Byzantine empire and Spain, the littoral of Mediterranean Europe, and Latin Christendom's crusader colonies of *Outremer* and the Holy Land, in Syria and Palestine. Over time, Saracens hardened into the international enemy-of-war *par excellence*, just as Jews congealed into the enemy-at-home in the heartlands of Europe.² Commercial competition was a complex arena, and is addressed in the last section of this chapter and in the section on Marco Polo in Chapter 6.

Enmity in itself need not be productive of race. In contact zones governed by either Muslim or Christian rulers, day-to-day lived practices often demanded pragmatic accommodations among enemies in order to sustain the survival of all. But where multiple lines of power converged – where, say, febrile propagandist polemics and political theology pushed military responses and fed the needs of war, and vice versa – a crucible could materialize in which racial pronouncements, thinking, and actions could thrive. Holy war – especially the extraterritorial mass military incursions we know today as the Crusades – is a matrix conducive to the politics of race, as we will see. Race is a product of instrumentalizations that occur in war, and is also produced by political theology's instrumentalizations in support of war.

Even in the contact zones, strategies of accommodation and creative acculturations among populations of unequal status living together cheek-by-jowl did not mean freedom from eruptions of violence, or from the sudden resumption of war. Where enemies live intimately in consort, stitching together mutual coexistence daily, peace is shadowed by violence. One lesson that issues from the spectacle of the so-called Martyrs of Córdoba in Umayyad-ruled Andalusia of 850–9, when some fifty Christians were executed, most at their own instigation, by order of the *qadi* of Córdoba is that *too much* acculturation – through interfaith marriage and sexual reproduction, linguistic adoptions, cultural mimicry, and stylistic adaptations – elicits violent response as a radical effort by some in the local populace (in this case, those who sought self-martyrdom) to etch clearer and more determinate identity boundaries between populations in close contact (Coope, *Martyrs*; Colbert; Wolf; Waltz).³

Indeed, the contact zones of Spain and the Mediterranean, as Norman Daniel, John Tolan, and others have shown, are in fact where the earliest and most febrile anti-Islamic polemics – scurrilous, lurid biographies of the Prophet; spurious accounts of Islam's emergence, doctrine, and historiography – were first manufactured. From as early as the seventh century, John of Damascus and other Byzantines, and later the author of the notorious, influential *Risâlat al-Kindi* (the Apology of Al-Kindi), furnished the Latin West with a compilation of exemplary falsehoods for future development (Daniel, *Islam and the West* 13ff; Tolan, *Saracens* 50ff).

A reasonable-sounding lie that hews fairly close to facticity, when offered as an explanandum that supports expediency, has significant motility across the centuries, sprouting like a fantasmic tree that laces its branches and shoots into the far corners of the imagination, and insinuating itself into the minds even of those committed to rationalist scholastics.

Modern scholars note that the Latin West was slow to recognize the scale of the threat posed by Islam – which some in the early Middle Ages held to be a temporary phenomenon intended by God as a scourge and a spur to Christians – until the onset of the First Crusade (Southern 13–18; Mastnak, "Muslims" 145–59; *Crusading Peace* 96–117). Yet the venerable Bede, ensconced in the far north of eighth-century Northumbria, already suspected that "Saracens had taken possession of the whole of Africa, a great part of Asia, and some of Europe" (Mastnak, "Muslims" 161). By the twelfth century, after the First Crusade, Peter the Venerable, the redoubtable Abbot of Benedictine Cluny, soberly concluded that Islam "occupied two parts of the world [and] did not leave the third (which is called Europe) whole to Christ or his Christians" (Kritzeck 142).

Even before Franciscan missionaries, fanning out into distant parts of the world in the thirteenth and fourteenth centuries, could confirm the global reach of Islam; before the eventual conversion of three of the four major Mongol khanates to the Muslim faith in the early fourteenth century; and long before the loss of the millennium-old bulwark of Christianity in the East, Greek Constantinople, to the Ottomans in the mid-fifteenth century, the global system of Islam stirred the Latin West into feverish alarm.

Churchmen at home, no less than crusaders abroad, were touched by Saracen fever before, during, and after the First Crusade, and, in the spheres they commanded, devised forms of theological militancy to combat the enemy. Through impassioned preaching, polemical tracts, meticulous translation projects, re/writing history, and innovating doctrine, the great minds of the Latin Church unleashed a slew of powers against the enemy they did not meet face-to-face in the killing fields of war. It was a churchman, and not a crowned head of Europe, who summoned pilgrims in the countries of the West with his eloquence and preaching and unleashed them as armed masses into the Near East, to conquer and occupy, in the headlong momentum we now call the First Crusade.

At the Council of Clermont in 1095, Pope Urban II delivered to the gathered throng a nightmare vision of defiling, polluting Muslims who tortured and eviscerated Christians in the Holy Land, raped women, and forcibly circumcised men, spreading the circumcision blood on church altars or pouring it into baptismal fonts, according to the report of Robert the Monk (Peters, *First Crusade* 2; *Recueil, Occ.* III: 728). Ordering Christians to cease internecine violence, criminality, and warfare in a Europe "too narrow" for its "large population," Urban unveiled the Holy Land (by then in Muslim hands for some four and a half centuries) as their rightful inheritance, ripe for the taking and urgently desiring liberation by the Latin West.

Detailing the abominations of the Muslims, Urban envisioned the armed Christian populace he was sending forth as the militia of God, acting out the will of God, and promised absolution for sins, and martyrdom, for the militant pilgrims he unleashed upon the East. The response, according to five major reports of Urban's address, was tumultuous and overwhelming. The eyes of some were bathed in tears, reported Baldric, Archbishop of Dol (Peters, *First Crusade* 10; *Recueil, Occ.* IV: 13); "God wills it!" cried out all who were present, reported Robert the Monk (Peters, *First Crusade* 4; *Recueil, Occ.* III: 728).[4]

The military success of the First Crusade established four core crusader colonies in the Near East: the County of Edessa, Principality of Antioch, County of Tripoli, and Kingdom of Jerusalem, along with cities, fortresses, ports, hinterlands, and other territories. "Christian holy wars before the Crusades were local affairs," Tomaz Mastnak wryly remarks, but the "Crusade was a world war" ("Muslims" 196).

After Edessa – the first crusader colony established – was recaptured in 1144 by Zengi, the Atabeg of Mosul, no less than the formidable St. Bernard, the Cistercian Abbot of Clairvaux, preached the Second Crusade in 1146 to a multitude at Vézelay, also to rousing acclamation. To support Hugh de Payen and his newly formed, highly unusual order of monks who were tasked as warriors dedicated to the full-time, permanent pursuit of holy war, the Order of the Temple, Bernard powerfully theorized and celebrated Christian militancy as a "New Knighthood" for the profession of holy war, a *monastic* warring knighthood embodied by the Templars whose champion Bernard became, and whose Latin Rule he cowrote in 1129.[5]

Crucial to Bernard's arsenal was his remarkable formulation in *De Laude Novae Militiae* (In Praise of the New Knighthood) that the enemy was not merely unspeakably vile, abominable, and accursed, as Urban II had said, and as the armed pilgrims of the First Crusade had understood. Muslims as the unclean, polluting, and abominable enemy had been the conceptual contribution of Urban in preaching the First Crusade. Bernard spliced in an ideational shift – that Muslims were *malefactors*, agents for the action of evil in the world. On Bernard's authority, then, whoever killed a *malefactor* was not a homicide, a killer of a human, "but, if I may say so, a *malicide* [malicida]," a killer only of evil ("Sane cum occidit malefactorem, non homicida, sed, ut ita dixerim, malicida"; Mastnak, *Crusading Peace* 125 n.262).

This is a theoretical formulation with profound consequences for the killing fields of war. On the authority of one of the great churchmen of the century, a killer of Muslims was not really a destroyer of human beings. In elevating war into a world contest against evil, human bodies had become epiphenomenal. A killer of Muslims was only a destroyer of evil itself.[6]

In the decade after the First Crusade, churchmen in Europe also busily concocted their own armchair accounts of the crusade, based on three eyewitness Latin chronicles written during and/or immediately after the crusade by participant chroniclers. The earliest, least embellished, and most utilized of these eyewitness chronicles was the *Gesta Francorum et aliorum Hierosolimitanorum* (the Deeds of the Franks and Other Pilgrims to Jerusalem) – likely begun by an anonymous vassal in the army of Bohemond at the siege and occupation of Antioch, and perhaps completed by the end of 1099, circulating in Europe shortly afterward (*Empire of Magic* 25).

The erudite Guibert de Nogent, Abbot of Nogent-sur-Coucy, reshaped the plain, straightforward, simple Latin of the *Gesta Francorum* into his own grand and polemical *Gesta Dei per Francos* (the Deeds of God through the Franks). With learned flourishes and newly invented content – including Guibert's devising of scapegoats for acts of cannibalism committed by the crusaders – Guibert's new calculus now made *God*, not humans, the performer of holy war (Heng, *Empire of Magic* 33–4, 319–21). Where at Clermont, God had only seemed to desire or to will particular actions ("*Deus vult*" had been the rousing cry of the audience's response to Urban), and where to the eyewitness chronicles of the First Crusade God had seemed to be the *spiritual* leader and guide of the crusaders, God now *performed* the crusade.[7] The sieving and honing of older dispensations, and the refinement of innovations after the First Crusade, thus conjured a cosmogonic theater in which God, as doer and actor, fought incarnated evil in the battlefields of the crusades.

The ideological universe of the most influential churchmen and theologians of the Latin West was not, of course, reducible to simple commensurabilities – the Abbot of Cluny, Peter the Venerable, another of the great ecclesiastics of the twelfth century, did not share St. Bernard's view that the "the cold-blooded murder or outright slaughter" of Saracens, as Peter put it, was willed by God ("Non vult enim Deus prorsus occidi, non omnino extingui," cited in Kritzeck 21). By contrast, Bernard of Clairvaux saw no difficulty in calculated genocide – in extirpating from the earth the enemies of the Christian name, as he put it ("Extirpandos de terra christiani nominis inimicos" [Epistola 457]; Mastnak, "Muslims" 188) – a lack of difficulty conduced by Bernard's political theology.

But in a world at war, even when the Abbot of Cluny saw that "The church has no sword ... but the staff of a shepherd," he nonetheless reasoned that "it may also be said to have a sword ... the sword of the Spirit, which is the Word of God (Eph. 6:17)"

(Kritzeck 22). For Peter the Venerable, as for others before him in the Near East and Iberia who had written polemical tracts on Islam and its Prophet, *the sword of the Spirit* was wielded via the manipulation of words. A war of words – ideological combat for hearts, minds, and souls across the world – thus interlocked with military politico-territorial war.

Peter the Venerable initiated the ambitious so-called Toledo translation project that in 1141–3 produced, for the first time, a full and complete translation of the Quran for the Western world, along with key texts on the life and traditions of the Prophet and Islamic doctrine: a collection that organized Islam as an object of knowledge that could be systematically opened up for scrutiny and aggressive refutation. Of the four translations Peter commissioned which comprise the collection, the translated Quran entitled *Lex Mahumet pseudoprophete* (the Law of Muhammad the Pseudoprophet) – painstakingly created by the English scholar Robert of Ketton – became "the most widely read Latin version of Islam's holy book," surviving in twenty-five manuscripts and printed in 1543 and 1550 editions. "When Europeans read the Qu'ran any time between the mid-twelfth and late seventeenth centuries, they usually read Robert's version" (Burman 15).[8]

Thomas Burman details the extent to which this translation – in a magisterial Latin that duly registers the importance of its subject, and with section divisions, colored initials, and paragraph marks to facilitate scrutiny – simultaneously grants the Quran "a kind of authority and prestige" even as the physical surrounding of the text by copious marginal notes and hostile commentary controls how the Quran is to be understood (60–3). Controlling the holy text of Islam by rendering it intelligible in Latin, and capturing its meaning inside a context of sustained refutation and dismissal, is, as Christopher Taylor pointedly suggests ("Global Circulation," "Prester John"), a way by which the literate in Christendom enclosed and surrounded the enemy's text in a form of epistemological capture, even as their crusader counterparts fought for territorial capture and control.

Combat against the revealed meaning encapsulated in the Quran was reinforced by the interminable retailing of scandalous, propagandist biographies of the Prophet, derisive representations of Islamic doctrine, and scurrilous rehearsals of *hadith*. The extra-Quranic translations, based on miscellaneous sources – especially the apparently inexhaustible *Risâlat al-Kindi* – assembled support for the view famously articulated by Peter the Venerable that Islam was the *summa* of heresies, and the Prophet the most dangerous of heresiarchs (Tolan, *Saracens* 159; *Ishmael* 56–7). The many elaborate fabrications about the Prophet's life and character, accruing from as early as the century that saw the emergence of Islam itself and continuing past the Middle Ages, are too numerous to rehearse (the most thorough summation is still perhaps Norman Daniel's *Islam and the West*, importantly supplemented by John Tolan's fine recent volumes).[9]

To understand racial thinking, however, it is crucial to note that specific elements of the Prophet's imagined biography are imported into *a general description of all Muslims*, and thereafter assigned as the collective personality traits of those who share a common religion. Practices of generalization, through which the personality of a singular individual becomes transcoded into the character of a collective totality of peoples, exemplify processes of race-thinking and racialization.

Invidious fables promulgated about the Prophet pivot on constructing Islam as a lie, and Islam's Prophet as a cunning, deceitful, ambitious, rapacious, ruthless, and licentious liar. In these accounts, the revelations received by the Prophet are construed as concocted messages invented by him, or by his advisors or cohort, to explain fits of epilepsy from which he suffered, and to authorize the expedient fulfillment of his personal desires and ambitions. Episodes from *hadith* which extol the Prophet as divinely gifted, because he is recognized at an early age (and thereafter at periodic junctures of his life) by key representatives of the Abrahamic faiths – representatives such as the Christian monk Bahira and Jewish interlocutors – are transformed into accounts in which Muhammad, a lowly camel driver, is variously tutored by wily heretical Christian monks, hermits, or Jews, who set him up as a false prophet, advocate his cause with the wealthy widow Khadijah, and aid him in constructing illusions of miracles and magic to deceive credulous Arabs into believing willy-nilly in his divinely appointed mission (Tolan, *Saracens* 139–41).[10]

Details vary. Some stories have the Prophet and/or his conspirators dramatically stage the appearance of the Quran as a book tied between the horns of a cow or bull, to awe the faithful (Tolan, *Saracens* 141). Others vilify the Prophet's possession of twelve or more wives, his conditional and hedged approval of polygyny for his male followers, and the expedient use of faked revelation to authorize his recruitment of Zaynab, originally the wife of his adopted son Zayd, into his expanding stable of women.[11] These constructions should be distinguished from the extravagant fantasies that pervade literary genres such as the *chanson de geste* or romance – genres in which Saracens, acting like pagans, crudely parade their pantheon of idols, futilely call on their "gods," and are luridly spirited off to hell by "Mahound" or devils when dispatched by Christian knights.[12] Different narrational modes exist for the racing of the enemy, with different kinds of effectivity.

In lieu of the outright literary fantasies offered by *chansons de geste* and romance, these more subtle constructions of a negative Islam use content from the extensive body of propaganda accumulated over the centuries in the contact zones where "Mozarabic authors base their caricature on knowledge of Islam and write for Christians who are in daily contact with Muslims" (Tolan, *Saracens* 152). Tracts such as the *Risâlat al-Kindi* – consulted by Peter the Venerable, Petrus Alphonsi, and others – "provide their readers with an image of Islam that seems realistic at the same time that it is repellent" by weaving together an intermixture of fact and fable that makes difficult the separation of one from the other (Tolan, *Saracens* 152).

They may also spin invidious interpretations out of historical matter. For instance, marriages entered into by the Prophet to cement political alliances, or to establish by personal example the dictum that widows, orphans, and divorcees should be provided for and protected under the aegis of marriage, become construed as nothing more than immoral acts of self-indulgence by a sexually rapacious leader.[13]

The variegated stories disseminated about the Prophet share the common thread of establishing him and his conspirators as superb masters of the lie: supreme falsifiers who connive through secrecy, deception, craft, and illusion. Even the Prophet's death occasions the conniving of fabrications. One such fabrication asserts that he mimetically anticipated a Christ-like resurrection, so that hasty dissimulation had to ensue when he did not in fact resurrect. Another fabrication spins a fanciful plotline of Near Eastern Christian pedigree into an anecdote in which the dead Prophet's body is encapsulated in a floating tomb or carapace levitated by magnets, in an elaborate hoax to hoodwink naive devotees (Tolan, *Saracens* 143–4, *Ishmael* 23–9).

Some stories tarred the Prophet by linking him to Persian magi and sinister magicians through cultural echoes, or, even worse, to heresiarchs such as Mani, Arius, and Nestorius. Other stories – such as Paul Alvaro's scurrilous but popular assertion that the Prophet died in a drunken stupor and was eaten by dogs or pigs – worked to puncture the aura of sanctity and righteousness with which Muslims associate the Prophet's life and deeds, even as they proffered canny explanations for why Muslims avoid alcohol, pork, and dogs.

The graphing of the Prophet's identity through accretions of miscellaneous tales is thus plotted along twin, intersecting axes. Along one axis runs a deep association of the Prophet with the masterful lie; the other axis identifies him with an insatiable sensuality. From the intersection of these axes spread the lineaments and patterning of a variety of stories. The twin identifiers of sex and lies are then extended by Latin Christian authors to characterize the group personality of Muslims in general. I examine one extreme example – a cultural fantasy of Islamic assassin-terrorists who intermingle sex, lies, and murder – later in this chapter.

Racialization of the Saracen is thus a multilayered phenomenon. At its most demonic – one might almost say ludic, or ludicrous – Saracens appear monstrous by being fused with animals, so that in the *Chanson de Roland* (Song of Roland) they have spiny bristles like a boar, or skin hard as iron, or they bark like dogs. No less damning, however, is to say that Muslims are monstrous in entirely *human* ways: that their "law" advocates unbridled, insensate lust and polymorphous perversity in this life and in the afterlife, monstrosifying human values. Equally monstrous would be a habitual embrace of lies, so that the relationship of Muslims to deception and falsehood – a relation that is offered as constitutive of their very identity and self-definition – hollows out and denatures their humanity at the core.

Holy War Redux: The Crusades, *gens Christiana*, *Malicide*, and Blood Races

Modern historians have been awed at the scale as well as the sheer human chaos of the First Crusade, the improbable success of which could not be replicated in the half-millennium of crusading that followed. Despite Pope Urban's injunction that only fit, able combatants should embark on the voyage to recapture Jerusalem – Urban forbade the old, the feeble, women without male guardians, priests not expressly authorized by bishops, and those unfit to bear arms to undertake the enterprise – all ages, genders, classes, ethnicities, and dispositions of humans, in all manner of physical condition, emerged from the villages, towns, cities, and countryside of Europe.

Coalescing in four or five contingents that merged, after the mustering at Constantinople, into one unwieldy "army" theoretically led by the major barons of the First Crusade under the Papal legate, they slogged their way to Jerusalem in nearly three meandering years.[14] This heterogeneous army of "pilgrims" (as they called themselves) encountered en route formidable geophysical barriers, wretchedly inhospitable terrain (made worse by the enemy's scorched-earth tactics), repeated starvation and unendurable thirst, disease and illness of many kinds, and slow or sudden death, as well as terrifying enemy forces and mistrustful, suspicious, and unreliable allies in the form of the Greek Christian "brothers" the Latin Christians were supposed to aid.[15]

Eyewitness chronicles narrated in detail the indiscipline, uncontrollability, and disorder of the crusade, which was not so much a united army of Christ (as the chronicles ringingly liked to proclaim) as it was a human swarm spreading across the East, a miasmic force lurching toward Jerusalem. One of their detractors, the Byzantine princess Anna Comnena, in her biography of her father – the emperor Alexius I, a supposed instigator of the First Crusade – announced that every contingent of crusaders that set out from Europe had been preceded by a vast swarm ("a plague") of *locusts*, "so that everyone, having observed the phenomenon several times, came to recognize locusts" as heralding crusaders – thus slyly tarring crusaders with a Biblical allusion that captured well the sense of awe and dread and the impression of formlessness and miasmic motility that the crusaders struck in the hearts of those who encountered them (310).

Whatever their intentions – and some crusade historians have liked to stress the best intentions of the crusade, the genuine piety, devotion, and earnestness of the pilgrim invaders – the actions of the pilgrims turned out not to be fully under their control, nor under the control of their leaders. Heinous deeds were performed during this holiest of wars-as-pilgrimage – not to mention the looting, rape, pillaging, killing, and sack common in medieval warfare – leading the eyewitness chroniclers to throw up their hands and inveigh against the sins of these pilgrims to the Holy Land.

The chroniclers feared the fury of God would descend for crusader sins, and the *Gesta Francorum* reports a vision in which Christ showed himself in person to excoriate the pilgrims (Hill 58–9). *Actions that are in excess of intentions* and the *meaning and effects of the actions*, generated by a human community that is sometimes overtaken (and taken aback) by its own actions, are what we will consider in tracking processes of race-making.

Tomaz Mastnak reflects on the degree to which the enemy that was encountered by the crusaders was not encountered by the crusaders as fully human. Beyond the startling alterity of first contact – Fulcher of Chartres relates the terrifying clashing of weapons and shrieking by the enemy, the thick hailstorm of arrows (the Seljuk Turks encountered by the crusaders used mounted archers extensively), and bizarre field actions involving pincer movements to surround the crusaders (Edwards, *First Crusade* 46)[16] – Mastnak argues that the repeated representation of Muslims as unclean, foul nations polluting the Holy Places congeals a view of the enemy as "dirt": in the words of Bernard of Clairvaux, "pagan dirt [that] had to be eliminated from the Holy Land (*a Terra Sancta eliminare spurcitias paganorum*)" (*Crusading Peace* 128).

Certainly, there is little sense that early crusaders felt Muslims ought to be treated as part of a universal fellowship of the living and sentient. Fulcher of Chartres, who is impressive for noticing the suffering of small animals who accompany the crusaders, such as dogs and goats, and for a profound sympathy toward beasts of burden who must carry heavy loads while starving, does not articulate similar compassion for the human foe.[17] Fulcher's sensitivity toward innocent animals who suffer and die simply does not extend to innocent humans on the other side – children, women, noncombatants – who also suffer in war, such as the Saracen women raped and slaughtered in camps overrun by the crusaders.[18]

The *Gesta Francorum* describes how crusaders outside Antioch, after the Turks had retrieved their postbattle dead and buried and entombed them at a mosque near the city, deliberately dug up the Turkish cadavers, destroyed the tombs, dragged the dead out of their graves, threw the corpses into a pit, and cut off their heads, trawling those heads back to the crusader camp (for purposes of counting, says the *Gesta*): actions that grieved the Turks "almost to death," and left them to "weep and howl" in daily lamentation (Hill 42–3).

Though both sides did abominable things in combat – such as beheading the enemy and lobbing the heads into the enemy's camp to horrify and demoralize – the cold-blooded, stage-by-stage desecration of the already dead and buried argues the reduction of human bodies to mere thinghood. *This* particular desecration – which may have begun as a rational act of tomb robbery (the *Gesta* says the dead had been buried with "cloaks, gold bezants, bows and arrows" and tools [Hill 42–3]) – evinces a gratuitous savagery and superfluity in excess of the need to count, to loot, or even to crow.

If a dead body becomes an object through piecemeal decimation (besides beheadings, bodies were also eviscerated; chronicles also notice scattered numbers of hands and feet), the most spectacular example of how the human enemy is reduced to a thing, I have argued, is to turn the enemy into comestibles. In December 1098, at Ma'arra an-Numan in northern Syria, after crusaders had sacked the city and put its inhabitants to the sword, they retrieved enemy corpses earlier flung into ditches, filleted them into pieces and slices, cooked these, and ate them.

Humans who had been turned into things by death and dismemberment were thus also turned into edibles to fortify the living. The eyewitness chroniclers report the events with constrained horror. Each invokes the rationale of extreme hunger yet elects not to mention that death on crusade ascends to the laurels of martyrdom, though the chroniclers laud death-as-martyrdom time and again in their chronicles.

Fulcher is tormented by the implications of cannibalizing the Muslim enemy – acts committed, he says, by *very many* crusaders – and shudders at the thought that the cannibals ate *raw* rather than adequately cooked flesh, as if a distinction between the raw and the cooked, nine centuries before Levi-Strauss, signaled an important difference:

> When the siege had lasted twenty days, our people suffered excessive hunger. I shudder to speak of it, because very many of our people, harassed by the madness of excessive hunger, cut off pieces from the buttocks of the Saracens already dead there, which they cooked and chewed, and devoured with savage mouth, when insufficiently roasted at the fire. And thus the besiegers more than the besieged were tormented.
>
> (*Historia Hierosolymitana* [History of the Expedition to Jerusalem] 266–7)[19]

As if hunger alone were insufficient, the *Gesta*'s author tersely adds an aside that makes eating the dead almost an inadvertency of looting the once-human bodies, a byproduct mechanical reflex:

> While we were there, some of our men could not satisfy their needs, either because of the long stay or because they were so hungry, for there was no plunder to be had outside the walls. So they ripped up the bodies of the dead, because they used to find bezants hidden in their entrails, and others cut the dead flesh into slices and cooked it to eat.
>
> (Hill 80)[20]

The account of Raymond d'Aguiliers, chaplain of Raymond de Saint-Gilles, Count of Toulouse, shows us how crusader cannibalism looks through other eyes, so we see that turning Saracens into food superordinates the crusaders into feared and seemingly invincible – if monstrosified – conquerors:

> Meanwhile, there was so great a famine in the army that the people [*populus*] ate most greedily the many already fetid bodies of the Saracens which they had cast into the swamps of the city two weeks and more ago. These events frightened many people of our race [*nostre gentis homines*], as well as outsiders. On this account very many of us turned back . . .

But the Saracens and the Turks said on the contrary: "And who can resist this people who are so obstinate and cruel [*crudelis*], that for a year they could not be turned from the siege of Antioch by famine, or sword, or any other dangers, and who now feed on human flesh?" These and other most cruel practices [*alia crudelissima*] the pagans said exist among us. For God had given fear of us to all races [*gentibus*], but we did not know it.

(Hill and Hill 101; Krey 214)[21]

Here we see that turning the human enemy into the less-than-human – into consumables – supercharges those who consume, so that they become *more* than human: Indeed, it transforms the crusader community into a race of feared *super*humans, even if these hypercharged, unstoppable vanquishers are grotesquely denatured. Cannibalism draws a line between those who eat – whose membership in a living race is implacably attested by their aggressive act of eating – and those who are eaten, the DNA and body parts of which disappear into the dominant bodies of the eaters, invisibly absorbed.

Crusader cannibalism may also have taken place at Antioch, a few months before Ma'arra. A letter to Pope Paschal II dated September 1099 from Laodicaea, signed by three leaders of the crusading forces (Godfrey of Bouillon; Raymond de Saint-Gilles; and Daimbert, Archbishop of Pisa) confesses the famine at Antioch to be so extreme that "some might scarcely restrain themselves from eating human flesh" ("*ut uix ab humanis dapibus se continerent aliqui*" [Hagenmeyer, *Kreuzzugsbriefe* 169]).[22]

Arabic chronicles by Ibn al-Qalanisi, Ibn al-Athir, and Kemal al-Din also direct attention to likely crusader cannibalism after the capture and sack of Antioch in June 1098, after a siege of seven and a half months (Gibb 46; *Recueil, Orientaux* 1: 194, 3: 583).[23] Finally, Anna Comnena cites a letter of Bohemond (which has not survived) in which Bohemond laments a famine at Antioch "so bad that most of us were even reduced to eating meats forbidden by the law" (358).

In "Cannibalism, the First Crusade, and the Genesis of Medieval Romance" and *Empire of Magic*, I discuss at length the devastation wrought by ingesting the unclean, infernal enemy, whose pollution of the Holy Places had now spread to the inside of Christian bodies thanks to crusader cannibalism: a contamination made especially problematic in an era of sanctified Eucharistic cannibalism where the Real Presence of God in the sacramental communion host rendered Latin Christian communicants one with the divine.

If you are what you eat, and if Eucharistic cannibalism sealed your oneness with God, what did it mean to absorb and disseminate the polluting, infernal enemy throughout your body? The outcome of these (no doubt unplanned and spontaneous) actions, I have argued, had significant consequences for the literary development of a mode of fantasy that we today call romance, and in particular for the efflorescence of the King Arthur legend in literary and narrative form.

Here, my interest is in matters of *race*: how cannibalism draws tight a community of the living who have reduced another human community to food. Two centuries or more later, when the initial horror at crusader cannibalism of 1098 had subsided – after these cannibalisms had been repeatedly processed and digested, having been worked on by a variety of cultural texts – the romance called *Richard Coer de Lyon* is able to manifest the crusader king of England, Richard I, as an unabashed, gleeful, and triumphant cannibal-imperialist.[24]

In this popular romance, Richard Lionheart as crusader-conqueror heartily devours a stewed, black-skinned young Saracen with relish, and later serves cooked black Saracen heads piping hot on platters to his dinner guests – who are the relatives of those heads-as-dinner – at a magnificent feast hosted by the English king, during which he himself showily carves up and lip-smackingly eats his own dish of Saracen.[25] Two or more centuries later, the knotting of epidermal race to religion, and to imperial conquest, by turning your enemies into comestibles, explicitly surfaces racial, religious, and geopolitical domination as aggressive acts that impart the collective identity of the Christian English.[26]

The crucible of holy war offered many opportunities for congealing a collective group identity beyond acts of eating the enemy. Tomaz Mastnak, for one, forcefully argues that the First Crusade brought a "new prominence of blood and torn flesh in defining Christian identity. Christians were defined as 'blood-brothers,' and Christendom by implication as blood-fraternity" ("Muslims" 192). Christ's shedding of his blood for the salvation of Christians – a doctrine at the heart of corporate Christian identity, and one that is perpetually renewed at mass and in communion wine – meant that "the shedding of *Christian* blood" by Muslims could become an occasion for consolidating Christian identity:

> References to the slaughter of "many thousands of Christians" like "cattle" by a "race of pagans" ... led to the appeal to "fraternal love" (*fraterna caritas*) that should impel Western Christians to lay down their lives for the "liberation of our brothers" [in the Byzantine empire and the Holy Land], for "as he had laid down his life for us, we also should lay down our lives for our brothers" ... "Christian blood, redeemed by the blood of Christ, has been shed, and Christian flesh, akin to Christ's flesh has been subjected to unspeakable degradation and servitude". That was a call on Western Christians to take up arms for their "blood brothers". And as Latin Christians adopted "the terms of race and blood to describe their group identity", their enemy, pictured as bloody and cruel, became the enemy of Christian blood, and a blood enemy.
>
> ("Muslims" 192–3)[27]

"Can there be a more existential, life-and-death definition of the existential enemy?" Mastnak asks ("Muslims" 193). We might add: In the contest of blood-letting, can there be a more succinct grasp of racial distinction than the articulation of fundamental blood differences in the identification of self from enemy? In this context, Bernard of Clairvaux's equanimity in calling for the enemy's extirpation through medieval-style genocide is intelligible, and indeed logical:

> Oriental Christians were Latin Christians' "blood-brothers." Such "ethnization" of Christianity, that is, "adopting the terms of race and blood to describe their group identity," was ominous. With the prominence of blood and Holy Land, the Crusade was formulated in terms of *Blut und Boden*. Urban II's speech can be read as harking back to the prohibition of the shedding of *Christian* blood, as formulated by the Council of Narbonne. Looking to the future, however, such particularization of redeemed blood opened the way to the uninhibited shedding of unredeemed blood. It opened the prospect of universal permissibility for the Christian fraternity to shed un-Christian blood, of universal Christian shedding of blood.
>
> (Mastnak, "Holy War" 36–7)

The massacre of Muslims and Jews in Jerusalem, when the pilgrims of the First Crusade finally arrived and captured the city – an unremitting orgy of slaughter, dismemberment, torture, and flowing blood that appalls and nauseates modern scholars – would seem a logical consequence, then, of the dynamics of race identity in a global holy war where religion is defined through categories of blood.[28] "No-one has ever seen or heard of such a slaughter of pagans," the *Gesta* says; "there was such a massacre that our men were wading up to their ankles in enemy blood" (Hill 92, 91). Raymond d'Aguiliers is more effusive:

> Some of the pagans were mercifully beheaded, others pierced by arrows plunged from towers, and yet others, tortured for a long time, were burned to death in searing flames. Piles of heads, hands, and feet lay in the houses and streets, and indeed there was a running to and fro of men and knights over the corpses . . . these are few and petty details . . . Shall we relate what took place there? If we told you, you would not believe us. So it is sufficient to relate that in the Temple of Solomon and the portico crusaders rode in blood to the knees and bridles of their horses. In my opinion, this was poetic justice . . . Jerusalem was now littered with bodies.
>
> (Hill and Hill 127–8)

Fulcher estimated that "ten thousand were beheaded" at the Temple of Solomon, and, in a curious moment, switches from his habitual use of first-person voice to third-person in describing the actions of the crusaders:

> If you had been there, your feet would have been stained up to the ankles with the blood of the slain. What more shall I tell? Not one of them was allowed to live. *They* did not spare the women and children.
>
> (Peters, *First Crusade* 77, emphasis added)

The *Gesta* recounts how the crusade leaders "commanded that all the Saracen corpses should be thrown outside the city because of the fearful stench, for almost the whole city was full of their dead bodies." When the corpses were piled high outside the city gates, the mounds of the dead "were as big as houses" (Hill 92).

The eyewitness chronicles seem awed at the magnitude and details of crusader carnage, but, unlike the anguish and horror they expressed at crusader cannibalism, they register little depth of concern, let alone horror, outrage, or condemnation, at the bloodletting in Jerusalem. Fulcher – perhaps the most sensitive of the three (he was also away in Edessa at the time) – registers the massacre, but quickly plants a vivid metaphor in our minds that likens the slaughtered enemy to "rotten fruit" that "falls from shaken branches," supplanting the carnage with an image of natural surcease:

> With drawn swords, our people ran through the city;
> Nor did they spare anyone, not even those pleading for mercy,
> The crowd was struck to the ground, just as rotten fruit
> Falls from shaken branches, and acorns from a wind-blown oak.
>
> (Peters, *First Crusade* 78)

Scholars sometimes contrast the bloodbath of the 1099 Jerusalem massacre to the relatively bloodless capture of Jerusalem by Muslims, first by the Caliph Umar in 637, then by Salah ad-Din in 1187. Tomaz Mastnak's argument that the First Crusade congealed Christians as a blood race under Christ – people who shared a common blood through their religion, and who attested their corporate blood-bond and identity by shedding the enemy's blood – is persuasive. Equally palpable in the chronicles is how the enemy is reduced to the status of thinghood, so that when they are hewn down in the massacre at Jerusalem, the vast carnage seems to happen to the less than fully human (despite their pleas for mercy, despite women and children being among the victims): It is just the fate of rotten fruit, as Fulcher tells it, or of acorns that must fall from a wind-blown oak; part of a natural, inevitable course of events.

*Super*natural events also confirm the crusaders as a virtual race in global war. Though their "army of God" (*exercitus Dei*) was internally multifarious – Fulcher counted some twenty-one different linguistic, regional, and ethnonational groups represented in the First Crusade – the abutting of internal European heterogeneity against an external foe saw a harnessing of resources to posit the crusaders as de facto and de jure one people. Among the dreams, signs, and visions experienced by the crusaders was an important visit by the Savior himself, to the priest Stephen of Valence.

As reported by Raymond d'Aguiliers, Christ comes in person and questions Stephen on the identity of the occupation army at Antioch: "*Homo, quenam est hec gens que civitatem ingressa est?*" ("Man, what race/people is this that has entered the city?") Stephen's reply presents the polyglot Latin forces as one entity: "*Christiani.*" (Hill and Hill 72–3). Indeed, again and again, crusaders reached across lines of country, region, ethnicity, tribe, and caste to constitute themselves as a people defined by their religion alone, highlighted by the cross blazoned on their clothing: *gens Christiana*, a Christian race.

Race-making of this kind is contingent and functional. Assembled in the field of war, when facing an external enemy that has itself been defined, over and over, by *its* religion, race is a glue in a crucial apparatus of support that shores up popular willpower, morale, hope, and survival. Under the circumstances of holy war, it is logical to nest the internal heterogeneity of the pilgrims within a superstructure of religious race – mirroring, in a sense, the religious racialization of the enemy, whose heterogeneity is also nested by the West within a superstructure of their detested faith.

Putting it another way, Robert Bartlett calls this "the 'ethnicization' of Christianity" and quotes "the French prelate Baudry de Bourgueil [Baldric, Archbishop of Dol], writing in the early twelfth century," who says, in his preface to his crusade chronicle, the *Historia Hierosolymitana* (History of the Expedition to Jerusalem), "I am a Christian and have descended from Christian ancestors" (Bartlett, *Making of Europe* 252). Like Chaucer's Prioress (as we saw in Chapter 2), the Archbishop hypothesizes Christian-ness as a biological inheritance of birth, blood, and genealogy, *as if he were raced as Christian* (Bartlett, *Making of Europe* 252). Bartlett concludes: "Latin Christians, as they encountered alien peoples in the course of their high medieval expansion, adopt[ed] the terms of race and blood to describe their group identity" (*Making of Europe* 252).[29]

The "high medieval expansion" touched on by Bartlett prominently includes crusader colonization of the Near East. A critical strain in medievalist scholarship has long acknowledged the crusades as twelfth-century colonial experiments in extraterritoriality, a *medieval* version of modern European colonial experiments. "Here was made the first step of teaching Europe how to colonize," says the redoubtable Joshua Prawer – an early model of the European colonial experience rooted in territorial occupation and political dominion, economic extraction, ideological reproduction, and evidence of a "colonial mentality" and colonial relations, legible in the records of the occupied territories of the Levant (366). "At their peak," Josiah Russell recalls, "the crusading states controlled about three fifths of the land and population of Syria" (56). Duncalf adds that "it is reasonable to believe that Urban did intend the westerners to keep the Holy Land" (55).

Indeed, writing his own crusade chronicle from his perch in twelfth-century France, Guibert de Nogent, the learned Abbot of Nogent-sur-Coucy, calls the Kingdom of Jerusalem a "new colony" ("*novae coloniae*") of Latin Christendom, self-consciously revivifying the memory of imperial Rome's colonizations as predecessor, in whose magisterial footsteps Christendom would now follow (*Recueil, Occ.*, 4: 245).

Importantly, Guibert's evocation of the Roman Empire as exemplar registers the twelfth-century West's engagement in colonialism as *Gesta Dei per Francos*, the deeds of God through the medium of the Franks: invoking *religion*, now, and *God*, as the authorizing discourse of the twelfth century's colonial enterprise, thus crucially altering Rome's antique imperialisms. Crusading militarism has set in place a creolized template of colonization indispensable to the later European colonial expeditions that would arrive – not like Rome, but like Christendom – wielding *both* the Book *and* the sword in the far reaches of the world.

Additionally, despite the eventual loss of all territories in Syria and Palestine after two centuries, Europe's adventurism shifted the economic calculus of early capitalism in favor of the Latin West. Through transfers of agricultural, industrial, engineering, and other knowledges from the Levant and Littoral, crusader colonization proved a crucial hinge not only for the growth of European industries, agriculture, infrastructure, and artisanry, but also for remaking the balance of payments calculus between East and West, so that by the end of the Middle Ages the East came to assume the erstwhile role of the West as exporter of raw materials over manufactures, in an ironic reversal of their trade roles early in the Middle Ages.[30]

How the dominance of Islamicate and Greek societies was eroded in export industries such as sugar, textiles, and even fine transparent glass is well documented. The economic consequences of the twelfth-century transfer of glass-blowing technologies from Tyre to Venice can still be seen in the twenty-first century, since today it is Venice's exquisite Murano glass, not Lebanese Tyrian glass, that is globally renowned and collected. As William Phillips wryly observes in his study of sugar production, while "the Crusades may have failed ... in economic terms they were successful, as the West wrested economic ascendancy from the East" (403).

Indeed, after his metaphors of rotten fruit and falling acorns have displaced the sanguinary vision of hewn-down Muslims pleading in vain for mercy, Fulcher's attention is immediately riveted by the *economic consequences* of the Jerusalem massacre. One outcome of the massacre, we learn, is the depopulation of Jerusalem, which then becomes an empty city ripe for repopulation by crusader-settlers:

> After this great massacre, they entered the homes of the citizens, seizing whatever they found in them. It was done systematically, so that whoever had entered the home first, whether he was rich or poor, was not to be harmed by anyone else in any way. He was to have and to hold the house or palace and whatever he had found in it entirely as his own. Since they mutually agreed to maintain this rule, many poor men became rich.
>
> (Peters, *First Crusade* 78)

The admirable cooperation described by Fulcher – a virtual communitarianism in apportioning houses and palaces among the crusader populace practicing its own version of settler-colonialism – quickly culminates in a paean of praise, an ecstasy of rejoicing, as Fulcher gives thanks to God for their attaining the prize of Jerusalem:

Oh, time so longed for! Oh, time remembered among all others! Oh, deed to be preferred before all deeds! . . . Cleansed from the contagion of the heathen . . . so long contaminated by their superstition, [Jerusalem] was restored to its former rank by those believing and trusting in Him.

(Peters, *First Crusade* 78–9)

By Book III of his chronicle, Fulcher is able to glory in the sustaining of a mature, settled, and prosperous colonial dispensation in Syria and Palestine, willing us a description of unmatched eloquence:

Consider, I pray, and reflect how in our time God has transformed the West into the East. For we who were Occidentals now have been made Orientals. He who was a Roman or a Frank is now a Galilaean, or an inhabitant of Palestine. One who was a citizen of Rheims or of Chartres now has been made a citizen of Tyre or of Antioch. We have already forgotten the places of our birth; already they have become unknown to many of us, or, at least, are unmentioned. Some already possess here homes and servants which they have received through inheritance. Some have taken wives not merely of their own people, but Syrians, or Armenians, or even Saracens who have received the grace of baptism . . . One cultivates vines, the other the fields . . . Different languages, now made common, become known to both races, and faith unites those whose forefathers were strangers . . . Those who were strangers are now natives; and he who was a sojourner now has become a resident. Our parents and relatives from day to day come to join us . . . For those who were poor there, here God makes rich. Those who had few coins, here possess countless bezants; and those who had not had a villa, here, by the gift of God, possess a city. Therefore, why should one who has found the East so favorable return to the West? . . . You see, therefore, that this is a great miracle, and one which must greatly astonish the world. Who has ever heard anything like it?

(*Historia Hierosolymitana* 748–9, *History* 271–2)[31]

Reading Fulcher's statement of twelfth-century European colonization gone native, recognition and surprise – difference *and* familiarity – jostle together queerly and in a disorienting way for those habituated to later European colonial empires. Fulcher's recitation theorizes the mobility of place, citizenship, identity, language, sexuality, economic labor, socioeconomic status, religion, memory, and race as a multigenerational project articulated in a seductive language of power. Reading Fulcher's *now* with the unavoidable knowledge of later, newer colonizations – accruing different moments of the colonial *now* – makes us alive to the modernity of the past, to the panoply of resources that can be amassed to mystify operations of power, and to the sheer parsimony and resilience of colonial dialect.

Those who work in postcolonial studies in the academy have heard this before, of course, albeit not issued as a twelfth-century paean of exultation. From the legacy of European maritime empires of the early and high modern eras, the details of colonial occupation to which Fulcher bears witness are startlingly familiar: expropriation of land and resources; the creation of colonial elites, a subject class ("servants"), and intergenerational transfers of colonial privilege ("inheritance"); a mystified politics of language and of sexual and ethnoracial relations; even the pleasures of going native, and complacent self-congratulation by colonial masters secure in the rightness of their destiny.

Race is only one factor here, in the twelfth-century colonial experiment of Outremer, and it is not, here, articulated as fractious or problematic. Race here is harmonious and orderly, a peaceful project that goes hand in glove with the blessedness of economic success. Who, indeed, has ever heard anything like it?

Sex, Lies, and Paradise: The Assassins, and the Fabulation of Saracen Pleasures and Civilizational Identity, or Deviance as the Definition of a Population

In the hydra-headed project of defining the Islamic Saracen and Islamdom in the European Middle Ages, a spectacular cultural fantasy of widespread dispersion knots together several strands of the cultural beliefs we have discussed thus far. European texts of many kinds, from chronicles to love poems, in Latin and in vernacular languages, exhibit a fascination with the legend of the *Assassins*: historically, a breakaway group of Ismaili Shiites who became infamous for targeted, highly public assassinations of their political, military, and religious enemies. First gaining a foothold in Latin crusade texts of the twelfth century, reports of the Assassins of Alamut spread so rapidly in Europe that by the second half of that century, or early in the thirteenth, five Provençal poems were able to refer to them and their leader alike – a shadowy "Old Man of the Mountain," in crusade lore – as ready metaphors that a public could understand without explanation (Chambers 245).

In due course, fabulations about the Assassins and their lair in the East overtook more historical accounts. Finally, in the second half of the fourteenth century, one of the most famous and popular literary works of the European Middle Ages, *Mandeville's Travels*, braided the Assassins' legend together with another absorbing cultural fantasy of the European Middle Ages, the legend of Prester John – a fictive Christian king presiding over an imaginary Christian empire in the Orient.

Mandeville's Travels – an extraordinary text that was transmitted in all the major European languages, of which some 300 manuscripts still survive (twice the number of manuscripts of Marco Polo's account of his travels), and possessing an extensive geographic reach and influence that continued for centuries – strikingly offers up the Assassins and Prester John as symbolic exemplars that point to essential differences in the corporate character of Islamdom and Christendom in its time. Though the *Travels* materializes the Islamic world variously, in dialogue and commentary, characters, and places, it also remarkably demonstrates how Islamic civilization can be compactly and economically summoned by means of a single cultural fantasy with which it was linked for centuries – the fantasy of the Assassins.

In fabulated and legendary accounts of the Assassins, male youths are fed a narcotic (usually *hashish*, hence their name, *Hashishiyya* or *Hashshashin* – users of hashish, the etymological derivation of the word *assassins*) and brought to a mountain fastness in the East, where a "sheik" or old man has connived a facsimile Islamic paradise: a garden resplendent with orchards, water, and pleasure-women, so that the youths are able to revel in polymorphous sensual pleasures. Told they can only return to this fake paradise by committing assassinations ordered by the old man, their master, the youths become assassins who perform sensational murders, their legend growing for nine centuries thereafter – continuing even in popular culture of the twenty-first century – and lending an infamous word, one that internationally signifies homicide, to the repository of human language.[32]

Beyond mass culture's fascination with their legend, the Assassins have also drawn the attention of scholars seeking a genealogy for "suicide terrorism" after the events of September 11, 2001, drew the world's attention to Al-Qaeda, a violent extremist group purporting to speak for Islam and all Muslims. "[T]he Assassins may indeed be regarded as the forerunners of the suicide bombers of today," the historian Bernard Lewis opined in a 2002 preface that accompanied the reprint of his well-known book *The Assassins: A Radical Sect in Islam* (xii):

> the connection[s] between the medieval Assassins and their modern counterparts are striking: the Syrian-Iranian connection; the calculated use of terror; the total dedication of the assassin emissary, to the point of self-immolation, in the service of his cause and in the expectation of heavenly recompense. Some have seen a further resemblance in that both directed their attack against an external enemy, the Crusaders in the one case, the Americans and the Israelis in the other.
>
> (xi)

Lewis' insistence on a direct connection between a 900-year-old past and the contemporary present is not atypical. Gérard Chaliand and Arnaud Blin, the editors of *The History of Terrorism*, a 2007 University of California Press anthology, agree that

> the case of the Assassins is not fundamentally different from that of Al Qaeda today. From his sanctuary in the mountains of Afghanistan, Osama bin Laden led a campaign against the West similar to that of Hasan against the Seljuks, with ... very similar tactics ... The propaganda drives and recruitment and training of terrorists in both cases were very much alike, often undertaken among the same social classes and in similar topographies (rural or mountainous regions with populations hardened by warfare).
>
> (69)

I have discussed elsewhere how this yoking of a 900-year-old phenomenon, forged in the crucible of Near Eastern Islamdom's roiling internal religious strife, to the global politics of today dangerously raises false identifications, and proffers the seductive lure of an oversimplified way to understand the politics of our time ("Sex, Lies, and Paradise"). Importantly, the Latin West's understanding of the Assassins was heavily colored by *fantasy*, so that facticity and legend became intertwined and inextricable in the Western imagination: a legacy that has survived to this day, and which colors the temptation to view a fractious Muslim minority as somehow representative of Islam. In European literature, the breakaway community represented by the Assassins – a community considered heretical by the Islamic populations of its day – came in time to stand in for Islam proper: a calculus we would not wish to reproduce in understanding the causes, proponents, and genealogy of "suicide terrorism" today.[33]

But who were the Assassins? Historically, a breakaway populace of Ismaili Shiites known to scholars today as *Nizaris* congealed communities in mountain fastnesses in Persia, Khurasan, and Syria for some 200 years, improvising a distinctive, territorially dispersed state formation out of chronically unstable conditions – a state formation remarkably adapted to the exigencies of regional existence – until extirpated by the Mongols in the thirteenth century.

Spread across Persia and Syria as a network of nodal points anchored by approximately 250 fortified mountain enclaves and their surrounding villages and towns (Willey, *Eagle's*

Nest 58) – with power loosely emanating from Alamut, the first site acquired in northern Persia, but not only from there – the decentered system was created after a critical split from the Mustalian Ismailis of Fatimid Egypt in 1094 over a succession dispute.

Under new leadership and their own imams, Nizari Ismailis improvised complex diplomatic and military affairs in the regional balance of power. Syrian Nizaris came to terms with the leader of the Sunni forces waging the countercrusade, Salah ad-Din Yusuf ibn Ayyub (Saladin), in the twelfth century, and conducted rapprochements with his successors in the thirteenth. They became tributaries of the orders of the Hospital and the Temple (that is, the military-monastic orders of Hospitaler and Templar knights); lent support to these orders on occasion; and were defended on occasion by the Hospital and the Ayyubid rulers of Aleppo and Damascus.

Rather than suggesting a rabid mob of the dazed and narcotically possessed, Nizari adaptations to the volatilities of regional power – coming to terms where necessary, using tribute, electing warfare, and improvising political assassination as a strategy of advantage against superior forces – suggested rationality and discipline.

The name *Assassins*, by which the Nizaris are popularly known, was attached to them by their enemies. The sobriquet first appears in a polemical epistle in 1123 by the Fatimid caliph, Al-Amir, leader of the Mustalian Ismailis, who, in refuting Nizari claims to the Ismaili leadership, vilifies the sect by tagging them as *"Hashishiyya"* – a term of abuse that has dogged the Nizaris for 900 years. In the thirteenth century, this epithet connoting Nizari degeneracy also appeared in rival Zaydi Shiite documents and miscellaneous Sunni documents, including Imad al-Din's chronicle of the Seljuks, Abu Shama's regional history of Syria (an important source for Silvestre de Sacy's nineteenth-century etymological deductions that tie the word to the use of hashish), and Ibn Muyassar's history of Fatimid Egypt (Daftary, *Assassin Legends* 37, 90; Hodgson 136–7).[34] Early non-Arabic sources who report this pejorative designation for the Nizaris include the Jewish traveler Benjamin of Tudela (who calls them *"Al-Hashishim"* [Marcus Adler 16]), the chronicler of the crusader states William of Tyre (*"Assissini"* [Migne 201: 31, col. 811a]), and the European chronicler Arnold of Lübeck (*"Heyessini"* [VII: 8, p.274]).

Today, scholars of the Nizaris think little of the claim that Nizari communities indulged in hashish as an inducement to, or preparation for, assassination by their *fedawis*, the specialized devotees within the Nizari state directed to the commission of assassination. Conceding that Nizari imams – especially their ascetic and erudite founder, Hasan ibn Sabah – imposed strict regimes of rigorous asceticism on their communities, most argue that the inflammatory name was circulated by their enemies – Sunni Muslims, Shiite rivals, Ismaili foes – to cultivate an association of the Nizaris with popular notions of social degeneracy and lower-class infamy (Daftary, *Assassin Legends* 91–2; Hodgson 135–6).[35]

Since they are a breakaway Islamic community, their *religious* degeneracy is summoned in the more common designation for Nizaris in Arabic texts: *malahida* or heretics, a designation as opprobrious in medieval Islam as it was in medieval Christianity, and referenced by Benjamin of Tudela as *Mulahid* (Marcus Adler 53), and by William of Rubruck as *Mulibet* (Wyngaert 287).

Archeologists tell us that Nizari enclaves constituted viable socioeconomic entities, cultivating innovations in technology, fortifications, and agriculture. Hasan ibn Sabah enlarged the mountain fastness of Alamut in northern Persia and had cisterns, underground chambers, and storerooms hewn from solid rock and a spring diverted for a permanent water supply (Willey, *Castles* 93, 222–4; *Eagle's Nest* 58). Alamut even had its own mint (Willey, *Castles* 219) and a renowned library, consigned to the flames in the Mongol invasion of 1256 (Hodgson 26; Daftary, *Assassin Legends* 39; Daftary, *Ismailis* 34; Boyle 666; Lewis, *Assassins* 13).

In the Alamut valley, Hasan extended irrigation and cultivation and had water canals dug and numerous trees planted (Daftary, *Assassin Legends* 32; *Ismailis* 130; De Sacy, "Memoir") – projects that insinuated the nucleus of an idea that Alamut might be an earthly paradise replete with wells, conduits, and orchards.

As the fortunes of the Nizari state fluctuated, one more element likely fed into a European fantasy of a profligate Assassin paradise. Nizaris were a theocratically organized polity based on a messianic creed vested in cycles of manifest and hidden divinely inspired imams who led the faithful through requisite devolutions of time along the path to eschatological fulfillment (*qiyama*). Not only did their creed require patient waiting and survival while being surrounded by demographically and militarily superior hostile forces and populations (consisting, mainly, of fellow Muslims), but theirs was a messianism committed to esoteric interpretations of sacred writ, and to strategies of dissimulation (*taqiyya*): defensive self-concealment through group behavior that deliberately obscured access to the lived realities of their communities and faith, and that sought to mislead and confound the uninitiated (Daftary, *Assassin Legends* 6, 13, 17, 20, 43; Hodgson 12, 155–6).

Under two successive Persian imams, the esoteric construal of eschatology led to a notorious period beginning in *c.* 1164 or 1165, when the rules of Islam proper were contravened for some forty-six to forty-eight years at Alamut (Daftary, *Assassin Legends* 41, 145–6; Lewis, *Assassins* 72–5; Hodgson 148–59; Boyle 688–90, 695–8ff.). This aberrant episode left a footprint in Latin texts: William of Tyre, for one, tells us that the Assassins were devout Muslims who followed the law and traditions of Saracens so strictly for forty years that all others seemed like prevaricators by comparison, but recently came to be led by an eloquent and subtle leader who absolved them from fasting, allowed indulgence in wine and pork, and ceased religious observances (Migne 201: 31, col. 811a–811c).

The aberration is also narrated by Muslim sources, among them Juvaini; Kashani, a Shiite of the Twelver sect; and the Sunni historian Rashid al-Din. Kemal al-Din reports how, in 1176, a faction of Syrian Nizaris misconstrued esoteric interpretations of doctrine and embarked on libertinism before being severely disciplined by their leader, Rashid al-Din Sinan (Daftary, *Assassin Legends* 42; Lewis, *Assassins* 73), the notorious "Old Man of the Mountain" of crusading lore and *chansons de geste*. Reports of this interval of "libertinism" likely helped to nourish tales of sensual excess by the Assassins of Alamut.

To Muslims, the Nizaris represented a breakaway population of heretics whose doctrines and esoteric traditions challenged Sunni orthodoxies – heretics who gave a face to troubling cleavages within Islam, Shiism, and even Ismailism. The very existence of Nizaris bore witness to a pluralized, unsettled, and unsettling Islam, a community of faith riven by counteruniversalist fragmentations that surrendered Islam to heterogeneity and division, with no end to discord in sight: Islam as the melodrama of an internally contradicted project.

Underscoring failures in the transmission of an unbroken line of religious authority, Nizaris also underscored grave propensities for more than doctrinal disorder, as their assassinations of key Muslim leaders spread regional disruption and chaos at a time when Muslim energies were directed toward the countercrusade being waged against the Latin

Christian occupiers of Syria and Palestine. For Islamic communities, vilifications of the Nizaris thus seem keyed to representing the Nizaris as *bizarre outcasts*, an aberrant heretical sect festering outside the broken circle of Islamic communal identity.

In their earliest European fabulations, the Assassins carried over the memory of their representing something strange within Islam, that might not be Islam altogether. Among the first, Arnold of Lübeck's *Chronica Slavorum* contains an account attributed to Frederick Barbarossa's envoy to Syria in 1175, in which the "*Heyssessini*" are described as *both* a race of Saracens in the mountains (*genus Sarracenorum in montanis*) *and* a breed or race of men living without law (*genus hominum sine lege vivit* [VII: 8, p. 274]).

Against the prospect that they are genuine Saracens (and not, say, feral indigenes of some kind) is the shocking knowledge that this bizarre community consumes pork, in direct violation of Islamic law: "*carne quoque porcine vescitur contra legem Saracenorum*" (VII: 8, p. 274). Its members were said to make use of all women without distinction, including their mothers and sisters (VII: 8 p. 274). Even Benjamin of Tudela, no fabulator, observed of *Al-Hashishim* that "they do not believe in the religion of Islam, but follow one of their own folk, whom they regard as their prophet" (Marcus Adler 16).[36]

By the end of the thirteenth century, however, Marco Polo's fabulation of Assassin history makes it plainer that Nizaris *are* Saracens. Indeed, Polo's account subtly closes a divide between Nizaris and Islam proper, so that it is easier to forget that this breakaway sect did not represent Islam, but merely their own very particular communities. In the oldest of the Polo manuscripts that have survived, the Franco-Italian redaction (B. N. ms. fr. 1116), "*Mulecte*" – from *mulhid*, or heretic – is demoted to the name of the *country* where the Old Man of the Mountain used to reside of old: "*Mulecte est une contree ou le Viel de la Montaigne souloit demourer anciennement*" (Ménard I: 166).[37] Telling us twice that *Mulecte* is a place name (Ménard I: 165, 166), the narrative stunningly insists that the Assassins' place is a faithful facsimile of paradise in standard Islamic doctrine.

The Prophet Muhammad, no less, is invoked by name to vouch for standards of fidelity, and we are told that the Old Man had the earthly duplicate made after the form that the Prophet had said paradise would take: "*l'avoit il fet de tel maniere que Mahommet dist que leur paradis [seroit]*" (Ménard I: 166). Like the real thing, this copy boasts a vast, beautiful garden, full of all the fruits of the world and with the most beautiful houses and palaces ever seen, all gilded and adorned with beautiful things (Ménard I: 166). There are conduits flowing with wine, milk, honey, and water, and the most beautiful pleasure-women in the world. Because the garden so exactly followed Muhammad's word of what paradise was like, the replica was believed to be paradise ("*pour ce croient il que ce soit paradis*" [Ménard I: 166]).

To this garden, youths from twelve to twenty were introduced by the Old Man via a sleeping potion (Ménard I: 167). Once there, they believed themselves to be truly in paradise (Ménard I: 167), for they had all that they could wish, and were pleasured all day by *dames* and *damoiseles* who did whatever the youths pleased (*femmes* whose age is never disclosed, but who knew how to play all instruments, sing, and dance, so that it was a delight [Ménard I: 166, 167]). The youths are transformed into assassins by being told they must commit murder in order to return: carried – in versions of the F-family texts – by the master's angels back to his paradise, if they should die in the commission of homicide (Ménard I: 167–8).

Created and furnished according to the Prophet's word, the Assassin paradise fools the young men *precisely because* it is exactly like the Prophet's description "in their law" (*en leur loy* [Ménard I: 168]). As an earthly instantiation of the real, this garden faithfully follows and enacts – does not contravene – standard Islamic doctrine, and is vouched for as genuinely Islamic, not the heretical creation of a breakaway minority sect. To be sure we understand this, the Prophet's name and word are thrice summoned to underscore the replicative exactness with which the Assassin garden delivers the promises of Islam (Ménard I: 167–8).

In stark contrast to Polo, a coterminous Arabic anecdote about the Assassin garden in the *Sirat Hakim* attributed to Ibn Khallikan (1211–82) reminds readers that the penultimate lord of the Assassins is Ali, from whom breakaway populations of Shiites and Ismailis trace religious authority and the lineage of their imams, and that the "*Fida'wiyyah*" serve "the Imam." Alluded to by Dorothee Metlitzki (226–8) and others (for example, Hodgson 134–5), this Arabic vignette repeatedly refers to the Assassin leader not as an "Old Man of the Mountain" (a Europeanized transliteration of "Sheik") but as "the Chief, Ismail." Even the name the Arabic tale attaches to the Nizari leader thus foregrounds the fact that Nizaris are not orthodox Sunnis but *Ismailis* – who are, to Sunnis, merely a deviant sect within a deviant religious minority, and not representative of Islam proper (Von Hammer 201–6).[38]

But if Polo's story, at the end of the thirteenth century, loosens for Europeans the memory of a fundamental distinction between Nizari Ismailis and Islam proper, it is in a later, fourteenth-century work purporting to relate the travels of one Sir John Mandeville from England to the Near East and Cathay that the Assassins come to stand in for Islamic civilization in a more general way.[39]

Before alighting on the Assassins, *Mandeville's Travels* sketches a description of the Quranic paradise in a lengthy exposition on the Quran and Islam. Paradise, the *Travels* says, is believed by Saracens to be

> a place of delights, where a man shall find all manner of fruits all times of the year, and rivers running with wine, milk and honey, and fresh water; and they shall have beautiful palaces and great and beautiful houses and good, after what they have deserved, and those palaces and houses are made of precious stones, gold and silver; and each man shall have four score wives of beautiful damsels, and he shall lie with them always when it is pleasing to him, *and he shall forever find them virgins*. This they all believe that they shall have in paradise; and this is against our law.
>
> (Warner 66, emphasis added)[40]

Arriving at the Assassins' lair, the *Travels* then describes the lair in vocabulary it has already established for the Islamic paradise: a beautiful garden with all manner of trees bearing diverse fruits, and even sweet-smelling herbs that bore beautiful flowers (Warner 137). The Assassin garden also has beautiful wells, three of which run with wine, milk, and honey, and many fair halls and chambers, painted with gold and azure (Warner 137). Precious stones and metals abound – jasper, crystal, gold, *inter alia* (Warner 137).[41]

But, curiously, the *Travels*' Assassin paradise also calls attention to marvels and feats of *engineering*. One marvel is intricate mechanical birds that sing most delectably, their motion animated by mechanical craft, so that it seemed as if they were alive ("bryddes that songen full delectabley and meveden by craft, þat it semed that thei were[n] quyke"

[Hamelius I: 185], "brides þe whilk semed as þai sang and turned by engine as þai had bene all quikke" [Warner 137]).[42]

Where Polo mentions in passing conduits of wine, milk, honey, and water, the *Travels* makes sure we understand that these are *subterranean* conduits, hydraulically laid down to supply the wells: wells that are highly ornamented, enclosed with jasper and crystal, and bound with gold (Warner 137; Hamelius I: 185). The halls and chambers of gold and azure are architectonically many stories high (Warner 137; Hamelius I: 185), and there is a high tower from which music issues, secretly played by "diverse minstrels" (Warner 137) or "diverse instruments" (Hamelius I: 185). The Cotton text of the *Travels* even emphasizes horticultural technique: The garden's trees bear all manner of fruits that *man knew how to devise* (Hamelius I: 185).

Uncannily, this garden's focal points recall not only Islamic eternity, but Islamic *civilization* at its apogee: the palatial, ornamented gardens and courts of the Umayyad and Abbasid caliphs, when tales of the glories of Arab civilization in the Near East and Andalusia made their way through Europe, along with exotic gifts and trade in luxuries.[43] The vista of a delightful garden with underground hydraulic conduits and gilded, decorated wells; a cultivated diversity of fruit trees, scented herbs, and beautiful flowers; ornately adorned multistory chambers and halls; exquisite automata that ingeniously blur the line between artifice and nature; the pleasures of music; and a high tower as a noted architectural element all famously point to the magnificent caliphal gardens of Al-Andalus and the Islamic East.[44] This false paradise even boasts a menagerie and aviary much like a caliph's, existing for the purpose of play and sportive delight (Warner 137; Hamelius I: 185).[45]

Unique among literary fabulations of the Assassin story, *Mandeville's Travels* places Assassin territory geographically cheek-by-jowl alongside the Christian empire of Prester John.[46] Side by side before our eyes are thus juxtaposed two extraordinarily contrastive societies. First, the *Travels* presents the vision of a Christian land led by a Christian ruler whose very name evokes priestly and evangelical functions. Then it presents the realm's neighbor, an Assassin territory recalling Islamic paradise and Islamic empire, and led not by the usual Old Man of the Mountain – too elusive a sobriquet? – but by "Gatholonabes" (Cotton) or "Catolonabes" (Egerton) – a latinization, Metlitzki suggests, of the Arabic "qatil an-nafs" (meaning "murderer"), or a transposition of "abu l-qatilin" into "qatilin abu'l," meaning "father of those who kill" (Metlitzki 298 n.35).

Prester John's fictive empire, as generations of scholars have emphasized, is an idealized society depicting Christianity at its best.[47] A utopia where wealth is conjoined to spirituality, the very objects attesting the realm's magnificence – a plenitude of gemstones, pearls, and precious minerals, named and paraded in turn – attest to both material grandeur *and* spiritual power, so that the sapphires and gold of the emperor's bed, we are told, have the virtue of making him sleep well, and keep away lechery (Hamelius I: 184; Warner 136). The inability of opulence to seduce king and subject into self-indulgence is a striking feature of this civilization's efficacy. Though a polygynous (because Oriental) king, the priestly John lies with his wives only four times a year, following the seasons of nature (Cotton), and only to beget children, in obedience to the ideals of Latin Christian reproductive sexuality (Hamelius I: 184; Warner 136).

In habits of sex and dining – the most primary of drives – a heightened abstemiousness underscores the realm's Christian values. Like their temperate, disciplined ruler, the 30,000 subjects at John's court dine so moderately, with their custom of partaking of only one daily meal, that they consume the equivalent of what 12,000 people in a country of Latin Christian Europe put away in a day (Warner 136; Hamelius I: 184). Eating 60 percent less, John's subjects conjure a memory of the Greek Christian empire of Constantinople, where, according to the English historian William of Malmsbury (2: 483), the custom of eating only one meal a day is also the civilizational practice. In its evocation of the best in Christian practices everywhere, West and East, John's realm is thus a model earthly paradise of the all-Christian kind. "In Prester John's kingdom," as Iain Higgins puts it, "spiritual and . . . temporal powers are one . . . and all . . . serve . . . under the fine cruciform banner of Jesus Christ" (*Writing East* 194–5).

By contrast, an earthly paradise of the all-Islamic kind is a place of sensory indulgence, empty materiality, cunning illusion, and lies. Like John's utopia, the Assassin paradise also has jasper, crystal, gold, precious stones, and pearls, but luxury here is all glittering surface, shorn of authenticity and depth. The mechanical birds, singing delectably, simulate life exquisitely, like the automata of the *Thousand and One Nights*, but there is no life in them. Indeed, the Islamic gardens after which the *Travels* patterns the Assassins' home were famously designed as places of illusion, where artifice and nature shadowed each other closely, with pleasure deriving from the fact that nothing was quite what it seemed.[48]

This fake Assassin paradise is serviced by the most beautiful maidens and stripling youths ("striplynges") in the world, younger than fifteen (Hamelius I: 185). Novitiates who are drugged and brought here to taste the delights of the Islamic utopia "in full blisse" (Warner 137) are then plied with the lure that, should they die while conducting assassinations, they would return and be evermore of the same age as the damsels, and have pleasure and intercourse with them at will ("dalyaunce" [Warner 138], "pleye" [Hamelius I: 186]), yet find their pleasure-companions perpetually virgin. Narrative insistence on the perpetual virginity of the *houri*-like companions, and the presence of beautiful *boys* as servitors – features conspicuously absent in Polo – show how attentive the *Travels* is to the template of the Quranic paradise, even as it conflates paradise with the caliphal pleasure gardens of Dar al-Islam.[49]

With *this* Islamic utopia's explicit focus on radical youth and virginity, we see that, by contrast to the responsible, orderly sexuality exercised to engender children in Prester John's Christian utopia, sexuality in the Islamic utopia is an endless orgy among near-children: a promised eternity of pleasure, puberty, and virginity without limit, without end, and without the goal of procreation. Indeed, the assassins are *themselves* the children they do not engender. Promised they will stay forever young and gratified in perpetuity by pubescent virgins, the youthful dupes are taught to want a delusive lie of arrested development, laid down by the law of a father who licenses bliss as an end.

The fantasy of youth and *eros* is doubly powerful, since regress to full pleasure is conjured within the Islamic garden, a space designed to impart the impression of perpetual springtime, where culture seemingly thwarts nature's seasons of change, age, and death.[50] Given that the real end of the Assassin paradise, and the father-of-those-who-kill, is in fact to spread unnatural death, a not-so-subtle allegory here is how ably psychic development performs the narrative drama of civilizational identity.

By abutting the world of John against the world of the Assassins – intercutting two absorbing European fantasies – the *Travels* shores up, in the starkest way, the stakes of civilizational identity in the fourteenth century. Like John's realm, Christendom is professedly built on *ascesis*, discipline, and postponement: the full or partial abdication of pleasure in favor of higher goals, and the deferral of bliss till after the end of time. Understood as the basis by which a civilization enters into maturity, the regulation of enjoyment in service to higher ideals in Christian society summons appropriate control of the body, so that orderly habits abide even in the most basic of human functions, at bed and at board.

Mature self-discipline, then, is the signature of Christian identity: rectitude that ensures the procreation and continuity of life. The saving rationality of Christian values locates Christian society's place in the developmental drama of civilizational maturity, and renders intelligible Christian collective identity's requisite sacrifice of pleasure in temporal life.

By contrast, the world of the Assassins is personified by an immature indulgence in a multitude of polymorphous pleasures, and driven by a wanton imperative of murder. Built on illusion and falsehood, *this* society hurtles toward the horrors of violence and the self-consuming suicide of its own youthful populace, some of whom sacrifice their young lives to carry out their society's homicidal regime. Organized around an infantile sexuality that appears to grant plenitude and fulfillment while in fact serving a drive toward death, the civilizational identity of this self-indulgent society is palpably *ir*rational, and so destructive that the society itself must be forcibly destroyed: not, it seems, by the historical fact of Mongol invasion, but by the purposeful rationality of neighboring rulers who defend themselves by banding together and razing the Assassin paradise to the ground, an unhistorical destruction the *Travels* simply makes up (Warner 138; Hamelius I: 186).

And so we have it: Christian society, pictured at its best by Prester John, is aimed at life, and moral and spiritual living. Islamic society, pictured at its worst by the false paradise of the Assassins and the father-of-those-who-kill, is aimed at homicide, suicide, and destruction. We see that embedded in the episodic narrative of *Mandeville's Travels* is *a project of distinguishing Christian and Islamic civilizational identities as absolutely different from each other, shorn of commonality, and denying the trace of any resemblance.*

Significant narrative pleasure is afforded to readers by this spectacle of opposed societies, with structures of identification inviting, simultaneously, fantasmatic enjoyment *and* renunciation, as well as allowing for a variety of readerly positions in between. Narrative insistence on the absolute difference of the societies, and denial of the trace, also works, of course, to undermine the immediate appeal of Islam's sensual gardens and civilizational delights – and perhaps the appeal of Islam itself, with its promises – even as these are being fantasmatically sampled and enjoyed in narrative.[51] In the end, places, actual or anticipated, that are geared to the full, utter pleasuring of the bodily envelope in all imaginable ways without proscription are dangerous, and best cast out as not-us, not-real, never.

Dramatically, the *Travels* insists that its allegory of opposite civilizations reports collective identities that are *factual* and *contemporary* to the fourteenth century. That is to say, its tale of Prester John is not an outmoded legend from crusade history of the twelfth and thirteenth centuries: John's empire exists and thrives in the present tense, and is in fact allied with the geopolitical empire of the Great Khan's Cathay through dynastic political marriages forged by women of royal blood, for each imperial house gives a daughter or a sister to the other emperor in marriage (Warner 134: "doghter oþer sister"; Hamelius I: 180–1: "doughter").

Similarly, the Assassins' homeland was not demolished during the tumultuous thirteenth-century history of Mongol invasion, a century ago, but persisted until just very recently: "it is not longes gon sith that place was destroyed" (Hamelius I: 186; Warner 138).

These stories are not offered as archaic fictions but as up-to-date field reports on the civilizations of the contemporary fourteenth-century world in dynamic interaction.[52]

Despite embellishing two societies to highlight their symbolic opposition, however, the *Travels* cannot quite prevent our suspicion that the border it creates between adjacent territories that touch might also be a seam that admits a mutual relation. John's empire and the Assassins' world share the fact, for example, that they are military societies committed to warfare, each organizing its mode of war according to its strengths. The Assassins specialize in the guerilla warfare of political assassination, while John goes into battle at the head of a traditional army, carrying before him three crosses of fine gold – great and high and full of precious gems – each cross being guarded by 10,000 men at arms and more than 100,000 foot soldiers (Hamelius I: 182; Warner 135). The economy of sex-and-gender in the two societies – circulating the serviceabililty of women – expresses another convergence. By the orthodoxies of their respective faiths, both are also heretical societies.

If John's mode of war seems to summon a wistful vision of vast crusading forces sallying into battle, not behind a single True Cross but behind a group of *three* great triumphal crosses that sign his forces as Christian thrice over – the True Cross having been lost since the ignominious crusader defeat at Hattin that preceded Saladin's recapture of Jerusalem in 1187 – we should remember that Prester John originally materialized, to quote Bernard Hamilton, out of "the thought-world of the crusades" in 1145, "a few months after . . . Edessa had fallen to Zengi of Mosul" in the first loss of the crusader colonies (Hamilton 256, 238).

Like a military avenger, the emperor John in the original Latin *Letter of Prester John* thunders, in first-person voice, that he vowed to visit the Sepulcher of the Lord with the greatest army to humble and defeat the enemies of the cross of Christ and to exalt His blessed name ("*humiliare et debellare inimicos cruces Christi et nomen eius benedictum exaltare*" (Zarncke 78). So keenly was John wanted by crusaders that at Damietta in July 1221, the leaders of the Fifth Crusade, and especially the Papal Legate, Cardinal Pelagius, based a disastrous field decision on the conviction that John, or his son, grandson, or nephew David, would imminently arrive to aid the crusaders. The Fifth Crusade surrendered to the Sultan of Egypt, Saladin's nephew, a few weeks later (*Empire of Magic* 451–2).

Even when not at war, the *Travels*' Prester John rides behind an upheld plain wooden cross, a promise of unwavering devotion (Warner 135, Hamelius I: 182). Unlike Assassin society, which came to a violent closure, John's Christian empire appears to have no end. Of greater longevity than the fake Islamic paradise promised as eternal, this Christian earthly paradise endures, and is considerably more puissant, for the *Travels* submits Assassin territory to the overlordship of the Christian empire of Prester John (Warner 137; Hamelius I: 184).[53]

If John personifies Christian military piety, dedication, and hope, the *Travels*' Exordium resonantly echoes Urban II's 1095 clarion call, at the Council of Clermont, to armed pilgrimage – a papal address that inaugurated the phenomenon later known as the First Crusade – and reissues Urban's words with vivid urgency. The Holy Land was promised to Christians as their heritage, the Exordium thunders, and every good Christian man who is able should exert himself with all his strength to conquer that inheritance, chase out the misbelievers, and wrest the land out of heathen men's hands (Hamelius I: 2; Warner 2; Letts II: 230).[54]

Ventriloquizing Urban's condemnation of the internal divisiveness and petty hostilities that misdirect the energies of lords in Europe and prevent the reconquest of Christians' rightful inheritance in the East, the Exordium proffers the standard excuse, traditional to crusade history, for why, after two and a half centuries of Christian holy wars against the infidel, the Holy Land still remained in infidel hands. The sins of Christians, such as pride, envy, and covetousness are to blame, says the Exordium; however, the *Travels* promises that Islam's domination of the Holy Land will end – and craftily vouches for this with an Islamic prophecy privately confessed by the Sultan of Egypt to the fictive Mandeville – when Christians come to serve their God devoutly and well (Warner 69; Hamelius I: 89).

I argued in *Empire of Magic* that *Mandeville's Travels* energetically reignites and sustains an intense desire for the Holy Land in the fourteenth century, and is signally alarmed by the vulnerability of key cities like Constantinople, bulwark of the Christian East for a thousand years, to invasive encroachment (264–5). I should add that the *Travels'* vision of the international contest between Christianity and Islam, and the meaning of civilizational identities and missions in the fourteenth century, is calibrated within the panorama of a global world – already well researched by Christian subjects in its time – that the *Travels* unfolds as its contemporary context of memory and decision.

In casting its eye over the world, the *Travels* minimizes the differences it finds dividing the branches of Christian faith – differences that, to the medieval Latin church in the *Travels'* time, would condemn all other branches of Christianity as heretical, including Prester John's (*Empire of Magic* 269–70, 274–5, 281). The *Travels'* concern for the vitality of the late medieval crusading movement is thus one element in its advocacy of a globalized and universal Christianity: a Christianity that reaches even into the empire of the Great Khan's Cathay, and embraces the rationality of new forces – including the technologies and methods of science, I've argued – without surrendering the centrality of Christian doctrine. A text passionately interested in scientific instrumentation and methods, azimuth, magnetism, the position of the pole stars, and global circumnavigation, and one that takes for granted the world's sphericity, the *Travels* nonetheless *insists* that Jerusalem is – as it must be, for Christians and crusaders – the center of the world (Hamelius, I: 2, I: 121; Warner 3, 91).[55]

The *Travels* was an important document in its time, with an extensive reach across the countries of Europe and an influence that continued for centuries. We've already noted that some 300 manuscripts of *Mandeville's Travels* exist – twice the number of Polo's manuscripts – in all the major European languages: a blockbuster dispersion that ensured this document would be consulted eventually by Christopher Columbus, Leonardo Da Vinci, early modern cartographers, the maker of the Behaim globe, and Martin Frobisher, *inter alia*, for how it understands and envisions the world (Higgins, *Writing East* 6, 8; *Empire of Magic* 239).

The *Travels'* weaving of two enduring European fantasies into a narrative that would intervene appositely in Christendom's and Islamdom's competitive relations in its time is, of course, shadowed by irony. Its selection of societies that would be condemned as heretical by the orthodoxies of their faith – one society with a historical tie to heretical Nizari Ismailis, the other with a quasihistorical tie to Nestorian Christianity – to feature as symbols imparting the civilizational identities and essential meaning of Christendom and Islamdom might seem perverse, were it not so extraordinarily inspired, resourceful, and economical.

Inheriting the cultural accumulation of centuries, the *Travels* merely – ingeniously – makes use of an age-old understanding that lies, deceit, unbridled sexuality, and violence were the characteristics of Islam and its Prophet from the beginning. Even the name *Saracens* was built around a lie. After seven centuries in which the Latin West saw Islam, the Prophet, and Saracens as intimately conjoined with lies, illusion, and violence, making the Assassins of Alamut symbolize Islamic civilization was merely a dramatic summation of centuries of cultural evidence.[56]

A Man for All Seasons: Saladin, and How the West Made New Races; or, Slavery, Sexual Mixing, and Slave Dynasties

Our discussion up to this point has centered on the racing of Saracens and Christians as communities that met in the international contest of ideology and war across several centuries. Yet history and literature in fact offered stranger spectacles than those we have considered thus far. Conditions of exigency and opportunity not only enabled race to be ideologically invented, or imagined, as need arose; such conditions also enabled race, and the intermixing of races, to be organically, *genetically*, reproduced in response to political, military, and economic incentives. We turn now to demonstrations of how biological reproduction was configured by exigent, opportunity-affording historical circumstances, and by the projections of imagination and desire, to see how history and literature have made strange bedfellows partnered in improbable relations of irony over time.

For instance: In the Middle English romance known as *The King of Tars*, a fair Christian princess is forced, through her kingdom's military defeat, to become a peace offering to a Muslim sultan. Marrying the sultan and faking conversion to Islam, the princess' sexual union to a black, "loathly" Muslim king results in the birth not of a mixed-race child, but of a monstrous lump of flesh without blood, bone, or human face – that is, until the lump is baptized, at which point it transforms into the conventional fairest child ever born. This transubstantiation also effects the baptism of his Muslim father, whose own skin color switches from "loathsome" black to all white "without taint" at baptism. After such potent baptismal miracles, the newly whitened, freshly christened sultan begins a bloody, crusade-like holy war against those in his own kingdom who refuse to convert to Christianity.

In the Old French trilogy of romances that culminates in the *Roman de Saladin* (Romance of Saladin), the sublime Saladin – favorite noble enemy of the Christian West – has a French ancestress, a great-grandmother who was ostensibly the daughter of the count of Ponthieu. In the trilogy's first romance, *La Fille du Comte de Ponthieu* (The Daughter of the Count of Ponthieu), the count's daughter, brought to Islamdom by merchants who find her adrift at sea, marries the Sultan of Andalusi Almería converts to Islam, and births a son and a daughter: Saladin descends through her daughter's line (the romance *Baudouin de Sebourc* [Baldwin of Sebourg], however, has *la fille* herself as Saladin's mother).

The King of Tars and *La Filled du Comte de Ponthieu* are representatives of a capacious category of literature in which a beautiful Christian princess or noblewoman is summarily forced by circumstances into marriage with a Muslim emir or sultan. This rich narrative motif of interracial, interreligious mixing has been thoughtfully studied as a striking species of invention that plays dramatically and productively with the cultural politics of gender, sexuality, race, and religion in the medieval period. Did lived realities bear any resemblance to cultural fantasy?

Not all cultural fantasies of Christian noblewomen marrying Muslim sultans treated their heroines as anonymous chess pieces in a larger world drama, neglecting even to name them. The beauty in Chaucer's *Man of Law's Tale*, famed for her constancy, is called *Custance*, or Constance. But seemingly all western cultural fantasies of this ilk – stories that flirt with the plot of mixed-race marriage between a Christian European noblewoman and a Muslim Oriental, Asiatic, or African king – are in love with the ripe possibilities of conversion and cultural capture.

Heathen kings and kingdoms become Christian through an elegant solution to holy war: The simple agency of a Christian princess, acting as a missionary for her faith and her people, obviates the need for large armies, territorial invasion, and bloody combat.[57]

To claim *Saladin* – the brilliant victor of Hattin, magnanimous conqueror of Jerusalem, undisputed leader of the countercrusade in the Near East, and a "virtuous Saracen" acclaimed in West and East alike for chivalry, generosity, *fraunchise*, and nobility – as in fact French *dans le sang* is an act of imaginative verve as audacious as it is recreationally entertaining.[58] Graciously granted a place in Dante's first circle of hell, along with "virtuous pagan" luminaries born before Christ and two esteemed Islamic philosopher-scientists to whom the West owed significant debts of knowledge – Ibn Sina (Avicenna) and Ibn Rushd (Averroes) – Saladin is the only "virtuous Saracen" welcomed into this favored location who posed a significant threat to Western military ambitions.[59]

Such was the extraordinary reputation of the man who wrested Jerusalem back for Islam that Latin and vernacular chronicles, as much as Sunni accounts, sang his praises, detailing anecdotes of how Saladin ransomed the infant child of a bereft Frankish mother who pleaded her case to him after her child had been taken as a spoil of war (a mere *girl* infant, at that); how he courteously forbore bombarding the corner of the fortifications at Kerak where crusader wedding festivities were taking place (in gratitude, the mother of the groom sent wedding delicacies out to him); how he was cheated by his own men when he himself ransomed the poorest Christians at Jerusalem after his capture of the city – reports such as these built high the glowing reputation of this lauded foe of Christendom.[60]

To impart some sense of how admired – and desired – this hero of Islam was in the European imagination, John Tolan relates the extraordinary account of how the lords of French Anglure came to name one son in each generation after Saladin until 1732, with the armorial bearings of their house attesting their fidelity to the sultan (*Sons of Ishmael* 80–1). The Islamic emir's "transformation over several centuries from the scourge of the lord into the epitome of chivalry" follows many paths, Tolan shows, with many factitious stories participating in the transformation (*Sons of Ishmael*, chapter 6).

Finally, to the inevitable question – how could such an honorable and magnificent hero, albeit a hero of the other side and a deadly foe to Christendom, *not* be *really* Christian under the skin, or not be French? – cultural fantasy invents the only proper answer: In fact, Saladin *was, really*, French and/or Christian. Both the *Roman de Saladin* and the *Récits* of the *Ménestral de Reims* relate how, on his deathbed, the Sultan asked for a basin of water, stealthily made the sign of the cross over it, and poured the water over himself, in a covert de facto baptism without the aid of clergy, and blessedly died a Christian.[61]

Saladin's essential European-ness in the *Roman de Saladin* – he journeys to France, excels at tournaments, handily champions ladies, distributes largesse, and, in true courtly love fashion, becomes the secret *ami* of the French queen – becomes instantly intelligible because we know that he is really part-French *dans le sang*, thanks to *la fille*'s fecund interlude in Islamdom. Saladin's ostensible conversion to Christianity on his deathbed is thus foreshadowed by the genetic determinist power of his mixed-race ancestry.

In stories of this kind, the Latin West has created new, hybrid races: men and women of mixed DNA whose behavior attests the desirability and supremacy of Western culture and the Christian faith – personages among whom Saladin stands out as a shining example of what racial mixing can achieve.

Medieval cultural fantasies of this ilk – affording pleasurable imaginary recompense for territorial losses and crusading failures – are not uncommon in the thirteenth through fifteenth centuries, when a dream of cultural capture through missionary activity, preaching, debate, and conversionary success coexisted with continued territorial militancy, as I argued in Chapter 1 (see also *Empire of Magic*, chapter 4).

But was cultural fantasy the principal – or the only – means by which new races were made?

Historians of medieval Iberia show us that the ideational premise of a romance like *The King of Tars* – where a Christian princess is given in marriage to a Muslim ruler to ward off war and guarantee harmony – is a premise deeply embedded in historical praxis. Simon Barton tells us that the *Chronicle of 754* reports the marriage of the daughter of Frankish Duke Eudo of Aquitaine to the Berber warlord Munnuza, "as a means to forestall further aggression" after Eudo of Aquitaine had "suffered several attacks by Muslim forces" ("Marriage" 6). Lampégie, this daughter of the Duke, was also famous for her beauty (El-Hajji 4).

In tenth-century Iberia, Barton suggests, "the decidedly weak political and military position in which the Christian monarchs found themselves . . . probably meant that at times they had little room for maneuver when Muslim rulers demanded Christian brides as the price of peace" (*Conquerors* 31).

Consequently, "noblewomen who belonged to Christian families of the highest rank and power" were joined in marriage to the Umayyads of Andalusian Spain. The *Roda Codex* records that the emir Abd Allah (888–912) married Oñega (the widow of Aznar Sánchez of the Arista family), whose grandson became the caliph Abd al-Rahman III (912–61); the Umayyad chief minister, Al-Mansur, married the daughter of Sancho Garcés II, King of Navarre (970–94), a princess whose Arabic name is given as *Abdah*; and princess Teresa Vermúdez, daughter of King Bermudo II of Leon, was married to an unnamed "Muslim king of Toledo" in the eleventh century (Barton, "Marriage" 8, 12; El-Hajji 4).[62]

The late tenth-century Christian *Roda Codex* also tells us that in 872 Musa b. Musa married "Assona, daughter of Íñigo Arista, founder of the Pamplonan royal dynasty," while the chronicler Al-Udhri records that Musa b. Musa's son, Mutarrif b. Musa, "married Velazquita, daughter of one Sancho, 'lord of Pamplona'" (Barton, *Conquerors* 26). There were clear military benefits to giving a Christian daughter to a Muslim leader in interracial, interreligious marriage: Barton tells us that in 918, "another such marriage pact" prompted Furtun b. Muhammad to "ally himself with King Sancho Garcés I of Pamplona (905–25)" against Abd al-Rahman III (*Conquerors* 26).

Simon Barton, Abdurrahman El-Hajji, and Fairchild Ruggles ("Mothers") conclude that marriages of this kind contracted at the highest levels between adversary populations to secure peace, political legitimacy, wealth, diplomatic goals, and territorial dominion occurred commonly in the four centuries after the Islamic conquest of Iberia, producing cultural memory of "a powerful resonance within Christian society thereafter" (Barton, "Marriage" 2).

By contrast, European romances and *chansons de geste* featuring Muslim princesses and queens who marry Christian knights and convert to Christianity have little historical basis: "it is notable that very few Muslim women are known to have crossed the [racial-religious] frontier in the opposite direction and taken Christian husbands ... cross-border marriages between Muslim women and Christian men occurred only in exceptional circumstances" (Barton, *Conquerors* 32).[63]

But unlike in the plots of European romances, historical Christian princesses who married Muslim emirs did not need to convert to Islam (nor even pretend to convert), since Islamic tradition permitted Muslim men to wed Christian and Jewish women if their children were raised Muslim. So commonplace did interfaith marriage at various levels of society become, Barton says, that a letter by Pope Hadrian (772–95) written between 785 and 791 "expressed dismay that so many daughters of Catholic parents in the Peninsula had been given in marriage to non-Christians" ("Marriage" 5).[64] Indeed, Barton suggests that interracial, interreligious marriage functioned as "a significant tool in the process of pacification and colonization that took place in the period immediately following the Islamic conquest" (*Conquerors* 21).[65]

But more remarkable and perhaps more enduring than interfaith royal marriages – a phenomenon which in Iberia "passed into desuetude from the mid-eleventh century onwards" (Barton, "Marriage" 2) – was the interracial mixing that occurred in sexual unions between high-ranking (especially caliphal) Islamic rulers and female Christian European *slaves*.[66]

In Iberia, Christian slave-concubines of the Umayyads, taken as war booty, purchased from traders, or born into slavery, birthed many emirs and caliphs. Qalam, "a woman of Christian Navarrese origin" (Barton, "Marriage" 7), daughter of an enslaved Basque Christian man (Ruggles, "Mothers" 76) and herself a skilled singer, dancer, calligrapher, and storyteller, joined the harem of Abd al-Rahman II (822–52) and became the mother of Muhammad I (852–86), winning "renown as a skilled singer and dancer, as well as an outstanding calligrapher and storyteller" (Barton, *Conquerors* 33).

Ailo, "a Christian woman from the northern provinces, perhaps Castile, Leon, or Basque country" (Ruggles, "Mothers" 71), in turn gave Muhammad I his successor, Al-Mundhir (886–8), while Muzna, a slave of either Basque or Frankish origin, gave the grandson of Muhammad I the first Iberian caliph, the famed Abd al-Rahman III (912–61). Best known of the slave-concubines (*jawari*) was the Navarrese woman known as Subh (d. 998), or "Dawn," "the Arabic translation of her Spanish name Aurora" (El-Hajji 4), "a fair-haired Basque" who bore the caliph Al-Hakam II (961–76) two sons – one of whom, Hisham II (976–1013), succeeded his father to the throne, reputedly through her influence (Barton, "Marriage" 8, *Conquerors* 33–4; Ruggles, "Mothers" 73, El-Hajji 4). "Such was her sway over the caliph, one source claimed, that he never opposed her will" and, after her son's accession to the throne, Subh retained "an influential role within the machinery of government in Córdoba ... with control over the state bureaucracy and treasury" (Barton, *Conquerors* 34).

Remarkably, "all the Umayyad males who came to assume the rank of emir or caliph in Al-Andalus between the eighth and the tenth centuries were born to slave consorts, many of them Christian, rather than to married mothers" (Barton, "Marriage" 10):[67]

> A female captive who bore a child to her Muslim master assumed the status of *umm walad* [mother of a child], which meant that she could not be sold, would enjoy permanent residence in her master's household, and would be manumitted on his death, if not sooner, while their child would be regarded as a free, legitimate heir, whose legal and social status was equal to that of any siblings born to their father's free wives.
>
> (Barton, "Marriage" 7)[68]

The Umayyad rulers of Al-Andalus, as Fairchild Ruggles wryly puts it, "in addition to being the proud sons of Arab men ... were the blond sons of northern, non-Arab concubines," so that "Ibn Hazm, writing in the early eleventh century, tells us that, with but one exception, all the Umayyad caliphs and their children were blond like their mothers and predominantly blue-eyed" ("Mothers" 69). That one exception, the caliph Abd al-Rahman III (An-Nasir), who "had red hair, light skin, and blue eyes ... is reported to have dyed his hair black, 'to make himself look more like an Arab'" (Kinoshita 184).

The practice of interfaith, interracial marriage between Christian princesses and Muslim rulers declined in Iberia after the mid-eleventh century, but "the recruitment of Christian slave women to the harems of Islamic potentates continued unabated," so that in later centuries "no fewer than five of the sultans of nasrid Granada were born to Christian slave concubines" (Barton, "Marriage" 18, 18 n.111). Phillips names Isabel de Solís, "captured in the town of Cieza," who became the wife of Abu al-Hasan Ali, the ruler of Granada, and Catalina de Linares, who "became the concubine of the brother of the king of Granada and had two children by him" (*Slavery in Medieval and Early Modern Iberia* 87).

Interracial sexual unions between Christian slave women and Muslim rulers were not a phenomenon only of medieval Iberia. Ruggles, citing Ibn Hazm, points out that from "750 to the early 11th century, all but three of the Abbasid caliphs were [also] born to slaves" ("Mothers" 74). The strategy of consolidating dynastic genealogies through the agnatic line "to construct a family tree without competition from the mother's genealogical family" meant that slave women (usually of unknown pedigree and thus able to guarantee the effacement of the maternal line) were sought out by Muslim rulers to birth heirs in Islamic dynasties all the way through the Ottomans:

> At a later time and place in the Islamic world, the harems of the Ottoman court in Istanbul contained Christian women of Polish, Greek, Balkan, Armenian, and Italian origins. In the Ottoman house from the mid-fifteenth century onward, the genealogical advantage of choosing slave-concubines to bear the Sultan's children and the Ottoman heirs was that the concubine, by virtue of her slave status, had no known bloodline to compete with that of the Ottomans. The concubine's only family was the Ottoman house that had adopted her, so that her interests concurred with theirs.
>
> (Ruggles, "Mothers" 74)[69]

By what means were such royal slave concubines acquired? Initially, fresh Islamic conquests furnished Christian European slaves as war booty: "just after the Muslim conquest [of Spain], the caliph in Damascus is said to have received 30,000 Christian slaves sent from Spain. As one fifth of all booty was owed to the caliph, the total bag must have been reported as 150,000 [slaves]" (Phillips, *Slavery from Roman Times* 70).[70] In the long run, however, after the first two centuries of Islam, war produced fewer slaves, and the slave trade gained great importance (Phillips, *Slavery from Roman Times* 71).

The slave trade also brought notable restrictions for Muslims. While ownership of slaves was allowed under Islam – the Quran enjoins followers to treat slaves with compassion; a hadith quotes the Prophet as saying that slaves should be given such food and clothes as their owners themselves enjoyed; and laws governed the proper treatment of slaves – Islam prohibited the enslavement of fellow Muslims (Phillips, *Slavery from Roman Times* 71–3). Slaves, then, had to be *non-Muslim*, at least at the time of their purchase, and tended to arrive from Central, Eastern, and Mediterranean Europe, Eurasia, and Africa.

Slave traffic in *women*, as historians such as William Phillips, Olivia Constable, and Steven Epstein like to emphasize, also witnessed a curious phenomenon: "White women were more prized and more expensive than blacks" (Phillips, *Slavery from Roman Times* 73; see also Phillips, *Slavery in Medieval and Early Modern Iberia* 105). A Genoese slave list examined by Constable confirms that among Spanish slaves, "White slaves appear to have . . . fetched higher prices" (275) and "Prices for women tend to be higher than those for men" (274).

Female slaves in the Muslim world were commonly employed as domestic servants, but Constable and others observe that "Islamic law also allowed their use as concubines" (270). Phillips reiterates, "after 800 not a single caliph was born the son of a free mother" (*Slavery from Roman Times* 74). Muslim rulers' slave harems were large: "the Fatimid viceroy al-Malik al-Afdal (1094–1121) . . . left eight hundred slave concubines in his harem when he died" (Phillips, *Slavery from Roman Times* 74).

How did this enormous traffic of non-Muslim, preferably white-skinned, women pass into Muslim hands in Dar al-Islam, fueled by Islamic civilization's "pull for high-priced female slaves" (Epstein, *Slavery* 187)? In the early Middle Ages, slave trafficking was unsystematic, though slaves were undoubtedly "one of the few commodities for which the West could find markets in the East and in the Muslim world" (Phillips, *Slavery from Roman Times* 60). Slaving brought important foreign exchange, and was "one of the few ways the West had for obtaining gold" (Phillips, *Slavery from Roman Times* 61).

In this early period, Marseilles was the nexus of the European slave trade, with Verdun functioning as an important castration center for the production of eunuchs headed for North Africa and Egypt (Phillips, *Slavery from Roman Times* 60–1; Heck 180).[71] "From Ireland the Vikings took slaves to be sold in Muslim Spain . . . some may even have been taken as far as Constantinople and the Muslim Middle East. The English also sold some slaves across the Channel to Frankish slave dealers" (Phillips, *Slavery from Roman Times* 63).

In this early eclectic phase, Italian traders had already begun to be active. In the eighth century, Venetians were selling slaves from central Europe across the Mediterranean (Phillips, *Slavery from Roman Times* 62, 103). By the eleventh century, "the bulk of [the Italian] slave trade was concerned with supplying third parties, especially the Muslims of Egypt, with slaves purchased in other regions (the Balkans and the northern ports of the Black Sea especially)," as popes attempted to curtail this trafficking in humans:

> In the eighth century pope Zacharias (741–752), pope Hadrian (772–795), and Charlemagne prohibited Venetian or other Italian slavers from going to Moslem lands and placed severe penalties upon such traffic. Several ninth- and tenth-century Venetian doges prohibited, under severe penalties, the sale of Christian slaves, yet Venice continued to be a market for slaves in these pre-crusading centuries."
>
> (Robbert 400)

The Genoese – whose "slave market seems to have come into full flowering around 1190" – were especially energetic in thirteenth-century slaving (Phillips, *Slavery from Roman Times* 103–4), and, for a confluence of reasons, the Black Sea formed the principal territory from which slaves were harvested in the thirteenth through fifteenth centuries. Citing Iris Origo's analysis of a sample slave list in Florence between 1366 and 1397 that records the transaction of 357 human chattels, Phillips notes that "329 of the slaves were female" and "only 4 of them were over the age of sixteen" (*Slavery from Roman Times* 105). The ethnic distribution on this list of largely prepubescent and pubescent girls included slaves who were Russian, Circassian, Bosnian, Slav, Greek, and Cretan, among others (Phillips, *Slavery from Roman Times* 105).[72]

We might soberly conclude, therefore, that from early in the Middle Ages, and increasingly in the twelfth through fifteenth centuries, *European slavers helped to create new, hybrid races in Dar al-Islam by supplying Islamic civilizations with slave women of procreative age who bred for their masters*, whether by intentional design – as in the case of the caliphal procreative regimes studied by historians – or inadvertently, as a result of their masters' spontaneous exercise of sexual recreation.

Nor were new, hybrid races created by European slavers *only* in Dar al-Islam. Italian slavers also brought Muslim and other non-European slaves *into Europe* for purchase and use. "In the twelfth and thirteenth centuries most slaves in Genoa were Saracens," though by the late fourteenth century Tartars were also an important species of slave in Genoa (Epstein, *Genoa* 267).[73] Constable too finds that "During the early Middle Ages, Muslims were only one among several varieties of slave available in Latin Europe, but they had become by far the predominant group by the later Middle Ages" (271). Female slaves again predominated. Epstein points out that a count of slaves in Genoa – where a slave "cost more than a house" – shows that in 1458, of 2,059 slaves in the city, 2,005 were women and only 54 were men, an "astonishing" gender imbalance (*Genoa* 267). Strikingly, Genoese law "punished rape with death except for the rape of a slave, which was punished by a fine of which the owner received half, becoming an accomplice" (Epstein, *Genoa* 269) – though presumably Genoese law did not punish the rape of a slave by her owner.

Sexual mixing of an interracial kind, we are forced to conclude, may be intuited from the domestic presence of myriad slave populations – disproportionately made up of young slave women – brought by Italian slavers into Italy for domestic use, a phenomenon that produced hybrid races *within Europe* even as Italian slavers also ensured the breeding of new, mixed, races within Dar al-Islam by supplying women to Islamicate civilizations.

History is silent on the private lives of these slave women who bred hybrid races. While cultural fantasy imagines them as princesses who handily convert the heathen, the reality as lived on the ground, Epstein grimly concludes, may have been "a lifetime of rape for some women" (*Slavery* 21).

In addition to securing genetic mixes of humans domestically and in Dar al-Islam through the sale of women, European slavers also furnished boy slaves from central Europe, Eurasia, and the Caucasus, among their procurement lands, for an Islamic military race built entirely out of enslaved boys who were brought into Islamdom to be trained, socialized, and raised for the profession of war – the Mamluks:

> The acquisition of slaves for the purpose of using them as soldiers is not . . . limited to Islam alone; but nowhere outside Muslim civilization was there ever created a military slave

institution which had been planned so methodically; which had been created for such a grand purpose; which succeeded in accumulating such an immense power, and in registering such astounding achievements; and which enjoyed such a long span of life.

(Ayalon, *Outsiders* 322)

The Abbasid caliphate used Mamluk warriors from the first half of the ninth century, and Mamluks as an institution continued to exist for a millennium afterward. Mamluks are also an attested institution in Islamic Spain of the eighth to the early eleventh centuries (Phillips, *Slavery in Medieval and Early Modern Iberia* 57, 120). But the apogee – and greatest triumph – of the Mamluk system was seen in the rise of the Mamluk Sultanate in Egypt, when the last Ayyubid sultan of Saladin's short-lived line, Turanshah, was assassinated by his father's Mamluk emirs in 1250. In a rapid, bloody series of succession struggles in which assassination featured prominently, the Bahri dynasty was established as the first ruling dynasty of the Mamluk Sultanate, followed in the late fourteenth century by the Burji dynasty made up primarily of Circassian Mamluks.

For Latin Christendom and the crusader colonies of Outremer, the creation of the Mamluk Sultanate in Egypt had devastating consequences. Egypt's Mamluk sultans completed what Salah ad-Din had begun, by reconquering for Islam all the remnant crusader territories in Syria and Palestine. Baybars retook the principality of Antioch in 1268, and Qalawun the county of Tripoli in 1289.[74] That last European foothold in the East, the crusader port of Acre (to which refugees flocked after each Mamluk reconquest of a once-crusader city), vanished when Acre fell to the Mamluks in 1291, thus finalizing the extirpation of crusader Outremer. The Mamluk Sultanate also successfully halted the advance of the Mongol empire into the Near East after the decisive Battle of Ain Jalut in 1260, and, until defeated by the Ottomans in 1517, was the supreme Islamic power of the region.[75]

Under the Mamluks at the height of their dominion, Egypt's economy and infrastructure – canals, bridges, irrigation, harbors, mosques, architecture – expanded, and individual sultans such as the exceptionally tall, fair-skinned, and bluish-eyed Baybars, who supported the arts, sciences, and medical research, became enshrined as heroes in the cultural memory of Islamdom.[76] In the second half of the thirteenth century and the first half of the fourteenth, the Bahri Mamluks oversaw thriving local agriculture and industries, increased demographic growth, lucrative trade in the Mediterranean and profitable monopolies in the Indian Ocean, and military expansionism over a vast swathe of the Near East.

For all this, historians give ample credit to Genoese human trafficking (Ehrenkreutz 342).

The success of the Mamluk system was erected on a shrewd understanding of human psychology exercised for military ends. Severed from his birth family and traded by slavers, a dislocated, disoriented young boy or adolescent was, after his purchase, raised among other boy slaves also cut off from social and kin networks, and the cohort was dedicated to the art of war in a system that rewarded them on the basis of individual merit – not for noble descent or family connections – so that a rigorous meritocracy ensued.

This meritocratic system, in which the fittest and most able rose to the top on their own abilities, was supported with patronage by the young Mamluks' purchaser and master – typically the sultan or a military commander who had himself been an owned slave in his time – who thus gained the lifelong loyalty of the Mamluk cohort that belonged to him.[77]

"The first Mamluk sultans bought perhaps 800 slaves a year," Eliyahu Ashtor reckons; as for emirs, "In the second half of the thirteenth and in the first half of the fourteenth century a rich and powerful amir would have 300, 600 or even 800 Mamluks" (*Economic History* 282, 283).

A young slave was manumitted on graduating from successful training, but his ties to his patron continued and assumed a filial cast, just as his fellow Mamluks also became a fraternal family-in-arms (Ayalon, *Outsiders* 327).[78] In this way, the psychological dynamic undergirding human relations in many military systems – in training recruits, militaries often try to inculcate family-like relations among soldier-comrades who may need to give their lives for their fellows – surfaced in Mamluk training with a distinctive, ruthless efficiency that bred spectacular military success in war and a remarkable military machine.[79]

Since the creation of Mamluks required the purchase of slaves from outside Islamicate societies – not only were Muslims forbidden to enslave fellow Muslims, but the isolation of a slave far from his country of origin was a significant psychological advantage, as was the absence of a biological family – it became especially desirable to recruit boy slaves from far-flung lands. Turks and Circassians were prized slave recruits (in medieval Mamluk records, more than one historian cautions, *Turk* was also a synonym for *Mamluk*, and could denote a wide range of races).[80] As David Ayalon wryly observes, "there is hardly any European country which was not represented in this or that Mamluk army" (*Outsiders* 323):[81]

> the Mamluk system was based on a very pronounced racial preference ... And, indeed, though the literal meaning of "Mamluk" is "an owned slave", its practical meaning is "white slave" ... There was no place for colored people among the Mamluks. Abyssinians, West Africans and Indians ... could join the Mamluk hierarchy only in one way: as eunuchs, who, incidentally, constituted a most vital part of Mamluk society.
>
> (324)

Historians contemplate how Mamluks formed an elite caste – a "military aristocracy" or "one-generation nobility" – who held themselves apart from the society in which they lived and on whose behalf they fought (Ayalon, "Muslim City" unpaginated). Many did not speak Arabic, but a Turkish dialect; their garrisoning in their own citadel (from which their dynastic naming derives) carefully isolated them from the surrounding population;[82] only Mamluks were allowed to purchase new Mamluk slaves; and Mamluks usually married "either slave-girls of their own provenance" or "the daughters of other Mamluks," so that the great historian Al-Maqrizi was driven to view intermarriage between Mamluks and daughters of the local populace as symptomatic of later Mamluk "decay and decline":

> Only seldom did the Mamluks marry the daughters of notable local *ulama*, of the great merchants or of high-ranking civil officials. It follows, therefore, that most descendants of Mamluks were of pure Mamluk blood, yet they were excluded from the upper class because they were not themselves born in the countries of origin of the Mamluks and had not been slaves.
>
> (Ayalon, "Muslim City" unpaginated)

This military caste of slaves whose members derived from miscellaneous ethnoraces sold as human chattel thus behaved as if the conditions of their procurement, the training they received, and the group culture they cultivated conferred upon them the de facto marks of race. Indeed, foreign provenance, military socialization, and slave status *ab origo* were privileged markers for entry into this virtual race whose manufacture rested precisely on nongenetic grounds. Mamluks, it seems, devolved a military race attesting that from the many can, in fact, come the one – *e pluribus unum* – when military imperatives intersect with sociocultural and economic imperatives in human manufacture.

Italian slavers are given substantial credit for the reproduction of this military race. "During the second half of the thirteenth century, Genoa [in particular] regularly supplied Mamluk Egypt with slave recruits for its army" (Phillips, *Slavery from Roman Times* 104). In the later fourteenth century and through the fifteenth and early sixteenth centuries – the era of the Circassian Mamluk sultans of the Burji dynasty that followed the Bahri Mamluks – recruits were sought from the Caucasus region and Caucasia.[83] Slavers in Europe thus helped to create the most ruthlessly effective army in the Islamic world, even as their crusader brothers-in-Christ were bloodily fighting that very Islamic army in the killing fields, often meeting with defeat at the enemy's hands.[84]

The irony of this Italian trafficking in human cargo was not lost on some in the Latin West. Steven Epstein recounts in detail the horrified response, in the period 1318–1322/3, of Bishop Guillaume Adam, a Dominican who inveighed mightily against one particular Genoese merchant of prodigious economic opportunism who called the Egyptian sultan his brother and friend: Segurano Salvaygo, a trafficker whose name appears in the records of Mamluk Egypt as *Sakran*. Segurano "was alone responsible for importing ten thousand boys into Saracen hands in Egypt ... all this naturally augmented Muslim military power" (Epstein, *Purity* 163; see also Ashtor, *Levant Trade* 28).[85]

In the eyes of the Dominican bishop, Segurano was "a traitor to all Christians" because his "pursuit of self interest had transformed him into a promoter of Islam – by Guillaume's standards, a renegade" (Epstein, *Purity* 162, 165). This Dominican bishop, who had visited Egypt and had also lived in the Muslim Ilkhanate of Persia, saw that Mamluk sultans were not merely formidable military foes: He also recognized that successful Mamluk control of "Indian ocean trade routes enriched the [Egyptian] state" (165). The bishop thus seemed to understand well the myriad ways that Italian supply of Islamic Egypt with young human chattels undermined the success of Latin Christian European power internationally in the thirteenth, fourteenth, and fifteenth centuries.

With insertion into Islamic society, young male slaves who were purchased to become Mamluks in the Egyptian Sultanate, like young female slaves imported into Dar al-Islam, procreated, produced children, and turned into the forebears of mixed races in due course of generational time.[86] DNA mixing, however, was not the only outcome of human trafficking and racialized slavery that accrued from transactions between European slavers and the Near East.[87] Ayalon, among others, is struck by how genetic race unexpectedly makes an appearance, after all, in dynastic governance in the Mamluk Sultanate of the later fourteenth century and after, when the Circassian Burji dynasty of Mamluk sultans and emirs supplanted the Bahri Mamluks:

> Barquq [the first of the Circassian Mamluk sultans] who made his fellow-Circassians the ruling caste in the Mamluk Kingdom, brought about one of, if not the greatest racial transformations ever witnessed in that state since its foundation. This transformation ... led to far-reaching changes in the organization of the state.
>
> (Ayalon, *Studies* 135)

Citing A. N. Poliak's use of Russian sources, Ayalon examines how "the decline of the Golden Horde [the Mongol Khanate spread across Russia and Eurasia] in the latter half of the fourteenth century and the internal wars that broke out there, were the main causes of the transfer of the Mamluks' purchasing-center to the Caucasus" (*Studies* 136). A decline in the Turkic Kipchak population also shifted the racial composition of slaves to Circassians.

Designated in Mamluk sources as *Jarkas* or *Jarakisa*, these Caucasians, according to the sociologist-historiographer Ibn Khaldun, lived "in poverty, and most of them are Christians" (Ayalon, *Studies* 136–7). Circassians were not newcomers to the Mamluk Sultanate – Qalawun, the successor of Baybars, had begun to purchase Circassians early in the Bahri dynasty, and Circassians formed "one of the more prominent racial groups" of the Bahri period – but the scale of their recruitment magnified in the later fourteenth century, and "in the wake of the males followed a considerable stream of women and female slaves belonging to the same races ... the emigration was confined to one age group, namely, adolescents" (Ayalon, *Studies* 136).[88]

These Circassians, according to Ayalon, brought about a game change in the Mamluk system, and closed ranks on racial purity, referring to themselves in exclusionist terms as "the People" (Ayalon, *Studies* 140). Instead of dislocation and isolation, they maintained close ties with their families in the Caucasus, "which they brought over in large numbers to the Mamluk Kingdom," so that "throughout the Circassion period no Turk ever became sultan" (Ayalon, *Studies* 142, 143).[89] Indeed, the Circassian Barquq bought Circassian slaves on such "an extensive scale" that he "effected the greatest and most far-reaching racial transformation in the entire history of the Mamluk kingdom" (Ayalon, *Studies* 139, 138).[90]

The race drama of Circassian Mamluks replacing Turkic Mamluks in the dynastic rule of Egypt and Syria and circling the wagons of racial exclusivity has a striking interlude in which Circassian *mentalité* is put on display. On ascending the throne in 1495, a young sultan, An-Nasir Muhammad, the fourteen-year-old son of the Circassian sultan Kayitbay, created a military corps of black slaves who wielded firearms – a new technology detested by the Mamluks – in an "attempt to create a new military base for his authority" (P. M. Holt 198).

An-Nasir Muhammad "was fascinated by firearms" and had his black slave contingent prominently march in front of him on official parades, a spectacle deemed by the Circassian emirs "foolish," "criminal," and "a shame for the state," according to contemporary sources (Ayalon, "Firearms" unpaginated):

> The young Sultan's habit of coming into contact with his black slaves, and with other socially inferior and contemptible folk of the population of Cairo, shocked the Mamluks. The climax was reached when, in 1497, the Sultan decided to bestow the dress of a Mamluk Amir on the commander of his unit of black slaves and let him marry a white-skinned Circassian slave girl ... The Mamluks could not endure this state of affairs any longer. They rebelled, killed the Negro commander and a number of his officers, and compelled the Sultan to disband his unit. Less than a year later, they assassinated the Sultan himself for his contempt of the throne.
>
> (Ayalon, "Firearms" unpaginated)[91]

The sanguinary Circassian response to what were viewed as multiple perversions in conduct – unacceptable behavior by the young sultan and his military corps at the intersection of race, class, female sexuality, and technology – trenchantly demonstrates the historical congruence of what might otherwise be assumed to be merely a nexus of modern concerns shorn of significance for premodern societies.

Circassian Mamluks in premodern Egypt, it seemed, troubled themselves deeply with race, class, gender, and sexuality as urgent categories that could undo or imperil their collective identity.[92] Here again is another instance of dramatic convergence between medieval and modern time, in the manifestation of deep anxiety over race, class, gender, and sexuality.

The race of Circassian Mamluks dominated the Egyptian Sultanate for over a century, a vivid example of how life on the ground was stranger than fiction. Medieval romance conferred on Saladin, the Muslim ruler of Egypt – a single ruler – an ancestress from Europe, and fictionalized him as a racial hybrid who was part-European. Two centuries later, history witnessed a dynasty of sultans, also Muslim rulers of Egypt – *many* rulers of Egypt – plucked from the Caucasus and Europe: a race of Caucasians governing an Islamic sultanate who were "insistent on racial purity" and warded off hybridity in their dynastic line and elite ranks, and who considered themselves an ethnoracial enclave, "the People" (Ayalon, *Studies* 140).

Among the earlier Bahri Mamluks there had been the occasional Caucasian or European sultan of Egypt – Al-Muzaffar Baybars was Circassian (P. M. Holt 139) and "Ladjin [1297–99] a Teutonic knight" – but in the Burji dynasty of Circassian Mamluks, "sultan Khushkadam [1461–67] was an Albanian"; there were also Greeks (Ayalon, *Studies* 143), and "European travelers who visited Cairo in the fifteenth century met there Mamluks of German, Hungarian, or Italian origin" (Ashtor, *Economic History* 282).[93] The European or Caucasian ethnoracial origins of these elite, culturally manufactured Muslim warriors thus suggest to us that in the long haul of imagining human relations, a factor that dependably surfaces is irony.

We saw earlier in this chapter that in holy war, concepts of religious race expediently emerged: Christians were theorized as a *blood race*, linked by the shedding of Christ's blood, and by the blood suffering of Christian bodies at the hands of the Islamic foe. That Islamic foe was an infernal race, a race incarnating evil, whose extirpation would be a form of *malicide*. Yet the phenomena of sexual mixing and racialized slavery that we are now contemplating show us that genetic race as such did not evanesce with such theologizings of race-as-religion.

Considerations of color, physiognomy, and genetic origins continued to inhabit human consciousness, in the cultural imaginary and in life lived on the ground. Cultural fantasy could merge genetic race and religion with admirable efficiency by arranging a simple equivalence: In a neat conflation of two kinds of sorting, a black, loathly, Islamic sultan in medieval romance turns spotless white at entrance into Christianity.

Life that was lived on the ground suggested a more intricate dance between religious race and genetic race as partners in human negotiations of difference. In the business of slavery, religion set the basic parameters – slavers could not sell humans of their own religion, and owners could not purchase and own humans who were co-religionists – but genetic race determined the prices and use of human chattel. Males channeled into war as Mamluks were selected from "white" peoples of varied Turkic and Caucasian genetic composition. Black-skinned and dark-skinned male slaves from Africa, India, and elsewhere were slotted into other uses, sometimes castrated as eunuchs, and ended up in other, equally indispensable roles in Islamdom's machinery of war and governance.[94]

A shocking factor in the historical drama of racialized slavery must surely be the gap between the intense, passionate commitments and ambitions of the Latin West – as voiced in its cultural productions, theology, and a range of documentary articulations – and the incalculable recklessness of the profit motive that drove Europeans to sell fellow Europeans and others to the enemy, filling the military ranks of Latin Christendom's international foe time and again, replenishing the Islamic leadership with sultans and emirs, and helping to secure Islamic domination of Egypt, Syria, and the Holy Land for centuries.

Despite the fact that popes "made great efforts to put an end to the close trade relations between the South European trading nations and the Mamluk kingdom," papal interdictions and prohibitions against the sale of slaves, arms, timber, iron, and other war materiel to the enemy proved futile (Ashtor, *Economic History* 298).

A number of Italian republics traded with the Mamluks, but Genoa is repeatedly singled out for special condemnation. "Authorities in the field of Genoese-Egyptian relations in the Middle Ages agree that Genoa was the most important supplier of Circassian slaves for the Mamluk army" (Ehrenkreutz 342). Ehrenkreutz grimly concludes that "Genoa's supremacy in the Black Sea [important Genoese colonies at Caffa and Tana made for efficient human trafficking], combined with Egypt's demand for slaves" meant that "[o]ne may go so far as to state that ... the Genoese held the key to the survival of the Mamluk sultanate" (342):

> Genoa's pro-Mamluk policy was instrumental in bringing about the extinction of Christian domination at the hands of Muslim warriors ... When compared with all the materialistic benefits obtained from the businesslike relations with the Mamluks, the final humiliation of the Cross in the Levant was of small concern to the hard-headed Christians of Genoa.
>
> (Ehrenkreutz 342)

A Christian princess of Tars, surrendered as a war prize to a sultan of Babylon/Cairo to buy peace for her kingdom in the late Middle Ages, would thus not have found a "loathly" black Muslim ruler *in situ* who needed to be Christianized, but a fair, once-Christian Caucasian who had become Islamized. His change of religion brought war not against Muslims, but against Christians, and in fact prevented Christians from ever possessing the Holy Land again.

Thanks to Italian slavers, especially the Genoese, whatever satisfaction was gained in the West from imagining Saladin, the master of Egypt, as a part-European who finally turned into a Christian is grimly ironized by the historical witness of a line of Caucasian masters of Egypt stretching across more than a century, the successors of Saladin – de facto Saladins all – who had turned into Muslims instead.

Such is the triumph of European mercantilism over European holy war, at the nexus of race, religion, and DNA.

Saracens, Inc.: Mercantile Capitalism and the Racial Economies of Global Islam

In the international contest between Christendom and Islamdom, it should not be supposed that Italian traders were uniquely aberrant historical agents who alone put economic opportunity above considerations of religion and race by transacting with the enemy.

Charlemagne, the first medieval Emperor of the Romans in the Latin West, crowned by the pope himself at St. Peter's on Christmas Day in 800 CE, had dispatched three separate embassies to the court of the Abbasid caliph Harun al-Rashid at Baghdad in the heyday of Arab-Islamic imperial dominion. Harun in turn sent two trade missions to the West, that famously brought the elephant Abu al-Abbas, a clock, a chessboard, aromatics, and robes and fabrics as luxury gifts, as well as "other marvels of the lands of the Orient," according to Charlemagne's biographer Einhard (Heck 180; Thorpe, *Einhard* 70). These embassies, active from 797 CE to 807 CE, have sometimes been thought of as designed to boost trade and the demand for products (Heck 179–80).

Gene Heck, citing the economic historian W. C. Heyd and others, suggests that selected European goods borne by Charlemagne's emissaries to Harun functioned "explicitly as enticements to develop new consumer tastes – and thereby, to promote commerce" (181).[95] Indeed, Einhard tells us Charlemagne selected gifts that included Spanish horses and mules; dogs chosen for their nimbleness and ferocity (an anecdote later tells of these Frankish dogs capturing a lion); and white, grey, crimson, and sapphire-blue cloaks from Frisia, because, we are told, Charlemagne discovered that such cloaks were in short supply in Harun's lands, and extremely expensive (Thorpe, *Einhard* 147).

Charlemagne – celebrated in Old French literature as the scourge of God visited on Islam (in the *Chanson de Roland* or Song of Roland, Charles is directly instructed by angels to perform holy war on God's behalf) – also sent ambassadors to Andalusi Córdoba and issued currency some of which "bore Arabic inscriptions, including a quote from the Qur'an" in praise of Allah (Heck 181, 185, 228).[96] Hailed in *chanson de geste* as the thundering avenger of Roland, Oliver, and the Twelve Peers of France at Roncevaux, Charlemagne had relations with Harun that seemed oddly amicable. Indeed, Harun even "offered to make Charlemagne the custodian of the Christian 'Holy Places' in Jerusalem" (Heck 180).[97]

Einhard affirms that Harun "went so far as to agree that this sacred scene of our redemption should be placed under Charlemagne's own jurisdiction" (Thorpe, *Einhard* 70). Charlemagne was also not the first in his family to initiate visits between adversary empires. His father, Pepin the Short (the son of Charles Martel, who is historically memorialized for beating back a Muslim raiding party near Poitiers and thus saving Western Europe from the Islamic empire), had sent a sizable delegation to the court of the Abbasid caliph Al-Mansur in 765 and 768. In 831, Harun's son and successor, the caliph Al-Mamun, sent an embassy to Charlemagne's son and successor, Louis the Pious (Heck 179 n.58).

Records in Arabic by Ibn Khurradadhbih, Ibn al-Faqih, Ibn Hawqal, Al-Istakhri, Al-Muqaddasi, Al-Tartushi, Al-Masudi, and others also testify more generally to a thriving trade between Christian Europe and Dar al-Islam (Heck 181–3). From early on, slaves featured prominently in the cargo originating from Europe. Ibn Khurradadhbih speaks of "Roman, Frankish, and Lombardi slaves," "Roman and Spanish maidens" (i.e., Greek Byzantine and Spanish female slaves), and eunuchs. Ibn al-Faqih also notes European slave cargoes, and Ibn Hawqal says that Frankish slaves were shipped to the Near East via Spain, a route confirmed by Al-Istakhri and Al-Muqaddasi. Al-Tartushi also records slave cargoes from Europe, while Liutprand of Cremona "claims astonishment at the incredible profits then being made by the merchants of Verdun in castrating eunuchs and then shipping them to Muslim Spain for reexport eastward, supporting a similar report by Ibn Hawqal" (Heck 181–2, 180).

Cargoes transiting through Europe, with origins in other lands, might evince a broad miscellany of content, but Europe itself until the "high" or "central" Middle Ages exported, in addition to human chattel, largely raw materials and primary products – furs, lead, iron, timber, and other "unprocessed commodities" – to Dar al-Islam. "Islamic 'counter-trade' with the Frankish West, in turn, appears to have primarily consisted of a traffic in luxury goods" – spices like pepper, ginger, cloves, spikenard, costmary, and galingale from India; musk aloes, camphor, and cinnamon from China; and "such 'Eastern' commodities as papyrus, paper, dates, olive oil, wines, ivory, crystal, art objects and assorted textiles (e.g., silks, purples, and brocades)" (Heck 182–3).

The sale of slaves, timber, furs, and raw materials brought Europe important currency in the form of gold and silver, supporting the development of a monetizing economy in the West, as many have noted. Yet the unequal nature of this international trade – Europe exporting raw materials and humans to pay for luxury goods and sophisticated products from more developed civilizations – lays bare a state of relations in which the Islamic empire appeared as "the premier economic superpower of the early Middle Ages" (Heck 260).

Islam as a religion, of course, was not ideologically hostile to mercantilism, profit, or capital accumulation, and in the first era of the Islamic empire, capital accruing from conquest nurtured a commercial dynamic that rapidly expanded the empire's economic base (Heck 322–4, 260). In the first three centuries, a network of trade thus accumulated "whose vast reaches stretched across the breadth of the then-known world – from Christian Europe in the West to Japan and China in the East," facilitated by the fact that "Muslim jurists, through their creative exegesis, were able to formulate carefully rationalized, capital-based solutions to their religion's ban on 'usury'" (Heck 260).[98]

Institutional structures that supported trade, such as the *commenda* contract system in which one party (or more) might supply capital while another party (or more) supplied labor – with permutations of this arrangement flexibly allowing an expanding number of small investors in merchant cargoes to partner with agents who accompanied cargoes and delivered goods, but did not make capital investments – also appeared early, in the form of the *qirad/mudarabah* agreements that some historians believe to be the precursor of the *commenda* system in the West (Heck 260, 243–5).[99]

The oldest extant Italian *commenda* contract, which is Venetian, dates to 1074, though references to *commendae* appear in Italian documents as early as the ninth century; the *commenda* system spread from Italy to the prime maritime cities of the Mediterranean, including, by the close of the fourteenth century, major entrepôts such as Marseilles, Barcelona, and elsewhere (Heck 237–8, 242).

By contrast, the *qirad-mudarabah* arrangement is centuries older, and may have predated Islam: The Prophet's first wife and first follower, Khadijah, a wealthy trader, is sometimes thought to have entered into a *mudarabah* arrangement with the young caravanist Muhammad, who contributed labor in overseeing her caravans and delivering her cargoes. Flexible and sophisticated economic instruments of this kind – which allowed for the sharing of risk and profit, even by those without capital for investing in ventures, and the pooling of human resources – could net "handsome rates of return" with a multiplier effect that vastly expanded commercial wealth and vitality (Heck 225).

Among the commercial actors of Latin Christendom, Italians traded actively with the Islamic Levant long before the holy wars of the West, and southern European commercial ventures in the Islamic Levant did not terminate during the crusading centuries of religious-territorial-ideological war. Indeed, priorities of religion, politics, territory, and trade were juggled and reshuffled in a shifting calculus for seven centuries of the post-Carolingian era, but the default of profit goals seemed to surface with healthy reliability. A hiatus in commerce arising from circumstances (such as war) where the calculus of priorities might skew toward disruption fortuitously only brought temporary suspensions.

> Venice, like the other Italian sea republics of Amalfi, Pisa, and Genoa, fought against Saracen sea power two centuries before the crusading epoch. In the ninth century Pisa and Genoa fought independently against Moslem sea powers in the western Mediterranean and the Tyrrhenian Sea, while Venetian fleets in collaboration with the Byzantines fought against Saracen encroachments in the Adriatic. Expeditions are recorded for the years 827, 829, 840, 842, and 846. A powerful Venetian fleet of sixty ships was destroyed in 840 as it attempted to drive the Saracens from Taranto ... [but] Venice won a naval victory over the Saracens based on Taranto in 871.
>
> (Robbert 382)

Pre-crusade struggles pitched Christians against Muslims, but incessant competition in the Mediterranean for territorial, political, commercial, naval, and strategic advantage, in addition to religious impulsions, meant that it was often difficult to disentangle and distinguish between the nested motives in each instance of warring conflict. Besides fighting Muslims, Venice also fought against the Latin Christian Normans of Sicily, to aid Greek Christian Byzantium in its territorial politics (Robbert 384, 386), and in the crusading period, internal rivalry among the Christian players became so intense that historians are led to concede that "Venice would far sooner help the Moslems than help Genoa or Pisa or Marseilles; and her rivals held similar views" (Runciman 2: 315).

Among intra-Christian struggles, Venetians fought and defeated Pisans at Modon and destroyed the Pisan naval base of Brindisi in 1195; they ravaged the Genoese quarter in Constantinople in 1162, when the Pisans also sacked the Genoese quarter; and from 1257, Genoa and Venice fought a series of wars lasting over a century (Robbert 413, 406, 407, 439). In struggles for dominance over bodies of water, port cities, and hinterlands, Mediterranean competitors – Latin Christian Italians and southern Europeans, Greek Christian Byzantines, Maghrebi and Syrian Muslims, and Shiite Fatimids – thus competed across a shifting tangle of grounds, driven by priorities that were reshuffled and recombined: priorities in which fidelity to religion, ethnorace, and tribe were important but not paramount in all circumstances.

These rivals, of course, also partnered across religious and ethnoracial lines for contingent advantage. Little proved a barrier to commercial interests, and even the family of one of the great canonist popes of the European Middle Ages, the Genoese Innocent IV, engaged significantly in Islamic commerce (Heck 241).

> The merchants of Amalfi, Venice and Genoa were foremost among ... Christian traders who came to the ports of Egypt and Syria. According to the account of a Syrian Arabic writer there were not less than 160 Amalfitans in Cairo in 996 ... In 991 Venice sent embassies to all the rulers of all the Moslem countries bordering on the Mediterranean. The Venetians carried on a very lively trade between Alexandria and Constantinople and,

in the twelfth century, between the ports of Syria and Palestine held by the Crusaders and the seaports of Egypt. Genoa too was very active in the Levantine trade in the century preceding the first Crusade ... By the end of the tenth century merchants of Bari and of Sicily visited the Near Eastern emporia, whereas the Pisans became prominent in the twelfth century ... commercial relations between Italy and the Fatimid dominions were continually increasing. The acts of the Genoese notary Giovanni Scriba disclose almost a hundred of his compatriots engaged in the trade with Alexandria in the years 1156–64.

(Ashtor, *Social and Economic History* 196)

Despite their commitment to profit, and "a considerable trade with the Moslem East" at stake, such ductile trading relations did not mean that the Italians stood aside from the rest of Latin Christendom, or objected to possible commercial disruptions, when crusading was launched willy-nilly in 1095 (Runciman 1: 55).

Genoese were active in the First Crusade, transporting armed pilgrims to the Levant mid-crusade and fighting in battles, their assistance being reckoned especially valuable at Jerusalem.[100] Pisans sent a fleet, also mid-crusade, headed by their archbishop Daimbert, who ascended to the position of papal legate on the death of Adhémar of Le Puys and became the second Patriarch of the Latin Kingdom of Jerusalem (Runciman 1: 299, 305).[101] Venetians were slower to realize the initiative; after the conquest of Jerusalem, they sent a fleet of thirty ships that aided crusaders besieging Haifa in 1100, and a larger force of 100 vessels in 1110 for the conquest of Sidon (Robbert 390).

Some have noted the time-lag before the Italian republics committed themselves to crusading. Runciman, for one, observes that though many individual Genoese immediately took the cross in 1095, Genoa prudently waited till 1097 to send ships, so that the republic "could tell whether the Crusade was a serious movement" (1: 112). But after the Latin victory at Antioch, Genoese hastened there, "eager to be the first to capture its trade. On 15 July Bohemond gave them a charter, allowing them a market, a church, and thirty houses" (Runciman 1: 251). Scholars recount in detail the extensive commercial advantages that accrued to the Italians for their participation in crusading:

> [Crusader] towns contained considerable Italian [merchant] colonies. The Venetians and the Genoese each possessed streets in Jerusalem itself. There were Genoese establishments, guaranteed by treaty, in Jaffa, Acre, Caesarea, Arsuf, Tyre, Beirut, Tripoli, Jebail, Lattakieh, Saint Symeon and Antioch, and Venetian establishments in the larger of these towns. The Pisans had colonies in Tyre, Acre, Tripoli, Botrun, Lattakieh and Antioch, the Amalfitans in Acre and Lattakieh.
>
> (Runciman 2: 294)

Italian gains from their participation in crusading were not minor.[102] Venetians acquired "extraordinary legal rights" in Acre and Tyre, and, through a grant issued by the Patriarch of Jerusalem, possessed one-third of the cities of Tyre and Ascalon. In Jerusalem, they had "astonishing tax exemptions" that freed them from all taxes and tribute, in contrast to the rest of the population, Latin and native alike (Robberts 390–1). When Venice sent a fleet to support the siege of Acre in the Third Crusade, all the Venetian privileges in the Holy Land were reconfirmed by Conrad of Monferrat on behalf of Philip Augustus, one of the two royal leaders of the Crusade (Robbert 392). The increasing reliance of crusading on Italian sea power meant that the merchant-cities had to be paid. They demanded trading facilities and rights, their own quarters in the larger towns, and the complete or partial freedom from customs-duties; and their colonies had to be given extra-territorial privileges … But the merchant cities were out not for the welfare of Christendom but for their own commercial gain. Usually the two interests coincided; but if they clashed the immediate commercial interest prevailed.

(Runciman 2: 315)

In addition to mercantile establishments in crusader ports and cities, country estates held around cities such as Tyre included agricultural lands – fields, orchards, and vineyards – cultivated by native workers, which contributed new products to the European market. Italian merchant colonists also gained direct access to Syrian artisans and local industries, a source of supply for fine goods, and, as importantly, for valuable, sophisticated skills:

sugarcane, unknown to Europeans until the First Crusade, was both cultivated and refined for export from Syria during the years of the Latin Kingdom of Jerusalem. In addition to the linen and silk products … from Egypt and from the Moslem cities inland, Syria itself also produced cotton and silk for sale to western merchants … Another fine finished textile produced in Syria was camels'-hair cloth. Syrian fabrics received special acclaim in western Europe because they were fabulously dyed in shades of indigo, Tyrian purple, and red. All these dyestuffs likewise were produced in Syria. Very fine, transparent glass from Tyre was also in great demand.

(Robbert 402)

One-third of the countryside surrounding Tyre belonged to Venice. Not only did Tyrian glass blowers produce exports for Venetian mercantilism, but "Some of them emigrated to Venice in the mid-twelfth century to found the Venetian glass industry" (Robbert 440). This mid-twelfth-century emigration of Tyre's glass blowers to Venice articulates a key moment in the transfer of knowledge and skills to Europe from the East, upon which later European artisans built. Crusader colonization can thus be seen as a crucial hinge for the growth of European industries and artisanry, which in later centuries bypassed the necessity of importing fine glassware from Dar al-Islam, thereby contributing to changing trade relations in favor of Europe. As I've noted above, today, of course, it is not Tyrian glass but Venetian glass, especially Venice's exquisite Murano glass, that is globally renowned.

Commitment to a passionate religious goal like holy war thus seemed to result in the expansion of business, and business, it seemed, was larger than religion, race, or other commitments. In the push–pull of mercantile capitalism, we have seen how the eagerness of southern Europeans to sell fellow humans of all racial stock to the Islamic world-rival and international foe, along with war materiel for enemy armaments and ships, bespoke a nonracist, solid business response to the forces of demand from Dar al-Islam, overriding other considerations. Just as holy war brought significant commercial profit, Italian best practices also triumphed over holy war.

Like Islamdom, Christendom too had forces of demand that called to be met, chief of which was a vast and ramifying European appetite for goods from the East – from the nearest East to the farthest – goods furnished by Saracens, Inc., acting as transit intermediaries for commodities from a global elsewhere, or as retailers and wholesalers of manufactures within Dar al-Islam itself. Doing business with the dispersed conglomerate that made up Saracens, Inc. meant that commercial establishments and rights should be sustained not only in crusader-held territories, but also in the enemy's homelands even after holy war had begun:

> Venetians engaged in vigorous trade with the Egyptian ports of Alexandria and Damietta between 1135 and 1147 and again between 1161 and 1168 ... Between 1173 and 1184 Venetian commercial voyages to Egypt greatly increased ... An official peace treaty was drawn up between the government of Saladin in Egypt and doge Sebastian Ziani of Venice about 1175. By its terms, Venetians could buy and sell their wares and also travel in safety in Egypt.
> (Robbert 396)

> Sometime between 1205 and 1217 Venice stabilized its position in Egypt by negotiating a series of six commercial agreements with the Aiyubid sultan al-Adil [Saladin's brother] ... The sultan agreed to honor and protect all Venetians and their Christian agents in his domains ... They were granted a *fundaco* [warehouse–office–hostelry] in the chicken market in Alexandria where they might live, and the right to come and go freely in Egypt. They were also given freedom to buy and sell any merchandise anywhere in Egypt without restraint. They were to be judged in their own courts.
> (Robbert 441)[103]

The Genoese notary, Giovanni Scriba, recording Genoese trade with the Levant for the period 1154–64, as we have noted, mentions nearly a hundred Genoese engaged in the Alexandrian trade. He also lists "fifty-eight commercial agreements concerning Alexandria, thirty-four [concerning] Syria" (Robbert 398). Robbert cites Vsevolod Slessarev's figures on the growth of Genoese trade in the period:

> The minutes of a single notary out of some twenty-nine active in Genoa ... indicate a flurry of investment to Ultramare (Syria and Palestine) between August 21 and September 24, 1191. The value of goods and cash destined for the Levant amounted to 8,570 Genoese pounds, which suggests [an annual] total of perhaps 80,000 pounds, a staggering sum for that time.
> (445)

What has been seen by scholars, then, as the lubricious infamy of the Venetians – their betrayal of the Fourth Crusade in 1204, when the Venetians successfully detoured the crusader army from its goal of conquering Ayyubid Egypt as a key base for the recapture of Jerusalem and unleashed the crusader forces instead on Greek Christian Byzantium – nests comfortably within the Italian republics' logic of business as usual, albeit spun out to a taxing degree.

The Fourth Crusade has been exhaustively documented and analyzed in all its complexity from all points of view. For our purposes here, the incalculable destruction visited upon Greek Christians by Latin Christians, so that the Byzantine Empire never fully recovered from its evisceration even after regaining a hollowed-out Constantinople in 1261, can be seen as a set of best practices in business that had not gone awry as such, but that had been ferried to a logical culmination.

Glossed by one scholar as "the apogee of Venetian participation in the crusading movement," the gains from the enterprise of the Fourth Crusade were again considerable, if not downright astonishing (Robbert 413).[104] In the initial contract to furnish fifty war galleys to transport the crusaders, the Venetian fee was 85,000 marks (bargained down from an original sum of 94,000 marks) and half the spoils of the venture.

A renegotiated second contract gave the Venetians three-fourths of the spoils as their transportation fee, with the remaining booty to be divided equally between crusaders and Venetians. Venetians were also to possess three-eighths of the Byzantine empire, with most of the areas promised Venice being coastal, to give Venetians control of sea routes (Robbert 414–18). Though the Latins never established control over the entire Byzantine Empire (they were now actively fighting enemy forces on two fronts, Muslim and Christian), "the Venetian control of Greek lands endured longer than any other result of the Fourth Crusade" (Robbert 419).[105]

It is worth repeating that through all the chaos and the mutable, changing conditions of the crusading centuries, mere enmity itself did not prove an insuperable obstacle to commerce. Venetian diversion of the Fourth Crusade to Constantinople helped to protect Venetian mercantile interests in Ayyubid Egypt, where the Genoese were keen competitors of the Venetians. The Genoese, allying in turn with the Byzantines to help them take Constantinople back from the Latins and Venetians in 1261, as a result of their alliance with Byzantium were then able to dominate the Black Sea trade, "a trade which was growing in volume and importance as the Mongol conquests developed the caravan routes across central Asia" (Runciman 3: 287). The Genoese alliance with Byzantium made the Genoese the chief supplier of slaves from the Black Sea region to the Mamluks, as we saw earlier.

Nor were Venetians and Genoese the only profit-bent Europeans during the centuries of holy war. Catalans established a *fondaco* (*funduq*) and a consulate in Alexandria in 1262. Notarial acts of Marseilles referred to active trade with Egypt in the 1270s and 1280s. The Pisans also had a *fondaco* in Alexandria; and Ancona, the coastal towns of Apulia, and Ragusa all appear in documentations of trading (Ashtor, *Levant Trade* 12, 14, 30, 31). The importance of this trade is witnessed by a 1308 Venetian order that assigned Venetian warships to escort and guard the five mercantile galleys making the voyage to Alexandria annually, "because of the danger of attacks" – not from the Islamic foe in holy war, we should note, but from Genoese rivals (Ashtor, *Levant Trade* 26)!

Trading with the religious-racial enemy had not ceased by the fifteenth century:

> Florence ... in 1422 obtained the right to have consuls in Alexandria and Damascus and obtained new privileges in 1489, 1496 and 1497 ... The Genoese had consuls and *fondachi* [warehouses–offices–hostelries] in Alexandria, Beirut and Damascus. They regularly sent their round ships to Egypt and Syria ... At the end of the fourteenth century the Catalans sent 3–5 galleys every year to Egypt and Syria ... The merchants of Marseilles were also very active in the trade with Egypt and Syria in the eighties of the fourteenth century and, after an interruption, at the beginning of the fifteenth century and in its fourth decade. In the second half of the fifteenth century ... traffic of the "galleys of France" was quite regular.
>
> (Ashtor, *Social and Economic History* 326)

Revenues flowing into the Islamic Levant from Latin Christian sources were sizable:

> The doge Tomaso Mocenigo (1414–23) maintained in a speech made before his death that Venice sent 300,000 ducats in cash every year to the Levant. In the Cronica Morosini one finds a greater sum, 460,000 ducats, referring to the year 1433 [when] Levantine trade was resumed after an interruption due to a military conflict. Statistics at the end of the fifteenth century also mention the sum of 300,000 ducats.
>
> (Ashtor, *Social and Economic History* 326)

The church, of course, did not sit idly by as humans, materials for war, spices, foodstuffs, finished goods, and fine luxury products were trucked between enemy populations in the midst of conducting holy war. After the alarming loss of Acre, the very last crusader foothold in the East, to the Mamluks in 1291,

> the pope made great efforts to put an end to the close trade relations between the South European trading nations and the Mamluk kingdom. He did so not only to cut off its supply of arms, timber, iron and other articles badly needed for the sultan's army and the fleet, but also to weaken [the] Mamluk economy ... [and lessen] the great profits made by Egypt and Syria from the trade with Southern Europe ... Pope Nicholas IV prohibited the selling of arms, timber and similar articles to the infidels. This prohibition was repeated by his successors time and again ... The Church did not content itself with the promulgation of these prohibitions, but sent out ships to capture transgressors and seize the ships and merchandise.
>
> (Ashtor, *Social and Economic History* 298)

Following the *ex cathedra* directives of the papacy, secular authorities also issued prohibitions of their own:

> The urban republics of Italy, which had carried on trade with Egypt and Syria for centuries, were compelled to promulgate decrees forbidding their subjects to contravene the papal prohibition. In 1291 Genoa forbade all trade with the lands of the sultan. Jacob II, king of Aragon and Catalonia, did the same in 1302. Pisa, in its decrees of 1302 and 1322, forbade the sale of arms and war material only ... Philip the Fair, king of France, in 1312, and Venice, in 1323, adopted the more rigorous attitude, prohibiting any trade with Egypt and Syria.
>
> (Ashtor, *Social and Economic History* 298)

Ashtor recounts at length the stage-by-stage efforts of the papacy and secular leaders to stem the tides of trade with the Levant time and again across the centuries, with the efficacy of such efforts always being mitigated by the complexities of intra-European politics, and the commuting of offenses through fines and the like, which came to be seen by mercantile interests as just another form of customs duty or tax – and which, it must be said, also "became a source of income" for the church (*Levant Trade* 17–48, 47). In the end, Saracens, Inc. proved too valued a trading partner for mercantile capitalism in the West:

> It proved impossible to stop the trade which was so profitable for both Christians and Moslems. The Europeans could not renounce the Indian spices, the Near Easterners needed the war material and the ducats ... the appeal of the *'turpe lucrum'* was too strong and the pope had to give in, granting temporary permits for trade, except for the sale of war material.
>
> (Ashtor, *Social and Economic History* 298)

But not only war materiel – "timber and iron for weapons, such as rams and other siege engines to batter the walls of towns" – found its way to the enemy. The enemy also successfully recruited skilled Latin Christian engineers for shipbuilding, bought ships from Christians, and employed Christian helmsmen and mariners to man their naval wars:

> The famous Arab scholar Ibn Khaldun (d. 1406) ... writing in the late fourteenth century ... says that the Moslems are no longer skilled in building good ships and

equipping war fleets, so that they need the assistance of European Christians. This statement is fully borne out by papal bulls ... [some of which] dwell on the fact that Christians sell the Moslems ships, serve them as helmsmen on their ships, and take part in their naval expeditions against other Christians.

(Ashtor, *Levant Trade* 9)

The international contest with the Islamic foe for geopolitical possession of the Holy Land and religious supremacy was not decided in favor of the West. Jerusalem – the earthly embodiment of the celestial city of Christian eschatology, and whose physical landscape was suffused with the auratic memory of the Savior's life and presence – flitted briefly into Christian hands after the final territorial loss of all the crusader colonies (as we will see in Chapter 4, Jerusalem was given to Frederick II by Saladin's nephew, the Ayyubid sultan Al-Kamil, in 1229 during the German Emperor's odd uncrusade), but was ultimately lost again. Fortifications and territories were captured and lost in skirmishes over the centuries in the interminable prolongation of crusading endeavor, but the masters of Christendom's Holy Land remained the Islamic enemy.

The location of this Islamic enemy also shifted, as Egyptian Mamluks gradually gave ground to the Ottomans – themselves also peoples from the steppe, and also Sunni Muslims – so that by the sixteenth century, Christian Europe faced a powerful religious-racial enemy much closer to its doorstep: the Ottoman Empire. The Mamluk decline is complex, and historians are not unanimous in apportioning responsibility and weight for the multiplicity of causes, whether of a governmental, economic, military, or technological kind. Most agree that the later fifteenth century witnessed rapacious Mamluk regimes in which Mamluk elites ruthlessly appropriated assets on a grand scale, devised ruinous monopolies, instituted widespread tax farming, and destroyed economic rivals, to the permanent detriment of the state, even as the Mamluk sultan lost control of his Mamluk emirs and Royal Mamluks, who were able to wreak violence and havoc on the population as they pleased.[106]

Other scholars emphasize technological decline and Mamluk slowness to incorporate firearms efficiently in warfare. Since Mamluks were contingents of proud elite horsed warriors, and guns could not be handled from horseback till later innovations brought changes, Mamluks used firepower principally for sieges and assigned firearms only to inferior, infantry troops, thus enabling the Ottoman empire – wielding firepower with unsentimental efficacy – to conquer and subjugate the Mamluk empire in the second decade of the sixteenth century (Ayalon, "Firearms" unpaginated).[107] Mamluk failure to continue earlier investments in sea power, navies, and warships also eventually lost Egypt control of the sea, including the all-important Red Sea route to India, the home of the spice trade.[108]

The failure in Egypt and Syria to maintain technological development in agricultural industries such as sugar, and in craft industries such as glassmaking, textiles and fabrics, and papermaking, is amply documented.[109] Such falling-behind is sometimes recited as parables in narratives about the "rise of the West," in which the failure of certain Islamicate lands – here, notably Egypt and Syria – to maintain their earlier edge and innovative superiority in agricultural production (which resulted in the "Green Revolution" of early Islamic civilization), in artisan and craft industries, and in finished goods manufacture, provides exempla for theories of *translatio imperii*, the transfer of rule from a declining East to an ascendant West.[110]

More important, perhaps, than the internal weaknesses in the Mamluk realms that have been ruminated over may have been external factors of massive bacterial visitation that wrought carnage on Egypt and Syria: the worldwide pandemic of the Black Death in the mid-fourteenth century, and a series of major post-Black Death epidemics that swept through Egypt and Syria, leaving death and depopulation in their wake. Ashtor counts a series of sixteen major epidemics in Egypt and fifteen in Syria, *after* the devastating predations of the Black Death:

> There were major epidemics in Egypt in 1363, 1367, 1381, 1416, 1430, 1438, 1444, 1449, 1459–60, 1468, 1469, 1476–7, 1492, 1498, 1505 and 1513, and in Syria-Palestine in 1363, 1369–70, 1373, 1381, 1385, 1411, 1437–8, 1459, 1460, 1468, 1469, 1476–7, 1492, 1497 and 1513. The accounts of the chroniclers show that in the second half of the fourteenth century Syria suffered from epidemics much more than Egypt. In Egypt they were frequent in the second decade of the fifteenth century, and later in its seventh and eighth decades, and about 1500 they raged very often in both countries. The plague had become so frequent that foreigners visiting Egypt were told that it broke out every seven years.
>
> (*Social and Economic History* 302; see also P. M. Holt 194)

Sheer densities of population in a premodern megalopolis like Cairo meant that plagues spread and ravaged with a far deadlier intensity and speed, and wrought greater destruction, than even in the largest cities of Europe, where the devastations of the Black Death were considerable. While London, Venice, and Paris may have had fourteenth-century urban populations of 100,000–200,000 inhabitants, historians reckon Cairo's urban population in the fourteenth century to be between 500,000 and 600,000, about three times the size of the largest European cities (Dols 401; Abu-Lughod 237). "The suburbs of the Mamluk city were [also] extensive in the early fourteenth century and greatly increase the figure for total urban population," and the total population of Egypt itself may have amounted to eight million people (Dols 403; Abu-Lughod 238).[111] Within a few years of the Black Death's arrival in 1347, "some 40 percent of Cairo's population was wiped out" (Abu-Lughod 237–8).[112]

Mortality was especially high among the Mamluks themselves. Some historians hazard that Mamluks, as non-native immigrants from foreign lands with little incidence of plague history, perhaps lacked some genetic immunities possessed by the indigenous members of local population groups (P. M. Holt 194). In the plague of 1429–30, which lasted four months,

> The severest plague was among the Sultan's Mamluks, those living in the citadel barracks . . . in the morning 450 of them might be sick and in the course of the day more than 50 Mamluks would die.
>
> (Dols 406)

"Royal Mamluks dropped in number from about 12,000 in the third reign of [An-]Nasir Muhammad to less than half as many under the Circassian sultans" (P. M. Holt 194) whose dynasty coincided with the long incidence of plague. For the plague of 1429–30, "assuming a figure of about 5,000 Mamluks, a plague mortality of 50 a day . . . would indicate a serious and costly destruction of the military elite" (Dols 406) that "must have necessitated very considerable expenditure by the sultans and amirs" who would need to purchase, train, and socialize new slave recruits almost constantly (P. M. Holt 194).

The plague centuries not only caused demographic decline but also began the depopulation of the country. Egypt did not recover its former growth after the Black Death:[113]

> A one-third loss [of the population] would have left the total population of the country at about five million, which was gradually reduced during the next fifty years as the plague periodically, albeit less virulently, reappeared. Further population decline is acknowledged to have occurred during the centuries of Ottoman rule. The population of Egypt was a scant three million when the French made their estimates at the time of Napoleon's invasion of Egypt in 1798.
>
> (Abu-Lughod 238)

> Villages were deserted, irrigation works neglected, and cultivated land went back to waste. Landed revenue ... steadily diminished: between 1215 and 1517 the land-tax of Egypt shrank from over nine million dinars to less than two million.
>
> (P. M. Holt 194)[114]

From the centuries of struggle with the international religious-racial enemy, Latin Christendom thus emerged with losses and gains. Jerusalem, and the Holy Land – the avowed reason for initiating the crusades, and the goal that fueled the determined tenacity of generations of Christian combatants who doggedly slogged their way to the East to oppose the heathen and wrest back their God-given inheritance – were irretrievably lost.

To add injury to injury, Constantinople, the bulwark of Christianity in the East for more than a millennium – Constantinople, which had held back the advance of the Islamic empire for eight centuries – succumbed to the Ottomans in 1453, never having fully recovered from the ravages of Latin Christian conquest and predation, and the Byzantine empire continued to be whittled away, and to attenuate. Centuries of religious-racial holy war did not succeed in repossessing Jerusalem, holiest of cities, for Christendom; instead Constantinople, the queen of cities in the European Middle Ages, became Istanbul, a city belonging to the Turkish Ottoman Empire.[115]

If sacred territory eluded the grasp of the Latin West, the conversion of the heathen – the other kind of global capture, which did not require militaries but could subjugate populations – also did not materialize. Instead, the opposite happened. The Ilkhanate of the Mongols, briefly the ally of crusade leaders like England's Edward I, and in the thirteenth century displaying occasional interest in joining Eastern and Western forces against the Mamluks, converted to Islam after the conversion of the Ilkhan Ghazan in 1295.[116]

History, we might say, thus reversed literature. Where in literature a single Christian princess handily converts a Muslim king and his kingdom to Christianity, in history, despite the efforts of missionaries and friars preaching conversion – the most poignant examples of which may have been St. Francis of Assisi preaching in Egypt to the Ayyubid Sultan Al-Kamil, and William of Rubruck trudging to Karakorum to preach to the Mongols – and despite royal political marriages, like the giving of the Christian Byzantine princess Maria Palaiogina, daughter of the emperor Michael VIII, to Abaga Khan of the Ilkhanate in 1265 (Runciman 3: 320), the Near Eastern swathe of the worldwide confederation of khanates that was the Mongol empire converted to Islam.[117]

Islam, moreover, spread even further east, and peaceably, from the seventh century CE, along the trade routes where merchants consorted with local populations in the marketplaces, towns, villages, and cities of archipelago Southeast Asia – which today attests the largest Muslim-populated country in the world. In maritime Southeast Asia, a globalized Islam dispersed through cultures of trade and human association, without the legacy of empire inextricable from the later advance of Christianity in these same regions – the legacy of the Portuguese and British in the Malayan archipelago, the Spanish in the Philippines, the French in Indochina, and the Dutch in the Indonesian archipelago.

In the international contest for religious supremacy and territorial dominion in the European Middle Ages, Christendom, for all its manifold efforts on different fronts, did not triumph. The failures of these avowed goals, however, did not daunt the West. Seeking a route to India – the home of the spice trade – that would bypass the Red Sea controlled by Mamluk Egypt, the Portuguese, led by Vasco da Gama, rounded the Cape of Good Hope and reached India in 1498. First Portugal, then others, found access to a farther East than the Holy Lands, and, bearing firearms, the Bible, and goals of economic expropriation, sought control of the oceans that launched European seaborne empires in India, Southeast Asia, and the farthest East.[118] For such colonial adventuring, the crusades had furnished the useful template of arriving both with the sword *and* the Book.

Thus began a new chapter of race-religion in Europe's history of racial empires and regimes.

Notes

1 On the name *Saracens*, see also John Tolan, "A Wild Man."
2 Jews and Saracens are thus the twin manifestations of what Kathy Biddick calls "the enemy's two bodies" ("Dead Neighbor Archives").
3 David Nirenberg also recounts violence against Jewish populations in contact zones where pragmatic coexistence was imperative: "In 'The Refutation' Ibn Hazm presents . . . a world in which Jews were becoming more powerful than Muslims, and the Muslim monarchs – or worse, all their Muslim subjects! – were becoming 'Jews' . . . The Granadans [] apparently agreed that this 'Judaism' had to be eliminated. Though Ibn Hazm did not quite live to see it, in 1066 the Muslims of Granada revolted against their *amir*'s employment of Samuel's son Joseph, killing him and three or four thousand other Jews" (*Anti-Judaism* 180–1).
4 Peters suggests that of the five major reports of Urban's address at Clermont, those by Robert the Monk and Guibert of Nogent are likely eyewitness reports (*First Crusade* 2, 10). Robert's and Baldric of Dol's accounts are the most virulent, studded with sensational images of Islamic pollution of Christian altars and holy places; the torture, mutilation, and profanation of Christian bodies; the wanton shedding of Christian blood; the portrayal of Christians as blood brothers; the rape of women; horrific invasion and depopulation of Greek Christian lands; the personification of Jerusalem as a pathetic damsel in distress, and as a desperate mother seeking succor from her children; the right of Christians to possess the Holy Land; the harsh realities of civil strife and violence in a Europe unable to sustain its growing population; the presentation of Jesus Christ as leader and battle commander in Christian warfare; and the promise not only of heavenly rewards and everlasting glory, but also of looting the possessions of the enemy (Peters, *First Crusade* 2–5, 6–7; *Recueil, Occ.* III: 728, IV: 13). The author of the anonymous *Gesta Francorum* (Deeds of the Franks) is characteristically bare and straightforward, while Fulcher of Chartres, in his *Historia Hierosolymitana* (History of the Expedition to Jerusalem), emphasizes aid to Christian brethren in the Orient, heathen occupation of Christian lands, Christ as the instigator of the armed expedition to the Orient, remission of sins for the expeditioners, and the transformation of erstwhile plunderers in the Latin West into the soldiery of Christ (Peters, *First Crusade* 5–6, 30–1). Guibert

of Nogent's account is characteristically prolix, with complex rhetorical circumlocutions and theological arguments not found in any of the other reports, but nonetheless reinforces the imagery of pollution and mutilation, and the idea of Jesus as battle-leader of the pilgrim troops (Peters, *First Crusade* 10–15). Eyewitness crusade chronicles thereafter repeat the conviction that the armed pilgrims of the First Crusade are the soldiery of Christ.

5 Intriguingly, Tom Sizgorich discusses *ghazis*, who, in the early centuries of Islam, were celebrated for being pious, monklike holy warriors – rigorous devotees who seemed Islamic precursors of the later monastic crusading orders: "a people staying up through the night . . . praying, and remaining abstinent during the day . . . commanding the right and forbidding the wrong, monks by night, lions by day" (909).

6 This insight is Tomaz Mastnak's, in his trenchant and powerful study, *Crusading Peace*. My thoughts on malicide and political theology, and on the instrumentality of blood in creating group identity, derive from Mastnak's arguments. The twelfth century was not the only era that witnessed the advocacy of killing Muslims as a kind of virtuous morality. Brian Catlos reminds us that after the fall of Acre in 1291, "a flurry of polemical tracts and essays . . . combined a spirit of *realpolitik* with proclamations regarding the moral virtue of killing Muslims" (334).

7 "Pope Urban's strength lay in his understanding . . . of how God's authorship of history translated into human action. God acted 'through Christian men.' When those 'Christian men' fought 'the Turks in Asia and the Moors in Europe,' God worked through them . . . But now, Christian men's deeds are not seen as helped by God but as God's deeds" (Mastnak, "Muslims" 199). Mastnak astutely reads this new distinction as indicating that "the Crusades were political theology in action" ("Muslims" 200) – a revealing example of how "some of the central concepts" of theology are in fact "theologized *political* concepts" ("Muslims" 200, my emphasis). "When action of man is seen as God's action, as deeds of God or work of God, as *gesta Dei* or *opus Dei*, we have to deal with a specific understanding of society and politics" (Mastnak, "Muslims" 199).

8 "As the title, *The Law of the False Prophet Muhammad* (*Lex Mahumet pseudoprophete*), shows . . . this was a political and polemical text, the aim of which was to contribute to the intellectual arsenal being assembled against Islam – one that included translations of Islamic law, *hadith*, and Arabic folklore also commissioned by Peter the Venerable. By the thirteenth century, indexed, pocket translations of the Qur'ran were circulating, apparently intended for missionaries and preachers, who needed to have easy and rapid access to the various 'errors' it contained" (Catlos 330). On the misnomer of the "Toledan translation project," see http://grupsderecerca.uab.cat/islamolatina/.

9 Since my writing this chapter, Brian Catlos' magisterial *Muslims of Medieval Latin Christendom c. 1050–1614*, surveying Muslim societies within Latin Christendom and medieval Christian societies' responses to the Muslims in their midst, and Suzanne Conklin Akbari's *Idols in the East*, presenting readings of European medieval literature in which Islam and Saracens are featured, have also appeared. See also the indispensable multivolume series by David Thomas et al., and Pohl and Gantner.

10 Catlos sums it up succinctly: "from the earliest Christian ideological engagements with Islam, whether by the likes of the Syrian Christian functionary, John of Damascus (676–749) in the eastern Mediterranean, or the eighth-century Mozarab chroniclers of Spain in the west, or the author of the apocryphal ninth-century *Risalat al-Kindi* at the Abbasid court. Latin thinkers from Baetica to Britain portrayed Islam as a Christian heresy, pagan idolatry, or a herald of the Apocalypse, and the Prophet Muhammad as a fraud, the Antichrist, a false prophet, magician, hypocrite, and letch" (327).

11 David Nirenberg sketches the antagonism between Judaism and Islam by recounting a different story of the Prophet's wives, seeing the acquisition of the Prophet's Jewish wife Safiya as an act of *droit du seigneur* that symbolized the Prophet's successful conquest of the Jewish fortifications of Khaybar in 629 CE: "Muhammad performed the subjugation of the community in the

time-honored way: by having sex with the daughter of its slain leader. In the political language of the day, his marriage to the Jewess Safiya, orphaned and widowed in the Muslim attack, was the most telling sign of his power. Hence it was vaunted in the announcement of his victory to his enemies in Mecca: 'Muhammad has conquered Khaybar, and has left married to the daughter of their king'" (*Anti-Judaism* 162). Nirenberg also articulates interreligious tension through another story of a woman's role – this time in the Prophet's death: "according to the traditions Zaynab, another captured Jewess of Khaybar, poisoned a roast lamb she prepared for Muhammad. One of his companions ate greedily, and died of the meal. Muhammad himself 'took hold of the shoulder and chewed a morsel of it, but he did not swallow it.' His prophetic prudence saved his life, though the poison began the illness that would eventually kill him" (*Anti-Judaism* 162–3). Though unflinchingly critical of Islamic "ambivalence about the inclusion of Jews in Islamic polity and policy," Nirenberg's accounts usefully exemplify critique that does not amount to race-making as such.

12 "Yet, even after the launch of the Crusade, when Latin polemicists had gained first-hand insights into the practice and tenets of Islam, they continued to present baffling mistruths, such as that 'Mahummet' was, in fact, a huge gem-encrusted cast-silver idol encountered by Tancred in the Temple of Solomon as Jerusalem fell, or the notion that Muslims imagined God as a sphere of solid 'hammer-beaten metal'" (Catlos 328). Such "baffling mistruths" suggest how romance and *chanson* tropes can leak into the accounts of chroniclers. Chapter 4 of Akbari's *Idols* usefully enumerates some Saracen typologies in medieval *chanson de geste* and romance.

13 Catlos remarks: "much of the personal vitriol against the Prophet of Islam was centered on the permissibility of polygamy, the practice of endogamy, the sensuous Qur'anic invocations of the afterlife, and the awkward aspects of Muhammad's relationship with Zaynab, wife of Zayn (Islam's 'Bathsheba moment')" (328).

14 Robert the Monk has Urban specify the combatants he envisages: "we do not command or advise that the old or feeble, or those unfit for bearing arms, undertake this journey; nor ought women to set out at all, without their husbands or brothers or legal guardians. For such are more of a hindrance than aid, more of a burden than advantage ... The priests and clerks of any order are not to go without the consent of their bishop" (Peters, *First Crusade* 4). I concentrate in this section only on the three attested eyewitness chronicles of the First Crusade: Fulcher of Chartres' *Historia Hierosolymitana* (History of the Expedition to Jerusalem), the anonymous *Gesta Francorum et Aliorum Hierosolymitanorum* (Deeds of the Franks and Other Pilgrims to Jerusalem) and the Provençal Raymond d'Aguiliers' *Historia Francorum Qui Ceperunt Iherusalem* (History of the Franks Who Captured Jerusalem). Fulcher is believed to have begun his chronicle between 1100 and 1102; Raymond d'Aguiliers is thought to have completed his before 1105 and possibly as early as 1102; and a copy of the anonymous *Gesta* already appears in Jerusalem in 1101, found by Ekkehard of Aura, who based his own chronicle on the *Gesta* (Munro, "A Crusader," 327; Runciman 1: 329; Peters, *First Crusade* 5, 23; Fink 20; Krey 7, 9; Raymond d'Aguiliers, *Historia* 7, Hill ix). For a discussion of these eyewitness chronicles, secondary chronicles and accounts of the First Crusade, crusader letters, the biography of Alexius I by his daughter, the Byzantine princess Anna Comnena, and Arab chronicles that detail the First Crusade, see chapter 1 of *Empire of Magic*. The terms "crusaders" and "crusade" were not yet invented at this early stage, and did not circulate until the late twelfth century; they are, however, conventionally used in scholarly discussion.

15 Fulcher of Chartres details the intimidation of mountainous terrain ("Vast mountains, on which no inhabitant was visible, towered over us on all sides"), ravines and precipices, "desert places," and rapid rivers treacherous to cross. Of one such river, "called the Demon by the inhabitants of the place, and deservedly," he wailed: "we saw many people, submerged unexpectedly by the strong current, perish when they hoped to wade through it step by step, and not one of the onlookers could help them" (Peters, *First Crusade* 40).

16 First contact was particularly traumatic, bringing the shock of an enemy fighting style that was, Fulcher says, "unknown to any of us" (Peters, *First Crusade* 46). The *Gesta* too recounts the diabolical sounds of the enemy, who seemed to howl, gabble, and shout devilishly in their own tongue as they fought (Hill 18).

17 "We saw the backs of . . . small beasts [goats, sows, dogs] chafed by the heavy loads" that the pilgrims placed on them (Peters, *First Crusade* 49). "[Y]ou would see goats and wethers . . . become very tired from the packs placed on them, and their backs chafed from the weight of the load" (Peters, *First Crusade* 85).

18 Fulcher notes noncommittally, "When their women were found in the tents, the Franks did nothing evil to them except pierce their bellies with their lances" (Peters, *First Crusade* 64).

19 "*Ubi obsidione per XX dies acta, famen nimiam gens nostra pertulit. dicere perhorreo, quod plerique nostrum famis rabie nimis vexati abscidebant de natibus Saracenorum iam ibi mortuorum frusta, quae coquebant et mandebant et parum ad ignem assata ore truci devorabant. itaque plus obsessores quam obsessi angebantur*" (*Historia Hierosolymitana* 266–7).

20 "*Fuerunt ibi ex nostris qui illic non inuenerunt sicuti opus eis erat, tantum ex longa mora, quantum ex districtione famis, quia foris nequiuerant aliquid inuenire ad capiendum, sed scindebant corpora mortuorum, eo quod in uentribus eorum inueniebant bisanteos reconditos; alii uero caedebant carnes eorum per frusta, et coquebant ad manducandum*" (Hill 80).

21 "*Interea tante fames in exercitu fuit, ut multa corpora Saracenorum iam fetentium, que in paludibus civitatis eiusdem .ii. et amplius ebdomadas iacuerant, populous avidissime comederet. Terrebant ista multos tam nostre gentis homines quam extraneos. Revertebantur ob ea nostri quam plures . . . Sarraceni vero et Turci econtra dicebant: Et quis poterit austinere hanc gentem qua tam obstinata atque crudelis est, ut per annum non poterit revocari ab obsidione Antiochie, fame, vel gladio, vel aliquibus periculis, et nunc carnibus humanis vescitur? Hec et alia crudelissima sibi in nobis dicebant esse pagani. Etenim dederat deus timorem nostrum cunctis gentibus sed nos nesciebamus*" ("*Liber*" 101). I have slightly modified Krey's translation (214).

22 The letter also attests to cannibalism at Ma'arra: "There was so great a famine in the army that the putrid bodies of the Saracens were now eaten up by the Christian people" ("*Tanta fames in exercitu fuit, ut corpora Saracenorum iam fetentium a populo Christiano comesta sint*" [Hagenmeyer, *Kreuzzugsbriefe* 170]).

23 Al-Qalanisi's account (see Gibb 46), written before his death in 1160, is the most contemporary of the Arab sources, the author having been resident in Damascus during the events of the First Crusade. Ibn al-Athir's is in volume 1 and Kemal al-Din's in volume 3 of the *Recueil des Historiens des Croisades, Historiens Orientaux* series. Ibn al-Athir says that after thirteen days had passed at Antioch and the Franks had nothing more to eat, the rich were reduced to eating their beasts of burden, and the poor ate dead bodies and the leaves of trees ("Treize jours s'étaient écoulés depuis que les Francs étaient entres dans Antioche. Ils n'avaient plus de quoi manger; les riches étaient réduits à nourrir de bêtes de somme, et les pauvres de corps morts et de feuilles d'arbres" [1: 194]). Kemal al-Din's thirteenth-century account, appearing in a history of Aleppo, similarly recounts that, confined within Antioch, the Franks were reduced to eating the flesh of cadavers and dead animals: "Les Francs, enfermé dans Antioche, en étaient réduits à manger la chair des cadavres et des animaux morts" (3: 583). Gibb's translation of Al-Qalanisi refers to "carrion" rather than cadavers, and the Arabic texts point to cannibalism at Antioch, but are silent on Ma'arra. The Arabic documents are, of course, late texts compared to the eyewitness Latin chronicles.

24 I argued in chapter 1 of *Empire of Magic* that historical cannibalism by Latin crusaders in 1095 at Ma'arra, en route to Jerusalem (and possibly at Antioch earlier), issued a cultural trauma that required stages of attenuation, displacement, and transformation processed through a historicized mode of cultural fantasy in Geoffrey of Monmouth's fabulous *History of the Kings of Britain*

(*Historia Regum Britannie*), which elicited the genesis of the magical genre we call medieval romance. The *Historia* transforms a traumatic memory of crusader cannibalism into a romance event through the heroism of King Arthur, a figure the *Historia* materializes to effect culture's rescue of history. The *Historia* also produces a *second* romance event in which Cadwallo, King of Britain, is restored to good health by his retainer Brian, who turns the king into an inadvertent cannibal in order to heal the king's malady: This is precisely the kind of restorative cannibalism that occurs in *Richard Coer de Lyon*. The two-stage processing performed by the *Historia*'s romance moments featuring cannibalism is exemplary of the kind of mediation and rescue that literature can offer to history, and that is performed with particular effectiveness by medieval romance.

The cannibalistic episodes in *Richard Coer de Lyon* thus have a long literary genealogy of predecessor moments and stages that make possible their production as an aggressive imperialist joke. After the eyewitness crusade chronicles first register the horror of crusader cannibalism, Guibert de Nogent's crusade history, written later in the first decade of the twelfth century, half-admits that certain Christians might eat Saracens under certain conditions ("secretly and rarely," Guibert says, if at all) when the Christians involved are "Tafurs," wild men who are desperately poor, ragged, and possibly foreign: *Tafurs* is Guibert's invented name for a subaltern group of impoverished underclass folk in the Christian forces, designed to shoulder responsibility for accusations of cannibalism directed at the First Crusade. Then, late in the twelfth century, the Old French *Chanson d'Antioche* embroidered on the guilt of these scapegoat-unfortunates, depicting *Tafurs* as unabashedly eating boiled and roasted Turk openly, to the amusement of the barons of the First Crusade (see Duparc-Quioc, ed., *Chanson d'Antioche*, laisses CLXXIV, CLXXV).

The *Antioche*'s contribution appeared after Geoffrey's *Historia*, in the first third of the twelfth century, had already interpolated the saving, healing cannibalism of the British king Cadwallo. The *Antioche*'s principal addition, then, to the genealogy of Christian cannibalism was to insert *laughter* as an ingredient (laisse CLXXV), suggesting that when it is a Christian underclass – the dregs of the crusading army – that turns cannibal, laughter by seigneurial onlookers is the appropriate response, thus paving the way for the depiction of cannibalism as a joke in *Richard Coer de Lyon*. The notion that cannibalism is an aggressive act of imperial warfare is of course already implicit in Raymond d'Aguiliers' eyewitness chronicle of the First Crusade, written in the opening years of the twelfth century, which suggested that the Latin crusaders' reputation for anthropophagy was tied to their reputation as aggressive and successful conquerors. For a historian's take on the original eleventh-century crusader cannibalism, see Jay Rubenstein.

25 In *Richard Coer de Lyon*, the two cannibal episodes are brilliantly positioned as *escalating* jokes: First, cannibalism occurs as a kindly joke played against King Richard by his loyal subjects, who heal their sick king by turning him into an inadvertent cannibal; later, cannibalism is in turn transmogrified by Richard into a muscular joke against Saladin's ambassadors, once the English king intuits the power of cannibalism for performing aggressive empire-formation.

26 A nationalistic joke is ideal for articulating international aggression, since aggression is the circuit of the joke when directed against a community of others. With humor, enemies become magically vulnerable – even the historically undefeatable Saladin, whose reputation for chivalry, magnanimity, and generosity extended beyond the Levant and into the heart of European history and culture, can be defeated with a joke. Thanks to a cannibalistic joke in *Richard Coer de Lyon*, national and colonial ambitions are seen as coterminous – logically partnered in war and power, a joke being an entertaining and witty way of showing how "the 'national idea' flourished in the soil of foreign conquest" (Brennan 59).

27 See also Anidjar's formulation of how Christianity develops over historical time as a blood community: "Blood is what the Christian community is made of, how the community comes to

be and understand itself" (44). "Ultimately," Anidjar concludes, "the exceptionality of blood in the Middle Ages has everything to do with the emergence, in ways that are both manifest and hidden, of a singular collective, a community of blood" (Anidjar 42).

28 The dynamics of identity in a global holy war where religion is served by bloodbaths resonates today with Jihadi statements of intent on shedding the blood of infidels, especially as demonstrated in the actions and the grotesque videography of the so-called "Islamic State." Nobody, it seems, has a monopoly on the instrumentality of blood when deployed in race-making or holy war.

29 Bartlett's oscillating attitudes to premodern race are discussed in Chapter 1. Here he says: "It is true that Christians are made – by baptism – not born, but the vast majority of those born in Christian Europe in the High Middle Ages underwent baptism as a matter of course. They could easily think of themselves, not as voluntary recruits to a particular community of believers, but as members of a Christian race ... when the Saxons were forcibly converted to Christianity by Frankish arms in the decades around the year 800, adoption of the new religion made them one *race*, as it were (*quasi una gens*), with the Franks. This ethnic sense of 'Christian' can be found repeatedly and perhaps increasingly in the High Middle Ages ... The expansion of the new millennium brought Christians 'where Christians had never come before,' and the circumstances of these new juxtapositions reinforced the sense that Christians were a people or tribe or race" (*Making of Europe* 251).

30 See, e.g., Abu-Lughod; Ashtor, "Economic Decline," *Social and Economic History*, "Levantine Sugar Industry," *Levant Trade*; Heck; Phillips, "Sugar Production". For the way in which the rise of European markets and cities is underwritten by "the hydraulic package" assembled earlier in Islamicate societies and transferred interimperially to the West, see Doyle.

31 I discuss medieval colonization of the Near East, and the intersection of colonization with crusader cannibalism of Muslims, in *Empire of Magic*. Because of a plethora of issues, including differences of religion, race, multinational militarism, and scale, overseas extraterritoriality of the crusader kind differs somewhat from local invasions of contiguous European territories, such as Anglo-Norman England's colonization of neighboring Ireland and Wales. For the colonial-racial politics of subjugating Christian neighbors, see Chapter 1.

32 Mass-market novels, video games such as *Assassin's Creed*, Hollywood movies, television – even the season three opener of the well-regarded NBC television political drama series *The West Wing*, an episode in which a so-called "suicide terrorist" threat to the White House leads to a little disquisition from the White House Communications Director on the Assassins as the world's first "suicide terrorists" – all famously testify to the enduring fascination with the Assassins of Alamut 900 years after their legend was promulgated. Ludicrous pretexts are even invented in order to feature these irresistible characters from the deep past: An episode in Netflix's fictional Marco Polo series, loosely based on Polo's and Rustichello da Pisa's *Le Devisement du Monde*, flimsily transports the Assassins of Alamut all the way to China, so that they can menace Kublai Khan in his imperial court at Khanbalik/Beijing!

33 Rather than speculate on the relationship between Islamic communities and "suicide terrorism" today, we would do better to consult Robert Pape's *Dying to Win*, a meticulous, data-driven study of many years that undoes easy suppositions about terrorist genealogies. With the rise of the so-called "Islamic State," or ISIS, we have a new example today of how a fractious Muslim minority can be manipulated to represent all Islam – aided, in this case, by ISIS' own self-representation.

34 De Sacy's nineteenth-century memoir linking the Nizaris to hashish is reproduced by, among others, Daftary (*Legends* 136–88) and Von Hammer and Wood (227–40).

35 I refer here to Islamic studies scholars. Europeanists often assume that De Sacy is correct and the Nizaris consumed hashish for purposes of assassination (see, e.g., Nowell's oft-cited "Old Man").

36 Though exact details vary, sex, the training of youths for assassination, an all-powerful leader, use of narcotics, secret places of delight, and the promise of paradise are elements that enter the story

very early, so that by the second half of the twelfth century or the early thirteenth, Provençal poems that deploy the Assassins, their paradise, and their master as ready metaphors already assume that "their public could understand the allusions without explanation" (Chambers 245).

37 The text adds that "Mulecte" means to say "of Saracens" ("*de sarain*," emended by Ménard to "*dieu terrien*" or "earthly god," an elevation tying the assassin leader even more closely to the Prophet [166]). Dating from the early fourteenth century, the Franco-Italian redaction is traditionally held to be closest to the lost original. I cite here from Ménard's 2001 critical edition, representing the French tradition likely to be familiar to literary authors in France and England, based on texts descended from F and following Moule-Pelliot's older stemma: FA, FB, FC, FD, and X (equivalent to FO in Moule-Pelliot). The discussion of Polo in Chapter 6 cites Ronchi's edition. For literary scholars, "Polo" is shorthand for a large body of texts whose original is believed to have been compiled by the historical subject known as Polo in collaboration with the romancer Rustichello da Pisa. See Gaunt for a recent argument on the original Franco-Italian of their collaboration and the complexity of the manuscript traditions. I discuss other aspects of Polo's/Rustichello's *Le Devisement du Monde* in Chapter 6.

38 Hodgson suggests both Polo's and Ibn Khallikan's accounts are rooted in stories current at the time in Persia and Syria (135).

39 Metlitzki suggests the *Sirat Hakim* as a source for *Mandeville's Travels*, a suggestion that has not been taken up in Mandeville scholarship. Scholars differ on whether the *Travels* first appeared in England or France, but generally concur that the Insular and Continental versions best represent the original work. Of the Insular, the elegant British Library MS Egerton 1982 (ed. Warner) and the slightly plainer and less complete (four missing leaves after folio 53) British Library MS Cotton Titus c. xvi (ed. Hamelius) are commonly cited. Egerton corresponds particularly well to the earliest extant dated manuscript, Paris, Bibliothèque Nationale MS nouv. acq. fr. 4515, copied in 1371, and representing the Continental version. I cite Egerton and Cotton in this chapter, and refer to Paris (ed. Letts) in notes. Iain Higgins has recently produced an elegant translation, with selections from source texts, of the important Anglo-Norman Mandeville, which I use in discussion in Chapter 6 (*Book*).

40 Egerton's original text reads:

a place of delytez, whare a man schall fynd all maner of fruytez all tymes of þe ȝere, and riuers rynnand with wyne, mylke and hony, and fresch water; and þai schall hafe faire palaycez and grete and faire housez and gude, after þai hafe disserued, and þase palacez and housez er made of precious stanes, gold and siluer; and ilk man sall hafe iiii^xx wyfes of faire damiselles, and he schall hafe at do with þam ay whem him list, and he sall euermare fynd þam maydens. þis trowe þai all þat þai sall hafe in paradys; and þis es agayne oure lawe.

Cotton is identical except for omission of the last line and the assertion that each man has sexual intercourse with the maidens "every day" instead of "when it is pleasing to him" (Hamelius I: 85).

41 On trees, herbs, wells, halls and chambers, and precious stones and metals in Cotton, see Hamelius I: 185. Paris has elaborate descriptions of gold and azure paintings of stories, tales, and diverse beasts on the walls of these chambers and halls, and says the fountains ("*fontaines*") display not only jasper, crystal, and gold but also pearls ("*grosses perles*" [Letts II: 388]).

42 Paris, too, says the birds perform "*par enging*" (i.e., by mechanical means) as if they were alive (Letts II: 388).

43 The Caliph Al-Mamun had a famed gold and silver tree in Baghdad where mechanical birds perched (Trapp 101; Terzioglu 3); the Caliph Al-Muqtadir also had a tree of gold and silver branches, where "gold and silver birds twittered and sang" (Ruggles, *Islamic Gardens* 78–9; Terzioglu 3). In Byzantium, the emperor Theophilos had a gold tree with mechanical singing birds (Ruggles, *Gardens, Landscape* 79); Liuprand of Cremona also saw gilded birds sing at the

Byzantine emperor's court a century later (Sherwood 571; Truitt 175). De Solla Price suggests that the thirteenth century is a high point for the transmission to Europe of knowledge on automata, after which "come many allusions to brass trees full of singing birds, set in motion by water power . . . wind, or . . . bellows" (19). As late as 1405, the court of Timur at Samarkand had a golden tree with golden birds pecking at gemstone fruit (Ruggles, *Gardens, Landscape* 83).

Sherwood pairs "the real automata of the Oriental courts and the imaginary ones" of European romances: bronze singing birds in an Emir's garden (*Floire et Blancheflor*), wind-worked singing birds in the Emir of Babylon's hall (*Aymeri de Narbonne*), the artificial singing birds of the *Roman d'Escanor*, and the 10,000 golden mechanical birds that sing and flutter in the *Roman d'Enéas*. The *Travels'* references are as likely, of course, to derive from literary as from other sources. Segol observes that a "tower motif is believed to be derived from Arabic literary sources," though a high architectural feature is also a motif of Islamic gardens (discussed presently).

Despite censure from theologians and jurists, Umayyad courts were famed for music, as were Abbasid courts, especially under Harun al-Rashid (786–809) and Al-Mamun (813–33). Rigorists objected in particular to the musical seductions of stringed instruments (Shiloah 17). Scent was also a key feature: Like the scented herbs of the *Travels'* Assassin paradise, Islamic gardens cultivated "perfume plants" (Husain 90).

44 Among the most studied are Al-Zahra, for its earliness, and the late Alhambra, for its excellent state of preservation. Ruggles emphasizes the importance of hydraulics in Islamic gardens – to simulate the rivers of paradise, and irrigate exotic horticultural hybrids and varied species of trees and plants – and the ubiquity of a high focal point in the *mirador* ("Gardens of the Alhambra" 164, 166). John Hooper Harvey observes that "the recovery of the pleasure garden . . . [and] . . . the higher techniques of cultivation, went hand in hand with the general rediscovery of science and technology through the scholars of Islam" (22).

45 Abd al-Rahman had a famous menagerie of rare animals in Al-Zahra (Ruggles, *Gardens, Landscape* 60), and Al-Muqtadir had a hunting park of wild animals (78). Colvin, discussing how features of "Hispano-Islamic gardens" filtered into Europe, notes the famed aviary at the park of Hesdin in Artois and aviaries at Winchester and Westminster, the latter "made or re-made for Queen Eleanor of Castile in 1277–8" (16). Henry I also had a park, Everswell, at Woodstock, near Oxford, with "semi-oriental luxuries" such as exotic animals – lions, leopards, lynxes, and camels – and "a water garden" (Colvin 18–19). Hesdin was famed for its water courses, fountains, aviary, and artifices, possibly also influenced by Islamic gardens via Sicily and Iberia (Van Buren). Cultural knowledge of European gardens with Islamic-style features may have served the *Travels* well.

46 The source for this episode in the *Travels*, Odoric of Pordenone's *Relatio*, narratologically moves from discussing Prester John to discussing the Assassins, but does not make their lands touch or geographically contiguous as the *Travels* does (Chiesa 155; Yule-Cordier 2: 329).

47 The original Latin *Letter of Prester John* dates to 1165, though the first reference to John occurs in 1145; the legend thereafter proliferated for more than 300 years, with late medieval vernacular versions offering vast elaborations. Scholarship on John is extensive; it is impossible to detail here the legend's complex development. See, however, Beckingham, de Rachewiltz (*Prester John*), Hambis, Hamilton, Kaplan (*Rise*), Nowell ("Prester John"), Olschki, Richard, Ross, and Slessarev. I cite from Zarncke's edition and Uebel's translation. Revealingly, the *Travels* prefers the high-fictional strain of John's legend, whereas Odoric and Polo endorse the mundane historical explanation of John's legend as the hyperbolized fable of a steppe tribal chieftain.

John's legend, I argued in *Empire of Magic*, figures the spoor of European desire as it moves across the world. Materializing in Eurasia and "India" in the twelfth and thirteenth centuries, this fictive Christian priest-king is relocated to Africa by the fourteenth and fifteenth centuries. John's reported presence beckons and invites Europe to explore and exploit, as Europeans say they are setting out to seek Prester John and his kingdom, so that for centuries, where Prester John went,

Europe was not far behind (*Empire of Magic* 285–7, 454–7). For other theorized interpretations of the Prester John legend, see Uebel and Christopher Taylor. I take up the discussion of Prester John's legend more fully in Chapter 6.

48 Analyzing the "desire to blur the distinction between the real and the artificial" in Islamic gardens – where "ruses" were "intended to delight, amaze" – Ruggles identifies the pleasure of "intentional ambiguity" as a form of mastery (*Gardens, Landscape* 84–8).

49 See Quran: 76:19, 56:17, 52:24 on *ghilman* and *wildan*, young male servants and boys of perpetual freshness who serve in the Islamic paradise. The *Travels* calls the novitiates "bachelors" (i.e., no mere riff-raff, but apprentices for knighthood). See also my discussion in Chapter 6 of the *Travels'* depiction of different levels of paradise – another indication of how the Mandeville author hews closely to the Quranic template.

50 Ruggles emphasizes, moreover, that "the creation of a permanent garden that did not fade seasonally and was unaffected by drought and frost embodied the concept of mastery, including control over the most frightening experience, death" (*Gardens, Landscape* 87–8). Such gardens, she adds, denoted power and "tremendous wealth" and were "expressions of cultural and economic status" (87).

51 Islam was seductive in many ways: "the Florentine Dominican, Riccoldo da Monte di Croce, an Arabist who traveled to Baghdad and studied the Qur'an in that 'garden of delights . . . watered by the rivers of Paradise' . . . was left 'stupefied, to ponder God's judgment concerning the government of the world. . .What could be the cause of . . . so much worldly prosperity for the perfidious Saracen people?'" (Catlos 327). Catlos adds that there were even "missionizing friars for whom the prospect of polygamy proved irresistible," and who converted to Islam (338).

52 Though the *Travels* endorses the hyperfictional version of John's legend, it proffers one salient detail from the more mundane historical version which it finds useful – dynastic intermarriage with the Great Khan of Cathay – to aggrandize John's status. For an argument that the fictional John represents an imaginary Christian threshold to the Great Khan and the splendors of Mongol Cathay, see Chapter 6 and *Empire of Magic* 282–4.

53 The *Travels* locates John's fictive palace at Susa in southwest Persia, playing ingeniously with history and geography: Nizaris had fortresses in northern and northeastern Persia. John's fantasy realm is thus literally placed cheek-by-jowl alongside actual Nizari strongholds, but in the opposite direction.

54 Robert the Monk's version – perhaps the most rousing of the accounts of Urban's address – has the pope thunder: "Enter upon the road to the Holy Sepulcher; wrest that land from the wicked race, and subject it to yourselves" (*Recueil*, Occ., 3:728).

55 For Jerusalem's place in the Western imagination during the Middle Ages, see Suzanne Yeager. I elaborate the themes here in Chapter 6, when discussing the pan-Christianity of *Mandeville's Travels*.

56 For how to avoid repeating today older cultural (mis)understandings in viewing Muslims and Islam, see my "Sex, Lies, and Paradise" and "Holy War Redux."

57 See Chapter 6, in the section on William of Rubruck, and *Empire of Magic*, chapter 4 for the Latin West's interest in an empire of culture through conversion, after geopolitical losses in the Holy Land and failures in military crusading. In *Medieval Boundaries*, Kinoshita offers a thoughtful historicized reading of *La Fille* in the context of Almería and Ponthieu.

58 While Sunni authors such as his biographer, secretary, and imam Beha ad-Din, and his secretary Imad ad-Din, narrated Saladin as a saintly figure of deep piety and gentle melancholy and a great military leader, Shiite authors were predictably less generous to the Kurdish sultan whose Sunni orthodoxy made him execute heretics. In the Latin West, Saladin was feared *and* admired: The tithe collected by churches to finance a crusade to retake Jerusalem was named for him, but his representation in literature varied from the palpably negative (the Middle English romance

Richard Coer de Lyon, spanning perhaps two centuries, shows Saladin as outmaneuvered and cowed by Richard) to the glowingly laudatory portraits surveyed by Tolan (*Sons of Ishmael*).

59 I adapt the term "virtuous Saracen" from Frank Grady's "virtuous pagan" in his *Representing Righteous Heathens*.

60 Stories of Saladin's generosity and magnanimity were legion among foe and follower alike. Beha ad-Din details how Saladin took the trouble to show mercy to a Frankish woman whose girl infant was taken by his men, and who sought the Sultan's help because of his reputation for kindness. Saladin had the child searched for, found, and restored to the mother, and himself reimbursed the man who had purchased the child. The whole affair took only an hour, Beha ad-Din relates matter-of-factly, with no comment on the Sultan's succor of an enemy (Ibn Shaddad 41–2).

Another typical anecdote: Despite the fact that the castellan at Kerak, the abominable Reynald de Châtillon, was someone Saladin had putatively sworn to kill with his own hands after Reynald's raid on a pilgrim caravan in which Saladin's sister had been traveling, the magnanimous Sultan, in attacking the castle, forbore to bombard the tower at Kerak where the nuptial couple was housed. Citing William of Tyre and Ernoul as Christian sources of the story, Runciman describes how the bridegroom's mother, Lady Stephanie, "herself prepared dishes from the bridal feast which she sent out to Saladin" (2: 441).

Beha ad-Din even recounts an incident in which Saladin heard a case against himself, adjudicating a complaint lodged against him: After listening to the plaintiff and witnesses, the Sultan judged himself in the wrong and submitted himself to penalty, showing how no one, not even the Sultan, was above the law (17–18). Runciman also recalls Saladin's compassion after his recapture of Jerusalem, allowing many of the inhabitants who could not afford their ransom to be freed (II: 466), while Imad ad-Din, another of Saladin's secretaries and chroniclers, recounts how Saladin was cheated by his own men at Jerusalem (Gabrieli 159).

61 The conviction that Saladin must somehow, at some time, really have been Christian or French took a number of inventive forms. Tolan remarks: "Another branch of the Jerusalem continuations makes Saladin into a renegade Christian" (*Sons of Ishmael* 181 n.76).

62 Barton lists a number of other marriages: the daughter of Theodemir of Murcia to Abd al-Jabbar ibn Khattab; Sara, granddaughter of King Wittiza of the Visigoths (702–10) to Isa ibn Muzahim; Sancha, the daughter of Count Aznar Galíndez II of Aragon to Muhammad al-Tawil, et al. ("Marriage" 4; *Conquerors* 26). Oñega or Iniga, is called Durr in Arabic ("pearl"); her son became the father of Abd al-Rahman III, the caliph of Al-Andalus, by a Christian slave concubine (see discussion below). Barton summarizes at some length the debate over the identity of the "pagan" king of Toledo to whom Teresa Vermúdez was given (*Conquerors* 27–31).

63 An anonymous reviewer suggests, however, that in Christian Spain, *sex* between Christian men and their Muslim *slaves* was common: See Tolan et al., part 1, chapters 3 and 4.

64 In the ninth century, not all the children of Christian–Muslim marriages were raised as Muslim (Barton, *Conquerors* 22). But so alarming was interfaith marriage that the assembled Christian clerics at an ecclesiastical council in Córdoba in 839 were moved to denounce "the impious marriage of various faithful with the infidel, sowing crimes among our morals" (Barton, *Conquerors* 11). Interracial, interreligious unions thus appear to have been contracted at all levels of society, not just at the highest levels (Barton, *Conquerors* 21).

65 "The cross-border interfaith marriage alliances that appear to have been relatively commonplace at the very highest echelons of peninsular society between the ninth and eleventh centuries came to be seen by later Christians as a sign of humiliation and weakness" (Barton, "Marriage" 19). "In April 1223 ... Pope Honorius III dispatched a letter to the archbishop of Tarragona and his suffragans, in which he denounced the custom of those Christian kings and nobles, who ... were in the habit of handing over their noblewomen to the Muslims" (Barton, "Marriage" 18).

66 Charles Verlinden's scholarship on the institution of slavery in medieval Europe is foundational: Both his 1955 *L'Esclavage dans l'Europe medieval I: Péninsule Ibérique – France*, focusing on the Iberian peninsula, the Balearic Islands, and France, and his 1977 *L'Esclavage dans l'Europe medieval II: Italie, Colonies italiennes du Levant, Levant latin, Empire byzantin*, focusing on Italy, Italian colonies in the Levant, the Latin Levant, and the Byzantine empire, are monumental studies, surveying a wealth of charters and notarial acts, displaying numerous tabulations, offering broad perspectives, and even reproducing whole original documents in the text and footnotes. Though Verlinden remains invaluable to scholars, I cite more recent scholarship in this section, particularly scholarship not only presenting statistical data but also offering sophisticated data-driven arguments invaluable for the understanding of ethnoracial politics in the contact zones discussed in this chapter. Verlinden's groundbreaking scholarship has, of course, enabled the more recent work by Barton, Constable, Epstein, Phillips, Ruggles ("Mothers"), and others. Interestingly, the later data by and large bear out Verlinden's earlier findings (such as the overwhelming preponderance of women slaves over men slaves in the Mediterranean, and the young age of these women). See also Rotman on slaves and slavery in the Mediterranean, and especially Byzantium.

67 Barton urges that "the Spanish Arabist Julián Ribera went so far as to claim that the degree of interfaith sexual mixing was so excessive in Iberia during the earlier medieval period that the proportion of Arab blood running through the veins of the tenth-century Umayyad caliphs of al-Andalus was in fact infinitesimal" (Barton, *Conquerors* 23).

68 Conquest made slave women readily available in this period: "The tenth century marked the apogee of the cross-border slave trade, as the Umayyad caliphate . . . exerted ever greater military pressure on the Christian states of the North . . . the fifty or so campaigns waged by al-Mansur from the 980s down to his death in 1002 produced such a glut of Christian slave women in the markets of Córdoba that prices collapsed, and the number of men deciding to take a free Muslim wife, as opposed to a slave concubine, slumped dramatically. The beautiful daughter of one Christian notable was said to have fetched only twenty dinars" (Barton, *Conquerors* 35). One later account claims that "when Barcelona was sacked in 985 some 70,000 women and children were taken into captivity; at Zamora (981) the figure given is 40,000 women; at Pamplona (999) 18,000" (Barton, *Conquerors* 35).

69 Barton agrees with Ruggles, seeing sexual unions with Christian slave concubines as "an important dynastic defense mechanism. Marrying a freeborn Muslim woman necessitated the paying of a dowry and even the providing of favors to her family, while divorce might lead to a costly property settlement. More dangerous yet, marriage ran the risk that a Muslim wife's own kin group might at some time in the future entertain its own competing dynastic claims. Marrying a Christian princess or, even more preferable, procreating with [a Christian slave woman], forestalled that danger" (*Conquerors* 42).

70 Barton, citing Bourdieu, makes sure we understand that sexual unions of this kind were "instruments of domination" (*Conquerors* 43). "The sexual dominance of a Muslim ruler over a Christian woman – be it a freeborn princess or a slave concubine – was portrayed by some as symbolic of Islamic political and military hegemony, as well as a humiliating reminder to the Christians themselves of their subordinate status" (Barton, *Conquerors* 39). Moreover, "the forcible deracination of Christian women and children to al-Andalus . . . was seemingly designed to encourage a process of assimilation which would hinder procreation among the Christians of the North and ensure a shift in cultural and ethnic loyalties in the future. Sex was, perhaps, the ultimate colonizing gesture" (Barton, *Conquerors* 40–1). Such historical scenarios are thus a far cry from the European medieval fantasy literature in which captive or coerced Christian heroines turn the tables on Muslims by converting their Muslim tormentors to the Christian cause through racial-religious recruitment.

71 In more recent work, Phillips adduces other castration centers: Besides Verdun in France, there was "Prague in Bohemia, Samarkand and Bukhara in the East, and Christian communities in southern Egypt, or in Muslim Spain, particularly the town of Pechina. Ibn Hawqal (tenth century) even wrote . . . that 'all the Slavic eunuchs that there are on the face of the earth are provided from Spain'" (*Slavery in Medieval and Early Modern Iberia* 121).

72 Reiterating that in Iberia, "Women were in the majority in almost every time and place where records remain to count the slaves," and "At almost every time for which we have price records, women commanded higher prices than men," Phillips adds that young women were the highest priced: "For Seville, the most expensive slaves were women between 15 and 25" (*Slavery in Medieval and Early Modern Iberia* 84, 85, 71).

73 "The only white slaves in Genoa were (by the fifteenth century) non-Italians from places like Bosnia, Muslim Spain, and the Caucasus . . . the Genoese enslaved everyone but themselves and their fellow white Christian western Europeans" (Epstein, *Slavery* 123). In Venice, where slaves "are mentioned in the documents of 1350 to 1450 far more often than in any other period" and where by 1379 "slaves were numerous enough to warrant the imposition of a special tax on slaveholders," Petrarch was "dismayed to see the lanes of Venice filled with a 'filthy populace' of slaves which 'infects with Scythian faces and hideous offscourings this most beautiful city'" (Kedar 127).

74 "It has been said that Baybars was a second Saladin . . . [but] As a soldier he excelled Saladin; he was more single-minded in his military objectives, as in yearly campaign after campaign he brought the great fortresses and towns of the Frankish states into his possession . . . unlike Saladin, he left to his successors a centralized kingdom, which retained its unity until the Ottoman conquest" (P. M. Holt 97). Baybars was apparently of Turkic origin, Kipchak or Cuman, though his name is also a common Circassian one.

75 Ayalon (*Outsiders* 335) also emphasizes "the overwhelming contribution of the Mamluk armies to the conquest of India, and the ensuing process of Islamization there (without the spread of Islam in India, the chances of its spread in South-East Asia and the Pacific islands would have greatly diminished)."

76 The city of Cairo "reached its zenith of greatness and wealth" under the Mamluks, who "erected religious and public buildings in it on a scale unknown till then . . . Ibn Khaldun . . . regards the Mamluks as the saviours of Islam and the Mamluk Sultanate as the paramount Muslim State of his time (for him Cairo was the most splendid Muslim city, the only one in the world where reality surpasses imagination)" (Ayalon, "Muslim City" unpaginated).

77 Ayalon estimates that slave boys bought for military training were between ten and fourteen years old (*Mamluk* 49). The meritocracy of deeds was also leavened by admiration of physical beauty "which has little to do with soldierly qualities," but could be a factor in advancement and promotion. Such beauty, according to Ayalon, was not intended for sexual use, though life on the ground sometimes proved complex: "Sultan Barquq (784–801/1382–1398), the founder of the Circassian reign, was known for his infatuation with boys and his preference for good looking Mamluks" (Ayalon, *Outsiders* 337, *Studies* 92, 100, *Eunuchs* 321). Even the pious Nuraldin once bought "a uniquely good looking Mamluk, for a price ten times higher than the ordinary one" and was "on the verge of satisfying his lust, but then God came to his rescue, and dispatched the beautiful Mamluk to the other world!" (Ayalon, *Eunuchs* 320).

78 The Mamluk's close personal loyalty to his patron (*ustadh*) and fraternal group loyalty to his cohort (*khushdashiyya*) was tempered, of course, by individual ambition and/or rivalry. Loyalty to a patron did not extend to the patron's son or a royal successor – who, on ascension to the throne, typically brought in his own royal Mamluks as replacements, thus setting in motion sanguinary factional rivalries. The breakdown of these close bonds of loyalty to *ustadh* and *khushdashiyya* in the Burji period of the later fifteenth century is seen as symptomatic of the decline of the Mamluk system.

79 Royal Mamluks, cohorts purchased by the Sultan himself, received "first-rate" military training, growing up and studying in "first-rate military schools." The Mamluks of the emirs, or military commanders, "attended the military schools of their masters" and were "necessarily less well trained than the Royal Mamluks" (Ayalon, *Studies* 460). In Islamic Spain, Mamluks also "began as slaves taken by slave traders from their places of origin and thus completely separated from the society of their birth. Legally, they were subject to the same laws and rules as other slaves … [but they] went through a military training program designed to reward loyalty. Once they were admitted to the ranks, they could rise as far as their ability and skill at intrigue permitted. They could attain freedom, and many Mamluks, once they were freed, rose to high office. In the eleventh and twelfth centuries, following the collapse of the Spanish caliphate, many of the successor *taifa* kingdoms had former Mamluks as their rulers" (Phillips, *Slavery in Medieval and Early Modern Iberia* 120). Phillips reckons that the rise of Mamluks in Spain came with Al-Hakam I (797–822), "who organized a permanent force of salaried and slave soldiers." By the time of Abd al-Rahman III, who declared himself caliph in 929, "their numbers in Córdoba are put at 3,750" (Phillips, *Slavery in Medieval and Early Modern Iberia* 57).

80 "The term [Mamluk] was applied only to white slaves, not negroes: at first especially to Turks from Central Asia, but later embracing slaves from western Asia, as well as from many parts of Europe, including the lands of the Baltic sea … whatever their origin, they all proudly called themselves 'Turks'" (Ziada, "Mamluk … 1293" 736), so that "The term *Turk* has sometimes very elastic and loose meaning in contemporary [Islamic] sources … Circassians may be called Turk [ ] so far as this term is synonymous with *Mamluk*" and "Mamluks of races other than Turkish were … given Turkish names" (Ayalon, *Studies* 136 n.13, "Muslim City" unpaginated). "The word *Turk* had two ordinary meanings in Mamluk times: (a) it was a synonym for the Mamluks … and (b) it was used as a generic name for the whole of that element coming from the Kipchak plain which predominated in the Mamluk kingdom during its earlier [Bahri] period" (Ayalon, *Studies* 137 n.19), and continued to be used "even when the Kipchaki Turks were superseded by the Circassians" (Ayalon, *Mamluk* 48).

81 Baybars was said to have had 4,000 Mamluks, and Qalawun between 6,000 and 12,000 "highly disciplined" Mamluks superior to those of any preceding sultan (Ayalon, *Studies* 223). "Each mamluk company was designated by the honorific of its owner" so that the Mamluks who belonged to Salah ad-Din, for instance, were the *Salahiyyah* (Ziada, "Mamluk … 1293" 737). "These mamluk companies had a considerable share in Saladin's wars before and after the battle of Hattin, and the roll of their dead and their casualties bears impressive witness to Saladin's dependence on mamluk soldiery, besides other troops of free status, mostly Kurds" (Ziada, "Mamluk … 1293" 737).

82 The Bahri dynasty of Mamluks takes its name from the location of the Mamluk fortress citadel on "one of the large islands of the Nile, facing the shore-line of Cairo … *al bahriyya*, after the Nile (*bahr al-Nil*)," though they later relocated from this river fortress to a mountain fortress "which commanded the city from the 250 foot eminence on which it stood" (Ayalon, "Mamluks" unpaginated).

83 "The Mamluk Sultanate drew its manpower … up to about the end of the fourteenth century, from the steppes of Southern Russia and Central Asia … Thenceforward, and up to 1517, from the Caucasus area and its vicinity. The Caucasus remained the main source of Mamluk manpower for Egypt until the extermination of the Mamluks … The Ottomans drew their manpower mainly from the Balkans and, to some extent, from Southern Russia" (Ayalon, *Outsiders* 323–4).

84 Before he even became Sultan, the Mamluk Baybars defeated St. Louis in the Seventh Crusade in 1250, crushing the crusader forces at the battle of Mansurah, where Louis's brother died fighting. Louis himself faced the ignominy of being captured, with a massive ransom being demanded for his and his men's release. Jean de Joinville's *Vie de Sainte Louis* (Life of Saint Louis) recounts a

poignant episode where, just after receiving the news of his brother's death, Louis is told to be grateful to God nonetheless for the accomplishments God had given him – swimming across a river, capturing enemy equipment and tents – and Louis humbly responds, "May God be worshipped for all He has given me"; then, Jean tells us, "big tears began to fall from his eyes" (Shaw 226). Baybars also halted the seemingly unstoppable Mongol advance at the famous battle of Ain Jalut, where he commanded the Mamluk forces against Kitbuka's Mongols (after the Ilkhan Hulegu's departure to support the ascension of his brother Kublai in the aftermath of the Great Khan Mongke's death); again, Baybars was not yet Sultan at this point (the Mamluk Qutuz was Sultan at the time), though he ascended to the throne shortly after.

85 Later in the century, another infamous Italian slaver, Gian Galeazzo Visconti – the Duke of Milan, no less – treacherously forewarned the Ottoman Sultan Bayezid of the Nicopolis Crusade of 1398; after their defeat at Nicopolis by Bayezid, many Christians and crusaders were subsequently enslaved. This Italian slaver's betrayal of his fellow Christians to Saracens has the dubious distinction of being memorialized in an extraordinary Middle English romance, the *Alliterative Morte Arthure*, where the Visconti is transformed into a heinous cannibalistic giant of vast wealth and loathsome appetites who preys on humans "in the country of Constantine" (l. 1187). For a discussion, see *Empire of Magic* 166–8.

86 Being of racially heterogeneous composition, Mamluks, even procreating only among themselves, can be assumed to have created mixed genetic races within their own military race. So-called "pure Mamluk blood" was also not sustained across the generations, though the later dynasty of Circassian Mamluks represented another attempt within this military race to circle the wagons (see discussion below) when whole families emigrated from the Caucasus (Ayalon, "Muslim City").

87 Besides the Italian slavers discussed here, other ethnoracial groups that included Muslims and Jews also trafficked in slaves, but attention to all would require a different book from this volume on the European Middle Ages. Simon Barton registers the activity of Muslim slavers in Al-Andalus who sold European slave women to other Muslims, adding that one source also refers "to the sale of a number of Christian women by Jewish merchants in ninth-century Mérida" (*Conquerors* 34). Phillips finds that of the slave traders supplying Andalusia, "Muslim and Jewish merchants predominated in the early period. Sale documents indicate that Christian merchants tended to replace Jews in the slave trade beginning in the twelfth century" (*Slavery in Medieval and Early Modern Iberia* 59). The European slavers however attract special attention for their spectacular ruthlessness in circumventing Latin Christendom's interests in the international arena of war.

88 "The Bahriyya [the originating dynasty of Bahri Mamluk sultans] ... had been recruited chiefly from Kipchak Turks, whose homeland at that period was in southern Russia and the Crimea" (P. M. Holt 139). There were also sporadic groups of Mongol immigrants – slave and free – from the lands of the Ilkhanate, but "of much greater and lasting importance was the change in recruitment from Turks to Circassians, begun by Kalavun [Qalawun] to form his Burjiyya garrison in the Citadel of Cairo. Turkish and Circassian Mamluks confronted one another in the struggle for power as long as the Kalavunic dynasty survived. The usurpation of the sultanate by the Circassian Barkuk marked the final ascendancy of his ethnic group" (P. M. Holt 139).

89 Ayalon's assertion that "no Turk ever became sultan" during the Circassian period is extreme and disputed by other Mamluk scholars. But Ayalon's magisterial status in Mamluk studies, and extensive analysis of documentation, lend weight to the overall trajectory of his account of racial transformation.

90 In Islamic Spain, the Mamluks came from North Africa, sub-Saharan Africa, and Europe, but "with the 'Slavs' (Europeans) the most important group among them" (Phillips, *Slavery in Medieval and Early Modern Spain* 57). "The predominant element," Phillips tells us, "consisted of Slavs and other Europeans ... [and] In time, many Slavs came to occupy important posts in

Islamic Spain, as freedmen or as slaves": *Slavery in Medieval and Early Modern Spain* 120). The ethnoracial apartness of these Iberian Mamluk Slavs – called "the silent ones" by the inhabitants of Córdoba, Phillips says, because of their lack of proficiency in Arabic – many of whom "attained freed status and formed families," is seen by Phillips as corrosive: "Their presence disrupted the balance of ethnic forces in the caliphate and hastened its decline. Their role declined with the end of the caliphate in the early eleventh century, when many of them migrated to certain of the *taifa* kingdoms, the city-states that replaced the unified caliphate, where they eventually became rulers of Almería, Badajoz, Denia, Mallorca, Murcia, Tortosa, and Valencia" (*Slavery in Medieval and Early Modern Spain* 57). In the *taifa* kingdoms of Al-Andalus, therefore, slaves or ex-slaves that we commonly think of as Caucasian Europeans also came to rule Islamic lands.

91 Ayalon elsewhere adds texture and detail to this story of a perceived insult to Mamluks through the gift of a Mamluk-style garment and a white slave bride: "Sultan al-Nasir Abu al-Sadat Muhammad ... ruled for little more than three years (901–4/1495–8), and ... was described as bloodthirsty, frivolous, though generous and brave. He set his mind on building a unit of black arquebusiers, to the great chagrin of the Mamluks. When the Sultan decided to have the black commander of that unit, Farajallah, marry a white Circassian girl, and bestow upon him a tunic usually worn by a Mamluk, the Mamluks revolted, killed Farajallah, and the unit was disbanded. Shortly afterwards the Sultan himself was murdered" (*Eunuchs* 192).

92 By contrast to the racial enclave created by the Circassian Mamluks of Egypt, Phillips shows how the rulers of Al-Andalus made simultaneous use of white European and black African Mamluks (*Slavery in Medieval and Early Modern Iberia* 57). Though the Caucasian element – "the 'Slavs' (Europeans)" – were "the most important group," "brought in as children, converted to Islam, and given an education in Arabic," nonetheless Al-Hakam II (ruled 961–76) not only made use of Slavs but also had "a unit of black soldiers as his personal guard" (*Slavery in Medieval and Early Modern Iberia* 57). "There was another group of slave soldiers, this one in Granada at the end of the Muslim period. Called *gacis*, they were black African slaves imported by Granada's rulers to help defend Granada at the very end of the Christian reconquest. After the Christians took Granada in 1492, many of the *gacis* went to North Africa, while others remained as dependents of prominent Muslim families" (Phillips, *Slavery in Medieval and Early Modern Iberia* 120).

93 P. M. Holt suggests that Ladjin of the Bahri dynasty was a Turk (*Age* 105, 139), and in the Burji dynasty the sultan Khushkadam was "possibly a Byzantine Greek," and Temurbogha an Albanian (195). Ziada calls both Khushkadam and Timurbogha Greeks ("Mamluk ... 1291–1517" 502, 504). P. M. Holt singles out Qalawun, Baybar's successor in the Bahri dynasty, as initiating the recruitment of Circassians "from the eastern coastlands of the Black Sea" to strengthen his position against the Turkish Mamluks, with Qalawun's successor, the sultan Al-Ashraf Khalil, continuing Circassian recruitment (105).

94 Assigned to the upbringing of Mamluks, and serving as tutors of future sultans, eunuchs were important in governance and the war machine (Ayalon, *Eunuchs* 9, 188–9). Ayalon retails a story about the eunuch-commander Bilal al-Mughithi: A "pitch black Abyssinian ... who served many rulers ... was the educator of ... [the] heir designate of Sultan Qalaun [Qalawun] ... was held in extremely high respect, and in official audiences ... used to sit above all the other amirs of the state ... Qalaun, on seeing him, would say 'I used to carry the slippers of that eunuch whenever he went to see Sultan al-Malik al-Salih [and kept carrying them] until he went out. Only then would I give them back to him' ... He was more than eighty years old when he died in 699/1299 accompanying the Sultan al-Nasir Muhammad b. Qalaun in his campaign against the Tatars" (*Eunuchs* 188–9).

Their indispensability meant that eunuchs were numerous: The Abbasid Caliph Al-Muqtadir had "11,000 eunuchs, 7,000 of whom were black and 4,000 were white" (Ayalon, *Eunuchs* 16). Slavs were also said to be prized as eunuchs, especially in Iraq of the ninth century (Murray 107).

Ayalon finds only four "races" of eunuchs in the Mamluk sultanate itself: "Greeks," "Abyssinians," "Indians," and West Africans, with "Greeks" being the only "white ('Caucasian') eunuchs … imported to that Sultanate," and says that unlike the Mamluks, "there is no indication that any of the racial or regional elements within that body [of eunuchs] ever acted as a group" (*Mamluk* 273, 282).

Ayalon traces the decline of Mamluk rule to the ascension to power of eunuchs at court, and what he calls "the effemination of the court" as favorite concubines, "slave girls," songstresses, and other women accrued power and influence (*Mamluk* 284–94). Since eunuchs were "essential not only for the upkeep of the harem … but also for the success of the Mamluk socio-military system … a great and formidable triangle was created in Islam, consisting of three elements: women, eunuchs, and Mamluks, with the eunuchs forming the connecting link between the other two elements" (*Eunuchs* 9).

95 From Carolingian court documents and capitularies and Islamic records, Heck argues that Islamdom "may have been a targeted beneficiary of Charlemagne's 'open market' economic policies – as sundry medieval Arabic geographies provide no small amount of evidence of ongoing trade between the Carolingian and Abbasid empires" (181).

96 "Charlemagne's last currency issue, struck at the onset of the 9th Gregorian century, precisely matched the Abbasid silver dirham in weight, and even bore Arabic inscriptions from the Qur'an that glorified Allah" (Heck 228).

97 An anonymous reviewer astutely points out that "Harun, as the ruler of the Abbasid empire whose capital was Baghdad, was the enemy of the Umayyad ruler of the Caliphate headquartered at Córdoba, and [] it was the Umayyad caliphate that was Charlemagne's mortal enemy along the Frankish-Iberian border. This Umayyad/Abbasid enmity makes Charlemagne's connection with Harun al-Rashid much less odd than it might otherwise appear. It was an example of the old adage that 'the enemy of my enemy is my friend.' And of course, the Abbasid empire was a critical source of the silver that fueled the late 8th and early 9th century Frankish economy." Though the Umayyad state in Al-Andalus would not actually become a caliphate until Abd al-Rahman III declared himself caliph a century after Charlemagne's death, this reviewer is shrewd to point out that what appears odd in geopolitics is really a canny political calculation.

98 Heck suggests that several of the Quran's precepts were "founded on the redeeming merits of trade," including the injunction that personal property and surplus capital ought to be put to "optimal productive use" (322). "The pursuit of private profit motive … was unquestionably a powerful driving force … doctrinal sanctions, and their implied encouragement of personal gain through productive private enterprise, were likewise strongly supported in medieval Islamic exegetical literature," and the "merits of earning a livelihood specifically through commerce is emphatically underscored" in *hadith* (322–3). Heck concludes: "The sources thus leave little doubt that the quest for trade-driven gain was to be among the foremost economic aspirations of devout Muslims" (323). "Such early attempts at free market exegesis would culminate in the monumental treatises of the renowned 8th–9th/14th–15th century economic historian Ibn Khaldun, whose cogent descriptions of the manifestations of medieval Arab 'profit motive' are defined in concepts that can only be described as *laissez-faire* in precept" (Heck 324).

In contrast to what Heck refers to as "such forward economic thinking," the medieval Christian Church censured the profit motive and the acquisition of wealth with moralistic denunciations. "As a consequence, while the Church was laboriously teaching that 'it is easier for a camel to pass through the eye of a needle than for a rich man to enter Heaven,' and 'you cannot serve God and mammon,' Muslim caravans were carrying merchandise to the distant corners of Asia – and ships bearing their commodities ranged from Japan to the furthermost reaches of Africa" (Heck 235). "This consolidation, combined with the rich natural resources that their conquered provinces contained, thus afforded great capital liquidity to the embryonic Islamic state … wealth produced by 'private sector productivity' . . . provided the financing that underwrote the private economic base that empowered the medieval Muslims to become pioneers of science and the contemporary masters of technological innovation. It was the 'leisure time' made possible by such wealth that propelled Islamic civilization to its cultural apogee in the early Middle Ages" (Heck 326).

99 Heck, Goitein and Friedman, Udovitch, and Abu-Lughod believe it likely that the idea of the European *commenda* system had its beginnings in Islamic contracts like the *qirad*, *muqarada*, or *mudarabah* (Heck 243–5). But even if the evidence here is inconclusive, "there is no question whatsoever that the Islamic 'double sales contract' was directly copied by the merchants of medieval Europe . . . it even took on the Latin technical term *mohatra*, after its Arabic equivalent: mukhatarah" (Heck 245). Abu-Lughod observes that documents "largely from Iraq" show that the *commenda* contracts had been "fully codified by the eighth and ninth centuries" (218).

100 Of the six Christian ships docked at the harbor of Jaffa to aid the crusaders at Jerusalem with food supplies, armaments, and siege materials, two were Genoese, and the skill of Genoese engineers was instrumentally useful in building siege engines at Jerusalem (Runciman 1: 282, 284).

101 Runciman, ever the Byzantinist, documents in detail the progress of this unruly fleet as it set forth in 1098 under Daimbert, raiding Byzantine ports and cities en route to aiding crusaders, and the role of Daimbert and the Pisans in politicking among the crusade barons – helping Bohemond to besiege Lattakieh, for instance, to the horror of Raymond of Toulouse – and notes the mendacity of Daimbert in particular (1: 299, 300–1).

102 Runciman sums up the consequences of such Italian gains: "the concessions they demanded and obtained meant that the Frankish governments in the East lost much of their potential revenue" (2: 16). In addition to Italian merchant colonies, there were also "establishments owned by Marseilles in Acre, Jaffa, Tyre and Jebail, and by Barcelona in Tyre" (Runciman 2: 294). Crusading also brought the more usual kind of gain: "Doge Domenico Michiel led a large Venetian fleet to Palestine" that in 1123 "won a great victory over the Egyptian fleet near the port of Ascalon . . . the Venetian ships captured ten Egyptian vessels loaded with rich spices, silks, tapestries, and precious stones" (Robbert 395).

103 "Tunisia was another area where Venetian merchant diplomats negotiated treaties . . . With Pisan merchants already firmly established, the Venetian doge Jacopo Tiepolo in 1231 made a formal compact with the rulers of Tunis to ensure the safety of Venetians, their merchandise, and their shipping. Although the treaty was to run for forty years, the Venetians and the Hafsid rulers of Tunisia renewed it in 1251" (Robbert 443). Venice in the thirteenth century had commercial privileges in Egypt, Tunis, Cilician Armenia, Konya, and the Black Sea coasts (Robbert 451).

104 Venice participated in crusading up to the Fifth Crusade, beyond which "except to further its quarrel with Genoa, Venice did not participate in any other thirteenth-century crusade . . . Of all the crusading expeditions before 1291, Venice had participated most fully and gained most from the Fourth Crusade" (Robbert 442).

105 "During these crusading centuries, Venice became in fact 'the queen of the Adriatic' and the ruler of the richest commercial empire in the Mediterranean" (Robbert 451). The Venetian colony's strength in Constantinople is "attested by the story, which appears [] in the Renaissance chronicle of Daniele Barbaro, that the Venetians debated at length whether or not they ought to transfer the seat of their government [from Venice] to Constantinople" (434).

106 For an overview of volatile conditions in the late Mamluk Burji dynasty, see, e.g., Ziada ("Mamluk . . . 1291–1517"), P. M. Holt (chapter 21), Ashtor, "Economic Decline" and *Social and Economic History* (chapter 8), and Abu-Lughod (chapter 7), *inter alia*. Ziada says that the Mamluks of Barsbey and Jakmak "mishandled the people and treated the women so insolently" that the Sultan was unable to "restrain them from molesting women on festive days," with the result that women "had to be forbidden to appear in the streets" ("Mamluk . . . 1291–1517" 496, 498). Nonetheless, Ziada reminds us, "with all the chaos . . . and notwithstanding the violence of

Mamluk factions and the incurable corruption of the government, the Circassian sultans contrived ... to enlarge its dominions and greatly extend its foreign trade in the Red and Mediterranean seas" ("Mamluk ... 1291–1517" 492).

107 "The last Mamluk Sultan, Tuman Bay, who ascended the throne after the defeat of August 1516 [by the Ottomans, wielding firearms in the field], and who, by the way, had been a Mamluk of [An-Nasir Muhammad] who had paid with his life for his interest in firearms, made every effort to equip the army of the Sultanate with firearms to be used in the open field ... [yet even] at this critical moment, when their existence was at stake, the Mamluks themselves did not use these weapons but entrusted them to units composed of semi-civilians and black slaves, exactly as in the past" (Ayalon, "Firearms" unpaginated).

108 Reynald de Châtillon is remembered in history and popular culture – dramatized in movies such as Ridley Scott's "Kingdom of Heaven" in the West, and Youssef Chahine's "Saladin" in the Middle East – for harassing pilgrim caravans in the Hijaz (the story goes that Reynald threatened and insulted Saladin's sister, for which Saladin later killed Reynald with his own hands). But Reynald's naval raiding on the Red Sea and his attacks on coastal cities of the Arabian peninsula (Runciman 2: 436–7) had the more important economic goal of challenging Egypt's control of the Red Sea and hence the lucrative India trade. Unfortunately, unlike their predecessors, the Mamluks of Egypt invested little in naval power: "there was never a permanent Mamluk navy. When the Mamluks launched a flotilla or fleet, this was done only to make possible a reprisal raid for some ... Frankish victory. During their rule the Mamluks built six or seven of these fleets, roughly one every 40 or 50 years. As the ships were constructed hastily, they became unusable in a short time, with the result that whenever a naval raid was planned, a new navy had to be constructed" (Ayalon, *Studies* 6).

109 See, in particular, Ashtor, "Economic Decline," *Social and Economic History*, "Levantine Sugar Industry," *Levant Trade*, and Abu-Lughod (chapter 7).

110 For an overview of the improvements in agricultural methods and systems, the expansion of varieties and strains of crops, and innovations in irrigation that produced the "Green Revolution" of early Islamic civilization, supporting rapid demographic growth and economic prosperity, see Watson.

111 The lower end of the Egyptian population estimate is four million. Dols's extensive and careful calculations, however, suggest that the actual figure was closer to the upper limit.

112 The great historian of the Mamluks, Al-Maqrizi, estimated that "from one-third to two-fifths of the combined population of Egypt and Syria died in the course of the plague" (Abu-Lughod 238). Dols's figures suggest that population mortality in Cairo may have been as great as 50 percent (400–1). Another historian of the Mamluks, Ibn Habib, says that two-thirds of Egypt's population died (Ayalon, *Outsiders* 9).

113 "In Europe the plague led to great shifts in the distribution of population, dislodging peasants and serfs from their land and causing an exodus of urbanites fleeing the worst conditions in their areas. In Egypt, the population was less free to move. Hemmed in by deserts and tied to the land as part of the Mamluk amirs' fiefs...the 'serfs' had no forests to which they could flee and urbanites had no untilled land to clear and cultivate ... the unforeseen positive consequences experienced in Europe after the plague were not paralleled in Egypt" (Abu-Lughod 238).

114 "Syria was even more impoverished than Egypt. Down to the end of the thirteenth century it had been the battleground of the Mamluks with the Franks and Mongols. It was subsequently the region in which Mamluk factional struggles were frequently fought out, and early in the fifteenth century it was once again devastated by the invasion of Timur Leng" (P. M. Holt 194).

115 For an argument that Constantinople is the model for King Arthur's glittering and brilliant court of Caerleon (and, later, "Camelot") when Arthur's legend materializes in literature for the first time in the European Middle Ages, see *Empire of Magic* 328–9.

116 Edward's crusade of 1269–74 and the overtures between him and Abaga Khan have been described as "the nearest thing to real Mongol-Frankish military coordination that was ever to be achieved" (Amitai 76). See Chapter 6 for a discussion of rapprochements between the West and the Mongols, especially in the section on Marco Polo.

117 Maria was originally intended for Hulegu, the first Ilkhan of the Iranian Ilkhanate, but was bestowed on Hulegu's son and successor, Abaga, the second IIkhan, because of Hulegu's death. More than one Greek Christian Byzantine princess – like the princess of Tars but in real time, we might say – was offered to the Mongols in the hope of securing alliances against various Muslim factions. Maria's sister, Euphrosyne, was betrothed to Nogai of the Golden Horde, and in the reign of Andronicus II a Byzantine princess was offered to Oljeitu, yet another Ilkhan (Van Millingen 272, 275). The grandson of Abaga and son of Arghun Khan, Oljeitu had been baptized and given the name "Nicholas," after Pope Nicholas IV (as we saw above), at the behest of his father Arghun, but later converted to Islam, like his brother Ghazan.

118 "Thus, a small number of European ocean-going ships of a new kind, armed with a new kind of weapon, succeeded in robbing the Muslims, almost overnight, of the absolute hegemony which they had exercised for hundreds of years over the most important international trade route of those days. The way was now paved for the building of the large empires of modern times, which drew their might from their dominions overseas, and within the confines of each of which were included millions of Muslims" (Ayalon, "Firearms" unpaginated).

4

Color

Epidermal Race, Fantasmatic Race: Blackness and Africa in the Racial Sensorium

[T]he normal medieval standard [is that] black is the color of hell and blackness of skin an outward pointer to heathen blackness of soul, just as the physical beauty of [European] courtly characters reflects their inner qualities. This association of black men with the devil and blackness of skin with sin is firmly rooted in early Christian exegesis, which continues a tradition of classical antiquity.

> D. A. Wells, "The Middle Dutch *Moriaen*, Wolfram von Eschenbach's *Parzival*, and Medieval Tradition" (263)

Augustine, in speaking of the universality of the Christian faith, says that even the Ethiopians ... are capable of receiving God's grace. [He] echoes Homer, who calls the Ethiopians *Eschatoi andron*, the "most remote of men."

> Kathleen Ann Kelly, "'Blue' Indians, Ethiopians, and Saracens in Middle English Narrative Texts" (43)

"For black women are hotter [a reference to the classical and medieval theory of humors], and most of all dusky women, who are the sweetest to have sex with, so lechers say ... because the mouth of their vulva is temperate and gently embraces the penis..."

> Peter Biller, "Black Women in Medieval Scientific Thought" (486), quoting Albertus Magnus in his *Quaestiones super De animalibus* (c. 1258)

"Why does *the Ethiopian* come among us?"

> Gay L. Byron, quoting from the *Apophthegmata partum*, relating the hagiography of Ethiopian Moses (sixth century CE), in *Symbolic Blackness and Ethnic Difference in Early Christian Literature* (129)

STUDIES ON premodern race have often focused on color as the paramount index of race – so that attitudes toward *blackness* are sought as the deciding factor adjudicating whether racial behavior and phenomena existed in antiquity and the Middle Ages.[1] To complicate our views on medieval race, I have thus far emphasized multiple locations of race over a singular epidermal focus: fanning out attention to how religion, the state, economic interests, colonization, war, and international contests for hegemony, among other determinants, have materialized race and have configured racial attitudes, behavior, and phenomena across the centuries. But attention to color, and physiognomy characterized in tandem with color, are now the focus of this chapter.

At the heart of scholarly interest in color – I have argued in articles over the years, and in Chapter 1 above – has lurked a spectacular enigma in the field of vision: the ascension of *whiteness* to supremacy as a category of identity in the definition of the Christian European subject (see Heng, "Jews"; "Invention … 1"; "Invention … 2"). Classicist James Dee, puzzling the enigma of color, has a vignette that tellingly gets to the point of color-as-race:

> In my classroom-teaching days, I used to hold up a blank sheet of paper and say, "Now *this* is undoubtedly white," then put my other hand in front of it, and add, "But if you *also* want to call *this* white, there's some serious semantic distortion going on that might be hard to explain to a visitor from outer space."
>
> (159)

The range of hues visible in Caucasian flesh tones – cream, pink, beige, and E. M. Forster's famous compound, "pinko-grey" – is only the starting point for Dee's question: "did the Greeks and Romans think of themselves as 'white people' or as part of a 'white race'?" (158). Surveying a host of documents attesting that virile, admired heroes in the Greco-Roman world, like the Greek Odysseus, are depicted as dark-skinned while women, sickly people, "pasty-faced philosophers, and cowards" are deprecated as pale, Dee finds that "the concept of a distinct 'white race' was not present in the ancient world" (162, 163).

Greco-Roman antiquity – revered and embraced by the Middle Ages as its superior in civilization and knowledge, and possessed of supreme cultural authority – did not enshrine whiteness of skin as an admirable, let alone a defining characteristic central to the authority of group identity, Dee finds. In the Mediterranean, where races, peoples, and dermal pigments intermixed for millennia, this is not perhaps so startling a conclusion.

But Madeline Caviness takes up the puzzle of when humans in Western Europe began to see their own flesh tones as identical to whiteness. In a remarkable article with fifty-nine full-color images, Caviness stresses the significant departure from traditions of antiquity that innovation of this kind entailed, especially for the visual arts. The visual arts are especially important, she asserts, because they "do ideological work more powerfully than texts": because we privilege sight over our other senses (Caviness 1), and also perhaps (though Caviness does not say this explicitly) because of visual art's beguiling sense of immediacy and intimacy – the impression visuality imparts of being more readily and easily accessed, without mediation, than literary texts which have to be read, word-by-word, and then painstakingly interpreted.

A picture, it seems to people, not only conveys more than a thousand words, but also offers less hindrance to immediate absorption and understanding. Not least of all, in the Middle Ages, visual art can be seen by a thousand times more people: While literacy is confined to a tiny percentage of elites, statues, stained glass, and frescoes literally reach multitudes.

A shift in thinking about the skin color of Europeans, Caviness finds, occurred in the Latin West in the second half of the thirteenth century (in this, we should allow her the courtesy of recognizing the likelihood of uneven development, as innovations occurred earlier in some regions and later in others, or were ignored in yet other regions):

In a tradition that stemmed from antiquity, Byzantine and early medieval painters applied heavy layers of pigment to faces and bodies, working up the relief contours to pinkish highlights. Typically, only the whites of the eyes are pure white ... Early twelfth-century European works that have little to do with Byzantine style – such as the great Catalan wall paintings or a famous service book from Limoges in France – also depict rich flesh tones, dramatically contrasted with white garments ... European artists adhered to these traditions through the early thirteenth century. Even in the north, they usually built a face up from a bluish or greenish modeling wash, through varied tones of brown and pink, to highlights, and much brighter whites of the eyes. These effects can be seen in English works of the late twelfth century; the Great Psalter from Canterbury, Paris, Bibliothèque Nationale MS lat. 8846, and the Bible in Winchester Cathedral Library provide good examples of this chromatic range in manuscript painting ... Layered modeling is also seen in contemporary glass paintings in Canterbury Cathedral ... The base color in this period was almost always a rosy-pink glass containing manganese.

(17)[2]

It thus seems that, for several centuries, in visual depictions the white of the human eye was seen as truly white, whereas European flesh was variously seen to range across rich tones of pink and pinkish brown, contrasting strongly with the whites of human eyes. Looking over an eleventh-century medical manuscript containing a commentary on Hippocrates, Caviness sees that "the nude figures are quite dark, and evidently still owe much to an ancient Greek or Roman prototype" (17). By contrast, in a fourteenth-century medical manuscript from France showing a sequence of physician–patient interactions, "all the faces and hands are opaque white, and the hair very light" (17):

> Two south Italian medical works, from the 12th and the 13th centuries, also provide a contrast in the depiction of bare skin. The earlier artists still adhered to rich flesh tints giving ruddy complexions, and variously black or brown hair ... By the second half of the thirteenth century this coloration had changed dramatically: In scenes of bathing in Peter of Eboli's tract on the curative baths at Pozzuoli the artist exposes pure white bodies and gold or red hair ... These examples in medical manuscripts are of particular interest because there is no reason for them to be impacted by theological ideas that elided the good with light and purity ... in fact, to be pallid was long recognized as a sign of ill health, as now in the phrase "dead white."

(17)

But by the late Middle Ages, Caviness shows us, "saints in paradise gleam as white as their garments, like [a] fourteenth-century Saint John from York Minster" (18). "A virginal saint might be celebrated...with a pearly complexion and 'pure' white garment ... At some stage, Christians appropriated this sanctity by depicting their kind as truly 'white'" (Caviness 18). Whiteness was also eventually equated with colorlessness: "By then it had become the norm for glass-painters to use colorless glass instead of flesh tints" (Caviness 18). That is to say, by the late Middle Ages, in their visual art, Latin Christian Europeans not only came to depict their skin color as white, but made whiteness literally transparent, invisible.

In order to "pinpoint the shift to a preference for 'white people'," Caviness moves from a broad survey of medieval visual art to a linked set of localized examples from France in the reign of Louis IX, the famed crusader king (18). She calls attention to the fact that the artists of the psalter made for Ingeborg of Denmark, Louis's grandfather's queen, circa 1195, still "modeled flesh in tones of pink and brown" (Caviness 18):

> Forty years later [Louis's] mother, Blanche of Castile who ruled during his minority, had much lighter colors painted in her Psalter ... The glass Louis IX and Blanche had painted in the 1240s for the palace chapel in Paris, the famous Sainte Chapelle, used colorless or barely tinted glass for the faces, and this became the norm ... Louis' own Psalter followed suit about 1255–70 ... For an older generation of art historians the predominant new complexion and facial type appeared to be no more significant than other stylistic changes, in accord with their notions of a Gothic era. I view it as a dramatic change in representational code, with broad ramifications.
>
> (Caviness 18)

The visual art made for one family across three generations thus compactly allows Caviness to localize to the second half of the thirteenth century Europeans' awareness of their skin tones as *white*, rather than pink, brown, cream, or a medley of tints, and then see that whiteness of skin as transparent – as no color at all.

For Caviness, the mid-thirteenth-century shift in artistic conventions – the "dramatic change in representational code" – that results in Latin Christian European flesh being imagined and visualized as *white*, and not flesh-colored, was an artistic response built up from accumulated encounters with palpably *non*-white peoples. Like many medievalists working in a variety of disciplines, Caviness sees the twelfth and thirteenth centuries as an expanded age of encounter:

> One reason that European Christians had come to regard themselves as white by 1250 may be that they had been coming in contact in large numbers with brown infidels, and with ... sub-Saharan Africans ... There are records of black so-called Ethiopians even in the north.
>
> (22)

Until the advent of that formidable period of prolonged, enforced mingling we know as the Crusades – the period of "the first European expansion," as Jean Devisse puts it (35) – Western Europe "no longer had any contact with blacks. All that was known about them was an abstraction – blackness itself" (Devisse 57).

If Caviness is correct, it seems such absence of substantive contact with black-skinned peoples did not lead Western Europeans to contemplate their own whiteness, nor to depict their own flesh tones as white. Scholars such as Devisse suggest that the relative absence of black-skinned peoples instead freed the European imagination to conjure with the meaning of *blackness*. Leaving aside for now the enigma of whiteness, we thus turn to the more traditional focus in discussions of epidermal race – blackness – in the centuries before the age of expanded encounter.

Out of Africa: The Good, the Bad, and the Piebald, or, Politics of the Epidermis, Part 2

Before the period of encounter that leads visual artists in Europe to meditate on whiteness, the relative absence of contact with black-skinned humans, Devisse and others suggest, offered Europeans fertile ground to muse on the meaning of the color black as "an abstraction" in discourses driven largely by theological imperatives:

> As human beings, the black and the African in general presented no direct problem, physical or metaphysical, to the Western European [in this time period]. Hence a total hostility to blackness could take root, apparently, without jeopardizing the fundamental idea of the vocation of all men to salvation. The fears and terrors of the Occidental were centered on blackness itself.
>
> (Devisse 57)

Devisse's insight that *blackness as a hermeneutic* was able to grow and thrive in Western Europe in the absence of substantial contact with living, black-skinned human beings – an absence that freed the hermeneutic development of blackness from being troubled by representatives in the flesh whose salvation would have to be considered – is supported by a parallel insight among scholars of medieval English Jews. After the expulsion of Jewish communities from England, in the absence of Jews of the flesh, there was a remarkable proliferation of imaginary and hermeneutic depictions of Jews, unbound by considerations of presence (see Heng, "Jews," for a bibliography).

The growth of an accumulating discourse on blackness from the end of the Roman era through the eleventh century – a discourse that made possible ingenious, paradoxical play with color that granted the great theological minds of the Middle Ages the satisfaction of subtle and witty meditations on the nature of salvation, as I noted in Chapter 1 – thus flourished in that relative absence of the real which conduces to the exploitation of possibilities inherent in fantasmatic race. "In Western Europe, at least until the twelfth century," Devisse flatly notes, "there were simply no black people except in some very limited areas" (51).

In contemplating epidermal race, it is thus useful to recognize a distinction between *hermeneutic blackness* in which exegetical considerations are paramount and often explicitly foregrounded, and *physiognomic blackness linked to the characterization of black Africans* in phenomena that extended beyond immediate theological exegesis. It is equally vital, of course, to recognize that distinct, and distinguishable, discourses on blackness might also at times converge and intertwine for ideological ends.

Devisse offers a prolonged meditation on how black became the theological color of sin and evil, tracing Biblical exegesis over the centuries to mark stages in discursive development of hermeneutic blackness (58–62).[3] But while duly noting that blackness per se "as a *sign* of evil" was not identical with "conscious hostility to black people," Devisse nonetheless observes that Ethiopians, as a symbolic construct personifying sin, invariably became indistinguishable from an African population whose blackness blazoned to all Christendom their innate sinfulness, and identified Ethiopia as the land of sin (59, 61, emphasis added).[4]

Dorothy Verkerk's study of the Ashburnham Pentateuch, one of the oldest illuminated manuscripts of Western Europe, suggests that "a transitional moment in the emergence of the pejorative representation of blacks in medieval art" might be the late sixth to eighth centuries (60). In the Ashburnham Pentateuch's illustrations of the tenth plague, the enemies of Moses and the Israelites are depicted as black, and Verkerk cites parallel examples in late antique and early medieval visual art, though, she cautions, artistic conventions "are not fully worked out" in this "intermediate stage" (60). Thanks to the authority of patristic exegesis, however, with its insistence on identifying blackness with sin and spiritual corruption, "black skin now becomes a metonym for evil . . . the sinful non-Christian now has a face and it is black" (Verkerk 63).

In Chapter 1, I carefully distinguished between the epidermal politics of *sin* and the epidermal politics of *the infernal*. A blackness linked to sin registers a state of abjection vitally important to the salvational discourse that is a cornerstone of Christian doctrine: The blackness of sin and sinners can function as a sign of potential future redemption and ultimate glory. By contrast, since the infernal is not redeemable in Christian doctrine, a blackness associated with the Devil and hell is a more damning kind of blackness.

Debra Strickland, however, implicitly suggests that an easy hermeneutic slippage occurred between identifying Ethiopians with sin, and identifying them with the Devil, pointing out that "Didymus the Blind (c. 313–98) reports that Ethiopians belong to the cult of the Devil," and "medieval exempla [narrate how] the Devil is fond of disguising himself as an Ethiopian in order to menace the faithful" (80).

An instructive example of how hermeneutic blackness performs in exegetical, allegorical, or symbolic ways in visual art might be Nicholas of Verdun's 1181 enameled plaque of an ambo at Klosterneuburg depicting the Biblical Queen of Sheba's visit to Solomon (Devisse 133 plate 103; see *Figure 10*). In the enamel, the Queen of Sheba's *skin* is colored black, but the refined, elegant lines of her *face*, carefully limned in gold like the rest of her person, cannot be distinguished from the standard iconography for European faces (by contrast, one of her attendants bearing the Queen's gifts to Solomon is shown with tightly kinked hair [Devisse 133]).[5] Chronologically preceding the era of Christ, the story of the Queen of Sheba – a popular symbolic and allegorical personage in the Middle Ages – is the story of a *virtuous pagan*: Her soul's as yet unredeemed nature, expressed by the Queen's blackness, is thus neatly twinned visually with the Queen's exalted Biblical status and potential for future redemption in eschatological time, expressed by her physiognomic indifference from Europeans.[6]

By contrast to Nicholas of Verdun's black-skinned but Europeanized Queen of Sheba, the mid-thirteenth-century Black St. Maurice of Magdeburg Cathedral – a figure who bears important sociocultural and political meaning, as Jean Devisse and Paul Kaplan ("Introduction") have separately argued – depicts a black knight-martyr of unmistakable African physiognomy. No less beautiful, and more vital, than the formal elegance of Nicholas' Queen of Sheba, the physiognomic realism and naturalistic expressiveness of Maurice's sensitive visage seem enigmatically to signal a panoply of interests not exhausted by theological exegesis (*Figure 9*).

In this, Maurice resembles, perhaps, the black African figures of thirteenth-century medieval literature – Moriaen, Belakane, Feirefiz – enigmatic others whose strikingly layered, thoughtful depictions seem to invite a range of reflections that extend beyond theological obsessions. I discuss these and other black Africans in medieval literature later in this chapter.

Exceptions like Maurice notwithstanding, *within* Christianity the color black accrued a slate of negative significations that yoked the "abstraction" of blackness (as Devisse puts it), to sin, ignorance, shame, error, and the state of unredemption preceding forgiveness and salvation, as well as – more perniciously and unforgivingly – to the devil, the demonic, the infernal, and the damned.[7] Color, of course, was also deployed to certify distinctions *between* religions and communities of faith. Just as the Queen of Sheba's pre-Christian, pagan status can be visually signaled through blackness, Saracens in

Figure 9. Face (detail) of the Black St. Maurice of Magdeburg. Magdeburg Cathedral, Germany, 1220–1250. Reproduced with permission from the Menil Foundation, Houston; Hickey and Robertson, Houston; and Harvard University's Image of the Black Project.

literature and in visual art are also sometimes depicted as black-skinned, as many scholars have noted.[8]

A more troubling development was the visualization of *black skin in tandem with a sub-Saharan phenotype*, in the portrayal of torturers and executioners, especially the killers and tormentors of revered people such as John the Baptist and Christ – a phenomenon Devisse meticulously surveys from the late twelfth century through the thirteenth century, a period of intense antiblack virulence in artistic thematics of this kind.[9]

"The executioner with 'Negroid' features survived for a long period" across the centuries, prompting Devisse to ask: "How many generations of Christians have been conditioned by looking at a grimacing black man torturing Christ or his saints?" (72, 80). Devisse and Caviness both intimate that such an artistic thematic may perhaps reverberate from close encounters of a local kind, and each points to a report by the Abbot of Nogent:

> In his autobiography, Guibert of Nogent tells of the fear inspired in the community of Laon in 1112 by an immense baptized Ethiopian hangman in the service of Bishop Gaudri, and it became common to represent one or more of the flagellants of Christ as black.
>
> (Caviness 22)

> What is the origin of this iconography? One might hold Guibert of Nogent responsible by reason of his story about Baudry, bishop of Laon, and his "black" laboring man, who terrified those who saw him.
>
> (Devisse 79)

In medieval European literature, black Saracens abound from the twelfth century on – in the shape of hideous giants, troops ranged in the battlefield against Christians, and enemies

Figure 10. Solomon and the Queen of Sheba. Nicholas of Verdun's enameled plaque of an ambo, Klosterneuburg, 1181. Museum des Chorherrenstiftes, Klosterneuburg.
Reproduced with permission from Erich Lessing and *LessingImages.com*.

whose bodies may also bear nonhuman characteristics such as horns, tusks, bristly spines, or skin as hard as iron, or who may issue animal-sounding speech (for example, Saracens who bark like dogs).[10] In the Middle English *Sultan of Babylon*, there is even a black giantess who is the mother of twin giant black babies, fourteen feet long – her infant sons of seven months. Saracen kings may be fully black, like the "loathly" Sultan of Damascus who turns spotless white without taint after his baptism in the *King of Tars*, or piebald, like Feirefiz, the offspring of racial miscegenation between Gahmuret, a fair European Arthurian knight, and Belakane of Zazamanc, a black African queen, in Wolfram von Eschenbach's Middle High German *Parzival*.

So fond is Wolfram, in particular, of imagining black–white racial mixing being played out on the epidermis of offspring that in *Willehalm*, Wolfram jauntily makes Josweiz, another product of sexual mixing across the color line – this time between Matusales, the king of Amatiste who had completely white hair and skin, and a Moorish woman – also black-and-white, like Josweiz' more famous counterpart Feirefiz.[11] David Tinsley shows us that not only do black Saracens like the Sultan of Damascus turn white after being converted to Christianity by a Christian wife white as a swan, but a reverse circuit also runs through the European imaginary: In the Middle High German *King of Moorland*, *Christian European knights turn black* when they are seduced by black women and converted to heathenry (90–1).[12]

Despite their status as the international enemy *par excellence,* however, Saracens are not consistently nor inevitably depicted as black. Jacqueline de Weever has shown us that Saracen princesses in Old French epics of the thirteenth century tend to be offered to audiences as lily white, a strategic bleaching that portrays the women as desirable and appropriate sexual companions for French knights, and conduces, also, to the women's eventual baptism and assimilation into Christian European polities.

Nor are admired Saracen "knights" such as Fierabras/Ferumbras in the French and English romances that bear their names, or the gallant Magariz of Seville in the *Chanson de Roland*, ever depicted as black. In the *Roman de Saladin*, the esteemed Saladin is also not portrayed as black. Indeed, Saladin passes easily for a European knight when he makes a prolonged visit to France, and there champions maidens, triumphs in tournaments, distributes largesse, and becomes the secret *ami* of the French queen. Some of Saladin's *men,* however, in the Middle English *Richard Coer de Lyon*, are black Saracens eaten with relish by the cannibalistic Richard; their black skin, grinning white teeth, and devilish appearance flash prominently before our eyes as the English king gleefully tucks into his human repast (see *Empire of Magic*, chapter 2).

Like the variety of Saracen skin color in literature, a broad color palette exists for the portrayal of Saracen skin tones in visual art, alongside variation also in iconographic markers – swords, shields, headwear, physiognomic features – that identify human figures as Saracens. The secondary literature on the depiction of Saracens is voluminous. In the sections that follow, I sample a few of the more provocative, or relatively overlooked, literary characterizations of black Saracens for what they might tell us about medieval race.

Variation in the visual depiction of Saracens – who may look like black Africans, Jews or Arabs, Indians, Tartars, or Europeans – well expresses a Latin Christian understanding that perhaps two-thirds of the world or more, as Peter the Venerable feared, swarmed with Saracens. Saracens seem to be everywhere in the lands Marco Polo traverses as he travels the world. Though they might under certain conditions be thought of as a single infernal race defined by their religion, or by their shedding of corporate Christian blood – as we saw in Chapter 3 – Saracens can be understood, in their internationalism, to *look* like the variety of the world's peoples. Like the Fourth Lateran Council's Canon 68, which mandated a difference of dress for Jews *and* for Saracens living in Christendom in order to prevent inadvertent sexual mixing between infidels and Latin Christian Europeans, literature and art can also acknowledge that it might sometimes be hard to tell apart the different populations of the Abrahamic faiths just by looking at them.

In the centuries after discourses on blackness-as-negativity had been established, more intriguing perhaps than the portrayal of Saracens as black is the portrayal of *black Christians* in medieval literature and art. Paul Kaplan's remarkable scholarship on the fourteenth- and fifteenth-century rise of the phenomenon of the Black Magus Baltazar (or, sometimes, Caspar) is a sustained study of how, in the context of extreme color virulence in medieval religious discourse, one of the Three Magi can be imagined as black in the visual art of the late Middle Ages (*Rise*). Kaplan and Devisse separately discuss at length the phenomenon also of the Black St. Maurice and briefly note the fashioning of another black African martyr, Gregory the Moor (whose cult, unlike Maurice's, was localized to Cologne).

I therefore end this chapter by taking up again a discussion begun in Chapter 1, on the thirteenth-century Black St. Maurice of Magdeburg. Before resuming the discussion of a black saint, however, I first consider the sudden, intriguing materialization of a Christian black knight in literature, a secular, literary companion to Maurice who, like Maurice, appears and is embraced in the heartlands of Western Europe. But the extraordinary thirteenth-century Middle Dutch romance known as the *Moriaen* is woven around a black knight who – unlike Maurice or the Magus – is not privileged as a sainted martyr or hallowed personage of nativity Christology, but merely arrives as a Christian knight from "Moorland" doggedly seeking social and economic justice.

With only two exceptions, I sample cultural exemplars from the thirteenth century – a period that, relatively early in the era of expanded encounter, posed key questions about epidermal race, and attempted creative and fertile responses in literature and art. By the time of the late Middle Ages, in the fourteenth and fifteenth centuries – as Jean Devisse and Michel Mollat amply demonstrate in their volume of *Image of the Black* that concentrates on the fourteenth through sixteenth centuries – a vast proliferation of exotica makes the depiction of blacks – especially in armorial bearings and heraldry – fashionable, and increasingly commonplace, so that the *topos* of blackness becomes in Europe a reflexive gesture denoting the exotic and foreign, like the late medieval enthusiasm for depictions of wild men and wild folk.[13]

By this time, courts, kings, and nobles played with blackness for purposes of spectacle in performances of masques, pageantry, processions, and balls; *morescas* were danced "as often as possible," and actors recruited to play "black Moors" and "white Moors" (Piponnier and Mane 145). Such fashions presided not only in fashionable France, but even in the far northwest of the European continent. In her discussion of entertainment at the court of James IV of Scotland and in Dunbar's sixteenth-century *The Masque of Blackness*, Louise Fradenburg remarks that

> Face-blackening was an important feature of early disguisings and dramas and of later folk-plays and processions: Chambers cites the Turkish knight, one of the combatants in the (late) Cheshire mummers' play, who is referred to as a "black Morocco dog." A play put on at Roxburghshire is reported as including "Gysarts" dressed in shrouds with faces painted black or blue . . . In the courtly morisco or morris-dance, face-blackening was also employed.
>
> (*City, Marriage, Tournament* 247)

With such proliferation and play, epidermal race is conscripted into the luxuriant vocabulary of court entertainments, and solicited for the sportive pleasures of masquerade by

Europeans donning blackface, even as black African heads and silhouettes became the domesticated familiars of heraldic and armorial signature. Late medieval and early modern epidermal race as masquerade and entertainment, and as collectible souvenirs for heraldic blazoning, makes for fascinating study, but my interest lies in the problems posed, and the responses delivered, when the enigma of epidermal race is fresh, and first rears its head in a culture where a negative discourse on blackness predominated.[14]

Black Knight/White Knight: Trajectories of Fear and Desire, or How Romance Figures Histories of the Outside/Inside

Medieval Europe had a long cultural memory of black Africans. Paul Edwards reminds us that there were black Africans in the auxiliary Roman legions dispersed across the Roman empire, and even in Britain, a small corner of the empire tucked away in the extreme northwest:

> [W]e know from . . . evidence that there were . . . African troops on Hadrian's wall around AD 200 at the time of [the Roman emperor Septimus] Severus's visit. A few miles from Carlisle a *numerous Maurorum* or auxiliary unit of "moors" was stationed at Burgh-by-Sands (*Abavalla*), and its presence is recorded on a stone inscription . . . Another inscription, on a tombstone found on the Wall at South Shields, records the death of "Victor, aged 20, of the Moorish nation, freed by Numerianus."
>
> (Paul Edwards 10)

Edwards repeats arguments arising from archeological analysis of the Roman Cemetery at Trentholme, York, said to furnish "evidence of an early Afro-Romano-British community" centuries before the arrival of "English invaders . . . from Europe" (10–11). If Africans were represented in the Roman imperial armies occupying territories in Europe, they were also in the armies and territories of the Islamic empire; and, after the eighth-century Islamic conquest of Spain, increased encounters with black Africans occurred.

> Evidence of continuing contact between the British Isles and Africa, and of the presence of Africans in the British Isles, is to be found in the records of the Scandinavian settlements in Dublin and Orkney. One of the fragments of ancient annals in Irish . . . records the landing of Black slaves in Ireland in AD 862, after one of the Viking raids in Moorish Spain and North Africa.
>
> (Paul Edwards 11)

Edwards wonders at the odd, anomalous passages in literature that sporadically hint at the scattered presence of Ethiopian-like peoples. A famed medieval Irish tale, *Mesca Ulad*, or "The Intoxication of the Ulster-men," set in the first century but probably composed in the ninth, describes King Conchobar's jester, Róimid, as a man with, "in literal translation, 'an Ethiop face, shiny blue-black' (Old Irish *ethiopacda slemangorm*) and 'short sharp-edged (?bristly) black hair' (*súasmáel dubrintach*)" (Paul Edwards 11).

Icelandic sagas described encounters not only with "Saracens (O. Icelandic *Sarazin*), whom we call infidels of Mohammed" but also with "a good many black men (O. Icelandic *mart blámanna*, literally 'blue men')" (Paul Edwards 12). By the early twelfth century, Geoffrey of Monmouth's semi-legendary history of the kings of Britain, the *Historia Regum*

Britannie, announces that Stonehenge had come *from Africa*, via Spain; and Geoffrey's history even imagines an invasion of Britain by Africans under an African king, which leads to alarming conversions among the local populace away from Christianity (*Empire of Magic* 50–1).

In the decades preceding Geoffrey's writing of British history, Africans did indeed come to Western Europe to defend Islam, in regions relatively close to the British Isles. In what can easily be imagined as an Islamic (re)invasion, the Maghrebi Berber dynasty of the Almoravids under the leadership of Yusuf ibn Tashfin arrived in Iberia at the request of the Taifa kingdoms of Andalusia, who were struggling against the Reconquista forces of Christian Léon and Castile.

Having already amassed territorial conquests in Sudanic/sub-Saharan Africa, the Almoravids brought large numbers of black Africans in their armies, as they began a new chapter in the history of Islamic Spain that included annexing the Taifa kingdoms, and holding back the tides of Christian reconquest. Peter Mark, citing the scholarship of Umar al-Naqar (with Ibn Khallikan as the original source), notes "the presence of 4000 Sudanese troops with Yusuf ibn Tashfin in the battle of al-Zalaqa [the Battle of Sagrajas] in Spain in 1087 A.D." (14 n.16).

Encounters with black Africans did not only take place in the peripheries of Europe: Europeans also made their way out of the Latin West, into the contact zones of Byzantium, the Maghreb, and Egypt. As we saw in Chapter 3, lively mercantile interests brought Latin Christian Europeans, along with cargoes and transshipments (that included, as we saw, cargoes of human slaves) to Byzantium and North Africa in the centuries before, during, and after that long period of encounter we know as the Crusades. There, Sudanic and Trans-Saharan African traders and caravaners were found alongside Arabs, Berbers, and miscellaneous ethnoraces in the markets, emporia, ports, funduqs, cities, towns, and hinterlands.

Ethiopia's conversion to Christianity in the fourth century and Nubia's in the sixth also meant that devout sub-Saharan Africans, just like devout Europeans, made pilgrimages to the Holy Land, and through their pilgrimages established "contact with the western world," as an Ethiopian scholar observes (Sellassie 254).[15] Ethiopian monks were found in Jerusalem – that most visited of international pilgrimage destinations – from the fourth century, admired for their "moral standard" and "purity of life" (Sellassie 112).[16]

Ethiopian pilgrims founded a religious community in Jerusalem from the late Aksumite period of the ninth and tenth centuries (Henze 109; Sellassie 112, 254), and "When the Holy Land was re-occupied by the Muslims led by Salahad-Din in 1189, the Ethiopian community in Jerusalem … migrated to Cyprus," establishing the monastery of St. Anthony in Famagusta and eventually moving to Nicosia, where they founded the church of the Savior of the World (Sellassie 262).

Ethiopian monks were even said to be in charge of the flame that burned continuously in the Church of the Holy Sepulcher in Jerusalem, so honored because an Ethiopian king, Caleb, during the brilliant Aksumite period, had "voluntarily abdicated the throne and entered monastic life in the hermitage of *Abba* Penteléwon, where he ended his days … [and had] sent his crown to Jerusalem to be hung on the Holy Sepulchre" (Sellassie 143).[17]

The impressive hagiography of Ethiopian Moses narrates scenes of dialogue that enshrine the holy man's humility precisely by playing movingly on his awareness of his skin color, and of how blackness is to be read in early Christian hermeneutics.

Most recently analyzed by Gay Byron, the hagiography of Ethiopian Moses soundly registers recognition of black African Christians as formative figures in early Christianity – just as, we might say, hadith about Bilal, the companion of the Prophet who performed the role of muezzin to the Companions, registers the importance of black African Muslims in early Islam.

A finer-grained view of contact between black Africans and Europeans thus refines our perspective of the half-millennium or so in which a discourse on blackness was accumulated before the expanded period of encounter we know as the Crusades. However, though sub-Saharan Africans could be found in the fringes of Western Europe, and though Latin Christian Europeans no doubt encountered Africans in commercial border zones and at Mediterranean pilgrimage sites in the centuries before the Crusades, from the twelfth century on, in the aftermath of the First Crusade, the documentary record registers significant recognition of expanded contact and encounter.

Guibert de Nogent's vignette of the enormous Ethiopian hangman working for Bishop Gaudri of Laon in the early twelfth century is a small example of Africans who appear in the historical record outside Italy, Sicily, Iberia, and Southern Europe – lands where the presence of black Africans is more usually attested, as we shall see later in this chapter. Africans are also markedly encountered in the battlefields, among the ranks of the enemy:

> The blacks who appeared frequently in the Islamic armies faced by the first Crusaders are often described as Ethiopians. Most likely these blacks were actually natives of the northern areas of the Central African steppe (the Sudan), or of the East African coast, but the Western chroniclers preferred to use the term which in classical times had designated all black peoples.
>
> (Kaplan, *Rise* 49)

Unsurprisingly, black Africans who appear in twelfth and thirteenth century European literature – especially the heroic epics and romances that are the staple narratives depicting martial encounter – are often rendered as Saracens or heathens, this formulation becoming something of a literary commonplace.

But the most discussed example of a text in which black African Saracens feature prominently is surely Wolfram von Eschenbach's *Parzival*, arguably the most famous German courtly romance of the European Middle Ages, and justly admired for its literary brilliance and imaginative verve. I now turn to this text, to refocus critical conversation anew in the context of issues of color raised by Madeline Caviness.

Parzival's first two and last two books – a remarkable addition to the rest of the narrative's creative refashioning of Chrétien de Troyes's *Perceval* – bookend most of the stories of epidermal-race-and-religion, and have been meticulously and ably analyzed.[18] In discussing *Parzival*'s cultural politics in this section and in the chapter sections that follow, my interest will center primarily on the checkered play between a white knight, a black queen, their piebald son, and a white queen, in the inside-out nature of the world carved out by the politics of color and religion. More precisely, my interest is to see what questions are raised in the politics of color and religion, and what investments are made, in this extraordinarily accomplished thirteenth-century literary artifact devised by one of the great authorial minds of the European Middle Ages.

Written in the first decade of the thirteenth century, Wolfram's *Parzival* inherits a color discourse sedimented across the centuries, so that the romance can issue standard moralizings on color – inconstancy's color is black, constancy's is white; sinful thoughts are black, chastity is white; Hell's color and Hell's lord are black, etc. (Cyril Edwards 3, 193, 23, 51; Lachmann I: 10, I: 758, I: 92, I: 204) – yet also offer the satisfying paradox of noncongruence between an epidermal surface and the interior meaning of human character: as, for example, demonstrated by the courtly black queen of Zazamanc, Belakane, whose epidermal blackness and internal virtue are twinned and coexist seamlessly in one person.[19]

Play with color in the first two books of *Parzival* is witty, highly memorable, and incessant. When Gahmuret, the white Christian European knight, goes to Zazamanc, land of the blacks, we are told, the people of Zazamanc were all dark as night, and in their company time seemed to him to pass slowly (Cyril Edwards 9; Lachmann I: 36). Many dark ladies did Gahmuret see on both sides of him, with complexions of the raven's hue (Cyril Edwards 10; Lachmann I: 40). When the black wife of the black burgrave in the capital city of Patelamunt kisses Gahmuret, he took little pleasure in it (Cyril Edwards 11; Lachmann I: 42). On her part, the queen Belakane hopes the fact that Gahmuret is a different color from her and her people does not displease him (Cyril Edwards 11; Lachmann I: 44). She can tell Gahmuret is handsome, however, because she had seen many a fair-skinned Christian before and knew how to judge pale complexions (Cyril Edwards 14; Lachmann I: 54). But if anything is brighter than the day, Belakane bears it no resemblance (Cyril Edwards 12; Lachmann I: 46). Belakane's black hand personally removes Gahmuret's arms and armor (Cyril Edwards 20; Lachmann I: 80), and finally, when Gahmuret and Belakane consummate their intense desire for each other, the narrative still cannot leave well enough alone, but must tell us (in case it's escaped our notice) that in the act of love their skins were unalike (Cyril Edwards 20; Lachmann I: 80).

This list by no means exhausts the gimlet-eyed focus on color in the first two books. Color is the pivot for praising martial prowess. It is also staged in the tale of Gahmuret's furtive exit from Zazamanc without its subjects' or his wife's knowledge – the seaman from Seville who helps Gahmuret escape is not like a Moor in color, and he warns Gahmuret to conceal his departure from those who have black skins (Cyril Edwards 24; Lachmann I: 96). Feirefiz's birth, of course, presents a delightful comedic-poignant opportunity to proffer a black-and-white, magpie-colored baby whose mother, Belakane, kisses him on his white parts (which no doubt remind her of her dearly departed Gahmuret [Cyril Edwards 25; Lachmann I: 100, 102]).

Gahmuret's return to Europe, however, brings a sudden shift in specular attention to color, as light-radiating *fair skin* now takes center stage. Gahmuret seems to be shedding light, his mouth shining and ablaze like a ruby, his hair bright and curly, and his person radiant; and Herzeloyde, the queen of Wales who will be his second wife, casts an equally bright sheen when she first appears (Cyril Edwards 28; Lachmann I: 112).

Since Gahmuret returns not only as an Angevin princeling who has finally come into his inheritance but also, we are told, as the King of Zazamanc, land of the blacks – and to make sure we are paying attention, the text calls him the King of Zazamanc nearly a dozen times – we may suppose an ironic comment to underpin the narrative description of the white knight's glorious brilliance here. His is a radiance, we notice, intensified by the gems, furs, and samite, the wealth and luxury, that he brings from the land of the blacks as its white king furtively gone AWOL – a wealth which festoons his radiant person (Cyril Edwards 28; Lachmann I: 112).

The shift of color attention when Gahmuret lands back in Europe suggests that *Parzival* is not only absorbed in the meaning of blackness and foreignness – an absorption the romance amiably flags with congenial explicitness – but is also keenly absorbed in what fair skin and radiance might announce or conceal, in the moral-ethical ratio of surface to depth *in Europe and among Europeans.* If Madeline Caviness is correct, the early thirteenth century, when *Parzival* is written, should be a time of intense interest in what the fairness of Europeans portends in signaling identity.

One of the meanings of lightness, Caviness suggests, is sanctity: and in *Parzival*, we see that everyone associated with the Grail radiates light, and is radiantly light in color. Grail maidens have light-colored hair, and the complexion of the Grail knight Parzival, the son of Gahmuret and Herzeloyde, vies in sheen with the radiance of candles. Ladies that Parzival encounters also have bright skin, very white in color, and luscious white breasts and bodies. The Grail itself imparts lightness of skin, so that the aged, sick Titurel has never lost his fair color but remains bright-skinned, because he sees the Grail so often (Cyril Edwards 98, 103, 108, 109, 211; Lachmann I: 386, I: 404, I: 428, I: 430, I: 828).[20]

Parzival's mother, Herzeloyde, is herself very, very white. Rhapsodized as resembling the sun in her brightness, Herzeloyde sheds such effulgence that even if all the candles around her had been extinguished, her skin alone would have supplied enough light (Cyril Edwards 44, 37, 28; Lachmann I: 174, I: 144, I: 112). The text is agog at her bare skin, white body, white hands, and especially her soft, white, little breasts. After Parzival's birth, those white breasts are generously offered to our gaze as Herzeloyde lyrically apostrophizes her breasts with their rosy nipples, presses her nipples to her red mouth, squeezes out their (white) milk, and finally, after rapt textual inspection of the red tips of those adorable breasts, pushes her breast tips into the infant Parzival's little mouth, in a *mise-en-scène* where the *virgo lactans* – Mary nursing the infant Jesus – is invoked to sanctify the avid gaze on erotic whiteness (Cyril Edwards 48–9; Lachmann I: 188, 190, 192).

With the invocation of the Virgin, voyeuristic excitement at the erotic white topography of a European woman's body is cleverly alibied as *hommâge* to nurturant maternity. But the slippage between sacred and secular that tends to occur – as Caviness has pointed out – is visible not only here. Whiteness may identify Grail-related sanctity, but it comes to characterize courtly elites in Europe too, so that even the secular young people at King Arthur's court, in this romance, have radiantly fair complexions (Cyril Edwards 320; Lachmann II: 306).

White thus appears to be a capacious, generous color. Offered as denoting sanctity, maternity, erotic female bodies, and secular aristocratic identity of the noblest (Arthurian) kind, the flexibility of whiteness in the text signals a keen textual interest in investigating what whiteness can accommodate, reveal, conceal, or mean.

White's flexibility as a signifying color returns us to Gahmuret: a white knight who is king of the blacks, and who fathers both the fair-skinned Grail knight Parzival and his half-brother the piebald heathen Feirefiz. However, Gahmuret's radiance and brightness presents something of a problem in the field of vision that ties whiteness to European identity. This is because in his actions, as well as in his loyalty and devotion, Gahmuret the fair-skinned, radiant Arthurian knight seems to act like a virtual Saracen.

Gahmuret's knightly deeds and prowess are plotted on a disturbing arc. We see him in action first as a mercenary serving the "baruc" (that is, Caliph) of Baldac (that is, Baghdad) against the Caliph's rivals, two brothers of Babylon ("Babilon"). This service wins the Angevin the prize in heathendom, where his courage and prowess garner him a dazzling reputation in Morocco, Persia, Damascus, Aleppo, Arabia, and Alexandria (Cyril Edwards 8–9, 10; Lachmann I: 32, I: 38).

After stellar performance for a Saracen potentate, Gahmuret goes to yet another heathen land, this time populated by *black* heathens – Zazamanc – where he defends the black land's heathen queen from the forces and allies of a deceased black knight who had been enamored with her, and that are now bent on exacting revenge for their dead lord, Isenhart of Azagouc, who had died endeavoring to prove worthy of her favor.

In this chessboard drama of race-and-religion, Black Queen fails Black Knight, and White Knight takes Black Queen and Black Knight's lands. Once a landless younger son and an economic casualty of European primogeniture, the Christian Gahmuret becomes the White King of two heathen lands populated by dark Moors and Mooresses. Could any postmedieval colonial fantasy, written for the grand ages of European colonial empire, offer a more productive outcome?

Having impregnated and married the black queen of Zazamanc, the White Knight now conjures up oddly uncompelling reasons for why he must desert his beloved Black Queen (who is dearer to him than his own life) and return to Europe, where – lavishly wealthy – he is repeatedly named as the King of Zazamanc, land of black Saracen Moors (Cyril Edwards 29, 30, 32, 33, 35, 36, 41; Lachmann I: 114, I: 118, I: 120, I: 126, I: 130, I: 138, I: 142, I: 160).

From Belakane's response to Gahmuret's letter informing her that his desertion was caused by her heathenness, it is patently clear that her conversion to Christianity was never raised between them as his desire, since she instantly declares she will gladly be baptized and live as he wishes (Cyril Edwards 25; Lachmann I: 100).[21] In fact, Gahmuret's own life has shown little allegiance to a missionary Christianity, and his return to Christian Europe is merely an intermission between military escapades in Islamdom for the benefit of Saracens.

Briefly back in Europe, Gahmuret impregnates and marries a white queen of Wales, Herzeloyde: White Knight, now King of the Blacks, takes White Queen. He then finds it urgent to leave again, once more in devotion to the Caliph of Baghdad, when that Saracen potentate is again menaced by his enemies from Babylon.[22] On this second dedicated war service to his lord the Caliph, Gahmuret loses his life.

His young corpse is embalmed and buried in Baghdad at the Caliph's expense, the tomb generously lavished with precious stones (Cyril Edwards 46; Lachmann I: 182). Though a cross is nominally erected, Gahmuret's Christian corpse is very palpably and inexplicably not returned to Herzeloyde and Christendom, but put instead into unconsecrated heathen ground in the heart of Saracendom (Cyril Edwards 46; Lachmann I: 182). Indeed, "His death grieved Saracens," we are told; we are also told that the heathens worship Gahmuret as their honored God (Cyril Edwards 47, 46; Lachmann I: 184, I: 182).

Stripped to its plot outline, Gahmuret's story is a strange tale in the Arthurian universe. If the symmetry of this bigamist-knight's abandonment of two pregnant wife-queens – one black, one white – is remarkable, more astounding, surely, is the deep homosocial devotion this Christian European knight shows to his lord the Caliph and his wars.

For all his protestation of longing for one of the wives he abandons, and his additional declaration moreover that the woman he does *not* marry, Queen Ampflise of France, is his true lady (Cyril Edwards 41; Lachmann I: 162), Gahmuret's real love and devotion – as seen by his *deeds*, not his words – belongs to the Caliph. This Christian knight's career begins and ends with devoted service to his lord the Caliph: the titular head of Islamdom and successor to Islam's Prophet (he is a Caliph, after all, and not merely a sultan).

Given the extraordinary brilliance of Wolfram's romance – with its elaborate pattern-ing and symmetries, delectable humor, trenchant wit, and creative inventiveness – we are forced to conclude that Gahmuret's characterization is likely neither a chance accident nor an afterthought. Color and religion are staked in that characterization. A *white Christian European knight* in mercenary service to Islamdom, Gahmuret's nominal subscription to the Christian universe zigzags in directions Europeans should fear, while his fair skin color seems less to advertise European identity than to conceal allegiances disturbing to Europe. This White Knight's color, it turns out, is an opaque surface that covers over a disquieting interior of deeply ambiguous moral, ethical, military, and geopolitical subscriptions.

Parzival is a text written in the early thirteenth century, after the horrific loss of the Kingdom of Jerusalem, the heart of the crusader East, to Saladin (Salah ad-Din Yusuf ibn Ayyub) in 1187 and after the disappointing failure of the Third Crusade in 1189–92, Richard Lionheart's and Philippe Augustus' crusade, to restore the Holy City to Christian hands. The romance even seems to show knowledge of the debacle of the Fourth Crusade of 1204, detoured from its military target of Egypt and avariciously ransacking Constantinople instead (Cyril Edwards 237; Lachmann I: 928, I: 930).

In a text rife with *orientalia* and Near Eastern place names, and obsessively fascinated with luxurious eastern silks and Syrian cloth, mentioning spices like cardamom, cloves and nutmeg; Arab gold and African gems; Arab astronomy and Arabic names for the planets; olive trees, heathen queens; Turks, Turcopoles, and templars (a name that appears nearly a dozen times), how should we judge a Christian knight who twice fights as a mercenary for the Caliph of Baghdad, a Caliph bearing affection for him and in whose service he dies (Cyril Edwards 8, 44, 46; Lachmann I: 30, I: 172, I: 180, I: 182)?

If this bright-sheened, dazzlingly fair European must leave Europe to adventure on the other side of the Mediterranean – *outremer* – why isn't he fighting on behalf of Christen-dom, in an honorable and holy cause, a cause as grand, noble, and just as it is urgent? That Wolfram was not unmindful of the imperative of holy war enjoined on Christian knights and rulers can be seen in his celebrated literary text featuring Saracens and Christians in combat, *Willehalm*: a text in which Christians and Saracens war over Gyburc, a once-Saracen queen liberated by her conversion to Christianity, and who possibly functions in *Willehalm* as an imagined figure for the lost city of Jerusalem.[23]

Indeed, Wolfram's repeated conjuring of "templars" in *Parzival* who serve the Grail in its temple at Munsalvaesche may lightly indicate that the successful Grail quest in *Parzival* is meant to be seen as a kind of fantasied compensation for a failed quest by those other Templars – Knights of the Order of the Temple – who served and guarded lost Jerusalem.[24]

Gahmuret's military service to Saracens not only deprives Christendom of a champion, but also means that he wars against Christians and Europeans. Defending the Moorish heathen queen, Belakane, Gahmuret wars against varied ethnic groups of Europeans led by Hiuteger, a Scottish duke in the retinue of Fridebant, the king of Scotland, and Gaschier of Normandy, avoiding only combat against Kaylet the Spaniard, because he was Gahmuret's kinsman (Cyril Edwards 17–18; Lachmann I: 68, I: 72).

This White Knight of ambiguous behavior is also habitually clothed in Saracen silk: His tabard, surcoat, and cloak are all made of prized green samite, "achmardi" – precious Arabian stuff that the narrative tells us is peerless, with no other clothing comparable to it. The boss of his shield is of Arabian gold, and a Saracen tent, and jewels and gem-studded gold goblets from Azagouc travel with him (Cyril Edwards 17, 28, 31, 37; Lachmann I: 68, I: 112, I: 123–4, I: 146).

Compounding his cagey geopolitical and military ethics are Gahmuret's personal ethical failings. Unlike Lancelot – an Arthurian knight famed throughout medieval European literature for his steadfast loyalty to his first love, Queen Guenevere – Gahmuret sheds his first love, Queen Ampflise of France, who educated him, counseled him, and conferred knighthood on him, giving him his shield, and receiving in return Gahmuret's ring (Cyril Edwards 41, 42, 33; Lachmann I: 162, I: 166, I: 132). Despite an announced great affection for and strong fidelity to Ampflise – who is his true lady, Gahmuret says (though the narrative is likely being arch here) – Gahmuret agrees to marry the virginal and younger Herzeloyde when the two white queens vie for him (Cyril Edwards 41, 42; Lachmann I: 164, I: 166, I: 168).

By this time, of course, he has also shed his pregnant black queen Belakane, whom he knew was pregnant when he left, a wife he says dearer to him than his life, and for whom he longs (Cyril Edwards 25, 41, 39; Lachmann I: 98, I: 160, I: 154). No Lancelot this, but twice married, with three women trailing in his wake and abandoning two while they are pregnant with his children, Gahmuret's confusedly mixed loyalties are dramatized in his personal life as sensationally as in his military career.

White on the surface of his skin and outwardly a Christian European, Gahmuret is morally and ethically *piebald* in his personal life, his military and geopolitical devotions, and his amassing of oriental wealth, kingdoms, and the impressive luxury wares that embellish his outward radiance. This White Knight's interior is as piebald as the exterior of his miscegenated son Feirefiz. In linking father and son, the text seems to say, skin reveals and conceals. Feirefiz's pied, parti-colored epidermis reveals his mixed genetic parentage. Gahmuret's whiteness and light-shedding radiance conceals a pied morality and ethics, mixed allegiances, and murkiness within.

For a nice contrast, Belakane's black surface – a sheen so unlike the dewy rose, the text laments – is pied with spotless virtue, chastity, a loyal disposition, outstanding courtliness, womanliness, sweetness, and a pure nature (Cyril Edwards 12, 14, 15–16, 39; Lachmann I: 46, I: 54, I: 62, I: 154). Inheriting a centuries-old discourse on color that the text shows it well understands, *Parzival* is a romance that plumbs surface and depth through the instrumentation of color and turns interiors inside out, to see if the inside of a human identity conforms to its outside.

Beyond a visual palette of color in this text, identity is what identity *does*: Therefore, actions and deeds are the other links between Gahmuret and Feirefiz. Like his father, Feirefiz faithlessly leaves three queens in his wake – Olimpia, Clauditte, and Secundille – one of whom, Secundille of Tribalibot, had instructed, inspired, and loved him, furnishing him with gifts in a role parallel to Ampflise's in Gahmuret's life (Cyril Edwards 316, 322–3; Lachmann II: 292, II: 310, II: 312, II: 316).[25] Father and son are also both exhibited to European eyes swathed in costly, showy magnificence – precious oriental gemstones blaze on their person, and the narrative is repeatedly agog at their wealth and their oriental treasures (Cyril Edwards 324, 307–8, 316, 318, 325, 328; Lachmann II: 318, II: 320, II: 258, II: 292, II: 300, II: 326, II: 338, passim).

Despite their dermal disparity, color indeed ties the one to the other, with skin acting as an interface – the father piebald on the inside, the son piebald without. Play with color also links Gahmuret and Belakane, but in a simple inversion that yokes each person's interior to the other's exterior. The white Christian European acts like a virtual Saracen knight, but the black Saracen queen acts like a virtual European queen in her hospitality, courtesy, and regal courtliness, and also like a virtual Christian in her chastity and virtue – indeed, the text tells us that her chastity was a pure baptism unto itself (Cyril Edwards 14; Lachmann I: 54).

Keenly interested in plumbing European identity – in exploring what a white, Christian identity signals on the outside and within – *Parzival* is also interested in a world of collective identity beyond Europe, where Zazamanc/Azagouc, virtual stand-ins for Ethiopia/Abyssinia/Nubia, mark the far reaches of the civilized world. Stepping into the land of the blacks, Gahmuret finds a world not different from the Europe he has left behind, except for the dermal hue and heathenness of its inhabitants. There are cities, armies, and chivalric armorial devices in Zazamanc; familiar rituals of martial combat, courtly manners, values, and hospitality, a kiss of greeting for noble strangers, and extravagant feasts. Language poses no barrier, and love is as familiarly intense – *more* intense – than in Europe.[26] Blackness of skin, plus religion, is what prevents this foreign corner of the world from looking like Europe.

I consider the implications of this below, in sections on the Black Queen and on mixed-race offspring, but it is useful to note briefly that in the cultural imaginary on display in this celebrated early thirteenth-century romance, oriental Africa looks a lot like Western Europe, but is the source of rare treasure, precious gems, and vast, untold riches. This land is accessible to a moral hybrid like Gahmuret, a knightly bigamist and mercenary with flexible ethics who is willing to dedicate himself to the causes of non-Christians, rather than pursuing the highest military goals and missionary endeavors of Christianity – wresting back Jerusalem from the infidel, and converting the unconverted in the person of Belakane and her people.

We thus see that, true to its rich complexity, *Parzival* has multiple fascinations. Well attuned to asymmetries of skin color and interior identity, and what color conceals and reveals, the romance's obsessive cataloguing of the Orient's wealth suggests that it's also very interested in what an ambitious knight of high martial caliber can accomplish. Gahmuret's ambitions and prowess are rewarded with the wealth of the Orient, heathen lands, two queens, and the birth of a Grail knight.

Parzival's fascinations with the global non-Christian world take many forms. They include an avid interest in Saracen stories, knowledges, and lore: The story of the Grail itself is traced back to a Saracen called "Flegentis" who descends from the Israelite stock of Solomon, but is heathen through his father's line. Flegentis is an astronomer who read the future of the Grail in the stars and wrote it down in Arabic (*in heidenischer schrifte*), where it was discovered and read by "Kyot" in Toledo, who then traveled through Europe's Arthurian lands amassing more scholarship, all of which forms the basis of Wolfram's own grail romance, which thus claims Saracen origins for itself (Cyril Edwards 191–2; Lachmann I: 750, I: 752, I: 754).

Tellingly, Wolfram's Grail messenger, Cundrie la Surziere, is not only a splendid loathly lady of the conventional romance kind, but also happens to speak Arabic and possess recondite astronomical knowledge that enables her to describe planetary bodies by their Arabic names (Cyril Edwards 132, 327; Lachmann I: 518, II: 334). Believe it or not, she is sent by Queen Secundille of Tribalibot, a land with the river Ganges, and with many rivers that carry precious gems rather than gravel, and that has mountains of gold (Cyril Edwards 218, 219; Lachmann I: 856, I: 858).

In this Grail romance, the global outside – all the far-flung lands of heathendom – leaches into Christian Europe, bringing knowledges, stories, gems, rare fabrics, sumptuous clothes, Arab gold, spices, aloe woods, and other exotic *orientalia* of incalculable worth. Saracen knowledge, Saracen lands, Saracen wealth, and at least one black Saracen queen are objects of intense absorption and desire. A White Knight of dubious morality, who ends his life in that global outside and never returns, has discovered that the rest of the world looks greatly like Europe, except for its extraordinary wealth, its lack of Christianity, and the presence of black-skinned peoples. This is how a celebrated and brilliant specimen of elite German cultural fantasy imagines the world of the early thirteenth century.

But later in the thirteenth century, literary culture in Europe fashions yet another response to foreign lands and black-skinned peoples, and envisions an alternate set of relations between Europe and them.[27] The Middle Dutch romance *Moriaen* reverses the trope of a White Knight adventuring in the lands of the Blacks, and offers instead a Black Knight from Moorland ("Moriane") who arrives in Arthurian Europe to search for his father – the knight Acglavael (Agloval), elder brother of Perchevael (Perceval/Parzival) – a father who sired him on a black Moorish princess Acglavael promised to marry before he went missing twenty-four years ago.[28] D. A. Wells persuasively urges that *Moriaen* is likely written after 1250, and does not derive from *Parzival* but is most probably a Dutch original in its own right ("Source" 46–7, "Middle Dutch" 260, 275; Claassens and Johnson 9).

Less well known than the German *Parzival*, the Dutch *Moriaen* is a freestanding romance within an immense manuscript compilation of ten romances in a series referred to by scholars as the Middle Dutch *Lancelot Compilation*: Some component romances are based on the Old French *Prose Lancelot*, while others are original Middle Dutch compositions (Claassens and Johnson 5–6).[29] In the *Compilation*, *Moriaen* appears after the romance *Perchevael* and before the *Queeste vanden Grale* (Quest of the Grail), and scholars have argued that *Moriaen* circulated independently before its incorporation into the massive manuscript (Wells, "Source" 40). No source texts are known to exist for *Moriaen*, but the romance draws widely on the beloved conventions, stories, characters, and motifs of Arthurian romance, especially from the French tradition, and possibly also the British (Besamusca; Claassens and Johnson 9; Wells, "Source" 32, 44).

This second contemplation of color offered up by thirteenth-century Arthurian literature is extraordinary. Its focus on blackness is a sustained meditation that shows awareness of what black signifies in the cultural milieu of its time, but also decisively shows how color difference can, and should, be bridged. Like Feirefiz, the Black Knight Moriaen comes to Europe looking for his missing father, but Moriaen is not a Feirefiz clone purged of white bits of skin. Though black, and from the equivalent of Zazamanc, *Moriaen is a Christian, not a Saracen.*

Despite Wolfram's portrayal of Zazamanc as a land of black heathens, by the end of the twelfth century and the beginning of the thirteenth, some knowledge existed of a Christian Africa:

> Richard of Cluny, writing in 1172, speaks of Christians in the kingdom of Nubia. Burchard of Strasbourg claims Nubia is Christian in 1175. The pilgrim Theoderich apparently met Nubian Christians at the church of the Sepulcher in Jerusalem, but this may be a later insert

into his account of 1172 ... Arnold of Lübeck refers to Nubia as Christian in 1209 ... Thietmar's account of his pilgrimage to the Holy Land mentions the Christian "Yssini" [Abyssinians, i.e., Ethiopians] located beyond Egypt. ...

(Kaplan, *Rise* 49)

Paul Kaplan's summary of thirteenth-century knowledge of a Christian Africa suggests an uneven but reasonable dispersion of that knowledge in Western Europe. Robert de Clari's chronicle of the Fourth Crusade records the arrival of a black Christian king of Nubia in Constantinople in 1204 (*Rise* 47). Oliver of Paderborn, writing of the capture of Damietta in 1219, says that Ethiopia has a large Christian population ruled partly by a Christian king and partly by Muslims, while Jacques de Vitry's *Historia Orientalis* (*c.* 1220) describes Nubians and Ethiopians as independent nations of Jacobite Christians. Even Matthew Paris "implies that both Ethiopia and Nubia are peopled with Jacobite Christians" (*Rise* 49–50). By the late thirteenth century,

Burchard of Mount Sion, a native of either Strasbourg or Magdeburg, composed in 1283 an account of his trip to and residence in the Holy Land, a narrative in which Christian Nubia and Ethiopia receive a good deal of emphasis ... The Christianity of these regions is also asserted on maps. The Hereford map of ca. 1285–1290 bears an inscription which refers to the "most Christian Ethiopians of Nubia"; the roughly contemporary Ebstorf map makes reference only to Nubian Christians.

(Kaplan, *Rise* 50–1)

It's thus possible that in the second half of the thirteenth century, the depiction of Moriaen as a Christian issues from cultural knowledge, or at least an intermittent cultural memory of Christian Ethiopia and Christian Nubia, but deliberately overlooks the eastern Christianity of these African lands which did not follow the Latin Rite. Whatever the case, *Moriaen* offers less historical specificity than *Parzival* with its panorama of references, place names, and *orientalia*: *Moriaen*'s global outside focuses specifically on color.

To be sure we are in no doubt that Moriaen is a Christian, the text has him calling on God the first instance he appears, and he calls on God repeatedly each time we see him (l. 483ff). Moriaen is thus that rare character in medieval romance: a black man and foreign other who's not a heathen but religiously invokes the Christian God. This romance is clearly not interested in the theme of how the heathen, virtuous or otherwise, can be converted – and not at all interested in Saracens or their religion, or the vast riches, knowledge, and power of the Saracen world. *Color alone* is the locus of difference in the *Moriaen*, so that blackness can be considered in its own right, without distractions. The text's attitude to color, and its Black Knight, is forthrightly simple:

> Moors are as black as a burnt torch.
> But in all things that one would praise in a knight,
> he was fair, after his own fashion.
> Though he was black, what harm was it?
> Nothing about him was unbecoming.
>
> (l. 768–72)

We see that fair skin is still the default category of valorization, since Moriaen is praised as "fair" *in his own way*. But there's a touch of defiance here: So he's black – so what? He's a fine knight in every way; nothing about him is unbecoming. Here is an unmistakable prompt: You should look past color, if color is the only difference.

In a romance of 4,716 lines, this explicit statement of the text's position on color difference occurs early, in the first sixth of the narrative. Thereafter, the romance shows how different people respond to Moriaen's blackness, attesting time and again that those who fear him, and believe him the devil on the basis of his color, are hopelessly wrong and clueless, while those who offer him respect are vindicated by his stellar martial performance, ethical behavior, and sterling personality. Having stated its view on color, the narrative proceeds to explicate and defend that view for the remainder of the romance.[30]

To dramatize its point, the narrative purposefully depicts Moriaen, in his physical appearance, as a stock figure of medieval romance and *chanson de geste*. Moriaen is "black as pitch" "except for his teeth" and – recalling the demonic black giants who populate these genres – he is exceptionally large, though "still a youth" (l. 766, 424, 773–5). People flee from him, so that as he travels he can find no lodging or shelter anywhere, no food or drink, nor transportation when he needs it – sailors on ships and boatmen at a harbor scatter in terror (l. 2363–6, 2375–8, 2408–23). People are affrighted "because he was both black and large," and "it seemed to them that Moriaen/had come straight from hell" and "was none other than the devil" (l. 2415, 2418–9, 2428). Even Gariet (Gareth), an Arthurian knight and brother of the great Walewein (Gawain), is taken aback at meeting him – the text registers Gariet's apprehension over eleven lines – and must be reassured by the wiser Walewein, who quickly introduces Moriaen and explains his quest, assuaging Gariet's discomfort (l. 2934–6; l. 2937–44).

By contrast, superior Arthurian knights such as Walewein, Lanceloet (Lancelot), and Perchevael, and the two hermits who shelter them, do not respond to Moriaen with dread, and Acglavael, on meeting his son and learning of Moriaen's mission, embraces him at once. Yet even the chief Arthurian knights are only human, and the narrative tells us when Walewein and Lanceloet first encounter Moriaen, Walewein would have thought "that it was the devil rather than a man/whom they had come upon/had he not heard him call upon God" (l. 481–3). Superior knights are able to look past a fellow's color – if he's a Christian: an example for others to follow.

Moriaen's frequent, trusting invocation of God is thus part of a textual strategy to present him as a sympathetic character who, unlike Feirefiz, has no real shortcomings. Indeed, "apart from his colour, great stature, and Moorish homeland, there is nothing to distinguish him from the traditional champions of Arthurian chivalry" (Wells, "Middle Dutch" 250).

Moriaen's portrayal is a flattering one: He fights Lanceloet (traditionally the best Arthurian knight) to a standstill, never giving way; he saves Walewein from torture and certain death; he's even half a foot taller than the tallest Arthurian knight (traditionally, again, Lanceloet); and he leads the vanguard in the defense of King Artur's (Arthur's) queen and castle, so that "Never had anyone seen a mortal man/deal such terrible blows" and "it seemed that he would put to rout/an entire army" (l. 4430–1, 4339–40). Moriaen is Lanceloet's equal in one-to-one combat, and Perchevael's equal in Artur's wars: As D. A. Wells notes, the man is a virtual Arthurian knight (l. 4541–2). Norris Lacy astutely adds that "failures by Artur's most indomitable knights, and Artur's own captivity, can only have been devised to point up Moriaen's precocious excellence: he is the only one ... never to have been defeated or captured" (130 n.13).

When he first appears, however, Moriaen is a little hotheaded, and so passionately bent on his quest that he offers to fight anyone unless they give him news of his father's whereabouts, battling Lanceloet to the ground as a result of this overeager insistence on news-or-combat. Counseled by Lanceloet to listen to Walewein, who advises Moriaen to try a more dulcet approach first, in sourcing for news, Moriaen absorbs the advice in an instant, and never again repeats his impetuousness (l. 432–606).[31] Thereafter, the Black Knight is a model of chivalry, courtesy, patience, and considerateness.

Though eager to be back on quest, after rescuing a badly wounded Walewein, Moriaen agrees to wait for his friend to recuperate before resuming his search for Acglavael (l. 2847–50). When he does find Acglavael and sees that his father also is badly wounded, and in no shape to travel to Moorland immediately, Moriaen in turn counsels his father to recover first; and, as he waits patiently for Acglavael to heal, he occupies himself with King Artur's cause, in which our Black Knight distinguishes himself (l. 3920–52).

The text's portrayal of Moriaen thus exhibits an empathy and warmth rare in medieval romance's portrayal of foreign others. Through the technique of *entrelacement* (the interlacing of plot trajectories), a narrative sequence directly contrasts the Black Knight's lonely journey, when he is shunned like a pariah, with the lavish hospitality Walewein receives at a castle where he has just killed the castellan's son but still must be feted according to chivalric hospitality's rules. Right after the depiction of Walewein's lavish reception, the narrative turns to the Black Knight, who, in stark contrast, finds no hospitality anywhere, though he has not committed a capital act like Walewein's.

Moriaen spends a lonely night with no sleep or rest, shorn of a civilized habitat where he can find comfort "beneath a roof." Yet, when the day breaks, with a clear, bright sky, he poignantly finds comfort in that simple fact of nature:

> *He had neither rest nor sleep that night,*
> *nor did he find any place where he might*
> *have lodgings, where he thought he could*
> *find some comfort for himself,*
> *a place inside, beneath a roof.*
> *Next morning, when daylight came,*
> *he was comforted greatly*
> *for the sky was clear and bright.*
>
> *(l. 2374–81)*

The touching simplicity of how Moriaen's spirits lift at so small a comfort imparts a fleeting glimpse of an inner life. Textual empathy for him also grants us an internal view of what it is like to *be* Moriaen – not only to see what Moriaen looks like to the Europeans he meets, but also to recognize his pained response to their reactions: a double consciousness that is the gift of this unusual romance.

After boatmen flee from him, at a crucial point in his quest for his father, Moriaen despairs: Unable to get to the other side of the sea, where his father is, he is forced to turn back, "lamenting all the while" (l. 2437). Up to this juncture, our Black Knight has been unselfconsciously doffing his helm (he wears armor as black as his skin), politely enabling people to see the face and facial expression beneath. But in learning how to view himself through European eyes, he has absorbed a bitter lesson of the white man's gaze:

> *They will not take me across*
> *because I am a Moor,*
> *and my countenance is different*
> *than that of those who dwell here.*
> *I have wasted this journey.*
>
> *(l. 2446–50)*

The text is not content with merely making us recognize the cruelties of epidermal racism. On his second day without shelter, food, or drink, the narrative shows us the *effects* of racial shunning, as the once resilient and ebullient Moriaen reels from repeated rejection. Not only does he suffer physically from hunger, so that he is feverish and his head hurts, but, with his morale at its lowest, he also suffers dejectedly from grief (l. 2454–7).

Narrative sympathy for Moriaen builds outward from the justness and decency of his cause. This Christian Black Knight doesn't swagger into Arthurian Europe backed by mighty armies and vast wealth, like the proud heathen Feirefiz, but poignantly comes alone, with no help, to seek social and economic redress. Because Acglavael did not return to marry the black princess after each had plighted troth to the other, the son she births is illegitimate, and by the law of their country, Moriaen's mother is deprived of her land, feudal rights, and great wealth, and she and her son are subjected to social opprobrium and shame (l. 707–719).

Unlike his uncle, Perchevael – whose mother died heartbroken because Perchevael had abandoned her, with her death being the "sin" that causes the failure of Perchevael's Grail quest, and necessitating penance on Perchevael's part – Moriaen's protective concern over *his* mother's welfare and rights registers him as ethically superior even to Perchevael, Arthurian romance's would-be Grail Knight.[32]

Moriaen's eloquent recitation of his backstory to Walewein and Lanceloet is scrupulously fair. He acknowledges that Acglavael did not know his beloved was pregnant, and details in stages mother and son's poignant suffering and shame and his own growing resolve. Economic disinheritance and social opprobrium are ample cause to move any knight, and Moriaen's quest – to restore his mother's dignity and his, and their rightful, legitimate place in their world – literally makes Walewein and Lanceloet weep.

> *Then neither of*
> *the two knights who stood there,*
> *– neither Walewein nor Lanceloet –*
> *could prevent great tears*
> *from falling from his eyes*
> *when they heard the story*
> *of what had befallen this knight.*
>
> *(l. 745–51)*

We see thus that this Black Knight is steadfast and ethical, and scholars have rightly insisted that the romance is fundamentally concerned with ethics.[33] Even Acglavael, that instigator of grief, exhibits none of the moral dubiousness of his counterpart in the land of the blacks, Gahmuret. Acglavael only left his beloved in order dutifully to resume his search for Lanceloet, whom he had been on a quest to find when he met the Moorish princess; he had not returned to Moriane afterward because a series of family obligations kept him away

(l. 3587–3611). No Gahmuret this, despite superficialities of plot resemblance: Acglavael was not in Moorland out of economic opportunism, and acquires no additional wives or sons afterward. The moment his son explains his mother's plight, Acglavael is instantly contrite, and swears to make amends:

> *That I have thus betrayed her*
> *and broken my vow*
> *is a crime that I intend to*
> *put right, with God's help.*
> *I shall yet win her grace.*
>
> *(l. 3641–5)*

The reunion of father and son is joyous, and we are invited to view the embrace of a white father and a black son without any narrative comment on the strangeness of the mixed-color pair. Unlike *Parzival*, which could not refrain from gleefully interjecting that the skins of Gahmuret and Belakane were unalike in their most intimate moment, *Moriaen* simply presents family happiness:

> *It would have done anyone's heart good*
> *who had heard them speak,*
> *to see how Acglavael and Moriaen*
> *embraced and kissed one another;*
> *Any heart would have been the gladder*
> *who had seen and heard*
> *their speech and their words.*
>
> *(l. 3652–58)*

This romance, you might say, has humbler ambitions than *Parzival*. If *Parzival* is eager to display knowledge of the wide world, *Moriaen* is content with a smaller canvas, which it paints with feeling and exactitude.[34] Indeed, the romance pins together all manner of telling details – especially psychological particulars – so that there is scarcely a loose thread in the warp and weave of narrative. For instance: At the castle where Walewein finds shelter, after having killed the castellan's son, the host's men plot Walewein's death once he is off their premises, but take care to feed well Gringalet, Walewein's horse, because they think the steed will soon be theirs (l. 2080–4). The psychological astuteness of this afterthought discloses how narrative attention alights on small, revealing particulars that add dimension, motive, and unexpected touches of realism.

This kind of psychological attentiveness leads the narrative to acknowledge a knight's dependence on his horse, and show us moments of warmth in human–animal relations. Walewein plunges his famed steed, Gringalet, into a wide, deep river where there is no bridge, and the animal gamely battles its way across "as best it could" against very strong currents, so that "it was a great miracle/that they were not both drowned" (l. 1268–74). When Gawain is ambushed and badly hurt by the castellan's men, the narrative movingly relates that on seeing Gringalet again "his heart soared so within him/that it seemed to him that he was completely healed" (l. 2636–7). We even have the horse's perspective. In a charming scene of animal–human attachment, Gringalet takes the injured Walewein by the sleeve in a delicate gesture of greeting and animal trust:

> *[Gringalet] came forward to meet his lord.*
> *That horse took him by the sleeve*
> *with his mouth, for friendship.*
>
> *(l. 2641–3)*

Quotidian details receive attention. When Gariet arrives at the hermitage where Walewein and Moriaen are recuperating, fortuitously bringing food and drink in the nick of time just as the hermit's small stores are depleted from feeding his knightly guests, the text troubles to account for why an Arthurian knight should be carrying victuals and wine on the road – when such explication is hardly standard procedure for a genre in which food and drink, magic devices and gifts, wealth, and nubile women routinely materialize with no bother of explanation.

Textual attention to detail is so scrupulous that even a ruse has to be explained: To hobble Walewein, the castellan's seneschal secretly makes "a deep gash" in Gringalet's stirrup leathers, so that they will break at a crucial moment when Walewein is riding. As to why Walewein doesn't notice this sly tampering, we are told that the cut is concealed "beneath the cover of the harness" – just in case we were wondering (l. 2066–9).[35]

The romance also has a wicked sense of humor. A terrified boatman who had earlier fled from Moriaen is given a second encounter with him, this time after Gariet has secured the boatman's services first, without telling him he would have Moriaen as a travel companion on the boat to Ireland. The text gleefully draws out what happens next:

> *[Gariet] put the money in the boatman's hand,*
> *who then made ready his rigging,*
> *the sail, and the tackle, too.*
> *He would soon regret it!*
> *When his [Gariet's] horse was on board*
> *and he was ready for the voyage*
> *Moriaen came riding up*
> *blacker than any other soul*
> *that a Christian man had ever seen;*
> *and the boatman wanted to run away*
> *as soon as he caught sight of Moriaen*
> *and as he rode even closer to him*
> *(He had seen him before)*
> *he thought that he would die of fright.*
> *He could hardly move a muscle.*
>
> *(l. 3421–35)*

With poetic, ludic justice, the glee here is aimed at a poor boatman who's been tricked into ferrying across the Black Knight, after having fled from him before. The text genially prolongs the joke about color – not against the man of color, but against the ignorant yokel who gazes on him. Gariet exclaims in exasperation – "Sir boatman, what is the matter with you?" (l. 3437) – fortifies the man's nerve with a belligerent threat – "Now, do not make it difficult for us / or this day will be your last" (l. 3440–1) – and waggingly lessons him:

> *By our Lord Almighty,*
> *what is it you are afraid of?*

> *This is not the devil;*
> *he has never seen the inside of Hell.*
> *I give you fair warning,*
> *Let him on board, he is my comrade.*
>
> *(l. 3442–47)*

After Moriaen's earlier suffering, the joke is too good not to be plumbed for all it's worth. When the Black Knight comes aboard, we are waggishly reminded that he is "so exceedingly large," and the boatman is "so very frightened," and "thought himself lost" (l. 3452, 3453, 3459). Worse yet, Moriaen decides to remove his helmet again:

> *When Moriaen had taken his seat*
> *he removed his steel helmet:*
> *then the boatman thought that he would die.*
>
> *(l. 3460–2)*

Luckily, the boatman gets a grip on himself and manages to relate much useful information on the whereabouts of Acglavael and Perchevael. Still, as a final jokey flourish, when Gariet and Moriaen go ashore, he "rejoiced greatly/that he was safely quit of them" (l. 3510–11).

When we consider how racial jokes can work in medieval romance – I have discussed at length the politics and psychology of the aggressive racial jokes in the Middle English *Richard Coer de Lyon*, where the English crusader-king Richard eats a black Saracen head with relish, then proceeds to host a feast for Saladin's ambassadors at which their captive sons and kinsmen are slain and served up as piping-hot platters of black Saracen heads to be consumed by king and guests – we see that the racial joke in this Dutch romance is amiably mild and *not* aimed at foreign communities of color (*Empire of Magic*, chapter 2).

Wolfram's *Parzival* also has its share of racial jokes, as we have seen, though the laughter elicited there can have a more uncertain timbre. Why do we smile at the thought of Gahmuret uneasily squirming at the hospitality kiss of the black wife of the black burgrave of Patelamunt, and who is the butt of the joke here? When the black queen Belakane kisses her piebald baby *only* on his white parts, is it funny, poignant, or mildly offensive? *Parzival's* winking racial jokes have a whiff of sly mischief about them that makes us hesitate to collude with their humor. By contrast, the Dutch romance's prolongation of the boatman's dismay seems mild and relatively innocuous.

Having noted the relatively good-natured circuit of this Dutch romance's racial joke, however, we should also note that courtly romance conventions direct the laughter here toward those who are *not* knights, but who are underclass folk in the courtly world, such as boatmen. Unlike lower-class yokels, a knight like Gariet can embrace Moriaen as "my comrade" despite the Black Knight's pitch-black skin, his white teeth, and his near-gigantic size, because chivalry is imagined as an international fraternity of men of like socioeconomic status. Everything that Moriaen does confirms him as an integral member of that privileged feudal class – his courtesy and prowess, and even the reason he is on quest in Arthurian Europe, searching for the restoral of feudal rights, lands, and position. The text imagines knighthood as a transnational institution that bonds a fraternity of elite men across borders, and across epidermal race.

Epidermal race and color difference can thus be bridged, if Europe shares in common with the lands of black-skinned peoples the *sine qua non* of Christianity and chivalry.

Christianity must needs be of a homogenous kind: Moriaen is devout, calling on God and His Mother with greater frequency than any Arthurian knight, and his faith is not marked in any way as different from the Latin Christianity of Arthurian Europe. If this thirteenth-century Dutch romance taps a deep cultural memory of Christian Ethiopia and Nubia (and Nubia, we note, became Islamized by the fourteenth century), it does not register any difference in the Christianity practiced by black Africans. To imagine relations between Europe and a global outside inhabited by people who are "much blacker . . . than any soot or pitch" (l. 3538–9), this thirteenth-century romance must theorize the strategic universalism of *Latin* Christianity.

The other strategic universalism is chivalry. Moriaen is welcomed into a circle of knights because he, too, is a knight, as he takes care to tell Walewein and Lanceloet from the outset: "I had myself dubbed a knight" (l. 720). The romance even emplots chivalric relations as a circle: *Lanceloet* advises *Moriaen* to listen to *Walewein's* counsel, and *Walewein* counsels *Moriaen*; *Moriaen* then rescues *Walewein*, who in turn rescues *Lanceloet*, bringing the actions of these knights back full circle. Chivalric relations engirdle the world, and the institution of knighthood exists even in far-off Moorland, where Moriaen has had himself dubbed a knight. For *Moriaen* as for *Parzival*, chivalry is a transnational network – an international brotherhood of the elite – that crosses all borders, enabling global relations between Europe and the vast outside.

Global relations of this kind, between communities of men who understand one another, share identical values, and support one another's rights, even across color and epidermal race, are cemented when kinship also unites races. The blood ties that link Moriaen to Acglavael, and thence to Perchevael and a web of kinfolk in Europe, attest that kin relations with black otherness are possible under universal Christianity and transnational chivalry. Together, the partnership of chivalry and Christianity can imagine a globality of kinship with otherness when men share socioeconomic interests and religion across skin color.

These are the conditions under which the text argues that epidermal race, by itself, should not matter. Moriaen is outwardly black, but his conduct, allegiance, and values are identical to any European knight's. Black outside, fair within: Or, as the text puts it, Moriaen is "fair, in his own fashion" (l. 770). The romance thus reverses the irony imbuing *Parzival*, where the White Knight, Gahmuret, is fair outside, murky within.

Textual accommodation does not go so far as to insist, of course, that blackness *per se* is beautiful, and should supplant or equal fair skin in our esteem. A creature of its time, the text says people think Moriaen ugly, but wise and brave: "Moriaen's counsel seemed good to them,/. . .although he appeared to be so ugly" (l. 4336–7). Textual generosity lies in the *attitude* toward that assumption of ugliness – a "so what?" which asserts that what matters is within, and not on a skin's surface.

Thus the narrative remarks that Moriaen "resembled his father/the noble knight Sir Aglavael" – a resemblance vested not in physical appearance, since Acglavael's handsomeness and fairness are remarked upon early, but vested in nobility, courage, and prowess (l. 648, 655, 2558–9). D. A. Wells sees thematic manifestation of the words of the Bride in Canticles I: 4 – *nigra sum sed formosa, I am black but beautiful* – presented here as "the contrast between outer blackness of skin and inner worth" ("Middle Dutch" 262).

The world beyond, represented by the land of the blacks, is more sketchily rendered in *Moriaen* than in *Parzival*, but like *Parzival's* Zazamanc, *Moriaen's* Moorland also resembles Europe. With Artur's return from Saxon captivity, and victory in the Irish war (thanks to Moriaen and Artur's principal knights), convivial celebrations follow; Walewein, Lanceloet, and Perchevael thereafter accompany Moriaen and his father to Moorland so that Acglavael can fulfill his pledge, marry Moriaen's mother, and make right earlier wrongs.

In Moorland, an *Odyssey*-like skirmish occurs at Moriaen's return, when some Moorish lords "wanted to refuse them entry/in order to be able to keep [Moriaen's] heritage." But after the Black Knight slays fifteen of the nobles "who wished to deny him his inheritance," the others quickly "sought mercy"

> *and yielded up to him all of his lands,*
> *and gave them into the hands of his mother*
> *and they became her men and from that time on*
> *they received their lands in fief from her.*
>
> *(l. 4619–22)*

We thus see a fully operational feudalism in Moorland, where Moriaen's mother is "proclaimed queen/of all the land" (l. 4624–5). The grand fourteen-day nuptial celebrations that follow are little different from great-occasion fêting and feasting in Europe's courts, with food aplenty; music, entertainment, and heralds; rich gifts of horses, clothing, and treasure; and "great largesse" (l. 4629–44).

At its end, after all the invited nobles have departed, Walewein, Lanceloet, and Perchevael make ready to return to King Artur's court, "for it was drawing nigh to Pentecost," when Lanceloet's son, Galaats (Galahad), the Grail Knight of the Old French *Prose Lancelot* cycle, would arrive at court and be knighted, signaling the start of the Grail Quest proper (l. 4661, 4665–7). Standing between the romance *Perchevael* and the *Queeste vanden Grale*, Moriaen's narrative obligingly prepares to segue into the next romance of the *Compilation*.[36]

Acglavael, Moriaen, and the new Black Queen remain in the land of the Blacks, an intact family at last. Europe has thus lost Acglavael, an Arthurian knight, to the great outside. Like *Parzival*, where Feirefiz leaves Europe for a country of black folk – India – *Moriaen*'s Europe is also evacuated of its sole black knight, as Moriaen returns home. Moriaen's home – what we see of it – looks a lot like Europe in chivalry, customs, values, feudalism, and even Christianity – almost an extension of Europe, but with black folk in it. The land of the Blacks and the land of European Arthurian knights are equal and alike, it seems, but separate.

The theorized universalism of chivalry, feudalism, and customs, in both *Parzival* and *Moriaen*, drives a hypothesis in which the world, for all its exoticism, wealth, and differently colored populations, mirrors Europe, and is in fact (might as well be) Europe. The identification with otherness on display here is thus a structure in which Europe identifies *itself* within the other – an Imaginary identification that is ultimately narcissistic, turning the circuit of attention away from otherness and back to Europe.[37]

Moreover, the chivalry on display in *Moriaen* seems of an emphatically homosocial kind. In the course of the knights' adventures, a damsel in distress and a princess turn up, but are never named; Moriaen's mother is never named – she's just a "princess" or a "queen" – and even Guenevere, Artur's celebrated queen is never named in this text, which refers to her merely as "Artur's queen." Unlike Feirefiz, Moriaen is given no lady of his own, and Acglavael's attachment to Moriaen's mother seems almost a pro forma plot necessity, occurring offstage, and is never dramatized, even at their reunion, when "each gave the other their promise in marriage" – an opportunity at last, surely, if ever there was one, for depicting the attachment between this White Knight and his Black Queen (l. 4628).[38]

The narrative expends several lines expatiating on the queen's feudal rights and Moriaen's dispatch of the lords who are tardy to surrender their usurped privileges, but no lines at all on the reunion of two betrothed lovers who spent twenty-four years apart. Instead, joy of a generalized, communal kind is perfunctorily invoked – "There was great joy and celebration there" – before the narrative quickly switches its attention to the feasting. Women, it seems, even exotic black women who prove irresistible to Arthurian knights, are shunted to the wings. For a more realized literary portrayal of a Black Queen, we must return to Wolfram's *Parzival*.

Black Queen/White Queen: The Geo-Erotics of Virtue, Flesh, and Epidermal Race

What difference does gender make to color? Or, to put it more precisely, if chivalry builds a bridge across epidermal race for elite men in literature, how do black *women* – who are palpably not knights – figure in the global chivalry theorized in romances like *Moriaen* and *Parzival*? In *Moriaen*, the black queen is presumably Christian, like her son – the text registers no religious difference for Moorland, nor are objections raised to the marriage between her and Acglavael – so Moriaen's mother faces no barrier by virtue of alien religion. Indeed, the universality of chivalric values enables this princess to become a queen, and regain social legitimacy and her economic rights. There's little to indicate, however, that Acglavael's return is driven by longing of the kind, say, that Gahmuret professes to feel for Belakane after his abandonment of her. Acglavael aspires to remedy his wrongs, and win the grace of Moriaen's mother, he says, but any suggestion that *fin'amor* is the driving force, rather than contrition at his chivalric inadequacies, must issue from readerly optimism.

Courtly love – a key animating fiction in chivalric culture and ideology – is not fleshed out in *Moriaen* in the way that it is in *Parzival*. The depiction of Moriaen's mother is so sketchy that the focus of courtliness lies in the chivalric behavior of two men, Moriaen and Acglavael, which restores her rights, elevates her to queenship, and ensures that marriage to an Arthurian knight is the proper outcome.

What emotional current exists flows from the black princess to Acglavael. She is roused by Acglavael's "great courtesy" and beauty ("he was so fair to look upon"): "attracted to his most handsome appearance,/a maiden fell in love with him:/that was my mother, by my faith," as Moriaen tells it (l. 648–9). There's a hint of Acglavael's desire in that "she did *his* will" after what sounds like courtly flirtation ("So far went the matter … through their words"), so that she "gave herself to him" after the precautionary initiative of securing a mutual pledge of troth:

> *So far went the matter*
> *between them through their words*
> *that she did his will*
> *on account of his great courtesy,*
> *and because he was so fair to look upon.*

She was ill paid for this,
and she suffered grievously for it.
Each pledged the other his troth
before she gave herself to him.

(l. 651–9)

In contrast to the chaste recitation of the facts by the son of this sexual union in *Moriaen* (we may sympathize, of course, with Moriaen's reluctance to elaborate on the primal scene of his conception, but the text also forgoes subsequent opportunities to portray a strong reunion between Acglavael and the Black Queen), *Parzival* shows us that courtly love is alive and well between the races, when a White Knight decides to go native with the local lovelies in Zazamanc, in the person of its Black Queen.

Intriguingly, Wolfram never explicitly acknowledges Belakane's beauty, though the narrative takes note of her body: Her black hand disarms and undresses Gahmuret; her black image is etched against white samite on her banners; and tears flow down from her eyes (Cyril Edwards 20, 15, 14; Lachmann I: 80, I: 58, I: 54). The romance seems almost afraid to *say* that she's beautiful, repeatedly turning instead to her color – if anything is brighter than the day, the queen does not resemble it; unlike the dewy rose, her splendor was black in hue – as if dutiful to the discourse on blackness it inherits in the thirteenth century. Or, as Jerold Frakes puts it, "Belakane's beauty is described in terms of how it does *not* conform to the norm" (82).

And yet, mysteriously, Gahmuret's desire for Belakane is powerful, rapid, and intense. It renders him sleepless at night, and causes him to swoon again and again, writhing and twisting like a bundle of willow twigs, his joints cracking, so that the night feels interminable, all the way till dawn breaks (Cyril Edwards 16–17; Lachmann I: 66). White is drawn to black, however taboo this attraction may be, and even if the discourse on blackness might judge it an inappropriate reaction. In the twelfth century, Peter Abelard's letter to his wife Heloise, as we saw in Chapter 1, reminds us that where *black women* are concerned, a counterdiscourse on blackness existed which admitted the desirability of black female partners for erotic purposes. In female, sexed-and-bodied form, color can afford special pleasures to be enjoyed and relished in privacy by a man:

it often happens that the flesh of black women is all the softer to touch ... and for this reason the pleasure they give is greater and more suitable for private than for public enjoyment, and their husbands take them into a bedroom to enjoy them rather than parade them before the world.

(Radice 140)[39]

We see the narrative gaze in *Parzival* follow Gahmuret and Belakane all the way into their bedchamber and onto their well-adorned bed with its sable coverlet: There, Gahmuret "was disarmed by the queen's black hand ... [and] intimate hospitality was granted him in increased measure...Then the queen practiced noble, sweet love, as did Gahmuret, her heart's beloved. Yet their skins were unalike" (Cyril Edwards 20; Lachmann I: 80). Fascination with the erotic contrast of skin, in this most intimate of encounters – black on white/ white on black – may lend a certain piquancy to that noble, sweet love practiced by the queen and Gahmuret which readers are invited to imagine. With satisfaction, the text adds a little later that she who was a maiden before was now a woman (Cyril Edwards 21; Lachmann I: 82).

Albertus Magnus' *Quaestiones super De animalibus* helps to supply a physiognomic and humoral basis for the gravitational pull exerted by black women (like Belakane) on white men (like Gahmuret):

> For black women are hotter [a reference to the classical and medieval theory of humors], and most of all dusky women, who are the sweetest to have sex with, so lechers say … because the mouth of their vulva is temperate and gently embraces the penis.
>
> (quoted by Biller, "Black Women" 486)

Peter Biller ("Black Women") thoughtfully surveys the long trail of scientific texts from antiquity – translated, annotated, interpreted, modified, and taught in university lectures and curricula – though which black women arrive in the Middle Ages as sexually superior objects of desire. We may also note the power and appeal of taboo: If black is the color of sin, shame, sinful thoughts, and unchastity, as *Parzival*'s narrator says it is, the blackness of Belakane's skin, so frequently pointed to by the text, is exciting by virtue of its embodying the forbidden. The excitement is intensified when the color of the forbidden, on female skin, is indivisible from a woman of such chastity, sweetness, and nobility as Belakane, a woman who is the very opposite of her enticing skin, inside her skin. Belakane literally embodies the most exciting contradictions.

Wolfram's *Parzival* carefully explains, however, that Belakane's allure is *internal*, not fleshly: It's her womanliness, great loyalty, womanly woman's ways, womanly and loyal disposition, chastity, good company, womanly bearing, true chastity, pure nature, sweetness, and nobility that draw Gahmuret like a magnet (Cyril Edwards 14, 24, 39; Lachmann I: 54, I: 96, I: 154). His attraction is swift and powerful, rendering him helpless, so we must concede great discernment to this White Knight's powers of interior inspection.

A victim of the lover's malady, Gahmuret is rendered sleepless and writhing, swooning and twisting, with his joints cracking all night long till morning all because of Belakane's *virtue*. Taking the text at its word, we see that color in female sexed-and-bodied form can also be bridged, if the black woman is virtuous, womanly, pure, sweet, and courtly, as Belakane unquestionably shows herself to be. This Black Queen's example attests that in matters of love, (feminine) *virtue* trumps (a woman's) *color*.

Sex, too, trumps color. Belakane's virtue would be more convincing as the sole factor in the White Knight's mesmerized passion if the text did not so often refer to her flesh and its sumptuous color, so vividly embodying all that good Christians must not touch or handle. Because the text *does* refer time and again to Belakane's dark flesh – always discreetly, without giving itself away, without disclosing the kind of voyeurism it allows itself in gazing on white women's flesh, like Herzeloyde's – we may be forgiven the suspicion that the Black Queen's internal virtue alone is not the sole powerful lure for Gahmuret. Gahmuret, a white Christian European knight, gets to touch and handle the dark flesh of an exquisitely sweet, virginal queen of great virtue – and also become, in the process, fabulously wealthy, with treasures and land, as the King of Zazamanc.

Belakane too is powerfully drawn to the White Knight, so that the lovers' passion is exquisitely mutual. Black is also drawn to white, but here we are to understand that this is normal, since white is the default category of beauty, and Gahmuret is described, like Acglavael, as handsome, and Belakane is described as a *connoisseuse* of the beauty of white-skinned men, whom she had seen before (Cyril Edwards 14; Lachmann I: 54). True to the best conventions of courtly love, an intense, almost unbearable desire instantly pounces as they gaze at each other, the woman gazing externally at male beauty, and the man gazing (ostensibly) at interior female goodness (Cyril Edwards 14; Lachmann I: 54).

Belakane's lack of Christianity is a barrier, of course, but the text devises an ad hoc solution when it tells us that her chastity was a pure baptism in and of itself, and so are the tears which flow from her eyes down her body, an effluvia likened to baptismal waters (Cyril Edwards 14; Lachmann I: 54). These makeshift modes of virtual baptism suffice for a sexual and marital union between the Black Queen and White Knight, but can conveniently be overlooked when Gahmuret needs a reason for abandoning his pregnant wife (whom he knows is pregnant, since his letter to her details an extensive genealogy for his unborn child). When Gahmuret needs a reason to be gone, Belakane is really still a heathen, despite her virtue and her 'baptismal' tears.[40]

By contrast to Belakane, the two White Queens who vie for Gahmuret on his return to Europe are not characterized as particularly virtuous. Through her messengers, Ampflise, the Queen of France, vaunts her superior claims to Gahmuret as his earlier love and his lady, and boasts of her greater beauty, power, and skills as a lover compared with Herzeloyde (Cyril Edwards 38, 34; Lachmann I: 134; I: 150).

Herzeloyde, the Queen of Wales, is not especially virtuous either; she claims Gahmuret against Ampflise on the basis of a chivalric technicality, and dismisses Belakane on the basis that the Black Queen is not a Christian (Cyril Edwards 41; Lachmann I: 160). Though a virgin, Herzeloyde woos Gahmuret aggressively, with "ruthless determination to secure him as a husband . . . ignoring the scruples he expresses and the claims of the other two women in his life" (Gibbs 17). She proffers a kiss (of welcome), has Gahmuret sit close by her, touches his bruises with her own white hands, and argues religion mightily as a weapon against Belakane (Cyril Edwards 36, 38, 41; Lachmann I: 142, I: 144, I: 152, I: 160).

Gahmuret, however, is shown to be far less quick to respond to Herzeloyde than to the Black Queen. It is Herzeloyde who finds him pleasing to look at, so that love oppressed her; she openly tells Gahmuret that she longs for his love (Cyril Edwards 36, 41; Lachmann I: 144, I: 160). In response, the knight tells Herzeloyde he can only accept her hospitality kiss if she kisses all the other lords too, and she accedes to this condition, kissing those she finds worthy and of sufficient rank (Cyril Edwards 36; Lachmann I: 144). At Kanvoleis, Gahmuret is shown to be quietly dejected and depressed, his heart wounded, troubled by his longing for his black queen and his wish to return home, and also by his brother's death (Cyril Edwards 39; Lachmann I: 154).

When it is clear that Herzeloyde has won him over Ampflise, we are told that grief still causes Gahmuret pain, and he takes the precaution of negotiating a prenuptial contract with Herzeloyde, to be allowed to go tourneying once a month (this actually being the reason, he now says, that he left Belakane) – and threatening to run away again if he's not allowed to tourney – before he finally accepts the lands and the royal maiden (Cyril Edwards 42; Lachmann I: 166). We see that the "passion-driven twenty-four hour courtship of Gahmuret and Belakâne may be contrasted . . . with Gahmuret's later marriage to Herzeloyde, where there is no depiction of excessive passion, but rather an almost excessive rationality, such that they [must] take their case for and against marriage (Gahmuret opposes it) to an arbiter" (Frakes 85).

It is a delicious romance conceit, of course, that a handsome knight habituated to amassing lands and women (Ampflise also offers a crown, scepter, and land) must be persuaded by slow degrees and burdensome arguments to accept a radiantly fair, sexually aggressive virgin queen and all her kingdom, and no doubt *Parzival*'s readers enjoy the conceit (Cyril Edwards 33; Lachmann I: 132). We are told that Gahmuret's sadness and grief finally vanish when Herzeloyde is bereft of her maidenhood, and we're treated to a lively description of their mouths kissing and the renewal of the knight's high spirits; we note that Gahmuret is now no longer referred to as the King of Zazamanc, but only as "the Angevin" and Herzeloyde's beloved (Cyril Edwards 43; Lachmann I: 168).

Given Gahmuret's history of infidelity, readers may cynically take his avowal of deep attachment to Belakane with a barrel of salt. After all, this is a man whose heart still lifts at the mention of Ampflise, whom he says is his true lady: Only the verdict of knights, he avows, keeps him in Herzeloyde's land (Cyril Edwards 42; Lachmann I: 166). Perhaps we are meant to imagine Gahmuret as a weak-willed, handsome, initially landless opportunist, who means what he says when he says it, yet whose behavior in the sphere of love shows that he moves on quickly.

In the sphere of war, as we have seen, his actions show a continuity of devotion to the Caliph of Baghdad, but his allegiance to women is shorter-lived. By way of excuse, the romance refers to Gahmuret's tacked-on, putative faery ancestry: His is a nature and lineage that compels him to love or desire love, the text says with sly charm (Cyril Edwards 42, 371 n.42; Lachmann I: 164).

Still, of the three queens in Gahmuret's short life, Belakane is the only beloved for whom Gahmuret declares longing, desire, and grief at being away from her (Cyril Edwards 39, 41; Lachmann I: 154, I: 160). Though he finds joy with Herzeloyde and his sadness disappears, there are no equal declarations of powerful passion and overwhelming desire for his White Queen as there are for Belakane. Albrecht Classen exclaims at how "profound and entirely unorthodox" Gahmuret's remarkable erotic relationship with Belakane is (88).

To Gahmuret, therefore, should go the last word on black–white interracial marriage in thirteenth-century medieval literature: Many an ignorant man believes that it was Belakane's blackness that drove him away, Gahmuret says to Kaylet, his kinsman, when they are in Kanvoleis, but he would rather look on her dark flesh than on the sun (Cyril Edwards 39; Lachmann 156).[41]

Mixed Babes and Haunting Presences: A Lump of Flesh, Piebald Offspring, the Giants' Infants, and the Return of the Black Knight

Like *Parzival* in the early thirteenth century, the *King of Tars*, a fourteenth-century Middle English romance, also highlights a black–white, interracial–interreligious marriage – a fertile union that also produces offspring – but in the English text, the man is the black heathen Saracen, and the woman is the white Christian European.[42] I've discussed at length the race and gender politics of this miscegenating pair (see *Empire of Magic*, chapter 4), and will confine myself here to noting primarily how much more conventional this romance's epidermal understanding is than *Parzival*'s or *Moriaen*'s in addressing the color line.

No special effort is expended to suggest the allure of dark flesh, or an alternative interior beauty paired with exterior blackness. Instead, the heroine, a nameless princess of Tars, is conventionally "white as the feather of a swan" (l. 12), with a complexion rosy as a "blossom on a briar," with the traditional grey eyes (l. 15, 941), sloping shoulders, and white neck (l. 16) of normative female beauty in medieval European literature – an image found in rhetorical treatises and repeated ad infinitum in manuscript illuminations.

It is thus no surprise that the Sultan of Damascus would demand this fair-skinned European beauty in connubial exchange for peace with her father, the King of Tars.[43] Nor does it surprise that the Sultan's own color is conventionally registered as "foul" (l. 393), black and loathly (l. 928), and hideous. By the fourteenth century, as Madeline Caviness points out, white has become the normative, definitive color of Latin Christian European identity, and, as Devisse and others point out, black has become established as the color of torturers of Christ and the Baptist, and the color of hell and the devil.

The exploration of what whiteness can mean – an interest, we saw, in *Parzival*'s early thirteenth-century characterization of Gahmuret – is thus superfluous. Whiteness can be counted on to deliver its racial-religious referent/s dependably. We see this highlighted in a theatrical way when the princess of Tars, in an unnerving plot twist, acts out the rituals of her conversion to Islam. Her conversion is stagey and elaborate, spun out in detail: The princess is made to kneel down and disavow the Christian God and faith; she verbally requests religious instruction in the new confession, makes an avowal of faith, ceremoniously kisses all the "Saracen idols" in a row, learns heathen prayers, and "said them openly" (l. 484–506). Though the narrative tells us that her actions are deceptive and she continued to pray to Jesus in her heart, the princess' simulated conversion has disturbed scholars, who have faulted her at the very least for hypocrisy.

This simulacrum of conversion is, indeed, deeply troubling on different levels. Heroines who bravely choose torture and death, over even pretend conversion, populate Christian hagiography, and Christian audiences are accustomed to admire the courage of honest martyrs. Furthermore, if we understand religion as an adherence to theological law, that is witnessed by conformity to a set of communal customs, gestures, and outward practices (an individual's private intent being otherwise unverifiable, as we said in Chapter 2), there's also little, visibly, to distinguish between the truth of an outward conversion to Islam and the truth of a supposed inner fidelity to Christianity.

Except, of course, for skin color. Because the princess' skin stays white and fair from beginning to end, never vacillating at any time, the romance is able to signal the continuity and stability of her Christian religious identity. If the princess prays like a Muslim, follows Islamic customs and law, and openly professes to believe in "Mahoun" (l. 847), there is nothing else to distinguish her from faithful, practicing Muslims, *except her color*. In a narrative sequence where acts are disturbingly disjoint from their inner reality, and words are uttered in order *not* to be believed, the guarantee of meaning via the witness of color is deeply reassuring.

The reliability of color in signaling true identity is affirmed again later with the somatic transformation of the Sultan, who changes from "blac & loply" to "Al white" without taint at *his* baptism, when he is granted a new epidermal race as part and parcel of a new Christian religious identity (l. 928–30). (Thereafter, the newly whitened Christian Sultan, at the behest of his pious wife, conducts crusading warfare against all Saracens who refuse conversion, behaving like a typical *chanson* leader, a veritable Charlemagne or Richard Lionheart.) For this fourteenth-century romance, whiteness as an index of piety, aesthetics, and Christian identity has become the *sine qua non* of how to tell the truth of someone's interior being. We are now a long way from Gahmuret and *Parzival*.

Before the Sultan's christening, the fertile sexual union of this black–white couple also produces offspring: not a whimsically piebald baby like Feirefiz, who bears race-and-religion on his surface, or a single-color child like Moriaen, black without but white within (belying his skin, Moriaen is a Christian and virtually European knight), but instead an inanimate, insensate wad of flesh, without blood, bone, limbs, or face – a true monstrosity that is, mercifully, not alive (l. 579–82).

Causative attribution is uncertain. The fleshy lump is the physical embodiment of an obscene union in which a Christian woman has done the unthinkable, either by going through public acts of conversion to Islam, or by joining with a Muslim without first converting him to her religion, or both (l. 604–5). Is it the Muslim man's (de)generative seed that fashions the monster which is birthed? Or does the terrifying spectacle of a Christian princess's avowed conversion to an infernal religion issue, *par consequence*, a fleshly horror, whatever her denial of the validity of her acts? Or is it the intimate metaphysical mingling of the warring essences of Islam and Christianity in the conjugal bed that so misshapes the infant flesh?

Despite the ostensible undecidability of cause and effect, the explicit lesson in this representational script of hideous birth is that religion can instruct biology – the lesson, also, in the Sultan's transubstantiation from black to white. As we saw in Chapters 1 and 2, political theology can understand religion to predispose somatic race: Jews, after all, were said to have a unique stench, to bleed congenitally and require Christian blood, to have a distinctive phenotype, and even to sport horns and tails. Cultural fantasy obligingly appends epidermal transformation and monstrous birth also as vocabularies manifesting the power of religion – power implicit in religious essences that are able to manipulate and instruct ontology.

When the fleshy wad is baptized by a priest and given the name "John" (on the feast day of the Baptist), it instantly transforms into a little infant, "with life and limb and face" as well as "skin and flesh," an infant who is now conventionally the fairest child ever born (l. 775–6, 778, 781). Not only does the sacrament of baptism possess a spiritual essence with the power to reshape ontology and fleshly matter but, we must assume, baptism also has the power to confer a divine soul in the process of making a human being.[44]

The lesson of progeny, in this romance, is that in matters of religious race, a child figures as the ground of contestation: not only in how his fate is decided – will he be a boy martyr slaughtered by the Jews, or will he lead Christians ringingly into a new future? – but also in his very flesh, which itself can manifest the contest of religions.

But the most whimsical illustration of how biracial–interreligious sexual mingling manifests itself on the flesh of offspring is no doubt the piebald Feifefiz, a literary curiosity about whom much has been written. Having someone's skin be a canvas that manifests his birth history and inner nature is a playful authorial decision that proffers lots of cues to an audience. Literally a black-and-white foil to his white-skinned, Grail Knight half-brother Parzival, Feirefiz is ably recognized by critics as a character whose color is "a mark of difference against and through whom the image of an ideal knight, the Christian and white Parzival, is developed" (Lampert, "Race" 405).

To be an adequate counterpart for his brother, Feirefiz is allowed many strong character qualities. The piebald knight displays great martial prowess and chivalric magnanimity, and like a true cosmopolitan, *he speaks French* (Cyril Edwards 311; Lachmann II: 272). He has a line of successful female conquests: Like his father, queens are eager to give him lands, love, treasure, and themselves. He is a king of lands in his own right, and arrives as the leader of twenty-five armies, assembled from such far-flung, diverse territories that none of these armies understood the others' speech; indeed, so many different lands served him that the constituent populations were not just Moors and blacks, but included Saracens of dissimilar aspect (Cyril Edwards 308; Lachmann II: 260).

This worldly, sophisticated romance knows Saracens come in all visages and guises, and speak many different tongues. Most of all, the text is just agog at Feirefiz's massive wealth: Narrative attention is glued to the display of dazzling gemstones and finery that accompany Feirefiz, his largesse in distributing treasure, and his unchallenged status as the wealthiest person who sat at the Round Table (Cyril Edwards 307, 308, 311, 316, 317, 318, 319, 324, 325, 328; Lachmann II: 258, II: 270, II: 292, II: 294, II: 300, II: 302, II: 320, II: 326, II: 338).

This parti-colored knight, true to his skin, is of mixed character. He is heathen, of course, and described as proud. Indeed, "wealthy" and "heathen" are the two choice epithets ubiquitously attached to him, raised by the narrative as often as his peculiar dermal coloration. Jerold Frakes additionally observes that Feirefiz's "lust" for the radiantly fair, lustrous Grail Maiden Repanse de Schoye makes him over into the male equivalent of the enamored Saracen princess who is a staple of European romance and *chanson de geste* – she who eagerly forsakes kith, kin, and creed, betraying all in a heartbeat, because she hopelessly loves a Christian European knight (who is sometimes a knight she has never met, and whom she can't tell apart from the other knights in the vicinity).[45]

Feirefiz willingly undergoes baptism in order to attain Repanse. There is a comic scene in which he mistakenly thinks baptism involves martial combat (which fires his eagerness), and must have his misapprehension corrected. Critics like to pounce on this scene as a display of poor racial politics and bad taste. Frakes sums up the critical opinion on "Feirefiz's lewd shallowness":

> In reviewing several scholars' evaluations of Feirefiz's baptism as shallow, external, flippant, and motivated strictly by lust, thinly disguised as (if) *Minne*, Henry Kratz comments: "When Feirefiz is baptized, he treats the whole thing as a joke." Hans-Joachim Koppitz also imputes humor to this construction of naïve and shallow blacks/Muslims: "[Wolfram] obviously has fun with the figure of Feirefiz."
>
> (Frakes 86)

Additionally, Lisa Lampert points out that "Feirefiz's rapid conversion stands in stark contrast to the slow education in religion through which so many key characters guide Parzival" (405).

Without a doubt, a piebald knight allows a narrator significant rein for playful mischief. Feirefiz is so smitten with Repanse that his white parts blanch, and turn even paler (Cyril Edwards 339; Lachmann II: 380)! The text also refuses to say how Feirefiz's black-and-white dappling is patterned, so that some critics believe he is speckled; others imagine him with a white surface and black markings (like writing on parchment, an analogy the narrative supplies), or with a black surface and white markings; or, like Jerold Frakes, they believe him to be striped like a zebra.

The text's favorite image for Feirefiz's intermingled black-and-white is the magpie: and, indeed, it's likely that animals and animal husbandry supply Wolfram the idea of mixed coloration. Besides magpies, dappled horses, dogs, and cats are a common enough sight across the centuries – yet biogenetics has shown us that piebald humans are also attested, if rare.[46] Feirefiz's piebaldism thus is not merely a fantasy invention shorn of all ties to reality – like pigs with wings – but textual reticence makes the bemusing fascination of Feirefiz's coloring a tease, playfully inviting speculation.

Whatever the impetus for Feirefiz' conversion to Christianity – often, medieval literature doesn't seem too particular about what the motivating reasons for conversion are, so long as conversion does in fact take place – Feirefiz turns into a paragon of Christian missionary zeal once he and Repanse move to India. With the plot closure of their removal overseas, Europe is thus emptied of its one black-and-white knight: Like Moriaen's departure and return to Moorland, Feirefiz's departure leaves Europe whole, and pristine once again in the European imagination.

In India, Feirefiz becomes the romance equivalent of the apostle Thomas, and cultural fantasy's stand-in for the historical Nestorian missionizing that took place on the subcontinent over centuries. Feirefiz's change at his baptism is thus *internal* – unlike the *King of Tars*' theatrically bleached Sultan of Damascus – but the change is equally effective and permanent, granting him entry into a new religious race, and transforming him into a missionary for Christianity. The converted Feirefiz's overseas actions thus fulfill what Gahmuret's pretext for leaving Belakane had *claimed* to want: conversion of the heathen. Like a latter-day Paul, Feirefiz begins an epistolary mission, sending letters all over India to tell people about the Christian way of life (Cyril Edwards 344–5; Lachmann II: 400).

Feirefiz and Repanse also become the genealogical birth parents of Prester John, the legendary Christian priest-king of India whose mid-twelfth century creation is thus ingeniously supplied with an early thirteenth-century prequel. I have written a good deal about Prester John in *Empire of Magic* (chapter 5) and also in Chapters 3 and 6 here, but it is worth noting for the moment how Feirefiz's trajectory of journeying – he starts in Africa, and ends in India – reverses the trajectory of the Prester John legend (John is found in India in the twelfth century, but by the fourteenth is relocated to Africa, where he begins to be sought).

This back-and-forth circuit that links Africa and India registers well the close associations of these lands, whose trade is documented in the archives of the Cairo Geniza, and in the Christian imaginary of missionary endeavor (see for example Goitein and Friedman). An icon created out of the "thought-world of the crusades" (Hamilton 256), Prester John of India will be eagerly awaited by the militants of the Fifth Crusade at Damietta in Egypt, later in the thirteenth century.

I've argued that Prester John is the moving figure of European desire in the Middle Ages, and where John goes, Europe is not far behind. Here, a brilliant thirteenth-century German romance represents John as really three-fourths European, so that the absorbing Western fantasy of a fabulously wealthy and powerful Oriental Christian potentate out there, beckoning Europe to come find him, is thoughtfully supplied a retroactive prequel that explains John's Christianity as *really originating in Europe after all*. John is not a Nestorian, nor any other heretical Eastern Christian, but the genuine article, a Latin Christian priest-king seeded by Europe out of Africa through the agnatic line.

The story that begins with Gahmuret thus seeds a fantasy of colonization that makes Indian lands really Europe's, through the paternal line. India – also known as Tribalibot, in this romance – is given to Feirefiz by his erstwhile (abandoned) lover and patroness, Queen Secundille, who conveniently dies, and is a land therefore legitimately ruled by Feirefiz and his radiant, lustrous European queen, the former Grail Maiden. Like the India of the twelfth-century Prester John legend, Tribalibot-India's rivers are encrusted with precious gemstones instead of gravel – a prize indeed. And here, too, Prester John – who is three-fourths European and all Latin Christian – figures the peregrinatory power of European desire: a desire birthing the tale of a sojourning European who sires John's father out of pliant, cooperative mother Africa.

Rewriting history, cultural fantasy offers global Christianity as emanating from Europe, not the Nestorian East, routing that Christianity through African darkness and heathenism, to emerge into the shining future in India in the form of the Prester John legend, a legend with substantial power to invite European exploration, settlement, and conquest for more than half a millennium. Out of the marriage of a European knight-adventurer and an African queen come the wonders proffered by the (now Latin) patriarch of Asia.

My discussion of raced offspring in medieval literature would be sorely remiss if it did not consider the black giant infants who make an odd appearance in the Middle English *Sultan of Babylon* (and the Middle English *Sir Ferumbras*) in the early fifteenth century. While gigantic black Saracens are a familiar *topos* in romance and *chanson de geste*, the *Sultan of Babylon* (*Sowdane of Babylone*) – perhaps the liveliest constituent in a well-known cluster of Charlemagne romances in Middle English representing rewritten versions (freely adapted "translations") of Old French *chansons de geste* – presents us with twin *babies*: the infants of a black giantess, Barrok (as the *Sultan* names her) or Amyote (as *Ferumbras* names her), and a black giant Saracen king of Ethiopia, Astrogote, who has the head of a boar (l. 346–7, 352–3, 2939–44).[47]

Astrogote, the father of the twins, is a conventional black Saracen giant, complete with animal characteristics to suggest his quasihuman, subnormal, heathen, foreign, monstrous nature. Barrok, the mother of the twins, is a little more unusual, since heathen black giantesses do not abound in medieval literature. Most unusual, of course, are these extraordinary, enormous, black giant babes. Indeed, the remarkable presence of these black infants in a *family* of giants intimates that the giants which are so common in medieval European romances are perhaps not singular aberrations *contra naturam*, as we are wont to imagine, but may represent whole *races* of giants, races more fully attested in Arabic than in European romance (where giants usually materialize as singular émigrés).

The massive black newborns, seven months old and fourteen feet long, are found after their parents are killed, but they do not survive, since they are nurselings unable to eat solid food – "neither butter nor bread" – and lack a mother to nurse them (l. 3020–3, 3031–4). Before their death, however, Charlemagne has them christened, optimistically naming them "Roland" and "Oliver" after his most famous knights, so that they would be mighty men of hand (l. 3027–8).

But why would a late medieval English romance conjure up a pair of giant black infant siblings? A lively, engaging text, the *Sultan of Babylon* also energetically conjures up other inexplicable strangenesses.

For instance: Early on, the romance presents us with a scene of rapturous celebration among the bivouacked and encamped Saracen armies after they have captured, sacked, and despoiled the city of Rome. The Sultan, Laban, and his son, Ferumbras, propitiate and make offerings to their heathen gods, burning frankincense whose smoky fumes linger strongly and long (l. 679–82). The festivities are triumphant and raucous, filling the air, ear, and nostrils, and making for "a fearful fascination" (Lupack 3): The men boisterously blow horns of brass and drink the blood of beasts, along with milk and honey that was royal and good; serpents are fried in oil and served to the Sultan (l. 683–8). In the midst of rowdy feasting, imbibing, and rejoicing; amid the brass horns, the din, and the smoky fumes, the men bellow out, "Antrarian, antrarian" (l. 689).

What is "Antrarian?" Why does the text pool attention around the Saracen army's shout, by explicitly telling us in the next line that the word "signifyed 'Joy generalle'" (l. 690) – that it signified communal joy? "Antrarian," Jeffrey Jerome Cohen responds, is "A nonsense word . . . introduced and glossed as if it were *Sarrazinois* – that is, as if the Saracens possessed a unifying, signifying language" ("Saracen Enjoyment" 130). Cohen's suggestion is part of a lucid and persuasive article on medieval race and racism which cites Alain Grosrichard's remark that "the West as a political system relies on a fantasy of a distant and despotic *subject supposed to enjoy*" ("Saracen Enjoyment" 130).

Cohen thus offers the *Sultan* as an example of how literature in the West dreams up Orientalist fantasies of Asiatic pleasures, complete with made-up nonsense words such as "Antrarian." This is an unexceptional and flawless reading, entirely legitimate and soundly grounded in a critical practice that remains of significant value: Cohen is absolutely correct.

Yet, what *else* might we find if we follow, offshore and out of England, the word *Antrarian*?

Antara ibn Shaddad, an African-Arab cultural hero equivalent in stature and fame to King Arthur or Charlemagne in the medieval Latin West, is the celebrated protagonist of one of the most famous, and largest, corpora of popular and literary Arabic cycles of heroic romances, accumulated through some eight or nine centuries of oral and literary narration. Stories of Antara, the "black knight," are still recounted today, sometimes by an *Antari* specializing in the aggregated corpus of the *Antarahya,* and are cited by Africanists and African Americanists such as W. E. B. Du Bois (4, 33, 104, 108).

A pre-Islamic warrior-poet of the sixth century CE, about whom little is known originally beyond the tradition that he was supposedly born in slavery, his mother an Ethiopian slave and his father an Arab prince, and who rose to become a towering hero of gigantic chivalry, courage, and prowess, Antara became the hero of his people, the Banu Abs, and was affectionately dubbed the "Father of Knights" in the Islamic Near East and Africa. In final literary compilations of the *Sirat Antar* (more than 5,000 pages in printed volumes, with the earliest extant 1466 manuscript of 919 folios representing less than half the total narrative material), Antara is diversely the foe, ally, friend, or rival of Greeks, Africans, Arabs, Franks, and crusaders.

Featuring tournaments; single combats; service to women, widows, and the poor; chivalry; feasts; adventures; extraordinary, named horses; heroic vaunting; the presence of ladies; giants; magical devices; the conquest of cities (including Rome); warriors who are poets; and boisterous humor, the expansive narrative tree of the *Antarahya,* with variant plot endings and episodes, has certain consistent features. *Antara's blackness of skin* is one focal point, for instance; another is his attribution of his prowess – his skill in the sword – to his lineage through his African mother (who is variously characterized as a slave or as a relative of the Ethiopian/Abyssinian *Negus*).

Worlds secreted inside the *Sultan of Babylon* delicately peel open when we see that its merrymaking Saracen armies are shouting out the name of their semilegendary hero, *Antara* – just as King Arthur's men might call out "Arthur!" or Charlemagne's men "Montjoie! Saint Denis!" – raucously and expectantly, calling for stories from the *Antarahya,* as they feast in communal triumph and joy.

The black knight himself in one of his vaunts encourages men to summon his great legend by name – "If you call aloud the name of Antar.../all will take you for a hero" (Norris 215) – a legend appositely recalled during feasting and celebration, social rituals at which stories are also retold with joy in the Latin West, whether in the Anglo-Saxon mead hall or called forth by Arthur's demand for a tale or adventure before the king sits down to his meat. *Antrarian* – the text winks – signifies communal joy and delight, "Joy generalle."

Following the trace of a famous name out of Africa and Arabia, we also glimpse a discontinuous tracery of global stories whose vestiges alight on some of the *Sultan's* characteristic and striking features. Like the Saracen Floripas in the *Sultan*, who chooses the Christian Guy of Burgundy as her lover and converts to Christianity, "Christian girls" in Arabic romances and heroic epics act "blatantly to seduce Muslims ... [and] must be converted" (Lyons I: 40). The Hilali cycle (*Taghribat Bani Hilal*) denigrates "Christian dogs who worship stones" (Lyons 1: 43), while the *Sultan's* Laban, who worships graven idols, denigrates his foes as "Crystyn dogges" (l. 956). Magic devices abound in Arabic cycles, some furnishing food and wine and others simply removing hunger, like Floripas' girdle which makes Charlemagne's Peers feel full and revivified (Lyons I: 51). In the *Sirat al-Amira Dhat al-Himma*, the Dailamis fight with clubs – so does the giant Alagolofur in the *Sultan*, who brandishes an oak log as his club (l. 2919) – and mountaineers wield sickles to mow down horses (Lyons I: 55); the giantess Barrok in the *Sultan* also wields a sickle to mow down all "like sheep in a fold" (l. 2940–1).

Beautiful, feisty Islamic princesses such as Ain al-Hayat in the *Qissat Firuz Shah b. al-Malik Darab* are larkily casual about killing their own – dispatching a slave and three of her father's guards (Lyons 1: 110) as nimbly as the *Sultan's* feisty Islamic princess Floripas drowns her governess and dispatches her father's jailor (l. 1578, 1605–6). Using extravagant diets to characterize a culture or personage, the cycle of Firuz Shah has a sorcerer eat reptiles and drink "noxious brews," while the *Sultan* has serpents fried in oil served to Laban, who has his men drink the blood of wild beasts to fire them up for battle (l. 1007).

In matters of conversion, the Arab cycles "show a mirror image of the choice between conversion and death offered to Muslims in the Chanson de Geste" (Lyons 1: 47), but there, of course, it is non-Muslim heathens, not Saracens, who break or strike their idols (cf. *Sultan* l. 2507). These homologies and echoes are not, of course, exact correspondences; nor are the sociocultural worlds, plots, themes, and characters featured in Arabic romances identical to those in European romance.

But in tracking a word – *Antrarian* – that unwinds back to other cultural networks, we are able to watch the *Sultan of Babylon* signal its participation in transnational circuits of exchange in which stories, traditions, goods, and motifs are globally traded. As a participant in such trading and exchange – and trading and goods, we note, are prime tropes dramatized by this narrative (l. 2863–4, 2885–8) – the romance signals itself as a globalized text marked by crisscrossing international traces, with the global tracery that accrues becoming an important part of the text's own symbolic capital.[48]

In summoning forth the black knight, Antara, through his name, called out by Saracens in celebratory feasting, we see a method of conjuring up a tracery of foreign worlds by intimating, through a small detail, the great beyond. In that context of evocation, those massive black twins christened "Roland" and "Oliver" by Charlemagne, so that, we are told, they shall become men who are mighty of hand (l. 3029), recall the famously black-skinned Antara and his brother Shaybub, both of gigantic prowess and stature, and who as the

Roland-and-Oliver of the *Sirat Antar* are indeed mighty of hand, amassing some nine volumes of adventures. Even Antara's daughter, the black-skinned Unaytira, is a giantess of sorts, "an exceptionally large baby" able to fight from the age of five and growing into a ferocious fighter as an adult woman, with the Prophet Muhammad himself being "astonished at her size" (Lyons I: III). It is well, perhaps, that the *Sultan*'s black Roland and Oliver do not survive.

The Saracens in the *Sultan of Babylon* have their own hero – just as their European counterparts have Roland, Oliver, Charlemagne, and Arthur – and a late medieval English romance is able to materialize Antara as an absent presence, when it has its Saracen armies summon their black knight by name. No piebald Feirefiz this, Antara is an authentically African-Arabian black knight, not a creation of Christian Europe who performs as a human curiosity invented in order to bless the desires and the cultural legends of Europe. Antara, the black knight, is no conscript of Europe at all, but an authentic presence from the global outside that haunts this European text.

The Racial Saint: Transporting Africa to Europe, or, Blackness and the Enigma of Racial Sanctity

Thus far, we've seen varying degrees of conditional acceptance for black African figures who are imagined in literary fiction to possess virtue, courtliness, chivalry, prowess, wealth, and, more rarely, Christianity. As carefully hedged exceptions to the dominant medieval discourse on color, these exemplars grant insight into the conditions imagined as mitigating blackness in circumscribed contexts.

But there remains to discuss the most extraordinary cultural phenomenon of all: the sudden, seemingly inexplicable appearance, in the heartlands of medieval Europe, of *a racial saint* in whom blackness of skin, African physiognomy, and venerable sanctity coincide. Some time after 1220 and before 1250, amidst a virulent, centuries-old discourse on blackness that was still producing horrific images in visual art of vicious black African torturers of Christ, brutal black African executioners of John the Baptist, and grotesque black African devils and demons, a Christian saint who had been venerated for nearly a millennium in the Latin West was suddenly portrayed as a black African knight – in an extraordinary, lifelike statue in Magdeburg Cathedral in eastern Germany, a cathedral where he was the patron saint.

This manifestation of St. Maurice – a martyr who hailed from the third century CE – suddenly as a black African was followed by another image of him, also from the thirteenth century, in a stained glass window at Naumburg Cathedral.[49] Then, a century later, more images of a black African Maurice arrive in visual art; the images proliferate and diversify in Europe till the seventeenth century, and accrue all manner of iconographic features, in all manner of styles. Catalogued by Gude Suckale-Redlefsen, art objects depicting an African St. Maurice have been found to total nearly 300; they are spread over Germany, Scandinavia, the Czech Republic, Austria, and Poland, as the maps of their diffusion show (Devisse 270–1; Suckale-Redlefsen 16, 17, 158–285; Kaplan, *Rise* 75).

Each instance where a black St. Maurice appeared, of course, had its own matrix of enabling circumstances, but the conjuring up of a black African saint for the first time in Germany remains an astonishing phenomenon. This thirteenth-century black Maurice is a *saint* and a *knight* – the most esteemed exemplars of the human in Latin Christian Europe, and the perfect marriage of Christian faith and warrior chivalry, seamlessly meshing secular and sacred prowess.

Unlike the fictitious Prester John, another medieval icon who conjoined military and evangelical goals, Maurice was not an elusive presence hovering somewhere in the great beyond, always anticipated but never materializing, and whose Christianity would likely have been a heretical kind, if he had existed. Nor was Maurice a black knight of the kind selectively depicted in European literary fantasy, like the black Christian knight Moriaen, or the piebald pagan knight Feirefiz – African sojourners who are ejected from Europe at the end of their fictional narratives.

We have seen the carefully hedged creation of such fictional characters: Wolfram von Eschenbach's *Parzival* early in the thirteenth century presented audiences with a pagan black virtuous queen, Belakane, and her son Feirefiz, a pagan black-and-white knight of great wealth and prowess. Later in the century, Dutch literature introduced a sole Christian black knight, Moriaen, riding into Arthurian Europe to seek socioeconomic justice and the reunification of his family. Yet the Black St. Maurice of Magdeburg is uniquely different from such characters – and not only because he arises in the medium of stone, rather than words, which allows him to be encountered by *all* classes of people, illiterates and elites alike.

Maurice was not a pagan, even one of great virtue or virtuosity, and, though a Christian knight like Moriaen, he was more than just a Christian knight: He was a saint and martyr who died for his faith. When he is suddenly seen as a black African, Maurice's hagiography is already a thousand years old, and his solid presence in the heart of medieval Europe is supported by the tangible evidence of his body and relics at Magdeburg Cathedral.

Maurice's hallowed martyrdom in the third century CE is chronicled first by Eucherius, bishop of Lyon, between 443 and 450 in his *Passion of the Martyrs of Agaunum*, and recounted in a contemporary letter to Eucherius' friend, bishop Salvius (Devisse 149; Suckale-Redlefsen 28, 29). But at the time of Eucherius' chronicle, a pilgrimage to the graves of Maurice and his men was "already in full flourish" (Suckale-Redlefsen 28, 29).[50] The events of the martyrdom are roughly as follows: Maurice, leader of the Christian Theban legion of imperial Rome, and his legionaries were summoned from Thebes in Egypt to Gaul to assist the emperor Maximian in a revolt in the third century CE. Ordered to persecute Christians or to make sacrifices to pagan gods, the Christian legionaries refused and were executed, either in stages (through the Roman system of selective culling known as decimation) or at once.[51] Maurice's fame spread from Agaunum to Tours to Auxerre and thence to the rest of Europe, where, over the centuries, he became the patron saint of various places, occupations, and kingdoms. His feast day in the Roman calendar is September 22.

Unlike fantasy characters in literature, the historical existence of saints is commonly attested by the presence of physical bodies and relics. Maurice's body was transported in 960 CE, at Christmas, from Saint-Maurice-d'Agaune (in Switzerland today), where his martyrdom is traditionally held to have taken place, to the Holy Roman Emperor Otto I at Regensburg, and sent on to Magdeburg (Suckale-Redlefsen 33). Maurice's skull, later found by crusaders in Constantinople and taken to Franconia, was subsequently purchased by Magdeburg in 1220 (Suckale-Redlefsen 41). The tangibility of a saint's presence, anchored by what is believed to be his actual body, places the power, and impact, of a saint in a different register from fictional characters in literature or art.

The lifelike statue in Magdeburg suddenly presented this sainted martyr, along with his body, as a physiognomic black African. The shocking boldness of the Magdeburg invention – a break with tradition lacking precedent – is justly admired by art historians and historians alike. Unlike Nicholas of Verdun's 1181 black Queen of Sheba enamel in an ambo at Klosterneuburg, the sandstone Black St. Maurice does not merely have the iconographic likeness of European physiognomy, accompanied by black skin, but is unmistakably *African* in his facial features. And unlike black Africans portrayed in European art before his appearance, Maurice is no mere African servant or attendant in the retinue of distinguished pagans from the East such as the Queen of Sheba or the Three Magi – he is not just an exotic servitor to mark the exotic provenance of Biblically important heathens.

To sum up the strangeness of this African saint: Maurice is not only black, but he is African; he is not a servant, but an important personage of high status, *a knight*; in fact, he's leader of the Egyptian Theban legion of imperial Rome. He is not a virtuous heathen, like the Black Magus who will appear later, after him, in fourteenth-century visual art: Maurice is a *Christian martyr*, movingly executed with his men for refusing the orders of Rome because of fidelity to Christ.

Maurice's uniqueness also stems from the *timing* of his appearance: A whole century before the Black Magus, and a half-century before St. Gregory the Moor, a black African martyr localized to Cologne, and possibly "modeled on the black Maurice though with a much lower profile" (Kaplan, "Introduction" 22).[52] Maurice also materializes considerably earlier than the Black Madonnas of Europe – fascinating images not "securely datable to the period before 1500" and that do not display "the characteristic hair, nose, or lips that have long been part of the European stereotype of black African appearance" (Kaplan, "Introduction" 25).

The Black St. Maurice of Magdeburg is so complex and multilayered a puzzle that it attracts continuing, vital scholarship attempting explanations. Who commissioned the statue, and why, and was it that person or persons who decided on the saint's portrayal as a black African? Who sculpted it, and did the sculptor make the decision of an African model? Who was the model? Were there a number of Afro-Europeans (as Paul Kaplan calls them) in medieval Europe ("Introduction" 25)? Ladislas Bugner sums up the enigma succinctly: "A black saint for whites . . . What for?" ("Foreword" 12, 13).

Last of all, and impossible to answer, are the questions that are asked, not top-down, but from the ground up. How might devotees feel, standing or kneeling before a black African saint, in supplication or prayer, in the heart of the Latin West in the thirteenth century? Must we assume that a Black Maurice would have been resisted by the faithful, or might a black African saint have unsuspected kinds of appeal? I end this chapter on epidermal race and Africans by considering answers to the enigma of the Black St. Maurice, and will at the very least attempt to engage speculatively with such questions as cannot ever be properly answered or confirmed, but that we continue, of necessity and curiosity, to ask.

To begin with, the statue itself: Gude Suckale-Redlefsen helps us understand that Maurice's lifelike naturalism is part of a new artistic fashion at the time, with the leaders of the artistic movement being resident in France (a country in which, however, St. Maurice was not portrayed as a black African):

> In the thirteenth century, the French were pioneers in the study of nature and its translation into artistic forms, setting an example to Europe. German stonemasons went to serve their

apprenticeship in France, or at least drew their inspiration from French models. Consequently, it is only natural that the first authentic figures of blacks are seen in the cathedral sculpture of France. [However,] all the African figures hitherto found there represent persons of subordinate position. In thirteenth-century France the age-old conventions of previous centuries are continued: the hangman's assistants in the Judgment of Solomon or the execution of John the Baptist are shown as Negroes. The cringing attitude of a figure with distinctly "Negroid" features below the white Queen of Sheba in the north transept portal of the cathedral of Chartres is symptomatic ... no portrayal of an African in a positive sense exists in France in the thirteenth century.

(44, 47)

Maurice is not only lifelike, but sculpted with sensitivity: He's a finely rendered life-sized knight who is realistically dressed in the armorial style of the day, with a beautiful, expressive face. The knight's bearing, dress, and posture, Suckale-Redlefsen reflects, suggest his calm poise and readiness for battle, while polychromy skillfully hints at the saint's aura of sanctity by surrounding the knight's face with a de facto golden halo created by his encircling coif. The statue is

approximately 150 centimeters, correspond[ing] roughly to the actual height of a thirteenth-century knight. The armor, firmly encasing the body, faithfully reproduces the fashion of the period: a cloth undertunic hanging down in deep folds, a mail hauberk, and a sturdy leather surcoat shaped like an apron at both front and back. We see the seams, rivet heads, reinforcement straps, and buckles for fastening the garment and belt at the back ... The mufflers covering the hands are of chain mail. Likewise the head covering, the coif, which terminates in broad flaps on the chest and back. In addition to the long sword in its sheath and the dagger belted above the right hip, the saint bore a lance in his right hand and a large shield reaching down to the ground in his left. Lance and shield and the lower part of the legs are now missing from the figure.[53] [See *Figure 8*.]

The African features are emphasized by the surviving remains of the old polychromy. The skin is colored bluish black, the lips are red, and the dark pupils stand out clearly against the white of the eyeballs. The golden chain mail of the coif serves, in turn, to form a sharp contrast with the dark face. Today the traces of color are no more than a mere shadow of their original intensity, so that the figure should be imagined as painted entirely in bright colors. [See *Figure 9*.]

A twofold function was fulfilled by painting the figure. The coloring of the face was faithful to nature and served to evoke the impression of a living presence. The choice of gold for the hauberk, on the other hand, did not correspond to reality, iron chain mail usually being represented in bluish grey tones. The precious gold framed the dark countenance with the radiance of a halo and heightened the religious connotations of the otherwise realistically depicted figure.

(Suckale-Redlefsen 18–19)

A millennium after St. Maurice of Agaunum's life and death, who suddenly decided the saint should be remembered as this vital, lively figure of a black African knight, "a sensational mutation in the field of iconography" (Devisse 158), and why? To address these questions, I begin by examining the evidence presented by art historians and historians who have studied the Black St. Maurice for decades. I then consider, step by step, the implications of a racial saint in the heartlands of medieval Europe, with each section that follows examining a different aspect of those implications.

The phenomenon of the Black St. Maurice has attracted considerable interest, but scholarship has been shaped principally by three major voices: Jean Devisse, Gude Suckale-Redlefsen, and Paul Kaplan.[54] Tracing the saintly cult of Maurice in Europe over the long centuries before Maurice turned into a black African, Devisse shows how from the tenth to the twelfth centuries, Maurice came to be seen increasingly as a knight, "one of the military saints to whom those close to the [Holy Roman Emperor] and those engaged in the profession of arms addressed their prayers" (153).

A martyr who elected to be put to death as his form of resistance to imperial authority might seem, to modern sensibilities, an odd choice for a military saint, but Devisse notes how Otto I (Otto the Great) founded a Benedictine Abbey at Magdeburg in 937 dedicated to Maurice and the Theban martyrs, and, after Otto's coronation as Holy Roman Emperor in 962, officially designated Maurice patron saint of Magdeburg, and of the Holy Roman Empire (153).[55] Otto began the construction of Magdeburg cathedral in 955, and later had the saint's body translated there.

Magdeburg was charged with evangelizing the Slavic lands, and in the eleventh century, under the Emperor Henry II, Maurice, the patron saint of the Empire, "became the symbol of the Germanic offensive against the Slavs" (Devisse 153–4). From having been a martyr slaughtered for resisting a pagan empire because of his Christianity, Maurice thus became a military saint who blessed the slaughter of pagan Slavs resisting Christianity imposed by a Christian empire.

Having established that "Maurice . . .was not a people's saint but a companion of those in power," Devisse hazards that a later Holy Roman Emperor, the infamous Frederick II (r. 1220–50), was likely the initiator of a black St. Maurice (160). In this, Maurice's traditionally attested geographic provenance proves important. Devisse (160) astutely notices the pull exercised by Egypt and North Africa in the thirteenth century.

Egypt was the original power base of Saladin, from which Saladin launched the countercrusade that eventually wrested Jerusalem back from Latin Christendom in 1187, after nearly a century of occupation by crusaders. Egypt – not Jerusalem – had been the target of the Fourth Crusade in 1204 before its armies were misdirected to Constantinople. Egypt was also the target of the failed Fifth Crusade of 1217; it was the destination of both St. Louis's crusades in 1248 and 1270, and the 1270 crusade of Edward I of England when he was yet a prince.[56] Significantly, Frederick II was keenly awaited by the armies of the Fifth Crusade in Egypt, where he failed to make an appearance.[57]

The history of crusading in the thirteenth century thus bears out Devisse's intuition that Egypt, from which Maurice issued, was on the minds of the military and imperial great in Europe. Given the abject failure of *all* the thirteenth-century crusades to Egypt, and Frederick II's lack of interest in disrupting commercial and political relations with Egypt's Ayyubid Sultan Al-Kamil (Saladin's nephew) and his successors by waging holy war, we can suspect that a saint from Egypt might usefully serve a compensatory, face-saving function in this time.[58]

Symbolism of this kind would say: While we cannot successfully capture and hold this Islamic land, we have proof, and an important visual reminder, that Christianity once triumphed here among its people. Maurice's blackness and Africanness would thus symbolically function as a trophy of a compensatory, apotropaic kind, warding off specters of military failure and the interminable postponement of Christianity's triumph. *The function of a racial saint can thus be to fill a vacuum imposed by military failure: art coming to the rescue of history.*

As to the choice of a saint for purposes of propitiatory symbolism, Devisse dismisses St. George, that most famous of eastern military saints in the Middle Ages, because he was "too compromised with Rome" (and no doubt also somewhat overused by this time), in favor of Maurice, "who was a Theban" (or at least led the Theban legion):

> Egypt was the land that drew the attention of Western Christians, Crusaders and merchants alike in the thirteenth century. If he could not conquer the country, Frederick could at least demand that it furnish him the geographic, and then the ethnic, origin of St. Maurice.
>
> (Devisse 16)

Black Africans might reasonably be expected among the populations of Egypt in the thirteenth century, as we have seen. And, given that the statue of Maurice had to appear in the standard accoutrements of medieval European knighthood, Maurice's far-off provenance would need to be signaled in some other way than through his dress.

Since he was a Christian, Maurice's foreignness could not be displayed through the iconographic vocabulary deployed visually to signify heathen foreignness, such as curved swords, insignia on shields, headdress, etc. One instantly intelligible way to announce Maurice's geographic provenance would thus be to specify this provenance with *racial* markings in the form of color and physiognomy. Here, then, a visible race serves as shorthand for geography, securing location and place.

Devisse and others emphasize Frederick II's attachment (like his imperial predecessors) to the cult of St. Maurice. Before the saint's transformation into an African, it was at Frederick's behest that Maurice's skull, a "costly relic" under the protection of the monastery of Langheim in Franconia, was sold in 1220 to Magdeburg. At Magdeburg, the relic was treated with great honor, set into a reliquary, and crowned with a crown belonging to Otto I; and "On the anniversary of Otto's death the crowned reliquary adorned the head-end of the dead emperor's tomb" (Suckale-Redlefsen 40, 41).

Devisse's hypothesis that Frederick was likely responsible for imagining the patron saint of the empire as a black African has been substantively improved by a new thesis expounded by Paul Kaplan, who persuasively demonstrates *why* the Hohenstaufen dynasty of emperors that begins with Frederick II's grandfather, Frederick Barbarossa (Frederick I, r. 1155–90), should particularly concern itself with Africans. Kaplan follows the trail of black Africans depicted in German and Italian art in the Hohenstaufen period, finding that the portrayal of these African figures was not necessarily negative, nor were the figures necessarily only low-status servants, but were sometimes images of an "egalitarian" kind ("Black Africans" 29).

Kaplan's decision to read visual art transregionally under the Hohenstaufen is a canny one: The 1186 marriage of Frederick II's father, Henry VI (r. 1191–7), to Constance, daughter of Roger II, the first Norman king of Sicily, and Henry VI's military successes in Sicily meant that the boundaries of the Holy Roman Empire in the thirteenth century had expanded from Germany and its adjacent northern territories, plus northern Italy, to subsume southern Italy and Sicily. The Empire now embraced a Mediterranean zone with significant multiracial, multiconfessional populations knitted into relationship with more northerly imperial lands.

Aggressive in his ambitions, Frederick II, Kaplan argues, adapted and *secularized* the Christian Pentecostal theme that all peoples of the earth are called to salvation – the early theological idea that "all races are equal before God, and ... the Christian mission is universal" ("Black Africans" 29). In visual art, the theme of universal salvation through converting the nations of the earth to Christianity was sometimes articulated by representing black Africans among the human populations of the saved. Suckale-Redlefsen notices that the one exception to her attestation that "no portrayal of an African in a positive sense exists in France in the thirteenth century" was "the idealized head of a black man in the throng of those risen from the dead in the Last Judgment tympanum in Paris" (44, 47). Devisse and Kaplan offer other examples of such art.

Under Frederick II, Kaplan argues, secular depictions of black Africans in Italian art and new roles for black Africans in sacred art in Germany and Italy arose in order to present a "more secular version of the evangelical universalism long promoted by both the Greek and the Roman Catholic Churches" ("Introduction" 12):

> The driving force in this iconographic transformation was the project of imperial universalism ... this ideological construct eventually asserted the Holy Roman Emperor's right to rule nothing less than all the earth. The vast political ambitions of Frederick II, an especially sophisticated and cosmopolitan ruler ... resulted not only in a number of evidently secular depictions of black Africans in Italian art but also in the introduction of important new roles for black Africans in sacred art in Germany and Italy as well.
>
> (Kaplan, "Introduction" 12)

Just as Christianity's dominion extended over all the earth, so too did (or should) the Holy Roman Empire, which had the right to encompass the entire world, whose farthest reaches are dramatically represented by black Africa. There, by tradition, lived the most remote of men. Visual art is then a means for articulating the Holy Roman Empire's assertion of universal power and the Holy Roman Emperor's right to rule the earth. *These depictions of black Africans are ideological statements in a visual medium: art in the service of empire.*[59]

Among visual art of this kind, the jewel in the crown is the fresco at the tower of the Church of San Zeno Maggiore in Verona, which cleaning and conservation rendered more readily legible in the 1990s. In this fresco,

> A seated figure with a crown accepts the homage of a line of twenty-nine men ... The figure at the head of the line is partly destroyed but he kneels as he approaches a podium and may have been presenting a gift. Behind him stretch nine groups of men; many of these groups are distinguished by headgear and/or facial hair, or the absence thereof ... The most distinctive group, and the only one made up of four rather than three men, are the figures with nearly black skin near the front of the line. Besides their complexion, the men are similar in their tightly curled hair.
>
> ("Introduction" 13)

The enthroned figure receiving homage is likely Frederick II:

> the most plausible and widely shared view about the fresco identifies it as Emperor Frederick II receiving the homage of his subjects. It is generally agreed that, from the

point of view of style, the work should be dated to the second quarter of the 1200s ...
Frederick ... actually stopped over in this very building on several occasions: the Monastery
of San Zeno [adjoining the Church] had long been used as a favored lodging by emperors
traveling into Italy.

(Kaplan, "Introduction" 13)

Frederick lodged at San Zeno in 1236, 1237, 1238, and 1239; in 1237, his consort Isabella of
England also lodged for some weeks at San Zeno, and in 1238, Frederick's natural daughter
Selvaggia was wedded to his vassal Ezzelino da Romano before the doors of the San Zeno
church on the feast of Pentecost – "that festival of universal evangelization often illustrated
with black African figures in nearby Venice and farther east" – a wedding Frederick
attended (Kaplan, "Introduction" 16):

> It has been suggested that the fresco was made as part of the preparations of this marriage
> or that it commemorated the lengthy imperial visit after the fact. If Frederick himself did
> not commission the fresco, Ezzelino or even Selvaggia might have been the patron.
>
> (Kaplan, "Introduction" 16)

Kaplan tells us that shortly after 1235, Nicholas of Bari addressed an elaborate encomium to
Frederick II in which he flatteringly likened the emperor to Christ and the Magi, even
quoting "a passage from Psalm 71 of the Latin Vulgate in which it is prophesied that
'Ethiopians shall fall down' before the Lord" – flattery, Kaplan wryly observes, that "must
have fallen on fertile ground [since] Frederick once referred to his birthplace at Jesi in the
Italian marches as 'our Bethlehem'" ("Introduction" 17). The San Zeno fresco, depicting an
enthroned Frederick – "the heraldic imperial eagle [even] appears in one corner of the
room" ("Introduction" 16) – receiving the homage of far-flung subjects who represent the
diverse nations and races of the earth, allows for an assertion of secular dominion that is
thus also remarkably redolent of sacred mythography.[60]

The artist's positioning of the four black Africans grouped together near the head of the
line manifests popular knowledge of Frederick's famed associations with black Africans.
The son of Constance of Sicily and Henry VI, Frederick grew up in his mother's Sicilian
domains, where he "absorbed the cosmopolitan pan-Mediterranean culture of the island,
which had previously been ruled by Byzantine emperors and (more recently) Muslim emirs"
(Kaplan, "Introduction" 14).[61]

Frederick's well-known admiration for Islamic culture, science, mathematics, and philosophy, his impressive grasp of Arabic epistolary and literary form, and his knowledge of
Arabic made him unique among Holy Roman Emperors.[62] Indeed, the Sixth Crusade of
1228–9 – Frederick's crusade, at last – was extraordinary, and something of an uncrusade.
Arriving in Palestine under papal excommunication, having fought no Muslims or any holy
war, Frederick was *handed* Jerusalem by the Ayyubid Sultan Al-Kamil, with no blood being
shed.[63]

Sojourning in the holy city, where he put the crown of the Kingdom of Jerusalem on his
own head before the altar in the Church of the Holy Sepulcher, the Emperor lightly jested
at the expense of Christians; chided his host, the Muslim *qadi* of Nablus, when that notable
had the muezzin refrain from issuing the call to prayer out of respect for the Emperor's
presence; and distributed money to the custodians, muezzins, and pious men of the Haram,
Arab chronicles reported (Gabrieli 275).[64] Resident in Jerusalem were some of the

traditional representatives of Christian sub-Saharan Africa: "among [Frederick's] new subjects were black monks from the kingdom of Ethiopia" (Kaplan, "Black Africans" 33).

In 1224, Frederick began the process of relocating Muslims in Sicily to a colony at Lucera in Apulia, which grew into a population of some 15,000–20,000 people (Julie Anne Taylor 89):[65]

> Among these Sicilian Muslims, there were people of black African descent, whom Frederick apparently selected for particular purposes: several boys were trained in wind instruments, and one man, known as Johannes Maurus (d.1254), became Frederick's chamberlain and the judge-administrator of Lucera. From his given name, it is possible that Johannes converted to Christianity. . . .. By mid-century Johannes obtained considerable power in Lucera and the southern Italian kingdom in general, acting as chancellor after Frederick's death.
>
> (Kaplan, "Introduction" 14)[66]

Frederick was fond of dramatic pageantry and processional spectacles with exotic elements as a mode of imperial display. The "conspicuous presence of black Africans in Frederick's train as he traveled through his northern Italian and German lands in the 1230s" is much remarked on, and a 1235 chronicle showed how Frederick approached Wimpfen in Swabia,

> "proceeding in great glory with numerous carriages laden with gold and silver, byssus and purple, gems and costly vessels, with camels, mules as well as dromedaries, with many Saracens, and with Ethiopians [that is, black Africans] having knowledge of rare skills accompanying apes and leopards and serving as guards bringing along money and treasure."
>
> (quoted by Kaplan, "Introduction" 15; see also Suckale-Redlefsen 22, 23)[67]

The racial elements of Frederick's imperial pomp – Africans with the knowledge and skill to care for fabulous animals like apes and leopards, and Africans who safeguarded money and treasure – and his black African chamberlain and governor, Johannes Maurus, are singled out and attached to Frederick's memory in the cultural record. More than three decades after the emperor's death, that memory of Africans is restaged in Europe, still attached to Frederick:

> An imposter claiming to be Frederick II appeared near Cologne in 1283. He had little to buttress his assertion, except for three black servants who followed him; one was his chamberlain, whose duty was simply to dispense treasure. Reminiscences of Johannes Maurus and of the blacks of the imperial retinue of 1235 are here combined.
>
> (Kaplan, "Black Africans" 34)

Africans were so distinctly identified with Frederick II that the "False Frederick" of 1283 paraded African retainers as proof to clinch his authenticity. To the question of who had the boldness and the motive to declare St. Maurice of Agaunum a black African, Devisse and Kaplan thus furnish a logical answer: that most unique of Holy Roman Emperors, Frederick II.

Devisse's early working hypothesis that "a command from the emperor caused St. Maurice to be depicted as a black in Magdeburg, the city where his relics were enshrined" (164) stemmed from Frederick's "Mediterranean policy," which required Frederick "to uphold the theory of his sovereign rights over the distant lands around the eastern Mediterranean" (160).[68] That working hypothesis of the 1970s is transformed, in Paul Kaplan's hands, into a thesis of how the Hohenstaufen used black Africans, and black

African visual images, to articulate his imperial claims to *universal*, not just Mediterranean, sovereignty – adapting the example of Christendom's Pentecostal mission to evangelize the earth and oversee all of humanity, and supporting those imperial claims "with evidence that people from remote lands acknowledged Frederick as their lord" (Kaplan, "Black Africans" 33).

The puzzle, however, of who had the black Maurice created, and why, is not unanimously considered settled. Suckale-Redlefsen, whose 1987 study *Mauritius: Der heilige Mohr* (Maurice: The Holy Moor) was announced by Devisse but not yet completed when Devisse's *L'Image du Noir* (The Image of the Black) appeared, disagrees with Devisse's and Kaplan's conclusions:

> Doubtless the public appearance of Moors in the train of the emperor Frederick II . . . played a part in promoting the new Maurician iconography. Through his magnificent ceremonies which greatly impressed the people and at which Africans were present not as slaves but as advisors – a fact remarked upon again and again – the Hohenstaufen emperor contributed largely toward accustoming Europeans to the characteristic appearance of this foreign people. But it would be erroneous to attribute the new iconographic conception of the black St. Maurice to the emperor himself, as Kaplan has attempted.
>
> (Suckale-Redlefsen 54, 55)

For an alternative to Frederick II, Suckale-Redlefsen proposes an archbishop of Magdeburg – either Albert II of Käfernburg, archbishop from 1205 to 1232, or his stepbrother Wilbrand, archbishop from 1235 to 1254 – as the person responsible for the "startling iconographic innovation" (52, 53). Devisse himself had raised this possibility, and had focused on Wilbrand, but ended up dismissing the idea because of what Devisse assumed would be negative psychological reactions on the part of the populace to the sudden arrival of a black African saint substituting for the old Maurice at an inopportune moment, and also because of the financial costs involved:

> Wilbrand . . . wanted to foster popular devotion to St. Maurice: was he perhaps responsible for the abrupt transformation of the saint's iconography. . .? Yet ordinary good sense would not induce the prelates of Magdeburg to make so spectacular a change as the blackening of Maurice at the very time when an effort was afoot to enlarge the patron saint's following in the province and to build up a pilgrimage that involved numbers of images connected with the relics. Public sensibility, as well as the cost of the necessary changes to be made in the familiar representation of the Magdeburg Maurice, argue against the idea that an archbishop of that city might have commissioned the splendid statue of a black.
>
> (Devisse 159–60)

Magdeburg cathedral in the thirteenth century presumably had other images of Maurice that did not represent him as an African, but with the exception of a statue from *c.* 1220, none has survived. Devisse's point – that all the statues of Maurice in the cathedral prior to his racial transformation would have had to be altered for consistency, at some cost – is driven home when we consider that surviving 1220 statue, which was sculpted in a style utterly unlike the artistic naturalism that allowed for the making of a lifelike black Maurice:

> A figure of St. Maurice which now stands in the choir . . . originally formed part of a cycle from ca. 1220. The saint triumphs over the Roman emperor who is seen cowering in a

grotesque attitude below his feet. Despite his full armor and the drawn sword in his right hand, he arouses no sense of martial prowess or human animation. This figure with its lifeless rigidity has the appearance of a columnar jamb statue from the west portal of Chartres, remote from reality. The armor is so overladen with ponderous ornamental detail that its protective function is obliterated . . . Unlike the statue of St. Maurice . . . this figure in the choir of the cathedral has neither "Negroid" facial features nor any other indication of the African origins of the Christian warrior.

(Suckale-Redlefsen 42–4, 43)

Suckale-Redlefsen favors Archbishop Albert II as the alternative to Frederick, which would date the commissioning of the black Maurice to before Albert's death in 1232 and presumably after the 1220 statue of a still European St. Maurice. She finds the prospect that Maurice was a black African raised for the first time in a chronicle of the third quarter of the twelfth century, noting that earlier chronicle references to Maurice, in Germany and elsewhere, had not raised his Africanness or blackness before.

But the *Kaiserchronik*, "a widely read book compiled by a cleric in Regensburg about 1160," explicitly describes Maurice "as 'the leader of the Moors' (*herzoge der swarzen Môren*) and his legionaries as 'black Moors'" (52, 53). Albert II presumably took cognizance of this new idea of the saint as a black Moor, and commissioned a black St. Maurice in the context of a new building program after a fire devastated the old cathedral in 1207 (Suckale-Redlefsen 42, 43).[69]

The 1220 statue of a pre-African Maurice was part of that sculptural program for the new cathedral, according to Suckale-Redlefsen; so also was the black St. Maurice, unlike as the two sculptures may be (42–4).[70] In the end, Suckale-Redlefsen's consciousness of archbishop Albert's shifting loyalties in the volatile politics of the Holy Roman Empire, where powerful rivals (Otto IV, Frederick II) contended to be emperor, and her consciousness that papal Rome's support of a candidate for emperor was mutable, leads her to conclude that "Archbishop Albert was an independent territorial ruler. In matters of art he was not guided by the court of Frederick II, but by French models which reached Magdeburg by way of Bamberg" (54, 55).[71]

By contrast, Kaplan emphasizes the ties of archbishop Albert to Frederick II.[72] Like Suckale-Redlefsen, Kaplan reads an artistic relationship between the statuary of Bamberg and Magdeburg, but comes to an alternate conclusion on their artistic connection:

> since 1979 new information has appeared attesting to Magdeburg's extensive political links to Frederick II. Albert II of Käfernberg, archbishop of Magdeburg from 1205 to 1232, was a relative of the Hohenstaufen, and Frederick II both donated money to the cathedral and helped Albert obtain the important relic of Maurice's skull. Virginia Roehrig Kaufmann has explained how Apulian sculpture made during Frederick's reign (and often for the emperor himself) had a potent influence on sculpture in Magdeburg and the other nearby imperial stronghold of Bamberg. There are two famous surviving equestrian statues in these cities, which may have commemorated imperial entries.

("Introduction" 15)

Virginia Roehrig Kaufmann, one of Kaplan's sources, points to documents in the Magdeburg archives analyzed by Berent Schwineköper to establish the working relationship between Frederick and Albert:

During the last ten years of his life, [the archbishop] was constantly in Italy in Frederick's service, a career that is first documented in 1221. In 1222 he was with the emperor in Naples and Capua, where he received the office of imperial legate for north Italy . . . the emperor then bestowed on him the countship of Romagnola, which yielded considerable revenue that could be put toward the archbishop's building projects in Magdeburg . . . He was in Pavia in 1226 as witness to a settlement of strife between the emperor and the citizens, which he had probably helped to negotiate. His association with the city was also strengthened by the troops from Pavia that the emperor supplied him and by the two imperial judges who helped him in his work. Of particular interest are Albrecht's [Albert's] activities at the very end of his life, when he was often with [archbishop] Eckbert [of Bamberg] and the emperor in Italy. In 1232 he was once again in north Italy, at Ravenna, Aquileia, Cividale, and Udine, where he and Eckbert, together with the German princes, worked out for the emperor the statute *in favorem principum*. After Albrecht's death in 1232, the building and decoration of Magdeburg cathedral proceeded only with great difficulty because of financial problems.

(Kaufmann 74)[73]

Archbishop Albert, Devisse had stressed in the 1970s, was extending the cult of St. Maurice. Having acquired the skull of the saint in 1220 for Magdeburg through the good graces of Frederick II, Maurice's relics thereafter "were brought out once a year for public veneration" (Devisse 159). Pilgrimage to Maurice was encouraged. To foster pilgrimage, when the Collegiate Church of St. Maurice at Halle was dedicated, Pope Honorius III "granted an indulgence of thirty days to those who visited the church" (Devisse 159). Paderborn, Trier, and Freising all "introduced Maurice into their diocesan devotional patterns," and at Albert's death in 1232, Pope Gregory IX showered the deceased archbishop with high praise: "Thanks to him, the pope wrote, Magdeburg had become one of the pillars of Christianity" (Devisse 159). Albert's successor, archbishop Wilbrand, also fostered popular devotion to Maurice (Devisse 159).

Would archiepiscopal fostering of pilgrimage and ambitions to extend the geographic reach of Maurice's cult in Germany have been hurt by the saint's delivery as a black African, as Devisse supposed (159)? Perhaps the answer is not as obvious as Devisse assumed.

It is not difficult to see how an Africanized St. Maurice could serve an ambitious emperor using art to articulate his imperial right to rule the earth, and the ambitions of an archbishop promoting pilgrimage and cult, without having to select between them. Indeed, we may find it useful to shift the focus slightly, from *who* originated an African Maurice to *what* the statue's African-ness tells us by calling attention to itself. Iconography that remains stable and is replicated without change does not issue an invitation to consider its meaning anew. The racial transformation of a saint, however, from a white European to a black African, invites attention to how reconceptualization of an old template produces new functionalities, and points to the functionalities themselves.

Kaplan has shown us that for Frederick, an African St. Maurice is art in the service of empire, a synecdoche for empire. The importance of Egypt in the failed crusades of the earlier thirteenth century also suggests that Maurice's racialization is an efficient means of marking his geographic provenance and to issue a propitiatory symbolism in the face of crusading failure. The luminous early tale of the Theban legionaries' heroic courage and selfless commitment to Christ, summoned through Maurice's origins made visible, retrieves Christianity's once and future presence in the heart of now-heathen North Africa – a recalling of the past, and future promise, that engages secular and church interests alike.

A signifier for an important crusade destination as well as the far-flung world, the visual medium of Maurice's racialized statue makes the saint's geographic origin readable instantly, and renders his body, relics, and cranium also readable as artifacts from Africa, lodged within Europe, where they are staged in a cathedral and displayed for all to see once a year.

Africa in Europe: Race here, in the person of an African saint, is a way of bringing a continent to Germany, the homeland of the Holy Roman Empire.

Maurice's Africanized statue is an exemplary model of how race can be used to make a place mobile, and transportable to the Latin West. The Africa the saintly Maurice issues is also the right Africa to have: not the medieval continent of sinful "Ethiopians" who are the torturers of Christ and the killers of the Baptist, but the hallowed ground of early Christianity.

Maurice's Africanization thus infuses his physical body and relics in the cathedral with a new aura and new meaning. Now understood as sacred artifacts from African shores, the relics collapse time and space: A deep Christian past in Africa, borne in these artifacts, is translocated into the European present, the immediate now, in the heartlands of Latin Christendom, where that Christian past is owned and displayed.

Race mobilizes and recruits Africa for Europe – an Africa of church fathers, desert ascetics, and the sainted martyrs of Latin Christianity in its formative, triumphant phase, the poignant early centuries of Christianity. This Africa, the matrix of Christianity, summons the faithful to prayer and pilgrimage through an African Maurice's physical and visualized body. A pilgrimage to Maurice's embodied remains in Germany is thus a journey through time and space: a way to travel to Christianity's luminous past and to African soil, collapsing geographies and temporalities. In the Africanization of Maurice, we thus glimpse a summary of the changing meanings of Africa for Europe, a mode of recruitment and ownership, and a process of selection that decides what Africa will give the West.

But Maurice was more than just an early martyr. Crusade historiography also depicted Maurice more recently as a *crusading* saint. During the First Crusade, Maurice is among the heavenly hosts inspiring crusaders in Antioch at a critical moment, when the ragged Christian army had captured the city but not the citadel. The crusaders were still fighting inside Antioch when they had to face the combined hosts of the Islamic East led by Karbuqa, the atabeg of Mosul, outside the city walls.

In the chronicle of Robert the Monk, Saints George, Maurice, Mercurius, and Demetrius materialize as the leaders of a heavenly army, lifting their standards, firing the spirits of the crusaders, and fighting alongside the Christians to dispel the might of the Saracen forces.[74] Crusade chronicles exult in how heavenly hosts garbed in white, led by Eastern saints, multiplied the ranks of the Christians, so that the crusaders seemed more numerous than they actually were. Is it any wonder that Karbuqa's military alliances fell apart in the field, that his allies retreated and his forces were routed, or that he himself fled, only to be found and beheaded while fleeing?

The First Crusade – that most militarily successful of the incursions into Syria, Palestine, and Egypt – wrested territory from the Islamic East, and established four crusader colonies: the County of Edessa, the Principality of Antioch, the Kingdom of

Jerusalem, and the County of Tripoli. At Antioch, during a debilitating siege of six and a half months, were found relics of Christ's passion, including the Holy Lance, when crusader morale was at its lowest. Thanks to confusions of tradition, statuary of Maurice, patron saint of the Holy Roman Empire, had the saint bear insignia that included a lance which tended to be conflated with the Holy Lance itself, a specimen of which had been found at Antioch.

Thus in his first life before his martyrdom, Maurice was from Africa. In his celestial afterlife, Maurice was also an Eastern crusader saint in the holy lands of the Littoral.

An Africanized Maurice by no means limits what is communicated to a single message, moreover. Signaling Egypt, Africa, and the Near East, Maurice's race is an aid to historical memory, but can also be a powerful instrument for eliciting more personal meanings in immediate context. For an archbishop promoting devotion and pilgrimage to the saint, Africanizing Maurice also furnishes the message that even the sinful Ethiopian, black from sin, and evoking a country of black humans that corporately personified sinfulness, could be saved – indeed, could be a saint.

To a Christian penitent undertaking pilgrimage to expiate sin, what more potent message could there be? Black, the color of sin, *on a saint,* elicits a powerful, tangible, *sensory* understanding of who can be saved. If Albert II and his successor churchmen were committed to promulgating pilgrimage to Maurice's relics, and extending devotion to Maurice's cult, a message of universal salvation carried in the very skin of a newly racialized saint, communicates hope in a powerful, tangible way to penitents and the faithful whose souls were most in need of intercession.

Blackness of skin and an African face can carry an emperor's message of his right to universal sovereignty, *and* an ecclesiastic's message of Christianity's sovereign promise of universal salvation. The vision delivered with an African saint is no less Pentecostal, evangelical, or universal than a Last Judgment painting in which Africans, too, are shown among the nations of the saved.

Secular and sacred functions thus dovetail readily in the genius that produces Maurice as a black African: *A racial saint is a gift to both Christian and secular empire.* Change away from the familiar – especially a radical change of this kind, when a saint is suddenly shown to be a black African – invites a dynamic relationship with the art object, and activates a process of response. A black African St. Maurice evokes, recalls, and summons.

Whoever imagined Maurice as a black African, Suckale-Redlefsen and Kaplan are in agreement on the likely sculptor of the black St. Maurice. Both art historians finger him as the "Master of the Magdeburg Rider," the sobriquet bestowed on the sculptor of one of two famous "equestrian statues" that may have commemorated an imperial entry into Bamberg and Magdeburg (Suckale-Redlefsen 42, 43; Kaplan "Introduction" 15). For Suckale-Redlefsen, the mounted figure of the Magdeburg Rider, a statue that is the sculptor's "masterpiece," is Otto the Great (42, 43); for Kaplan, the mounted figure may be either Otto *or* Frederick II:

> The Magdeburg rider was originally equipped with an enormous Gothic baldachin and located in the Old Market Square of the city. At the very top of the frame and canopy was a statue of St. Maurice that is now lost, and the only surviving visual record of it is too small to show anything of the saint's physiognomy. Nevertheless, it is apparent that Magdeburg was an active supporter of Frederick's (and vice versa) and that Maurice was associated with

a major public imperial image there in the 1230s. Indeed, it is likely that the sculptor of the Magdeburg rider and the cathedral's St. Maurice are one and the same.

(Kaplan, "Introduction" 15)⁷⁵

Virginia Roehrig Kaufmann reasons that Albert II had the Magdeburg Rider made and installed in a prominent, public space in the city of Magdeburg as an important reminder. The equestrian statue, which "depicts an imperial entry, an *adventus regis*, of a medieval emperor into Magdeburg," is a strategic visual confirmation of the archbishop's legal authority, issuing from the emperor, over the city populace, with whom the archbishop's relations had become tense because the citizenry of Magdeburg "wanted a greater share in legal and political matters and seem to have grown restive in the first half of the thirteenth century" (66, 67). The life-sized Magdeburg Rider, with a naturalistically carved face and wearing thirteenth-century clothing, has a "real-life appearance"; his "open mouth suggests, moreover, that he was in the process of speaking" (Kaufmann 66):

> The archbishop would have had good reason to want to demonstrate his authority in the major public space of Magdeburg, the Old Market Square. The depiction of an imperial entry with the emperor uttering the grant of confirmation of privileges to the archbishop would have been a most effective way of demonstrating to Magdeburg's citizens his ultimate authority over them, and the source of that power. Schwineköper has demonstrated convincingly that the Rider monument served this function in Magdeburg, where it was situated before the archiepiscopal court of justice. There the archbishop himself, or his representative, sat facing the gesturing and "speaking" equestrian emperor, seemingly in the process of granting or reconfirming the archbishop's powers.
>
> (Kaufmann 67)

The capacity of stone statuary for dynamic action is striking. The Magdeburg Rider brings the original grant of privileges and authority conferred by Otto I on Magdeburg's archbishop *out of* the tenth century and *into* the thirteenth century, where it visually confirms Albert II as the recipient and bearer of those archiepiscopal rights. If the imperial Rider is Otto I, the monument collapses time, transporting the past to the present, and creates a temporal mobility in the way an African Maurice makes Africa mobile and transportable.

If the Rider is Frederick II, Archbishop Albert's canny use of the monument's activity in the present context strikingly parallels Frederick's use of black African visual images to attest *his* authority and privileges. The extraordinary, lifelike naturalism of these stone figures – Maurice, the Magdeburg Rider – sustains, moreover, a "real-life appearance" that works to elicit human response. These lifelike faces and human forms beckon to audiences and issue a sense of immediacy, even intimacy. They "speak" to us through pathways more direct, perhaps, than narrative hagiography.

For the enigma of Maurice, this may be one of the few clues supporting our quest to imagine how a supplicant or pilgrim might feel before the image of a black African saint in the heart of German Europe: Stone statuary, it seems, in mimicking life and summoning the past or distant lands, has a dynamic ability to issue an invitation to transact with it, and initiate a living dialogue with its viewer.

These meticulous efforts of recovery, of course, tell us little about the sculptor himself. But Suckale-Redlefsen's admirable account of the stonemason's style tries to explain why French artists, the leaders in naturalistic portrayals, themselves did not portray Africans "in a positive sense," whereas in Germany, "especially in the eastern parts," art patrons who commissioned work, and artists who executed their commissions, were allowed a freedom to create unusual forms. Because of

> the comparatively consistent development and enormous density of sculptural productions in France ... This led to an early fixing of the iconography and within it of social and hierarchical graduation. The sculptors certainly possessed the skill to portray non-Europeans precisely, but the representation of saints as black persons would have constituted an unthinkable affront to established norms. In Germany, especially in the eastern parts, the situation was entirely different. Here there were hardly any established traditions to which the sculptors could refer. The local art patrons who commissioned their works were also less conventional than elsewhere, and the specified tasks less strictly defined. This is doubtless the reason for the striking richness of invention.
>
> (Suckale-Redlefsen 44, 47)

German stonemasons who were furnishing Magdeburg cathedral with new statuary in the first half of the thirteenth century were thus able to apply French "innovations with astonishing independence" (Suckale-Redlefsen 54, 55). In Germany, then, we may suppose, "the representation of saints as black persons" would *not* "have constituted an unthinkable affront to established norms" either to the patrons commissioning the art, who were "less conventional" than patrons elsewhere, or to the masters executing their commissions, who had "astonishing independence." A black St. Maurice, we may gather, was made whose creation fell within a window of opportunity – an interval of time in cultural creation – that was opened. That window of opportunity thereafter closed:

> Soon after the middle of the century artists turned away from the realistic approach of their predecessors and created stylized ideals of beauty which had little in common with the actuality which had seemed so desirable only a short time before.
>
> (Suckale-Redlefsen 50, 51)

Paul Kaplan, citing Kaufmann, has an alternate view of the artistic models influencing Magdeburg's black Maurice and the Magdeburg Rider. To Kaplan's mind, southern Italy, rather than France, provided the examples and influence. From southern Italy came also "egalitarian" depictions of black Africans in visual art.[76] The evidence of masonry thus leads Kaplan to trace artistic influences from *within* Frederick's empire, rather than without, linking two geographic extremities of the empire into cultural relationship. Kaufmann acknowledges that sculpture at Reims cathedral in France "has generally been considered the source for the German sculpture at Bamberg and Magdeburg" (81), but she too suggests – referring not specifically to Maurice, but to Magdeburg's and Bamberg's imperial monumental sculpture around the time of Maurice – that we consider "revising our idea of the direction of influence" (82):

> We might consider the possibility that Italy, as well as France, was a major source of influence on sculpture in Bamberg and Magdeburg. We have found evidence of the presence of a German artist associated with Bamberg and Magdeburg working in Apulia.
>
> (82)

Is it possible that sculptural forms in Magdeburg benefited richly from *both* France *and* Italy? Does artistic creation issue from singular sources of influence or multiple resources, and can the question of influence be decided on the basis of relative emphasis and degree? Whatever we conclude from the thoughtful arguments of art historians on the enigma of Maurice's creation, Suckale-Redlefsen's summary of the shift in European visual art, after the mid-thirteenth century, toward idealized forms and away from naturalism is valuable for those of us interested in questions of epidermal race.

Suckale-Redlefsen's midcentury shift is borne out by one singularly crucial feature, also the result of a midcentury shift, which the art historian Madeline Caviness has detected in medieval visual art. As we have seen, Caviness argues that after the mid-thirteenth century, we find depictions in European visual art of European skin tones as *white* – white like the whites of the eye, like the whiteness of clothing – and no more the naturalistic flesh tones of the preceding centuries.

Like the shift toward physiognomic idealization and away from naturalism, stylizations of this kind, depicting European skin as white, also "had little in common" with "actuality." As we saw at the beginning of this chapter, change in the depiction of European skin color, which Caviness localizes to the middle of the thirteenth century, *idealized* a medley of human flesh tones in a variety of tints (pink, cream, ruddy, light brown, greyish, and E. M. Forster's famous "pinko-grey") as *pure white*.

The stylizations and idealizations of the later thirteenth century that closed the window on naturalistic depiction thus not only renovated earlier ideas of beauty, but also supported *the emergence of whiteness* as a *stylized, idealized representation of Western European human beings*. After all, white is the color of beauty and sanctity in the thirteenth century – except, of course, for Maurice. Maurice's African naturalism, and the stylized whiteness that followed, thus seem to stand as two moments of epidermal depiction that virtually touch in the racialized art of thirteenth-century Europe.

I have suggested gains to be had from racialized art in the form of an African St. Maurice for those who wielded power – emperor, archbishop – by considering functionalities that are gained with this particular racial saint, at this particular time. For the penitent, pilgrim, or devotee standing or kneeling before an Africanized Maurice, however, naturalizing explanations are less easily to be had. Ladislas Bugner states the case baldly: "How can one reconcile saintliness and blackness? Impossible. Maurice is white and handsome. Because a saint" (10, 11). A black St. Maurice is a contradiction in the very meaning of sanctity, a paradox incarnate.

Yet Bugner himself introduces a possibility that does not offend commonsense sensibility and everyday Christian thinking:

> Compared to more familiar figures, Maurice's African features and black complexion express in a more blatant fashion the insignificance of a world of appearances and the preeminence of an ideal reality ... It was the genius of the Magdeburg sculptor to give material expression to this veritable spiritual about-face in which, through holiness, blackness is changed into light.
>
> (10, 11)

Maurice is black but a saint: someone who visually embodies the early Latin Christian theme that blackness sometimes coexists with beauty as a resounding paradox – *nigra sum sed formosa*, says the bride in Canticles, I am black but beautiful. We have detected a similar arc in Moriaen's depiction as a chivalrous Christian black knight: Look beyond his blackness, *Moriaen*'s narrative urges; he is fair in his own way, and in all other ways except surface visuality. Moriaen is black but chivalrous, and Maurice is black but a saint: A paradox of this kind directs attention to "the insignificance of a world of appearances" and points to the importance of attending to "an ideal reality" beyond.

For sinful laity, I've suggested, a penitent can see his own sin, hidden away within him, visually externalized in the skin of the saint, and can thus understand God's generosity to embrace him, an ordinary sinner, since it embraces even those who are the very color of sin itself. Maurice's is thus an apotropaic blackness that positions a consoling paradox: *representing sin and forgiveness, blackness on a saint wards off the prospect of infernal damnation.*[77]

Intuition of this kind on the part of a penitent only requires a small leap of identificatory sympathy with Maurice, with little of a barrier to faith: It is amply helped by the fact that, as a martyr, Maurice's sanctity is of the most hallowed and traditional kind, his martyrdom wholly orthodox and reassuringly familiar in its pedigree. Indeed, the absence of a racialized subjectivity attached to Maurice's original hagiography has allowed a millennium of pious responses by devotees to be sedimented, on which the new iconography could draw. Maurice's sanctity, attested by a thousand years of veneration, anchors and secures the invitation of identification.

But a less naturalizing way to think of Maurice's blackness is to treat the possibility that *blackness itself holds a power to counter the dominant medieval discourse on its meaning.* In this, popular devotion to the Black Madonnas of Europe – a later phenomenon than Maurice, to be sure, but an equally persistent phenomenon over *la longue durée* – may supply a guide of sorts.

Explanations differ for the efflorescence of black images of the Virgin Mary at the close of the Middle Ages or in the Renaissance. Church explanations center on how candle smoke, accumulated over the centuries, inadvertently blackened the Virgin's face, turning her images black in some instances (critics who resist this explanation point out that atmospheric blackening of this kind should be less selective in recoloring statues, or parts of a statue only).[78]

Some scholars proffer a more anthropological perspective: that the images are in fact Christianized incarnations of ancient pagan goddesses such as Isis or Ceres, goddesses especially of fertility and abundance, whose aspect of black soils and dark mysteries sometimes found expression in their being colored black. Whatever the explanation/s, scholars remark on the deep attachment of devotees to their black Madonnas – their devotion not just to the Virgin, but to the Virgin *as black.*

A color that embraces all other colors, black's appeal on the Madonna may indeed testify to a memory of ancient power associated with it. Equally, we note that contradictions in how color is bound to meaning appeal to the great minds of the church as exquisite ways to articulate subtleties of theology and afford erudite play, as we saw in Chapter 1. Common church teaching also thrived on contradiction and paradox. Mary, the mother of Jesus, *is* and *must be* a *virgin*, despite her conception of a child and her parturition. Original sin is borne by all humanity out of the disobedience of Adam and Eve, *except* for Mary, who, contradictorily, remains without original sin. Cannibalism is heinous and abhorrent, forbidden to all, *except* when the faithful consume the consecrated host that is the transubstantiated body of God, sacramentally eating God: Then, cannibalism is not only permissible, but highly recommended and salvific.

Acknowledging that contradiction and paradox are harnessed and used by the church, and disseminated in church teaching, does not, of course, clearly suggest how the faithful actually responded to incarnated paradoxes – except when popular heretical movements were seen specifically to reject the contradictions and paradoxes of church teaching, such as the eating of a transubstantiated host-that-was-god.

For a black St. Maurice, the recognition that blackness may have an ancient allure that is not negated in its entirety by a rationalizing theological discourse on the meaning of blackness has implicit appeal. This is because *blackness on a saint or the Virgin can be safely embraced*, whereas in other contexts it is to be shunned, feared, and abhorred. Attraction and revulsion are affective responses that can exist as alternating – reversible – currents.

Laid upon a holy figure, blackness is imbued with a capacity for protective homeopathy, and doses of sacred blackness, embraced in protected contexts of safety and reassurance, such as the privacy and inwardness of devotional moments, can help to defend against larger, more frightening contexts in which the otherness of blackness is called into play.

To put it another way, as Ladislas Bugner has: "the representation of St. Maurice offers here a *space* where darkness, rather than threatening and swallowing up, is dissipated" (10, 11). For color to work apotropaically in *this* way, blackness must be coupled with safety and reassurance – conditions that are realized in a black St. Maurice and black Madonnas.

There's an uncanny aura, then, possessed by a racial saint which marks him off from, say, a blind saint, an animal-loving saint, or a saint who blesses the crops. *Able intimately to mingle familiarity and alienness, the body of a racial saint offers up the power of a queer sanctity that can shock and shelter. The queerness of racialized sanctity lies in both the jolting unexpectedness and strangeness of its manifestations, and the ability of racialized sanctity to comfort and reassure.*

In medieval courtly literature, we have seen that an admixture of blackness, courtliness, and gendered virtue figured by the black queen Belakane allows the attraction of otherness to surface and to be enjoyed by the European Arthurian knight Gahmuret and by *Parzival*'s readers. Blackness that is coupled with chivalric prowess, as figured by the black knight Moriaen, similarly manifests otherness as familiar and welcome, affirming an international fraternity of knighthood, of courtly behavior, and of aristocratic kinship.

Might not the epidermal blackness of a saint or a Madonna offer a similar degree of protective sheltering, in which the lure of otherness can be embraced and welcomed, while the fear of otherness is disengaged and dissolved, within a proffered context of safety and reassurance?

Since it's impossible to recover with any clarity or sureness the affective devotional response of pilgrims and penitents to Maurice, and equally impossible to prevent ourselves from wondering, with human curiosity and sympathy, what that response might be, the push to ask our questions, and the effort to think about the unanswerable, at least tenders some small measure of affective optimism in the readerly imaginary.

But the closing of the window of opportunity in which a sympathetic African naturalism was able to take hold in visual art of the thirteenth century, it turns out, coincides with the end of the Hohenstaufen dynasty in 1268 with the death of Conradin, Frederick II's grandson. Suckale-Redlefsen appropriately cautions that "We will never know whether the ideas for these programs were dictated entirely by the patrons who commissioned them, or whether perhaps the artists themselves had a greater share in their conception" (46, 47).

Nonetheless, Kaplan finds links for nearly all the Hohenstaufen family – Henry VI (Frederick II's father), Manfred (Frederick II's natural son), Conradin (Frederick's grandson) – with black Africans and/or black African depictions in visual art, and this coincidence helps to provide a double accounting for why so large an interval yawns between the first appearance of a black Maurice and the subsequent late-medieval reappearance of black Maurician images only in the fourteenth through sixteenth centuries ("Introduction" 13–14, "Black Africans" 33).

In the remainder of the thirteenth century itself, Suckale-Redlefsen remarks,

> It may at first seem surprising that the conception of the black St. Maurice which had evolved in the stone sculpture of Magdeburg did not meet with general acceptance, and that in later works the allusions to the saint's African origins remained at most extremely discrete [i.e., discreet], indeed almost veiled, if present at all.
>
> (50, 51)

If Maurice's thirteenth-century transformation into a black African was at the behest of the emperor Frederick II, the archbishop Albert II, or archbishop Wilbrand, there is little incentive for us to suppose that the black St. Maurice "did not meet with general acceptance" by the laity, whose devotional responses are unknown and unknowable, and greater incentive for us to suspect that changes – of a political, theological, aesthetic, socioeconomic, or other kind – on the part of those commissioning statuary and those executing their commissions shifted the depiction of racialized sanctity.

Suckale-Redlefsen points, after all, to the midcentury turn away from naturalism in visual art, toward increasing idealization and "stylized ideals of beauty" (50, 51), while Caviness points to a midcentury shift that portrayed the flesh hues of sainted figures and Europeans as pure, pristine, idealized white. Not surprisingly then, in the second half of the thirteenth century, racial saints were ultra-whitened Europeans, and Maurice's race is alluded to only discreetly in subsequent visual representations and "almost veiled, if present at all" (Suckale-Redlefsen 50, 51).

The stained-glass black Maurice *c.* 1250–60 in the west choir of Naumburg Cathedral is the only other surviving image from around the period of Magdeburg's black Maurice, and Naumburg is a suffragan diocese subordinated to Magdeburg and under Magdeburg's influence (Suckale-Redlefsen 48, 49). A black St. Maurice only reemerges a century later when another Holy Roman Emperor, Charles IV of Bohemia, resurrects the iconography of the saint as a black African in a series "of approximately one hundred thirty panel paintings executed by Master Theodorik and his workshop between 1359 and 1365" in the Chapel of the Holy Cross in Karlstejn castle in Bohemia (Suckale-Redlefsen 56, 57). This "deliberate reversion to the older Magdeburg iconography," Kaplan and Suckale-Redlefsen agree, issues from imperial ideology:

> The choice of saints reveals that careful attention was paid to representing all the nations of Europe and the various parts of the empire. Precedence is given to the saints of Bohemia and the German Empire. This program is not only religious, but also political, expressing very cogently the aspirations cherished by Charles IV. Although his claims had no basis in the actual balance of power, Charles IV regarded himself as a world sovereign whose domain encompassed East and West.
>
> (Suckale-Redlefsen 56, 57)

Devisse and Kaplan emphasize how the Luxembourg emperor follows in the footsteps of the Hohenstaufen Frederick: "Once again those in power drew attention to Maurice: thereafter he was black" (Devisse 169). Devisse tells us that Magdeburg "welcomed [back] the black saint in its episcopal sees, monasteries, and humble rural churches," and he follows the trail of an African Maurice in Halle, Jüterbog, Stendal, Halberstadt, and across Germany and to the north and east (174).

Kaplan points to a salient difference, however, in this second, late-medieval efflorescence of an African Maurice:

> Although many of these Bohemian images seem to reproduce or extend approaches first developed in the time of the Hohenstaufen, in one respect there is a substantial difference between these two eras: there is no evidence of the actual presence of people of black African descent at Charles IV's court or in Bohemia. Instead, part of the appeal for Charles, and for Bohemian artists and audiences, may have rested on the notion that the Czechs, like the Ethiopians, were a group at the edge of the Christian world. The fair skin and golden hair of the Czechs, emphasized by Giovanni dei Marignolli, one of Charles's court intellectuals, may have been seen as defining one extreme of human physical appearance, just as the black Ethiopians embodied the opposite extreme.
>
> ("Introduction," 19)

Kaplan's intuition of the symbolic potential of crossrace identification continues the trace of an affective logic that makes identification with a black African Maurice possible by the lay faithful, by the sculptors themselves, and by the great who commissioned an African Maurice with an eye to ideology. Instantiating Africa inside Bohemia of the fourteenth century, a black African Maurice allows all who feel themselves insecurely situated in some way – on the periphery, or set apart by their sin, by nature, or by geography – to identify with an extremity that so eloquently dramatizes how an insecure position can be thoroughly secured through sanctity, across the opposite ends of epidermal race.

Thereafter, on the heels of Bohemia arrives a wondrous diversity of art objects depicting a black Maurice that accrues over the centuries and across regions and countries. The marvelous color and monochromatic plates in Devisse's sumptuous volume (a volume now reissued by Harvard University Press, with a new introduction by Kaplan, in a multivolume reprinting of *The Image of the Black in Western Art*) show us a profusion of black Maurices, large and small, in two and three dimensions: displayed on a bishop's miter, covered in dazzling plate armor, with loop earrings, crowned with jewels and sporting jeweled collars, sprouting a goatee and mustache, even materializing as tiny statuettes atop a ciborium and a drinking horn (Devisse figures 142, 147, 150, 151, 160, 162, 163).

Kaplan contemplates Maurice's legacy in the emergence of the Black Magus in the fourteenth century and beyond, and scrutinizes the portrayal of *Afro-Europeans* all the way into Renaissance visual art, where vital, confident male and female Africans beckon, "lively and alluring," manifesting "a part of the past that reads as modern" ("Introduction" 30). To Devisse, then, who first brought the attention of scholars to the extraordinary enigma of the Black St. Maurice of Magdeburg, belongs the final word:

> There remains the masterpiece in Magdeburg . . . one would search in vain in medieval art and probably in Western art as a whole for a representation of the African as faithfully and powerfully rendered as this one. Beyond its realism and historicity this statue, in the plenitude of its expressiveness, embodies the ultimate vocation to offer a blackness through which the light of sanctity might shine.
>
> (205)

Notes

1 For studies on antiquity, see, e.g., Snowden, Goldenberg; for studies on the Middle Ages concentrating on blackness, see, e.g., the special issue of the *Journal of Medieval and Early Modern Studies* edited by Hahn, and also Biller ("Black Women"), Epstein (*Speaking of Slavery*), and Hahn ("Difference").

2 Caviness' article and arguments are supported by numerous lavish, full-color images impossible to reproduce here, but that may be found at: http://differentvisions.org/issue1PDFs/Caviness.pdf

3 Verkerk, Byron, and Strickland are also among those who discuss the growth of a negative discourse on blackness in patristic and exegetical traditions. Buell discusses early Christian rhetoric on whiteness in the formation of Christian community in the Mediterranean.

4 A "few partisans" of an "optimistic exegesis see Ethiopia as a symbol of humanity in quest of salvation," but St. Jerome dooms the Ethiopians by suggesting that their "barbarous, bloody ways" earn them their name, while their land "symbolizes all the earthly attachments that chain men to the blackness of sin" (Devisse 61). Jerome "admits in theory that [Ethiopians] are called to salvation through the gift of grace" but his comments are "generally harsh. His texts were repeated again and again and it is undeniable that they inspired the later interpretations that invariably identified blackness with sin, Ethiopia with the land of sin, and the Ethiopian with the collective sin of a people" (Devisse 61). Jerome, as we saw in Chapter 3, is also responsible for the lie that designates Arabs – who call themselves Saracens (*Saraceni*) he says, because they are ashamed to be descended from the bondwoman-concubine Hagar, and instead pretend to be descended from Sarah, Abraham's legitimate wife – and, later, Muslims as a race of liars.

5 Devisse reads the queen's hair as "blond" and her stance as significant: She has "a protective arm over a kneeling servitor who presents gifts" (129).

6 The queen has important allegorical significance for unredeemed humanity: "Isidore of Seville . . . saw the queen as symbolizing those who pass from paganism to Christianity by their own volition . . . [For] Rupert of Deutz . . . the queen symbolizes *the Gentiles* who desire to follow Christ – or, still more exactly, she stands as the symbol of the *nations of the whole world*, the Jews excepted" (Devisse 129).

7 Devisse points out that in the Book of Isaiah, "the color of sin is not black but red" and there is a "rivalry between red and black that runs through all Oriental, Jewish, Christian, and Muslim exegesis and symbology" as the color to designate evil (58). Devisse's genealogy of how blackness accrued negative meanings fingers Jerome as key to the preference for black as the color of sin and death in the Latin tradition (59).

8 Just as Caviness muses on the colors used to convey European flesh tones in visual art, Strickland muses on the colors that convey black skin: "In pictorial works of art, the correspondence in color between demons and Ethiopians is more readily apparent if brown, dark blue, purple, and sometimes even dark green are read as substitutes for the color black . . . There are technical, aesthetic, and symbolic reasons for the choice of some other dark color over black in these cases. First, unmodulated blackness in portraits that seek to emphasize physiognomical difference is problematic because other important stereotyped facial features, such as large eyes, flat noses, and everted lips, would not be visible against a completely black background. Second, the color black is inappropriate in certain monumental contexts, such as stained glass. Third, if communicating the strangeness and exoticism of the imaginary Ethiopian was an artistic objective, the use of non-natural colors is a very effective way of achieving this goal" (83).

9 The "*Passion of Perpetua* written by Tertullian in the second century constitutes our earliest witness of the presence of an 'African' headsman [but] it was not until the twelfth century that iconography began to portray the type. Thereafter we cannot dispel the thought that once contact

with areas where there were blacks was renewed, artists who chose the black as the type of the executioner knew exactly what they were doing. The date [of the twelfth and thirteenth century] explains why we find personages whose features are "Negroid" rather than simply dark in color. It was the time when ... contacts of all kinds were reestablished between Western Europe and Africa and the Africans" (Devisse 72). Devisse's twelfth-century examples of the African torturer-executioner motif are drawn from the *later* twelfth century; Debra Strickland points to a few *early* twelfth-century examples, including an illustration of the flagellation of Christ in the Winchester Psalter (*c.* 1150), where a phenotypic black African flagellator pulls tight Christ's fetters with his left hand as his right hand is raised to strike with a multitailed whip (82).

10 In these sensational creations, cultural fantasy may well have been responding to historical encounters: "to medieval anthropology, Eastern 'giants' were verifiable phenomena, like black-skinned men, described by geographers, naturalists, and travelers, and realistically associated with tall Africans in Saracen armies" (Metlitzki 197).

11 Wolfram hints that Josweiz may be picturesque in a different way from Feirefiz, since Josweiz is likened to the swan – whose image is blazoned on the banners of Josweiz' armies – which Wolfram says is white, with black beak and feet, perhaps suggesting that we should imagine Josweiz also with white skin, and with a black mouth and feet (190–1).

12 Interestingly, medieval Islamic writers discoursing on black Africans did not associate blackness with sin, the infernal, or a religion; however, as the fourteenth-century sociologist-historian Ibn Khaldun shows in his *Muqaddimah*, the depiction of black Africans by Islamic writers may be no friendlier: "Negroes are in general characterized by levity, excitability, and great emotionalism. They are found eager to dance, whenever they hear a melody. They are everywhere described as stupid" (63). A subscriber to climate theory, Ibn Khaldun attributes the character properties of black Africans to their residence in the hot zone, and believed that were they to settle in more temperate zones, they would "produce descendants whose colour gradually turns white in the course of time" (60).

13 Lorraine Stock's work on representations of wild men and wild folk suggests that forms of alterity meeting with fear and loathing earlier in the Middle Ages – whether it is epidermal race, or the primitive uncanny associated with wildness – were by the late Middle Ages welcomed; incorporated for personal, family, and social use; and manipulated for public attestations of identity and group play: "In the early Middle Ages the Wild People were considered monstrous examples of otherness to be feared and loathed [but] in the late Middle Ages the attitude toward the Wild People exhibited by the cultural elite included both identification with and impersonation of them. Identification was revealed in the incorporation of the Wild People in heraldic shields, family crests, and other signifiers of personal identity ... As exemplified in the Bal des Ardents [of 1393, in which Charles VI of France and his lords were dressed as wild folk], impersonation took the form of representation of wild people by civilized humans, such as a king, publicly enacted in ritual performance and pageantry" (138–9).

We noted in Chapter 3 how cultural processing over *la longue durée* has the capacity to domesticate the unspeakable, repackaging this into social utility and pleasurable recreation. Even appalling acts of crusader cannibalism committed on the cadavers of the infernal Saracen enemy in the late eleventh century – acts at which eyewitness Latin chronicles expressed horror and revulsion – can be transmogrified into cannibalistic jokes at the expense of the enemy two to four centuries later, as we saw in Chapter 3 (see also *Empire of Magic*, chapters 1 and 2).

14 Devisse and Mollat's volume of the multivolume *Image of the Black in Western Art* offers a comprehensive selection of epidermal race in visual art of the late medieval period. The volume by David Bindman et al. in the recent reissue of the *Image of the Black* series spans the sixteenth and seventeenth centuries. On blackness in early modern England in particular, with a focus on gender, see Kim Hall.

15 Sellassie suggests that Lalibela, the famous Zagwean king of Ethiopia, was inspired to build some of Ethiopia's famed churches after his own visit to Jerusalem (272), and that he might have ordered churches built at Roha because of the dangers faced by Ethiopian pilgrims "in the deserts of the Sudan and Egypt or in passing through Muslim countries on their way to the Holy Land" (273). "Roha then was intended to be a substitute for Jerusalem, a place of safety for pilgrims" (Sellassie 273).

16 Sellassie cites a letter of Jerome, who was in Bethlehem in 386, "to a certain lady, Marcella," in which Jerome mentions that "from Ethiopia we welcome crowds of monks every hour" (112).

17 "The Ethiopian monks long held a special privilege regarding the Holy Sepulchre which they no longer retain today. They were entrusted with the custody of the light which burns continuously on the tomb of the Lord, and, on the night before Easter, they offered the light to the Patriarch to celebrate the Feast of Resurrection" (Sellassie 143).

18 I cite Cyril Edwards' translation in English, and Karl Lachmann's edition for the Middle High German. The scholarship on *Parzival* is large, and, with apologies to the many scholars who have written on *Parzival*, I am only able to cite a sampling of the most recent scholarship focusing on epidermal race in this section. The scholars cited, however, furnish bibliographies that may be consulted by readers interested in literary criticism of this romance.

19 Jerold Frakes samples the negative discourse on blackness in medieval German literature: "In Reinmar von Zweter's poems, Johann von Würzburg's *Wilhelm von Osterreich*, and Konrad von Megenberg's *Buch der Natur*, black skin signifies evil and the devil. In the *Millstätter Exodus*, Pharoah and the Egyptian army are black ... In Albrecht von Scharfenberg's *Jüngerer Titurel*, one of Parzival's relatives is attacked in the East by opponents who are black as Hell, as the battle-cry *kampf den weisen* [battle the whites] is raised" (*Vernacular* 65).

20 Frakes totals up references to color in Gahmuret's adventures in Zazamanc and in Europe and finds that when Gahmuret is with Belakane and her people, heathenism and blackness are mentioned "forty-five times in some twenty-five pages of text," while in Europe "there are thirty references to brightness, light, and whiteness in twenty-four pages. Likewise images of light are practically absent from the first *aventiure*, as are images of darkness from the second" except when they refer to Belakane (*Vernacular* 83).

21 D. A. Wells dryly remarks "Gahmuret's cavalier desertion of Belakane after three months of marriage, knowing her to be pregnant ... In the light of his other amorous adventures one can hardly take seriously his promise that she might be able to win him back if she is converted" ("Source" 34).

22 Gahmuret's dedication to the Caliph means, in effect, that in the internal politics of medieval Islamdom, Gahmuret sides with the Caliph of Baghdad against the Ayyubids of Cairo ("Babilon"), since *Parzival* was written before the rise of the Mamluks in Egypt. Given *Parzival*'s early thirteenth-century provenance, after the infamous loss of Jerusalem to Saladin at the end of the thirteenth century, the two brothers of "Babylon" here may well be fabulated stand-ins for Saladin and Sephadin (the transliterated name for Al-Adil – *Saif-ad-Din* – Saladin's brother who appears in a number of European chronicles).

23 In *Willehalm*, Christians "take the cross" when they go to war. The insight that Gyburc/Orable might figure the lost city of Jerusalem is Jason Escandell's.

24 The knights of Munsalvaesche are called "templars" several times, translated by Kühn in Lachmann's edition as "Templeritter" (see, e.g., Cyril Edwards 188, 197, 294, 332, 334, 336, 337, 342, 343, 344; Lachmann I: 736, I: 776, II: 204, II: 350, II: 352, II: 358, II: 366, II: 370, II: 388, II: 390, II: 392, II: 398). The Grail King Anfortas, released from his agony by Parzival, decides to serve his order and fight in the Grail's service (Cyril Edwards 343; Lachmann II: 394). The Grail, it thus appears, continues to need military service by "templars."

25 "[I]t is apparent from the narrator's comments and from subsequent events that [Feirefiz] takes after Gahmuret ... and that his chief interest is the opposite sex" (Wells, "Source" 34).

26 Wolfram is conscious of multilingualism, however, as his characterization of Cundrie later makes plain: His Cundrie speaks three languages – Latin, "heathen" (i.e., Arabic), and French. She speaks *en franzoys* to the Arthurian court, but discourses knowledgeably on the planets and Arab astronomy in Arabic (Cyril Edwards 132, 326–7; Lachmann I: 518, II: 334).

27 While other thirteenth-century European literary texts exist that depict epidermal difference, my choice of *Parzival* and *Moriaen* for discussion in this section stems from the sustained, self-conscious, and thoughtful explorations of the meaning of color, and of the relationship between color and quintessential identity, in both texts. Both these texts are thus unusually fine exemplars of how questions on color can be raised, examined, turned on their head, and answered with some intricacy and nuance in a key modality of cultural creation. Later in the chapter, I examine statuary and visual art in the form of the Black St. Maurice of Magdeburg.

28 *Moriaen*'s narrator remarks in the prologue that some books actually identify Moriaen's father as Perchevael, while others say his father is Acglavael, Perchevael's brother. But since it is held as the truth that Perchevael and Galaet (Galahad, whose name is also spelled *Galaats* in this romance) both died virginal knights, the narrator therefore maintains that Moriaen could not have been Perchevael's son, but was instead Acglavael's. This intriguing disclaimer has led scholars to speculate that the original source may well have had Perchevael as Moriaen's father. For a detailed examination of the arguments – including a discussion of Acglavael's dream, the significance of which seems to relate more to Perchevael than to Acglavael – see Lacy.

29 "This immense manuscript [The Hague, Koninklijke Bibliotheek, 129 A 10], dating to ca. 1320, now comprises 241 folios written in three-column format. It contains the lion's share of the surviving Middle Dutch Arthurian romances. Five scribes, under the leadership of one of them, the so-called scribe B, were responsible for transcribing no less than 10 texts into this codex" (Claassens and Johnson 5). Claassens and Johnson, the editors and translators of *Moriaen* and other texts in the *Lancelot Compilation*, believe that "the *Moriaen* is an original Middle Dutch romance" (9). All references are from their edition and translation in progress, and I am deeply indebted to them for their generosity in sharing their work.

30 Lacy observes that the narrator "comments incessantly" on Moriaen's color, "a near obsession on the narrator's part" (129, 130). Moreover, the "author of the *Moriaen* . . . shows his full awareness of the stock equation of physical and spiritual blackness" and "takes pains to make him appeal to the Christian God on every conceivable occasion. He is a civilised Christian knight *in spite of* his black skin – this is the true significance of the 'nigra sum sed formosa' theme" (Wells, "Middle Dutch" 263, 264).

31 Moriaen's muscular impatience, which is channeled by Walewein into more dulcet chivalric ways, is thus a microcosm of the multistage instruction undergone by Parzival himself, who is a boisterous *rusticus* until he learns to be a proper knight. Moriaen, however, is already a knight when he appears, and D. A. Wells attributes Moriaen's "impetuous oath . . . to fight any knight who refused to disclose whether he had knowledge of Moriaen's father" to "shame at his illegitimacy and lost inheritance" rather than to hotheaded youth ("Middle Dutch" 250). Lacy, moreover, casts some doubt about who is being taught what here, by pointing out the irony of Walewein's admonitions to Moriaen about chivalry, since later "it is the neophyte who must save the life of Artur's greatest knight" (130).

32 Unlike Parzival, Perchevael's failure in the Grail quest springs not from failing to ask the Grail King the right question, but "because of the sin/that he committed against his mother/by his own volition and in that place/where he left her in the forest/when he abandoned her/and no longer wished to remain with the woman;/it was then that she died of sorrow./Those sins prevented him/ from achieving the lance and the grail" (l. 3064–772). The boatman who ferries Perchevael and Acglavael across the sea later reports that "one of them [i.e., Perchevael] was weeping/so that the tears fell thick/down his face" (l. 3492–4). Perceval's twelfth- and early-thirteenth-century role as

Grail Knight is later displaced, of course, by Galahad in the Old French *Queste del Saint Graal* romance, a knight designed to be a more perfectly Christian and less secular chivalric quester for the Grail, now sacralized as a precious relic of Christology in the aftermath of the loss of Jerusalem.

33 D. A. Wells contrasts Acglavael with Gahmuret, pointing out that Acglavael is "ignorant of Moriaen's conception," "leaves his betrothed … apparently with reluctance," and "can give a reasonably plausible excuse for his failure to return, and is willing to make amends through marriage. All this forms a sharp contrast to Gahmuret's cavalier desertion of Belakane" ("Source" 33). Wells also contrasts how each son characterizes his errant father: Feirefiz's "praise of Gahmuret's positive qualities, and heartfelt sorrow on learning of his death" is a courtly attitude wholly unlike "Moriaen's hope that, if dead, Acglavael may have his sins forgiven" ("Source" 34). Wells concludes: "the author imposes an ethical, as opposed to a purely thematic and formal, unity on his disparate material" ("Source" 48).

34 Scholarship has noted the remarkable intricacy, attentiveness, and care on display. Wells calls the *Moriaen* "one of the most lucid and readable of the Dutch romances" ("Source" 48), while Lacy observes that, "with its three heroes separating for adventures that are recounted sequentially, and with its multiple quests that diverge, reconverge, and cross, the romance … appears to be characterized by an usual density of texture and comparative tautness of structure" (126 n.4).

35 This seneschal also steals Walewein's sword and substitutes a poor-quality replacement, cuts halfway through his reins, and damages the saddle girths (l. 2061–71). The torture to which the host's men plan to subject Walewein – hewing off his limbs, spearing him, roasting him over a fire, and breaking him on the torture device of a wheel before finishing him off – seems queerly reminiscent of hagiographic features imported into a romance. In a delicate touch later, the text's fidelity to psychological realism has Lanceloet, Walewein, Moriaen, and Gariet ride "gently forth" to rescue Arthur's besieged queen, because Lanceloet is badly wounded and Walewein must tend to Lanceloet's many wounds as they ride (l. 4162–3).

36 The three romances in series – *Perchevael*, *Moriaen*, and the *Queste vanden Grale* – thus move their chivalric protagonists incrementally toward knightly perfection. *Perchevael*'s grievous fault, in failing his mother, is viewed through the looking glass of the Black Knight *Moriaen*, who protects and restores his mother; and the successful culmination of Moriaen's quest brings the start of the quest of the perfect, infallible knight of the Grail, Galaats.

37 In seminar discussion of this text, moreover, a graduate student – Rebecca Liu – pointed out that *Moriaen* is ultimately an assimilationist narrative, in which a protagonist who is an epidermal outcast gains respectability by being better than virtually everyone else in Arthurian Europe, because "if you're black, you have to be better than anyone else."

38 "The attitude to sex is noticeably different from that of works written in the dominant period of aristocratic culture; both Walewein and Lancelot are unrewarded by the ladies they serve, a contrast to traditional versions of the same episodes. The girl Walewein rescues disappears from the story" (Wells, "Source" 46–7). Wells also points out that the adulterous relationship of Lancelot and Guenevere is a motif "almost entirely suppressed" by the text, and adds that Acglavael's marriage to Moriaen's mother, which fully exonerates him for his earlier treatment of her, is "arguably a middle-class, as opposed to an aristocratic trait" ("Source" 47). Moriaen's service to his mother seems to obviate the necessity of service to other courtly ladies; this Black Knight is his mother's champion and no one else's.

39 For a survey of fourteenth- through mid-sixteenth-century portrayals of sex with black women, see Groebner. Peter Abelard's insights on the erotic appeal of black women are paralleled, William Phillips shows, by some Islamic writers who also enjoyed contemplating the pleasures afforded by black female bodies. Delighting in black African slave women, the Iberian Muslim writer Al-Sharishi "in the early thirteenth century praised the qualities of the slave women of Ghana. 'God has endowed the slave girls there with laudable qualities, both physical and moral, more than

can be desired, their bodies are smooth, their black skins are lustrous, their eyes are beautiful, their noses well shaped, their teeth white, and they smell fragrant'" (*Slavery in Medieval and Early Modern Iberia* 87).

40 Frakes is among the many who deprecate this convenient, flimsy fiction. He also observes that Dido and Aeneas are the template: "Obviously the first marriage was illegitimate for Wolfram (as also for the Catholic Church), for much the same reason as the Trojan and proto-Roman hero Aeneas's marriage to the Semitic Dido in Virgil's *Aeneid* was routinely deemed illegitimate (by both Virgil and, with few exceptions, two millennia of Virgil commentators) . . . it was a legitimate marriage only as long as it was convenient for Aeneas's libido and his divinely appointed *fatum*, before his abandonment of his Asian African bride and his move on to Europe and his destined Italic bride" (*Vernacular* 85).

41 Critics, however, are not always convinced by this smooth-talking white knight: "Ebenbauer suggests that Gahmuret's abandonment of Belakâne stems in large part from *rassistische Vorurteile* [racist prejudices] and *rassisches Ressentiment* [racial resentment] and notes that in Gahmuret's later excuses for abandoning her, where he claims that it was not because of her black skin, he reveals 'the true motivation for his actions, in that he unnecessarily rejects it.' Eva Parra Membrives similarly argues that ultimately, it is the foreignness (race, skin color, religion) of the Muslim queen Belakâne that makes it impossible to integrate her into the European courtly system despite her otherwise normative courtliness" (Frakes, *Vernacular* 84).

42 The fourteenth-century *King of Tars* is preserved in three compendia-manuscripts: the Auchinleck, Vernon, and Simeon. Judith Perryman's fine edition, based on the Auchinleck, is used in all references to *King of Tars* here. Perryman has an excellent, detailed introduction on the tangled skeins of legend, folklore, hearsay, mythology, and literary motifs intertwined in the fabrication of this romance. *Tars*, in the romance, has been variously identified as *Tarsus* in Armenia, or *Tauris*, the modern Tabriz (Hornstein 405–6), or *Tharsis*, originally linked "to a region of the Levant" (Kaplan, *Rise* 64), *Tharsia*, or *Tartary* (Perryman, introduction, and *Empire of Magic* 418 n.72). Despite the exoticized foreign locale named as the homeland of the Christian princess, however, the text's insistence that the princess is a classic Western European beauty whose whiteness of skin and thoroughly conventional Latin Christianity is constantly paraded makes the foreign locale hardly distinguishable from the Latin West, and suggests the place-name *Tars* functions merely as a proxy for Western Europe. Since the appearance of *Empire of Magic* a number of scholars have published on this romance, which has also become a popular Middle English text to analyze in PhD dissertations; there are now many talented discussions of the black–white epidermal politics of the romance. *The King of Tars* and *The Sultan of Babylon* are the only non-thirteenth-century examples I analyze in this section.

43 For historical analogues of how freedom from harassment by Muslim warlords in Andalusian Iberia could be purchased by proffering the tribute-bribe of a fair European (and Christian) maiden for a wife or a concubine, see Chapter 3, in the section "A Man for All Seasons."

44 Though epidermal race is the vocabulary for this romance articulation of absolute and fundamental differences between two human groups, color in this text also functions as the visible manifestation of absolute and fundamental *religious* differences: color here being the dramatic *signum* of religious race, signaling the intractable war between Christianity of a palpably Western European kind and Islam, portrayed here as a pagan polytheism centering on idol worship. To that end, the conventional, dogmatic Christianity featured in this text concentrates the utmost significance on rites, sacraments, holy days, catechism, and priests. We saw in Chapter 3 that the *Roman de Saladin* has Saladin self-baptize on his deathbed, suggesting that the *fact* of conversion, for the French romance, was of paramount importance. By contrast, the Middle English *King of Tars* requires *a priest* to perform baptismal rites for the miscegenated lump of flesh that the princess of Tars births and for the Sultan of Damascus (a priest, of course, is conveniently found

among the Sultan's captives). The princess of Tars delivers a pious homily in the form of a catechism to instruct her husband before his baptism; the fleshy wad she births happens to be baptized and transformed into a child on a holy feast day; and Biblical numerology is conspicuously scattered throughout the text. The crusade-like war that the freshly converted and whitened Sultan visits on his own people is thus only the military counterpart of the ideological, cultural war waged by this romance, wielding all the weapons of Christianity – rites, sacraments, catechism, priests, feast days – to subdue the infidel foe.

45 On the whitening of the "enamored Muslim princess" – as this *topos* has been dubbed – to render her an appropriate mate for a European knight, see Jacqueline de Weever. Converted Saracen queens such as Bramimonde in the *Chanson de Roland* and Orable in the *Prise d'Orange* of the Guillaume cycle of *chansons* famously and early, but only typically, lead the cast. F. M. Warren's 1914 article on the fantasy of the treacherous (and libidinous) Eastern woman, always royal, is an oft-cited classic. For more recent examples see Weiss, de Weever, and Kinoshita ("Courtly Love," "Pagans"). The Saracen princess Floripas in the *Sultan of Babylon* avers a passion for Guy of Burgundy, but cannot pick him out from a company of peers when she encounters him for the first time.

46 See, e.g., Fleischman's National Institutes of Health article on human piebaldism, and google "piebald humans" and "human piebaldism" for a variety of images. Human piebaldism results from depigmentation or hypopigmentation of the skin and hair, so that a black-and-white person would be a black-skinned human who has lost color, for genetic reasons, in patches across the body; a white forelock that stands out from the surrounding dark hair on the scalp is a striking characteristic. Piebald animals are far more common than humans, of course, as searching on Google Images attests.

47 References to the *Sultan of Babylon* in this section are from Alan Lupack's edition in *Three Middle English Charlemagne Romances*.

48 Norris, Lyons, and others emphasize the multidirectionality of such interchange. For other examples of global textual circulation, see Amer, *Empire of Magic*; Kinoshita (*Medieval Boundaries*); Lasater; Metlitzki; and Menocal.

49 The Naumburg black Maurice "does not appear as an armed knight, but as a duke clad in a long robe with a girdle, a cloak with fur collar, and the ceremonial headdress denoting ducal rank ... The crisp curls and the bluish shade of the hands indicate the African origins of the saint. Unfortunately nothing can be ascertained concerning the physiognomy because the face has been destroyed ... The Naumberg figure of St. Maurice as a duke is also without an iconographic precedent" (Suckale-Redlefsen 48, 49).

50 "On the basis of archeological findings the date of the first church dedicated to the Theban Legion could be fixed at approximately A.D. 380" (Suckale-Redlefsen 28–31). Between 470 and 500 CE, an anonymous author added a supplementary account of some length to the *Passion* (Suckale-Redlefsen 28, 29; Devisse 149). Marbod of Rennes wrote an eleventh-century verse account of the *Passion*; Sigebert of Gembloux wrote twelfth-century commentary; and anonymous authors at different times wrote poetry in honor of Maurice and his companions (Devisse 149). Devisse (chapter 3) and Suckale-Redlefsen (chapter 1) have lengthy accounts of the transmission of Maurician hagiography and the spread of the legend.

51 Suckale-Redlefsen supplies one of the more detailed versions: "At the time the emperor Diocletian (284–305) ruled the Roman empire in association with his coemperor Maximian. As supreme commander of the Roman army in Gaul, Maximian had crossed the Alps on a campaign against the insurgent Gauls. Having pitched his camp at Octodurum (now Martigny in Switzerland), he exhorted his subordinates to participate in a sacrifice to the Roman gods before the battle. Maurice and his legionaries, who were baptized Christians, attempted to avoid blasphemy by moving their camp to Aganaum (Saint-Maurice-en-Valais). On being ordered to return to the rest of the army

and perform the heathen sacrifice, Maurice refused. Maximian retaliated by having every tenth man of the Theban Legion executed. But even in the face of this signal example the faith of the Theban Legion remained unshaken. A second bloody punitive expedition met with just as little success. Maurice and his officers Exuperius, Candidus, and Innocent attested their willingness to submit to discipline in military affairs but continued to insist on their right to freedom of religion. Thereupon Maximian, who demanded unconditional obedience, had the rest of the Theban legion massacred together with their commander Maurice" (28, 29). Suckale-Redlefsen adds, "The authenticity of the martyrdom of the Theban Legion in this place is generally doubted today" (28, 29). Variant accounts exist of the events in the martyrdom.

52 Suckale-Redlefsen presents one version of Gregory's legend: "According to a variant of the legend current in Cologne, part of the Theban Legion chanced to escape the massacre at Saint-Maurice-d'Agaune through being absent on military operations outside the camp. Upon hearing of the murder of the main body of the legion with its commander Maurice, this unit, which included Gereon, Candidus, Exuperius, Victor, Cassius, Florentius, and a group of Moors under the command of Gregory, fled to the Rhine. Ultimately these Thebans also suffered martyrdom in various parts of the lower Rhine region (Bonn, Cologne, Xanten). After the discovery of the relics of Gregory the Moor and his 360 companions in 1046, Archbishop Anno of Cologne declared the saint co-patron of the ancient Church of St. Gereon, which was dedicated to the Thebans" (124, 125). Gregory begins to appear as black in the fourteenth century, "in a repainted but physiognomically African reliquary bust of about 1300" and "a magnificent portrait in stained glass of about ca. 1320 ... In the stained glass image, Gregory stands next to Gereon ... An altarpiece of ca. 1400–1425, also from this church, again pairs a very black St. Gregory with a white Gereon" (Kaplan, *Rise* 74). "In the person of St. Gregory the Moor, Cologne now had a saint who appears to have been consistently depicted as a black from the fourteenth century on. The other Thebans always remained white" (Suckale-Redlefsen 124, 125). Devisse adds, "neither he nor the Holy Moors, whose leader he was, were prominent in the city's devotions" (176).

53 Devisse, citing a PhD dissertation at the University of Paris as his source, says that Maurice's right hand once held a banner (166).

54 Devisse's chapter in *L'Image du Noir* appeared in 1979, Suckale-Redlefsen's *Mauritius: Der heilige Mohr* was published in 1987, and Kaplan's publications range from 1983 to 2010. Their work forms the context of critical summary and discussion and guides my thinking in this chapter.

55 "From the time of the Ottonian emperors the cult of St. Maurice in the German Empire was closely bound up with the coronation ritual. The king-elect kept his vigil in the chapel of St. Maurice in the cathedral of Aachen. Before the coronation he was invested with the spurs of the late saint, and the lance [of St. Maurice] was carried in front of him in the procession. After the coronation ceremony the new emperor laid aside the insignia in the chapel of St. Maurice before ascending the throne of Charlemagne. After the second half of the twelfth century the emperors were anointed by the pope in front of the altar of St. Maurice in St. Peter's in Rome" (Suckale-Redlefsen 36, 37). Conrad II and Henry III followed their imperial predecessors in embracing the patron saint of the Empire, and Maurice's cult spread throughout the entire imperial territory: "The many castle chapels dedicated to St. Maurice indicate that he was much favored by the high nobility. The title of *totius regni summus patronus* ('highest patron saint of the whole realm') [was] recorded by Abbot Hermann of Niederaltaich in the second half of the thirteenth century" (Suckale-Redlefsen 38, 39).

56 In 1270 the Eighth Crusade, led by Louis IX of France, intended Egypt again as destination, but made first for Tunis as a base from which to attack Egypt; St. Louis died in Tunis shortly before Edward of England arrived. Louis's brother, Charles of Anjou, abandoned the siege of Tunis, and Edward proceeded to Acre, the last crusader colony in the Levant, arriving in 1271.

57 As we saw in Chapter 3, the other potentate awaited along with Frederick – the fabled Prester John of India – also did not materialize. For not joining the crusade to Egypt and his subsequent failures to honor his pledge to go on crusade, and for other misdeeds, Frederick was excommunicated by Pope Gregory IX in 1227. David Abulafia observes that Frederick "had set a date, and agreed to his own excommunication if he did not fulfill his pledge by then" (*Frederick II* 167), though Arab chronicles claimed that the Hohenstaufen dynasty was prone to excommunication largely because of their Islamophilia. The chronicler Ibn Wasil says of Frederick II, his son and successor Conrad, and Conrad's successor Manfred (Frederick's natural son), that "All three were hated by the Pope – the Frankish Caliph – because of their sympathy with the Muslims." Ibn Wasil believed the Pope "excommunicated Manfred for his Muslim leanings and for having dishonored Christian religious law. His brother and his father the Emperor had also been excommunicated by the Pope of Rome for the same thing" (Gabrieli 277, 278).

58 Ibn Wasil reports that Frederick in fact tried to dissuade Louis IX from initiating a crusade to Egypt, and had sent "a secret embassy" to the Sultan "to put him on his guard and advise him to prepare to resist the attack, which [the Sultan] al-Malik as-Salih did ... the Franks never realized that the Emperor was intriguing with the Muslims against them" (Gabrieli 276). When "the King of France met the fate he deserved – the defeat and destruction of his army by death and capture ... the Emperor sent to remind him of the advice he had given him and of the sorrow he had brought upon himself by his obstinacy and disobedience and reproached him harshly for it" (Gabrieli 277). If the Arab chronicler is correct, Jean de Joinville's account of Louis's poignant grief at the loss of his brother at Mansurah, Louis's genuine piety, his abstention from extravagance and self-indulgence, and his quiet dignity in captivity suggest that Frederick was remarkably harsh to his fellow Christian monarch.

59 Kaplan offers other art in which such "universalist objectives" are detectable: e.g., a striking Apulian capital sculpted in the first half of the thirteenth century, discovered in 1954 in the sacristy of the cathedral at Troia, which is "decorated with four heads of varied types, including a woman, an Asian, and, most remarkably, a black" ("Black Africans" 30; see also Devisse, figure 91). A second carved capital also bearing four human heads, from the same time period and now in the Metropolitan Museum of Art in New York, exhibits similar human variety, and also features a lifelike, naturalistic black African face – a face that even sports a mustache (Kaplan, "Introduction" 14; see also Devisse, figures 89 and 90).

60 Unlike the two capitals sculpted with African faces and the Black St. Maurice in Magdeburg, which have come down in "decontextualized settings," the San Zeno fresco, Kaplan stresses, is an example of visual art that has valuably retained its original contextual markings ("Introduction" 16).

61 Frederick's cosmopolitan worldview and mozarabic familiarity with Islamic culture and learning brought him the admiration and friendship of the sultans of Egypt. Ibn Wasil reports that the "Emperor was a sincere and affectionate friend of al-Malik al-Kamil, and they kept up a correspondence till al-Kamil died"; with Al-Kamil's son and heir, too, "the Emperor was on sincerely affectionate terms and maintained a correspondence. When al-Adil died in his turn and his brother al-Malik as-Salih Najm ad-Din Ayyub [the last of the Ayyubid sultans of Egypt] succeeded him, relations were unchanged: al-Malik as-Salih sent to the Emperor the learned shaikh Siraj ad-Din Urmawi, now qadi of Asia Minor, and he spent some time as the Emperor's honoured guest and wrote a book on Logic for him. The Emperor loaded him with honours" (Gabrieli 276). Frederick was especially fond of Fakhr ad-Din, one of Al-Kamil's most trusted emirs. Runciman relates a traditional and doubtless apocryphal story in which Fakhr ad-Din, who was instrumental in Frederick's bloodless regaining of Jerusalem, received a knighthood from Frederick (III: 185).

62 One scholar describes him like this: "He was attested as knowing Arabic; he drew directly on works of Arab science and learning; he patronised Muslim and Jewish scholars and translations from Arabic; he employed Muslims in his armies; he maintained an exotic menagerie whose leopard-breeders were Muslims; and even dispatched philosophical questions in Arabic ... to Muslim thinkers in the hope of enlightenment from beyond the realm" (Metcalfe 280). A contemporary chronicler referred to him as the wonder of the world (*stupor mundi*); Pope Gregory IX, more belligerent a churchman than Honorius III, under whose protection Frederick had spent his minority in Sicily, referred to Frederick as the Antichrist. Muslim chronicles spoke admiringly of him, but wondered at his faith (Gabrieli 275).

For divergent views of this complex man, two of Frederick's letters may be contrasted. One, in Arabic and addressed to his beloved friend Fahkr ad-Din, Al-Kamil's emir, is recorded by the Arab chronicler Tarikh Mansuri; the other, addressed to his brother in Christ, Henry III of England, to inform the English king that Frederick had regained Jerusalem for Christendom, is recorded by the English chronicler Roger of Wendover.

The letter to Fakhr ad-Din shows Frederick's command of Arab epistolary rhetoric and aureate literary form, and begins in Arabic verse alternating with rhymed prose: "In the name of God, the merciful, the forgiving/We departed and left behind us our heart, which stayed (with you) detached from our body, our race and our tribe./And it swore that its love for you would never change, eternally, and escaped, fleeing from its obedience to me./If we set ourselves to describe the great desire we feel and the sorrowful sensations of solitude and nostalgia we endure for the high excellency of Fakhr ad-Din – may God lengthen his days and extend his years, and make his feet firm in power, and keep the affection He has for him and do him honour, and give his desires fulfilment, and direct his actions and his words and heap him with abundant graces, and renew his safety night and morning – we should exceed by far the limit of an exordium and err from the path of reason. For we have been smitten, after a time of tranquility and ease, with a bitter anguish, and after pleasure and peace with the torment of separation; all comfort seems to have fled, the cord of strong-mindedness is cut, the hope of meeting again turned to despair, the fabric of patience slashed. At our parting/If I had been given the choice between life and death I should have said:/'It is death that calls me.'/Death is tired of us, he has taken others in our place; he has chosen to leave us and seems to have forgotten our love" (Gabrieli 280–1).

The letter to Henry III is written *ex cathedra* in the persona of the Holy Roman Emperor, in Latin prose, and deploys the Christian rhetoric of divine miracle: "Frederick, by the grace of God, the august emperor of the Romans, king of Jerusalem and Sicily, to his well-beloved friend Henry, king of the English, health and sincere affection. Let all rejoice and exult in the Lord, and let those who are correct in heart glorify Him, who, to make known His power, does not make boast of horses and chariots, but has now gained glory for Himself, in the scarcity of His soldiers, that all may know and understand that He is glorious in His majesty, terrible in His magnificence, and wonderful in His plans on the sons of men, changing seasons at will, and bringing the hearts of different nations together; for in these few days, by a miracle rather than by strength, that business has been brought to a conclusion, which for a length of time past many chiefs and rulers of the world amongst the multitude of nations, have never been able till now to accomplish by force, however great, nor by fear" (Peters, *Christian Society* 162).

These two letters hint at Frederick's mercurial capacity for alternate personas, and may impart a better idea of his talents and personality than even learned scholarly arguments. In a revisionary swing of the pendulum, after Kantorowicz' 1927 account of Frederick's life, historians are now more inclined to suggest Frederick's similarities to his European counterparts, rather than his differences. David Abulafia's 1988 account of Frederick (*Frederick II*) may be contrasted with Kantorowicz'.

63 In the 1229 treaty of Frederick and Al-Kamil, Frederick gained Jerusalem, the third most important city in Islam after Mecca and Medina (leaving only the Haram/Temple Mount, with the Dome of the Rock and Al-Aqsa mosque, in Muslim hands), Bethlehem, Nazareth, "and a strip of land running from Jerusalem to the coast, further Sidon and Caesarea, Jaffa and Acre, and some other places" (Kantorowicz 187). "The Christians had thus regained control of the three holiest shrines of their religion, the places of the Annunciation, Nativity, and Crucifixion" and Al-Kamil also agreed to the refortification of Sidon, Jaffa, and Caesarea (David Abulafia, *Frederick II* 183). On his part, Al-Kamil gained a ten-year truce "with no guarantees on either side save the personal good faith of Emperor and Sultan" (Kantorowicz 187). This lopsided bargain sometimes strikes historians as "most obviously colored by the personal desire to please on al Kamil's side" (Kantorowicz 187). Frederick, who "did not even maintain the pretence of a war for the faith," had "accomplished more than all the mighty Crusaders of recent times," whereas the "Sultan's advantage in this pact was slight" (Kantorowicz 191, 188).

Al-Kamil had begun discussions with Frederick as a move against his brother, Al-Muazzam; Al-Muazzam's death subsequently rendered a pact with Frederick unnecessary, but Al-Kamil nonetheless kept faith with the Emperor, who asked for Jerusalem so that "he could 'hold up his head among the [Christian] kings'" (David Abulafia, *Frederick II* 182). As outraged Muslims across Dar al-Islam learnt of Al-Kamil's gift of Jerusalem to Frederick, dismay swelled: "The Khalif of Baghdad called him to account, the other Sultans were wroth with him, and mourning for the loss of the Holy City, which was felt to be a most bitter blow to Islam, rose to open demonstrations against al Kamil" (Kantorowicz 188). Registering the loss, the chronicler Ibn Wasil bitterly recalls Saladin: "The news spread swiftly throughout the Muslim world, which lamented the loss of Jerusalem and disapproved strongly of al-Malik al-Kamil's action as a most dishonorable deed, for the reconquest of that noble city had been one of al-Malik an-Nasir Saladin's most notable achievements" (Gabrieli 271).

Ibn Wasil shows how Al-Kamil's deed was exploited by his enemies and rivals: "When news of the loss of Jerusalem reached Damascus al-Malik an-Nasir began to abuse his uncle al-Malik al-Kamil for alienating the people's sympathies, and ordered the preacher, shaikh Shams ad-Din Yusuf ... to preach a sermon in the Great Mosque in Damascus. He was to recall the history of Jerusalem, the holy traditions and legends associated with it, to make the people grieve for the loss of it, and to speak of the humiliation and disgrace that its loss brought upon the Muslims ... It was a memorable day, one on which there rose up to heaven the cries, sobs and groans of the crowd" (Gabrieli 272).

There were negative consequences in Christendom as well. David Abulafia points out that since "the emperor's objective was the winning of Jerusalem rather than the winning of glory on the battlefield," and this was an expedition led by an excommunicate – shorn of the usual papal indulgences – and not a holy war, the Emperor's Crusade was also seen "in the Christian world as a betrayal" (*Frederick II* 183–4). A day after Frederick's crown-wearing in the Church of the Holy Sepulcher, Jerusalem was placed under an interdict by the archbishop of Caesarea, which meant that "pilgrims were denied the opportunity to earn the remission of sin they would gain from visiting the Holy Places" (David Abulafia, *Frederick II* 189).

64 Al-Jauzi says that Al-Kamil had thoughtfully ordered the Qadi of Nablus, Shams ad-Din, "to tell the muezzins that during the Emperor's stay in Jerusalem they were not to go up into their minarets and give the call to prayer in the sacred precinct" (Gabrieli 275). On the first day, the *qadi* forgot, and at the midday prayer, as the "muezzins' cry rang out, all [Frederick's] pages and valets arose, as well as his tutor, a Sicilian with whom he was reading (Aristotle's) Logic in all its chapters, and offered the canonic prayer, for they were all Muslims" (Gabrieli 274–5). Not hearing the call to prayer on the second day, Frederick chided the *qadi* for silencing the muezzins, reportedly saying: "My chief aim in passing the night in Jerusalem was to hear the call to prayer by the muezzins, and their cries of praise to God during the night." "He must have been very

familiar with the sound of the muezzin from Sicily and Lucera," David Abulafia observes, adding that the story is probably apocryphal (*Frederick II* 185). Al-Jauzi cites a custodian of the sanctuary who reported that Frederick wrathfully knocked to the ground a Christian priest sitting disrespectfully by the Dome of the Rock, near the imprint of the Prophet's foot; Abulafia's account of this offense, by way of explanation, has the priest entering Al-Aqsa mosque carrying a Bible (*Frederick II* 185). Frederick's jest at the expense of Christians involved punning in Arabic (Gabrieli 274). Al-Jauzi concludes, perhaps unfairly – Frederick II was a complex man – that Frederick's "Christianity was simply a game to him" (Gabrieli 275).

65 "In the early 1220s, the Emperor Frederick II began transferring the Muslim population of Sicily to Lucera, creating an inland Muslim colony not far from Christian towns and cities in Apulia . . . A diverse economy was created . . . Muslims farmed lands at Lucera and elsewhere in Capitanata. The Muslim community provided Frederick's armies with skilled archers, crossbowmen, and arms. The establishment of the colony created a controlled resource . . . [and] did not jeopardize his relations with Muslim rulers such as Sultan al-Kamil of Egypt" (Julie Anne Taylor xv). Historians sometimes find two phases of relocation to Lucera, one in 1223–5 "involving the Muslim population of Agriegento and another taking place at Iato and Entella between the years 1243 and 1246" (Julie Anne Taylor 12); none of this jeopardized "the long established and friendly ties which existed between Frederick and al-Kamil" (Julie Anne Taylor 13).

66 Julie Anne Taylor cautions, however, that while "most Muslims used Arabic names," there were "some signs of assimilation, such as the adoption of Christian names," which did not necessarily indicate conversion (xix).

67 Frederick II's propensity for exotic wild animals is well documented. Al-Kamil apparently once gave Frederick the gift of an elephant, resuscitating the cultural memory, perhaps, of Harun al-Rashid's gift of the elephant Abu al-Abbas to that first Holy Roman Emperor, Charlemagne. Frederick arguably topped the Sultan by giving Al-Kamil a polar bear "which to the amazement of the Arabs eats nothing but fish" (Kantorowicz 196). Notably, "Lucera, along with the island of Malta, was chosen by Frederick II as a spot for the raising of wild animals, particularly leopards, by Muslim keepers" (Julie Anne Taylor 100). North Africa and Malta "were the centers of the animal trade" and proceeds "from grain sales in '*Barbaria*' were used by Frederick to purchase leopards in 1239" (Julie Anne Taylor 101). Frederick also introduced camels into Italy. "If the request made by Giovanni Moro [i.e., Johannus Maurus, or John the Moor, Frederick II's black African chamberlain, and judge-administrator of Lucera] in 1240 that eighteen saddles for camels and 200 saddles for beasts of burden be made at Lucera is any indication, Frederick's project for bringing camels to Capitanata was a success. Camel keepers were working in Melfi, Canosa, and Lucera that same year" (Julie Anne Taylor 102).

68 The theory "that the whole circuit of the world was by right under the tutelage of the Roman Imperator" was also held by Frederick's father and grandfather (Kantorowicz 7). Frederick's grandfather, "Barbarosa . . . had once commanded the Sultans to place their lands under his rule as heir of the Augusti, because these eastern territories had of old been conquered by the generals of his Caesar ancestors" (Kantorowicz 7). Frederick's father, Henry VI, "had laid claim to Denmark and the Polish East; England had become a tributary vassal state" with the capture of Richard I upon that crusader king's return after the Third Crusade (Kantorowicz 8). Henry's pacification of Sicily extended Hohenstaufen hegemony: "Since the days of Roger II the Normans had styled themselves 'Kings of Africa,' and the Muslim princes, from Morocco to Tripoli, were now compelled to render to the German emperor – the new Lord of Sicily – the tribute heretofore paid to their Norman masters" (Kantorowicz 9). To David Abulafia, Frederick II's crown-wearing ritual in the Church of the Holy Sepulcher in Jerusalem was thus his declaration of "Roman imperial universalism," "the idea that the monarch has been called by God to rule *all* mankind" (*Frederick II* 188, emphasis original).

69 Archbishop Albert also "brought back the finger of St. Catherine" acquired during "his journey to Rome to receive the pallium," and nominated St. Catherine co-patron saint of Magdeburg cathedral (Suckale-Redlefsen 40, 41). Both Maurice and Catherine remain co-patron saints of the cathedral today. For an incisive argument on the cultural politics of their functions as co-patron saints, see Hammond.

70 Devisse, who dates the black Maurice to 1240–50, somewhat later than Suckale-Redlefsen's dating (she dates it before 1232), does not intimate that both statues belong to a single sculptural program for the new cathedral.

71 Suckale-Redlefsen emphasizes that the archbishop shifted political positions a number of times, and was not always loyal to Frederick II. "Amidst the confusion of the rivalry between the Hohenstaufens and the Welfs for the German throne [Albert II] was chosen to fill the most eminent diplomatic posts by three emperors and the pope. He was in the service of the Hohenstaufen Philip of Swabia [the uncle of Frederick II] and endeavored to effect a reconciliation at the meeting of the rival emperors [i.e., the Welf Otto IV and the Hohenstaufen Frederick II] in Magdeburg in 1208. No agreement was reached at this meeting, and Philip of Swabia was assassinated immediately afterward. Now Albert gave his support to the Welf Otto IV, who had hitherto been antiemperor. But this change of allegiance did not last long. From 1211 on he again espoused the cause of the Hohenstaufens under the rule of Frederick II. In the same year, in his capacity as archbishop of Magdeburg, Albert promulgated the excommunication of Otto IV by Pope Innocent III, whereupon the deposed emperor invaded the Magdeburg territories in a series of campaigns which ended only with his death in 1218" (Suckale-Redlefsen 38–41). The archbishop's shifts in loyalty between Otto IV and Fredrick II thus suggest to Suckale-Redlefsen the unlikelihood of a close relationship between archbishop Albert and Frederick II.

72 Archbishop Albert II was among the archbishops and princes present to elect Frederick II Holy Roman Emperor at Nuremberg in 1211 (the election was subsequently reconfirmed in 1212, and Frederick was crowned in 1220). In 1220, as we saw, Frederick enabled Magdeburg to buy the important relic of Maurice's skull; Frederick also made donations to the archbishop and cathedral "beginning at least in 1221" (Kaufmann 74). Kaufmann (85–6 n.56) points to the entries of payment in the *Regesta Archiepiscopatus Magdeburgensis*, 2: 291, no. 639 (September 17, 1221) and 2: 293, no. 641 (September 20, 1221).

73 "Albrecht's successor eventually had to appeal to the pope to cover debts, and the pope in turn put the fiscal management of the cathedral chapter in the hands of others. Albrecht's successors, including his half-brother Wilbrand, traveled less in Italy and had less contact with the emperor" (Kaufmann 74).

74 "As battle raged, and there was a risk of flagging in such a long fight with the number of enemies never growing less, an innumerable army of white soldiers was seen riding down from the mountains. Its standard bearers and leaders were said to be St. George, St. Maurice, St. Mercurius, and St. Demetrius. Once the Bishop of Le Puy saw them, he exclaimed loudly: 'Soldiers, here comes the help God promised you!' Our men would most certainly have been terrified had it not been for the hope they placed in God. The enemy began to tremble violently; they turned away, covered their backs with their shields and each one fled wherever he could" (Sweetenham 171–2). Robert the Monk's chronicle – not an eyewitness account, but among the wave of secondary chronicles of the First Crusade written in Europe in the decade afterward – is based on the *Gesta Francorum*, an eyewitness account written while on crusade and completed by 1101, by an anonymous vassal of Bohemond of Taranto, the landless Norman baron of the First Crusade who became the first prince of Latin Antioch. In the *Gesta*, the saints in heavenly white are George, Mercurius, and Demetrius (Hill 69). Robert's addition of Maurice suggests Maurice's growing popularity and helps to build Maurice's association with the crusader East. If Maurice once carried a banner in his right hand (as Devisse intimates) as well as a lance (as

Suckale-Redlefsen suggests), the statue shows him as a standard bearer, like Robert the Monk's crusading saint. For a comparison of eyewitness and secondary chronicles of the First Crusade, see *Empire of Magic*, chapter 1.

75 "The medieval baldachin is known from a late sixteenth-century drawing from Pomarius' *Chronika der Sachsen und Niedersachsen* (Wittenberg 1588) (*Figure 6*). It was composed of eight towerlike gables, four of which had female figures leaning from windows. It was crowned by a pointed metal roof, on the top of which a sculpted image of Saint Maurice was placed at some time. Maurice was the patron saint not only of Otto I, who founded Magdeburg, but also of the archbishop and Magdeburg cathedral" (Kaufmann 63). Kaufmann presents a meticulous and detailed argument on Frederick II's interest in reviving Roman imperial art forms, and his special interest in monumental equestrian statues of the *adventus regis* variety, marking the emperor's entry into a city. Her balanced survey of the likelihood that the Magdeburg Rider is a representation of Otto I, or of Frederick II, concludes that if the Magdeburg Rider represents Frederick II, the figure is "not meant to be a true-to-life portrait of the emperor but to show him in the way he wanted to be remembered for eternity" (80).

76 Kaplan argues that the stone capital found in Troia and the other now in New York, both of which display expressively lifelike and naturalistic black African faces, were fashioned in Lucera, Frederick II's Muslim colony. Since both capitals "display a range of human types" in the faces they depict, Kaplan considers them "briefer versions of the Verona fresco," and similarly designed to drive home the ideological point of the Emperor's universal dominion over the far reaches of the earth ("Introduction" 14). From Lucera comes yet another extraordinary sculpture – a beautiful, naturalistic African head, made in the 1240s, and now gracing the museum at Lucera. The stone face bears a prominent scar rising from below the lips to the upper left cheek, which suggests to Kaplan that this may be an image of Johannes Maurus himself, Frederick's chamberlain who was described as "deformatus" ("Introduction" 14–15).

77 In an early version of this section on the Black St. Maurice, that appeared as a contribution to the volume *Sainthood and Race: Marked Flesh, Holy Flesh*, edited by Vincent Lloyd and Molly Bassett, the volume's editors asked contributors to consider the question: How is a racial saint different from other saints – from a saint, say, who sustains the poor, loves animals, or blesses the crops? My understanding here (and below) of the apotropaic character of epidermal blackness on a racial saint is a partial answer to their question.

78 For an introduction to the Black Madonna, see Scheer; Begg; Cassagnes-Brouquet; and Oleszkiewicz-Perabala.

5

World I

A Global Race in the European Imaginary: Native Americans in the North Atlantic

The smaller the number of Indians ... the easier it is to regard the continent as having been up for grabs. "It's perfectly acceptable to move into unoccupied land," [Leonore] Stiffarm says, "And land with only a few 'savages' is the next best thing."

In the long run ... the consequential finding is that ... The Americas were filled with a stunningly diverse assortment of peoples who had knocked about the continents for millennia.

> Charles C. Mann, quoting Leonore Stiffarm, a Native American education specialist, and paraphrasing Elizabeth Fenn, author of *Pox Americana*, "1491"

OUR DISCUSSION of race has thus far centered on the Abrahamic faiths and epidermal binaries of black and white. But what happens to race when Europe encounters a world of differences, in which non-Abrahamic religions and a variety of skin colors proliferate, and few coordinates exist to make sense of a plethora of humans previously unaccounted for?

The Latin West's representatives to the Mongol empire in the thirteenth century found religions as bewilderingly unfamiliar as Shamanism, Buddhism, Taoism, ancestor worship, and animism, even as they again encountered Islam and familiar "heresies" such as Manichaeism and Nestorianism. The pragmatic Mongol conquerors of the steppe visited by Western Europe's representatives made few distinctions of an absolute kind in sorting and distinguishing among the humans of the world, and a stew of polyglot cultures and practices, sometimes in inextricably syncretic forms, coexisted among the peoples they ruled.

In a world of differences, physiognomic taxonomy's categories had to make room for the physiology of indigenes in the Americas (the paleo-ancestors of the First Nations, Inuit, and Native Americans of today); myriad ethnoraces in the Mongol confederation; Han and non-Han Chinese of the Middle Kingdom; and the Jat, Rajput, or other races of India, groups of whom made their way westward in the Middle Ages – dark-skinned peoples who turned into "Gypsies" and "Egyptians" in the course of their migrations.

The last chapters of our multifaceted foray into premodern race also bring environments beyond the temperate zones of the Latin West and Mediterranean conditions. On the one hand, Greenlanders and Icelanders discover a verdant, abundant land in pre-Columbian North America of the early eleventh century, rich in food sources and timber, Edenically fertile, and mild in weather – an ideal home for new settlement, were it not for the native races already there. On the other hand, a scrubby grassland on the Eurasian steppe breeds cultural responses among the locals that are so alien to the sedentary societies of Europe that a barefoot Franciscan monk who braves inimical weather, near starvation, hopeless translators, and an eerie, forbidding landscape in order to preach the faith, minister to far-flung Christians, and report back to the King of France, believes that he has, in truth, stepped into another world.

These last chapters allow us to consider what happens to race and race-making encountered at the extremities of climate and environment, and also at the extremities of power.

The Europeans who ventured across the world discovered that power assumes many forms. A clutch of Norse colonists – 65 or 160 people, the number varies according to the sources – weigh their ability to settle and occupy land where the dew is sweet, and assess their chances of fighting and holding their own against large numbers of the indigenous population who do not possess the iron smelting and metal weapons of Greenland, Iceland, and Norway. After a decisive pitched battle, the settlers conclude that power resides not only in their own putatively superior technology, but also in the vast numbers of the native population, and they withdraw back to northern Europe. But the Norse also find that power can manifest itself in the ability to shape the terms of trade between unequal, miscommunicating partners who meet for the first time on the American continent: a contingency that enriches the shrewd among the sojourners who return to the European homeland.

For the subaltern Asiatics who today call themselves the Romani, journeying to Europe without power, without the possession of armies or economic wealth, means they are preyed on and become a slave race exploited and owned by monasteries and landowners in parts of Southeastern Europe. In stark contrast to Jewish communities in diaspora, Romani inability to fend off catastrophe through bribes and economic negotiation transformed them into one of the most abject ethnoraces of the European Middle Ages.

At the other end of the scale from Romani abjection, the absolute power exercised by the Mongols – the terrifying alien race ruling over the largest land empire in the history of the human species – helped popes to imagine that the soft power of conversion, and not military adventurism, was perhaps the way to advance Christendom's interests in the thirteenth and fourteenth centuries. The crusader monarch Edward I of England even aspired to engage the Ilkhanid khans of the Mongol empire to forge a military alliance with Christendom in its continued struggle against the Mamluks of Egypt and Syria.

Revealingly, the *meaning* of the Mongol race, an alien race of empiremongers, shifted and altered in the perception of the West across two centuries of Mongol power. From the time the Mongols exploded onto the consciousness of Latin Christendom, up to their apogee of power – when they ruled the greatest civilization of the European Middle Ages, the "Middle Kingdom" of China – the West recalibrated its attitude to Mongols as it became increasingly aware of the Mongol empire's many forms of power – military, political, strategic, and economic.

The Invention of Race in the European Middle Ages ends with a consideration of peoples from India, focusing not on the literary, fabled India of the Alexander legends – that exotic, ancient land inexhaustibly elaborated in travelogues from the *Indika* of Ctesius to *Mandeville's Travels* and beyond – which the European Middle Ages so avidly desired for gems, spices, and Christianization, but rather on the people who departed their fabled homeland and began the long trek across the world, in a journey that, for many, ended in slavery and subjugation. *The Invention of Race in the European Middle Ages* thus begins and ends with peoples in diaspora – Jews, Romani – races that spread across the face of their known world.

Questions we've asked ourselves in the earlier four chapters continue, but are of necessity modified, in construing the global races treated in the last three chapters of this book: Is race in a world of differences still fundamentally *religious* race, as we saw in Chapters 2 and 3 with Jews and Muslims? Under what conditions can racial divides be bridged – a question we asked and explored in Chapter 4, on Africans and epidermal race? Are there new configurations of the racial that we have yet to see in Europe's encounters with alien otherness across the globe? Finally, in a global economy of mercantile capitalism, might race itself become irrelevant: When profit is the driving force, and trade capitalism webs the world in a network of intertwined relations, is race shunted aside as no longer of import?

First Races of the Americas: "Skræling" in the Land of Abundance

In the *Greenlanders' Saga* (*Grænlendinga saga*), one of only two existing Vinland Sagas that embed cultural memories of the "discovery" of North America during the first decade of the eleventh century, the first encounter between an expedition of Greenlanders and Icelanders from northern Europe and indigenes living in the Americas is swiftly homicidal.[1]

The expeditioners discover a small group of nine natives on a beach and immediately kill eight of them, but the ninth escapes.[2] Vinland ("wine-land") is extraordinary: a country where grapes grow naturally in the wild, salmon are fat and plentiful in river and lake, "wild wheat" sprouts without cultivation, grass for pasture hardly withers even in winter, and tall, magnificent trees proliferate in abundant forests – a land rich in everything that home-steaders in Greenland and Iceland could possibly want.[3] With such magnificent natural resources beckoning for extraction, more expeditions follow, and at least one settlement, perhaps more, is established on the North American coast.

The 1960 discovery by Helge Ingstad of a Norse settlement at L'Anse aux Meadows in Newfoundland, followed by extensive excavation of the site since, confirms the value of the Vinland sagas as historical records of a special kind.[4] The material evidence at L'Anse aux Meadows shows us that in North America in the early eleventh century, people from Greenland built houses, smelted iron, hewed trees, repaired ships, slept, socialized, threw away their trash, and even did single-needle knitting. One object found might have been a child's toy.[5]

Scholars are divided only as to whether the complex of buildings at L'Anse aux Meadows is the archeological record of what is described in the Vinland sagas, or whether L'Anse aux Meadows represents another, anonymous expedition or expeditions not recorded in any saga. Nordic journeying to the Americas half a millennium before Columbus is not itself disputed.

In the past two decades, considerable information has surfaced on climate conditions in the maritime Arctic and sub-Arctic and the native habitats and cultures of coastal Canada,

Greenland, and North America, and archeological finds have denoted far-flung mobility and trade.[6] In a series of studies, Birgitta Linderoth Wallace, in particular, has argued with increasing sway that the substantial size and strategic location of the settlement at L'Anse aux Meadows created too important a staging post – she calls the base a "gateway" to the North American continent – for the settlement to have been ignored by cultural memory's narrational record; Wallace believes L'Anse aux Meadows to be the archeological evidence of the cultural memories the sagas encapsulate.[7]

Archeology, however, is silent on the relations between these northern European expeditions and the indigenous populations the expeditions encountered. For such relations, we must turn to the Vinland sagas themselves.

The *Greenlanders' Saga* describes voyaging that takes place in stages, occurring first as exploratory visits by reconnoitering crews of hale, adventurous men in their prime, and only later by a mixed group of men and women who bring with them farm animals. This saga, which only exists in a manuscript compilation called *Flateyjarbók*, attests to *four* expeditions to Vinland. The first expedition of thirty-five men, led by Leif Eiriksson (the son of Eirik the Red), comes to explore unknown territory that was accidentally sighted to the west of Greenland by Bjarni Herjolfsson, when Bjarni was blown off course.

Historically, sightings of this kind, followed by exploratory voyages, led to the settlement of Iceland, then Greenland, by the Norse, with the creation of homesteads through land taking (*landnám*). Eirik the Red, a famous example, comes from Norway to settle in Iceland, but, after he is outlawed in Iceland for the kind of violent outburst and killing often depicted in saga literature, and which had driven his father to settle in Iceland in the first place, sets off to search for new territory that has been sighted (Magnusson and Pálsson 50; Sveinsson and Þórðarson 241). Eirik finds, names, and explores Greenland, settling there with a community of followers who emigrate from Iceland with him (Magnusson and Pálsson 50–1; Sveinsson and Þórðarson 242–3). The sagas thus show us that accidental sighting, followed by exploration, is how folk who are Norse colonize new lands.

In his turn exploring land accidentally sighted previously, Leif, the son of Eirik, gives names to the distinctive ecoscapes of the North American continent – in Labrador, Newfoundland, and possibly New Brunswick or Nova Scotia – and erects a base camp with "booths" (*búðir*, temporary shelters) and larger, more permanent houses at a site which the saga calls *Leifsbúðir*, Leif's "booths," or, by extension, Leif's camp (Sveinsson and Þórðarson 261).[8]

Tyrkir, a German-speaking southerner who's a part of Leif's family's household (Leif calls Tyrkir his foster father) excitedly finds wild grapes, and the expedition is able to return to Greenland with a valuable cargo of timber, grapes, and vines.[9] No natives are encountered in the first expedition. The second expedition, made up of thirty men and this time led by Thorvald Eiriksson, Leif's brother, are thus able to use Leif's camp and Leif's houses as their base, and, in the following two summers, to explore from there the coastal regions.[10]

In the second summer, at a forested promontory between two fjords (or what look to the Greenlanders like fjords), Thorvald and his men discover three mounds on the sandy beach of the headland – mounds which turn out to be boats made of or covered with skin, each boat sheltering three men (presumably sleeping) underneath.[11] The Greenlanders at once divide up their forces, seize the natives, and kill eight of them; the ninth manages to flee in his skin-boat (Jones, *Norse* 196; Magnusson and Pálsson 60; Kunz 642–3; Sveinsson and Þórðarson 255–6). Not surprisingly, the natives soon return in force, now in innumerable canoes, as the Greenlanders prepare to defend themselves.

In a hail of arrows from these indigenes which the *Greenlanders' Saga* calls *Skræling (Skrælingar)*, Thorvald Eiriksson receives a deadly wound and dies, his last utterance exhibiting the kind of ironic, stoic black humor for which the saga genre is justly famous.[12] Thorvald's men wait out the winter at their camp: The warmer global climate in 1000–1250 CE known to climatologists as the Little Climatic Optimum (sometimes also called the Medieval Warm Period) supported voyages between Greenland and Vinland, but only in summer, the season when the passage was navigable.[13] The men gather grapes and vines for cargo, and sail back to Greenland the following spring/summer (Jones, *Norse* 197; Magnusson and Pálsson 61; Sveinsson and Þórðarson 257).

The instant violence and homicide committed by the Greenlanders in this first encounter augur poorly for subsequent encounters. Since the first two expeditions have reaped cargoes of precious timber and an unexpected harvest of grapes, and brought renown through exploration and adventure, a third, larger expedition is launched, this time headed by a wealthy Icelandic merchant trader, Thorfinn Karlsefni, who has married Leif's widowed sister-in-law, the beautiful and intelligent Gudrid Thorbjarnardóttir. Karlsefni is also given permission to use Leif's houses at the base camp, houses which continue to remain Leif's property.[14]

Greenlanders' Saga reports that Karlsefni brings sixty men and five women to the Americas, along with livestock of all kinds, including a bull, because their intention is to make a permanent settlement there if possible (Jones, *Norse* 200; Magnusson and Pálsson 65; Sveinsson and Þórðarson 261). The presence of women this time, plus the addition of livestock, augments the impression that a longer stay is envisioned. At Leif's camp, presumably because of the pasture's rich sustenance, the male livestock grow frisky and hard to handle. The settlers fell trees and set the timber out to dry; they hunt game, fish, gather grapes, and make good use of all the natural resources of the country (Jones, *Norse* 200; Magnusson and Pálsson 65; Kunz 646; Sveinsson and Þórðarson 261).

In the summer after Karlsefni's expedition's first winter at Leif's camp, a great many *Skraeling* suddenly appear out of the woods, carrying bundles containing sables, furs, and pelts of all kinds. They proffer their wares – neither side can understand the other's speech, we are told – and the saga announces that *Skraeling* particularly want the Greenlanders' metal weapons in trade (Karlsefni, of course, forbids his men to trade any weapons). In a single gesture, the narrative has deftly characterized the expeditioners as a community with advanced metal technology keenly desired by the locals.

Karlsefni has a brainwave: He offers food instead, telling the womenfolk to bring out milk (*búnyt*). Once the *Skraeling* see this food, we are told, they want nothing else, and trade away all their furs and skins. So that was what became of the *Skraelings'* trading, the saga tells us with satisfaction: The *Skraeling* carried away what they bought in their bellies, while Karlsefni and his men gained their furs and skins (Jones, *Norse* 200–1; Magnusson and Pálsson 65; Sveinsson and Þórðarson 261–2).

In Settler Colonization, Two Lessons on How to Bilk the Natives

Thus far, the first European settlement in the Americas, as narrated in the *Greenlanders' Saga*, has performed steps in land taking (*landnám*) – the beginnings of colonization, with Iceland as a historical example – of an aggressive kind. Leif Eiriksson and his men find an apparently empty land, ripe for resource extraction. They duly extract resources they assume are there for the taking. Thorvald Eiriksson and *his* men, on finding the land not empty after all, meet a few local inhabitants and instantly kill them, thus provoking retaliation and hostilities between two populations depicted as meeting on the continent for the first time.

By contrast to the Greenlanders, the native races that make their way to Karlsefni's camp offer *peaceful* contact by initiating trade. Studies have shown that ancestors of the Mi'kmaq, Beothuk, Maliseet, Eastern Abenaki, Penobscot, and other Algonquian-speaking communities annually frequented the eastern Atlantic coast during summer for hunting and trade (Odess et al. 204, Sutherland 238, McAleese 356). The *Greenlanders' Saga* mentions no aggressive behavior on the part of the natives. Indeed, while trading, the natives are so startled by the settlers' aggressively bellowing bull that they flee in panic, looking for protective shelter in the houses of the camp, and running toward Karlsefni's house.

Proffering sables, grey furs, and pelts, the natives are bilked into desiring foodstuff they have never seen before (and for which, in fact, most of them nutritionally lack the genes to process) in an unequal exchange that the saga fully understands to be exploitative.[15] In a second round of trading – the natives return after the first exchange in much greater numbers (we do not learn if these are the same natives as before, or different tribes) – Karlsefni shrewdly *again* instructs the womenfolk to bring out the same foodstuff as before, but no other goods. The natives are so eager to trade, they at once throw in their bundles over the protective wooden palisade the settlers have now erected around the houses of the camp (Magnusson and Pálsson 66; Sveinsson and Þórðarson 262).

Though we might say that in a sense each side got what it wanted most in barter – after all, the natives had the novelty of new food, and the settlers gained richly valuable furs and skins – the smug comment of the saga narrative, with its condescendingly superior knowledge that food soon evanesces in the body while furs are valuable commodities in the international trading network of Europe and beyond, suggests that it understands well the exploitative and unequal nature of this transaction between races (Magnusson and Pálsson 65; Sveinsson and Þórðarson 262).

Tellingly, at the close of the saga, the resourceful Karlsefni takes his Vinland cargo first to Norway – gateway to continental Europe's markets – where he disposes of his wares. Karlsefni's report of adventures in Vinland must have had a sensational reception, since we are told that he and Gudrid are made much of by the most notable people of Norway (Jones, *Norse* 205; Sveinsson and Þórðarson 268). Indeed, the *Greenlanders' Saga* tells us that Karlsefni more than anyone else is responsible for recounting the story of all the voyages (Kunz 652, Magnusson and Pálsson 72, Sveinsson and Þórðarson 269).

Profit from the Vinland trade must be handsome, for Karlsefni next proceeds to Iceland where he buys land, builds a house, and establishes a permanent family homestead and farm at Glaumbær which continue in the family line for generations to come (Jones, *Norse* 205; Sveinsson and Þórðarson 268–9).[16] Karlsefni even makes one last handsomely advantageous trade as a postscript at the saga's end, when he sells a ship's figurehead made of North American wood (*mǫsurr*) to a Saxon for half a mark of gold, a small fortune (Jones, *Norse* 205; Sveinsson and Þórðarson 268).[17]

In the other saga embedding cultural memory of journeying to Vinland – *Eirik the Red's Saga* (*Eiríks saga rauða*) – the first encounter is less brutal, with each side mostly evincing surprise at the first, brief glimpse of the other. Here, the unwieldy account of four separate voyages is done away with, and Leif's expedition is just a perfunctory landing when he is blown off course, finds land where none is expected, and takes back to Greenland specimens of wild wheat and vines (Kunz 661; Jansson 48).

Eirik the Red's Saga's two manuscripts neatly focus on Karlsefni and Gudrid's expedition instead, and make Thorvald Eiriksson part of this expedition (Thorvald still dies by a native's arrow – narration is consistent in this regard – though the display of saga humor here has Thorvald uttering a different ironic remark at his wounding and death). This saga, some scholars have noted, is more genealogically oriented than *Greenlanders' Saga* to the distinguished line that issues from Karlsefni and Gudrid, three of whose descendants become important bishops – a lineage that the *Greenlanders' Saga* also acknowledges at its close (Kunz 652; Magnusson and Pálsson 72; Sveinsson and Þórðarson 269; Jansson 80–1).[18]

Unlike the *Greenlanders' Saga*, *Eirik the Red's Saga* – existing in two manuscript recensions, *Hauksbók* and *Skálholtsbók* – has 160 members in Karlsefni's expedition, including women; in this saga too, the expedition brings along livestock of all kinds, including a bull (Magnusson and Pálsson 94, 95; Jones, *Eirik* 146; Jansson 61, 64). But Karlsefni has a business partner and coleader in the enterprise, Snorri Thorbrandsson, and it is *this* expedition, not Leif's, that gives the names *Helluland* ("rock-slab land"), *Markland* ("forest-land"), and *Vinland* ("wine-land") to the coastal and interior territories of the North American continent. In *Eirik the Red's Saga*, the Greenlanders and Icelanders make *two* settlements: a base camp at a place they call *Straumsfjord* (*Straumfjörðr*, "current-fjord" or "tide-fjord" (Magnusson and Pálsson 95; Kunz 667; Jansson 64) and a second camp further south, at a place they call *Hóp* ("tidal-pool"), near a lake/lagoon (Kunz 669; Jones, *Norse* 224; Jansson 68).

It is at the southern location, Hóp, where first encounter occurs. During the fortnight of the expedition's stay, one morning a number of skin-boats appear (*Skálholtsbók* has nine boats, *niu hud keipa*; *Hauksbók* mentions a multitude of boats, *mykinn fiolda hudkeipa* [Jansson 69]), on board which staves are being brandished that make a swishing sound as they are twirled in a circular, "sun-wise" (i.e., clockwise) motion, sounding like threshing flails. Snorri Thorbrandsson, the coleader, suggests they meet the visitors by raising a white shield, a sign of peace in Norse culture. The natives row toward the settlers, astonished; they land and stay a while, marveling, then row away southward, around the promontory (Kunz 669–70; Magnusson and Pálsson 98; Jansson 69).

We see these natives – who are not yet called *Skraeling* by the text – through the settlers' eyes. The natives are short-statured men (*smair men*, according to *Skálholtsbók*), dark men (*suartir men*, according to *Hauksbók*), with malignant features (*illiligir*), evil hair on their heads (*illt hár á höfði*), large eyes (*mjök eygðir*), and broad cheeks (*breidir i kinnunum* [Jones, *Norse* 226; Jansson 69]). Despite their unprepossessing appearance, no violence is visited on them – perhaps because in this first encounter the natives are not palpably outnumbered or asleep – and the settlers decide to winter at Hóp, a locale so far south that there is no snow at all that winter and their livestock is able to find food for itself, grazing outdoors (Jones, *Norse* 227; Magnusson and Pálsson 98; Jones, *Eirik* 150–1; Jansson 70).[19]

Any sense of disquiet that their first encounter may have brought the colonists is undercut by the substantial advantages at Hóp: an idyllic Eden where every brook teems with fish; fields of self-sown "wheat" grow on low ground and grape vines on high ground; the woods are filled with plentiful game of all kinds; and halibut appear in trenches scooped out at the high-tide mark when the tide goes out (Magnusson and Pálsson 98; Jones, *Norse* 226; Jones, *Eirik* 150; Kunz 671; Jansson 68–9).

The second encounter in this saga, like the second encounter in *Greenlanders' Saga*, involves trade – but unlike *Greenlanders' Saga*, *Eirik the Red's Saga* only has one episode of trade. At Hóp after the first winter, a great multitude of skin-boats appear from the south and round the promontory one morning in spring, with staves whirling again on every boat. Karlsefni and his men again raise their shields, and trading begins.

In *this* Vinland saga, the natives want most of all to buy red cloth (in exchange for furs and skins, *Hauksbók* adds [Jansson 70]), but they also want to buy swords and spears. Both Vinland sagas thus signal native recognition of the desirability of Europe's superior metal weaponry, suggesting universal acknowledgment of iron's efficacy and an innate understanding that the colonists represent a civilization with advanced technology. Karlsefni and Snorri prudently forbid any sale of weapons, just as in the *Greenlanders' Saga*. No mention is made about bilking the natives with milk in exchange for furs. Instead, *Eirik the Red's Saga* has its own version of exploitative exchange.

The natives offer a pelt for each span of red cloth, and tie the cloths they acquire around their heads.[20] When this goes on for some time, and the supply of red cloth is much reduced, Karlsefni and company arrive at the inspired idea of cutting up the cloth into pieces no wider than a finger's breadth: yet the natives (*Skrælingar* now) continue to pay just as much, or more, for these diminished goods. The text offers no comment at this – it merely registers the credulous willingness of the locals to tender a pelt for each diminished strip of red cloth (Magnusson and Pálsson 99; Kunz 670; Jones, *Eirik* 151; Jansson 70–1).

If *Eirik the Red's Saga* is silent on the natives' apparent naiveté, scholars have been less reticent:

> Aborigines have no idea of the "real" (European) value of things and willingly give away their most valuable wares in exchange for cheap luxury articles, minute quantities of unfamiliar foodstuff or stimulants. Thus, Columbus notes in his log on 22 October 1492 that the Indians would exchange pieces of gold for small glass beads, while on 5 November 1492 he states: "All that these people have they will give for a very ridiculous price: they gave one great basket of cotton for the end of a leather strap" ... Similarly in *Eiríks saga rauða* ... we learn that the Skrælings traded their valuable furs for small strips of red cloth ... this is matched, and indeed bettered, by what *Grænlendinga saga* tells us of the Skrælings giving away their most valuable possessions for a drink of milk.
>
> (Almqvist 26)

Though each of the two Vinland sagas takes cognizance of different goods traded to the natives, milk in one saga, strips of red cloth in the other – these sagas were written down, after all, over two centuries after the voyages, and details may be expected to change in their oral transmission before they were set down in writing – the singular recognition remains, in both sagas, that the settlers' trade with the natives is satisfyingly unequal, with palpably superior results for the settlers. Half a millennium before Columbus set foot on the continent, it seems that Europeans were already congratulating themselves on bilking the native races of the Americas.

In *Eirik the Red's Saga*, the trading ends in chaos when the colonists' bull suddenly runs out from the forest and bellows loudly. At this the locals take fright, scatter to their boats, and row away, back to the south. Both sagas, we notice, register the impact of a bellowing bull that terrifies the natives: a large, bellicose creature foreign to their shores. Three weeks pass with no incident, then a multitude of native boats issue from the south, this time with staves whirled counterclockwise and men shouting aloud (Jones, *Norse* 227; Jones, *Eirik* 152; Magnusson and Pálsson 99; Jansson 71).

Karlsefni and company take the reversed motion of the whirled staves and the shouting to be a battle challenge, so the settlers now take up red shields instead of white, and both sides engage in a protracted, fierce struggle. Though the natives lack the metal weapons they have tried to buy, it turns out that they have war slings, or catapults (*ualslongur*). When they rain down on the settlers a large, dark, spherical object (the size of a sheep's gut, *Hauksbók* adds: *iafna sem saudarvomb*) that makes a horrific din when it lands, it is the settlers' turn to be terrified and flee (Jones, *Norse* 227; Jones, *Eirik* 152; Magnusson and Pálsson 99–100; Jansson 71). Native war technology deployed by Stone Age peoples, it seems, can be superior to the advanced metallurgy of Europe after all, especially when the natives seem able to launch their own equivalent of Europe's ballista or trebuchet.

In each Vinland saga, the narration of a final and decisive pitched battle is precipitated by something that occurs during trading. The *Greenlanders' Saga* assigns responsibility to an incident that happens during the second episode of trade, when a native is killed by one of Karlsefni's household servants – for trying to steal weapons, the saga says (although, given the narration of native curiosity about the colonists' strange metal technology, we might also wonder if the native was merely examining them inquisitively).

Upon the killing of the native, trading ends, and the indigenous visitors scatter in such haste that they leave behind clothing and wares: more profit for the expeditioners. Karlsefni understands however that they will soon return a third time, to avenge their own, and prudently identifies a battleground to the settlers' advantage, to which they plan to lure their attackers. In making their stand, the settlers also plan to strategically deploy their bull, which had earlier so frightened the locals (Magnusson and Pálsson 66; Jones, *Norse* 201–2; Kunz 647–8; Sveinsson and Þórðarson 263).

In *Eirik the Red's Saga*, the return of the natives in war mode is precipitated by the sudden appearance of the settlers' bellowing bull during the one trade episode narrated. This untoward incident of a rampaging bull is apparently understood by the natives as a gratuitously hostile act aimed at them while they are peacefully trading, and they return three weeks later whirling their staves in reversed motion to signal a reciprocally hostile intent.

The three-week interval, we note, may indicate the length of time it takes the affrighted natives to consult with their home communities, amass forces, and launch their counter-attack. This, at least, appears to be the saga's understanding in narrating the sequence of events, since the saga does not distinguish among any of the native groups encountered by the colonists, nor does it specify that some tribes might be friendly and interested in trade, while others might gratuitously mount sudden surprise attacks.

The sagas thus show us that even peaceful contact through trade is risky when vastly different races are meeting with no language, background, or culture in common, and with no intermediaries or translators to facilitate communication. The settlers' bull, which suddenly appeared from the forest, bellowing, in *Eirik the Red's Saga*, is unlikely to have been set upon the natives deliberately, since the saga indicates that trading was proceeding smoothly to the settlers' great profit, as each small strip of red cloth garnered a pelt in exchange.

Moreover, the *Greenlanders' Saga*, which also features a bellowing bull, confides the information that male animals brought to Vinland became restive and hard to manage. The bull's bellicosity thus likely derives from the animal's response to the lushness of Vinland, rather than instigation by the settlers. Also, the native killed by Karlsefni's man in the *Greenlanders' Saga* may only have been examining the settlers' weapons with curiosity when he was killed outright for attempted theft.

But misunderstandings are rife when no common language or translators exist to ease the incomprehension of communities alien to each other and depicted as meeting for the first time, and where only signs of a rudimentary kind – staves whirled clockwise or counter-clockwise, white or red shields being raised – sketch the parameters of anticipated behavior. In *Eirik the Red's Saga*, the settlers were able to hazard a lucky guess as to what the clockwise whirling of rattling staves might mean, and make another lucky guess that their own white shields would be understood as emblematic of their peaceful intent. But these two signs specify the limits of guesswork in communication.

The only shared cultural commonality between these alien races narrated as meeting on the North American continent for the first time is barter. Yet even when trade is the basis of encounter, one side registers its triumph in securing advantageous, exploitative terms, while the other returns in force to avenge slights or hostile actions it does not deem accidental or inadvertent. From as early as the beginning of the eleventh century, the European literature of encounter and colonization shows race relations to be fraught, exploitative, and volatile, ending – seemingly inevitably – in violence and war.

Women Make a Difference: Not War or Trade, but Linguistic Exchange

The *Greenlanders' Saga*, however, does relate one extraordinary encounter of a peaceful kind that occurs when two individuals from these ill-communicating, mutually alien races meet in a *domestic* setting, an encounter that differs considerably from all the occasions when men from both sides meet in public settings.

Gudrid Thorbjarnardóttir, Karlsefni's wife, gives birth to a son, Snorri, the first European child (so far as we know) to be born on the North American continent, and is quietly sitting in the doorway of her house, by the cradle of her infant son, when the natives return for a second round of trading. As Gudrid sits by her child, a shadow falls across the doorway and a woman enters. The woman is small of stature, pale, and has the largest eyes ever seen in a human head. She has light reddish-brown/chestnut hair with a headband around it, and wears a dark, close-fitting garment.

> She walked to where Gudrid was sitting and spoke.
> "What is your name?" she said.
> "My name is Gudrid. And what is your name?"
> "My name is Gudrid," she said.[21]

> *Hon gekk þar at, er Guðríðr sat, ok mælti: "Hvat heitir þú?" segir hon. "Ek heiti Guðríðr; eða hvert er þitt heiti?" "Ek heiti Guðríðr," segir hon.*
>
> (Sveinsson and Þórðarson 262–3)

Gudrid, the mistress of the house (*húsfreyja*), motions with her hand to the woman to come and sit down beside her, but at that very moment a great crash is heard outside, and the woman disappears: In that moment, we are told, Karlsefni's man has killed the native who had apparently attempted to steal some weapons.

This remarkable episode of two women meeting in a domestic setting has provoked considerable scholarly disagreement as to its meaning. There is a touch of the uncanny about its details: The unknown woman's sudden appearance in Gudrid's doorway and her just as sudden departure when the crash occurs, betokening the native's death by Karlsefni's servant's hand, are suggestive of something out of the ordinary. Some scholars understand the woman to be a spirit related to anticipation of the native's death, or to be a supernatural figure from Norse lore transported to the Americas.[22] The paranormal is not alien to this narrative, nor to the saga genre, and long before this, the *Greenlanders' Saga* and *Eirik the Red*'s Saga have already narrated other episodes in which men and women – but especially women – have a touch of the uncanny about them.[23]

Scholars who believe this unknown woman to be human, and not a revenant or spirit, have had to contend with the words spoken by the two women. Some have suggested that the woman with the strange features and appearance is a Greenlander or Icelander who also happens to be called Gudrid (which is not a noticeably Native American name), and that somehow, after all this time together in North America, Karlsefni's wife is meeting her fellow settler with the same name for the very first time, and doesn't yet know her name.

Perhaps more reasonably – given that the woman's large eyes and small stature are native features also described in the first encounter in *Eirik the Red's Saga*, and given that her other descriptive attributes also appear in anthropological literature characterizing early indigenous populations in the Americas – Bo Almqvist suggests that the episode more likely registers an encounter between Gudrid and a Native American woman.

Almqvist does not claim that the episode reports in precise detail an actual, historical encounter between a northern European woman and a Native American woman. The historicity of this, Almqvist understands, would be impossible to verify, given that the sagas only set down, centuries later, cultural memories transmitted orally for generations. Rather, Almqvist suggests, the episode imagines an encounter considered important enough to be transmitted, and finally set down in saga form (20).

To make sense of the verbal exchange between the two women, Almqvist makes one small emendation to the dialogue, and suggests that "*ok mælti*" is an addition by a copyist, the result of a scribe's error in interpreting how the exchange should be read. Without the pointer that the unknown woman walked up to Gudrid *and spoke*, the dialogue is sufficiently ambiguous – when shorn of the punctuation that is editorially added to the medieval manuscript – as to suggest that it is *Gudrid* who speaks first, and the woman's utterance merely repeats Gudrid's words:

> Let us suppose, therefore, that it is Guðríðr Þorbjarnardóttir, and not the visiting woman, who says – slowly and clearly, much as one might speak to a small child – *Hvat hettir þú*? "What is your name?" With no answer forthcoming, she continues – we might imagine that she points to herself – *Ek heiti Guðríðr*, "My name is Guðríðr", and then adds (now pointing to the Skræling) *eða hvert er þitt heiti*, "and what is your name?" Totally baffled the Skræling woman repeats like a parrot what she has just heard, uttering the words (perhaps imitating Guðríðr's voice) *Ek heiti Guðríðr*.
>
> (Almqvist 27)[24]

Sensitive to the politics of cultural encounter between Europeans and native populations, Almqvist stresses foremost the kind of slight (well-meaning) condescension that inhabits the speech of Europeans who encounter natives and try to speak to them.

Gudrid, thus, is speaking *as one might speak to a small child*, slowly and clearly – as, even today, Westerners in trying to make themselves understood are wont to speak to foreigners: slowly and clearly, articulating their phonemes well, as if talking to children still in the process of learning their syllables. In similar fashion, to Almqvist the native woman doesn't repeat Gudrid's words experimentally and musingly, sounding out on her tongue a new, alien language for the first time, but *repeats like a parrot what she has just heard* (27).

Almqvist's sensitivity to the politics of cultural encounter is admirable, and unquestionably correct on its own terms. Gudrid may be speaking slightly condescendingly, as if to a small child, and the Native American woman is perhaps portrayed as mindlessly parroting her.

But might it be possible, in this strange, undecidable episode where there's an aporia in meaning – an episode that presents an encounter so unlike the other saga encounters of sudden homicides, the flailing of axes and hurling of catapults, and sheer glee at swindling the natives – that the saga is also trying to imagine, for whatever reason, for whomever in its audiences wants this episode to exist, an alternative scene in which two people – *women*, not trading, warring men – meet *peacefully* and on equal terms in the home of the one who is a mother with a small child?

The native woman here can then be read as trying out, with curiosity, the strange syllables of Old Norse on her tongue – the first indigenous person in the Americas to sound out one of Europe's languages. Astonishingly, she would also be the only Native American in the Vinland Sagas who ever speaks, her voice the only indigenous voice we ever hear.[25]

Whether partly imagined, partly historical, or an inextricable mélange of reportage and cultural desire, the episode offers a meeting of two individuals in an unthreatening environment – not the risky context of trade, where misunderstanding can lead to violence in an instant or where a multitude of boats land ashore a host of men of uncertain intent, but a domestic interior where a mother sits by her infant's cradle and shows no sign of fear when a strange woman enters her home, but invites the woman to sit down beside her, after asking her name.

No unequal trade, no violence, and no war are here, just a woman and a child, welcoming another woman in an intimate, domestic environment. Gudrid Thorbjarnardóttir – Almqvist observes – has already been described by the saga as "an intelligent woman who knew how to conduct herself among strangers" (*vitr kona ok kunna vel at vera með ókunnum mǫnnum*), and "her well-mannered behavior" is precisely on display in her fearlessly welcoming an unknown indigenous woman into her home (26 n.26).

The encounter is carefully presented in gendered, intimate terms – one woman offering hospitality to another in her home – and it is the saga's *only* portrayal of direct linguistic communication, of verbal dialogue, between European and native races. All other attempts at speech between the races is reported, not portrayed. Sadly, however, the communication here is not a two-way circuit – the saga has already told us in the first trade encounter that neither side can understand the other's language – and Gudrid's name is reflected back to herself as an echo, an aural mirror of the European woman's attempt to communicate, in asking for the name of the other. The peacefulness of this brief domestic encounter also quickly evanesces, disrupted by the horrific din outside which signals that a native has been killed by a colonist, and the unknown woman departs in that same instant.

The Vinland sagas, moreover, do not allow us room sentimentally to imagine peaceful intercultural relationships that might accrue between foreign races if only women, instead of men, were meeting in transcultural encounter. In the *Greenlanders' Saga*, the fourth expedition to Vinland is in fact led by a woman, Freydis, Leif Eiriksson's sister, along with two male partners, Helgi and Finnbogi: and Freydis, the text tells us, commits homicide by having her partners, and their men and women, killed through her crafty manipulations to keep all the resources of Vinland for herself. No natives are encountered by Freydis' expedition (which again has permission to use the houses at Leif's camp), but Freydis herself personally slaughters the women in Helgi and Finnbogi's groups (Magnusson and Pálsson 68–9; Sveinsson and Þórðarson 266).

That is to say, in the one expedition to Vinland led by a woman, all the homicide committed is endogenous and occurs because of the woman who initiates the expedition. This saga essentializes neither female conduct nor female nature, nor does it rhapsodize over the reliability of female virtue: Gudrid, the good woman who is beautiful, wise, and hospitable, and has a distinguished line of descendants who are bishops, is countered by a foil in the unruly, greedy, ambitious, and sanguinary Freydis whose progeny, her brother Leif Eiriksson (who doesn't have the heart to punish her as she deserves) predicts, will come to no good (Magnusson and Pálsson 70; Jones, *Norse* 205; Sveinsson and Þórðarson 268–9).

Eirik the Red's Saga, the other Vinland saga, does not give us a peaceful encounter between a European woman and a Native American woman. Instead it gives us the vision of a pregnant Freydis – who in this saga is apparently part of Karlsefni's and Gudrid's expedition to Vinland – fiercely challenging the natives during the all-out battle that occurs three weeks after the bellowing bull has interrupted trading. As the Greenlanders and Icelanders flee from the large spherical missile hurled at them by the natives, Freydis enacts the traditional Nordic and Germanic female role of shaming the men, shouting at them to fight and to cease acting like cowards.

She herself is unable to keep up with them because she is pregnant (presumably in her third trimester, if she is burdened sufficiently to be slowed down), and the natives close in on her. Undaunted, she snatches up the sword of a dead settler as the natives close in, pulls out her breast from under her clothing, and dramatically slaps her sword on it (*beru suerdinu*, the *naked* sword, *Hausbók* adds), in a splendid gesture of defiance that merges the epic image of a Norse woman warrior with the folkloric image of a Celtic mother shaming her unruly offspring by baring her breasts.

This spectacle frightens the natives so much that they flee back to their boats and row away, and Karlsefni praises Freydis for her courage (Magnusson and Pálsson 100; Jansson 73).[26] *Eirik the Red's Saga* thus has its own episode in which a European woman shows presence of mind and acts without fear – with the effect, here, that she intervenes between warring races, routs the natives, and saves the day. But the saga's rendition of female prowess here hardly resembles peaceful encounter.

Native Boys, Foreign Animals, and Zoonotic Disease: Race, DNA, and Historical Ecology

Intriguingly, *Eirik the Red's Saga* also apportions attention to children. Both sagas register the birth of Snorri, the son of Karlsefni and Gudrid in Vinland, but *Eirik the Red's Saga* offers the additional information that Snorri is a toddler, three years old when the colonists finally leave Vinland (Jones, *Norse* 230; Sveinsson and Þórðarson 262; Jansson 76). The first native-born Caucasian in the Americas, Snorri is subsequently raised at Glaumbær, the farm his father buys in Iceland, where his family's history becomes well established in the historical record.

In *Eirik the Red's Saga* the colonists also *abduct two native boys* from Vinland and kidnap them back to Europe, in an interlude that occurs after the battle at Hóp. The battle is not the last encounter with the indigenous population, though it is the trigger for the decision by Karlsefni and company to leave Vinland – an admirable land, but one in which there is no safety, because of the indigenous inhabitants already there. Disappointingly, North America is not an empty land ripe for the taking. The settlers do not leave Vinland immediately, however, but retreat to winter at Straumsfjord – their more northerly base, where Skraelings never seem to intrude – and only after their third winter in Vinland (a winter of some discontent, because the unmarried men are restive and pester the married men over their wives) do the settlers finally sail back to Northern Europe (Magnusson and Pálsson 102; Jansson 74).

As they retreat from Hóp back to Straumsfjord, along the way Karlsefni and company kill five more natives whom they find asleep, because, *Eirik the Red's Saga* says, the expeditioners believe these indigenes to be outlaws from their tribal groups (Magnusson and Pálsson 101; Jones, *Norse* 229; Jansson 74). The episode however resonates queerly with the *Greenlanders' Saga*'s narration of first encounter, when Thorvald Eiriksson and his men also summarily and without explanation kill the sleeping natives on whom they chance. In the Vinland sagas, sleeping natives who are chanced on, it seems, are never allowed to live.[27]

From the more northerly Straumsfjord, the settlers then explore land and sea, using Straumsfjord as their base; in one of their voyagings, Thorvald Eiriksson dies, shot with an arrow by a one-legged native, a *Skraeling*-uniped (*einfætingrinn* [Magnusson and Pálsson 102; Jansson 75]).

Finally, the settlers begin the journey back to Northern Europe, but en route, reaching Markland – the forests of Labrador – they prey on five more natives they encounter: a bearded man, two women, and two boys. The adults escape by sinking into the ground, but the children are captured, and the expedition kidnaps the boys and transports them to Europe, baptizes them, and teaches them language (i.e., Old Norse).

Once they have European speech, the children then serve as native informants, volunteering the names of their parents and describing the social structure of *Skrælingaland* (it has two kings, whose names the boys also surrender) and the habitat of its people, who live in caves or holes, not houses (Magnusson and Pálsson 102–3; Jansson 77). The boys also describe another human population or tribal group in an adjacent region. Beyond this, the saga is silent on the fate of these stolen native boys. Whether the children become fosterlings, slaves, or something in-between back in Greenland, Iceland, or Norway is apparently not of sufficient interest or importance to mention.

If the saga's report of two boys snatched from the North American continent by Karlsefni's expedition has any historical basis, genetic mixing may be one inadvertent result of the expeditions to Vinland. In 2011, anthropological geneticists from Iceland and Spain published their discovery of a DNA feature (C1e) in a subgroup of Iceland's population today, which apparently does not issue from European or Asian origins. While carefully noting a lack of certainty, their study nonetheless concludes: "the most likely hypothesis is that the Icelandic voyages to the eastern coastline of the Americas resulted in the migration of at least one Native American woman carrying the C1e lineage to Iceland around the year 1000" (Ebenesersdóttir et al. 98). Might the abducted children memorialized in *Eirik the Red's Saga* have passed on the distinctive C1e DNA element?

If ancestral Native North Americans were indeed forcibly deprived of two of their children, at least the natives were fortunate not to have been afflicted in the first decade of the eleventh century with the bacterial epidemics that would later decimate whole indigenous populations, post-Columbus. Alfred Crosby notes that smallpox did not even reach Iceland till 1241 or 1306: "The Norse in Iceland and even more so in Greenland were so remote from Europe that they rarely received the latest installments of the diseases germinating in European centers of dense settlement, and their tiny populations were too small for the maintenance of crowd diseases" (Crosby, *Ecological* 52).[28]

But if Greenlanders and Icelanders did not spread disease on the American continent in the eleventh century, what of the many kinds of *animals* the sagas say the colonists brought with them? That livestock included a bellicose bull notorious for creating havoc among the natives, and lactating animals who produced the milk the settlers in the *Greenlanders' Saga* used for trade. In a provocative article in *The Atlantic* on the size and composition of pre-Columbian populations in the Americas, Charles Mann points to how easily disease exchange – communicated through animals, not humans – can occur when "Old" and "New" worlds meet. Mann's examples relate to post-Columbian encounter, but carry an uneasy undercurrent when we consider the many kinds of animals the sagas tell us the eleventh-century colonists brought to Vinland:

> When human beings and domesticated animals live close together, they trade microbes with abandon. Over time mutation spawns new diseases: avian influenza becomes human influenza, bovine rinderpest becomes measles. Unlike Europeans, Indians did not live in close quarters with animals – they domesticated only the dog, the llama, the alpaca, the guinea pig, and, here and there, the turkey and the Muscovy duck. In some ways this is not surprising: the New World had fewer animal candidates for taming than the Old. More-over, few Indians carry the gene that permits adults to digest lactose ... Non-milk-drinkers, one imagines, would be less likely to work at domesticating milk-giving animals ... what scientists call zoonotic disease was little known in the Americas. Swine alone can disseminate anthrax, brucellosis, leptospirosis, taeniasis, trichinosis, and tuberculosis. Pigs breed exuberantly and can transmit diseases to deer and turkeys. Only a few ... pigs would have had to wander off to infect the forest.
>
> (Mann 8)

We do not know, of course, exactly what species of animals were among the many kinds the settlers brought to Vinland – other than a bull and milk-producing beasts. Nor do we know if any animals wandered off, whether any rats were shipped to the American continent as stowaways, or if all the animals returned to Greenland and Iceland.[29] We only know that the settlers' animals thrived in Vinland, where pasture was available even in winter. Crosby, who notices how sixteenth-century European livestock flourished in the Caribbean – "goats, dogs, cats, chickens, asses grew faster, brawnier, reproduced at unheard of rates, and often went back to nature" (*Columbian* 76) – also notices that in the eleventh century, "Scandinavian livestock" showed great promise in Vinland during their few seasons there. Grass in America was plentiful and lush, and the climate was certainly more moderate than they were accustomed to . . . It is worth noting for later reference that these Old World animals began to go wild in the Vinland wilderness, despite centuries on centuries of domestication. "Soon," reads the saga, "the male beasts became very frisky and difficult to manage."

(*Ecological* 47)

In the half millennium separating the Vinland expeditions from the forays of Columbus, any impact that animals from Northern Europe might have had on native populations and native animals went unrecorded. The sagas, of course, are not concerned with what might have happened to the natives or local animals after their departure. Their main concern is how the settlers' bull – a large, ferocious, bellicose creature – secures the intimidation of the natives in the final battle.

However, a few scholars have raised the prospect that disease from European sources may have been a factor that contributed to the long-term decline of Dorset Paleoeskimo culture in Labrador and its environs. The Dorset were a Paleoeskimo subset who originated from Northeast Asia, migrating across the Arctic 4,000 years ago and spreading eastward to coastal North America and Greenland. From the thirteenth century, the Dorset began to disappear (they are not ancestral to any living peoples today), leaving a paucity of skeletal remains – displaced, it is thought, by the Thule, a population migrating from Alaska around 1000 CE who are the ancestors of modern-day Inuit (McAleese 355–6, Odess et al. 193–8, Sutherland 242).

The Dorset were still in northern Labrador at the time of the Vinland expeditions but had ceased to inhabit Newfoundland and southern Labrador. A Late Dorset-style soapstone lamp found in the smithy at L'Anse aux Meadows and a spindle whorl made from a fragment of a Dorset soapstone vessel recovered in a L'Anse aux Meadows house are thus believed only to signal the European settlers' scavenging of Dorset sites, or their acquisition of such objects through trade intermediaries (Sutherland 241). Nonetheless, a range of Norse artifacts recovered from Dorset sites suggests to some that it is difficult to rule out the possibility that "saga descriptions of *skraeling* whom the Norse encountered in Markland while on their Vinland voyages may refer to Dorset people" (Sutherland 242).[30]

Indeed, Birgitta Linderoth Wallace suggests that when the two children captured from *Markland* – forested regions of coastal Labrador that were distinguished by Leif Eiriksson and the Greenlanders from the tundra-and-rock ecoscape of Labrador and Baffin Island which they dubbed *Helluland* – tell of "another nation on the other side of their land where people wore white clothes, whooped loudly, and carried poles with flags," this is a reference to "the Dorset people, who then inhabited most of northern Labrador . . . especially if their clothing, like that of the later Thule Inuit, included polar-bear fur and sealskins with the fur side in" ("An Archelogist's Interpretation" 231). Archeologists have been perplexed at the extinction of the Dorset, and have wondered if competition and conflict with the incoming Thule or assimilation into Thule culture played the larger role.

It has also been suggested that the Norse might have precipitated Dorset decline by introducing European diseases. . . . While disease clearly did not wipe them out completely, it may have eliminated them from some areas. . .and reduced their ability to withstand the onslaught of Thule people from the west.

(Odess et al. 197–8)[31]

The two boys themselves are usually thought to be ancestral Innu, a native people who shared Labrador with the Dorset and the Thule.[32] Yet the boys' report that their people lived in caves and holes in the ground queerly recalls the winter habitations of the Thule people who replaced the Dorset. The adult man and two women who managed to elude capture when the children were abducted escaped, we are told, by *sinking into the ground* (Magnusson and Pálsson 102; Jones, *Norse* 230; Jansson 77). Though the first decade of the eleventh century is early for Thule settlement in Labrador, Thule winter houses were indeed sunk into the ground:

> Thule winter dwellings were pithouses made from stone, turf, and whale bones ... Each was dug down below the ground level and had an entrance tunnel ... The entrance tunnel of the house was set lower than the floor.
>
> (Odess et al. 199)[33]

But what we should notice here is that the salient features memorialized in the story of the two boys focus on the abduction and transfer of two Native North Americans – young boys have resonant symbolic potential in European cultural narrations, as we saw in Chapter 2 – back to Europe, the forcible conversion of these two child-captives to Christianity, their compulsory linguistic assimilation into European society, and their service as informants delivering news of primitive modes of existence elsewhere. Underground cave-habitations or hole-in-the-ground dwellings reinforce the impression of the native populations as primitive, while the mysteriousness of how the adults are able to sink into the ground and escape reinforces a motif of magic associated with the natives seen in earlier episodes of encounter in both Vinland Sagas.

Distinguishing among the *Skraeling* they encountered was not, of course, of particular importance to the expeditioners. Certainly, this would be no easy task for folk in "their first encounter with true aliens, groups of humans who were totally outside their experience and who were not known from legend or history" (McGhee, "Skraellings" 43). But we glimpse the sagas reaching out for a frame of reference through which to understand the indigenous population of the Americas when *Eirik the Red's Saga* names as a *uniped* the one-legged native who fires the arrow that kills Thorvald Eiriksson: This is a demonstrable and striking view of local people filtered through the Plinian grid of monstrous races ostensibly found in the world outside Europe, and especially in Africa, as we saw in Chapter 1.[34]

Debra Strickland's contention that medieval belief in the existence of monstrous races created an "ideological infrastructure" for understanding "other types of 'monsters,' namely Ethiopians, Jews, Muslims, and Mongols" (see Chapter 1) can thus be stretched to include North American native peoples, who are here identified as belonging to the constellation of misshapen, freakish, and deformed semi-humans that make up the Plinian races (42). The primitive one-legged creature that kills Thorvald is palpably not a singular freak but part of a race of the one-legged kind, since *Eirik the Red's Saga* tells us the settlers could see Uniped-Land (*Einfœtingaland*) toward the north but prudently chose not to go there in order to avoid risking more loss of life (Magnusson and Pálsson 102; Jones, *Norse* 230; Jansson 76).

Trying to understand unknown new races through a cultural grid of familiar monstrosities is one narrative strategy. Sverrir Jakobsson further argues that the sagas may also try to make sense of the natives the settlers encounter by reflexively recalling the Finns, a pagan enemy the sagas associate with sorcery, since their "Skraelings seem to be endowed with supernatural powers, like the *Semsveinar* (Finns) known to the Icelanders from Norway" (Jakobsson 98).

In the *Greenlanders' Saga*, after Thorvald Eiriksson and his men have gratuitously slain eight of the nine men they find sleeping under canoes, the Greenlanders are suddenly stricken by intense drowsiness, and fall asleep. The expeditioners awaken in the nick of time when a mysterious voice tells them to get to their ships at once, just as the natives are returning in force to enact vengeance for the earlier homicides.

Jakobsson urges that the voice be seen as divine agency protecting these northern Christians against the local heathen: "The Lord looks after his own. This sleep that overcomes them is clearly not natural, and seems likely to have been caused by sorcery. Finnish sorcery often took the form of causing sleepiness, according to old northern writings" (Jakobsson 98). As further support, Jakobsson points to another episode, this time in *Eirik the Red's Saga*, where, during the final violent confrontation, it seems to the settlers that the natives appear far more numerous than they really are, implying that the natives created an illusion to fool the settlers (98). To these examples of heathen sorcery, we might add the adult natives' mysterious sinking into the ground in *Eirik the Red's Saga* when the two native boys are successfully kidnapped.

Jakobsson points out that people like the Finns "were not only heathens, but active opponents of Christianity" and were "regularly 'slátrað sem búfé' [slaughtered like beasts] by Christian kings, while those who converted to Christianity were presumably accepted by the community, like the two boys who were able to tell Þorfinnr Karlsefni and his men about the customs of the cave-dwellers" (98). If the Vinland Sagas' characterization of the indigenous in the Americas is implicitly cast in the image of the Finns, then the unprovoked slaughter of sleeping natives and the abduction and forcible baptism of native children may be understood by saga audiences as justified, with little need of explanation, even though killing those who are asleep, without provocation, is usually seen as an act of cowardice and villainy in saga culture (Jakobssen 97).

If Jakobsson is correct – and Jakobsson's readings make sense of the odd mention of drowsiness in the *Greenlanders' Saga* and the odd mention of illusory magnification of the enemy's numbers in *Eirik the Red's Saga* – we are perhaps not so distant after all, even in the new world of the Americas, from the race-as-religion that we've seen among the warring communities of the Abrahamic faiths. It would appear that even with "true aliens, groups of humans who were totally outside their experience and who were not known from legend or history," religion as a master discourse can justify, for Europeans, wanton slaying of the other and abduction of their children in establishing appropriate relations between two races, one Christian and the other heathen.

After all, as the *Song of Roland* so pithily put it, Christians are right and pagans are wrong. The Vinland sagas do not explicitly moralize either the slaying or the child abduction as Christian allegory (saga narratives are notoriously taciturn), but their narratives show an awareness of the continuing tussle between Christianity and the pagan precursor past of the Nordic peoples, in episodes acted out in Vinland, and in the homesteaders' own societies in Greenland, Iceland, and Norway.[35]

Bodies, and the Limits of Technology, or How Demography Trumps Metallurgy

Observations of native physiognomy are made and repeated in the Vinland sagas – such as, for instance, that Native Americans have large eyes, broad cheeks, and are short-statured – but variations abound: The man with the children is bearded, the only mention of a bearded male (*eirn skeggiadr*), and *Hauksbók* describes the natives in the first encounter as dark (*suartir menn*), yet the woman who visits Gudrid is described as pale (*folleit* [Jansson 77, 69; Sveinsson and Þórðarson 262]).

The sagas thus depict Native Americans as varied in physiognomy and color, and do not elide differences to suggest a racial homogeneity of appearance. In fact, the *Greenlanders' Saga*, in the final struggle between settlers and natives, shows Karlsefni distinguishing a tall and handsome man among the natives as their leader, clearly an exception to the short-statured local peoples elsewhere (Magnusson and Pálsson 67; Sveinsson and Þórðarson 263–4). As Jakobsson wryly remarks, "Leaders are always identifiable, and they always recognise each other. This class or rank consciousness transcends all differences of race and creed" (99). Indeed, class identification across ethnoracial differences is a phenomenon we've encountered before, especially in the literary genre of medieval romance, as we saw in Chapter 4.

Like physiognomy, cultural details do not always help to distinguish among the varied ethnoraces of the Americas. Skin-boats were used by many populations. The Thule had the *umiak*, a multipassenger skin-clad boat; ancestral Innu and Beothuk peoples had a variety of skin, bark, and wooden craft; and the Mi'kmaq Indians in Nova Scotia, Prince Edward Island, and eastern New Brunswick had skin canoes (Odess et al. 198, 200–1; Birgitta Linderoth Wallace, "An Archeologist's Interpretation" 229).

> A Mi'kmaq named Arguimaut told Abbé Maillard, around 1740, that in his ancestors' time the canoes had been of "moose skins, from which they had plucked the hair, and which they had scraped and rubbed so thoroughly that they were like your finest skins."
>
> > (Birgitta Linderoth Wallace, "Vinland and the Death of Þorvaldr" 383)
>
> "They soaked [the skins] in oil and then placed them on the canoe frame."
>
> > (Aguimaut to the Abbé Maillard; qtd. by Birgitta Linderoth Wallace, "An Archeologist's Interpretation" 229)

Some scholars today have found a few clues in the native weapons the sagas describe. Birgitta Linderoth Wallace, who believes Hóp, the more southerly camp in *Eirik the Red's Saga*, to be in eastern New Brunswick, identifies the stave-twirling natives in the saga as Mi'kmaq,

> who have inhabited the rivers and lagoons of New Brunswick ever since the lagoons were formed 2,500 to 3,000 years ago. The Oxbow area, twenty miles … up the Miramichi River from the bay (today the Red Bank First Nation), was a prominent gathering place to fish for salmon and hunt sturgeon. The Micmac had skin canoes, arrows, and slings for shooting stones. ES [*Eirik's Saga*] tells us that the *skraeling* had staves, which they swung clockwise ("sunwise") when they were friendly and the opposite direction when they planned an attack. Staves in the hands of Micmac were reported in Cape Breton in the sixteenth century by Richard Hill of Redrife in England who wrote in 1593 that, "Thereupon nine or tenne of his fellowes … came towardes us with white staves in their hands like halfe pikes" … ES also tells of a formidable weapon consisting of a big blackish object mounted up on a pole, which they shot off toward the Norse, scaring them greatly. This could have been a throwing weapon known from other Algonquian tribes, a large boulder wrapped in skin and mounted on a pole.
>
> > ("An Archeologist's Interpretation" 230)

But whatever their technology, the native populace is consistently depicted in the sagas as made up of simpletons and primitives. The sagas make much of the fact that those who come to trade are easily swindled; they are also terribly keen to acquire Norse technology in the form of swords and axes – presumably because, the sagas imply, steel and iron weapons are superior to their stone-tipped projectiles and stone axes.

After all, Europeans have entered the modern era of metal; the natives of the Americas are still Stone Age primitives, situated at a moment in time that is long in Europe's past. In the *Greenlanders' Saga*, native covetousness of advanced metal technology is in fact made the cause of the sudden breach in trading relations, as a native is killed by one of Karlsefni's men ostensibly for trying to steal weapons.

Another episode in *Greenlanders' Saga* registers native wonder at the superior efficacy of metal. During the final battle, a native picks up a Norse axe, examines it a moment, then swings it experimentally at his fellow standing beside him, who instantly drops dead. The tall and handsome indigenous recognized by Karlsefni as a leader because of the man's telltale height and handsomeness then takes hold of the infernal weapon, looks at it briefly, and flings the doomsday device as far as he can into the water (Magnusson and Pálsson 67; Sveinsson and Þórðarson 263–4).

The *Greenlanders' Saga* deems it unnecessary to comment on his act: perhaps we are to understand that the natives find the technology to be so terrifying in its efficacy that their leader judges the axe a doomsday weapon not to be handled by mere mortals. Such are the limitations of the Stone Age mind.

Eirik the Red's Saga offers a counterpoint to this moment in which the locals also demonstrate utter ignorance of metallurgy, in an episode that also takes place during the final hostilities. *Hausbók* tells us that the natives find a dead settler with his axe beside him, and, picking up the weapon, each in turn experimentally hacks at a tree, admiring the instrument and believing it a marvelous find because of its sharpness – until one of them hacks at a rock, whereupon the axe breaks and the natives fling it away, now believing it useless because it cannot chop stone (Magnusson and Pálsson 100; Jones, *Norse* 228; Jansson 73). In both sagas, the primitive simplicity of the native mind is put on display.

The primitivism of the local populace thus situates them at a moment in time that is long in Europe's past. One Vinland saga registers native wonder at, and fear of, metal weapons technology, while the other registers native ignorance of how that technology performs. But while both sagas register the childlike naivety and primitiveness of indigenous peoples, and their intense desire for the settlers' modern, iron-era weapons, they also inadvertently suggest the efficacy of the indigenous peoples' own weapons.

After all, the giant spherical object hurled by a native catapult strikes terror into the settlers, who flee from the shock of artillery they did not anticipate. Moreover, in *Eirik the Red's Saga*, the triumph of stone over metal is quietly demonstrated when the steel axe breaks on the rock and is deemed useless, auguring that, in some circumstances, stone can be more efficacious than metal. Most pointedly of all, Alfred Crosby reckons, though "the Norse had metal and the Skraelings did not," Thorvald Eiriksson received "a mortal wound from a stone-tipped Skraeling arrow" (49):

> Flint points can pass between ribs as easily as metal, and a stone ax can crumple a shoulder
> or smash a skull quite as neatly as anything made of iron or steel. Metal weapons are better
> than stone, but in hand-to-hand combat between desperate men this may be only an

example of the proverbial distinction without a difference. So much for Norse advantages over the Skraelings.

(Crosby, Ecological 49–50)

Stone projectiles even follow the Greenlanders home to Greenland. In 1930, a chipped-stone arrowhead – a Ramah chert projectile point quarried from the highly prized, oft-traded stone of northern Labrador around Ramah Bay and associated with the natives of southern Labrador and Newfoundland – was found in the churchyard cemetery at Sandnes in the Western Settlement of Greenland, raising the prospect that "The projectile may have accompanied a Norseman – who had been shot by a Native North American – to his burial at home" (Seaver 275).

Another projectile point, made of quartz, was recovered from rocks on the shore below the ruins of Brattahlid – Eirik the Red's and Leif Eiriksson's family homestead in Greenland's Eastern Settlement, from which Thorfinn Karlsefni had launched his Vinland expedition, leading some to ask: "Were these projectile points from stray arrows lodged in the deck of a Viking boat [from Vinland] or in one of the [expeditioners] themselves?" (Odess et al. 203).[36]

Both the Vinland sagas and the historical record suggest in their own ways that the Native North Americans of the continent were more than a match for the northern European would-be colonists of Vinland. As Thorvald Eiriksson and the settlers discover, native technology answers well in battle, and Native American stone proves as efficacious as Europe's iron and steel.

> Karlsefni's followers coveted Vinland – the land was rich, game plentiful, the streams full of salmon, the grass to the taste of their livestock, and already one child, Snorri, son of their leader and Gudrid, had been born there – but the Norse realized they could never live in that land safely. Vinland was already thoroughly occupied. The Norse needed an "evener," something to compensate for their inferiority in numbers to the Amerindians. Their military technology was not it, as we have seen.

(Crosby, Ecological 51)

Larger expeditions from Greenland to bolster the size of the settlement at Straumsfjord or Leifsbuðir, as an equalizer to balance out the ratio of Norse to natives, were not feasible. Greenland, closest to the Americas, never held more than a few thousand people throughout its existence, unlike Iceland or Norway, and possibly held only as few as two thousand settlers (Birgitta Linderoth Wallace, "L'Anse aux Meadows: Gateway to Vinland" 233). Excavation at L'Anse aux Meadows suggests that the settlement at L'Anse likely took some 10 percent of men and women from the communities in Greenland:

> It took about one-tenth of the entire population [of Greenland] to run L'Anse aux Meadows and exploit the Vinland resources. Although some of the labor crew might have been Icelandic, the drain was hardly acceptable for a still-marginal, new settlement [as Greenland was], especially as the Vinland crews consisted of people of prime working age ... [and] an isolated settlement of less than about five hundred people is simply not viable.
>
> (Birgitta Linderoth Wallace, "L'Anse aux Meadows: Gateway to Vinland" 233)

By contrast, the Mi'kmaq alone in the northeastern Atlantic may have numbered "up to 35,000" strong (Birgitta Linderoth Wallace, "L'Anse aux Meadows: Gateway to Vinland" 216):

> Recent demographic studies suggest that aboriginal populations of the New World were much higher than had been previously thought. Scholars have now realized that earlier estimates had been based on accounts of populations in which up to 95% had disappeared as a result of European disease. It is now thought that, at the time of the Vinland voyages, population densities in the New World were approximately the same as those of similar environmental regions in the Old World. Most of the estimated 100 million New World people lived in areas of the great Mesoamerican civilizations, but an estimated 15 to 20 million people are thought to have occupied the area of what is now the United States and Canada.
>
> (McGhee, "Skraellings" 51–2)

The colonists never encounter very many natives in the northerly regions of the North American continent, in Markland-Labrador – only small, isolated groups who are easy to kill or capture – and no natives ever seem to appear at Leifsbuðir or Straumsfjord. Birgitta Linderoth Wallace argues that if Leifsbuðir or Straumsfjord is L'Anse aux Meadows in Newfoundland, as she believes, the base camp merely functioned as the gateway "at the edge of a hinterland serving as a collection point and transshipment station for goods from various parts," and *Eirik the Red's Saga* in fact shows the expeditioners exploring the surrounding regions, with Straumsfjord as a base encampment ("L'Anse aux Meadows: Gateway to Vinland" 228).

But farther south, at the camp called Hóp, the native populations encountered are shown to be substantial, arriving in a multitude of boats – always from the south – to trade or for more bellicose reasons. Based on the evidence of butternuts and a burl of carved butternut wood found in the middens at L'Anse aux Meadows, Birgitta Linderoth Wallace suggests that the St. Lawrence Valley and northeastern New Brunswick, "along the Miramichi and other New Brunswick rivers issuing into the Gulf" – the northernmost boundary where butternuts grow – were among the southerly regions visited by the expeditions.[37] These regions were the ancestral homelands of numerous native populations who followed herds of caribou inland into the interior in winter, and when summer came,

> shared a common focus on the sea as a provider of foods, material goods and social exchange. Norse voyagers appearing in any of the territories south of the Gulf of St Lawrence during the summer boating season would have discovered these coasts to be filled with Indian villages in nearly every bay and river mouth.
>
> (Odess et al. 204)

In addition to ancestral Mi'kmaq, Maliseet, and others, Iroquois – more formidable people – "occupied the St Lawrence valley upstream from the present location of Quebec City [and] may have made summer visits to the Atlantic coast, as did their sixteenth-century descendants" (Sutherland 238).

After the settlers' withdrawal from Vinland, sporadic expeditions to harvest lumber likely continued to Markland/Labrador, which was only a couple of days' journey from Greenland. This may help to account for the discovery of Norse artifacts in Dorset and Thule sites, though only L'Anse aux Meadows – and possibly a secondary site on Baffin Island described by Patricia Sutherland in 2015 (Pringle) – has been found.[38] This is hardly surprising, perhaps. North America at the beginning of the eleventh century may have been Edenic, as the Vinland Sagas tell us, but the natives were too restless, and too many, for Europe to plant itself successfully upon the world it found just yet.

Another half-millennium would need to pass first.

Notes

1 The two Vinland Sagas stem from separate traditions with, it is believed, common origins. Their manuscripts are from the late thirteenth or the fourteenth and fifteenth centuries, but scholars believe the sagas themselves to have been set down earlier in the thirteenth century, after accounts of the expeditions to the Americas had been orally transmitted from the time of the expeditions. I provide more than one translation, since there are sometimes noteworthy variations in how the principal translators of the Vinland Sagas interpret narrative elements or prioritize manuscripts. The *Greenlanders' Saga, Grænlendinga saga*, appears in the saga of Olaf Tryggvason, *Óláfs saga Tryggvasonar* in *Flateyjarbók* (Codex flateyensis, MS Gks 1005). *Eirik the Red's Saga, Eiríks saga rauða*, is in two manuscripts, *Hauksbók* (MS AM 544 4to) and *Skálholtsbók* (MS AM 557 4to).

   Icelandic sagas are a unique genre, and are held to be grounded in considerable historicity, even if particulars in their narratives may be embellished or synthesized, or may vary from manuscript to manuscript. Icelandic family and community sagas narrate the histories and social relations of families, kinship groups, and communities, as well as the lives of remarkable individuals who left their stamp on group relations and genealogies; sagas of this kind thus encompass historiography and literary endeavor of a distinctive character, unique to the culture of medieval Iceland and Greenland. Birgitta Linderoth Wallace sums up how best to understand our two sagas: "[a] characteristic of all the versions of the *Vinland Sagas* is events, places, and persons have been collated, collapsed, and stylized. This is a common pattern in oral traditions" ("L'Anse aux Meadows and Vinland" 211). For ease of reading, I have modernized the spelling of names: e.g., Guðríðr Þorbjarnardóttir's first name is given as "Gudrid" and Þorfinnr Karlsefni's is given as "Thorfinn."

2 Ethnically and culturally, Greenlanders and Icelanders are Norse, though I avoid the term "Norsemen" in this chapter, since the name tends to conjure images similar to the term "Vikings" – the Norse maritime raiders who caused such havoc and destruction to coastal Europe of the eleventh century. I prefer "Greenlanders," a term that evokes the expeditioners' status as home-steaders and colonists in Greenland, after their migration from Iceland. Some of the seafarers in these expeditions, of course (such as Thorfinn Karlsefni), were Icelanders, and settled back in Iceland eventually.

3 Not everyone agrees as to what this wild wheat was, but "American dune grass, *Elymus mollis*, looks very much like Norse wheat . . . It is common in both coastal and inland locations in eastern North America. It is related to Icelandic lyme grass, *Elymus arenarius* . . . which has always been a flour substitute in Iceland, but sufficiently distinct from it . . . that the Norse would have noted the difference, so this plant is a strong contender for self-sown wheat" (Birgitta Linderoth Wallace, "Vinland and the Death of Þorvaldr" 382). Wallace observes that wild grapes grew in the St. Lawrence River Valley west of St. Paul Bay, on the Miramichi and the St. John River ("Vinland and the Death of Þorvaldr" 382). Wild grapes were also "recorded in 1535 by Cartier on Isle d'Orleans just east of Quebec, where they were in such abundance that he named it 'Bacchus' Island . . . Grapes were also noted in that vicinity by Lescarbot . . . in 1606" (Birgitta Linderoth Wallace, "L'Anse aux Meadows and Vinland" 228). The Miramichi, Wallace points out, "has been the richest salmon river in eastern North America at least since the seventeenth century, in spite of industrial development and changes to the river bed. In 1672 Nicolas Denys . . . complained that he could not sleep because of the noise created by the multitude of salmon jumping in the Miramichi, and an eighteenth-century fisherman took 700 salmon in a 24-hour period. In the 1960s about 30,000 salmon were caught yearly in the Miramichi" ("Vinland and the Death of Þorvaldr" 383).

4 As archeological verification of events narrated in the Vinland Sagas, only the sizable settlement found at L'Anse aux Meadows has been universally accepted as proof of the existence of a Norse

colony in North America. However, in 2015 the archeologist Patricia Sutherland urged the existence of a second Norse settlement at Baffin Island (named *Helluland*, or "rock-slab land" in the Vinland Sagas), which she had been excavating since 2001, and which possibly stemmed from the fourteenth century and may thus have constituted a later site than the sites of the Vinland Sagas (see Pringle).

5 Other notable items that were found include "a bronze pin of West Norse type dating from the late tenth or early eleventh centuries," a spindle whorl, and a whetstone for sharpening needles, knives, and scissors, a glass bead, and the fragment of a small ring "of gilded brass and decorated with striations ... which indicates that it must have belonged to someone of relative affluence" (Birgitta Linderoth Wallace, "L'Anse aux Meadows and Vinland" 139; "L'Anse aux Meadows: Gateway to Vinland" 187). A small burl of carved butternut wood was also found in the middens. Smithing slag, ninety-nine nail fragments, a wooden arrowhead of Eastern white cedar, birch bark rolls and a birch bark cylinder, wood fragments and wood debris, pieces of a twined rope of spruce roots, possible fishing net weights, and a possible stone forge were also among the artifacts recovered from the site (Birgitta Linderoth Wallace, "L'Anse aux Meadhows: Gateway to Vinland" 177, 183–7).

6 I discuss studies on archeological finds and native habitats and cultures throughout this chapter. For studies on climate in the North Atlantic based on tree rings, ice cores, and other scientific data see in particular Hughes; Ogilvie, Barlow, and Jennings; Ogilvie and Jónsson; and Ogilvie and McGovern.

7 Wallace confesses she originally believed L'Anse aux Meadows to be "an anonymous site, perhaps not mentioned in the sagas," but became convinced, after extensive archeological research and archeological anthropology had accumulated over the decades, that it "is far too substantial and complex a site not to be mentioned in the sagas ... Calculations based on post moulds in combination with material requirements to build the replicas in the A-B-C complex [at L'Anse] give an estimate that at least 86 tall trees had to be felled for the posts of the three large halls plus large amounts of wood for the huge roofs and all the smaller buildings. Calculations based on wall widths and lengths, their estimated heights (average of 1.5m) and estimated size of roofs give an estimate that about 1100 cubic meters of sod were used in the construction. Based on the amount of labor expended on the three house replicas at LAM, we can estimate that it would have taken a labor crew of sixty at least two months to build the whole settlement, or a crew of ninety at least a month and a half, not including the time spent on the actual cutting and transportation of the sod. This is the better part of summer" ("Vinland and the Death of Þorvaldr" 380).

Wallace cites Niels Lynnerup's demographic estimate of the population of the Greenland colony in its first decades (at the time of the Vineland expeditions) to amount to no more than 400–500 inhabitants. L'Anse aux Meadows, built to shelter seventy to ninety people, would have depopulated Greenland of 14–22 percent of its people if all the expeditioners in Vinland were Greenlanders. "Even if two-thirds of the crew were Icelanders, the remaining third constituted at least five percent of all Greenlanders" ("Vinland and the Death of Þorvaldr" 380). L'Anse aux Meadows "thus represents a major effort on the part of the Greenland colony," Wallace concludes: "For demographic and economic reasons, the Greenlanders would simply not have had sufficient labor to form additional settlements of this magnitude" ("Vinland and the Death of Þorvaldr" 380). The size and substantial nature of L'Anse aux Meadows, according to Wallace, urges that the site is memorialized in the Vinland Sagas.

8 "Booths" are temporary shelters, "a cross between a tent and a house" built for short-term occupation, e.g., at "the *things* [law-giving assemblies] or market ports" (Birgitta Linderoth Wallace, "L'Anse aux Meadows: Gateway to Vinland" 168). In this phase of colonization, Wallace suggests, Leifsbúðir functions as a base camp from which further exploration and resource extraction can take place. For Wallace, either Leifsbúðir or Straumsfjord (the name of

the northern settlement in *Eirik the Red's Saga*) or both Leifsbúðir and Straumsfjord point to the site we know as L'Anse aux Meadows ("Vinland and the Death of Þorvaldr" 386).

9 "In Norse society, wine was an exotic luxury of great value and the type of product a chieftain would use in the feasts which were essential mechanisms for negotiating social relationships and maintaining power ... Normally, all wine had to be imported. The potential for an unlimited source of domestic wine would have rivalled the finding of gold" (Birgitta Linderoth Wallace, "L'Anse aux Meadows: Gateway to Vinland" 213). Wallace suggests that lumber and grapes are harvested in one fell swoop: "Where grapes grow wild, the vines look nothing like that in a vineyard. Instead they wrap themselves around any tree or bush that happens to be nearby, often all the way to the top of the trees. These are the *vinvið*, the grapewood-trees of the sagas, the lumber harvested and brought back to Greenland by every Vinland expedition" ("Vinland and the Death of Þorvaldr" 383).

10 The importance of Vinland for resource extraction leads Leif Eiriksson to retain control of his camp and houses. "In a society such as that of Norse Greenland, the power of the chieftains depended in large measure on wealth and an ostentatious display of status goods, exotic items, brought in from abroad. Thus the *control* of trade and imports was essential ... the sagas are clear that [Leif, who had succeeded his father Eirik the Red as the paramount chief of Greenland] maintained ownership ... of Leif's Camp and Vinland. His siblings and his in-law Karlsefni were trusted as deputies, but Leif only *lent* the camp to them. With *ownership* of Leif's Camp came control of Vinland and its resources, and these Leif presumably wished to keep for himself" (Birgitta Linderoth Wallace, "L'Anse aux Meadows: Gateway to Vinland" 232, emphasis original).

11 Wallace, among others, tells us that skin boats were common among the ancestors of Algonquian-speaking communities like the Mi'kmaq: "Although made of birch bark in later times, a Mi'kmaq named Arguimaut told Abbé Maillard, around 1740, that in his ancestors' time the canoes had been of 'moose skins from which they had plucked the hair, and which they had scraped and rubbed so thoroughly that they were like your finest skins'" ("Vinland and the Death of Þorvaldr" 383). McGhee tells us that "Indian canoes such as those described [in the *Greenlanders' Saga*] were appropriate to three-man crews who traditionally slept beneath their craft when making temporary camps" ("Skraellings" 48).

12 Scholars agree that *Skrælingar*, "a term with no single accepted definition and with unclear origins," is likely derogatory: "It seems plausible that the name was derived from 'Karelian' and refers to the Saami, the small, dark hunting peoples whom the Norse knew as occupants of northern Europe" (McAleese, 353; McGhee, "Skraellings" 45). McAleese wryly observes: "the sagas have reified Viking Age *skræling* for all indigenous people of the circumpolar, northwest Atlantic" (353). Magnusson and Pálsson's translation has Thorvald announce earlier, "It is beautiful here ... Here I should like to make my home," and then ironically declare, as he dies from a native arrowhead, "I seem to have hit on the truth when I said that I would settle there for a while" (60–1; Sveinsson and Þórðarson 255–6).

13 Later, gradual cooling after 1250, followed by the Little Ice Age in 1500–1750, eventually resulted in the abandonment of Greenland to the Inuit, whose hunter-gatherer economy was better adapted to climate change than Norse farming and homesteading. Astrid Ogilvie's extensive work on medieval climate importantly reminds us that the "Medieval Warm Period" was not uniform everywhere; northern Europe, for instance, experienced its effects more readily than, say, the countries of the Mediterranean. To imagine the Medieval Warm Period (and, by extension, the Little Ice Age) as universal would thus be erroneous. See Ogilvie, Barlow, and Jennings; and Ogilvie and McGovern.

14 This summary of expeditions in the *Greenlanders' Saga* only accounts for the expeditions that arrived in Vinland, not those planned but aborted or unsuccessful, such as that of Thorstein, another of Eirik's sons and Gudrid's first husband.

15 "Scandinavians, like other northwest Europeans," Alfred Crosby observes, "are among the world's champion milk digesters," whereas the indigenous folk with whom the colonists traded might not have fared well: "We can be quite sure the latter were miserably sick within hours" (*Ecological Imperialism* 48). Nonetheless, the saga insists that the locals returned in greater numbers (of the same people? Other local populations to whom the news had spread?) for more of this novel food.

16 Glaumbær has also been extensively excavated. For an introductory bibliography, see Nancy Marie Brown's lively biography of Gudrid.

17 Scholarship has speculated on what the North American wood referred to as *mǫsurr* might be, with some translations offering the wood as maple. Since butternuts were found at L'Anse aux Meadows – including a carved butternut burl discovered in the middens – Birgitta Linderoth Wallace suggests Kalsefni's figurehead made of *mǫsurr* may have been carved from a butternut burl ("L'Anse aux Meadows and Vinland" 228). Interestingly, the northernmost areas where butternuts, *Juglans cinera* – also called white walnuts – were found are the St. Lawrence Valley and north-eastern New Brunswick, where wild grapes also were found. "Whoever picked the butternuts found at L'Anse aux Meadows could hardly have avoided seeing grapevines" (Birgitta Linderoth Wallace, "L'Anse aux Meadows and Vinland" 228–9).

18 Besides her eminent line of descendants, Gudrid is also given a worthy ancestry by *Eirik the Red's Saga*. Gudrid's father, Thorbjorn, is the son of Vifil, a well-born man of noble descent who had been taken captive in the British Isles and enslaved till freed by Aud the Deep-Minded, who had married the warrior-king Olaf the White (son of the king of Dublin), and who later founded settlements in Iceland (Magnusson and Pálsson 75–6, 78; Sveinsson and Þórðarson 195–7, 202–3). Gudrid is described as "a most beautiful woman and distinguished in everything she did" (Jones, *Eirik* 130; Jansson 33).

19 Even in the twentieth century, snowless and mild winters have occurred at L'Anse aux Meadows, the site Birgitta Linderoth Wallace believes to be Straumsfjord in *Eirik the Red's Saga*, which is further north than the southern settlement at Hóp. "In 1998 . . . when the average temperature was a couple of degrees higher than normal, there was no snow at all, and very little in 1999 – it arrived only in April and disappeared shortly thereafter. This means that in the early eleventh century, when the average temperatures were one to two degrees Celsius warmer than in our era . . . the winters could have been snow-free, and livestock could indeed have grazed outside all winter" (Wallace, "L'Anse aux Meadows and Vinland" 138).

20 McGhee finds "the use of red cloth as hair decoration" echoed in the earliest written account of Labrador coastal Amerindians by an early eighteenth-century Dutch writer, who says the natives have "long black hair which they plait with red pieces of cloth into long tails or spouts" ("*Skraellings*" 48). See also Moorehead for the importance of the color red for a native population in Maine, and DeBoer for colors associated with pre-Columbian symbolism in North America.

21 The translation is from Jones, *Norse* 201, amended slightly here, since Jones omits "ok mælti." For the original Old Norse see Sveinsson and Þórðarson 262–3.

22 Almqvist concedes that "most scholars have been inclined to regard her [the unknown woman] as a supernatural being, either a ghost or some more ordinary type of revenant, so to say, or an ancestral spirit of the kind referred to as *fylgja* or *hamingja* in some Icelandic sagas" (18). But he quickly dismisses the suggestion that the native woman might be "a kind of guardian spirit of one of the Skraelings": If this is a native spirit, Almqvist snorts, it should not be speaking Norse (18). Nor would a revenant fit the description of Nordic ghosts in Icelandic sagas: "If a ghost speaks at all . . . it always has an important message to convey. One might also object that it would be strange for a ghost to cast a shadow and for a living person to invite it to sit down! Furthermore, ghosts are likely to possess supernatural knowledge and consequently they have no need to inquire about the names of those to whom they appear. In addition, ghosts are often previously known to those whom they visit, in which case there would be no need to ask for their names; and even if a

ghost were not recognised, a living person encountering one would be more likely to inquire 'Who are you?', rather than 'What is your name?'" (Almqvist 18). Almqvist goes on to demonstrate at length that the woman could not possibly have been a *fylgja*, and also dismisses the notion that she might be Norse, but somehow "unbeknownst to Karselfni and the other settlers," concluding, "why should [a Norse woman] disappear in the fashion described in the saga?" (19).

23 In the *Greenlanders' Saga*, the corpse of Gudrid's first husband, Thorstein Eiriksson, had reanimated itself after death and talked to Gudrid familiarly, asking for his body to be buried in consecrated ground, and prophesying Gudrid's future (Magnusson and Pálsson 63–4; Sveinsson and Þórðarson 259–60). *Eirik the Red's Saga* featured an uncanny prophetess, Thorbjorg, who was treated with great honor when she was invited to the house of Thorkel of Herjolfsness in Greenland, the chief farmer in the district, to disclose when the evil fortunes of the season would end, and what the future portended for all. Arriving at Thorkel's appareled in curious, exotic splendor, she is feasted, sleeps overnight, and performs spells and sorcery for all assembled (Magnusson and Pálsson 81–3; Jansson 39–43).

During her visit, Gudrid is enjoined, reluctantly, to sing spells known as warlock songs, which Gudrid had been taught in Iceland by her foster mother Halldis. Gudrid's initial reluctance to comply with Thorbjorg's request for assistance loudly attests Gudrid's Christian piety and faith – this is the sort of knowledge and ritual she wants nothing to do with because she is a Christian, she says – even as Gudrid's knowledge of pagan rites and spells establishes her as a woman of power and knowledge in the old ways, locating her at an important seam in culture where old and new meet (Magnusson and Pálsson 82–3; Jansson 42–3). But Gudrid sings the songs so well and beautifully that the spirits are charmed, the prophetess says, and the assembly is rewarded with news of good fortune to come – Gudrid herself being personally rewarded with a prophecy of a great and eminent family line that will issue from her (Magnusson and Pálsson 83; Jansson 43).

Eirik the Red's Saga also offers us another uncanny woman, Thorgunna, said to be of noble birth, who has an affair with Leif Eiriksson when he is in the Hebrides and who becomes pregnant with his child. When Leif refuses to take her back with him to Greenland, Thorgunna prophesies that she will give birth to a son, and that Leif will not enjoy the outcome when she sends her son to him in Greenland. The saga tells us that Thorgunna's son, Thorgild, did indeed come to Greenland, and there seemed to be something uncanny about him all his life (Magnusson and Pálsson 84–5; Jansson 47).

24 Gunnar Karlsson, who also argues for "the Indian identity of the visiting woman," suggests that "the native woman's name was the result of scribal error," which would make the dialogue between the two women more reciprocal in the exchange of names (Almqvist 29 n.30). However, the suggestion that it is Gudrid who speaks first is possible even without Almqvist's emendation. There are no quotation marks to denote speech in the saga manuscripts, and punctuation and paragraphing have been normalized in editions. Adjusting our modern expectations of syntax, it is timely to remember that in medieval literature, the last person to whom the text refers is frequently the referent of the next unattributed remark. Thus: "She walked to where Gudrid was sitting. And [Gudrid] spoke: 'What is your name?' she said." The native woman then repeats Gudrid's question wonderingly, sounding out the syllables of this strange foreign tongue experimentally.

25 Later, when the colonists abduct two native boys and teach them Norse, *Eirik the Red's Saga* reports that the boys furnished them with information of various kinds. The children's voices are never directly heard, however – only reported. In both instances – the encounter between the native woman and Gudrid, and the text's report of what the kidnapped boys tell the expeditioners – the only language we hear or that's reported to us is Norse.

26 Scholars have sometimes insisted that it is not Freydis but Gudrid who acts here, noting that Gudrid is the one woman mentioned as pregnant, since she gives birth in the saga to Snorri. Given that *Eirik the Red's Saga* has not mentioned Freydis at all, pregnant or otherwise, up to this

point (though the saga earlier says that Freydis' *husband* is part of Karlsefni's and Snorri Thorbrandsson's expedition), scribal error may indeed be responsible for switching the names here. *Skálholtsbók* says that according to some other men's accounts, Freydis remained behind at Straumsfjord, while Karlsefni and Snorri Thorbrandsson sailed south to Hóp with forty men, spent barely two months there, and returned the same summer – which would indeed mean the heroine at Hóp was not Freydis. *Hauksbók* however says it is Gudrid who remains behind at Straumsfjord, while Karlsefni and Snorri Thorbrandsson with their forty men sailed south to Hóp (Magnusson and Pálsson 101; Jansson 74).

But if indeed Freydis, and not Gudrid, is the heroine of this episode, then the expedition may witness more than one birth in Vinland, since one more winter passes – the settlers' third winter in Vinland – before they return to Europe, giving a pregnant Freydis perhaps enough time for parturition. Gudrid, we are told, gives birth to Snorri the first autumn that the settlers arrive, and Snorri is three years old at the settlers' departure (Jones, *Norse* 230; Jansson 76). Perhaps two European children were born in the Americas in the early eleventh century?

27 Jakobsson remarks that both Vinland Sagas "clearly express the view that Skraelings could be killed with impunity wherever they were found, even without their having offended in any way against the Norse," although in "medieval Icelandic writings it is generally regarded as cowardly to kill anyone in his sleep, let alone to attack without cause. Thus the inference is clear that the Norsemen regarded the Skraelings, for some reason, as being people who could be killed with impunity" (97). In the killing of the five sleeping natives, *Eirik the Red's Saga* at least offers the explanation that the expeditioners believed the five to be outlaws, and outlaws, by Icelandic law, could be killed with impunity. *Greenlanders' Saga* offers no explanation for the slaughter of the natives the expeditioners find sleeping under their skin-boats. Magnusson and Pálsson suggest that the containers full of deer marrow mixed with blood that the five sleeping natives had beside them is pemmican, "cakes of dried meat mixed with marrow-grease" which Amerindians "used as iron rations on hunting expeditions" (101 n.1).

28 Consequently, when smallpox arrived, Icelanders would prove almost as poorly resistant as the indigenous peoples of post-Columbian America: In two years from 1701 onward, smallpox wiped out 18,000 of Iceland's 50,000 inhabitants (Crosby, *Columbian* 44).

29 Gwyn Jones (*Norse Atlantic Saga*) suggests that the livestock would have included "cows and a bull, mares and a stallion, ewes and a ram, and maybe goats and pigs" (119). Two bones found at the L'Anse aux Meadows site were originally identified as those of the domestic pig, but one – a scapula – was later reidentified as a seal bone. The other "has since been lost in the mail" (Birgitta Linderoth Wallace, "L'Anse aux Meadows: Gateway to Vinland" 176).

30 A Norse penny, minted during Olaf Kyrre's reign (1065–80), "probably reached North America on a Norse ship and passed into Dorset hands somewhere on the coast of Labrador, either through trade or as the result of a skirmish with a shore party" (Sutherland 241). But "Norse contact with Dorset people was not limited to Labrador. A nearly ten-foot (three-meter) length of yarn spun from the fur of arctic hare was recovered from a Late Dorset dwelling at a site on northern Baffin Island. Spinning was not a part of the technology of northern aboriginal peoples, suggesting that this specimen originated in a European community. This supposition is supported by the identification of several goat hairs in the yarn and by the discovery of very similar cloth made of yarn spun from hare fur and goat hair from Gård Under Sandet (Farm Beneath the Sand), a Norse farm site in the Western Settlement of Greenland ... The acquisition by the Dorset people of a length of spun yarn hints at a form of contact more complex than a simple trade in useful metal objects" (Sutherland 241).

Among a number of Norse artifacts found at Dorset sites, Sutherland also lists a piece of smelted iron linked to "the Late Dorset occupation of a site on Axel Heiberg Island on the extreme northwestern fringes of Dorset habitation" (241). William Fitzhugh finds "an amulet made of reworked, European-derived copper … in the late Dorset site at Gulf Hazard-I in Richmond Gulf, radiocarbon dated to between 1095 and 1315" (Seaver 275). More curious is "the occasional representation of Europeanlike faces" in the art of the Dorset, who fashioned "small sculptures in ivory, antler, or wood representing a wide range of animals and humans" (Sutherland 241). Among the relief carvings, "a distinctive long and narrow face with a prominent straight nose and occasional hints of a beard appears on several specimens, one of which came from the same Baffin Island winter house that produced the piece of Norse yarn. It is tempting to suggest that these portrayals may represent the strangers who occasionally landed on the coasts inhabited by the Dorset people" (Sutherland 242).

31 Odess et al. cite Robert McGhee's reply (590) to a comment by Douglas R. Stenton in McGhee's 1994 *American Anthropology* article, "Disease and the Development of Inuit Culture," in which McGhee agrees with Stenton's contention that Dorset Paleoeskimos may have been reduced by disease introduced through contact and encounter. Stenton's suggestion, however, is that the Dorset may have acquired diseases from the Thule, not the Norse. Odess et al. thus extrapolate from McGhee's argument in extending it to the Norse.

32 "In the eleventh century, the only natives present in central Labrador (Markland) would have been the Indian ancestors of the Innu (Montagnais and Naskapi)" (Birgitta Linderoth Wallace, "An Archeologist's Interpretation" 230). "At the time of the Vinland voyages, ancestral Inuit [i.e., the Thule] had begun to expand their occupation eastwards from their Alaskan homeland, but had not yet reached the eastern Arctic. The Inuit displaced their Palaeo-Eskimo predecessors from most of the eastern Arctic during the eleventh and twelfth centuries A.D." (McGhee, *"Skraellings"* 46).

33 It is timely to recall that since the Vinland Sagas set down retold memories of expeditions to the Americas orally narrated over centuries, we are likely to find composite details in them that might have accrued from different periods of time. Archeological evidence suggests that Greenlanders encountered the Thule repeatedly in various contexts. Patricia Sutherland lists Norse artifacts recovered from Thule sites, such as part of a bronze balance used by traders throughout the medieval Norse world ("a type of artifact we would expect to find in the possession of a medieval Norse trader"); a Thule driftwood carving of a human figure "in what is apparently European clothing"; and smelted iron objects, including specimens composed of meteoric iron "that originated in northwestern Greenland, the only known source of meteoric iron in Arctic North America" (244–5). It is not inconceivable, therefore, that the anecdote of the native boys retrieves details gleaned from encounters with the Thule not otherwise recorded, or that the anecdote relays a composite inventory of details remembered from encounters with more than one set of ancestral Native North Americans.

34 Sverrir Jakobsson (99–101) suggests that the saga author may have believed Vinland to be coterminous with Africa – a land where, as we saw in Chapter 1, medieval world maps commonly situate the monstrous races. The *Hausbók* manuscript of *Eirik the Red's Saga* describes the natives as dark, swart men (*suartir men*) with malignant features (*illiligir*), evil hair on their heads (*illt hár á hǫfði*), and large eyes (*mjǫk eygðir*), which might be a description of Africans, Jakobsson says, though Africans are more usually described in Norse texts as *blámenn*, "black men" (Jones, *Norse* 226; Jansson 69).

35 The *Greenlanders' Saga* tells us that Christianity was still in its infancy in Greenland (Magnusson and Pálsson 62; Sveinsson and Þórðarson 257–8), and we have already seen in *Eirik the Red's Saga* the welcoming of the prophetess Thorbjorg, during a season of ill fortune, by Thorkel of Herjolfsness and the community in Greenland, and the old spells of warlock songs that Gudrid, depicted as a good Christian, is reluctantly compelled to sing. Signs of recidivism to pagan practices in conditions of ill fortune are noticeably not confined to Greenland. In *Eirik the Red's Saga*, the first winter faced by Karlsefni's expedition is a harsh one, and food is scarce. When a whale washes up ashore, the cooks boil its meat, consume it, and become ill. Thorhall, one of the

expeditioners who has composed a poem in honor of Thor, his patron, considers the whale a reward from the pagan Norse god who, Thorhall says, seldom failed him, and Thorhall goes on to mock Christ as less successful than Thor in succoring them.

At this, the saga avers, the others refuse the whale meat, throw it over a cliff, and commend themselves to God's mercy. True enough, a break in the weather arrives, and they are enabled to go fishing; after that there is no scarcity of provisions (Magnusson and Pálsson 96; Jones, *Norse* 224; Jansson 66). Written centuries after the events they narrate, after Christianization had long been secured, the Vinland Sagas allegorize the triumph of Christian over pagan belief in episodes like this, but also register the power of the old ways in the communal response to uncanny figures such as Thorbjorg.

36 The people "who shot the arrow into Þorvaldr," Birgitta Linderoth Wallace intimates, would have been "the ancestors of the Algonkian-speaking Innu, formerly known as the Montagnais and Naskapi and related to the Newfoundland Beothuk" ("Vinland and the Death of Þorvaldr" 389). Wallace adds: "So will we find Þorvaldr's grave? I think not. In GLS [*Grænlendinga saga*] Þorvaldr asks that he be buried with a cross at his head and one at his feet ... the sole purpose given for his brother Thorstein's expedition the following year was to collect Þorvaldr's body. ESR [*Eiríks saga rauða*] does not mention either burial or removal, but if we assume that Þorvaldr was Christian, it would have been a necessity to bring his body back to consecrated soil in Greenland" ("Vinland and the Death of Þorvaldr" 389).

If the Ramah chert projectile point found in the churchyard cemetery at Sandnes and the quartz arrowhead recovered below Brattahlid are any indication, Thorvald may not have been the only Greenlander who returned home for Christian burial with Native American stone in his body.

37 As we have seen, butternuts – *Juglans cinerea*, a North American variety of the walnut – grow "in the same areas as wild grapes, in this case *Vitis riparia*, riverbank grapes. Other larger grapes were recorded in 1535 by Cartier on Isle d'Orleans just east of Quebec, where they were in such an abundance that he named it 'Bacchus' Island ... Grapes were also noted in that vicinity by Lescarbot ... in 1606. In 1749 the Finnish traveller Peter Kalm ... recorded that grapes growing near St. Paul east of Quebec were the larger and sweeter fox and frost grape, *Vitis labrusca* and *Vitis valpina* (species which now only grow in New England), and that butternuts grew in this vicinity as well. Whoever picked the butternuts found at L'Anse aux Meadows could hardly have avoided seeing grapevines" (Birgitta Linderoth Wallace, "L'Anse aux Meadows: Gateway to Vinland" 229). "It is of some interest," Wallace adds, "that the butternut wood was a burl, burls being the *másr* of the sagas" ("L'Anse aux Meadows: Gateway to Vinland" 228). We recall that Karlsefni later sells a ship's figurehead, made of *másr* or *mǫsurr* wood, to a German for a handsome sum.

38 Robert McGhee's excavation of Thule winter houses stemming from the late eleventh or early twelfth centuries at Brooman Point on Bathurst Island in the Canadian High Arctic "yielded several Norse artifacts" that suggest sporadic contact continued after L'Anse aux Meadows was abandoned (Seaver 277). More than fifty items of Norse origin were also discovered off the coast of Ellesmere Island in thirteenth-century Thule ruins – including chain mail – the evidence of occasional trade, conflict, or shipwrecks (Seaver 277). From a Late Dorset ruin in Smith Sound near the end of the thirteenth century comes a fragment of a bronze pot (Seaver 277). Sporadic contacts seemed to continue through the end of the Middle Ages. In an indication that "Norse Greenlanders did not just wait for expensive shipments of lumber from Norway," Seavers remarks, "three entries from 1347 in the *Icelandic Annals* note that a small ship with seventeen or eighteen Greenlanders on board had made it to safety in Iceland after drifting off course on its way home to Greenland from a voyage to Markland ... There was no elaboration, which suggests that to the Icelandic contemporaries of the annalists, both the place-name and the purpose of the trip would have been self-explanatory" (Seaver 275).

6

World II

The Mongol Empire: Global Race as Absolute Power

Their food consists of everything that can be eaten, for [the Mongols] eat dogs, wolves, foxes and horses and . . . they feed on human flesh . . . They eat the filth which comes away from mares when they bring forth foals . . . I have even seen them eating lice.

> John of Plano Carpini, *History of the Mongols*, in *Mission to Asia*, ed.
> Christopher Dawson (16)

When we arrived among those barbarians, it seemed to me as if I were stepping into another world.

The men surrounded us and gazed at us as if we were monsters.

> William of Rubruck, *Journey*, in *Mission to Asia*, ed. Christopher Dawson (106, 150).
> See also *The Mission of William of Rubruck*, ed. Peter Jackson and
> David Morgan (97, 173)

I forbear to speak of the wealth and magnificence and glory of this great Emperor [the Mongol Khan of Yuan Dynasty China], of the vastness of the empire and the number of its cities and their size; and of the government of the empire, in which no man dares to draw sword against another; for it would be too long to write and would seem unbelievable to my hearers. For even I who am on the spot hear such things and I can hardly believe them.

> Andrew of Perugia, Bishop of Zayton (Quan-zhou, in Fujien province),
> in a 1326 letter to the Minister General of the Franciscans, in
> *Mission to Asia*, ed. Christopher Dawson (235)[1]

IN THE two centuries after the encounters with Native Americans in Vinland, the alien races that drew the attention of Latin Christendom's communities were Jews at home in the towns and cities of Europe and Muslims overseas, as we've seen in the discussions in Chapters 2 and 3. The thirteenth century, however, saw the arrival of a new alien race at the doorstep of Europe: At Europe's northern and eastern corridors, steppe peoples whom the Latin West referred to as *Tartars* adventitiously made an appearance.[2] The arrival of Mongols threw Christendom into disarray, since Mongols materialized as relentless, devastating conquerors, inexorably overrunning all in their path.

In the course of half a century, Europeans therefore toiled mightily to render intelligible this new global race, hitherto unknown to them.

This chapter registers the early shock of Europe's encounter with Mongols, and the first European attempts to explain Mongol alterity by recourse to inherited systems of knowledge that traditionally accounted for alienness and monstrosity. Mongols were imagined early as heinous, bloodthirsty *cannibals* issuing from among the monstrous races of the world whose existence had been theorized by the natural histories of Pliny and Solinus.

We then consider the expeditions that were hastily cobbled together for on-the-ground reconnaissance and attempts at converting the Mongols – domesticating the alien through religion – and the dawning consciousness of the Mongol empire's power and reach, as reports arising from more extensive and intimate contact accrued. By the end of the thirteenth century, with the Mongol empire encompassing the largest geopolitical landmass in human history in four major khanates that together spanned the vast diversity of the world, the Mongol empire's power, wealth, and sophistication became a lure and a promise to Europe, beckoning opportunity.[3]

Late in the century, we thus see an inventive development: The crusader King of England, Edward I – famed for surviving a Nizari Ismaili's blade in Acre in 1272, and infamous for expelling England's Jews in 1290 – attempted a rapprochement with Abaga Khan of the Mongol Ilkhanate of Persia against their common enemy, the Muslims, forging military plans with Abaga, who sent troops against Aleppo in response to Edward.[4]

From the farthest east of the Mongol empire, Rabban Sauma, a Nestorian monk of Uighur or Ongut descent, journeyed with companions from Beijing in the Mongol Khanate of Cathay to the West, visiting the holy places and relics of Latin Christendom, discoursing on differences between Eastern and Western Christianities with the Curia in Rome, and performing a mass of the East Syrian rite at Bordeaux in 1288 at the behest of Edward I: a mass at which Edward, who had expelled the domestic infidel and fought the Near Eastern infidel, improbably took communion from the hands of this heretic Mongol missionary from the farthest, predominantly pagan East, in an extraordinary gesture of welcome and acceptance. In just half a century, the meaning of the alien Mongol empire had changed for Europe.

At the end of the thirteenth century, a Venetian merchant named Marco Polo, who had spent most of his adult life with his father and uncle in East Asia, recorded a narrative with the help of a romancer-collaborator, Rustichello da Pisa, which eloquently expressed admiration of what the Mongol empire had come to represent for a merchant from the West. Finally, in the fourteenth century, the fabulous simulacrum of world travel encapsulated in that timeless classic *Mandeville's Travels* vaunts the Mongol East as an object of desire, splendor, and fabulousness, and reconfigures the centuries-old fiction of Prester John as an imagined threshold to the great, historical East of unimaginable wealth and puissance – an East that the letters of fourteenth-century Franciscan missionaries residing in China found impossible to capture with adequacy for an audience in the West.

How did the West's responses to the historical arrival and meaning of this alien global race become so extraordinarily transformed in just half a century? Chapter 6 traces significant moments in European racialization of the Mongols, in order to examine the astonishing evolutions in European response.

From 1236 to 1242, medieval Europe's understanding that the international contest for control of the known world was between two great powers – Christendom and Islamdom – received an unpleasant jolt when an Asiatic race from the Eurasian steppe invaded

Northeastern and Eastern Europe, spreading carnage and terror. The invasions of 1236–41 had been preceded by Mongol raiding and reconnaissance in the Caucasus after Genghis Khan's successful 1219–21 campaign against the Khwarezmian empire in Central and West Asia. Exploring the area, Genghis' generals, Subutay and Jebe, had encountered and crushed the Georgian army, making Georgia the first European vassal state of the Mongol empire. The generals also defeated the combined forces of a number of princes of the Kievan Rus and their Cuman allies in 1223 at the River Kalka, in what is now the Ukraine (Jackson and Morgan 13).[5]

Before the decision for the invasion of Europe was formally made in 1235, the Mongol empire had thus become aware that unknown lands further west and northwest were ripe for the taking. Once invasion began, the Mongol military policy of rewarding resistance with massacre and wholesale destruction spread horror in the wake of their campaigns, so much so that even in the far northwest corner of Europe, the English chronicler of St. Albans, Matthew Paris, registered the domestic shock by reporting that in 1238, German fish merchants were so terrified to leave their homes that there was a glut of herrings at Yarmouth that year, and herrings were of no value at all even in places distant from the sea (Luard, *Mathaei Parisiensis . . . Chronica majora* III: 488).

By this time, Genghis Khan, the extraordinary creator of an expanding confederation of steppe peoples led by the Mongols, had been dead for more a decade, but his grandsons Batu and Mongke and his old general Subutay led the invasion of Europe, conquering Russia and the Ukraine; demolishing Ryazan in 1237 and Kiev, the capital, in 1240; overrunning Poland and Bohemia in 1240–1; and devastating Hungary in 1241.[6] In 1246, John of Plano Carpini – a Franciscan monk sent by Pope Innocent IV to bring diplomatic and ecumenical messages to the Mongols and learn the nature of the enemy – witnessed the investiture of Guyuk (son of the Great Khan Ugedey, and grandson of Genghis), as Guyuk became the third Great Khan and emperor.

The papal envoy warned the West that the new Great Khan was planning yet another invasion of Christendom: John, who had seen the killing fields of Russia littered with the skulls and bones of the slain and Kiev a ruined shell of a city, grimly warned that Livonia and Prussia were next (Dawson 29–30, 44–5; Wyngaert I: 71–2, 94–5; see also Dawson 58; Wyngaert I: 112).[7] The Mongols had destroyed the whole of Russia (*"destruxerunt totam Rusciam"*), he lamented (Dawson 30; Wyngaert I: 72). When John arrived at the camp of Batu, Genghis' grandson who ruled the Khanate of the Golden Horde, the papal envoy duly noted the large, beautiful pavilions of linen that Batu possessed, which once had belonged to Béla IV of Hungary, but were now Mongol trophies (Dawson 57; Wyngaert I: 110).

Fortunately, Europe was not the only, or even the primary, focus of the Mongol confederation's territorial ambitions, and internal rivalry between Ugedey's and Guyuk's branch of the Golden Family and the family of Jochy and Toluy, Genghis' other sons, worked to protect the West from further advance. Central and North Asia, West Asia, South Asia, East Asia, and Southeast Asia, however, became part of the largest land empire in human history, stretching from Iran and Iraq in the west to China and Korea in the east, subsuming Russia in the north, and Tibet, Burma, and Vietnam to the south. Even a distant kingdom of maritime Southeast Asia, Java, felt the lash of Mongol invasion.

The relatively brief invasion of Europe, moreover, was not without productive results for medieval Europe both in the short and the long term. In the short term, the Mongol obsession with arts, crafts, technology, and inventions meant that Mongols had learnt to use gunpowder from their earlier invasions of China, and at the 1241 Battle of Mohi in Hungary they deployed gunpowder weapons against the forces of King Béla IV – including bombs hurled by catapults – and thus introduced Europe to the sensational efficacy of gunpowder (Chase 58).

What Are Mongols? Animals, Diet, and the Limits of the Human in Global Imperium

But Europe's first encounters with Mongols required making sense of a people so alien in appearance and habits that the West could scarcely decide if they were human at all. Matthew Paris is repelled by what he sees as the abnormally large heads of the Mongol people – so disproportionate to their bodies, he says – and by the belief that they were cannibals who fed on raw flesh and human beings ("*carnibus crudis et etiam humanis vescuntur*" [Luard, *Chronica majora* III: 488]).

The chronicler of St. Albans excitedly offers graphic accounts of Mongol cannibalism, his imagination alighting on the rapacious hands, bloody teeth, and eager jaws of the "Tartars." Recording events under the years 1238, 1241, 1242, and 1243, Matthew assures us that not only did these animalistic and inhuman beings drink blood, but they also fed on the cadavers of those they slew in war and served up the mutilated paps of virgins, savagely slain through repeated rape, as delicacies for their chieftains (Luard, *Chronica majora* IV, 76)!

Attributing cannibalism to a people is always a powerful, instantaneous way to set them apart from the rest of humanity, and to point to the subhuman and bestial nature of the unfortunates in question.[8] Writing in Hertfordshire, England, Matthew Paris did not himself come into contact with Mongols, of course – and he is notorious, moreover, for his fascination with lurid and sensational imaginings (as we saw in Chapter 2) – so it little surprises that he gives imagination free rein in relishing the subhumanity of the new enemies of Europe.[9]

But even Latin Christians who came into contact with the Mongols, lived among them for a time, and painstakingly advised the Latin West on how to deal with them insisted on the historical reality of Mongol cannibalism, which, of course, they also did not witness. John of Plano Carpini's *Ystoria Mongalorum*, the most important of the early eyewitness European accounts of the Mongol empire that we have, is written by a papal envoy who directly experienced the society and culture of the Mongols, yet insists that during the prolonged Mongol invasion of China (at which John was not present) the invaders ran out of food and Genghis Khan himself personally ordered one out of every ten men to be sacrificed and eaten by their comrades – a utilitarian improvement, it seems, on the ancient Roman punishment of culling human groups through a similar decimal practice sans cannibalism (Dawson 21; Wyngaert I: 56). Needless to say, the Mongols' *Secret History*, detailing the life and death of Genghis Khan and the founding of the empire, makes no mention at all of supervised cannibalism by Mongols, of Mongols, through order of the imperial founder during the invasion of China.[10]

If the humanity of enemies somehow always seems in question, John of Plano Carpini also clearly proved unable to resist some of the more tenacious cultural traditions in the medieval West that recommended ways in which enemies, foreigners, and aliens should be understood. In addition to his conviction that Mongols were cannibals, John accepted the cultural tradition that the Plinian (monstrous) races were located in Central Asia and dutifully recounts tales about them in his *Ystoria*, though he does not claim to have personally encountered these monstrous races in his time on the steppe.[11] We are reminded again of Debra Strickland's admonition that the Latin West's inherited traditions of imagining monstrosity, rather than affording only harmless, exuberant entertainment for their audiences, also "provided the ideological infrastructure" for ruminating on and understanding "other types of 'monsters,' namely Ethiopians, Jews, Muslims, and Mongols" (42).

Fidelity to tradition aside, John's detailed, thorough, and for the most part down-to-earth description of Mongol life and society is uniquely valuable, and represents the earliest full, concerted account in the Latin West to make sense of the people and the empire – an account that survives in its entirety.[12] Like Matthew Paris, John is struck by the physical appearance of Mongols, who do not resemble the other races that had become familiar to the West. Mongol faces are broad, with more space between the eyes and across the cheekbones; the cheekbones are prominent; the eyes are small, with hardly any room between the eyelid and eyebrow; and male faces rarely have facial hair – at most a little on the upper lip and chin (Dawson 6; Wyngaert I: 32). The strangeness of this Asiatic face – so vastly different from the faces of Europeans and the bearded Muslims of the Near East – confirmed the alienness of a people whose habits and behavior were nothing like what the West had known.

Framing the Mongol face, moreover, were the peculiar appurtenances of culture: weirdly tonsured haircuts with side braids for the men, and ludicrously towering, storied headgear for married women (Dawson 7–8; Wyngaert I: 32–4).[13] However, as the Franciscan monk learns of more and more Eastern races in his travels, the Mongol face becomes John's template for describing other Asiatic faces. We are told, for instance, that the people of Cathay (that is, northern China, ruled by the Jurchen of Manchuria, who formed the Jin dynasty until conquered by the Mongols in 1234) have a physiognomy that resembles the Mongols, but Chinese faces are not so broad, and are more likely to be beardless (Dawson 22; Wyngaert I: 58).

John's account of how Mongols looked, behaved, and lived their lives carried supremely authoritative weight: These are the observations and judgments of the first official envoy from the West who reached the heart of the unknown, alien Mongol empire. John's consciousness that he is conducting the affairs of Christendom, as he put it (Dawson 52; Wyngaert I: 104), and his status as the Latin West's official envoy leads him to announce early in the *Ystoria* that his words are addressed to *all* the faithful in Christendom who read him, and that his mission is undertaken by command of the Supreme Pontiff himself (Dawson 3–4; Wyngaert I: 27–8). The papal envoy is fully aware of the critical importance of his embassy, and the weight his words carry.

As he might wish, the *Ystoria Mongalorum* became the most widely known early account of the Mongols and their empire. Surviving as a full, complete version and shorter recensions (Dawson 71–2; Wyngaert I: 130), and incorporated into Vincent de Beauvais' immensely popular encyclopedia, the *Speculum Historiale*, John's description of who Mongols were, and his advice to the West on how to think about Mongols, circulated far more extensively than the later narrative of his fellow Franciscan, William of Rubruck, who went to the empire eight years after John in 1253, bearing a letter from the King of France, Louis IX, on an informal mission to preach and convert that did not amount to an embassy.

It is significant that it was the Pope in Rome who dispatched the first envoys to the Mongol empire, and not any European monarch or the Holy Roman Emperor. Innocent IV sent three or four embassies to the Mongols in 1245, of which only John's, which came to include Benedict the Pole and a few other companions, succeeded in reaching the court of the Great Khan himself.[14] The number of ambassadors Innocent dispatched, bearing copies of two *ex cathedra* papal bulls and taking different routes to the Mongols, allows us to glimpse something of the sense of urgency that impelled this medieval pope.

The impression that Innocent IV saw himself as the de facto and de jure leader of the European West is hard to avoid. After all, it was also a pope, Urban II, who initiated the First Crusade in 1095, a century and a half ago, and not the crowned heads of Europe or the Emperor. Military and political initiatives such as this – when a series of official representatives, or hosts of armed pilgrims, were sent into foreign places to deliver actions – indicated the range of statecraft of which the Apostolic See was capable, as it functioned like a global state, a state without borders – or a state whose borders, rather, extended to all of the Latin West.

Unsurprisingly, John's report of his diplomatic, political, and ecumenical mission to the Mongol empire in 1245–7 discloses the extent to which his journey is a reconnaissance mission from the West to ascertain the nature of the Mongol threat, and to ascertain how to defeat the Mongols in war. Systematically organized into sections, John's narrative reports on the physical environs, the people, the religion, the customs, the empire, the wars, and the subjugated territories and vassal states of the Mongols, culminating in a detailed treatise on how war should be waged against them, followed by a final section recounting the journey he and his companions made. The aim of the *Ystoria*, the papal envoy tells us at the onset, is to prepare the Christian West for war (Dawson 3; Wyngaert I: 28).

Thus, 40 percent of the *Ystoria* concentrates on the Mongols' machinery of governance and war, Mongol battle array and battle tactics, and Mongol treatment of subjugated territories and peoples. By contrast, William of Rubruck's account of the Mongols less than a decade later casts a more anthropological eye over the alien peoples whom William hoped to convert to Latin Christianity, and whose habits and mores he duly set down for the edification of the French king who sent him forth – Louis IX, the sole addressee of William's narrative.

The passionate urgency that imbues the sections in which John details the war machine of the Mongol empire; his barely concealed sense of panic when explaining the precise nature of the dangers posed by Mongol ways of fighting; and the intense effort John's narrative makes to ensure his words are heeded and understood, and thus able to correct contemporary western ways of waging war: All this frames the earlier sections of the *Ystoria* as a preliminary, background preparation for the most important sections of narrative, the sections in which he teaches the West to understand and defeat the Mongol threat.

John's mission is thus one of unconcealed espionage, mingled with political diplomacy and ecumenism. The very letters written by Innocent IV and conveyed by John and others to the Khan direct themselves to both political and ecumenical ends, simultaneously urging the Khan and his Mongols to convert to Christianity, and embedding veiled threats of reprisal for continued bellicose behavior.[15] In the twin aims of espionage and reconnaissance, John's account even suggests it has secret advance knowledge of future revolts being planned against the Mongol empire. According to information he has acquired, John confides, the Georgians intend a rebellion against their steppe masters (Dawson 41; Wyngaert I: 88). The *Ystoria* also warns of an imminent reinvasion of Europe, beginning with invasions of Livonia and Prussia (Dawson 44–5; Wyngaert I: 94–5).[16]

The *Ystoria Mongalorum* is a complex narrative. Not least of all, it is the first-hand report of an eyewitness ambassador attempting to scent out the weaknesses of the society he visits, so as to render it vulnerable. But the *Ystoria* is also invariably part travelogue, the account of a remarkable journey made by a Franciscan monk and his small group of companions, soldiering onward for the Pope and the Latin West. And it is part anthropological study, an interested historical and contemporary ethnography of the Mongol empire as seen through the eyes of its enemies.

The upshot of the papal envoy's observations and judgments is that Mongols were an impossibly alien people, sharing far less in common with the West than Saracens and Jews, and inexplicable in customs and habits. Mongols had alien faces that set them apart from the other races of the world, and unisex clothing for men and women (Dawson 6–7; Wyngaert I: 32–4). They put to death anyone who stepped on the threshold of a chieftain's yurt on entering or leaving (Dawson 11; Wyngaert I: 40). They practiced an economy antithetical to sedentary societies, and they were monotheists who nonetheless made idols of felt and reverenced the elements and the sun and moon. They even seemed to turn dead Mongols into gods in their practice of ancestor worship, transmuting the deceased founder of their empire, Genghis Khan, into an idol (Dawson 9–10; Wyngaert I: 37–9).

Mongols were polygynists who practiced what looked, to the eyes of the papal envoy, like incest, including levirate marriage, and they lived in an alien, remote, and forbidding landscape – a world seemingly almost devoid of trees, the unimaginable opposite of heavily forested, lush, green Western Europe (Dawson 7, 5; Wyngaert I: 33, 30–1). Even their climate was perplexing, with heavy snowfalls, hailstorms, and hurricanes of bitter cold *in summer*, when extreme heat also alternated unpredictably with this extreme cold (Dawson 5–6; Wyngaert I: 31–2).[17]

Their dietary habits were execrable, scarcely deserving the name of human eating. Above all, the close association of Mongols with their animals – the horses on whom they depended for everything, as well as the oxen, goats, sheep, and camels they bred and herded – made Mongols themselves seem less than human.[18] The *Secret History of the Mongols* even tells us that Mongols believed their founding ancestors to *be* animals – a grey wolf and a fallow deer: the totemic primordial parents of the Mongol race (de Rachewiltz I: 1).

John's report to the Pope and Christians of Europe makes plain that a civilization, to the official envoy of the Latin West, is defined by what it eats. Bread, a universal staple made from a variety of grains in sedentary societies around the world practicing agriculture, was not routinely part of the nomad diet; nor were vegetables, fruit, nuts, or herbs; and alcoholic beverages fermented from grain or fruit had to be imported if they were to be consumed. Instead, a society practicing the animal husbandry of pastoralism lived off its animals, and what its animals produced.

Mongols drank the milk of their animals, and they fermented mares' milk into *koumiss*, a dietary staple and an alcoholic beverage which William of Rubruck, if not John, came to enjoy. Mongols ate the meat of their animals, including horsemeat, but in such sparingly small quantities that John is astonished they could survive on so little; they also ate whatever creatures they were able to catch in the austere environment of the steppe, including wolves, foxes, dogs, and – John reports with revulsion – even lice. The papal envoy says they even ate the afterbirth of mares (Dawson 16; Wyngaert I: 48).[19]

The dietary habits of Mongols who practiced transhumance thus seemed as extreme and bewildering as the climate and the ecoscape in which they had to survive. The harsh, gravelly, treeless land in which John and his companions found themselves had little water; woods were few, small, and scarce; and rivers and oases that sustained life were far apart and rare (Dawson 5–6; Wyngaert I: 30–1).

The conditions of nomad existence did not conduce to niceties such as tablecloths or napkins, or the washing of dishes (dishes were rinsed in meat broth, which was then returned to the cooking pot): All this is observed and reported by the papal envoy with a palpable air of superiority and mild disgust (Dawson 16–17; Wyngaert I: 48–9).[20] The lack of water also meant that Mongols did not normally bathe themselves.[21] Rather, in the human habit of turning necessity into virtue, they developed cultural taboos to prevent wasting the precious resource of water.

So rudimentary, then, did Mongol dietary habits and hygiene seem to the emissary from the West (even by the standards of hygiene-deficient medieval Europe, let alone the hygiene-conscious Near East) that Mongols scarcely seemed to exist along the same continuum of human culture as the rest of the world. John marveled that Mongols ate so parsimoniously that they did not even give bones to their dogs until all the marrow had been extracted and consumed (Dawson 17; Wyngaert I: 49). No part of an animal was wasted: Mongols ate even the entrails and the blood, refraining only from consuming the animal's dung (Dawson 25; Wyngaert I: 63–4). A people with so peculiar a diet, and a people moreover without bread – the universal food of sedentary civilizations – could not possibly be civilized.

Beyond diet, there were other circumstances that indicated to the envoy that Mongols lived beyond the pale of civilization. In Chapter 2, we saw how medieval English Jews who handled money and monetary transactions for all classes of their society became heavily stigmatized as coin clippers – a hazard of being too intimately associated with the currency they handled.

Mongols, who handled horses and herds, lived in daily proximity to animals, and depended on animals for their existence and survival, were implicitly stigmatized by the papal envoy's report to the West as some hybrid species of the human, a variety of folk who were de facto part human and part horse, deeply colored by the horse culture they cultivated. Mongols had more horses and mares, the emissary believed, than existed in all the rest of the world (Dawson 8; Wyngaert I: 36). The Latin West had not before seen the like of a population so intimately intertwined with horses that the relationship between human and horse forged the identity of the group, in everyday life and at war.

Medieval Europeans were cognizant of an armored knight's dependence on his charger, of course. This was a relationship that undergirded the identity of the elite class of warriors that European knights constituted, a relationship sentimentalized and celebrated in chivalric literature. In Chapter 4, we saw how the Dutch romance *Moriaen* even attributed to the famous horse of Sir Gawain, Arthur's knight, a feisty personality, and poignant emotions of loyalty and love for his master. But knights made up only an elite stratum that did not represent all of society, and knights did not depend on their horses for food, drink, tools, footwear, fuel, or funerary customs.

By contrast, Mongols eat, drink, and wear their horses. Horses' hide becomes shoes and boots for wearing, or is made into cuirasses; horses' hair becomes rope and tools for use;

horse flesh can be eaten in a shortage of food; and fermented mare's milk is a dietary staple. In times of necessity, during war or long-distance travel, a Mongol rider might even open a vein in his horse's body, and temporarily sustain himself on its blood (thus perhaps inducing Matthew Paris' nightmare vision of vampire-Mongols with bloody teeth). Horse dung becomes fuel and energy: Fires for cooking are made from the dung of horses and oxen (Dawson 5, 97, 101, 133, 172; Jackson and Morgan 79, 86–7, 141, 204; Wyngaert I: 30, 176–7, 181–2, 221, 272).

Horses are even important in burial rites, and some are buried with the deceased, including mares to ensure a supply of milk in the hereafter. Horses are also killed, hollowed out, and turned into funerary totems to mark the graves of the deceased (Dawson 13; Wyngaert I: 42).[22] Such clear-eyed, pragmatic, and multifarious use of the horse might suggest to some that Mongols were callous or unsentimental about their horses – and certainly, the *Secret History* exhibits nothing of the sentimentality lavished in European literature on horses like Gawain's Gringolet. But the incorporation of the horse into Mongol religious ceremonies, art, music, and culture – into emotional and spiritual life – suggests high Mongol esteem for the horse, and a reverence of its own kind.

In the *Secret History*, horses are mentioned in the same breath when human individuals are introduced, the narrative tying each person to the horses he possesses or rides, or is identified by, or that come to accrue to him – linking humans and horses in intimate relationship (see, for example, de Rachewiltz, *Secret History* I: 1, 6, 26, 27). Indeed, a Mongol's sense of the world's immensity and extent is measured by where a horse can go (Dawson 202; Jackson and Morgan 248; Wyngaert I: 307).[23]

Horses also functioned as currency, and the *Ystoria* reports that Mongol chiefs paid feudal rent and tribute to their Khan in the form of mares (Dawson 28; Wyngaert I: 69).[24] Astonishingly, infants and toddlers of two or three years old could shoot and ride; women were as able riders as men, and also went to war, though according to John, the work of women for the most part involved every activity that sustained life and society outside of war (Dawson 18; Wyngaert I: 50–1).[25] But women and children were also deployed in war to swell the numbers of horsed warriors seen by the enemy, and to intimidate the enemy with an illusion of the collective strength of Mongol numbers (Dawson 36; Wyngaert I: 81–2). A people organized to be on the move, grazing its herds, hunting, and at war, every member of society could shoot and ride.

Unlike European militias, Mongol armies only consisted of horsed troops who fought from horseback, with no infantry to slow them down. Each rider, John explains, was equipped with five horses, could switch between steeds when a horse tired, and never rode the same horse twice over a number of days: This was an entire horsed army, with tremendous advantage in speed and mobility and, thanks to their weapon of choice, able to reduce their enemies from a distance.[26] The seamless melding of rider and horse meant the rider could shoot even when his horse was racing, and he could shoot *backward*, when necessary.

Valued as much as the humans who ride them, Mongol horses are protected by armor, like their riders. They are also honored like humans, John reports, and at the *kuriltay* or general assembly at which Guyuk is elected Great Khan, when the Mongol chieftains are splendid in magnificent robes of red, white, and blue velvet and rich brocade, the horses are resplendent with twenty marks' worth of gold on their bits, breastplates, saddles and cruppers (Dawson 61, 62; Wyngaert I: 117–18).

The shaggy Mongol horse that is the backbone of the Mongol armies, moreover, had none of the limitations of bulky, rapidly tiring Western chargers. Small, hardy, and resilient, Mongol horses can endure long stretches without food or drink, like their riders. Amazingly, they can even dig up grass and roots from under the snow with their hooves, as if they were human (Dawson 52; Wyngaert I: 104). Indeed, to onlookers, these tough, durable beasts must have seemed uncannily human-like with their strange, unequine skills and ability to fend for themselves under harsh conditions.

Their riders, bred to horseback from infancy, in turn must have seemed part horse, blended into their steeds like centaurs, man and horse together forming a single moving composite entity. With horses that seem half human and humans that seem half horse, a Mongol rider's inseparability from his animal, we might say, is the thirteenth century's equivalent of the posthuman as a fighting unit in a war machine.

The *Ystoria*'s description of Mongol armies as a whole suggests that Mongols functioned like a kind of sentient swarm or herd that surrounded its victims, lured the victims into foolish pursuit, then cut them down when their horses tired, or when the victims could be pincered with the arrival of concealed, fresh Mongol reinforcements. William of Rubruck's later account showed how much even Mongol hunting techniques – encircling, surrounding, and hemming in a target – resembled a rehearsal for war (Dawson 100–1; Jackson and Morgan 85; Wyngaert I: 181).

Fast and efficient in the battlefield, Mongols nonetheless had a preference for siege warfare, the *Ystoria* says – penning their hapless victims inside their own fortifications, encircling them only to flush them out by damming a river, or swarming into their interiors through sapping and underground tunnels (Dawson 48–9; Wyngaert I: 99–100). In sieges, Mongols fought tirelessly, by day and by night, dividing up their forces so that different forces could rest and battle alternately, and they could sustain a siege for several years (Dawson 37; Wyngaert I: 82–3). The *Ystoria* portrays Mongols in their indefatigable efficiency as a relentless war machine, an army that seemed to move as with one mind, like a single entity.[27]

Mongols so confounded and upturned the military expectations of the West that the envoy from the West felt he needed to detail, earnestly and with a touch of panic, how unique Mongol forces were. John's advice to the Christians of Europe on how to defeat Mongols in war thus ultimately rested on one salient piece of wisdom: European armies would need *to become like the Mongols themselves* in war – tough, resilient, fast, disciplined, and wily – and they would need to emulate the battle formations, technologies, and field strategies of the Mongols. In short, to defeat the Mongols, European armies would themselves need to become virtual Mongols. Even as this alien race – Europe's newest alien other – is being defined, we notice, Europeans are being asked by the *Ystoria* to reimagine themselves militarily in the alien other's terms.

The envoy urges Europe to use weapons like those the Mongols use – bows, lances with hooks to drag riders off, arrowheads tempered in the Mongol fashion, a good supply of arrows (Mongols had specialized arrows for different usages, and carried files for sharpening them), and armor to protect horses as much as men (Dawson 35, 46; Wyngaert I: 79, 96–7).[28] He urges a Mongol-style division of European troops into units of ten, a hundred, a thousand, and ten thousand – a decimal system of fighting in which the group is made responsible for the action of each individual, with an entire group being punished for the misbehavior of *any* of its members (Dawson 33, 46–7; Wyngaert I: 77, 97–8). He points out the military rationality of a Mongol system that, unlike the customs of chivalric warfare adhered to by European knights and Muslim emirs, did not offer captive enemy nobles and leaders to be ransomed, but instead efficiently executed them all (Dawson 38; Wyngaert I: 83–4). He recommends severe punishment for deserters, and prevention of looting before a battle is over: standard disciplines in Mongol military culture.

The emissary also advises copying Mongol battle formations – forming many lines of attack instead of advancing as a single army, and sending scouts in all directions, since Mongols liked to surround their enemies. European leaders should only watch and direct their forces, like the Mongol chieftains, rather than engaging in combat themselves: an instruction requiring a self-restraint no doubt excruciating to glory-hungry European knights (Dawson 46–7; Wyngaert I: 97–8). The Franciscan's admonitions to imitate the Mongols are followed by detailed instructions on what type of battleground to select, the need for supply of water and provisions, and how to maintain a siege for several years, if necessary – one Mongol siege of the Alans had already lasted twelve years (Dawson 48–9; Wyngaert I: 99–100).

To combat the Mongols, then, European forces in the field of battle would need to become Mongols themselves. There is no indication in the *Ystoria* that the papal envoy considered the tactics, weaponry, military discipline, technology, or leadership of Europe's forces, fighting in their usual way, as at all adequate to the exigencies at hand. The courage of knights is not extolled, nor the efficacy of the heavy cavalry charge in scattering the enemy. Indeed, the only European weapon that halfway meets with John's approval is the crossbow: a weapon which, John says, Mongols fear – not a distinctively chivalric weapon at all, but one that enabled a simulacrum of the kind of warfare at which Mongols excelled.

John issues his instructions to copy the Mongols with great earnestness and exactitude, with minute, detailed specifications. Indeed, John's *over*-specification, and his repeated injunctions to perpetual vigilance, discloses a touch of hysteria. Europeans must be equally alert by night as by day, he says; they are never to undress to sleep, or sit at table enjoying themselves; they are always to look to danger, never let their guard down, eat in moderation, hide their corn in secret pits, never be without water or wood, burn all hay and straw when retreating in order to deprive Mongol horses of food, and so forth – a stream of microinstructions that more than hint at an undercurrent of panic (Dawson 48; Wyngaert I: 99).

Unfortunately, in his anxiety to get everything right, and to get everything down, John ends up exhorting Latin Christians to opposite and contradictory ends. He warns Christians not to stint on money when purchasing weapons, because these are "for the defense of souls and bodies and liberty," but he also warns them to beware of "their usual tendency of over-expenditure," lest they be forced to withdraw for lack of money "and the Tartars destroy the whole earth and the name of God be blasphemed on account of their extravagance" (Dawson 46, 48; Wyngaert I: 97, 98–9).

Either way, it seems, Europe will not be able to get it right. But to underscore the absolute urgency of getting it right, John reiterates *five times* in the *Ystoria* that Mongols intend to rule the world (Dawson 25, 38, 39, 43, 45; Wyngaert I: 64, 84, 86, 93, 95). And according to his intelligence, John tells us thrice, Guyuk, the Great Khan at whose election and enthronement John was present, intended to raise his banner against the whole of the West soon after his ascension to office (Dawson 44, 45, 65; Wyngaert I: 94, 95, 122).[29]

A formidable characteristic of the Mongol military machine, John indicates, is that like the army of Alexander, Mongol forces comprised not only people of their own ethnorace –

who were fewer in number and weaker in body than the Christian peoples, John says (Dawson 44; Wyngaert I: 94) – but a confederation of assimilated subject peoples. War and conquest thus increased the size of the Mongol army, so that Mongol forces had local informants within their ranks who were familiar with the territory they traversed, and the forces grew larger with the assimilation of able-bodied locals, despite any losses in war.[30]

The pragmatic Mongol response to enemies – why not turn them into one's own troops? – was of a piece with other kinds of Mongol pragmatism, such as the depopulation and repopulation of conquered cities, the translocation of peoples Mongols found valuable to other parts of their empire, and the transplanting of artisans and craftsmen great distances from their original homelands for the purpose of making use of their skills.[31] Pragmatism also shaped the historically famed Mongol attitude of religious tolerance, the distinctive configurations of Mongol foreign policy, Mongol esteem for craftsmen and artisans, Mongol use of foreigners such as Marco Polo for diplomatic and other tasks, the Mongol tendency to deploy non-Mongol surrogates in local governance, and the dynamics of Mongol geopolitics, as amply attested in Western and Eastern records that depict Mongol rule.

A masterpiece of diplomacy, Guyuk Khan's response to Innocent IV itself showcases Mongol pragmatism, opening a window onto the kind of pragmatist logic that drove Mongol thinking. To Innocent's call for him to convert to Christianity, the Great Khan answers by saying that it made no sense for him to become like the trembling, weak Nestorian Christians he knew when his great success in conquest was already a sign of God's favor, since nothing could be accomplished without the will of God. In turn, he poses a question to Innocent: How could the pope be so certain that he knew to whom God showed mercy and absolved, or know that he was speaking words with God's sanction, since from the rising of the sun to its setting, all lands had been made subject to the Great Khan? How could this have been accomplished, if it were contrary to the command of God (Dawson 85–6; de Rachewiltz, *Papal Envoys* 213–14)?[32]

Mongol Women, the Asiatic Gift Economy, and Mongol Political Alterity

Mongol pragmatism also meant the acceptance of women as rulers and counselors, and the historical record is impressively punctuated by the deeds and governance of powerful women regents, ambassadors, governors, advisors, and the like. Indeed, our papal envoy pronounces "Sorocan" – Sorghaghtani Bekhi, a Kereit princess of Nestorian Christian faith and the wife of Toluy, Genghis' youngest son, and mother of Mongke, who became Great Khan after Guyuk's short-lived reign – the most powerful and renowned personage among the Tartars, after Batu himself (Dawson 26; Wyngaert I: 66).

Nomad society did not waste the talents of half its population, and John tells us that, like men, women were appointed to control Mongol courts and received tribute (Dawson 60; Wyngaert I: 115). Before he was allowed to meet Guyuk in person, John was sent first to meet the Great Khan's mother, Toreghana Khatun, the wily Naiman empress-dowager who had ruled as Great Khatun in the five-year interregnum between her husband Ugedey's death and her son Guyuk's ascension (Dawson 61; Wyngaert I: 116).

The papal envoy's experience of powerful Mongol women was by no means unique. In 1248, when the Dominican Andrew of Longjumeau was sent by Louis IX of France to Guyuk Khan with letters from Louis and a lavish tent-chapel of scarlet cloth, figurines illustrating the New Testament, and all that was necessary to celebrate mass, Andrew found Guyuk Khan already dead, and Oghul Gamish, the Great Khan's principal wife, ruling as regent in his stead. It was she, as Jean de Joinville relates with chagrin in his *Histoire de Saint Louis* (History/Life of Saint Louis), who infamously assumed that Louis's gifts constituted tribute and amounted to an acknowledgement of vassalage, and who issued a haughty reply to the French king ordering his continued obeisance and provision of tribute (Shaw 198, 283, 287).[33]

William of Rubruck, journeying to the Mongols, would also remark on the high-ranking women, including Oghul Gamish, who exercised influence and authority in the Mongol society he found, some of whom continued to be honored even after death.

The *Ystoria* shows how Mongol pragmatism also issues in a kind of radical meritocracy that raises the hackles of the papal envoy. The ambassador from the West is aghast that Mongols did not stigmatize illegitimacy of birth, but afforded equal status and opportunity to the sons of concubines as well as the sons of legal wives. To show how this lack of respect for proper status misshaped Mongol foreign policy, John recounts a story – slightly garbling the historical details to make a point – of how the Mongols favored an illegitimate younger son of the King of Georgia, "David," over his legitimate half-brother, "Melic," and shockingly made the legitimate heir subordinate to the bastard (Dawson 40–1; Wyngaert I: 87–8).

The lesson therefore that John takes away from Mongol appointment of the corulership of two claimants to the Georgian throne, David VII Ulu (the older, illegitimate son of the late king, George IV Lasha) and David VI Narin (George's younger, legitimate son), is that Mongols did not in all decency honor the claims of birth, inheritance, and class that formed the cornerstone of the feudal West. The very fact that Mongols *elected* their Great Khan during a vast assembly of leaders – a procedure originating with Genghis Khan's own election in a *kuriltay* – must have seemed to the envoy from the West another denaturing political institution.

It comes as little surprise, then, that John perceived the Mongol threat to Europe not only as the geopolitical threat that it certainly was, but also as the threat of a worldwide class war. It is the object of Mongols, the papal envoy grimly concludes, to wipe from the face of the earth *all princes, nobles, knights, and men of gentle birth* (Dawson 44: "*Intendunt etiam delere omnes principes, omnes nobiles, omnes milites et honestos viros de terra*" [Wyngaert I: 94]). Favoring women, illegitimate sons, the election of overlords – seemingly all and sundry, instead of proper degree – through a pragmatism that conduced, in effect, to the creation of a kind of radical meritocracy, Mongols must have appeared an alien race indeed in the eyes of the emissary from the West.

Compounding the alienness of their physiognomy, personal habits and social mores, religious beliefs, bizarre diets, totalizing horse and animal culture, alien landscape and forbidding climate, and absence of European standards of decency in matters of hygiene, marriage, inheritance, and rule was also an incomprehensible economy based not only on transhumance, trade, and plunder, but also a system of supernumerary gifts supplementary to a tributary economy.

A tributary economy was by itself, of course, not unfamiliar to Europeans, since the necessity of ameliorating invasion and threat from the powerful with propitiatory tribute was a worldwide phenomenon. We saw in Chapter 3 how some kinds of tribute even took the form of appeasing the mighty with tributary gifts of *humans*, in the form of beautiful women of noble blood for concubinage or marriage. The political economy of tribute – exercised by empires over vassal states and subject peoples to secure some measure of non-interference for such states and peoples from their imperial overlords – was a time-honored system in the management of human relations of power.

But the papal envoy's incredulity at how gifts were solicited ad hoc from him and his cohort *by all and sundry* during their travels signals the extent to which the Asiatic gift economy, as distinct from the political economy of tribute, was a concept alien to the emissary from the West. Though the papal envoy is warned by Boleslaus, the Duke of Silesia, that he would need to have prestige gifts to present, and though John makes a show of purchasing valuables such as pelts and skins with money he says was given to him and his fellows as alms, the envoy is overwhelmed by the incessant demand for gifts, especially on the part of the *minor* Mongol officials he encounters (Dawson 51–4; Wyngaert I: 102–7).[34]

A *formal* system of tribute officially paid to the rulers of empires was one thing, but the *informal* expectation of petty officials, captains of military contingents, local governors, and the like that John and his fellows would participate in the Asiatic gift economy which conventionally lubricated all human encounters and exchange strikes the papal envoy as outrageous.

Envoys should bear tribute, yes, and at the *kuriltay* of Guyuk, John duly describes the magnificent gifts lavished on the Great Khan by tributary states and kingdoms near and far.[35] The *kuriltay* is in fact the occasion at which John indicates he understands a distinction to exist between official tribute and prestige gifts. There were 4,000 envoys present, the papal emissary reports, to honor the Great Khan, and John divides these 4,000 representatives into five categories: those who were bringing tribute; those who were bringing gifts; sultans and chieftains attending to offer their submission; people summoned by the Mongols; and the governors of territories (who were presumably obliged to attend [Dawson 62; Wyngaert I: 118]).

But the emissary from the West is outraged and defeated by how he is also expected to participate in low-level and mid-level exchange relations with subordinates and surrogates, including men of lower rank (Dawson 28; Wyngaert I: 69) such as captains of a hundred or a thousand, and exclaims testily and with hyperbolic annoyance that even the slaves of the Mongols expected gifts (Dawson 39, 51–4; Wyngaert I: 86, 102–7).[36] The envoy rails mightily at the extortionate Mongol pyramid of gifting expectations, which he moralizes into a system of individual greed and extortion.

The pervasiveness of the Asiatic gift economy, weighing upon the papal envoy at all levels of encounter, was so little anticipated by him that when the emissary from the West finally arrived at Guyuk's enthronement and met the new Great Khan, to John's chagrin his store of gifts had been depleted, and the papal envoy had to introduce himself and his fellows to the Great Khan embarrassingly empty-handed (Dawson 64; Wyngaert I: 120).

To his credit, by the time he finally meets the Great Khan, the papal envoy has come to understand the meaning and importance of the Asiatic gift economy (while continuing to inveigh mightily against its extortionate demands): Not only is social exchange and communication eased by the proffering of gifts, but, potlatch-like, an envoy's status and importance, and the status and importance of those he represents and the lands from which he comes, are measured in the eyes of the recipient by the quality and quantity of the gifts the envoy tenders (Dawson 28; Wyngaert I: 68–9).

When he accounts for his need to bestow as gifts a great part of the things given by the Christian faithful for the expenses of his cohort and himself, John communicates the tart Mongol response to his paucity of gifts, which resembles, in Mongol eyes, a Scrooge-like miserliness and niggardliness: "You come from an important man and you give so little" (Dawson 28; "*A magno homine venitis et tam modicum datis*" [Wyngaert I: 69]).

By contrast, the Great Khan, who has received no gifts from the papal envoy to honor him, has John and his fellows received with courtesy and "great honor" (Dawson 62; Wyngaert I: 117). The envoy and his men are specially served with mead and wine because they refuse to drink *koumiss*; they are seated in a location of honor, on the right-hand side of the Great Khan's court; and they are given robes of honor, each man receiving a lined, fox-skin cloak and a length of velvet from the Great Khan's mother (Dawson 57, 62, 64, 69; Wyngaert I: 110, 117, 120, 126). The irrationality of Mongol social customs and the barbarity of Mongol personal habits, it seems, is ameliorated somewhat by the Great Khan's hospitality and his one-sided tendering of gifts.

The Mongols, who were visited by envoys and ambassadors from all regions of the world, must have been perplexed by these strange men from the West, who brought no gifts to signal respect, nor to signal the importance of the lands and leaders the men claimed to represent. As the rulers of an ever-expanding empire, Mongols were no doubt used to myriad visitors who claimed to be envoys of some kind – at Guyuk Khan's *kuriltay* alone, John had counted some 4,000 official envoys, Benedict the Pole some 3,000 – and doubtless had methods to distinguish between authentic ambassadors and mere charlatans and poseurs (Dawson 62, 81; Wyngaert I: 118, 139). Perhaps as an authenticating measure, a suggestion is made to the papal envoy that he should request return envoys from the Great Khan to Europe – a suggestion, however, that John rejects out of hand (Dawson 68; Wyngaert I: 125).

The papal envoy lists five reasons in the *Ystoria* why it would be imprudent to escort Mongol envoys back to Europe, including his trepidation at assuming responsibility for their safety, given wide knowledge that Mongols visited punitive vengeance when their envoys were harmed (Dawson 68; Wyngaert I: 125). But the first reason the papal envoy gives for rejecting out of hand the suggestion of Mongol envoys is his fear, he says, that the envoys' real purpose might be to spy out the land, and that seeing the dissension and wars that are rife in Europe, they might encourage their leaders to attack the West (Dawson 68; Wyngaert I: 125). With this acknowledgement that espionage and reconnaissance might be the real purpose of envoys, the emissary from the West circles back to the reason for his own voyage to the Mongols: reconnaissance and espionage.

Late in the narrative, John rounds up his account of precisely such reconnaissance and espionage by listing some of his sources in his project of information gathering. Russians, Hungarians, and others who had been with the Mongols for between ten and thirty years – men who knew the language of the Mongols, and had lived with them through wars and other events – had shared "private information" ("*alia multa secreta*") with the papal envoy – willingly, and sometimes without being asked, he says, for they knew what John and his fellows wanted – so that with the help of these men, the emissary from the West was able to gain a thorough knowledge of everything (Dawson 66; Wyngaert I: 122–3). One bit of private information we've already learnt, of course, is that the Georgians intend to revolt against their Mongol masters, a plan the papal envoy says the Georgians confided to him.

John's account ends soon after a detailed description of the process of exchanging letters and translations between Guyuk Khan and Innocent IV, in lieu of escorting Mongol ambassadors back to the West. Unlike William of Rubruck, the Franciscan who would later arrive, John has the good fortune to secure adequate translators: an indispensable precondition to a mission's success. Though John's Russian interpreter from Kiev proves insufficiently competent to translate Innocent IV's letters, translators are found at the *orda* of Batu Khan, who have Persian and Uighur ("Saracenic" and "Tartar"); and at Guyuk's *orda*, Duke Jerozlaus' knight Temer (Timur) and two clerics, along with Guyuk's secretaries, prove adequate to the task of multilingual translation, enabling the Great Khan's reply to Innocent to be translated, and acting as interpreters for John and his cohort (Dawson 55–6, 66–7, 70; Wyngaert I: 107–9, 123–4, 128).

John's embassy to the Mongols therefore might be counted as something of a success. Official letters have been exchanged between heads of state, and information acquired from knowledgeable local informants and personal observation. Innocent IV's envoy valuably tenders a full accounting of the enemy in all its individual and social irrationality and barbarism, and also a full account of the rationality and efficiency of the Mongol military machine: twin faces of the Mongol paradox for the West. While this new alien race might not be fully human or explicable to the West, the papal envoy's detailed, complex account effectively transforms the Mongol race and empire into an object of knowledge through which the West can scrutinize the nature of a race that has so successfully specialized in warfare.

John's journey also has other, perhaps nearly as important, achievements. Meeting with a warm reception and welcome on his return journey into Poland, Bohemia, and Russia, the papal envoy effects a reconciliation of Eastern Orthodox Christians to the Latin Church when Daniel of Galicia (later the first King of Rus) and his brother Vasilko, following discussion with their bishops and notables, decide to accept the authority of the Pope and the Roman Church (Dawson 70; Wyngaert I: 127). John's mission thus achieves a number of goals, not least of which is the accomplishment of an important milestone on the path to the Second Council of Lyons in 1272–4, at which Eastern and Western churches became reunified.

The *Ystoria* concludes with an authentication of John's account, by his naming of witnesses for his journey to the Mongols (Dawson 69–72; Wyngaert I: 127–30). Significantly absent from the narrative is any ill feeling toward Christians who fall outside the umbra of the Latin Church. Though John notices and mentions Eastern Christians he comes across in his journey, who are unquestionably heretics from the standpoint of the thirteenth-century Roman Church, he has no words of animosity for these Christians.

There is a clear enemy in the *Ystoria Mongalorum*: a race so alien that all efforts are focused on rendering them intelligible, with little energy to direct toward other forms of alterity that were of concern to Latin Christendom. Eight years after the journey of John of Plano Carpini, however, another Franciscan, William of Rubruck, would arrive at the heart of the Mongol empire, and see enemy aliens not only outside the borders of Christendom, but also infesting Christendom from within. He would express attitudes to these internal – Christian – aliens that visualize them in virtually racial terms.

"As if we were monsters": The Ethnoracial Empire Gazes Back

In the years after the valuable reconnaissance embassy of John of Plano Carpini, the Latin West accrued a most important piece of knowledge about the Mongols: *There were Christians among them.* These Christians were not merely captives from Europe living among the Mongols, and not only Eastern Orthodox Christians like those John met, but *Mongol Christians*. In the context of the thirteenth century, when the imperative to Christianize the world and extend the umbra of the Latin Church was a driving force, the knowledge that *Mongol Christians* existed on the steppes of Eurasia altered the meaning, and the West's understanding, of the new alien race.

The thirteenth century, as we saw in Chapter 1, was a remarkable period that witnessed a ramification of extraterritorial projects by the West, casting a long shadow over the centuries to come. In the aftermath of Christendom's loss in 1144 of Edessa, the first crusader colony established in *Outremer*, to Zengi of Mosul; and the loss in 1187 of the Kingdom of Jerusalem to Salah ad-Din Yusuf ibn Ayyub ("Saladin"), military expeditions to the Levant for territorial recapture and expansion urgently continued.

But energetic, activist popes also began to diffuse a "soft power" vision of Latin Christianity worldwide, seeking to extend Christendom's reach not only through geoterritorial military enterprises like crusading, but also through missions, conversionary preaching, chapter houses, churches, and foreign-language schools for proselytes.[37] In these latter endeavors, the new orders of mendicant friars established in the first quarter of the thirteenth century – the Order of the Friars Minor, or Franciscans, and the Order of the Preachers, or Dominicans – "represented the newly founded intellectual and evangelistic shock-troops of the Latin West" (Jackson and Morgan 47). "In the thirteenth century," as one scholar puts it, "the overall strategy of Christendom underwent modification": The battle now was "not only military but doctrinal" (Burns 1387).

James Muldoon's survey of Vatican registers traces the efforts of some sixteen popes in the thirteenth century and half a dozen in the fourteenth to extend the purview of Latin Christianity to North Africa, Mongol Eurasia, Eastern Europe, India, and China through a range of initiatives, including conversionary preaching, papal fiefs, papal treaties, and even economic threat (*Popes, Lawyers, and Infidels*). This is not to say, of course, that the hope of expanding Christendom's borders and purview through crusade and military adventure ended.[38] Even after numerous crusading failures in the thirteenth and fourteenth centuries, and after the last major gathering of international forces foundered at Nicopolis in 1396, the practice and ideology of crusading did not die (Atiya, *Nicopolis*; see also Atiya, *Later Middle Ages*, on late-medieval crusading).

It was Pope Innocent IV himself (1243–54), whose initiatives to the Mongols cast him in the role of leader of the Latin West, who developed the theoretical and legal basis for interventions worldwide: "the pope's responsibility for the souls of all men, Christian and non-Christian alike, justified papal intervention in the functioning of infidel societies" and "authorized him to send missionaries into their lands to instruct the nonbelievers in the proper way of worshiping God. Should an infidel ruler block the entry of peaceful Christian missionaries, the pope could order him to admit them or face an invasion by Christian armies" (Muldoon, *Popes* 9, 11).

Despite the legal and canonist basis for extending Christianity worldwide to the heathen, however, Europe was not in a position to dictate to the Mongol empire with military force. The papal bulls composed by Innocent IV and conveyed by John of Plano Carpini to Guyuk Khan thus only threaten the Great Khan with the prospective wrath of Divine Majesty in this world and the next, hinting darkly at nonspecific vengeance, not the might of Christian armies (Dawson 76; Rodenberg 75). Other methods were needed to bring the Mongol heathen into the fold. Where force was impractical, conversion had to be voluntary, the fruit of persuasion and preaching. In this, the conversionist project for the heathen multitudes would be greatly aided if Christianity, projected as universal, was already universal, and existed in some form in the far corners of the world.

Culture, always the rescuer of history, fanned the hope that Christianity was indeed always already universal. In Chapters 3 and 4, we noted the rise and international diffusion of one remarkable story that affirmed Christianity's manifest destiny of enfolding the planet. A brilliant fiction written in first-person voice, the *Letter of Prester John* asserted the existence of an avenging, puissant, Christian priest-king of India, who would come to help the West humble and defeat the enemies of the Cross of Christ ("*humiliare et debellare inimicos cruces Christi et nomen eius benedictum exaltare*"), his Christian empire in the Orient proving beyond the shadow of a doubt the truth of Christianity's universalism (Zarncke 78).

Invented in the mid-twelfth century after the fall of crusader Edessa, the Prester John legend acquired a luminous backstory and distinguished parentage in the early thirteenth century, courtesy of the genius of Wolfram von Eschenbach.[39] Slightly later in the thirteenth century, conviction in Prester John, we saw, helped to bring about the defeat of the Fifth Crusade, when the crusaders based a disastrous field decision on their belief in John's imminent arrival. And in Chapter 4, we examined yet another extraordinary cultural assertion of Christianity's universalism, when a sainted martyr venerated in the Latin West for a millennium – St. Maurice – was suddenly racialized into a black African in Magdeburg, Germany, diffusing thereafter through the countries of the West the memory that Africa, too, was a matrix of Christianity.

Without contradiction, then, the thirteenth-century drive to Christianize and evangelize the world went hand in glove with the belief that parts of the world *already were Christian*, thus rendering the project of converting the world into something that better resembled Christian Europe less of an impossible task.[40] I take up the discussion of Prester John's legend in greater detail in the section on *Mandeville's Travels* later in this chapter. For the present, we should note the role played by the myth of Prester John in contributing to an altered sense of the Mongols soon after the completion of Friar John's mission.

Despite John of Plano Carpini's prudent refusal to allow Mongol envoys to accompany him on his return to Innocent IV, the Mongol commander of West Asia sent two envoys in 1248 – a Turk, and Sergius or Sargis, a Nestorian Syrian – back with Innocent IV's Dominican envoys, Ascelin of Lombardia and Simon of St. Quentin – emissaries who did not reach the heart of the Mongol empire or the Great Khan, but who had delivered Innocent's bulls to Bayju, a West Asian regional subordinate (Dawson xix; de Rachewiltz, *Papal Envoys* 117).[41]

In the same year, Aljigiday, the senior Mongol official who had arrived at Bayju's camp in time to ensure the safety of Ascelin and Simon (unlike the Franciscans led by John of Plano Carpini, the Dominicans had severely antagonized the Mongols they met), sent a remarkable letter and two envoys, David and Mark – also Nestorian Christians – from Mosul to the King of France, Louis IX, who was at Nicosia in Cyprus, en route to undertake what history would call the Seventh Crusade (de Rachewiltz, *Papal Envoys* 120).

Aljigiday's letter, a masterpiece of diplomacy, magnanimously affirmed that "Latins, Greeks, Armenians, Nestorians, Jacobites and all worshipers of the Cross" were "one in the eyes of God and the Mongol emperor" (de Rachewiltz, *Papal Envoys* 120).[42] The distinguished Eurasian studies scholar Igor de Rachewiltz notes that the letter intriguingly added that Aljigiday's envoys were carrying an oral message that the King of France should heed (*Papal Envoys* 120).

Aljigiday – whom Guyuk Khan had appointed the supreme commander of the Mongol forces in West Asia, replacing Bayju – appears to have had reason not to commit the contents of the oral message in writing, since it apparently volunteered advance notice that Aljigiday was planning to besiege Baghdad the following year (de Rachewiltz, *Papal Envoys* 120). The envoys told Louis that Aljigiday hoped "the Franks would carry out a simultaneous attack on Egypt and, in this way, prevent the [Ayyubid] sultan [of Egypt] from coming to the aid of the Caliph [of Baghdad]" (de Rachewiltz, *Papal Envoys* 120).

If the report of Aljigiday's Nestorian emissaries, David and Mark, is trustworthy, the Mongol chieftain's orally delivered message suggests that John of Plano Carpini's mission had borne additional fruit, since the message raises the prospect of a de facto military alliance between Aljigiday and the crusader King of France (whose 1249 crusade did in fact target Egypt) against their common enemy, Islamdom. De Rachewiltz observes that Aljigiday knew of John's mission and the Great Khan's reply to the letters of Innocent IV delivered by John (*Papal Envoys* 117).

Mongols, it seemed, were now seizing the agency and the initiative after Christendom's embassies. Guyuk's surrogates were sending Christian emissaries to Christendom's Pope and to the sainted crusader King of France; and this regional commander, Aljigiday, not only made overtures suggesting joint military action, but was willing, it appears, to confide details of a military action being planned.

Louis IX was so buoyed by this overture, his crusader-biographer Jean de Joinville tells us, that he inducted the Dominican Andrew of Longjumeau, who was serving as translator for the interview between Louis and the Nestorian emissaries, to proceed to the Great Khan in a return embassy, bearing the famous and costly red tent-chapel, figurines relating the Christian story, fragments of the True Cross, and implements for mass (Shaw 198, 283; Jackson and Morgan 35).[43]

Louis's encouragement was likely fueled not only by the foreknowledge of Mongol intent against Muslims and the suggestion of a military partnership; David and Mark – perhaps on their own initiative – also informed the crusader king that *Guyuk Khan's mother was the daughter of Prester John*, and that both Guyuk and Aljigiday had converted to Christianity and intended to help the Christians recapture Jerusalem.[44]

Naïve as St. Louis's optimism might seem – Guyuk Khan's mother, after all, was Toreghana Khatun, whom John of Plano Carpini had met, and the Franciscan envoy had not remarked on any traces of Christianity, let alone a relationship to Prester John[45] – the Nestorian envoys' insistence on Christian Mongols at the apex of the Mongol empire buttressed an earlier shard of information from Sempad of Armenia (brother of King Hethoum I of Cilician Armenia and brother-in-law of the King of Cyprus), who had himself been an envoy to the Mongols in 1247–8. The letter Sempad wrote from Samarkand to his brother-in-law in Cyprus "stressed the importance of the Christian element among the Mongols. From these sources St. Louis learnt that Sartak, the son of Batu, was himself a Christian" (Dawson xxi).

It appeared that Christians were everywhere among the Mongols, and Andrew of Longjumeau's embassy for Louis produced the additional information that in Kazakhstan there survived a group of German slaves belonging to Buri, the son of Chagatay (another of Genghis' four sons), who were subsisting far from any Latin Christian ministry (de

Rachewiltz, *Papal Envoys* 123). However, Andrew's embassy for Louis did not itself meet with success. Guyuk Khan had died; his appointee Aljigiday sent Andrew on to Guyuk's widow, the regent Oghul Gamish, who, as we have seen, arrogantly treated Louis's gifts as tribute that signaled the French King's submission, and issued imperious demands for future tribute and obeisance.

Aljigiday himself would soon be replaced, and it would be Hulegu, the son of Toluy, Genghis' youngest – not Aljigiday – who would end the 500-year-old Abbasid Caliphate and destroy the strongholds of the Nizari Ismailis.[46] Jean de Joinville registers Louis's profound dismay on Andrew's return in 1251, and tells us the King of France bitterly regretted that he had ever sent envoys to the Mongols (Shaw 288).

We therefore see how the 1253 journey of the Franciscan William of Rubruck to the Mongol empire – a scant eight years after John of Plano Carpini's pathbreaking embassy – took place against a changed horizon of expectations.[47] The West now possessed the hopeful knowledge of Christians among the Mongols: Latin Christian captives from Europe, like Buri's German slaves; Eastern Christians, like those John had encountered; and, most importantly, Mongol Christians. An alien race that had seemed scarcely human to Matthew Paris and John of Plano Carpini even appeared to have Christians at the apex of their society: a discovery that softens and humanizes the alien, and brings Mongols closer to the rest of Christian *societas*.

However, the rude reception of Andrew of Longjumeau's embassy, and Louis IX's bitter disappointment on Andrew's return, did not encourage the French king to send further ambassadors bearing costly gifts. William of Rubruck therefore repeatedly tells every Mongol official he meets who asks after his purpose that his journey is *not* an embassy. Unfortunately, the nonofficial nature of his journey confers on William a different status from the papal envoy John, and will color William's reception by Mongol power. Without the privileges that are bestowed on official envoys, William will be more vulnerable than his predecessor, who had already keenly felt his expedition's vulnerability (Dawson 3; Wyngaert I: 27–8).

Mongols took the status of envoys with the utmost seriousness, seeing in envoys the leaders and lands they represented, and ensured that envoys to their empire were received under protection and were able to address Mongol rulers whenever they wished, and at whatever length they needed. In his *Itinerarium*, written for the benefit of Louis IX (unlike John's account, William's narrative is not addressed to all Christians but has only one addressee, Louis), William tells the French king that Mongols considered envoys to be so important they executed those who falsely claimed to be ambassadors (Jackson and Morgan 94, 187; Dawson 105, 160; Wyngaert I: 186, 256).[48] William assures the French king that he himself took great care never to say that he was Louis's ambassador (Jackson and Morgan 97; Dawson 106; Wyngaert I: 188).

But precisely because William was *not* an envoy, his access to the great personages he met – Sartak, Batu, and the new Great Khan Mongke – was narrowed, limited only to the times at which he was specifically sent for. On those occasions, moreover, he tells the French king, he had to keep silence till he was bidden to speak, and then he was only allowed to speak briefly (Jackson and Morgan 131; Dawson 127; Wyngaert I: 213). William's unofficial status thus unfortunately invites calamities early in his journey.

For example: At Sartak's court, after William and his fellow traveler, the Franciscan Bartholomew of Cremona, have been given an audience with the Khan and shown the

Khan the vestments, thurible, and holy books the missionaries had with them, Sartak's men decide to suborn the objects by insisting that they constitute gifts from William and his group (Jackson and Morgan 116, 119–20; Dawson 118, 120; Wyngaert I: 201–2, 204).[49] Despite the friar's terrified and strenuous efforts to prevent this, a number of vestments and books are taken from them, including a most beautiful illuminated psalter given them by the Queen of France (Jackson and Morgan 116, 119–20; Dawson 118, 120; Wyngaert I: 201–2, 204).

William laments that because they did not enjoy free access to Sartak, and there was none to show them justice, they had to endure the confiscation with patience (Jackson and Morgan 120; Dawson 120; Wyngaert I: 204).[50] John had complained about Mongol demands for gifts, of course, but the papal envoy and his men had not suffered the humiliation of having their treasured possessions stolen from them by their hosts. William's inability to protest to Sartak or petition the Khan thus affords a quick lesson in powerlessness early in his journey.[51]

In an alien land, William of Rubruck is an individual who represents neither king nor pope, striving to maintain dignity in the face of massively unequal relations with a foreign power to whom he and his men have to submit, and bearing only the authority of the faith he possesses, a faith he had mistakenly supposed already to be entrenched at high levels in the Mongol empire. Not being Louis's envoy, William cannot count on the respect shown to the representative of a king. Louis IX sends with William only one letter, and it is addressed to Sartak, the putatively Christian son of Batu, a letter which asks only permission for William "to preach the Gospel and give spiritual help to the Christians scattered in [Sartak's] domain" (de Rachewiltz, *Papal Envoys* 126).

Igor de Rachewiltz suspects the French king was not enthusiastic about William's journey, though no doubt sufficiently astute to see the value of further reconnaissance (*Papal Envoys* 126). There were no letters for William to convey to any higher authority than Sartak, the intended target of missionary zeal, not to his powerful father, Batu, nor to the Great Khan, Mongke. We are to see William's journey only as individual missionary endeavor, undertaken in the spirit of the thirteenth-century dream of making Christianity global by ministering to far-flung Christians and converting the native heathen everywhere.[52]

Peter Jackson and David Morgan suggest that one reason why the *Itinerarium* circulated so little – "Apart from the . . . use made of it in the geographical sections of [Roger] Bacon's *Opus Maius* [Greater Work] there is no evidence that anyone read it" – is "doubtless one more consequence of Friar William's unofficial status" (51). In contrast to the "numerous manuscripts of the standard version of Carpini's report . . . we may well have [Roger] Bacon to thank that [the *Itinerarium*] survived at all" (51).

A certain poignancy thus hovers over the efforts of William and his small group of men, who bravely make their way into what seems to them another world, seizing opportunities and improvising as best they can for their faith (Jackson and Morgan 97; Dawson 106; Wyngaert I: 187–8).[53] The grievous loss of vestments and books is soon compounded, moreover, by palpable disappointment when Sartak's representative, a Nestorian called Koyak, tells William that Sartak, to whom the Franciscan had come to minister, did not wish to be known as a Christian. William concludes from this that Sartak likely was not a Christian, though he says it is impossible really to know (Jackson and Morgan 120, 126; Dawson 121, 123; Wyngaert I: 205–9). And because Louis's letter contains certain matters which Sartak's men say Sartak dare not act on without the advice of his father, the Franciscans are sent on to the court of Sartak's powerful father and khan-maker, Batu (Jackson and Morgan 119; Dawson 119–20; Wyngaert I: 203–4).

There, as William stands waiting to be received by Batu – he's told not to speak until allowed, and then to be brief – William grows conscious that he and Bartholomew must present quite a spectacle to the Mongols. Unlike the papal envoy John, who, the *Itinerarium* says, had changed out of his habit and robed himself in accordance with his official position and status as papal ambassador, William and Bartholomew stood there in their Minorite habits, "bare-footed and heads uncovered, and we were a great gazing-stock for their eyes" (*"nudis pedibus in habitu nostro discoopertis capitibus et eramus spectaculum magnum in oculis eorum"* [Dawson 127; Wyngaert I: 213]).[54]

Shorn of the stature of the ambassador who is appropriately garbed and whose gaze upon the foreign produces an object of knowledge, William becomes more aware than his Franciscan predecessor of an exchange of gazes: Not only does he gaze upon the strange culture and society of the Mongols, but he also feels the gaze of the Mongol empire upon him and his men, staring back.[55]

William's sensitivity to the great spectacle he must form for Mongol eyes – barefoot, head uncovered, robed in the habit of the Minorites – discloses a capacity for self-consciousness. His *Itinerarium*, scholars agree, is an exceptionally rich document: Simultaneously travelogue, ethnography, cultural geography, and natural and social history, William's narrative maps geographic sites and natural features with close attention, and brings to life social environments and an entire cultural *habitus* on the steppe through thick description of an unparalleled kind in the thirteenth-century West.[56] His eye for the telling detail, his painterly eloquence, his ear for tone and irony, and his deft summation of character and event attest the literary genius of this Franciscan friar as singular indeed.[57] It is a pity the *Itinerarium* circulated so little in the Middle Ages.

However, one aspect of William's sensitivity – the ability to see through the eyes of the other – needs to be contextualized within the arc of his journey's trajectory, and historicized by the new receptivity in the West to reconceptualizing the Mongols. Tellingly, William's ability to visualize himself through Mongol eyes increases as his understanding of his own powerlessness also increases. At his first meeting with a powerful Mongol personage, Sartak, the Franciscan has honeyed words for the khan, but shows no interest in Sartak's position as the khan wrestles to make sense of this strange traveler from the West who bears a letter, but claims not to be the envoy of the king who issued that letter.

But by the time William reaches Batu's *orda*, after the keenly felt loss of vestments and treasured books and the anxiety he feels on seeing Batu's vast encampment, which looked like a great city stretching out into the distance (Jackson and Morgan 131; Dawson 126; Wyngaert I: 212–13), he becomes more attuned to the subject position of the next khan who is seated before him. William tells of an exchange of gazes from *two* subject positions, (first) Batu's and (then) his own: "He eyed us attentively and we did him" (Dawson 127; Jackson and Morgan 132; Wyngaert I: 214).[58] It has become profoundly in William's interest to understand what the gaze of the Mongol means.

When Batu tells William to raise his bowed head, the Franciscan quickly troubles to search out why: Either Batu Khan wished to scrutinize them more intently with a further look, or else perhaps he interpreted a bowed head as an evil omen (Jackson and Morgan 133–4; Dawson 128; Wyngaert I: 215). Whatever the reason, this vignette is striking for the

Franciscan's attempt to fathom the khan's motives and subjectivity, and underscores the need to continue the effort to see through the eyes of the other, as more dangers and ordeals arrive in William's journey.

However, William's ability to render Batu Khan scrutable is limited, and the Franciscan has no explanation when Batu decides to divide up the missionaries, sending William and his interpreter onward to Mongke – the new Great Khan – and sending back to Sartak's *orda* other members of the Franciscan group: a decision that fills William's fellows with dismay and fear (Jackson and Morgan 134; Dawson 128–9; Wyngaert I: 215–16). William requests that his companion, Bartholomew of Cremona, should accompany him to Mongke, and Batu assents to this but requires the French clerk from Louis IX, Gosset – the member of the party who handles the group's purse – to remain behind, a de facto hostage to fortune. When William tries to plead on Gosset's behalf, he is peremptorily told that Batu has made his decision.

At Batu's *orda*, then, a *second* demonstration of William's powerlessness and his inability to effect outcomes for his group has occurred, and he tells Louis that the members of his mission separated with tears (Jackson and Morgan 134; Dawson 129; Wyngaert I: 216). Insult follows injury. After Gosset's return, the Nestorian priests at Sartak's *orda* impudently adorn themselves in Sartak's presence with the vestments that belong to the Franciscans (Jackson and Morgan; Dawson 129; Jackson and Morgan 134; Wyngaert I: 216).[59] No longer able to hold his mission together, William embarks on a journey of severe tribulations and ordeals, including near-starvation, en route to the *orda* of the Great Khan Mongke.

William, who is a corpulent man despite the rigors of Minorite discipline, endures the privations of the three-and-a-half-month journey to Mongke with extreme difficulty (Jackson and Morgan 140; Dawson 132; Wyngaert I: 220–1). Food is rationed to one meal a day, Mongol-style, and meat is sometimes eaten half-cooked or almost raw because of the lack of fuel for cooking. Bartholomew is so hungry, he tells William – almost with tears in his eyes – that it seems to him he has never had anything to eat at all. There is no end to hunger and thirst, cold and exhaustion, and the guide given them by Batu is disgusted at having to conduct such insignificant men and shows the greatest disdain for the non-envoys he escorts (Jackson and Morgan 135, 141; Dawson 129, 133; Wyngaert I: 216, 221). Adding to the burden of disappointments, William has also been unable to acquire news of Buri's German slaves (Jackson and Morgan 145–6; Dawson 135–6; Wyngaert I: 224–5).[60]

When the Franciscans finally arrive at Mongke's *orda*, they are given a tiny hut as their dwelling; meanwhile their guide from Batu is honored by being assigned a large dwelling and given rice wine, and he receives many visitors (Jackson and Morgan 172; Dawson 149; Wyngaert I: 244). Light is shed, however, on the mystery of why William has been shuttled from one khan to another, up the hierarchy, when William is summoned and questioned closely at Mongke's court. Unconvinced that the friar's journey bears no diplomatic import of any kind, Sartak and Batu have somehow misconstrued Louis's letter as embedding a request for an army for help against the Muslims, a misconstrual that accounts for why Sartak felt unable to act on the letter's contents and why he and his father in turn sought counsel up the hierarchy (Jackson and Morgan 172; Dawson 149; Wyngaert I: 244).

William, who knew the gist of Louis's letter, tells the French king that he suspects the Armenian interpreters, with their intense loathing for Muslims, had rendered an aggressive translation of Louis's polite request to Sartak to be a friend of all Christians and an enemy of all enemies of the Cross, so that what should have sounded like a conventional formula in the rhetorical style of a crusader king famed for piety and saintliness had sounded instead like a bid for military aid (Jackson and Morgan 172; Dawson 149; Wyngaert I: 244).

William tends to blame translators and interpreters, of course, because of his experience with the incompetent translator the Franciscans have brought with them, *Omodeo* (*Homo Dei* = Abdullah), who is ineffectual and, indeed, dangerous because of his mistranslations and spontaneous fabrications.

But the episode also reveals William to be unable to enter Sartak's and Batu's *mentalité* and think from the perspective of the Mongols, who are driven by military pragmatism, just as William and Louis, as signaled by Louis's letter, are driven by religious ideology. The Mongols find it hard to believe that William's journey is without any diplomatic import at all, and we see later from the *Itinerarium*'s description of their shamans ("soothsayers") that their own holy men would never undertake a journey to the West like William's to the Mongols.[61] Two widely divergent perspectives and value systems are thus neatly characterized in this episode, which shows us the extent to which William is unable to think himself into the skin of the other.

The unanticipated outcome that the Mongols have not understood William's journey and intent thus signally alarms the Franciscan. He has repeatedly insisted that he is not an ambassador, and his hosts had not accorded him an ambassador's privileges. He was not required to perform an ambassador's gestures, such as genuflecting on being introduced to Batu Khan (Jackson and Morgan 132; Dawson 127; Wyngaert I: 214).

Yet when he arrives at the Great Khan's court, William is repeatedly asked – as if he were *still* Louis's representative – if Louis IX wants to make peace with the Mongol empire: the desire to "make peace" being code, as we saw from Guyuk Khan's and Oghul Gamish's replies to overtures from the West – and as Mongke's letter to Louis will make plain once more – for whether one wanted to offer submission and vassalage, and accept the suzerainty of the Mongols (Jackson and Morgan 172, 250; Dawson 149–50, 203–4; Wyngaert I: 244, 309).[62] Mongol pragmatism simply cannot grasp the concept of a journey driven by religious fervor alone: Why else has he come here if he does not wish to make peace, William is repeatedly asked with amazement (Jackson and Morgan 172; Dawson 150; Wyngaert I: 244).[63]

William takes shelter in a taciturn logic – he replies that he came because he was sent to Mongke by Batu – and, like the friar he is, shelters in the comfort of familiar gestures: He goes barefoot to see the Great Khan, not realizing he would have a long way to walk from his horse to the Khan's dwelling (Jackson and Morgan 173; Dawson 150; Wyngaert I: 245). It is midwinter – late December 1254 – on the frozen steppe, and the Mongols cannot believe their eyes. In his discombobulated state, William again becomes aware of how he and Bartholomew must look in the eyes of the other. Men gazed at them as if they were monsters, William tells the French king, and asked if they had no need of their feet, because they supposed the friars were going to lose their feet right away.[64]

To explain the bizarre spectacle of barefoot Europeans on the frozen midwinter Eurasian steppe, a Hungarian servant or slave of Mongke's tells the Mongols about the rules of the Minorites, but it is uncertain if the Order's rules make any sense to the listeners. Mongke's chief secretary and chancellor, Bolgay, a Nestorian Christian, interrogates the Franciscans closely, plies the Hungarian with many questions, and decides to send the friars back to their lodgings (Jackson and Morgan 173; Dawson 150; Wyngaert I: 245). They get to meet Mongke only on January 4, 1255.

We thus see that each time William shows an ability to look through the eyes of the ethnoracial other and understand how he looks to them, it has occurred in circumstances after he has been subjected to humiliation, ordeal, or terror.[65] This is not to say that William is without the capacity to understand the other at all – and I will discuss William's adaptive responses to Mongol culture, including "going native" in his consumption of *koumiss,* a beverage reviled by John of Plano Carpini – but only to acknowledge the circumstances that condition William's circumscribed ability to see through the other's eyes.

When you are not representing king or pope, but only yourself, in a mighty foreign empire far from your homeland, *the ability to see through the eyes of the ethnoracial other who possesses absolute power over you* – the power to take your belongings, hold your people hostage, supply or withhold food and drink, grant liberty or incarcerate you, and put you to death – *is an important skill in the interest of survival.*[66] That William has the astuteness to acquire important survival skills on the steppe can be seen, I will suggest, in his display of limited kinds of acculturation to Mongol society. For now, it is critical to note that to a European traveler from the West, *encountering the Mongols in their homeland is to encounter race in the form of absolute power:* a global race administering a global imperium, with the power of life and death at their command.

Prayers as Currency: The Gift-and-Service Economy of an Empire of Pragmatism

The ordeal of William, who has no official status or power to call on, is palpably greater than the ordeal of the papal envoy John of Plano Carpino, whose early mission to terra incognita had already been terrifying, as John made plain (Dawson 3; Wyngaert I: 27–8).[67] But William's exigent circumstances and his resilient personality eventually elicit from him a kind of saving resourcefulness, so that by slow degrees, the Franciscan friar learns yet another skill that never troubled John: how to enter the Asiatic gift economy of the Mongols when lacking material goods, and render himself and Bartholomew more intelligible and more valued to the masters of Eurasia.

The way that William enters the Mongol gift economy is to use *prayer as currency.* After he's delivered his modest gifts of Muscatel wine, biscuits, and fruit to Sartak (who immediately orders the gifts distributed to his men), and after Sartak's men have helped themselves to additional "gifts" in the form of the Franciscans' vestments and books, nothing remains to be presented to others. Arriving at Batu's *orda,* there's no mention of offering any gifts to the khan. But in the course of the journey from Batu to Mongke, their escort and guide (who begins by despising his charges, as we have seen) develops the enterprising habit of taking the friars to the *ordas* of wealthy Mongols to pray for them (Jackson and Morgan 141; Dawson 133; Wyngaert I: 221–2). Unlike his master, this guide from Batu seems to accept at face value that the Franciscans are what they say they are, that is, men dedicated to religion, like the monks of Asia, and not ambassadors. The narrative does not say if the guide profits from his deployment of the friars to wealthy clients, but we should observe that an idea has been planted which we will later see bearing fruit.[68]

Further along the journey, when the caravan must pass through a defile thought to be inhabited by demons who spirit men away, their Mongol guide again requests prayers, asking William and Bartholomew to recite some auspicious words that could put demons to flight (Jackson and Morgan 166; Dawson 146; Wyngaert I: 240). The friars loudly sing the *Credo*, and the party passes through safely. Thereafter, William says, the Mongols ask the friars to write down words that they could carry on their persons, and William obliges by writing down the *Credo* and the *Pater Noster* (Jackson and Morgan 166–7, Dawson 146; Wyngaert I: 240). William and Bartholomew have thus accidentally stumbled upon a commonplace of Far Eastern religions: the committing to script of words that are believed to possess power, which believers then carry on their persons, or commit to places of honor in their homes.

The prayer economy proceeds apace. On their journey, they also encounter the widow of one of Guyuk Khan's brothers, and she detains them a whole day, so that the friars can go to her home and "bless her" ("*benediceremus ei*"), that is, pray for her (Dawson 147; Morgan and Jackson 168 ["give her a blessing"]; Wyngaert I: 241). With all this prompting by the Mongols and with such cumulative requests for prayers, by the time the Franciscans arrive at Mongke's *orda*, a dynamic is in place that enables the friars *to see that they can bestow prayers as if they were gifts*. At his first audience with Mongke, William accordingly shows he has learnt an important lesson well: He begins by calling down a blessing on the Great Khan for a good and long life, proceeds to tell the Khan why he had left his homeland to go on a journey to see Sartak, and ends by requesting permission to stay in the Khan's domains to serve God *on behalf of the Khan, his wives, and his children* (Jackson and Morgan 179; Dawson 155; Wyngaert I: 250).[69]

Naming the Great Khan and his wives and children as beneficiaries of Franciscan spiritual labor, as well as the patrons of that labor, may or may not be what Louis IX had in mind, but William and Bartholomew are a long way from Europe and have come to the heart of the Mongol empire without, as William says, gold or silver or precious stones to present to Mongke – they can present only themselves, to serve God and pray to Him for the Khan (Jackson and Morgan 179; Dawson 155; Wyngaert I: 251). It is an inspired declaration, from a gifted, silver-tongued Franciscan. The effect is slightly undermined by Abdullah, the Franciscans' inept and intoxicated translator – Mongke replies a mite testily that he has no need of their gold or silver, because his power and Batu's are everywhere, like the sun – but William smoothly recovers with a declaration that he meant only to say he wanted to honor the Great Khan with both temporal and spiritual gifts (Dawson 155; Jackson and Morgan 180; Wyngaert I: 251).

Spiritual gifts: What better treasure could Franciscan friars offer to Mongol men of power? An imperishable and durable commodity, unnecessary to purchase with coin – and the specialty, moreover, of the religious – such gifts could be an infinite resource, infinitely renewed, and truly a godsend. The supernatural economy of prayer can even be made materially visible, since we have already seen that prayers can be written down for the recipient, materialized in script. John of Plano Carpini perhaps had little need to offer such gifts, and might have deemed it undignified to be the prayer-servitor of heathen barbarians who were scarcely human. But in the interval between John's mission and William's, the Mongols were in the process of becoming more human, if still barbaric, and William was more exigently in need than John of a way to negotiate with absolute power.

William's adaptation to the social system of the Mongols is thus measurable by innovative, if not conversionary, achievements. The most striking achievement is his success in entering and participating in the socioeconomy of the steppe. Once he has made himself intelligible to Mongol men of power in this way, like the other holy men – Nestorian,

Armenian, Buddhist, Taoist, Shamanist, animist, Muslim – who are in attendance at Mongke's *orda*, William and Bartholomew are allowed to stay, travel with the *orda*, and deploy prayers as the Mongols see fit in daily life.[70]

They are obliged to say a blessing and sing when the Great Khan's chief wife ceremonially imbibes alcoholic beverage, and they pray for a second *khatun* when she is sick and help to heal her with rhubarb, holy water, and prayer (Jackson and Morgan 191, 198–9; Dawson 163, 168–9; Wyngaert I: 260, 267). They pronounce blessings on Mongke repeatedly (Dawson 154, 164; Wyngaert I: 250, 262). Traveling with the *orda* as spiritual camp-followers, the Franciscans even turn into weather-workers at one point, when they are asked to pray for a storm, with its severe cold and wind, to abate – and they do, and it does (Jackson and Morgan 211; Dawson 177; Wyngaert I: 278).

The friars integrate well into the gift-and-service economy of the steppe, and they are paid for their work with garments and tunics because they will not accept gold or silver (Jackson and Morgan 251; Dawson 205; Wyngaert I: 310).[71] As they receive this thoroughly Mongol medium of compensation, they are of course required to say a prayer for the Great Khan (Jackson and Morgan 251; Dawson 205; Wyngaert I: 310).[72] Finally, after an extended stay of more than six months, and many acts of prayer and blessing, the Mongols accept that William is not an ambassador after all, and Mongke's scribes tell him the Great Khan sees that he has only come to Karakorum to pray for him, like many another priest (Jackson and Morgan 230; Dawson 190; Wyngaert I: 293).[73]

Besides his deft entry into the economy of exchange relations, William's acculturation to Mongol society can also be traced through his gustatory adaptations. Though he never seems to acclimate to the Mongol diet beyond a liking for meat broth, William does come by degrees to enjoy *koumiss*, the fermented mare's milk that is a Mongol staple, and can even – like a connoisseur – identify the different kinds of *koumiss* he comes across; describe at length how *koumiss* is made and what one version of it, *airak*, tastes like; and note how that taste lingers and transforms pleasingly on the tongue into the taste of almond milk, greatly delighting the inner man (Jackson and Morgan 81–3, 98, 99, 135; Dawson 98–9, 107, 108, 130; Wyngaert I: 177–9, 189, 217).

So accustomed does William become to *koumiss*, in fact, that during his return journey from Mongke's, on reaching the encampment of Baachu – the commander of the forces stationed at the Aras river – and being given new and special wine by Baachu (who himself drinks *koumiss*), he tells Louis he would have preferred *koumiss* instead, which he found a more satisfying drink (Jackson and Morgan 264; Dawson 212; Wyngaert I: 321).[74]

Overall, William seems to notice a far greater range of alcoholic beverages on the steppe than had ever impinged on the consciousness of John of Plano Carpini. John mentions mead and wine, but William notices rice ale, red wine (like the wine of La Rochelle, he tells Louis), rice mead, white *koumiss*, black *koumiss*, a honey drink called *boal* or *bal*, another rice mead or wine called *terracina*, and a beverage made from rice, millet, wheat, and honey, which is clear like wine (Jackson and Morgan 76, 178–9, 191, 209; Dawson 96, 154, 163, 176; Wyngaert I: 175, 249, 260, 276).[75]

The bacchanalian centerpoint that dramatizes Mongol procurement of and delight in the world's variety of alcoholic beverages is a magnificent silver tree at the entrance to Mongke's palace in Karakorum, the capital of the Mongol empire, made by the Parisian master goldsmith and Mongol slave William Boucher, which cunningly positions pipes issuing from four silver lions and other pipes guarded by gilded serpents, from which flow four kinds of alcoholic liquid into silver basins (Jackson and Morgan 209–10; Dawson 176; Wyngaert I: 276–7).[76]

This large silver-tree-magic-fountain – an extravagant drink-dispensing automaton that features not only lions and gilded serpents, but also an angel holding a trumpet at its apex (a trumpet that sounds) and branches, leaves, and fruit all fashioned of silver – composes a new image to guide how a reader of William of Rubruck's *Itinerarium*, along with Louis IX, might view the Mongols. That is to say, while the *Itinerarium* continues to vilify Mongols as barbaric in their habits, eating all manner of foul things, and frequently inebriated, intertwined with the *Itinerarium*'s descriptions of their execrable social habits are also descriptions of the *art* and *artistry* that are a part of Mongol cultural life.

For instance: William relates group drinking in which men and women vie with one another in ways of imbibing that the friar finds truly disgusting and gluttonous (Jackson and Morgan 77; Dawson 97; Wyngaert I: 176). But he also emphasizes the fact that *music* accompanies the drinking: Indeed, he tells Louis that by the entrance of each dwelling is found not only *koumiss*, but also a musician positioned with his instrument, and when the master of the house begins to drink, the musician strikes up his instrument and plays (Jackson and Morgan 77; Dawson 96–7; Wyngaert I: 175–6).[77]

Feasts are accompanied by music, hand-clapping, and dancing, and when William and his men first meet Sartak, the Mongol khan is sitting in state with a lute-like instrument being played and people dancing before him (Jackson and Morgan 77, 115; Dawson 97, 117; Wyngaert I: 176, 200). Another chieftain he meets is holding a stringed instrument when William is allowed into his presence (Jackson and Morgan 100; Dawson 108; Wyngaert I: 190). While William did not see actual European instruments such as lutes and viols, he tells the French king that he saw *many* other kinds of musical instruments unknown to Europe. For all their unhygienic and immoral habits, can Mongols still be not-quite-human, bestial animals if music and artistry have an integral place in their culture?

We also see prominently featured in the *Itinerarium* the importance of *fabric and robes* in Mongol society. Just as nomad culture privileges movable art like music, treasure in nomad society tends to take the form of what is readily movable, and can serve multiple functions. In the sumptuous silks and brocades (*nasij*) and the rich garments so highly esteemed by the Mongols, art and treasure efficiently converge. For Mongol society, fabric can serve as currency, constituting acceptable coin in trade relations, and also as tribute.[78] Fabric is also valued as art, for its intricacy and beauty, resplendently lining the ceiling and walls of a *ger*: Mongke's *ger*, William tells Louis IX, is completely covered on the inside with cloth of gold (Jackson and Morgan 177; Dawson 153; Wyngaert I: 249).[79]

Silks, velvets, brocade, and other precious weaves can be made into prestige-enhancing garments that confer status and recognition on the wearer; they can also be used to reward loyal service, and enable the retinue of a chieftain or khan to be distinguished at a glance through color and type of cloth. Cloth – simultaneously art, treasure, livery, and more – thus comprises a far more pragmatic kind of wealth than vaults of gold and silver. So while an Anglo-Saxon king might earn his kenning-name of *ring-giver* by distributing treasure in the mead hall to his *comitatus* in the form of metal ornament, at his feast in Karakorum the Great Khan Mongke distributes treasure to his nobles in the form of rich robes (Jackson and Morgan 209; Dawson 175; Wyngaert I: 276).[80]

At the same time that we see music and art highlighted in a Western description of Mongol society, moving that society in the direction of humanized civilization, we also see that William, unlike John of Plano Carpini or Matthew Paris, tellingly does not impute *cannibalism* – that most distinctive criterion for distinguishing between social groups that are human and civilized, and those that are subhuman and uncivilized – to Mongols. Instead, William shifts the attribution of cannibalism to another steppe people, the Cumans or Kipchaks, a Turkic nomad confederation defeated by the Mongol empire – which suggests that while the West has to find cannibals somewhere, as an aid to defining levels of civilization, who gets to play the role of the cannibal shifts (Jackson and Morgan 70; Dawson 93; Wyngaert I: 171).

Admirably, in his encounters with race on the steppe, William shows an ability to disaggregate the capacious group designation of the Latin West, "Tartars," into a number of constituent ethnoracial groups: Tartar, Karakitay, Kereit, Merkit, Uighur, Mongol, Tangut, Naiman, and Kirgiz (Jackson and Morgan 120, 122–4, 157–60, 167, 200–1; Dawson 121, 122, 142–3, 147, 170; Wyngaert I: 205, 206–8, 233–5, 240, 269).[81] William understands that Mongols are not, in fact, Tartars (Jackson and Morgan 120, 124, 125; Dawson 121, 122, 123; Wyngaert I: 205, 207–8), and finds identifying markers for some groups through their written script (culture) and for others, such as the tall and swarthy Tanguts (Jackson and Morgan 154, 159, 203–4; Dawson 140, 142, 172; Wyngaert I: 231, 234, 271), through their physiognomy (nature). Unlike John of Plano Carpini, William is also highly skeptical that Pliny's, Solinus', and Isidore's monstrous races exist in Eurasia, and, when told a tall tale of similar ilk – of a country beyond Cathay where a person who enters remains the same age forever – he dismisses it with disbelief (Jackson and Morgan 201–3; Dawson 170–1; Wyngaert I: 269–70).[82]

The Franciscan also debunks the myth of Prester John, identifying the puissant emperor so beloved of the West as merely a Nestorian chieftain among the Naimans, a brother to the Ong Khan, a pastoralist-herder chieftain defeated by Genghis.[83] Revealingly, William raises the topic of Prester John as an opportunity to castigate Nestorian Christians, whom he blames for hyperbolically enlarging the myth of Prester John, making of it ten times more than the truth and fabricating a great rumor out of nothing, which, William says, the Nestorians "from these parts" typically do (Jackson and Morgan 122; Dawson 122; Wyngaert I: 206). Those villainous Nestorians, he tells Louis, are also to blame for spreading the belief that Sartak, Mongke, and Guyuk Khan are Christian, when the truth is that they are not Christian (Jackson and Morgan 122; Dawson 122; Wyngaert I: 206).

William also remarks on a panorama of other races and peoples, and the internationalism of the steppe in the wake of *Pax Mongolica* (Jackson and Morgan 144–5, 146–7, 173–4, 182–3, 212, 213; Dawson 135, 136, 151, 157, 177, 179; Wyngaert I: 224, 225–6, 245–6, 252–3, 278–9, 280).

The "European colony" comprised Frenchmen, Germans, Hungarians, Slavs and at least one Englishman, called Basil.[84] They intermingled with Alans, Georgians, Armenians, Persians, Turks, and Chinese. All these people worked for the Mongols in various capacities: Europeans, West Asians, Persians and Turks mostly as craftsmen, merchants and scribes; the Chinese as artisans, especially potters and builders.

(de Rachewiltz, *Papal Envoys* 134)

John of Plano Carpini also noted an internationalism of races on the steppe, especially at the *kuriltay* of Guyuk Khan, but William's ability to see a variety of steppe ethnoracial groups rather than a single monolithic population of "Tartars" or Mongols arises in part from the ways in which his mission differs from that of John. Unlike John, the ambassador from the West who was treated as a visiting envoy, William lives and travels with the Great Khan's *orda*, serving as one of the *orda*'s religious camp-followers – an intimacy that grants an inside–outside position more favorable than John's for participant-observation, and for imparting finer-grained, on-the-ground details of Mongol society.

We should also remember that William's mission to the Mongols, following in the footsteps of others in the course of eight years, has none of the critical urgency of John's, whose task it was to ascertain, gauge, and describe the Mongol threat in order to prepare the Latin West for war. Precisely because his voyage is *not* a reconnaissance mission, William is in a position to cast a more leisurely eye and to offer a more nuanced view of lived Mongol reality than John, including a finer-grained appreciation of gender-based divisions of labor.

"Heretics," a Virtual Race in the Thirteenth Century: Racing Nestorian Christians

That sense of lived reality to which William, more than John, has close-up access results in unexpected developments. For instance: Even as the Mongols continue to represent *absolute power* on the steppe, the *absolute alterity* that Mongols incarnated for John of Plano Carpini is attenuated for the Franciscan missionary who lives among them and travels with them, dispensing prayers and blessings for his Mongol hosts. Instead, as Mongols become increasingly familiar to William – whose accumulation of data on their society is the largest, most detailed, and most impressive before Marco Polo's account at the end of the thirteenth century – the *Itinerarium*'s sense of the alien, and of otherness, shifts and adapts. The place of the other gradually enlarges to become inhabited by *Christian* otherness as well, when William discovers the horrifically mixed hybridities of steppe Christianities, which mingle practices considered heretical in the thirteenth-century Latin West with what appear in Franciscan eyes to be pagan darkness and even demonism.

Creepily, William finds Nestorian priests participating in divination, reciting psalms over twigs (Jackson and Morgan 199; Dawson 169; Wyngaert I: 268). At the dwelling of the *khatun* the Franciscans help to heal, he discovers an evil thing, a silver chalice hanging on the wall (pillaged from some church in Hungary, William supposes), full of ashes, on top of which is a black stone (Jackson and Morgan 199; Dawson 169; Wyngaert I: 267). Intermixtures of Christian and shamanist practices infect the behavior of all sorts of Christian religious men on the steppe. A Russian deacon practices divination, and Sergius, the Armenian monk who is first introduced by the *Itinerarium* piously wearing a hairshirt and chains, and with whom William and Bartholomew come to share a dwelling, also has a shaman perform divination for him (Jackson and Morgan 220; Dawson 183; Wyngaert I: 285).[85]

Igor de Rachewiltz is surprised at the Franciscan's condemnation of his fellow Christian clerics for these and other offenses:

> During the several months spent at Möngke's *ordo* and at Karakorum the Franciscan friars often found themselves in the company of Nestorian clerics, taking part in their ceremonies and in the religious services for the imperial family ... But at heart [William] resented being assimilated to the Nestorian clergy, whom he severely criticized both on account of their ignorance and of their morals. His bitter complaints about their corrupt practices,

such as bigamy, simony, usury and drunkenness, fill page after page of the *Itinerary*. It is true that the Nestorian beliefs and practices noted by William show the influence of the Mongol milieu and also some contamination by Buddhism (apparently one of the monks accepted the doctrine of transmigration of souls in animals); however, most of his criticism is far too severe. Considering that Mongol Nestorianism had been cut off from its source in Mesopotamia for so long, it is remarkable how little it had departed from its fundamental teaching. William's complaints stem chiefly from the frustration he experienced in carrying out his ministry and in reforming what he mistakenly regarded as a debased form of Christianity.

(*Papal Envoys* 136)

William's condemnation of the Nestorians is indeed extreme: founded both on moral objections, and on detestation of Nestorian doctrine and practices deemed heretical by the Roman Church. Nestorians did not abide by the Latin Church's proscription of marriage for priests, and moreover practiced simony (a century later, of course, Latin churchmen themselves would be condemned for simony, and Chaucer's *Canterbury Tales* would famously dramatize the fact that priests with children also infested the Latin West, but William is a thirteenth-century purist). William inveighs mightily against the Manichean coloration of Nestorian beliefs, Nestorian differences of liturgy and ritual, the acculturation of Nestorian priests to Mongol customs such as the frequent consumption of alcohol, and even the fact that the Nestorian cross is not a crucifix proper (Jackson and Morgan 196, 207; Dawson 166, 175; Wyngaert I: 264, 275).[86]

Those miserable priests, William intones, sang and howled, got drunk, know nothing, and are completely corrupt (Jackson and Morgan 163, 191, 196, 199; Dawson 144, 163, 167, 169; Wyngaert I: 238, 260, 264–5, 267–8). Even the wisest priest among them, William snorts derisively, has asked him about the transmigration of souls, a concept that clings tenaciously to religions in the East (Jackson and Morgan 232; Dawson 192; Wyngaert I: 295). All this heresy and syncretism amount to divergences from the proper path of Christianity that are so profoundly disturbing to William that he reserves for the Nestorians a condemnation more absolute and fundamental than even his condemnations of the Mongols themselves. *The lives of the Mongols,* William tells Louis, *and even the pagan* tuins (Buddhist and/or Taoist monks), *are more innocent than the lives of the Nestorians* (Jackson and Morgan 164; Dawson 145; Wyngaert I: 238).[87]

Heretical Christians, it seems, can constitute a kind of virtual race, set apart by absolute and fundamental differences within Christianity. The setting-aside of people as separate, alien, and other here seems not to require differences *between* Christianity and other religions such as Islam (as we saw in Chapter 3) or Judaism (as we saw in Chapter 2). In Chapter 1, with the example of the Irish – a people who were among the earliest in Europe to embrace Roman Catholicism – we saw how distinctions of a fundamental kind could be posited, even among Christians. The Anglo-Norman perspective articulated by Gerald of Wales insinuated divisions even *within* the Roman Catholic community of faith. Postulations of this kind, we saw, are made on the basis of behavior, habits, and customs, and do not require physiognomy, color, or the attribution of somatic essences to establish a sense of the target group's difference and otherness. It should surprise us little, then, that if absolute and fundamental differences can be posited even within Latin Christianity, Nestorian Christians should then be absolutely and fundamentally set apart – virtually racialized – by their differences from the Latin Christian norm.

Most vexing of all, perhaps, was the fact that Nestorians were ubiquitous in Eurasia. Dispersing into West Asia in the fifth century, after the arguments of Nestorius, the former patriarch of Constantinople, were declared heretical by the Council of Ephesus in 431, adherents of the Church of the East spread throughout Eurasia, East Asia, and South Asia, reaching northern China in 635 during the Tang dynasty, as Chinese and Syriac inscriptions on the famed Tang-era Nestorian Stele, rediscovered in the seventeenth century, attest. The St. Thomas Christians of India are the result of Nestorian missionary efforts, which also gave teeth to the idea that the evangelical and bellicose Prester John was the emperor of India.[88]

Nestorians were everywhere in the world that Franciscans and Dominicans had begun to explore. The *Itinerarium* reports that Nestorians already had a presence in fifteen cities in China, including a bishopric in Beijing (Jackson and Morgan 163; Dawson 144; Wyngaert I: 237). On their way to Mongke, William and his group come across a completely Nestorian village (Jackson and Morgan 165; Dawson 145; Wyngaert I: 238–9). The Nestorian church at Karakorum, the Mongol capital, is impressively large and beautiful, its ceiling covered with silk brocade (Jackson and Morgan 213; Dawson 178; Wyngaert I: 279). Thanks to centuries of missionary efforts by Nestorians, in the thirteenth-century Christianity is, indeed, global.

As importantly, though Louis IX may have been misled by Nestorian and Armenian emissaries into believing Guyuk and Sartak to be Christian,[89] Christians were indeed to be found in the Golden Family of Genghis Khan's descendants, especially among the mothers, wives, and children of the khans. William witnesses John of Plano Carpini's "Sorocan" – Sorghaghtani Bekhi, the Nestorian Christian mother of the Great Khan Mongke – continuing to be honored after her death and receiving blessings for her soul, with her youngest son, Arik-Boke – Mongke's youngest brother – continuing to live in her *orda*, and being raised in Christian practices (Jackson and Morgan 212, 223; Dawson 178, 185; Wyngaert I: 279, 287). Arik-Boke knows the Gospels, makes the sign of the cross when he sees William approach carrying the cross, and silences Muslims who blaspheme against Christ with the declaration that the Messiah is God (Jackson and Morgan 212, 224–5; Dawson 178, 185–6; Wyngaert I: 279, 288).

Mongke's eldest son, too, is tutored by a Nestorian, David, and shows deep respect for the cross, prostrating himself before it in adoration and honoring it with an elevated position (Jackson and Morgan 194, 207; Dawson 165, 174; Wyngaert I: 262–3, 275). A deceased wife of Mongke who had been deeply loved by him had been a Nestorian Christian, and her daughter was honored by being made the mistress of her mother's court (Jackson and Morgan 178; Dawson 154; Wyngaert I: 249). This daughter receives the Franciscans with joy, reverently adores the cross, and places it in a prominent position on a cloth of silk when William visits (Jackson and Morgan 195; Dawson 166; Wyngaert I: 263).

Not surprisingly, the Great Khan's current chief wife herself attends services at the Nestorian church, showers Christian religious men with gifts, and shows great respect for Christian ritual; William tells Louis that she may have been baptized according to Nestorian rites (Jackson and Morgan 189; Dawson 162; Wyngaert I: 258–9). The wife who is ill, and whom the Franciscans help to heal, also shows deep respect for the cross, kneeling and prostrating herself before it six times (Jackson and Morgan 195; Dawson 165; Wyngaert I: 263).[90]

Of even greater strategic importance than the infiltration of Christianity into the Great Khan's family is how Christianity is rooted among the officials of the Great Khan's administration. Mongke's chancellor, chief secretary, and chief scribe, Bolgay, is a Nestorian Christian – like his predecessor whom John of Plano Carpini met, Chingay, who was the chancellor and chief secretary of the previous Great Khan, Guyuk (Jackson and Morgan 173; Dawson 150; Wyngaert I: 245).[91] Immensely influential in the empire, Bolgay's counsel is followed in almost all matters (Jackson and Morgan 173; Dawson 150; Wyngaert I: 245).

Bolgay judges and sentences capital offenses, and, fortunately for the Franciscans, it is this Nestorian Christian chancellor who makes the decision not to execute or punish Bartholomew of Cremona for stepping on the threshold of the Great Khan's dwelling – a capital offense in the belief system of Mongol culture, as both the *Ystoria Mongalorum* and the *Itinerarium* make plain (Jackson and Morgan 194; Dawson 165; Wyngaert I: 262). When a distinguished Nestorian monk comes to visit, Bolgay houses him in a place of honor, in front of Bolgay's own *orda*, and the Great Khan sends his children to receive the monk's blessing (Jackson and Morgan 252; Dawson 205–6; Wyngaert I: 311). Mongke's interpreter is also Nestorian, and is in charge of raising one of his daughters (Jackson and Morgan 179, 180; Dawson 154, 155; Wyngaert I: 250, 251).

Nor were Nestorians prominent only in Eurasia. The chief wife of Hulegu – Mongke's brother, who destroys the 500-year-old Abbasid caliphate in Baghdad and the strongholds of the Nizari Ismailis to found the Mongol Ilkhanate of Persia – is Dokuz Khatun, a Nestorian Christian famed for her piety and goodness, with a reputation as a second St. Helena. Dokuz Khatun is the mother of the Ilkhan Abaga, who famously sought alliances with Edward I of England against the Mamluks of Egypt and who himself married a Christian, the Byzantine princess Maria Palaiologina, a natural daughter of the Byzantine emperor Michael VIII.[92] One of Hulegu's chief generals, Kitbuka, was also a Nestorian Christian.

The thirteenth century thus bore witness to the ubiquity and dispersal of Nestorian Christianity across the Mongol world. From Cathay, two distinguished Nestorian Christian monks, one of whom became Patriarch of the Nestorian Church, and the other of whom was known for his saintliness and piety – Markos, or Mar Yaballaha III, and Rabban Sauma – made journeys westward. Later in this chapter I discuss Rabban Sauma's account of his extraordinary voyage to visit the holy places and relics of Christianity and meet the crowned heads of Europe and the Roman Curia – a remarkable record of how the Latin West appears in the eyes of a Nestorian Christian monk and envoy from the farthest East (Budge).

To the missionaries of the Roman Church who were beginning to make journeys of great hardship to distant lands for their faith, however, the ubiquity of such Christianity was not always welcome. The entrenchment of Nestorian churches, priests, monks, and followers across the world proved that Christianity was, indeed, global. But this global Christianity, which confirmed the universality of Christendom, was the *wrong kind of Christianity*: a heretical, deviant, syncretist travesty of the faith.

William is thus alternately elated and repelled in his encounters with eastern Christianities. On the one hand, he tells Louis he is overjoyed when he finds a church in the Nestorian village en route to Mongke's *orda*, and he and Bartholomew loudly sing *Salve Regina* (Hail, Queen [of heaven]) as they enter it (Jackson and Morgan 165; Dawson 145; Wyngaert I: 239). On the other hand, William is deeply disturbed at having to associate with Nestorian and Armenian coreligionists when they collectively attend on Mongke and his family, and only after distressed deliberation does he decide to say mass in the beautiful Nestorian church at Karakorum on Maundy Thursday for the benefit of the international community of Christians loyal to the Roman Church who are gathered at the Mongol capital (Jackson and Morgan 214–16; Dawson 179–80; Wyngaert I: 281–2).

On that uneasy occasion, William tells Louis, he used a very large Nestorian silver chalice and paten, in a baptistery assigned to him by the Nestorians, at an altar sanctified with Nestorian chrism; and he said mass and gave Holy Communion to the people with, *he hoped* ("*sicut spero*"), the blessing of God (Jackson and Morgan 216; Dawson 180; Wyngaert I: 282).

The discomfiting *convivencia* of William's performance during Holy Week witnesses another factor in the Franciscan's intensely negative reactions to his Nestorian coreligionists. William tells Louis that the Nestorian priests at Karakorum baptized *sixty people* on Easter eve (Jackson and Morgan 216; Dawson 180; Wyngaert I: 282). By contrast, over the course of their six-month sojourn with Mongke, the Franciscans manage to baptize only *six people*, one tenth of what the Nestorian priests accomplish in one day (Jackson and Morgan 253; Dawson 206; Wyngaert I: 312).

We see thus that not only were Nestorian priests heretical, they were also *successful* compared to the Franciscan missionaries. Igor de Rachewiltz is astute to recognize that part of William's condemnation of Nestorian priests likely issues from a sense of his own limited accomplishments, his intense rivalry with the Nestorians, and what looked to the Franciscans like the failure of their mission.[93]

The deep rivalry between Franciscans and Nestorians is replayed at the end of the thirteenth century and the beginning of the fourteenth when the indefatigable, courageous, and redoubtable John of Monte Corvino makes his way to China as the legate of Pope Nicholas IV, and there singlehandedly builds a church at Khanbalik (Beijing), the northern capital of the Mongol Yuan dynasty; learns the "Tartar" language (either Mongolian or Uighur); translates the whole of the New Testament and the psalter into that language; and in the course of a dozen years baptizes some *six thousand people* by 1305 (Dawson 224–7; Wyngaert I: 245–51).[94] Later made Archbishop of Khanbalik by his successors, Bishop Andrew of Perugia and Bishop Peregrine, John of Monte Corvino even converts to Roman Christianity and baptizes a Nestorian Ongut princeling by the name of George who is putatively of the family of Prester John (Dawson 225–6; Wyngaert I: 348).[95]

For John of Monte Corvino, even more than for William of Rubruck, the place of the alien other is not so much occupied by Mongols as it is by the Nestorian Christians who are his rivals and antagonists. John's second letter from Khanbalik admiringly tells the Pope that no king or prince in the world is the equal of the Mongol Khan of Cathay, and his third letter says the Khan esteems and honors John before all other prelates and envoys (Dawson 227, 230; Wyngaert I: 350–1, 353–4).

But the Nestorians, he complains, behave in a very un-Christian manner, persecuting him grievously, bribing and corrupting people against him, and slandering him over the course of more than five years, which put him in jeopardy of his life and prevented him from baptizing 30,000 more souls (Dawson 224–5; Wyngaert I: 346–7).[96]

By the greatest irony, therefore, for the mendicant Franciscans of the later thirteenth and fourteenth centuries – a period in which the dream of a universal Christendom is most intensely alive and vital – it is the (heretical) *Christians* they meet in the far reaches of the world whose otherness makes them over into a foreign and condemned virtual race.

The highlight of William's sojourn at Mongke's *orda*, modern readers of the *Itinerarium* sometimes feel, is the disputation that is staged at Karakorum toward the end of the sojourn, a debate among the representatives of three faiths, in which the Franciscan participates at the request of the Great Khan. The irony and queerness of this disputation on the steppe cannot be emphasized enough.

Interreligious disputations that were staged in the thirteenth-century Latin West between representatives of Judaism and Christianity have long been recognized as Christian "set-ups" that did not involve "intellectual confrontation on an even footing," but favored the scholar or Dominican debating on behalf of Christianity over the rabbi attempting to argue for Judaism (Kruger, *Spectral Jew* 177–80). In Christian Europe, especially in Catholic Spain, the consequences of defeat for the rabbis, and their families and communities, could be punitive and deadly.

Here, however, was a Franciscan debating the faith in a context where he did not have the might of state power or church power behind him, but instead found himself in an environment of religious pluralism and tolerance where other religions – shamanism, Buddhism, Islam – were already well entrenched. Unlike the staged performances in Europe, the debate here was instituted at the behest of an alien potentate with no vested interest in the outcome, but with a curiosity consonant with the culture of religious toleration for which the Mongol empire was famed.[97] Uncannily familiar in one way, yet queerly estranged and defamiliarized by context and lineaments of power, *this* particular disputation – a historic occurrence – was not skewed in favor of Christianity.[98]

Nonetheless, William tells Louis he won the debate handily against the *tuins* (Buddhists and/or Taoists) and Muslims, and reports on his own excellent rhetoric, arguments, and words at length. He does not report in equal detail and at similar length the arguments made by the representatives of the other faiths, but we must accept his judgment of his victory as accurate. After the main disputation, the Nestorians expound the Christian faith, and everyone listens intently and without contradiction, William reports – but, disappointingly, no one says that he believes, or wants to become a Christian (Jackson and Morgan 231–5; Dawson 191–4; Wyngaert I: 294–7).[99]

William's disappointment at the little that his arduous and brave mission to the steppe manages to accomplish is poignant to any sympathetic reader of the *Itinerarium*. Sartak did not welcome his mission, did not want to be known as a Christian, and might not even have been a Christian (Jackson and Morgan 120, 126; Dawson 121, 123; Wyngaert I: 205, 209). The Franciscans baptized only six new souls for the Latin faith, and reconciled one Nestorian priest to Catholic last rites and communion on his deathbed (Jackson and Morgan 219, 253; Dawson 182–3, 206; Wyngaert I: 284, 312).

Despite William's eloquence, nobody was converted as a result of his successful participation in the historic first interfaith disputation on the steppe. And when he finally gains news of the German slaves to whom he had hoped to minister, and William asks the Great Khan for permission to return to serve them and their families, Mongke considers the request in silence, but returns no answer. Lacking even permission and support to travel freely in the Mongol empire and to minister to Latin Christians who are far from their homelands, William makes the long trek back to Louis IX, without the French queen's beautiful illuminated psalter or the equipment and vestments lost to Sartak's men.[100]

The Franciscan's sense of a failed mission is keenly palpable on his homeward journey, when he encounters five Dominican friars in the city of Ani in Armenia who have come to see him. Newly on their way to the Mongol empire, the Dominicans are carrying letters from the pope addressed to Sartak, Mongke, and Buri, requesting permission for the friars to stay, travel, and preach. But instead of welcoming the newcomers with advice and the hard-won knowledge he has gained from his own mission to the steppe, William discourages the new missionaries from journeying on, warning them of the extreme hardships ahead and the little they would be able to accomplish if they were not official envoys, but merely there to missionize.

They would be held of little account, he tells them, especially as they lacked an adequate interpreter. At this disappointing discouragement, the Dominicans turn aside, and decide to take advice from other friars in their order as to what to do. William adds that he has no idea what became of them, and exhibits little further interest in their hopes or mission (Jackson and Morgan 270–1; Dawson 216; Wyngaert I: 326).[101]

Modern readers of the *Itinerarium*, however, have judged William's mission less harshly than he himself appears to have done. Today, readers are charmed by the liveliness, expressivity, and eloquence on display in the *Itinerarium*, and William has been praised for everything from his passionate enthusiasm and acuity (de Rachewiltz, *Papal Envoys* 126, 141) to the excellent "scientific quality of his report" (Jackson and Morgan 51), his attentive ethnographic and artistic eye (Dawson xxii–xxiii), and even his fine, un-Orientalist commitment to equality and his high devotion to Christian salvational evangelism (Khanmohamadi).

Some of the praise heaped on the *Itinerarium* may owe something to how the *Itinerarium* looks in contrast to the *Ystoria Mongalorum*. John of Plano Carpini's succinct narrative, with its anxious descriptions of weapons and war tactics and its sense of critical urgency, is significantly less charming than William of Rubruck's long, musing account, which hardly mentions weapons at all but offers instead lengthy, colorful descriptions of yurts and intriguing accounts of divination with sheep bones, or how exotic beverages such as *koumiss* are made.[102]

But for all William's keen observational powers, insight, and expressivity, we should note that his powers do not in the end conduce to eliciting from him what might be called *relative tolerance*, let alone *cultural empathy*, for either his fellow coreligionists or the Mongol other. William may be fed, housed, and clothed by the hospitality of Mongke and his *orda*. He may enjoy *koumiss*, and the meat broth of the Mongols, and gain respect for ministering to Mongke's wives – one of whom even cozily gives him instruction in Mongolian (Jackson and Morgan 198, 199; Dawson 168, 169; Wyngaert I: 266, 267).[103] He may have the freedom during his sojourn to preach, say mass, perform the sacraments, and attempt conversion as he pleases, thanks to the tolerance of Mongols for all religious faiths.

Yet William tells Louis IX that *if he were permitted, he would preach war against the Mongols, to the best of his ability, throughout the whole world* (*si permitterretur michi, ego in toto mundo pro posse meo predicarem bellum contra eos* [Jackson and Morgan 173; Dawson 150; Wyngaert I: 244]). If we are startled by these sanguinary intentions – a Franciscan friar who wishes to undertake a global mission to preach war? – they are of a piece with William's other judgments against the Mongols in the *Itinerarium*. Citing Deuteronomy xxxii:21 to condemn them, for William, the Mongol other is a people "which is no people" and "a foolish nation" (Jackson and Morgan 139; Dawson 132; Wyngaert I: 220).[104] He tells Louis that had he the power to work miracles, like Moses, he would have humbled the Great Khan (Jackson and Morgan 239; Dawson 197; Wyngaert I: 300).

As if this were not enough, William astonishes at the close of his narrative with an even more sanguinary vision of bellicosity. He suggests to Louis it would be easy for an army of the Church to subjugate Hungary, Armenia, Greece, and other countries en route to the

Holy Land (Dawson 220; Jackson and Morgan 278; Wyngaert I: 331). *An army of the Church* (*exercitus Ecclesie*): and if gratuitous aggression against the neighbors of the Latin West, including Christian nations, were not sufficiently astounding, William adds that if just Louis's *peasants* – to say nothing of kings and knights – were willing to travel and do as the Tartars do, *they could conquer the whole world* (*possent acquirere totum mundum* [Jackson and Morgan 278; Dawson 220; Wyngaert I: 331]).

It would seem that for all his commitment to saving souls and preaching the faith, this Franciscan friar after all dreams of universal Christendom as a world-empire founded on military invasion and conquest, like Matthew Paris's Bishop of Winchester, and like the Mongol empire itself – to be accomplished by hardy peasants, kings and knights, and an army of the Church bearing the Book, but also the sword.[105] We see thus that William of Rubruck, the sensitive ethnographer and missionary, is not so distant in his intentions and ambitions, in the end, from John of Plano Carpini, the envoy intent on instructing the West on how to wage war.

To step beyond such sanguinary visions perhaps we would need to consider travelers of a different sort to the Mongol empire, who saw differently from bishops, friars, and religious ideologues with their ambitions of territorial conquest and religious domination. We consider next a representative from the West less invested in spreading the power of Christian ideology, and who had interests of a more secular and worldly kind. From religious men, we turn now to Marco Polo for a merchant's-eye view of global race.

Marco Polo in a World of Differences; or, Mercantile Capitalism as the End of Race?

Afortuitous happenstance in 1298 – when the Venetian merchant Marco Polo and a well-known author of Arthurian courtly romance, Rustichello da Pisa, found themselves sharing captivity in a Genoese prison – brought the world an extraordinary narrative composition called *Le Devisement du Monde* (The Description of the World) and *Milione* (Million): an account of the travels of Polo, his father Niccolò, and his uncle Maffeo, in the many Asias from west to east to south, with the Mongol khanate of Cathay and its environs occupying pride of place in the narrative.[106]

This complex composition, arising from the collaboration of Marco and Rustichello, narrates in first- and third-person voice, treating Marco now as an authorial speaker, now as a character in his own story, and is redacted and translated with additional or variant material many times, so that the account of Polo's travels winds its way through some 150 surviving manuscripts in most of the languages of Europe.[107]

Unsurprisingly, the name *Marco Polo* has long since become a famed touchstone for travel, the exotic, and adventure in foreign places, especially the East, and it is a name therefore suborned in our time by restaurants, vendors of carpets and furniture, and ships and spacecraft alike. Perhaps the thirteenth-century bearer of that name, so alive to the importance of commodities everywhere in the world and to his own important relationship to the greatest possessors of wealth and power in the world, would not have been displeased.[108]

Le Devisement is a complex, hybrid text, and scholars have remarked that it is influenced by conventions, content, and stylistic devices found in merchants' manuals, medieval romance and *chanson de geste*, encyclopedias, missionary narratives, ethnographic and geographic accounts, books of marvels, miscellaneous travel writing, and chronicles, *inter alia*.[109] Complete scholarly agreement on the priority of its most important redactions, in Franco-Italian, French, and Latin, and their precise relationship to the lost original does not exist.[110]

There is general agreement, however, that the oldest and most complete of the most important manuscripts is BNF f.fr.1116 (Bibliothèque Nationale de France fonds français 1116), dated to 1310, representing what is referred to as the "Franco-Italian" redaction written in an Italianate French and, it has been recently argued anew, probably nearest to the original composition.[111] BNF f.fr.1116 is dated remarkably close to the time of the original composition – a mere twelve years later – and this is the account we will use for discussion here.[112]

In 1269, Marco Polo left Venice as a very young man of fifteen, accompanying his father and uncle on their return journey to the East, and the merchant trio returned to Venice only in 1295, after Marco had been away for twenty-six years – seventeen of which he spent in the Great Khan's Cathay, undertaking missions for the Khan, as we are told by the "prologue" of *Le Devisement* (Moule and Pelliot I: 81, 73, 93, 87; Ronchi 313, 306, 324, 319). A youth when he departed and a middle-aged man when he returned, Marco Polo thus grew to adulthood and lived the prime years of his life as an expatriate in foreign lands: a singular circumstance that no doubt marks his narrative in singular ways.

The prologue, which is narrated in third-person voice and treats Marco as a character in his own story, confides that Marco knew languages and four scripts (without specifying what these were). Scholars have surmised that one was likely Persian, the language of international commerce and a *lingua franca* at the Great Khan's court (Larner, *Marco Polo* 60), and another Mongolian, given Marco's extended time in the Cathay khanate – since these languages would have been most useful to him (Moule and Pelliot I: 86; Ronchi 318).[113]

The prologue lavishes praise on Marco's wisdom and prudence, and especially his skill for enlivened description of the curiosities he encounters: a talent, it says, which the Great Khan finely appreciates in his messengers and envoys (Moule and Pelliot I: 86; Ronchi 318). It seems that the Khan, like King Arthur, enjoys hearing a good tale, with descriptions of new things and the customs and usages of the places to which he sends embassies – information that, we might note, can serve a double function as pleasurable entertainment and useful reconnaissance (Moule and Pelliot I: 86; Ronchi 318).

Alas, however, the Khan's usual envoys are fools and ignorant. In steps Marco Polo to remedy this. After the Venetian youth returns from his first embassy for the Khan, all who hear Marco's report of what he had seen praise the youth as someone who will become a man of great sense and great valor, and from here on for seventeen years, Marco was repeatedly sent on missions by the Great Khan (Moule and Pelliot I: 86–7; Ronchi 318–19).

With Marco enlisted as a valued factotum of the Mongol empire, one keen to demonstrate his skills, the stage is set by this prologue for what the world looks like through a Venetian merchant's eyes as he grows from youth to middle age.[114] The canny use of the third person enables the prologue to recommend Marco to us without unseemly self-praise by the principal witness of the tale, who then has the freedom, in *Le Devisement*, to function flexibly sometimes as the subject of what is enounced, and at other times as the subject articulating the enunciation.

The Great Khan or *Khagan* ("Khan of Khans") whom Marco serves is of course Kublai, the Mongol emperor of China immortalized for the modern West, along with his "pleasure-dome," by Samuel Taylor Coleridge. Kublai and Genghis Khan, Morris Rossabi reasons, were the two most important personages in Mongol and Eurasian history, towering figures in their time and after (*Khubilai* 1). Kublai had been elected Great Khan by a *kuriltay* in Cathay in 1260, after the death of his brother Mongke the year before, though a rival *kuriltay* in Karakorum also in 1260 designated his younger brother, Arik-Boke, Mongke's successor.

Arik-Boke, if we recall, was the youngest of the four sons of Sorghaghtani Bekhi and Toluy, and was described by William of Rubruck as having been raised in Christian practices and familiar with the Gospels (Jackson and Morgan 212, 214; Dawson 178, 185–6; Wyngaert 279, 288). But Kublai was supported by his other brother, Hulegu, who founded the Ilkhanate of Persia; and, successfully fending off challenges from Arik-Boke and from other relatives in due course, the Great Khan of Cathay crushed the last resisters of the Southern Song dynasty in 1279 and reunified all of China, north and south. Even before the surrender of the Southern Song, Kublai had announced the establishment of the Yuan dynasty (Da Yuan, or "Great Origin") of China, in 1271.

When Marco Polo came to serve the Mongol emperor of the Yuan, in a land which had not been unified since the close of the Tang dynasty more than three and a half centuries earlier, the empire was thus ruled by a Sinicized Mongol whose second son and heir apparent had a Chinese name, Zhenjin ("True Gold"), rather than a Mongol one. This first Yuan emperor also did not govern from the Mongol capital of Karakorum, in the traditional Mongol homeland, but rather from Khanbalik (*Le Devisement*'s "Cambulac" [Moule and Pelliot] or "Canbaluc" [Ronchi]), or Da-Du ("Great Capital") in Cathay, which Kublai caused to be rebuilt largely on the site of the old Beijing, with Shang-Du ("Upper Capital," Coleridge's "Xanadu") to the north as his summer capital.[115]

Our Venetian expatriate's admiration for this Mongol *Khagan* and the wonders of the empire he ruled appears to be boundless, as many scholars of *Le Devisement* remark. Kublai is adored for the glories that accrue to his position – for his puissance, and the unimaginable wealth and power of the Mongol empire – but his personal qualities also receive mention (Moule and Pelliot I: 192–3; Ronchi 405). We are told by the text in first-person voice that he is the most powerful man, in people, in lands, and in treasure, that ever was in the world and that now is, from Adam, our first father, till this moment; and he had the rule by his valor, and by his prowess, and by his great knowledge (Moule and Pelliot I: 192–3; Ronchi 405).

With such fulsome accolades articulated in the witness of a first-person voice, we see that we are a long way from Matthew Paris's demonization of a Mongol leader as a rapacious cannibal-barbarian who savagely relishes the paps of captive virgins as delicacies. We are also a distance from William of Rubruck's Mongke, Kublai's brother, who is shown by William to be wealthy and powerful, but whose imperial capital, Karakorum, was not as large even as Saint Denis, the Franciscan friar had said. The monastery of Saint Denis was worth ten times more than Karakorum, William had sniffed (Jackson and Morgan 221; Dawson 183–4; Wyngaert 285).

By contrast, *Le Devisement* presents the new Mongol capital of Khanbalik, an architectural sign of Kublai's puissance, as one of the world's great urban centers. Built on a square, with a circumference of twenty-four miles, Khanbalik is massively walled and gated, with a great clock and bell in a palace sounding the nightly curfew; the city teems with beautiful palaces, mansions, houses, and inns (Moule and Pelliot I: 212–13; Ronchi 420). Large suburbs spill outward from the city's walls and gates, also filled with mansions and houses as fine as those in the city, but containing even more people.

In these suburbs are merchants' lodgings, and even quarters for prostitutes (who number 20,000, in case we wondered); and beyond the suburbs are places for cremation and burial (Moule and Pelliot I: 235–6; Ronchi 437–8). The Mongol empire now has a capital that the sedentary civilizations of the West can admire unstintingly. Khanbalik's importance is also measured in trade: Dearer things and items of greater value come into Cambulac than into any other city of the world, we learn; indeed, more than 1,000 cartloads of silk enter the city daily (Moule and Pelliot I: 236–7; Ronchi 438).

Kublai's imperial residence and the residence of his heir, Zhenjin (*Le Devisement*'s "Cinchim"), are situated in a palace complex in Khanbalik that surpasses the city in magnificence. In a square enclosed by a wall four miles in circumference, with a second wall inside, this complex has some sixteen palaces reserved just for armaments and equipment (Moule and Pelliot I: 207–8; Ronchi 416–17). Kublai's imperial residence is the greatest palace that has ever been seen (Moule and Pelliot I: 208; Ronchi 417).

The walls of its rooms are covered in gold and silver, and display dragons, animals, birds, and knights; gold and paintings cover the ceiling (Moule and Pelliot I: 208–9; Ronchi 417–18). The hall alone can accommodate 6,000 diners at feast, while the roof is so cleverly glazed in colors that it is bright like crystal and its sheen can be seen from afar (Moule 209; Ronchi 417–18). Zhenjin has a palace similar to his father's (Moule and Pelliot I: 211; Ronchi 419).

Besides these fabulous edifices, the palace complex has lawns and grounds where stags, deer, and beautiful animals of various kinds roam, and a large lake teems with many types of fish. A river flows into the lake (Moule and Pelliot I: 210; Ronchi 418). A manmade hill is populated with gorgeous evergreen trees sourced from different regions, and the hill itself is covered in green gemstones, its summit crowned by a green palace (Moule Pelliot I: 210–11; Ronchi 418–19). Everything appears designed to delight the eye and the senses with color, brilliance, and variety. These extravagant constructions of landscape and architecture – and the exorbitant artificial prominence, in particular – bespeak fabulous wealth and aesthetic deliberation, and gesture at the ability to marshal unimaginable resources for their accomplishment.[116]

We should recognize that the architectural, topographic, and landscape opulence of Kublai's palace complex, and the impressiveness of Khanbalik, are *Mongol* accomplishments. Later, *Le Devisement* will gawk at the incomparable Hangzhou (or Kinsai, *Le Devisement*'s "Quinsai") in southern China, arguably the greatest city of the thirteenth-century world, and offer us Hangzhou as one of the world's great wonders. Where the city limits of Khanbalik encompass twenty-four miles in perimeter, we learn that Hangzhou has an urban circumference more than four times larger, at 100 miles (Moule and Pelliot I: 327; Ronchi 513).

A city surrounded by water, like Venice, but a premodern megalopolis, Hangzhou has 12,000 bridges, a pleasure lake thirty miles in circumference, 3,000 public baths, and 1,600,000 houses (Moule and Pelliot I: 327, 334, 339; Ronchi 513–14, 516, 518–19).[117] Still, Hangzhou is the capital of the Song, and the accomplishment of *Chinese* rulers, not the Mongols, and it is praised only after Kublai's conquest of South China (*Le Devisement*'s "Mangi") has been related, when Hangzhou has become a Mongol prize.

Indeed, *Le Devisement* will guide us through the cities, provinces, and assets possessed by the far-flung Mongol empire – everything important that Mongols built, and everything important they seized – as seen through the eyes of the narrator represented as Marco. The use of the first-person voice at such moments – when extolling the Great Khan, or inventorying the empire – vouches for the authenticity of the act of witnessing. Occasionally, the speaker presumed as Marco will augment his narration with lively self-admonishments to remember to tell us something; scold himself for having forgotten to narrate a detail, an omission which he will then correct; halt to expatiate at some length on a feature; or make an impromptu decision to skip over a city because it offers little of interest. These simulations of a speaking voice augment the impression that we are being led on an intimate tour of the empire and beyond by an especially knowledgeable and enthusiastic personal guide.

As he winds us through China, Yunnan, and further south, the narrator offered as Marco will also check off an inventory list when he alights on each new city and province and begins its description, always making sure to note whether the place (1) is subject to the Great Khan, (2) uses the paper money issued by the Khanate, and (3) has products that bring revenue to the Khanate's coffers.

Other details, of course, will also be checked off – such as the religion of the inhabitants, noteworthy flora and fauna (especially when these can be commoditized into goods), and peculiar habits and customs (especially the sexual mores of local women, and execrable regional practices which the Great Khan in his civilized superiority has tried to extirpate). But the political and economic interests of the Mongols in each location are the most important factors to set down, if you are acting like a mendicant factotum of the Mongol empire, and seeing through the empire's eyes and from the empire's point of view.

Such identification with the Mongols on the part of a Latin Christian European is something new and unusual, if not downright astonishing, in the thirteenth century, especially when we consider how little time has lapsed between John of Plano Carpini's description of the Mongols and Polo's. Not only is praise lavished on the Great Khan, but members of his family (that is, those not opposed to Kublai or in rebellion) are also idealized as good, wise, and just.

Kublai's son Manggala (*Le Devisement*'s "Mangalai"), governing the city of Quengianfu, keeps his kingdom well, in great justice and great right, and is much loved by his people (Moule and Pelliot I: 264; Ronchi 457). Kublai's son Essen-Timur (*Le Devisement*'s "Esentemur"), who rules Karajang ("Caraian"), is similarly a very great king and rich and powerful; he keeps his land well, in great justice, and is wise and experienced (Moule and Pelliot I: 276–7; Ronchi 469). Indeed, the seven sons of Kublai who are mentioned all rule provinces and kingdoms well, and are wise and prudent (Moule and Pelliot I: 207; Ronchi 416).[118]

If such praise in *Le Devisement* hits the ear as somewhat formulaic, Kublai himself is lauded as the wisest man, and the greatest ruler of people and of empire, and a man of greater valor than ever was in all the races of the Tartars (Moule and Pelliot I: 207; Ronchi 416). Discerning readers can come to their own conclusion as to which of *Le Devisement*'s authorial pair bears greater responsibility for such conventions of praise in the text.

Marco's identification with Mongol interests makes him a participant in *Le Devisement* not only in Mongol diplomacy and administration, but also in Mongol *military affairs*. *Le Devisement* claims the Polos accompany Kublai's armies to Xiangyang (*Le Devisement*'s "Sayanfu"), and help Kublai capture this key city of the Southern Song by teaching the Mongol forces the siege technology of mangonels and trebuchets.

This episode is related with the Polos as third-person characters, perhaps to mitigate a sense of immodest self-praise and to assuage readerly incredulity, since the episode improbably features our merchants-as-heroes transmitting superior European military know-how to the East, *contra* John of Plano Carpini's *Ystoria Mongalorum*. We should also take note of the fact that scholars agree the Polos did not arrive in Cathay till a couple of years after the Mongol seizure of Xiangyang.

At Xiangyang, *Le Devisement* says, the Polos tell Kublai they have in their household men skilled in constructing trebuchets. After they explain to Kublai what trebuchets are, and what such catapults can do, the Great Khan gives them the go-ahead, and a German and a Nestorian Christian of the Polos' make three trebuchets that each hurl 300 lb. boulders. *Le Devisement* says the trebuchets seem to the Mongols to be the greatest wonder in the world, and when they are deployed, all hell breaks loose in Xiangyang (the Chinese, apparently, have never seen such advanced technology before either). The Song surrender in confusion (Moule and Pelliot I: 319; Ronchi 505–6).[119]

Historically, of course, Mongol forces led by Kublai's handpicked commanding general, Bayan, did use heavy missiles to batter the walls of Xiangyang and force a surrender after they had cordoned off the city with a naval blockade for nearly five years.[120] But the engineers who built the missile technology of the Mongols at Xiangyang were not Latin or Nestorian Christians, as we will see later.

Nonetheless, *Le Devisement*'s narrator resumes the first-person voice at the end of the episode to conclude with satisfaction that the capture of Xiangyang happened through the kindness of Master Niccolò, and Master Maffeo, and Master Marco (Moule and Pelliot I: 320; Ronchi 506). The narrator makes sure we understand Xiangyang's conquest to be a major accomplishment (as indeed, historically, it was): not because Xiangyang was the last great military obstacle to the subjugation of Hangzhou, the Song capital, but because Kublai derived great revenue and great profit from the city and its province (Moule and Pelliot I: 320; Ronchi 506).

Revenue and profit, after all, are what matter to merchants. And several centuries before Hollywood's romances of Westerners who go to Asia and transform themselves into samurai or Shaolin kung-fu experts and save the day for the locals, we are afforded a spectacle in thirteenth-century European literature of merchant-heroes who romantically save the day for the Mongols, by instructing the empire how *finally* to overcome the Song, and seal the conquest of elusive southern China.

While Latin Christian *merchants* might identify with the Mongols and Mongol military ambitions, we do not see Latin Christian *missionaries* identify with the Mongol empire or the Great Khan. The letters of John of Monte Corvino, Peregrine, and Andrew of Perugia indicate that the Franciscan bishops and archbishops who live and proselytize in Khanbalik in the years following the Polos' departure attest to the empire's majesty and opulence, and the Khan's generous munificence to them, but although they are financially supported by the generosity of Kublai's successor, Timur, the missionaries never identify with the empire, with its Khan, or with Mongol ambitions (Dawson 224, 230, 234, 235, 236; Wyngaert 345–6, 353–4, 368, 373–4, 375–6).[121]

Marco's singularity, then, owes much to the fact that he is a trader by profession, and not a proselytizing missionary. The Venetian's assessment of human greatness, *Le Devisement* shows, is grounded in the powerful tug of material goods, in displays of wealth, and in the important relationships and status conferred by wealth and conduced by the control of material abundance. In assessing Mongols, the Franciscan missionaries to the empire before Marco tended to focus on moralizing Mongol *behavior*, rather than on the material abundance the Mongols controlled. Thus John of Plano Carpini and William of Rubruck judged the gift rituals of the Mongols to be a sign of avarice and greed, the heterogeneity of Mongol eating a sign of repulsive barbarity, and the superstition of Mongol behavior a sign of savage ignorance.

By contrast, Marco is dazzled by material abundance, and his assessment of Mongols, from a mercantile worldview, sees the control of abundance as inextricable from such moral attributes as wisdom, valor, and the like held by Kublai, the possessor of abundance. Material-minded equivalence of this kind, of course, also undergirds the Mongol world-view. We saw earlier that when Pope Innocent IV had exhorted the Great Khan, Guyuk, to cease his predations and convert to Christianity or else face the wrath of God, Guyuk had responded that God was already on his side: Guyuk's success in conquest was a sign of God's favor, since it was impossible to be successful against the will of God (Dawson 85–6, de Rachewiltz, *Papal Envoys* 213–14).

In mercantile as in Mongol thinking, material success and moral righteousness are intermeshed in a calculus of equivalence and correlation. Kublai's personal virtues – his valor, prowess, knowledge, and wisdom – can be extrapolated from the fact that he has dominion over more peoples, lands, and treasure than anyone in the world who ever lived. *Le Devisement* is agog at Kublai's wealth, and repeatedly tells us that the Mongol emperor is the wealthiest man in the world, as if mesmerized by Kublai's immense resources. Not only does the great lord have more treasure than any man of this world, the narrator breathes, but *all the lords of the earth combined* have not so great riches as the great lord has alone (Moule and Pelliot I: 240; Ronchi 441).

In the eyes of Marco the merchant narrator, the Mongol empire is a vision of the economic sublime, and Kublai is its master.

Like moral values, aesthetic values also seem inseparable from material success, and with Mongol possession of China – arguably the greatest civilization of the thirteenth-century world – Mongol physiognomy is also no longer seen as ugly. Unlike John of Plano Carpini's description of an alien and alienating Mongol face in the *Ystoria Mongalorum, Le Devisement* offers Kublai's physique as a kind of golden mean, and Kublai's face as actually beautiful.

Kublai is of fair size – neither too small nor too large, but of middle size. He is covered with flesh in a beautiful manner, and more than well formed in all parts. His face is white and red like a rose, the eyes black and beautiful, the nose well made and well set (Moule and Pelliot I: 204; Ronchi 414). The Mongol face is finally a human face, and even a beautiful and well-made one. With overwhelming success comes admission to the society of *huma-nitas*. The Mongol race has been welcomed into civilization.

Le Devisement's Mongols, moreover, do not appear as anything other than Mongols. While modern historians appropriately emphasize Kublai's sinicization, *Le Devisement* shows behavior by Kublai that falls securely within the traditional style of Mongol chieftains, albeit on a scale so lavish that it beggars the performances of Kublai's predecessors. Kublai's feasts to commemorate his birthday and the New Year are massive affairs, replete with vast quantities of wine, gold and silver vessels, lacquered bowls, and multitudinous crowds of feasters of all ranks, including foreign dignitaries bearing precious gifts: The Great Khan tends to feast more than 40,000 people at a time (Moule and Pelliot I: 217–18; Ronchi 422–5).

Yet among all this gorgeousness and plenitude, *Le Devisement* alights on a small, familiar detail of Mongol custom that we have seen before in the *ger* of Mongol chieftains on the steppe: When the Great Khan wishes to drink, musical instruments play for him – although now, there are a great quantity of instruments, as barons and others all kneel down to reverence the *Khagan* (Moule and Pelliot I: 220; Ronchi 423).

Like every Mongol Khan, Kublai is also enamored of sumptuous fabric, and treats fabric and luxurious garments as forms of treasure. He dresses in cloth of gold, and gives livery of silk, cloth of gold, and girdles of gold to 12,000 of his retainers – robes that are ornamented with precious stones and pearls. Anglo-Saxon and Germanic kings are ring-givers; Mongol khans give fabric and garments. Some of the robes Kublai confers are worth more than 10,000 gold bezants, we learn, and the Khan's robes, of course, are considerably costlier (Moule and Pelliot I: 221, 226; Ronchi 424, 428).

At his great New Year's feast, Kublai and all his subjects ceremonially dress in white (white being, both *Le Devisement* and *The Secret History* tell us, a supremely auspicious color), as the Great Khan receives gifts of gold, silver, pearls, precious stones, and white fabric, as well as 100,000 fine white horses (Moule and Pelliot I: 223; Ronchi 426). Fabric is even for animals: Kublai's 5,000 elephants are draped in white cloths festooned with beasts and birds; and camels are also covered with cloth (Moule and Pelliot I: 223; Ronchi 426).

There is reverencing and obeisance to the emperor aplenty, and bowing and kowtowing ("just as if he were God") at this splendid "white" feast of the New Year, but the feast is only one of thirteen the emperor gives annually (Moule and Pelliot I: 224; Ronchi 427).[122] For these thirteen feasts, Kublai generously confers on each of his 12,000 barons thirteen robes, each vestment of a different color, and a belt of gold and boots worked cunningly with silver thread, so that at every feast during the year, Kublai and his nobles are all garbed in a single color – a sweeping visual spectacle of corporate unity composed with fabric (Moule and Pelliot I: 225–6; Ronchi 428).

To make certain we understand the magnitude of such gifting, *Le Devisement* tallies the count and reminds us it is a total of 156,000 robes – all of which are worth so great a quantity of treasure that the number could hardly be told, not accounting even for the belts and boots, which are also worth considerable treasure (Moule and Pelliot I: 226; Ronchi 428).

Kublai's behavior is so much that of a traditional Mongol leader – not the behavior of someone sinicized and acculturated to China – that even his imperial harem, we learn, is recruited from only his own race. *Le Devisement* observes that Kublai's coterie of four wives and innumerable concubines comprise only Mongol women recruited from a tribe known as *Ungrat* (Moule and Pelliot) or *Ungrac* (Ronchi) – that is, Kungurat – reputed for their very handsome people.[123] Every year a hundred maidens, the most beautiful there are in all that race, are chosen and brought to the Great Khan (Moule and Pelliot I: 205; Ronchi 414). These fortunate ones undergo a rigorous process of intimate scrutiny supervised by the ladies of the palace to determine if they are fit to service the emperor, a process that confirms the sweetness of their breath, the intactness of their virginity, and other personal traits that the narrator is happy to detail (Moule and Pelliot I: 205–6; Ronchi 414–15).

We may have noticed in these summaries of goods and people a certain preoccupation with numbers – with quantity – and with the fineness and quality of the goods and the people. A kind of quantitative reasoning and inquisitiveness in the mechanics of determining quality is on display in the *mentalité* of the text. Kublai's hawking expeditions are a case in point. For this enjoyable recreation, Kublai takes 10,000 falconers and 500 gerfalcons, peregrine falcons, and saker falcons with him (Moule and Pelliot I: 229–30; Ronchi 432), as well as four elephants, a pavilion for holding court that can house 1,000 knights, and pavilions for himself; his retinue of physicians, astrologers, and officials; and his sons, his barons, and his harem, so that the pavilions number 10,000 in all (Moule and Pelliot I: 231, 233; Ronchi 433–5). Kublai's retinue even includes a keeper of lost property, placed in charge of lost-and-found (Moule and Pelliot I: 230; Ronchi 433).

Though the Great Khan's pursuit of falconry staggeringly assumes the proportions of a city on the move, Marco's interest in such vastness of scale does not occlude an equal fascination with fine-grained particulars, and he also scales down to descriptions of individual objects, to give us granular details that impart a sense of comparative value and quality. The principal pavilions and the Khan's bedchamber have carved poles of spice wood, and are all covered outside with tiger skins striped black, white, and red (*Le Devisement* calls these "lion" skins). Inside, the pavilions are lined with ermine and sable – and ermine and sable, Marco the narrator tells us, are the most beautiful, rich, and valuable furs in the world.

In case we were wondering just what their value might be, he adds: Of the kind of sable that would be used for a man's robe, the fine kind is worth 2,000 bezants, and the common kind is worth 1,000 bezants (Moule and Pelliot I: 232; Ronchi 435). *Le Devisement* routinely contemplates and assesses items in this way, and their cost, relative value, scarcity, or abundance are ascertained in a tallying system that is reflexively, automatically, calculated as an integral part of narration.

If the mercantile imaginary of *Le Devisement* seems obsessively fascinated with diverse goods and commodities, and with tagging and tallying their value, what implications are there for how this famous and important thirteenth-century text sees *human* diversity, in the large world through which Marco travels?

First of all, it is important to emphasize that a reflexive mechanism of identifying, tagging, and tallying the things he sees, and quantifying their value, affords Marco an important means of taxonomizing the world, so that the inexhaustible variety he encounters in the globalism of his travels is not overwhelming, but is reducible to units that can be sorted and categorized in an orderly, routinized way that renders even inexhaustible variety manageable.

The sheer diversity of the world is thus filtered into lists of what industry, agriculture, or trade is practiced in each place Marco visits, and what goods and services are consequently derived. A random sample: Lesser Armenia manufactures the most beautiful carpets in the world; Greater Armenia makes the best buckram; Basra grows the best dates; Baghdad makes *nasij* (brocade) richly decorated with birds and beasts; Persia's eight kingdoms raise fine horses for export to India; Kerman has steel ore and manufactures armor and weapons; Rudbar raises wheat and cereals, fruit and nuts, and large white oxen that are good for eating; Kuhbanan manufactures large steel mirrors of high quality; Shibargan grows the best melons; Talikhan has mountains of salt, the best in the world; Badakhshan produces rubies of great beauty and value; Kashgar produces cotton, flax, and hemp, Pem's rivers yield jasper and chalcedony; Sinju offers the best musk in the world; Kalachan exports the finest camlets of camel hair and white wool; Sindachu manufactures accoutrements for armies; Ydifu has rich silver mines; Kungurat exports concubines to the Great Khan; virtually all the cities and towns of southern China produce silk and cloth of gold; Tibet has giant bamboo, gold dust in lakes and rivers, cinnamon, and coral; Jiandu has a lake that yields pearls; Karajang has gold dust in rivers and gold nuggets in mountains; Bengal exports eunuchs, slave girls, cotton, and spices; Malabar and Ceylon are responsible for most of the pearls and gems in the world; Motupalli produces the only diamonds in the world; and India and the Indies deliver a variety of different spices and condiments (all itemized): The comprehensiveness and detail of *Le Devisement*'s itemization are impressive and habitual. Such is the world of the mercantile imagination: a world made up of commoditizable raw materials, markets, supply and demand, manufacturers and producers, consumers and importers.

We cannot help but observe that people, religions, allegiances, and sometimes languages are accounted for in a parallel system. Take, for instance, *Le Devisement*'s itemization of the religious affiliation of the world's peoples: Mosul's Arabs worship Muhammad ("Mahomet" in *Le Devisement*); Kurds are Nestorians, Jacobites, and also Saracens who worship Muhammad; Yazd's inhabitants worship Muhammad; Kala Atashparastan's inhabitants are idolaters who worship fire; Hormuz' inhabitants are black and worship Muhammad; Balkh's inhabitants worship Muhammad; Pashai's inhabitants are brown-skinned idolaters who have sorcerous arts; Kashmir's inhabitants are brown-skinned idolaters who have idols that speak; Kashgar has Nestorian Christians; Samarkand is inhabited by Christians and Saracens; Uighuristan has idolaters and some Nestorians and Saracens, and the Christians often intermarry with the idolaters; Ganzhou's inhabitants are idolaters, Muhammadans, and Christians, and the Christians have three fine, large churches but the idolaters have many monasteries and abbeys and very many idols; Kalachan's inhabitants are idolaters but there are three churches of Nestorian Christians; the people of Cathay (i.e., the Chinese of Mongol-ruled northern China) are all idolaters; and idolaters fill the many cities, towns, and villages (all named in the text) and the agricultural countryside west of Khanbalik.

The list goes on, but I will set aside a discussion of *Le Devisement*'s treatment of religion for later. At present, it is important to see that with religion as the example here, the mercantile imaginary's tendency to create a taxonomy of the world's different goods conduces also to taxonomizing the differences of the world's peoples in a routinized habit of sorting and categorization without, necessarily, the principal aim of establishing a hierarchy for critique or condemnation (I will discuss exceptions to this later).

In global transversal, taxonomies of this kind help to make intelligible and manageable the inexhaustible variety that is encountered, so that the world's diversity can be processed. Formulas that serve to inventory the panorama of different goods and products around the world then also serve to inventory the panorama of human differences. A parade of goods and a parade of humans are delivered through similar narrational practices.

So the world is seen as gridded by a diversity of goods that constitute units of capital, assets: Differences among the goods – their very diversity – are a necessary condition for the goods to yield value. The world is also seen as gridded by a diversity of peoples: And, just as with merchandise, differences among the peoples can also be a necessary condition for their yielding of value.

That is to say, in the *mentalité* that is fashioned by commerce, human otherness and difference may design conditions of possibility that can yield advantage for those who see opportunity in difference, and know how to profit from difference and otherness. Key examples illustrate this when Marco the narrator shows us differences of custom and morality in varied regions of the world that design conditions of sexual opportunity for traveling men, who can then take carnal advantage of available local women and profit from otherness.

Profiting from Difference: Sex, Race, and Exchange in the Global Economy

In Pem, where the people worship Mahomet and belong to the Great Khan, when a woman's husband leaves for a journey of more than twenty days, she is able by local usage to take another husband until his return; and the man who is away is likewise entitled to do the same (Moule and Pelliot I: 147; Ronchi 368–9).

In Kumul ("Camul"), where the people are all idolaters, when a stranger arrives and comes to lodge, a man tells his wife to do all that the stranger wishes and then leaves his home for two or three days, so that the stranger stays with the man's wife in the house, does as he likes and lies with her in a bed just as if she were his wife, and has great enjoyment (Moule and Pelliot I: 154; Ronchi 374). The narrator confides that the women of Kumul are fair, gay, and wanton.

When the Great Khan learns how those of Kumul make their wives commit adultery with strangers, he commands them to end the disgusting practice, but they propitiate him with a great gift and implore him to permit the continuation of the custom, because their ancestors had said that their idols held them in great favor for the pleasure which they made for strangers with their wives, and their corn and labor on the land multiplied greatly because of it (Moule and Pelliot I: 155; Ronchi 375). Kumul's sexual difference from Latin Christian European norms thus does not meet with censure in the mercantile imaginary, but seems terrifically advantageous for the international traveler (who is gendered as male).

But differences in Tibet furnish even better conditions for sexual tourism. Here, where the people are all idolaters, virginity is actually abhorred: So when male strangers arrive and pitch their tent, the old women of the villages and hamlets bring out their daughters by twenty and by forty and give them to the visitors, who do their will with them, and lie with them, and enjoy themselves with them, and keep them as long as they wish (Moule and Pelliot I: 270; Ronchi 463).

When the travelers leave, it is the custom to give some jewel or token to the woman with whom they have lain, so that when she comes to be married she can show that she has had a lover. In this way, it is the custom for each young woman in Tibet to have more than twenty tokens around her neck, to show that many men have lain with her, and those who have more tokens and can show that more men have lain with them are esteemed higher than others (Moule and Pelliot I: 270–1; Ronchi 463–4).

Human otherness and difference of this sort so delights Marco that it excitedly prompts him to exclaim a recommendation: Young gentlemen from sixteen years to twenty-four will do well to go into that country (Moule and Pelliot I: 271; Ronchi 464)!

Jiandu ("Gaindu"), where the inhabitants are idolaters subject to the Great Khan, has a custom similar to Kumul's, but with greater flexibility in the offering of women. When a foreigner comes by, a man offers his wife, daughter, sister, or any other woman who resides in his house to the foreigner, and goes off to his field or his vines, not to return as long as the stranger lodges in his house. Marco confides that often the stranger remains for three days, lying in bed with the wife; to keep away the man of the house, the visitor hangs up his hat or some other token outside to indicate that he is within, and the poor wretch stays away as long as the visitor remains (Moule and Pelliot I: 273–4; Ronchi 466–7).

In this way, the narrator shows us a world where not absolute, but relative values prevail: one in which the relative values of commodities around the world run parallel to the relative values of human behavior and female sexuality around the world, and both commodities and humans can be entered into exchange relations that yield profit for all. Everyone wins when something is traded: A woman receives a jewel or token; a traveling merchant receives pleasurably prolonged sexual favors and lodgings; a region receives good harvests, abundant return for labor, and agricultural prosperity.

All participants who are willing and able to take good advantage of human differences can profit. In a world gridded by commerce and trade relations, not only are goods exchanged, but people also circulate in relations of exchange that produce profit calculable by the participants: This is how a mercantile imaginary sees the world. All human relations are economic relations of a sort where participants seek to profit from trading, including intimate kinds of trading.

But profit, of course, can be unequal for the participants in exchange relations, since those in control often decide the conditions of trading. The value of Badakhshan's rubies is kept artificially high by the king, who controls the monopoly and limits their supply; and the Great Khan controls the monopoly over Jiandu's pearls, to ensure their scarcity and keep their value high (Moule and Pelliot I: 137, 273; Ronchi 360, 466). Marco, who is acutely sensitive to forces of supply and demand, usually sees how profit can be extracted ad hoc from local conditions: In Karajang (*Le Devisement*'s "Caragian"), a region that has gold in abundance, the exchange value of gold relative to silver has fallen, and in Cangigu even precious spices can be bought cheaply because the place is so far inland that the inhabitants cannot control transportation by sea (Moule and Pelliot I: 278, 296; Ronchi 470–1, 485–6).

Le Devisement is silent, however, on how the women of Kumul, Tibet, and Jiandu – women who are not portrayed as assertive and purposeful agents who control their own self-insertion into exchange relations – might feel about being offered to strangers by their husbands, brothers, fathers, mothers, heads of households, and villages and hamlets for hospitality sex. If these women seem to be treated like merchandise, perhaps it is because the world of *Le Devisement is* saturated with merchandise that governs how humans behave toward one another.

In the mercantile imaginary, the world is a supply chain where even people – women – serve as goods to be exchanged. Such lack of interest in how female participants in the trading of sex might feel doubtless owes less, then, to any deliberate and conscious misogyny in the text than to the nature of the world that is presented in *Le Devisement*: a world governed by the endless generation and regeneration of capital in the form of goods, commodities, objects, produce, material resources, and treasure.

The mercantile imagination turns even otherness into units of capital, to be entered into calculated exchange for advantage. In a universe where capital is mighty, and constantly transforming and retransforming itself – gold being exchanged for silver, the Great Khan's vaunted paper money being exchanged for goods and services, cowrie shells and salt bricks being exchanged for other currencies – gender and sexuality also become subsets of capital.

Does *race* become a subset of capital in a universe gridded by flows of capital? For *the dominant race* that controls capital, and the world's assets – the Mongols – there is only admiration and awe. Make no mistake: *Le Devisement* shows that this awe-inspiring race controls *unimaginable* capital in the premodern world.

From the city of Hangzhou and the lands under Hangzhou alone, *Le Devisement* calculates revenues for the Mongol empire in the millions. Revenues from salt are worth 5,600,000 *saggi* of gold annually, a saggio of gold being worth more, the text says, than a florin of gold or a ducat of gold (Moule and Pelliot I: 341; Ronchi 520). Spices of every kind pay a tax of 3 1/3 percent; from rice wine and charcoal also come large revenues; and miscellaneous goods also pay 3 1/3 percent (Moule and Pelliot I: 341; Ronchi 520). The 12,000 craft and artisan workshops pay duty on everything (Moule and Pelliot I: 342; Ronchi 520). Silk, and many other items, bring revenues of 10 percent each, amounting to untold money, our witness says. The witness vouching for the numbers is of course Marco ("I, Marc Pol, who several times heard the count of the revenue" [Moule and Pelliot I: 341; Ronchi 520–1]).[124]

Not counting the revenue from salt, the gross revenue from Hangzhou and its lands is usually 15,700,000 *saggi* of gold – an incalculable amount of money, Marco says – and this is just income from *one* of the nine parts of the province of Mangi or south China (Moule and Pelliot I: 342; Ronchi 521). The great port city of Zayton (Quanzhou, or *Le Devisement*'s "Çaiton") also yields immense revenue: Duties from ships' cargoes, including gems and pearls from India, yield 10 percent and the hire of the ships yields anything from 30 to 44 percent depending on the types of cargo, so that the merchants who frequent Zayton really give over half the value of what they bring, and the Khan has a very great quantity of treasure from here (Moule and Pelliot I: 351; Ronchi 528). Marco does his best to tally specific sums of revenue for us, but his frequent invocation of the inexpressibility *topos* also renders the wealth of the Mongols as the embodiment of the fiscal ineffability of the economic sublime.

Mongol Modernity, Mongol Woman: The Transformation of Fear and Desire

Yet even more remarkable than its immense revenues is how the Mongol empire's vast wealth is used in ways that craft a vision of the ideal modern state in premodernity: a state that is astonishing in efficiency, forward-looking in its institutional innovations, and admirable for benevolence to the poor.

Le Devisement presents the Mongol communication system as a marvel of its time: Trunk roads traverse the provinces and realms of the empire, and at every twenty-five or thirty miles of each main highway, a post-station is located with well-appointed lodgings and 400 horses, where those who carry communications may rest comfortably, and find fresh mounts (Moule and Pelliot I: 243; Ronchi 443). The lodgings at these posts are so luxurious, Marco says, that if a king arrived, he would be well lodged (Moule and Pelliot I: 243; Ronchi 444). Off the main highways, in areas of sparse population, stations of equal splendor and horses are also located, but at greater intervals of thirty-five or forty miles (Moule and Pelliot I: 243; Ronchi 444). In all, more than 200,000 horses and 10,000 stations interlace the empire, to engineer swift and efficient communications.

Under exigent circumstances (such as a rebellion), riders on horseback are furnished with the Great Khan's gerfalcon tablet as a sign that they must go at express speed. Riding post haste from station to station without stopping to rest, they exchange exhausted steeds for fresh horses at every station: In this way, the riders can cover 250 to 300 miles a day, and bring news to the Khan at tremendous speed (Moule and Pelliot I: 246–7; Ronchi 445–6). The Mongol system of riders is even supplemented by messengers on foot: Every three miles, between one post and another, are hamlets of about forty houses where fast runners reside who carry messages on foot. Each runner swiftly runs three miles, then hands over what he carries and a ticket to the next runner, and the relay continues, so that in a day and a night, the Great Khan can receive correspondence and news from places that are ten days away (Moule and Pelliot I: 244–5; Ronchi 445).[125]

Part of the stunning impressiveness of the Mongol communication system is its scale: the way vast resources are marshaled and organized for the ends of efficiency and speed. Indeed, we may be forgiven for seeing this state-of-the-art communications system as a kind of Internet of the premodern age. But more important even than the vision of organization that the system installs is the way such organization *systematizes* and *routinizes* communication, breaking communication down into constituent parts that function in a routine and automatic way, without haphazardness, but in engineered dependability.

The marvel of Mongol efficiency and innovation, here, is the marvel of *modernity* – a glimpse of what the future might hold. *Le Devisement*'s readers need not possess teleological hindsight, retroactively imported from the twenty-first century, to wonder what might happen if the world elsewhere, or everywhere, could look like this: where important services are delivered in a system of engineered routinization and systematicity.

Another vision of Mongol modernity is the empire's use of paper money as universal legal tender. Though the Mongols did not invent paper currency but inherited it from the Chinese, the use of paper as the standard and regular medium of exchange in the empire ensures that money in this form is universalized across the vast territory of *Pax Mongolica*. Marco may wonder at the spectacle of paper money – his fascination extends to telling us in detail how it is made from bark and trees, cut into different sizes for various denominations, and stamped with the Great Khan's imperial seal (Moule and Pelliot I: 238; Ronchi 439) – but he instantly recognizes the efficacy and advantages of such currency.

Marco assures us that the notes are universally accepted in trading and business and are not cumbersome to carry, unlike other currencies in *Le Devisement* such as gold, silver, cowries, or salt (the sheet of paper that denotes ten bezants weighs not one, Marco observes); and when they are torn or spoilt beyond use, the bearer can exchange his old notes for freshly minted notes at Khanbalik's mint for a fee of 3 percent (Moule and Pelliot I: 239–40; Ronchi 441).[126] Marco understands that the credibility and stability of paper has to be secured by precious metals, and assures readers that one can bring paper money to the mint and receive gold and silver from the master of the mint in exchange (Moule and Pelliot I: 240; Ronchi 440–1).

We might wish to observe that the issuance of standardized paper money, by doing away with everyday dependence on metal, also does away with accusations of short weight and coin clipping. The Jews of thirteenth-century England, whose fiscal activity also conjured a vision of economic modernity (but in the Latin West, not in China), as we saw in Chapter 2, would have benefited greatly from this other vision of fiscal modernity – the Mongol kind – at the opposite end of the world.

Mongol paper money thus ushers in a vision of a world where fiscal exchange is done differently from before, with a lightweight, uniform currency that is regulated, standardized, and put into universal circulation. Modernity here resides in how paper, unlike gold or silver, renders an *abstraction* of money. Unlike precious metals, recognized as valuable for their scarcity, or salt, recognized as valuable in some places because of its usefulness or scarcity, the success of paper money depends on a universal willingness to accept *currency in its pure form – as an abstraction, as a medium with no intrinsic value, but only symbolic and exchange value.* Unlike cowrie shells, notes of paper cannot even be worn as jewelry.

Such acceptance, Marco understands, is only possible in the thirteenth century when currency that circulates in so abstract a form is backed by power. That is to say, paper money is a *signum* here of the *real* wonder – which is that Kublai Khan has the power to make everyone accept it as legal tender, as if it were gold or silver.[127] None dares to refuse such money, Marco says, on pain of his life (Moule and Pelliot I: 239; Ronchi 440).

Among its innovative institutions, the Mongol empire also has a disaster relief and social welfare system that sustains people during agrarian emergencies and crises. Kublai sends out messengers throughout his lands, realms, and provinces to gather data on whether people have had agricultural losses in summer (because of bad weather or locusts, Marco says), or loss of flocks in winter (Moule and Pelliot I: 248; Ronchi 446–7). Tax is commuted that year for those who have lost their corn or their animals, and the state gives them corn to sow and eat, and also animals (Moule and Pelliot I: 248; Ronchi 447).

Moreover, Kublai maintains great silos of grain (Marco lists wheat, barley, millet, rice, and panic, *inter alia*) purchased when harvests are abundant, and has such grain carefully preserved, so that it can keep without spoilage for three or four years (Moule and Pelliot I: 250; Ronchi 449). Then, when there is a grain shortage, the Great Khan releases his stores, giving four bezants' worth of grain for what a bezant will usually buy, and he takes out so much that each person has an abundance of grain, and in this way so provides that none has a dearth. The emperor does this through all the lands where he has rule (Moule and Pelliot I: 250; Ronchi 449).[128]

In Khanbalik, the Mongol capital, the state additionally supports families of six, eight, or ten members, who are poor and have nothing to eat: Very great numbers of such citizens are supplied with wheat and corn (Moule and Pelliot I: 251; Ronchi 449–50). Such forward-looking, large-scale, and well-planned state beneficence is complemented by more traditional, ad hoc benevolence such as charity at court. Bread is refused to none at the Khan's court, so that more than 30,000 people go there every day to be fed (Moule and Pelliot I: 251; Ronchi 450). All this, we learn, makes the people so fond of the *Khagan* that they worship him as God (Moule and Pelliot I: 252; Ronchi 450).

This ideal state created by the Mongols has other markers of good governance that the Latin West would find familiar, such as the maintenance of roads. But even here the Mongols go one better: Kublai has had trees planted beside highways so that messengers, merchants, and other travelers do not lose their way, since these large trees can be seen from afar. Through all the provinces and kingdoms, even by lonely ways, we are told the trees stand as a great comfort to merchants and to wayfarers (Moule and Pelliot I: 248–9; Ronchi 447).

The Mongols' welfare system of providing grain and flocks in times of need depends, of course, on information gathering – on benevolent state surveillance and paternalism – but Marco also shows us other kinds of surveillance that may seem closer, in their thoroughness and inexorability, to modern state apparatuses. Historians estimate that perhaps a few hundred thousand Mongols resided in thirteenth-century China, but the Chinese population of northern China alone perhaps amounted to *ten million* people, with that of southern China accounting for another *fifty million* (Rossabi, *Khubilai* 71–2).

The Mongol state exercised surveillance over this large subject population, *Le Devisement* relates, through an ingenious system of self-maintained, self-perpetuated census by the state's subjects.

The immediate example is Hangzhou, but we are told that the system is institutionalized through all the provinces of southern China ("Mangi") and northern China ("Catai").

Every burgher in Hangzhou has to have his name, and the name of his wife, his sons, the wives of his sons, his slaves, and everyone in his household (because, presumably, he may have daughters and sons-in-law living with him too – though it would have been more usual among Kublai's Chinese subjects for a daughter to leave the familial household on marriage and enter her husband's familial household), as well as the number of horses he keeps, written on the door of his house (Moule and Pelliot I: 340; Ronchi 519).

If anyone dies, their name is erased; if anyone is born, their name is added.[129] In this way, we learn, the authorities in each city know all the people who live there. Inns and hostelries also have to register all who lodge there, by the day of the month, so that through the year the Great Khan can know who comes and who goes throughout his land (Moule and Pelliot I: 340; Ronchi 519). This panopticon of surveillance – which is praised by Marco as a thing which befits the wise – is the obverse, then, of the benevolent welfare system of the Mongols.[130] State scrutiny by a perpetual-motion census machine in the thirteenth century?

A state that can get its citizens to exercise instrumental surveillance over themselves on an ordinary, everyday basis without fuss and update the records of self-surveillance regularly is a marvel indeed, in whatever era. And so we have these extraordinary markers of the modern state in premodernity, painstakingly described to us by *Le Devisement*: a Mongol state that issues standardized paper money, regulates a welfare system for disaster relief and for the poor, plants tall trees along highways to facilitate travel for state purposes, commerce, and communication, innovates a state-of-the-art postal system, collects census data that is regularly updated by its own citizens, and routinizes demographic surveillance on an everyday basis.[131] It is little wonder that the Mongols as a race dazzled Marco Polo.

Just how exceptional a race Marco thought the Mongols were may be indicated, perhaps, by his anecdote about an exceptional Mongol *woman*, Khutulun (called in *Le Devisement* by one of her other historically attested names, Aiyurug, "Aigiaruc"). In direct opposition to how the women of Kumul, Tibet, and Jiandu are represented in *Le Devisement*, this Mongol woman, the daughter of Kaidu (the grandson of Ugedey, Kublai's uncle and the Great Khan who succeeded Genghis), is shown to be wholly in control of her sexuality and refuses marriage to any man who cannot defeat her in hand-to-hand physical combat – in wrestling, a favorite Mongol competitive sport. Lest we imagine that in relating this longish tale *Le Devisement* will be obliged to hew to narrative conventions laid down by mytho-literary characters such as Atalanta or Brünhilde, and eventually show Khutulun being tricked by or succumbing to a man who will take her virginity, *Le Devisement* in fact surprises us by showing Khutulun to be in command of her body and sexuality indefinitely.

More than this, Khutulun is shown in control not only of her sexuality, but also of her relations with others. First of all, she has wrested an agreement from her father, Kaidu, the khan who was the de facto ruler of Central Asia, that it would be she, not he, who would decide the conditions under which she would consider marrying. Like other women in *Le Devisement*, Khutulun thus participates in exchange relations, but unlike other women, she gets to set the terms of the deal. The price is simple: Every suitor who would contest with her will deliver her 100 horses if he loses. In this way, we are told, Khutulun has won more than 10,000 horses, which suggests she has defeated more than one hundred men in fights (Moule and Pelliot I: 454; Ronchi 619). Khutulun is thus a wealthy and successful economic entrepreneur *par excellence*.

The denouement arrives when a princely suitor – comely, young, strong, powerful, and right in every way – brings with him a very fine company and 1,000 beautiful horses as his stake (Moule and Pelliot I: 454–5; Ronchi 619). Everyone in the court, Marco says, excitedly roots for him, including Khutulun's parents, who would love nothing better than to see their daughter lose to this desirable paragon. Kaidu even takes his daughter aside and tells her she *must* allow herself to be vanquished (Moule and Pelliot I: 454; Ronchi 619).

With such expectations stacked against her, not to mention story conventions that incline toward the happy ending of female defeat followed by grand marriage festivities, Khutulun still refuses to comply. She handily defeats this paragon of perfection and throws him onto the palace floor, winning his 1,000 beautiful horses (Moule and Pelliot I: 455; Ronchi 620). None in all the hall was not sorry for it, Marco says ruefully (Moule and Pelliot I: 455; Ronchi 620).

Remarkably, this indomitable young woman who is so wealthy in horses is never criticized in any way – not by those around her, and not by the text. Although it mentions the disappointment of everyone in the hall when she beats the 1,000-horse suitor, *Le Devisement* never comments negatively on Khutulun's choices, but shows instead that her story does not end with (or without) marriage – which simply drops out of sight and seems to become irrelevant – but just goes on. We learn that Khutulun accompanies her father Kaidu into many battles, and in all the fighting, he never had a knight more valiant than she. Fearless and undefeated, she had a practice of charging into enemy lines many times and seizing and bringing back a captive by force (Moule and Pelliot I: 455; Ronchi 620).

The historical Khutulun is thought eventually to have married, and some sources even offer the conventional explanation of love. Rashid al-Din, for example, insists in his chronicle that Khutulun fell in love with Arghun's son Ghazan, the Ilkhan who converted to Islam (Boyle, *Successors* 26). But *Le Devisement* makes the narrative decision to let Khutulun be, so that we have the image of an exceptional woman who is unlike any other woman in *Le Devisement*: an assertive and purposeful female participant in exchange relations who successfully, repeatedly controls the terms of exchange, and the outcomes of exchange.

Even among the remarkable Mongol women of the thirteenth century acknowledged by Eastern and Western authors, Khutulun is an exceptional figure: a woman who did not politick for power through her sons or the men of the Mongol clans, as shown by *Le Devisement*, and who did not achieve wealth, power, and reputation in history through the traditional feminine route of marriage and childbirth.[132] A wealthy, confident, strong, independent, and undefeated woman who does what she likes without hindrance, and confounds expectations with no repercussions, Khutulun in *Le Devisement* iconizes in the register of *gender* – a different register from Kublai – just how exceptional a race the Mongols are.

For *Le Devisement*, the Mongol race is exceptional and held up for admiration *not* because it has acclimated to the wonderful sedentary civilizations it has conquered. Instead it is admired for the very same qualities that John of Plano Carpini had described with trepidation and foreboding some five decades earlier: Mongols are hardy, resilient, excellent warriors with astonishing horses, heterogeneous dietary habits, and many wives who are excellent managers, and they sustain themselves at very little expense. They are good men in battle and mightily valiant, exceedingly good archers, and people who are most in the world to bear work and hardship with least expense: In short, they are the best suited to conquer lands and kingdoms (Moule and Pelliot I: 171; Ronchi 389). Their horses are so well trained that they wheel as readily as a dog would, and fight as well and as stoutly even when faced with the enemy (Moule and Pelliot I: 174; Ronchi 390–1).

These qualities in men and horse, instead of being horrifying to the Latin Christian European author/s making the observations, are embraced. So what if they lead to the conquest of lands and kingdoms by Mongols? Mongols are the race best suited to conquest. Mongol qualities are even moralized positively: For nothing in the world would a Mongol touch the wife of another, we learn, because they hold it an evil thing and exceedingly vile. Concomitantly, Mongol women are also good and loyal to their lords, and do their household duties very well (Moule and Pelliot I: 169, 170; Ronchi 387).

In fact, it is only when Mongols *cease* to be Mongol-like in their behavior that the race comes in for criticism. The Mongols in Cathay who have assumed the manners, mores, and customs of the Chinese, we are told, are much debased (Moule and Pelliot I: 174; Ronchi 391).

From being a race that was reviled and abhorred, Mongols have become an exceptionally fine race of peoples, admired from a number of perspectives, their economic and material success breeding unreserved admiration. If the Mongols are now to be admired, their Great Khans, of course, are inviolate. Genghis Khan ("Cinghis Kan"), the founder of the empire, is lauded in the same terms as Kublai ("Cublai"). Just like Kublai, Genghis is a man of great valor, great wisdom, and great prowess (Moule and Pelliot I: 162; Ronchi 381).

But Kublai is greater and more powerful than *any* of the Great Khans before him (*Le Devisement* counts five Great Khans before Kublai, instead of four, and names them incorrectly). Indeed, all the previous five put together will not have so much power as this Kublai, *Le Devisement* affirms, because all the emperors of the world, and all the kings of Christians and of Saracens, would not have so much power, nor could they do so much as this Kublai Great Khan could do (Moule and Pelliot I: 167; Ronchi 385–6).

And there we have it: In the glorious spectacle of Kublai Khan, and the empire he ruled, is lodged the extraordinary transformation of Mongols from an object of fear and loathing into an object of admiration and desire by Latin Christian European authors.

But the dynamic of that newly hatched desire requires some adjustment to be made as to how the *object* of desire might perceive the new *subject* of desire, the corporate form of which is the Latin West. When Mongols were still an object of fear and loathing, William of Rubruck had not been impressed by rumors of Mongol friendliness to Christianity, the religion of the West, and was skeptical of ostensible converts among high-level Mongols; and we recall that William had decided from the evidence of personal encounter that Sartak, reputed to be Christian, probably was no Christian at all.

Remarkably, by contrast, *Le Devisement* bends over backward to suggest Kublai's friendliness to Christians and his lively interest in Christianity. After Kublai had crushed the insurrection of Nayan ("Naian"), a descendant of Genghis Khan's half-brother Belgutey, and Nayan had been executed, *Le Devisement* tells of how Christians were mocked by Saracens, idolaters, Jews, and many other people who did not believe in God (Moule and Pelliot I: 200; Ronchi 411). This was because Nayan had been a Christian, and had carried the Cross of Christ on his standard (Moule and Pelliot I: 199; Ronchi 410). See how the Cross of your God has helped Nayan who was a Christian, the non-Christians jeer, making great fun and great mockery (Moule and Pelliot I: 200; Ronchi 411).

Astonishingly, Kublai comes to the rescue of the beleaguered Christians, calling together the Christians who were there and comforting them, and saying: "if the Cross of your God has not helped Nayan, it has done right, because the Cross is good. Nayan, who had opposed his lord, was both disloyal and treacherous, so there is great right in what happened to him, and the Cross did well by not helping Nayan against right" (Moule and Pelliot I: 200; Ronchi 411–12). When the Khan spoke evil in this way to those who had made fun of the Cross and the Christians, the Christians were heartened and agreed that the Khan spoke truth, for the Christian Cross would not have supported a traitor who was disloyal to his lord (Moule and Pelliot I: 200–1; Ronchi 411–12).

Race-as-Religion Returns: Christian–Saracen Enmity in a World of Differences

Kublai's casuistic logic in the intriguing episode of the beleaguered Christians might seem startlingly ingenious and unaccountably generous if we did not suspect that *Le Devisement* would like to suggest that Kublai was sympathetic, even amenable, to the religion of the Latin West.

It is satisfying when the object of your desire is seen to respect your religion and defends it against its detractors; and, fortuitously, the famous tolerance of the Mongols for all religions can be exploited here to suggest that Kublai might possess the kind of warmth and kindliness toward Christianity that William of Rubruck did not find among Mongol khans. Significantly, this episode also refers to *Christians*, rather than *Nestorians*, as the target of mockery – though Eastern Christians were of far greater ubiquity than Latin Christians in the Mongol empire – whereas elsewhere in *Le Devisement,* the text often refers to Nestorian Christians in the Mongol empire simply as *Nestorians*. Blurring the distinction here between Eastern and Western Christians augments the impression that Kublai was supportive of the religion of the Latin West.

Kublai's enthusiasm for the religion of the Latin West is also intimated by *Le Devisement*'s prologue, which asserts that Kublai had asked Niccolò and Maffeo to request of the Pope in Rome 100 Latin Christian clerics, wise men of the Christian religion who should know the seven arts and know well how to argue, so that the Latins could show Kublai and the "idolaters" of Cathay (Buddhists, Taoists, Confucianists) that their beliefs were erroneous and their idols devilish things, and demonstrate by clear reason the superiority of the Christian religion (Moule and Pelliot I: 79; Ronchi 311).

As an addendum, Kublai also asks for oil from the lamp that burns above the Holy Sepulcher in Jerusalem, demonstrating a reverence for Christendom's holiest shrine (Moule and Pelliot I: 79; Ronchi 311). In response, the prologue says, Pope Gregory X sent two Dominican friars, William of Tripoli and Nicholas of Vicenza, with the Polos for their return to Cathay, but both friars went no further than Ayas ("Laias"), because they were daunted by the perils of travel (Moule and Pelliot I: 83–4; Ronchi 315–16).

The men of God having proven less hardy than the men of mercantile capital, the Polos did not return to Kublai with a hundred men of learning, but only with Marco: a result that would cause deep regret among authors in the Latin West for the next two centuries, as word of Kublai's putative request and its nonresults spread, snaking its way notably in the fourteenth century into the popular travelogue *Mandeville's Travels*, and in the fifteenth century into Christopher Columbus' journal.

Not surprisingly, the historical record outside of *Le Devisement* does not mention Kublai's desire for 100 Christian men of learning from the West at all, let alone that he wanted them for the purposes of proving wrong the beliefs of all his officials, administrators, military officers, and courtiers. Indeed, Kublai is known to have depended greatly on Confucians and Buddhists among his officials, especially Zen Buddhists and the Tibetan Buddhists favored by his chief wife, Chabi (Rossabi 16).

If in fact Kublai *had* made a request of the kind *Le Devisement* suggests, it would probably have been one more indication of Kublai's shrewd efforts to diversify his administration, so that no single constituency among the officials serving his empire became indispensable or overpowerful. That is to say, if Kublai Khan had wanted 100 Christian religious men from the West, he would likely have wanted them for administrative service, not for demonstrating the superiority of the Christian religion to the detriment of Eastern philosophies.[133]

We thus see that even a medieval text so thoroughly imbued with the materialist *mentalité* of commerce as *Le Devisement* bears the marks of Christian religious allegiance. But unlike missionaries such as William of Rubruck and John of Monte Corvino, *Le Devisement*'s allegiance to Latin Christianity does not require the condemnation of other Christianities and Eastern Christians. *Le Devisement* inveighs against neither heresy nor Nestorians, nor does it view Nestorian Christians as competitors with Latin Christianity.

But it is true that religion is one of the chief categories by which *Le Devisement* habitually taxonomizes human difference – and in this, the text is a creature of its time. Specifically, there is *one* group of humans, defined by their religion, which is set apart for distinctive treatment, a treatment that bears the marks of race: Muslims. But such treatment occurs for reasons, I will suggest, that are more complex than the religious-racial fanaticism of Christian missionary ideologues aiming to end human difference by reducing it to the same, through religious conversion of the racial-religious other.

Traveling across large territorial swathes of the Near East, and West and Central Asia, the Polos could not have avoided noticing how widely dispersed the religion of Islam was: The inhabitants of city after city, town after town, and through many regions, provinces, and realms, *Le Devisement* announces, "worship Mahomet." Editors and translators of the text have noticed, with surprise, how this catalogue of Saracen ubiquity curiously *insists* that the devotees of Islam *worship Mahomet*, as if Muslims were pagans and idolaters.

After all, the merchants of Venice and the Mediterranean, as we saw in Chapter 3, were hardly unsophisticated rustics who were never exposed to the basic commonplaces of the Islamic religion, such as monotheism; indeed, we saw how Venice and Genoa, and the other Italian republics, continuously profited from trading with Muslims for centuries, against repeated papal prohibition and through every kind of disruption, including the Crusades.

Le Devisement is a worldly text, voiced by a merchant traveler who claims global transversal, and demonstrating a sophisticated understanding of commerce and economics. The text is not an example of insular literary fantasy written by a cleric ensconced in remote parts of the European continent, who had never encountered Muslims before but could fantasize the religious enemy's idols and gods to his heart's content.

We are urged to consider the possibility, therefore, that *Le Devisement*'s repeated, casual proclamations that Muslims "worship" Muhammad are falsifications of a deliberate kind, to set Islam apart from the monotheisms of the other Abrahamic faiths. We noted in Chapter 3 that *Le Devisement* also adjusts the sensational story of the Assassins of Alamut and the Old Man of the Mountain to make these Nizari Ismaili Shiites – a breakaway religious minority denounced as heretical in its time and abhorred by orthodox Sunni Islam – stand in for mainstream Islamic civilization.

Practices such as these perjure Islam: They make it into a religion that, unlike Christianity, practices idolatry by worshiping a prophet, and a religion that, unlike Christianity, is obsessed with a sensual paradise in the afterlife geared toward pleasuring the bodily envelope, and whose practitioners ruthlessly lie and deceive their young for murderous ends.

Islam in *Le Devisement* is also shown to persecute Christians, and Islam's leaders as desiring the conversion of Christians into Muslims, or else the death of the Christians. Around the year 1275, the narrator/s say/s (narration here switches between the first-person plural and singular), the Caliph of Baghdad, after spending all day and all night scheming as to how to coerce the Nestorians and Jacobites in his land – who were a very great number – to convert back to Islam or die, decides to make use of the Gospel tale of the mustard seed that affirms how faith can move mountains (Moule and Pelliot I: 105–6; Ronchi 332–3).[134] The Christians are given ten days to find a Christian who can move a mountain in the vicinity, or else come back to the law of Mahomet, or die an evil death (Moule and Pelliot I: 106–7; Ronchi 333).

These persecuted Christians of Baghdad are explicitly identified as Nestorians and Jacobites, not Christians of the Latin Rite. They are also represented as apostates from Islam, called by the Caliph to return to the faith. The Christians pray day and night for eight days, after which their bishop has a vision in which a messenger tells him of a pious shoemaker who fasted, committed no sin, went to church and mass daily, and had only one eye, because he had destroyed the other after having been tempted at the sight of an attractive woman customer's foot and leg (Moule and Pelliot I: 108–9; Ronchi 334–5). The story is teased out at length, and readers are given blow-by-blow details of the shoemaker's perfect piety that are milked for all they are worth, accompanied by commentary.

Finally, on the day in question, the Christians go to mass and gather in the plain of the mountain, with the Cross of the Savior before them. There are 100,000 Christians, as well as a multitude of Saracens who had come to kill them because they did not believe the mountain could be moved (Moule and Pelliot I: 110; Ronchi 336). The shoemaker kneels before the Cross, holds his hands toward the sky, and prays. The mountain moves. Many Saracens became Christians that day, and the Caliph himself became a Christian, but only secretly. When the Caliph dies, they find a cross around his neck, and do not bury him with the other caliphs, but set his body apart (Moule and Pelliot I: 111–12; Ronchi 337).

This miracle story, elaborated at some length and in some detail, culminates in a warning: Saracens are evildoers whose law permits them to commit every kind of evil against those who do not share their religion. Their prophet Mahomet has given them commands that all the evil that they can do to all people who are not of their law, and all that they can take from those not of their law, does not constitute sin, the narrator/s say/s (Moule and Pelliot I: 112; Ronchi 338).

This characterization of a people according to their putative religious code is then generalized to apply to *all* Muslims universally, so that we have a virulent characterization of an entire group of humans extended by a logic of religious racialization: All the other Saracens of the world behave themselves in this manner, *Le Devisement* smugly concludes.

Lest we imagine this miracle story of persecution and conversion in Baghdad to be an isolated instance of how Muslims and their leaders are negatively portrayed, *Le Devisement* later recounts the dynastic history of Hulegu's descendants in the Ilkhanate of Persia as an epic struggle between a pernicious Muslim usurper, Ahmad Sultan ("Acmat Soldan"), and his nephew, Arghun ("Argon"), the son of the Ilkhan Abaga.

Arghun is away from the Ilkhanate when his father, Abaga Khan, dies, and Ahmad Sultan bribes the barons and knights into supporting him by giving them a vast, indeed unbelievable, quantity of treasure (Moule and Pelliot I: 457; Ronchi 623). The fact that Ahmad has converted to Islam is pointedly highlighted at the outset. Ahmad then issues a spurious statement about how, as Abaga's brother, he should rightfully have had a half share of the Ilkhanate, but he had generously given the realm in entirety to Abaga. Now that Abaga is dead, it is right that he should have a turn as Ilkhan. With such fulsome bribes, the barons and knights decide that Ahmad is a very good ruler, and wish for no other lord than he, but – the narrator adds in first-person voice – this is a wicked thing for which Ahmad was much blamed by many people (Moule and Pelliot I: 457–8; Ronchi 623).

Arghun, of course, challenges the usurper, and Ahmad and Arghun's armies, each numbering 60,000 men, journey to meet in combat to decide the outcome. Ahmad's horsemen rather viciously and gratuitously declare they would like nothing better than to kill Arghun, or else to capture and torture him (Moule and Pelliot I: 458; Ronchi 624–5). Again, the wily Ahmad dangles vast material largesse before his men, telling them that he is only interested in honor and renown, and would be happy to give over the profit, possessions, and domains of all the lands and provinces to them. Again, the barons, knights, and others enthusiastically acclaim their unswerving loyalty to Ahmad to the death (Moule and Pelliot I: 459; Ronchi 625).

Le Devisement spiritedly portrays Arghun's determination to show valor and courage (Moule and Pelliot I: 459; Ronchi 626). Gathering his barons and wise men, Arghun reminds them of the companionship they had shared with his father in conquest and battle, and how his father had treated them like his own brothers and sons (Moule and Pelliot I: 459; Ronchi 626). Arghun then proceeds to make an astounding declaration: Ahmad, he tells his men, is not of our law, and has become a Saracen and worships Mahomet.

Goadingly, he adds: See now, how worthy a thing it would be that a Saracen must have rule over Tartars (Moule and Pelliot I: 460; Ronchi 626)! Arghun then urges each man to fight valiantly and exert himself beyond his powers so that the rule remains with them, and not with Saracens. Finally, he concludes: We shall win the battle because we are right, and our enemies are wrong (Moule and Pelliot I: 460; Ronchi 627).

Historically, Ahmad Teguder did indeed convert to Islam, and his brief reign of only two years as Ilkhan served to interrupt the relationship with Christians that Hulegu's dynasty had forged – a relationship that continued till the conversion of Ghazan (Hulegu's great-grandson and Arghun's son) to Islam. As we have seen, Hulegu's mother, the extraordinary Sorghaghtani Bekhi, was a Nestorian Christian, as also was Hulegu's favorite wife, Dokuz Khatun, who was sometimes hailed as a second St. Helena. Hulegu's chief general, Kitbuka, was also a Nestorian Christian. Hulegu's son and heir, Abaga, married the Greek Orthodox princess Maria Palaiologina, as we've noted, and is famed for his attempted rapprochements with Edward I to combine forces against the Mamluks of Egypt and Syria. Abaga's son Arghun, whose mother was also Christian, in his turn sent embassies to Europe for alliances, and even had his own son Oljeitu baptized as a Christian and named Nicholas, after Pope Nicholas IV.[135]

A text with Christian allegiances might therefore be forgiven for finding Ahmad Teguder something of a thorn in the side of dynastic history before the accession of Ghazan in the Hulegid dynasty, after which the Ilkhanate became decisively and permanently Islamized. But *Le Devisement* is more than just annoyed.

It relates the history of Ahmad's reign, and Arghun's revolt, as a cautionary parable of the dangers of religious difference, *as if a change of religion would produce a de facto change of race.* Arghun tells his men that it is improper for a Saracen to rule over Mongols – as if Ahmad, a Mongol, had ceased to be a Mongol by converting to Islam, and was now only a Saracen. Postconversion, Ahmad is not a Muslim Mongol ruling over other Mongols of diverse religions – Buddhist, Shamanist, Christian, and Muslim Mongols – but has instead become a kind of race traitor by virtue of his conversion, and unfit to rule over true (that is, non-Muslim) Mongols.

Continuing his logic of religious transformation as racial transformation, Arghun then goes on to describe the coming battle with Ahmad for the governance of the Ilkhanate as if Arghun had read *La Chanson de Roland*, a text whose proclamation *Christians are right, Pagans are wrong* is justly infamous. Arghun's words – we are right, and our enemies are wrong – echo the *Roland* eerily. Mongols are right, and Saracens are wrong – as if Mongols here were a placeholder for Christians (Moule and Pelliot I: 460; Ronchi 627).

Alas, in the battle between the armies, Arghun is bested and taken prisoner. The description of the battle itself has highly conventional elements: Arrows fly but are dispensed with quickly; then swords (and clubs) come out and there is stabbing and hacking, and body parts (hands, arms, shoulders, heads) are cut off, and many proven men die there, and many ladies will be forever in wailing and in tears for it (Moule and Pelliot I: 463; Ronchi 631).[136]

Upon Arghun's capture, Ahmad puts his best emir, a *malik* ("melic") and fellow Muslim by the name of Sultan ("Soldan"), in charge of his prisoner-nephew Arghun, and then goes off to pleasure himself with all the fair ladies of the court, since he is a man "of very great indulgence" (Moule and Pelliot I: 463–4, Ronchi 631). Well, he is a Muslim, after all, and we know from *Le Devisement*'s earlier tale of the Old Man of the Mountain and the Assassins what that means about his sexual appetites. By contrast, *Le Devisement* never refers to Kublai Khan – a man of many wives and concubines, who recruits 100 new Kungurat virgins annually for his harem – as a man of very great indulgence.

Fortunately for Arghun, an old Mongol baron called Boga who is *not* a Muslim emir, because he's explicitly called a *Tartar* (and we know that Tartars who convert to Islam are no longer Tartars, but *Saracens*), has second thoughts, repents, and decides to free Arghun, convincing many barons to join him. After Arghun has sworn to these barons that they will not be punished for their initial disloyalty to him and he will treat him as his father the Ilkhan Abaga did, the barons release him. Before he escapes, however, Arghun kills the Saracen *malik* Sultan (Moule and Pelliot I: 464–5; Ronchi 632–3).

When Ahmad the usurper receives the unwelcome news of this turn of events, he decides to appeal to a fellow Muslim, the Sultan of Babylon ("Babilonie"), for help and inexplicably sets off on his own for Babylon (Cairo), without an escort. At a defile through which he must pass, the man guarding the pass captures Ahmad and brings him to Arghun, who has his uncle executed and his body cast where it would never be seen again (Moule and Pelliot I: 465–7; Ronchi 634–5).

Unlike the miracle story of the mustard seed, the parable of Ahmad Sultan the usurper does not round off with a condemnation of all Muslims. Instead, condemnation focuses on a single individual, the Islamic convert Ahmad, who is shown to be wily, scheming, traitorous, disloyal, and sexually self-indulgent, and who trusts only his own kind, fellow Muslims. We learn from *Le Devisement* that Ahmad's own kind changes from Mongol to

Saracen with conversion to Islam. In the opinion of *Le Devisement*, race and religion –
when it comes to Muslims – are equivalent categories in the taxonomy of difference.

If we were inclined to attempt to sort out the messy skeins of responsibility for portions
of text, we might be tempted to view these two stories in *Le Devisement* – the tale of the
mustard seed, and the tale of Ahmad Sultan – as the work of Rustichello the romancer, and
not Marco the merchant traveler. The story of miracle and mass conversion, after all, has a
whiff of elements that seem to leak in from medieval hagiographic romance, and the story
of Ahmad's conversion and racial-religious war, with its conventional sentiments and
depictions of martial combat, has a whiff of elements that leak in from *chanson de geste*.

Still, in the authorial collaboration between Marco and Rustichello, it would be difficult
to apportion to Rustichello alone all responsibility for the Christian allegiances exhibited by
the text and all textual signs of animosity to Muslims and Islam. While a merchant's
attitude to religious difference might be more pragmatic than a romancer's or a religious
ideologue's, there are in fact pragmatic reasons for why even Christian merchants from
Venice might wish to sideline, critique, and negatively portray Muslims.

For one, though *Le Devisement* never mentions this, medieval Muslim traders whose
networks crisscrossed the world for centuries were inevitably to some extent the mercantile
competitors of Christian traders. Trade in the global Middle Ages was often synonymous
with Muslim trade, and the *lingua franca* of international commerce was Persian, not Latin
or Hebrew, despite the existence of Christian and Jewish merchants. European medieval
literature even acknowledges the ubiquity of Muslim mercantile internationalism, when we
notice how frequently the merchants who appear in literary narratives turn out to be
Saracen merchants.

Accommodations made by Mongol rulers also acknowledged the importance of Muslim
traders. We learn from William of Rubruck that the Mongol capital of Karakorum has two
districts: one for the Cathayans (Chinese), who are all craftsmen, and one for the Saracens,
where the all-important markets are situated (Jackson and Morgan 221; Dawson 184;
Wyngaert 285–6). The court of the Great Khan is *always* near the Saracens' quarter, we
are told, and many merchants flock there on account of the court, with its many envoys
(Jackson and Morgan 221; Dawson 184; Wyngaert 285–6). Muslim merchants in Karakorum
are so important that they are allocated one of the two divisions in Karakorum.

Muslims also have two mosques in Karakorum, whereas Nestorian Christians only have
one church situated at the far end of the town. Where you are situated in Karakorum and
how far your location is from the Great Khan's *orda*, William had observed, spoke volumes
for your relative importance or unimportance, and for your access to power. In the Mongol
capital, Saracen merchants are important, close to the Great Khan's court, and monopolize
the quarter with the markets.

Historians tell us that Muslims and Central Asians were also of importance to Kublai's
empire and administration. The story of Ahmad the Bailo, the corrupt governor of
Khanbalik, is in Ramusio's redaction of *Le Devisement* and not the Franco-Italian, but
the account of Ahmad's misrule is corroborated in Chinese and Muslim sources, and
treated not only in *Le Devisement*. From the early 1260s to his death in 1282, this Ahmad
(said to be from Banakat, southwest of Tashkent in Uzbekistan) labored mightily and
successfully to increase the Mongol empire's revenues from agricultural and mineral
production, tariffs, and taxation, to finance Kublai's military commitments and the empire's
needs – one reason for the continued favor Ahmad found in Kublai's eyes for more than two

decades (Franke 539). It was the wily and ruthless Ahmad, so reviled in *Le Devisement*, who worked to produce the massive imperial revenues of which Marco was in awe.

Ahmad also recommended more comprehensive census surveys of households throughout the empire; contrived to increase the grain reserves of the state; and had Chinese Song paper money taken out of circulation in southern China and replaced with Mongol Yuan paper money, the imperial currency that had so dazzled Marco.[137] His successful fiscal measures, coupled with relentless politicking, meant that Ahmad rose to become more powerful than *Le Devisement* admits, controlling not just the imperial capital of Khanbalik but also one of the four administrative-institutional pillars of Kublai's government, the Presidential Council, and with extensive influence over the other institutions. The purge after Ahmad's assassination disclosed that Ahmad's vast powers had allowed him to place 714 appointees to positions in his networks, favoring members of his family and other Muslims (Franke 552, 555–6).[138]

Muslims served in various capacities in Kublai's administration, just as – Marco says – Marco also served. In the *Yuan Shi*, the official Chinese history recording the Mongol Yuan dynasty, an examination of the eleven commissioners of one state agency showed that "five ... had Muslim names, two Jurchen names, and ... four were Chinese" (Franke 546). Muslims were well intercalated into Kublai's government and administration.

Despite this, the Franco-Italian redaction of *Le Devisement* has something of a preference for *absent* Muslims. It is willing to inventory and describe the many parts of the world where the inhabitants "worship Mahomet" – and we see that fully a third of the world *is* Islamic, as Peter the Venerable had feared – but the Franco-Italian redaction rarely describes the actual *business* and *activity* of Muslim merchants per se – though we should no doubt extrapolate that in the many Islamic regions it inventories, the people involved in the export of horses to India, or carpets, or brocade, are Saracen traders who "worship Mahomet."

But notwithstanding stories of anti-Christian Caliphs and Saracen usurpers, Muslims are something of an absent presence in *Le Devisement*. In addition to the lack of Muslim merchants actively trading or doing business in the world traversed by Marco, the accomplishments, activity, and service of Muslims in the Mongol empire also fail to be acknowledged by *Le Devisement*, or are actively suppressed by the text.

For instance: The narrator takes pains to describe Khanbalik at length, as we have seen, even explaining in detail that there used to be an older city here but the Great Khan had decided to rebuild the new city of Da-du/Khanbalik slightly to the side of the old site because of a prophecy. Yet Marco the narrator never cares to tell us that a Muslim architect, supervising an international team, was responsible for rebuilding Khanbalik (Rossabi, *Khubilai* 131).

In similar fashion, the two engineers who built catapults that hurled great missiles at the walls of Xiangyang for the Mongols in Kublai's successful conquest of this key city were not Christians – *not* a German and a Nestorian in the retinue of the Polos, as *Le Devisement* claims, but Ismail and Ala al-din, two Muslim engineers from the Middle East, a fact *Le Devisement* suppresses (Rossabi, *Khubilai* 83).[139] In the episode of the missile engineers, we also see *Le Devisement* referring to religion and ethnicity as if these were proximately equivalent and synonymous categories. The Polos' putative engineers are a German (identified by ethnorace/nationality) and a Nestorian (identified by religion).

There are other conflations of religion with race in the narrative. *Le Devisement* tells us that Tenduc has a mixed-race people who are called "argon," which is to say a people born of two races, from the lineage of the inhabitants of Tenduc (who are idolaters) and those who "worship Mahomet" (Moule and Pelliot I: 182; Ronchi 398). In *Le Devisement*, racial categories based on religion are more frequently invoked than racial categories based on skin color or physiognomy, and when the religion is Islam, as we have seen, warnings of persecution and danger are issued, dynastic history is turned into racial-religious allegory, and the presence and accomplishments of Muslims are suppressed.

Le Devisement's response to skin color is more varied, spanning a range from curiosity and interest to admiration, neutral observation, and revulsion. Fairness of skin is usually praised as beautiful, but darkness of skin can also be considered attractive in a relative sort of way, except when it is accompanied by physiognomic features the text considers ugly, such as the facial features of the poor unfortunates of Zanzibar ("Çanghibar").

So: The people of Japan ("Çipingu") are white, fair-fashioned, and beautiful, yet the women of Kashmir ("Chesimur") are very beautiful *for dark women* (Moule and Pelliot I: 357, 140; Ronchi 531, 363). Blackness can be a neutral description: The people of Hormuz ("Curmos") are black and worship Mahomet (Moule and Pelliot I: 124; Ronchi 348). But the dark-skinned people of Pashai ("Pasciai") are idolaters who are very malicious and cunning in their customs (Moule and Pelliot I: 139; Ronchi 362).

At the opposite end of the spectrum from the white-skinned, fair-fashioned Japanese are the people of Zanzibar, who are large limbed and immensely strong, and seem like giants: These people are black, with curly hair, and so great a mouth, and so flat a nose, and lips and eyes so large that they are a very horrible thing to see, for whoever should see them in another country would say of them that they were devils (Moule and Pelliot I: 432; Ronchi 596). Kashmiri women pass muster; black Africans get short shrift.

Le Devisement sees however that valuations of skin color can be relative, depending on place and the eye of the beholder. In India, we are told, people oil their infants with sesame oil once a week, so that their babies' skin becomes considerably darker than when they were born, and they paint the idols of their gods black, whereas their devils are portrayed as white as snow (Moule and Pelliot I: 400; Ronchi 566). Even the St. Thomas Christians of India say that God and all the saints are black, whereas devils are white (Moule and Pelliot I: 400; Ronchi 566). With this, we come full circle back to the contrariness of customs around the world: a world in which female virginity and chastity, and whiteness, can be abhorred by the local populace, whereas female profligacy and blackness of skin can be extolled.

What happens then to race in a world of differences? With rare exceptions, such as the highly conventional aesthetic views on display in descriptions of the people of Japan and Zanzibar, race-as-skin-color ceases to be assigned fixed values. Blackness is not evil or moralized; whiteness is not the color of goodness, saintliness, or purity. Indeed, purity itself can be undesirable in a world of differences, as we saw in the sexual customs of Tibet and other places.

Even theories of climate make little sense, and seem not to compel human behavior or predispositions with any reliability. In Maabar, India, people go naked except for a little cloth to cover their privates, because all the seasons are so temperate, and there is neither hot nor cold (Moule and Pelliot I: 383; Ronchi 553). But people also go naked there because of the great heat, heat so great that it is a wonder (Moule and Pelliot I: 390; Ronchi 559). Such are the contradictions of India.

Does race disappear altogether, then, in the global Middle Ages of Marco Polo, world traveler, mercantile capitalist, diplomat, and administrative factotum of the Mongol empire? Religious race does not disappear. Jews are among those who jeer at the Christians of Khanbalik when the Christian Nayan loses to the pagan Kublai. Muslims are evildoers permitted by their religious code to practice every evil to others not of their religion; and Caliphs viciously persecute Christians.

Kublai Khan, of course, is virtually a prospective Christian, who desires oil from the Holy Sepulcher and 100 learned Latin Christian religious men who can prove all the idolatrous certitudes of his own people wrong. The internecine contest of the Abrahamic faiths is alive and well, even in a world of differences visualized by a mercantile imaginary.

The alien race known as the Tartars, however, has been given a new role: Now admired and served by a representative of the Latin West, the Mongol empire has become an object of desire, and imagined, once again, as highly receptive to Christianity. And so, the story continues.

Mandeville and Fantasies of Race-and-Religion, China, and "India": The Prester John Legend, and the Return of the Jews

Not long after the earliest recension of *Le Devisement* was written, some time in the middle decades of the fourteenth century – around 1356 or 1357, "closer to 1360 than to 1370" – a remarkable travel narrative appeared that described the peregrinations of an English knight, Sir John Mandeville, around the world (Higgins, *Book* xvi). Voiced in the "I" of a first-person witness, this travel narrative – conventionally called *Mandeville's Travels, The Travels of Sir John Mandeville*, or *The Book of John Mandeville* – was so extraordinarily attractive to audiences that it became a medieval blockbuster: Some 300 manuscripts survive in all the major languages of Europe, showing the *Travels* to have substantially outperformed *Le Devisement* (which has only half as many surviving manuscripts) in its dispersion and popularity.[140] One modern translator of the *Travels* expresses awe:

> When Leonardo da Vinci left Milan for France in 1499, he had an inventory made of his library. His books reflected his wide interests, and the depth of his reading. He owned several books on natural history, on the sphere, on the heavens. But out of the multitude of travel accounts Leonardo could have had, in MS or from the new printing press, the list records only the one: Mandeville's *Travels*. At about the same time Columbus ... was treating Mandeville with great seriousness as a source of information on China and the East while he prepared for his voyage; and in 1570 a copy of the *Travels* was with Frobisher as he nosed into Baffin Bay.
>
> (Moseley, *Travels* 9)

Part of the glamor of the *Travels* was its aura of authoritative verisimilitude. Mapmakers of the fourteenth and fifteenth centuries scrupulously consulted it: The *Travels* was a source for Abraham Cresques' incomparable Catalan Atlas of 1375, made for Peter III of Aragon; the Andrea Bianco map of 1434 (which eschewed *Le Devisement* as a reference); and the earliest known globe of the world, devised by Martin Behaim in Nuremberg *c.* 1492, which very respectfully documents its debt in a legend on the globe to the "würdige doctor und ritter Johan de Mandavilla" ("worthy doctor and knight, John of Mandeville"; Moseley,

Travels 31–2, "Behaim Globe" 89). As late as 1577 Gerard Mercator used the *Travels* as a source for his own map (Moseley, *Travels* 33).

While the state-of-the-art geographic resources of the day took the *Travels* as an authority on the world and its peoples, it was also used as a guide by actual travelers. Sir Walter Raleigh's 1596 *Discoverie of the Empyre of Guiana* quotes Mandeville by name, and

> When the native Amerindian myth of the regenerative land of Bimini reached the ears of the first Spanish settlers, they eagerly grafted on to it the story of Mandeville's Well of Youth, of which Mandeville had drunk three times, and Ponce de Leon led two expeditions, in 1513 and 1521, to look for it.
>
> (Moseley, *Travels* 32)

One owner of the Cotton recension of the *Travels* tore out the pages that could be taken for a pilgrim guide to the Holy Land – "perhaps so to use them," Moseley suggests (*Travels* 22). Moseley adds, "It is indeed a curious coincidence that right up to the end of the sixteenth century there are noticeable increases in the frequency of known editions of the *Travels* coinciding with major voyages of exploration" (*Travels* 32):

> It may ... be that Columbus's determination to sail west to Cathay was fuelled by Mandeville's story of circumnavigation. Frobisher, in his attempt on the North West Passage, took with him a copy of Mandeville for its information on China ... [and] Columbus seems, from surviving letters, to have died believing he had found islands off Mandeville's Cathay.
>
> (*Travels* 32)

Not for nothing, then, has the *Travels* been called "the single most popular European work of secular literature in the late medieval, early modern period" (Braude 106), a period in which "it was regarded as the most authoritative and reliable account of the world" (Braude 116).

When printing arrived, the *Travels*' popularity and dispersion only increased. Moseley points out the profit to publishers from demand for this popular text: "before 1500 eight German printings are known, seven French, twelve Italian, four Latin, two Dutch and two English. There are Czech and Spanish editions before 1520. Clearly there was money as well as interest in Mandeville" (*Travels* 30). There was even an all-illustration, no-text version – a kind of early graphic novel, we might say. Iain Higgins – perhaps the foremost scholar on the *Travels* today – succinctly sums it up: "If any medieval book can be called an international best seller, [*The Book of John Mandeville*] can" (*Book* xiii).[141]

It might thus come as a shock to the medieval and early modern audiences enamored of the *Travels* to learn that their English knight, "Sir John Mandeville," likely did not exist. After generations of scholars searched earnestly for *Sir John Mandeville, auctor*, a scholarly consensus has emerged that "Mandeville" is a fictitious personage most likely created by an erudite cleric in possession of an excellent library, fine literary skills, and a lively desire to bring the world to the doorstep of Europe.[142]

The success of the Mandeville author's efforts to render a totalized planet for audiences in Europe – those who did not travel as well as those who did – meant that for "over two hundred years, courtiers, priests, and ordinary people as well as explorers, mapmakers, artists and writers" were deeply absorbed in the world summed up for them by a non-existent, fictitious English knight whose account was so compelling that its authenticity was not doubted before two centuries had elapsed (Higgins, *Book* xii).

The runaway success of the *Travels* surely prompts our asking a version of Freud's old question: "Was will das Buch?" *What does Mandeville's Travels want?* And, more important, what was it able to give to so many in Europe that its prolific survival was ensured for over two centuries? Unlike Freud, who found only a single answer to his infamous query, in *Empire of Magic* I suggested that the *Travels* wants many things, and coaches its readers also to want its objects of desire. Here, where my topic at hand is medieval race, I want to concentrate on one skein of narrative desire that powers an organizing principle of unquestioned importance to the *Travels*: how to think about religion in the disposition of human differences.

The *Travels* has been called many things – a "mendacious romance," "satire," the "popular encyclopedia" of a "marvel monger" or "philosophical fabulist," "a map" or "series of maps," or in "e-jargon . . . a 'mash-up'" (Higgins, *Writing East* 11; *Book* xi). Moreover, while it recounts some of the fantastical marvels expected of travel literature, the *Travels* also evinces a deep fascination with contemporary knowledge in science and technology – presenting us with a spherical world that can be circumnavigated; tracing imaginary latitude and azimuth to help locate one's position on the globe and what one can see in the sky; discussing magnetism, the Pole Star, compass, astrolabe, and a gemological test to ascertain true diamonds; and even exhibiting interest in the replicability of empirical experience (*Empire of Magic*, chapter 5).

Yet, for all its investment in a scientific or quasiscientific worldview, the *Travels* never wavers from a bedrock allegiance to Christian cosmology. The world may be a sphere, but this sphere nonetheless has to have a center, the city of the Lord: "Jerusalem is in the middle of the world" (Higgins, *Book* 113; Deluz 336). The center itself has a paramount focal point, the Church of the Holy Sepulcher, and the Holy Sepulcher too has a center:

> a circle where Joseph of Arimathea laid the body of Our Lord when He was taken down from the cross, and in the same place he cleaned His wounds. It is said that this circle is right in the middle of the world.
>
> (Higgins, *Book* 48; Deluz 192)

If Jerusalem is the center of the world, and the circle where the Lord's body lay is the center of the center, it is no wonder that in the *Travels'* purview, all roads lead to Jerusalem. If one begins from "the regions of the West – as from England, Ireland, Wales, Scotland, or Norway," one can travel to Constantinople, the Mandeville author shows, to get to Jerusalem (Higgins, *Book* 7; Deluz 95). From Jaffa, the "closest port to the city of Jerusalem," the holy city is only a day and a half away; or one could go from Tyre by land to Jerusalem (Higgins, *Book* 20; Deluz 125). From Damascus, there are three ways to get to "the holy city of Jerusalem," either by sea or by land (Higgins, *Book* 77; Deluz 258). In short, "one route and the next all lead to the same destination" (Higgins, *Book* 80; Deluz 264–5).

There are reasons why the Mandeville author wanted his audience to go to Jerusalem. First and foremost, even after two and a half centuries of crusading endeavor, Jerusalem was still in the hands of the infidel, the miscreant Saracens:

> – which is why every good Christian who has the power and the means ought to take pains and do great work to conquer our . . . right inheritance and take it from the hands of the miscreants and appropriate it to us, for we are called Christians after Christ, who is our Father; and if we are true sons of God, we ought to reclaim the inheritance our Father left to us and wrest it from the hands of the foreigners.
>
> (Higgins, *Book* 4; Deluz 91)

The *Travels*' Exordium exhorts the faithful to seize Jerusalem back from "the miscreants," and the Mandeville author entices his audience and builds resolve by imbuing the landscape and topography of the Holy Land with auratic wonder. Under his care, the very landscape itself bespeaks the body of the Savior, and becomes a vibrant witness to Jesus' life immanent in rock and water. At the mount of Calvary, there is a rock, "colored white with a little red mixed into it in some places" where "the blood from Our Lord's wounds dripped when He was hung from the cross" (Higgins, *Book* 46; Deluz 189).

Nearby is an altar where the column lies "to which Our Lord was tied and . . . scourged," and four stone columns always drip water, because "some say they weep for Our Lord's death" (Higgins, *Book* 47; Deluz 190). Above the valley of Jehoshaphat is the Golden Gate where "Our Lord entered . . . on Palm Sunday" (Higgins, *Book* 49; Deluz 193). A rock named Bethel, where the Ark of the Covenant was kept and Jacob had his vision of angels ascending and descending on a ladder, is redolent with His presence:

> On this rock Our Lord was presented to Saint Simeon; and on this rock Our Lord often preached to the people . . . and He set himself on this rock when the Jews wanted to stone him, and the rock split in the middle and He was hidden in that cleft; and a star came down to Him there that gave Him light and served as a lamp. On this rock Our Lady sat and learned her Psalter. There Our Lord pardoned the sins of the woman taken in adultery, there he was circumcised, there the angel announced to Zacharias the birth of his son John the Baptist, and there he first offered bread and wine to Our Lord as a sign of the sacrament to come.
>
> (Higgins, *Book* 52; Deluz 203–4)

The toposcape of the Holy Land is saturated with the aura of Jesus' life, vibrant with affect. Moreover, Jerusalem beckons with a chiaroscuro that mingles the hierophantic and the quotidian in intimate proportions. Not only do we encounter there the awe-full, storied places of the New Testament, but we are also able to experience homelier sites closer to His personal daily life: Here is Our Lord's bath, with water from Paradise, and there Our Lady's bed; here Our Lady sat and learned her Psalter (Higgins, *Book* 53, 52; Deluz 205, 203).

Everywhere you turn is a place numinous with poignancy and summoning awe. Our Lady was conceived here; Our Lord healed the paralytic man there; Our Lady dwelt here; here is the place Saint Peter denied Him three times before cockcrow; this is the stone that the three Marys saw on the day of the Resurrection; here is where Our Lord washed His disciples' feet; there Our Lord first appeared to His disciples after His Resurrection; here He celebrated Passover; there Saint John the Evangelist slept on His chest; here is where He made the blind man see, and Judas hanged himself, and so forth, ad infinitum (Higgins, *Book* 53–6; Deluz 205–10).[143]

The land is also graced by objects that Jesus touched, where the very rock bears the intimate imprint of His body, His hands, His feet.[144] At Gethsemane, "the fingers of Our Lord's hand are still visible where He leaned on the rock when the Jews forcefully seized Him" (Higgins, *Book* 58; Deluz 213). From the Mount of Olives, "Our Lord rose to Heaven on Ascension Day and [the imprint of] His left foot is still visible in the rock" (Higgins, *Book* 58; Deluz 214).[145]

The *Travels*' description of the Holy Land is thus a pilgrim brochure that invests Jerusalem and its environs with the radiance of the palpable life of Christ – offering rocks you can reverently touch, water you can dip your hand in, grooves and imprints you can trace, that Jesus also touched, dipped in, felt.[146] The *Travels* offers you a motive for why it takes such pains to describe "the noble city of Jerusalem" for "those who have the will and desire to visit": "it has been a long time since the general passage over the sea" – that is, it has been a while since there was a mass crusade to the Holy Land, and, the *Travels* adds coyly, "many people delight in hearing the said Holy Land spoken about and take pleasure in it" (Higgins, *Book* 5; Deluz 92).

In Chapter 3, I pointed to how the *Travels'* Exordium issues a clarion call to the Latin West to recapture Jerusalem by ventriloquizing some of the sentiments, and evoking the powerful affect, of Pope Urban II's address at the Council of Clermont in 1095, a conciliar address that summoned the mass movement of armed pilgrims later known as the First Crusade. In its own appeal, the Exordium explicitly singles out the elites of Europe:

> Today pride, greed, and envy have so inflamed the hearts of the lords that they seek more to disinherit others than they do to reclaim and conquer their own and lawful inheritance [the Holy Land] ... And those commoners who with goodwill have given their bodies and possessions to conquer our above-mentioned inheritance can do nothing without their sovereign lords. For a gathering of the commons without a chief lord is like a flock of sheep without a shepherd: it spreads out and does not know where it should go or what it should do. But if it pleased our holy apostolic father [the Pope] – for it would please God well – that the landed princes were reconciled and with each of their commons would undertake the holy voyage overseas, I believe it to be certain that in a short time the Promised Land would be restored and placed in the hands of its rightful heirs, the sons of Jesus Christ.
>
> (Higgins, *Book* 4–5; Deluz 91–2)

Urban's address, too, had made mention of the violence and unruliness of elites in the Latin West, whose confines he pronounced too narrow for knightly ambitions and energies, and Urban had urged the outward direction of those energies toward the goal of conquering Jerusalem. But the Mandeville author goes one better when he tells us why the *Travels* will be written in *French*, not Latin, though Latin would produce a briefer account: "I have put it into French so that everyone can understand it, and the knights and the lords and the other noble men who know no Latin, or a little, and who have been beyond the sea know and understand whether I speak the truth or not" (Higgins, *Book* 5–6; Deluz 93). This is to say, *Mandeville's Travels* explicitly "singles out the courtly estate" (Higgins, *Book* xvii) and is linguistically fashioned to encourage its successful reception among knights and lords, for whom French, not Latin, is the literary lingua franca.

Knights, and lords, and other noblemen who know no Latin or only a very little, are a key constituency of the "everyone" that constitutes the *Travels'* target audience – the class of elites indispensable to the recapture of the Holy Land, the *Travels'* Exordium says. To ensure the attention of these elites, the author offers a point of identification, making the narrator of his eyewitness account himself a knight, "Sir John Mandeville," putatively "born and raised in England in the town of St Albans" (Higgins, *Book* 5; Deluz 92).

The route to Jerusalem along which the knight Mandeville – as "tour guide" – takes his readers just happens to be the route of the First Crusade, derived from Albert of Aix's twelfth-century crusade chronicle (Higgins, *Book* xxiii, 7; Deluz 95).[147] It's been "a long time since the general passage over the sea," and if the lords of Europe with "their commons would undertake the holy voyage overseas," the Mandeville author assures his readers, it is "certain that in a short time the Promised Land would be restored and placed in the hands of its rightful heirs, the sons of Jesus Christ" (Higgins, *Book* 4–5; Deluz 92).

The Mandeville author seems to understand well, however, that an exhortation to rise to a great challenge needs to be sweetened, and the *Travels* is wisely filled with many inducements – not only the allure of a Holy Land suffused with the aura of the Savior, but also intriguing stories of an exotic world that beckons, because the unfamiliar and the new, the narrator slyly acknowledges, "give pleasure" (Higgins, *Book* 185; Deluz 479). *Pleasure* is a wonderful cue: It tells us that *Mandeville's Travels* is too wise a text, and wants too many things, to function only as a crude ideological instrument for reinvigorating European crusade. Indeed, the *Travels* has a larger vision it wants to impart to Christendom, not a single narrow ambition, and it will leaven that vision with pleasure.

What the *Travels* presents to its audiences is an expansive view of the world for Christendom to consider: a world that might be Christianity's oyster, under the right conditions – none of which would be unattainable, the *Travels* shows, including the retaking of the Holy Land. Beginning with the pull of the Holy Land, the narrative ranges farther and farther afield, always discovering religions that share some basis with Latin Christianity – "some articles of our faith," as the text puts it (Higgins, *Book* 184; Deluz 477) – even among heretical Christians, and even if that shared basis is, minimally, a belief in some kind of God.

And when a religion is incommensurable and impossible to reconcile to Latin Christianity, that religion can still serve Christians by the example of its adherents' devotion, since Latin Christians need to emulate devotional fervor.[148] For as it sketches a world that is ready to become, or that already is, more Christian than Europe realizes, the *Travels* in tandem takes aim at the shortcomings of Christianity at home – critiquing, shaming, and urging more true adherence to the Latin Christian faith within Latin Christendom itself. *Mandeville's Travels* dreams of a truly expansive, global Christianity – projective or actualized, involving crusade when necessary, or persuasion where people already have "some articles of our faith" – but a genuinely global Christianity also requires Christians at home to be more genuinely Christian.

Written in the optative mode, *Mandeville's Travels* is thus the finest kind of medieval travel romance – filled with optimism and desire, not fully concealing its aims, but conjuring with the real and the imaginary seamlessly and to best advantage, and sweetening the reception of its vision by giving its audience pleasure.[149]

Conquering the Worlds of Islam, Regaining the Holy Land

But what of the problems posed by Islam, that formidable international competitor whose adherents have held Jerusalem "for the space of one hundred and forty years and more" (Higgins, *Book* 45; Deluz 188)? Remarkably, the *Travels'* view of Islam and Saracens is an instrumentally pragmatic one. Islam, the *Travels* suggests, presents a *phenomenological* problem, not an epistemological challenge.

A religion originating with a man who had fits of epilepsy that he disguised as visitations by the angel Gabriel and who was consequently hailed as a prophet, Islam is an Abrahamic faith that accepts many tenets of the New Testament: Its adherents "have many good articles of our faith and of our belief" (Higgins, *Book* 85; Deluz 277). The *Travels* is therefore optimistic that despite its origins in duplicity, Islam does not pose an epistemological obstacle to converting Muslims to the Christian faith, for "they have many good articles of our faith and of our belief, although they do not have perfect law and faith according to Christians."

The way to optimism is through a sunny generalization: "all those who know and understand the Scriptures and the prophecies are easily converted" (Higgins, *Book* 85–6; Deluz 277). Insistently, the *Travels* more than once urges the ease of converting Muslims:

> Because they come so close to our faith they are easily converted to Christian law when one preaches to them and shows them clearly Jesus Christ's law and explains the prophecies to them. They also say that they know by the prophecies that Machomet's law will fail, just like the Jews' law, which is a failure, and that the Christian people's law will last until the world's end.
>
> (Higgins, *Book* 84–5; Deluz 276)

The seriousness with which the *Travels* treats the question of Islam can be seen in how it meticulously tries to describe the Islamic religion with accuracy. Handling its sources (which include Christian authors familiar with the Near East) deftly and skillfully, the *Travels* conjures up not the demonized "Mahound" or polytheistic caricature of medieval romance and *chanson de geste*, but close-to-accurate renditions of the Islamic faith, its Prophet, and its history – colored, of course, to some degree by conventions sedimented by earlier Christian polemics, such as the Prophet's putative epilepsy, drunkenness, and ruses, which the *Travels* inherits from its sources.[150]

The *Travels* is even that rare literary text from Northwestern Europe (England?) which quotes the Islamic *shahada* – the profession of faith that is the core of the Islamic creed, the pronouncement of which accompanies entrance into the religion – in not-too-badly garbled Arabic (Higgins, *Book* 89; Deluz 283).[151] The text even graciously allows that "Saracens are good, faithful, for they entirely keep the command of their holy book Alkoran" – evincing in this, as ever, the narrative's respect for adherents who are devout and pious, whatever their faith (Higgins, *Book* 87; Deluz 280).

But what excites the *Travels* most is the extent to which Islam might be interested in Christianity – how Islam acknowledges Jesus as a prophet, gives credence to His bodily Ascension into heaven, and reveres His life (Higgins, *Book* 83; Deluz 274–5). In its excitement, the *Travels* somewhat exaggerates the extent to which Jesus is revered by Muslims: It misleadingly declares, for instance, that Muslims, like Christians, believe in the Incarnation, and that the Quran states that "amongst all the prophets Jesus is the most excellent, and the closest to God" – the use of the superlative here intimating that the Quran presents Jesus as more excellent, and closer to God, than even the Prophet Muhammad himself (Higgins, *Book* 85, 83; Deluz 277, 274).

The narrative's buoyant insistence on Islam's theological receptivity to the central tenets of Christianity is essential, of course, to narrative optimism that the Islamic problem can be resolved without too much difficulty. Islam does not pose theological obstacles because – with one possible exception I discuss below – its epistemological apparatus is not significantly different from Christianity's. The Islamic problem is then a military one, to be resolved by crusading endeavor, and the success of crusading can be ensured by a solution that is readily at hand, as the *Travels* takes pains to show.

The *Travels* effervescently seals its optimism with prophecy, that old trusty standby. "They also say that they know by the prophecies that Machomet's law will fail, just like the Jews' law, which is a failure, and that the Christian people's law will last until the world's end" (Higgins, *Book* 85; Deluz 276). Better yet, the *Travels* puts the prophetic statement proclaiming the future triumph of Christian crusading in the mouth of the august leader of the Saracens, the Sultan of Egypt, who expatiates to Mandeville on why the Holy Land was lost by Christians, and how and when it can be regained:

> [Christians] break the entire law that Jesus has given them and set out for their salvation. Thus for their sins they have lost all this land that we possess, for because of their sins your God has put them [the lands] in our hands – not through our strength, but for their sins. For indeed we know truly that when you serve God well and he wants to help you no one can counter you, so we know well through our prophecies that Christians will win back this land when they serve their God more devoutly.
>
> (Higgins, *Book* 87; Deluz 279)

Thanks to the Sultan, we learn that Saracens, after all, might not even be much of a military challenge. The solution is plain, and it lies in the hands of Latin Christians themselves, for Christians are destined to win back the Holy Land merely by becoming better Christians. The time-honored crusade explanation for why Jerusalem remained in the hands of the infidel is thus handily called into service again, this time accruing all the greater persuasiveness for being voiced by the chief enemy himself, no less: the Sultan of Egypt.[152] With one narrative stroke, two critical exigencies find an answer: the problem of Jerusalem's recapture, and the problem of goading Christians in Europe to be better Christians.

Mandeville's loquacious Sultan appears like a veritable romance Saladin (who, we recall, was also Sultan of Egypt). Mandeville's Sultan speaks French (as, presumably, also does Saladin in *Le Roman de Saladin*, when Saladin adventures in France), and he is magnanimous to Mandeville (like the legendary Saladin might have been), allowing our knight into the sacred places of Jerusalem closed off to visitors, and benevolently offering Mandeville a Saracen princess for a bride (Higgins, *Book* 23; Deluz 134).[153] The Sultan even invites Mandeville into his personal quarters, alone and in private – with no protective bodyguard, counselors, courtiers, "lords and others, whatever their rank" present – for a private conversation in his chamber.

This important if improbable conversation between the puissant leader of the mighty Islamic empire of the Mamluks and our knight-narrator allows the Mandeville author to stage, with pomp, an extended harangue excoriating Christian Europeans for their sins, with the Sultan acting like a virtual scourge of God, who righteously accuses Christians of hypocrisy and abject failure to be adequate Christians (Higgins, *Book* 86–7; Deluz 278–9).[154]

Showing an astute grasp of human psychology, the *Travels* then positions the Sultan's reassuring prophecy at the end of his harangue. Significantly, it is not the first time that a prominent member of the Saracen foe prophesies victory for the Christian side, in a moment when reassurance is needed; crusade chronicles have deployed the narrative strategy before.[155] To arrive at this narrative moment, however, *Mandeville's Travels* has had to enact what at first glance appears a queer contradiction.

Urging on readers the reconquest of Jerusalem, the *Travels* nonetheless makes its English knight take military service with the Sultan of Egypt, the very Saracen foe who possesses Jerusalem (and not, apparently, for purposes of espionage – Mandeville merely confides, "I dwelt with him as a soldier in his wars for quite a while against the Bedouins" [Higgins, *Book* 23; Deluz 134]). The text's noble Christian goal – Jerusalem's recapture from the infidel – is thus queerly married to a narrative gesture that makes its knight-narrator a

Christian mercenary who serves the very infidel from whom Jerusalem must be wrested. Does Mandeville's example suggest that advancing a Christian goal first requires advancing the enemy's goals?

In and of itself, the prospect of a Christian knight serving a Muslim ruler is a romance trope of some duration. We saw in Chapter 4 that in Wolfram von Eschenbach's early thirteenth-century romance *Parzival*, the Arthurian knight Gahmuret faithfully and more than once serves the Caliph of Baghdad. Literature in fourteenth-century England later than the *Travels* also did not hesitate to deploy the trope: Chaucer's knight in the *Canterbury Tales* was a mercenary in foreign lands, with a hint of dubious allegiances. Beyond literature, the *Travels'* narrative decision is borne out by historical developments: Not long after the First Crusade's establishment of crusader colonies in the East, Christian knights did indeed on occasion serve Muslim leaders in the Levant in various regional wars and conflicts.

Mandeville's service to the infidel in the *Travels* is instrumentally useful for several narrative ends, moreover. It authenticates Mandeville as a genuine eyewitness in the places he claims to have visited, and positions our knight as a participant-observer able to record details close at hand to his ostensible experience. Mandeville's service also allows him access to the Sultan, and makes possible the intimate conversation in the Sultan's chamber which in turn enables the author to deploy the Sultan as a mouthpiece to accuse, critique, and shame the Christians of the West, while also declaring the future victory of Christians over Muslims.

If the leader of the enemy, who has no reason to look forward to defeat, subscribes to the truth of Christian victory, should not the knights, lords, and other noblemen of the Latin West find his confession of so-called Islamic prophecy profoundly reassuring? Not least of all, the *Travels'* invocation of the romance trope of the Saracen princess – the Sultan offers to marry Mandeville "very highly to a landed prince's daughter" and to give him "great inheritances" if Mandeville is willing to convert to Islam – allows the text to confirm Mandeville's credentials as a faithful, Christian, and trustworthy narrator by the English knight's refusal of the seductions of sex, rank, and wealth extended in the Sultan's offer (Higgins, *Book* 23; Deluz 134).

There is one constituency of Muslims, however, that must be dealt with differently from the generality of Saracens represented by the urbane Sultan of Egypt – the Assassins of Alamut (or "Milstorak," the place-name *Travels* inherits from its source), whose leader is Gathalonabez (Higgins, *Book* 164; Deluz 440).[156] This group is used by the *Travels* to dramatize the logic of a putative Islamic desire for a sexual exorbitance that might prove a serious obstacle to the conversion of Muslims: the Quranic promise of a supremely sensual paradise of delights filled, the *Travels* admits, with "fruit in all seasons, and rivers flowing with milk and honey and wine," where one can have beautiful and "noble houses" of "precious stones and gold and silver," and "where each man will have ninety wives, all virgins, and will have relations with her [sic] every day, and will always find them virgins" (Higgins, *Book* 82; Deluz 273). The *Travels* says that "all Saracens believe" in this sensational Islamic paradise "of delights," which is described in the "Alkoran" given to Saracens by their Prophet (Higgins, *Book* 82; Deluz 273).

Though relegated by the Quran to the afterlife, the salacious Islamic paradise, the *Travels* shows, seems also to leak into Islamic life on earth, since the "book of Alkoran" allows every Muslim to have "two wives or three, or four," and "now they take up to nine, and as many concubines as they can maintain" (Higgins, *Book* 85; Deluz 276). Such conjugal liberality – an early foretaste of the ninety (*sic*) virgins awaiting male Saracens in the Islamic paradise? – has no equivalent in Christian doctrine, and is not one of the shared "articles of faith" between Islam and Christianity.

But ingeniously, the *Travels* decides to unpack the underpinning logic of such lubricious salaciousness by allegorically retelling the old fable of the Assassins of Alamut – the legend fabricated by the West, and that I discuss in Chapter 3 – of youthful dupes who are lured into a false paradise of sensual delights created by an "Old Man of the Mountain" and told they can only return if they commit murder for their master.

The *Travels'* account of this legend, I argued in Chapter 3, is careful to have readers understand that "Milstorak" (Alamut) is a faithful copy of the Islamic paradise in every way. The facsimile features "the most beautiful garden with trees bearing all kinds of fruit," "sweet-smelling herbs," "beautiful flowers," "diverse animals," "birds that sang," beautiful halls and rooms "in gold and azure," and beautiful fountains flowing with milk, wine, and honey (Higgins, *Book* 164; Deluz 440–1). As the body's senses are diversely pleasured, lovely female prepubescent and pubescent virgins under the age of fifteen are at hand to enable "love-play" to the body's content. These *houri*-like companions, whom Gathalonabez calls "God's angels," remain perpetual virgins, so that *love-play* with the dewily pubescent and virginal can be perpetually refreshed and enjoyed anew (Higgins, *Book* 164–5; Deluz 440–2).

The outcome of this elaborate duplicity, with its proffer of orgiastic pleasure and sensual indulgence, however, is death: both the death of enemies targeted by Gathalonabez and, more like as not, the death of the youthful dupes for whom the fake paradise is made, who die in the commission of their murderous tasks (Higgins, *Book* 165; Deluz 441–2). While seeming to offer life in its most exquisitely intense and pleasurable form, therefore, the terrestrial paradise in truth only hurtles men toward death and destruction (Higgins, *Book* 165; Deluz 442). The fable's intertwining of two motifs – wanton enjoyment of full sensual pleasure, and the horrors of death and destruction – congeals a sobering allegory that intermixes sexual profligacy with death. Sex and death: The one is twinned to the other, and they are intimate companions in this story of an Islamic paradise on earth, a warning that the offer of full sexual license is never what it appears to be.

This dramatic episode, which concedes how Islam is, after all, not very like Christianity, is treated with a certain narrative tact. The *Travels* does not say that Milstorak's paradise is a replica of Islam's, nor does it need to: As a facsimile, Milstorak so faithfully copies the Quranic paradise the *Travels* earlier presents, down to detailed particulars like the perpetual virginity of the pleasure-maidens, that an announcement can be waived (Higgins, *Book* 82, 164–5; Deluz 273, 440–2). Moreover, not only are there *houri*-like prepubescent and pubescent female "angels" to serve as sexual companions, but like the Quranic paradise, Milstorak also has beautiful *boy* servitors under the age of fifteen, mimicking the *ghilman* or *wildan* of the Quran – a detail conspicuously absent in the Mandeville author's source, Odoric of Pordenone's *Relatio*, and missing also from Marco Polo's *Le Devisement* – predecessors that recount the story of the false paradise of the Assassins (Higgins, *Book* 164; Deluz 441).

Impressively, the *Travels'* familiarity with the Islamic paradise also includes knowledge that Islam posits the existence of *more than one level of paradise* (or *Jannah*, literally, "garden") and has superior, higher levels of paradise, including *Firdaws*, the highest level of all, which is attained by martyrs and is where God dwells. Thus the Mandeville author has Gathalonabez tell his dupes that should they die in the commission of murder, he would place them in yet "another paradise a hundred times more beautiful" than the one they were currently enjoying, and "in a still more beautiful paradise where they would see God . . . visibly in his majesty and in his glory" (Higgins, *Book* 165; Deluz 442).

Apparently, Gathalonabez slyly intimates to his youthful dupes that their death while committing assassination would transform them into martyrs, guaranteed entrance into *Firdaws* by his patronage. Such remarkable attentiveness to the infrastructure of the facsimile paradise, which meticulously copies the edifice of paradise in the Islamic afterlife, also has no equivalent in Odoric's *Relatio* and Polo's *Le Devisement*.

Gathalonabez' visualization of a terrestrial foretaste of the Islamic paradise is disturbing, and the *Travels* is careful to proffer two kinds of narrative containment. In yet another departure from its source, Odoric's *Relatio*, the *Travels* places the land of Milstorak under the overlordship of Prester John (Higgins, *Book* 164; Deluz 440) – the sublime priest-king of the Christian utopia in whom the *Travels* is deeply invested, and a personage I discuss later in this chapter. A Christian emperor thus has dominion over the unsettling Milstorak. Even more reassuringly, Milstorak and its master have been destroyed by neighboring lords, and no longer exist (Higgins, *Book* 165; Deluz 442). Only the Sultan of Egypt and the Saracens, who can be easily converted, since they share articles of the Christian faith, remain to bear witness to an Islamic prophecy that Jerusalem will once again be Christian.[157]

But if, for the *Travels*, Islam and Muslims will pose little impediment to a victorious Christianity in the Near East, thanks to prophecy and apparent Islamic embrace of the central tenets of Christianity, how does the *Travels'* vision of an expansive Christianity handle religions and peoples much farther east?

Fully a third of the *Travels* is dedicated to teaching readers how to think about the Mongols, those peculiar people who had drawn intense European scrutiny for over a century, and whose meaning, as a race, underwent dramatic change, as we have seen. Iain Higgins traces the *Travels'* sources on the Mongols to primarily three texts: Odoric of Pordenone's *Relatio*, an account by a pious Franciscan monk of his fourteen-and-a-half-year-long mission to India and China that began in 1314 or 1315; a redacted version of John of Plano Carpini's *Ystoria Mongolarum* and Simon of Saint Quentin's (lost) account of the Mongols copied into Vincent of Beauvais' *Speculum Historiale*; and Hayton (Hethum) of Armenia's 1307 *Flor des estoires de la terre d'Orient* (Flower of the Histories of the Land of the East).[158]

From its sources, the *Travels* thus inherits a bifurcated view of Mongols – one that sees Mongols as the savage barbarians we encountered in mid-thirteenth century Franciscan missionary reports, but also as the puissant rulers of a supercivilized Cathay led by the greatest emperor in the world – which Odoric of Pordenone's more recent fourteenth-century account readily attests. The *Travels* accordingly looks at Mongols with something like stereo-optic vision. The narrative deftly assigns Tartars-as-savages to the thirteenth-century past, where they are still led by Batu ("Batho") in the peripheries of the Mongol empire (Higgins, *Book* 80; Deluz 266).

In that space-time continuum, such thirteenth-century-style Mongols inhabit "a most miserable land," where scarcely anything grows, and eat "only meat without bread," drink "milk from all animals," and devour everything that moves (as we saw in John's *Ystoria*); they are "extremely filthy people" of "a wicked nature," who use the dung of horses and other animals for fuel (as we saw in William of Rubruck's *Itinerarium*). Even the princes of these mid-thirteenth-century-type Mongols subsist on little (Higgins, *Book* 80; Deluz 266). Mongols of this sort, if we remember, inhabit a barren ecoscape with hostile, contradictory extremes of weather – storms, lightning, and thunder, with intense heat inexplicably alternating with intense cold in summer, as the early Franciscan missions to the Mongols had reported (Higgins, *Book* 80; Deluz 266).

When retelling Mongol history, beginning with Genghis ("Chan Guys") Khan, in a chapter that Higgins says is based on Hayton's chronicle, the *Travels* once again evokes the bestial nature of thirteenth-century Mongols: "they were all animal-like and did nothing but keep animals and lead them to pasture" (Higgins, *Book* 135; Deluz 380). But the *Travels'* account of Mongol-ruled Cathay stereo-optically also offers readers a fourteenth-century view of Mongols who live in a state-of-the-art civilization governed by the greatest ruler on earth, the Great Khan. Released from the shackles of mid-thirteenth-century descriptions, these fourteenth-century Mongols inhabit the greatest civilization on earth, their lords dressing "in clothes of gold," wearing "rich gold crowns with precious stones and large orient pearls," and sharing the magnificent feasts of the Great Khan (Higgins, *Book* 140; Deluz 390).

Securely nested in the fourteenth century, the Mongols of Cathay are shown to be the Mongols of Marco Polo and Odoric, not of John of Plano Capini and William of Rubruck – a privileged race inhabiting a superior fourteenth-century civilization. At the Great Khan's feasts, 4,000 lords ("dukes, counts, and marquises and commanders") are identified by the color of their robes – green silk and red silk, purple/indigo silk and yellow silk – which are embroidered with gold and precious stones and pearls (Higgins, *Book* 140; Deluz 390). We are regaled with spectacles of staggering opulence and magnificence, and the vast numbers of courtiers, animals, and entertainments to which *Le Devisement* had accustomed us.

Minstrels, magicians, and beautiful young female dancers abound as court entertainers, and, extravagantly, tame lions, eagles, vultures, "and many kinds of birds, fishes, and snakes" are brought before the emperor "to honor him, for they say that every living creature must obey and honor him" (Higgins, *Book* 142; Deluz 394). All creation, it seems, must bow before the Great Khan, whose imperial household includes "officials who keep birds: ostriches, gyrfalcons, sparrowhawks, peregrine falcons, lanners, sakerets, talking parrots, and singing birds, and also wild animals and tame elephants . . . baboons, monkeys, marmots and other diversities" (Higgins, *Book* 143; Deluz 395–6).

Because the *Travels* is fascinated with science and technology, to signal the sublimity of this Mongol civilization, the Mandeville author has the Great Khan's elites exhibit knowledge of what the narrative considers to be state-of-the-art fourteenth-century science. In attendance at court is an array of "philosophers" specializing in diverse "sciences," who parade their "instruments" and technologies:

> To one side of the emperor's table sit many philosophers learned in many sciences such as astronomy, necromancy, geomancy, pyromancy, hydromancy, augury, and many other sciences; and some have gold astrolabes in front of them, or spheres, some a dead man's skull, others gold vessels full of sand, others vessels full of burning coals, others gold vessels full of water and oil, and others very nobly made clocks and many other kinds of instruments suited to their sciences.
>
> (Higgins, *Book* 141; Deluz 391–2)

The Great Khan also has 130,000 servants, spends "an incalculable amount" of money (which he prints on bark or paper), and has at court 50,000 horsed warriors and 200,000 foot soldiers (Higgins, *Book* 146; Deluz 402).¹⁵⁹ When he travels between his summer capital of Shang-du ("Saduz") and his winter capital of Khanbalik ("Camaalech"), four armies travel with him, the least numerous of which comprises 500,000 warriors (Higgins, *Book* 142–4; Deluz 397–9).

This emperor, of course, like Polo's Kublai, also travels in pomp and luxury, in a chariot-borne "beautiful room" made of fragrant wood ("lignum aloes") from the Earthly Paradise, covered with fine gold plate, precious stones, and large pearls (Higgins, *Book* 144; Deluz 398). Naturally, he travels with gyrfalcons, and hunts along the way for sport. Four elephants and four large white charges, richly caparisoned, draw the entire appurtenance, attended by mounted lords who ride alongside (Higgins, *Book* 144; Deluz 398). In "the same way go the empresses, each having with her four armies just like the emperor," and "his eldest son goes by another route . . . in this same manner" (Higgins, *Book* 144; Deluz 399). Just like in Polo's *Le Devisement*, when the Great Khan travels, a city appears to be on the move, so that "it is a wonder to see and no one would believe the number if he did not see them" (Higgins, *Book* 144; Deluz 399).¹⁶⁰

If the Great Khan is overwhelmingly impressive, so is his empire, which is divided into twelve provinces with more than 2,000 cities each and countless towns (Higgins, *Book* 144; Deluz 399). A king rules over each of the twelve provinces, with many subsidiary kings under him, "and all are obedient to the Great Chan. His land and his lordship extend so far that to go from one end to the other both by sea and by land would take more than seven years" – the "kingdom of Cathay," the *Travels* stresses, "is the largest kingdom there is in the world, and . . . the Great Chan is the strongest emperor there is under the firmament" (Higgins, *Book* 144, 139; Deluz 399, 386).

The Mongol empire of the *Travels*, like the Mongol empire in *Le Devisement*, has a state-of-the-art postal and communications system, with a network of way stations, hostelries, riders, and couriers to ensure efficient, high-speed communications (Higgins, *Book* 145; Deluz 399–400). In short, "Under the firmament there is no lord so great or so strong as is the Great Chan, neither above earth nor below" (Higgins, *Book* 146; Deluz 402). But, wistfully, the *Travels* concludes: "he surpasses all the earthly princes – which is why it is a great harm that he does not steadfastly believe in God" (Higgins, *Book* 146; Deluz 402).

What the Mandeville author acknowledges here in a sad, honest moment is that the Great Khan of mid-fourteenth-century Mongol Cathay does not believe in Europe's *Christian* God. Higgins reminds us that the narrative had already contradictorily pro-claimed earlier, in a cheerier moment, that Mongols believe in "immortal God": an immortal God, presumably, who might be imagined as the immortal God of Christianity, since, according to the Mandeville author – and the *Travels* really insists on this – two earlier Mongol emperors, Mongke Khan ("Mango Chan") and Kublai Khan ("Cobila Chan"), *had actually been Christians* (Higgins, *Book* 139; Deluz 386)! Mongke "was a good baptized Christian and gave letters of perpetual peace to all Christians," and Kublai "was also Christian" (Higgins, *Book* 138, 139; Deluz 385, 386).¹⁶¹

Such is the *Travels'* desire for the magnificent Great Khan of the fabulous Mongol empire to be Christian that it larkily revises the religion of two previous historic Khans: Mongke (who, William of Rubruck had derisively attested, was most certainly not Chris-tian), and Kublai.¹⁶² We thus see how Marco Polo's claim that Kublai Khan favored

Christians, and desired 100 Christian men of learning for purposes of instruction and conversion, has come to teleological fruition – in the *Travels'* inventive insistence that Kublai Khan was, in fact, *actually already Christian.*

With two former Great Khans confidently claimed for global Christianity, the *Travels* then does its best to recruit the current mid-fourteenth century Great Khan and his court into Christianity's fold too, because unfortunately the Mongol emperors since Kublai's time, the narrative laments, "are not now Christians" (Higgins, *Book* 139; Deluz 387). But shunting aside its source, Odoric of Pordenone's *Relatio*, which reports that the fourteenth-century Mongol emperor whom Odoric visits keeps in attendance 400 pagan physicians, 8 Christian ones, and a single Saracen (Chiesa 140), the *Travels* sunnily declares that the Mongol emperor is attended by 200 *Christian physicians*, 210 *Christian medics*, and 200 Saracens, "for they put much more faith in the work of Christians than of Saracens" (Higgins, *Book* 143; Deluz 396).

The Great Khan's court is also populated with Christians: "many lords and servants who are Christian and converts to the faith through the preaching of the Christian monks who dwell there," and there are even covert Christians who, despite the fact that the Khan puts such store in "the work of Christians," "do not wish it to be known that they are Christian" (Higgins, *Book* 143; Deluz 396). The Great Khan of Cathay sure seems to be surrounded by *a lot* of Christians.

To suggest reverence for Christianity on the part of the Great Khan himself, the *Travels* regales its readers with a story it adapts from an addendum to Odoric's *Relatio*, attributed by some manuscripts to the Franciscan friar Marchesino of Bassano. Christian monks dwell in many cities of the empire, the *Travels* says, and walk in procession with the cross and holy water, chanting "*Veni Creator Spiritus*" [Come, Creator Spirit] in a loud voice (Higgins, *Book* 145; Deluz 401). When the Great Khan hears them,

> he orders his lords who are riding beside him to make the monks come; and when they approach and he sees the cross he takes off his *galahoth* – which sits on his head like a felt hat, [and] which is made of gold and precious stones and large pearls, and it is so rich that it would be worth a kingdom in this country – and bows to the cross. Then the chief priest of these monks says his prayers in front of him and then blesses him with the cross and he bows most devoutly to the blessing.
>
> (Higgins, *Book* 145; Deluz 401)[163]

In addition to proclaiming the Great Khan's deep respect for the cross and for the blessing of monks, the *Travels* also mines the famed religious tolerance of Mongol rulers for glimmers of hope: Though the emperor "does not steadfastly believe in God," nevertheless "he very willingly hears God spoken about and continually allows that there are Christians who go throughout his whole country, for no one is prohibited from holding such law [religion] as he likes" (Higgins, *Book* 146; Deluz 402).[164]

Two Great Khans of the past might be claimed by the *Travels* for Christianity, but the Mandeville author refrains from transforming the contemporary, real-time ruler of mid-fourteenth century Cathay also into a Christian. For one, this would openly contradict Odoric of Pordenone's still-circulating and widely popular *Relatio*, a chief source of the *Travels*. For another, Franciscan missions are still active in Khanbalik and Zayton in fourteenth-century China, and the letters from China written by John of Monte Corvino, Peregrine of Castello, and Andrew of Perugia, citing fellow Franciscans by name

(Peter of Florence, John of Grimaldi, Emmanuel of Monticulo, Ventura of Sarezana, Gerard, bishop of Zayton, et al.) and testifying to the generous stipendiary charity of each Great Khan on which they live, make it obvious that the fourteenth-century Great Khans of Yuan Cathay are not Christians (Dawson 224–37; also see Moule for more on the Franciscan missions in northern China).

Ingeniously, however, the *Travels* proposes a fantasmatic solution to the "great harm" that the Mongol emperor of Cathay does not believe in the Christian God: The *Travels* devises a *romance* answer to the problem, to bolster Christian hope and optimism in the face of intractable historical facticity. The *Travels* offers its readers a facsimile emperor of the East who *is* a devout Christian and *does* "steadfastly believe in God," an emperor whose empire, though not as wealthy as the Mongol Khan's, can serve as an imagined threshold to the great Mongol empire against which it abuts. That mirror-emperor, a Christian doppelganger of sorts for the Great Khan, is the legendary priest-king the West knows as Prester John.

An Emperor for All Reasons: Prester John Triumphs over the Great Khan

By the time the *Travels* was written, European belief in the fictitious priest-king Prester John was 200 years old, and John's legend had gained its ever-enlarging traditions through two distinct strains of development. One strain was more historically inflected than the other, and linked "Prester John" to actual personages of Kara-Khitan, Kereit, Ongut, or even Naiman ethnicity in Central Asia and Eurasia, with the name "Prester John" surviving over time to lend luster to the pedigree of later generations of Nestorian Christian chieftains associated with him.

The other strain was more fantasy-based, identifying John as the emperor of a fabulous, opulent "India" filled with marvels ("India" itself being the name of an exotic, flexible territory with shifting locations in the medieval European imaginary).[165] Belief in Prester John of India survived longer than belief in Prester John of Eurasia – up into the eighteenth century – and served as an inducement, or at least a pretext, for European voyaging into foreign lands long past the medieval period. The two lines of development in the Prester John legend, of course, intertwined, converged, and separated at various historical junctures.[166]

Both these traditions of the Prester John legend stemmed from historical events that occasioned the opportunistic literary production in the Latin West, c. 1165, of the *Letter of Prester John*, a Latin epistle composed in first-person imperial voice to Manuel I Comnenus ("Emmanuel"), ruler of the Romans (i.e., of Greek Byzantium, the latter-day Eastern Roman Empire), by a putative potentate of "India" who claimed to be both a priest and a king of kings, and who vowed in the *Letter* to "visit the Sepulcher of the Lord with the greatest army" to "humble and defeat the enemies of the cross of Christ and to exalt his blessed name" (Zarncke 78).[167]

The legend of Prester John, as Bernard Hamilton, Charles Beckingham, and others have persuasively shown, came to life as a consolatory fiction to buttress Latin Christian optimism in the face of territorial loss, and materialized out of "the thought-world of the crusades" as early as 1145, "a few months after ... Edessa had fallen to Zengi of Mosul" in the first recapture of the crusader colonies of Outremer by Islamic countercrusades ("Continental Drift" 256, 238). That is to say, the *Letter of Prester John* began its life as a literary, mid-twelfth-century romance answer to a historical disaster.[168] The path to the *Letter*'s appearance was paved by an important and fortuitous rumor. In the 1145 chronicle of Otto, Bishop of Friesing, the *Historia de Duabus Civitatibus* (History of Two Cities), Otto claims in Book VII chapter 33 that when he visited the court of Pope Eugenius III, he had met a Viterbo Bishop Hugh of Jabala, who

> related that not many years ago a certain Iohannes [John], a king and a priest, living in the Far East, in *extremo Orientale*, beyond Persia and Armenia, who like all his people was a Christian though a Nestorian, made war on the brothers, the kings of the Persians and Medes, the Samiardi, and stormed the capital of their kingdom, Egbattana ... [T]hey fought for three days ... At last Presbyter Iohannes – for so they are in the habit of calling him – was victorious, putting the Persians to flight with most bloodthirsty slaughter.
>
> (Beckingham, "Achievements" 2)[169]

In 1165, the anonymously authored *Letter of Prester John* materialized, and elaborated on the idea of an Eastern potentate who was a devout Christian and would labor mightily in the service of the Lord, vowing to visit the Lord's Sepulcher with the greatest army to destroy utterly the enemies of the cross. To ensure its appeal and circulation, the *Letter* shrewdly harnesses a wealth of exotic, fabulous material from travel literature, romance, bestiaries, lapidaries, folklore, legends, and the like, to describe Prester John's realm as a vast utopian empire that was an ideal social and ethical polity – shorn of sin, vice, and crime; flowing with milk and honey; proliferating with precious gemstones, exotic beasts, and the marvelous races of the Plinian tradition; evincing palatial architectural wonders and extraordinary edifices (including a giant, panopticon-like all-seeing mirror for the realm's defense); inhabited by diverse, multireligious subject populations governed by subsidiary kings; and with Prester John, the overlord of the realm, majestically ruling over all in stable, good governance and dramatizing his Christian piety through processional ritual:

> When we proceed to war against our enemies, we have carried before our front line, in separate wagons, thirteen great and very tall crosses made of gold and precious stones in place of banners, and each one of these is followed by ten thousand mounted soldiers and 100 thousand foot soldiers ... when we ride out unarmed, a wooden cross, ornamented with neither paint, gold, nor gems, proceeds before our majesty, so that we may always be mindful of the passion of our lord Jesus Christ, and [so does] a golden vase, full of earth, in order that we may know that our body will return to its proper origin, the earth. And another silver vase, full of gold, is carried before us in order that all may understand that we are lord of lords.
>
> (Uebel, *Ecstatic Transformation* 157; Zarncke 84)

The *Letter of Prester John* was embraced with great enthusiasm in the Latin West. Over a hundred manuscripts in Latin survive, and the *Letter* was translated into multiple vernacular languages, including French, Italian, German, English, Hebrew, Serbian, and Russian, to reach a variety of audiences, with later iterations substantially expanding and elaborating on its spectacular fictions. The desire in the Latin West for Prester John and his Christian kingdom to exist, and be real, was exorbitant, and unquenchable for 600 years (*Empire of Magic* 276–87).

For the mid-fourteenth-century *Mandeville's Travels*, with its desire to reinvigorate crusade and its vision of a triumphal Christianity that will be practiced by genuinely pious, devout Christians, the allure of Prester John, though by now a 200-year-old legend, must have been well nigh irresistible. But in order for John and his empire to offer some kind of purchase on Mongol Cathay and its Khan, the *Travels* first had to establish a link between the ideal Christian emperor it imports from European epistolary fiction and the pagan Great Khan of Cathay. To effect that link the *Travels* resorts to the other, alternative tradition of the Prester John legend – the view of John as a ruler on the steppe whose history is intermingled with that of the Mongols.

The Mandeville author joins the two emperors by means of marriage, making Prester John's daughter the Great Khan's first and chief wife: "Of his three wives the first and the foremost (who was Prester John's daughter) had the name Serioch Chan" (Higgins, *Book* 147–8; Deluz 406). "Serioch Chan," Higgins correctly informs us, is "Seroctan" (*Book* 148 n.487) – or John of Plano Carpini's "Sorocan," as we saw in the *Ystoria Mongalorum*, the Latinized name of Sorghaghtani Bekhi, the highly influential Kereit and Nestorian Christian mother of Kublai, Mongke, Hulegu, and Arik-Boke, and the wife of Toluy, Genghis Khan's youngest son.

Not content with establishing Sorghaghtani Bekhi as the hinge between the two emperors, the *Travels* also insists there is a *mutuality* and *equivalence* between the emperors in the register of matrimony, an equivalence that is signaled by a *mutual exchange* of royal women. For the *Travels* insists that "This Emperor Prester John always takes the Great Chan's daughter as his wife, and the Great Chan [takes] Prester John's daughter as well" – a narrative innovation, Higgins points out, that reconfigures the *Travels'* source, Odoric's *Relatio*, which only mentions Prester John's marriage to the Great Khan's daughter but not its corollary (Higgins, *Book* 161, 161 n.523; Deluz 435; Chiesa 150). This marital exchange doubly cements relations between the two emperors.

In plucking Sorghaghtani Bekhi from the thirteenth century with the help of redacted Franciscan missionary documents and making her into the seam that joins Prester John and the Great Khan, the *Travels* thus nods in the direction of the tradition that places "Prester John" in nomad Eurasia, rather than exotic, fabulous India. The legend of "Prester John" in Eurasia, scholars have argued since the late nineteenth century, likely began with Hugh of Jabala's misrecognition of a historical event in which Yelu Dashi, a Kara-Khitan who, leading the remnants of the Khitan (Liao) dynasty of China westward, had roundly crushed Ahmad Sanjar, the Seljuk sultan of Persia, at Qatwan in Samarkand in 1141. The story of an Islamic Seljuk sultan's defeat at the hands of a conqueror from farther East happily signaled to Latin Christendom that there was an "unknown aggressor, who shared with the crusading West an hostility to Islam" and "was transmuted by the Catholic world into a powerful Christian ruler" (Hamilton, "Continental Drift" 238):

> Prester John symbolized the hopes which western Christians in the twelfth century derived from the certain knowledge that there were in the lands beyond Islam Christian communities who might potentially be useful allies, and those hopes were focused on the region where allies were most needed, the lands to the east of Mosul, whose Zengid rulers were threatening the Crusader States. It is no coincidence that Prester John first appeared in 1145, a few months after the holy city of Edessa had fallen to Zengi of Mosul. This was the first serious loss of territory which the Franks in the East had suffered, and so severe was the

psychological shock to western Christendom that it led to the preaching of the Second Crusade.

(Hamilton, "Continental Drift" 238)

As one crusader colony after another, including Jerusalem, was recaptured by the infidel, the thirteenth-century desire for Prester John to exist kept him in the sights of the Latin West, and we have seen how Armenian emissaries who had visited the Mongol empire, and Nestorian envoys sent by the Mongols, fed rumors that Christians were part of the Mongol nomad confederations. We encountered earlier in this chapter the extraordinary claim made by David and Mark, Nestorian envoys dispatched by Aljigiday to Louis IX at Nicosia in 1248, that Guyuk Khan's mother was the daughter of Prester John: this despite the fact that Innocent IV's papal ambassador to the Mongol empire, John of Plano Carpini, had met Guyuk Khan's mother, Toreghana Khatun, face-to-face.

But the "Prester John" of the steppe who gave a face to rumors of Christians among the Mongol confederations bore little resemblance to the Prester John of India described by the twelfth-century Latin *Letter*, and did not rule a magnificent, marvelous empire of palaces and gems. William of Rubruck's mid-thirteenth century *Itinerarium* makes sure that his addressee, Louis IX, understands that "Prester John" is a mere Nestorian pastoralist, "a mighty herdsman and the ruler over a people called the Naiman" who "set himself up as king" after the death of the Gur-Khan ("Coir Chan") – that is, Yelu Dashi, who had assumed the title of Gur-Khan (Jackson and Morgan 122; Dawson 122; Wyngaert 206). William is unusual in making John a Naiman – Prester John is more often linked to the Kereit and Ongut, tribes commonly associated with Christianity – but takes care to puncture the inflation of John's legend:

> The Nestorians called him King John, and only a tenth of what they said about him was true. For this is the way with the Nestorians who come from these parts: they create big rumors out of nothing ... In this way was broadcast the impressive report about King John; and when I myself crossed his pasturelands, nobody knew anything about him except for a few Nestorians.
>
> (Jackson and Morgan 122; Dawson 122; Wyngaert 206)

William's *Itinerarium* also shows us how Sorghaghtani Bekhi enters into the story of Prester John of Eurasia. When this King John died without heirs, the *Itinerarium* adds, his brother (William calls this brother "Unc"), who was "likewise a mighty herdsman" ("*potens pastor similiter*"), took over, had himself proclaimed Khan, and entered into war with Genghis. Unc Khan was roundly defeated; his daughter was taken prisoner by Genghis, was given to one of Genghis' sons for a wife, and became the mother of Mongke, William concludes ("Mangu," Jackson and Morgan 123–5; Dawson 122–3; Wyngaert 207–8).

The *Secret History of the Mongols* confirms the broad outlines of the *Itinerarium*'s story, if not its details. Toghril Khan of the Kereit, who was known as the Ong Khan, was an erstwhile ally of Genghis but later warred with Genghis, in part, the *Secret History* shows, because the Ong Khan had been poorly advised by his son Senggum that a marital exchange proposed by Genghis – between the Ong Khan's daughter and Genghis' eldest son Jochy, and Genghis' daughter and the Ong Khan's grandson Tusaka – would end up lowering the Ong Khan's dignity (de Rachewiltz I: 84).

After defeating the Kereit, Genghis then gives Sorghaghtani, the Ong Khan's niece – his younger brother's daughter – to Toluy, Genghis' youngest son (de Rachewiltz, *Secret*

History I: 108). Sorghaghtani Bekhi, of course, becomes the mother of two Great Khans and the Ilkhan Hulegu, and a famous historical figure in her own right. John of Plano Carpini respectfully estimates that she is the most powerful personage in the Mongol empire of its time, second only to the khan-maker Batu (Dawson 26; Wyngaert 66; see also de Rachewiltz, *Secret History* II: 669–70).

Narrating events similar to those that appear in the *Secret History*, Marco Polo's *Le Devisement* announces that the Ong Khan ("Uncan") is in fact Prester John, "of whom all the world talks of his great rule" (Moule and Pelliot I: 162; Ronchi 380). *Le Devisement* amends the details of the proposed marital alliance, making Genghis Khan request the Ong Khan's daughter *for Genghis himself*, not for Genghis' eldest son, in the year 1200 (Moule and Pelliot I: 163; Ronchi 381–2). Thanks to Polo, the Ong Khan is thus identified as Prester John, and a tradition is established that the Great Khan of the Mongol empire wanted Prester John's daughter for a wife.

Le Devisement announces that Prester John was killed in the battle that followed and lost all his land, but the story doesn't end there: John's descendants now live in the province of "Tenduc" (Ongut), subject to the Great Khan Kublai, with Tenduc being ruled by a king in the lineage of Prester John, called George, and who himself is also a priest (Moule and Pelliot I: 166, 181–2; Ronchi 385, 397–8). Thanks to *Le Devisement*, we now have a Prester George. Furthermore, *Le Devisement* adds, the Great Khans have always given of their daughters and of their kindred to the kings who are of the lineage of Prester John (Moule and Pelliot I: 182; Ronchi 397).

And there we have it: a solid narrative platform for the *Travels'* claim that Prester John and the Great Khan of Cathay each gives a daughter to the other for a wife. But *Le Devisement's* narrative gifts do not end there, and the text continues to expatiate on John's descendants. *Le Devisement* says that King George of Tenduc is the *sixth* lord in the lineage of Prester John, but later it also says that George, the *grandson* of Prester John, fought alongside Kublai Khan's son Nomogan (that is, Nomukhan) against Kaidu (Moule and Pelliot I: 182, 449–52; Ronchi 398, 613–17). In the alliance between John's grandson George (the same priest-king George of Tenduc? An earlier descendant also called George?) and Kublai's son Nomogan, this George is repeatedly called "the son to the son of *the* Prester John," as if "Prester John" has now been transmuted into a status title (Moule and Pelliot I: 449–52; Ronchi 613–17).

The name *George* is prominent again in the fourteenth century, when the second letter of John of Monte Corvino from Khanbalik in northern China, dated January 8, 1305, relates how he, the Archbishop of Khanbalik, had converted to the Latin faith a Nestorian ruler of the lineage of Prester John:

> A certain king of these parts, of the sect of the Nestorian Christians, who was of the family of that great king who was called Prester John of India, attached himself to me in the first year that I came here. And was converted by me to the truth of the true Catholic faith. And he took minor orders and served my Mass wearing the sacred vestments, so that the other Nestorians accused him of apostasy. Nevertheless he brought a great part of his people to the true Catholic faith, and he built a fine church with royal generosity in honour of God, the Holy Trinity and the Lord Pope, and called it according to my name "the Roman church." This King George departed to the Lord a true Christian, leaving a son and heir in the cradle, who is now nine years old. But his brothers who were perverse in the errors of Nestorius perverted all those whom King George had converted and brought them back to

their former state of schism. And because I was alone and unable to leave the Emperor the Chaan, I could not visit that church, which is distant twenty days' journey. Nevertheless if a few helpers and fellow workers were to come, I hope in God that all could be restored for I still hold the grant of the late King George.

(Dawson 225–6; Wyngaert I: 348–9)

Two and a half centuries after the legend of Prester John arose, a flesh-and-blood descendant of that fictitious potentate was claimed for Latin Christianity by a remarkable, dedicated Franciscan missionary; this historical, non-fictitious "Prester George" (so to speak) had even converted his own people, if only for a brief flicker of time.[170]

However keenly the Nestorian King George might have interested the Franciscan missionaries of Cathay, Odoric of Pordenone's *Relatio*, the source for much of the *Travels'* material on the East, is, like William of Rubruck, dismissive of Prester John of Eurasia:

Departing from that land of Cathay and traveling westward for fifty days . . . I arrived at the country of Prester John, but as regards him not one hundredth part is true of what is told of him as if it were undeniable. His principal city is called Tozan, and chief city though it is, Vicenzia would be reckoned its superior. He has, however, many other cities under him, and by a standing compact always receives to wife the Great Khan's daughter.

(Chiesa 150)

Unlike Prester John of India, the fabulous potentate whom many sought over the course of half a millennium but none ever found, Prester John of Eurasia was found, along with his descendants, but did not impress those who record his existence. Nonetheless, the repeated refrain either that the Great Khan wished to have a daughter of Prester John for his wife, or that the Great Khan gave John his own daughter for John's wife, forged a solid narrative bedrock for the Mandeville author's claim that Prester John's family and the Great Khan's family were intimately linked by royal women.[171]

The *Travels'* portrayal of John and his empire weaves together material from both the Eurasian and the Indian skeins of the Prester John legend. From the Eurasian yarns, the *Travels* picks out the important exchange of wives and daughters that conjoins John's house and lineage and that of the Great Khan's, so that the descendants of both families share a genetic intermingling of bloodlines and kinfolk. John and the Great Khan are family, with intimate blood ties. The *Travels* also takes care to establish similarities between the two emperors' realms. We learn that socially, Prester John's kingdom shares a distinctive custom with the Mongols that the *Travels* conjures for the Mongols out of one of their identifying characteristics – the abstemiousness and hardiness of the Mongol race:

Throughout [Prester John's] country . . . they eat only once a day, just as one does at the Great Chan's court. More than thirty thousand people dine every day at his court, without [counting] guests and visitors, but the thirty thousand of his country or of the Great Khan's country do not consume as many goods as would twelve thousand from the country over here.

(Higgins, *Book* 163; Deluz 439)[172]

Like the Mongols, a hardy race shown by the Franciscan missionaries to be capable of eating very little – Mongols ate only one meal a day, according to William of Rubruck, during his escorted journey from Batu Khan's to Mongke's court – Prester John's kingdom is also abstemious and disciplined in dining, despite the realm's abundant resources.[173] The Khan's Mongols and John's kingdom even share an ethical resemblance: Mongols "do not fight with or scold one another; and there are no thieves in the country and they greatly respect one another," while John's people are "truly loyal to one another" and "do not care for disputes, or tricks, or fraud" (Higgins, *Book* 148, 161; Deluz 408, 435).[174] The realms are thus twinned in their distinctive social customs and their ethical character, just as their rulers are joined in ties of kinship.

But the virtues in John's kingdom are distinguished by their *Christian* coloring, for much of the kingdom, unlike the Mongol Khan's, is a utopian Christian polity, where it is the shaping force of Christianity that ensures there is no dispute, fraud, or disloyalty:

> This Emperor Prester John is a Christian and a large part of his country as well ... they do not have all the articles of the faith such as we have. They indeed believe in the Father and the Son and the Holy Spirit and are very devout and truly loyal to one another ... they do not care for disputes, or tricks, or fraud.
>
> (Higgins, *Book* 161; Deluz 435)

The good behavior in John's kingdom comes from devotion to Christianity, and in this sense John's empire is actually *superior* to Mongol Cathay. Unlike Polo's *Le Devisement*, which is agog at the matchless superiority of the Mongol empire, *Mandeville's Travels* has found a way to modulate its admiration of, and desire for, the greatest civilization of its time: by materializing a facsimile empire resembling the Mongol empire in key ways, but intimating that the simulacrum in fact surpasses the original in desirability.

If Gathalonabez can conjure up a facsimile paradise for his youthful assassins, so can the Mandeville author conjure up a facsimile empire and emperor for his readers, thanks to the wonderful gifts of history, legend, and inherited traditions. Prester John's empire is as worth having as the Mongol empire – in fact it is even *more* worthy of admiration and desire than the Khan's, because it is devoutly Christian.

So keen is the *Travels* to exploit the possibilities of comparison between its two empires and emperors that even its description of Prester John's and the Great Khan's *bedchambers* manages somehow to intimate the superiority of John's environment. As part of its opulence, the Great Khan's bedchamber features gold pillars, in one of which is "a ruby carbuncle a foot long that lights up the whole room at night" (Higgins, *Book* 143; Deluz 397). John's equally opulent bedchamber also has pillars "of fine gold with precious stones and carbuncles that give much light at night," but additionally,

> The frame of his bed is of fine sapphires trimmed with gold to make him sleep better and to restrain his lust, for he will sleep with his wives only four times a year according to the four seasons, and that is only to beget children.
>
> (Higgins, *Book* 163; Deluz 439)

In their power to anchor moral conduct, the very *gemstones* in John's bedchamber are superior to those of the Khan's bedchamber. The Great Khan's giant ruby carbuncle might light up the room, yet John has not only room-lighting carbuncles but also sapphires with the wondrous power to govern sexual desire and subject desire to the ideal Christian goal of sexual performance – begetting children – and in perfect rhythm with the seasonal cycles of nature, no less. John's very bed signals his subservience to Christian ideals.

A Christian doppelganger for the Great Khan, John thus makes up in ideal kingly behavior what his empire might lack in wealth when compared to Mongol Cathay. Interestingly, the *Travels* is willing to admit that the Mongol empire surpasses John's in wealth, but quickly offers naturalizing reasons for why this is so: John's empire is much farther away, the narrative says, and "merchants do not go there as commonly to buy merchandise as they do in the Great Chan's land, for it is too far" (Higgins, *Book* 160; Deluz 433). Merchants already find in Mongol Cathay "all that they need: silk, and spices, and gold cloth, and all goods sold by weight" (Higgins, *Book* 160; Deluz 433). And even though the merchants would "get a better bargain in Prester John's land," they are daunted by the long journey and also the great dangers, for "in the sea in these regions" there are huge rocks of adamant with magnetic properties that would sink ships by drawing out their nails (Higgins, *Book* 161; Deluz 434).[175]

With such an overdetermination of reasons, including an ingenious recourse to the perils of magnetic rocks, it seems that we have to take John's empire on trust and accept only Sir John Mandeville as witness for its existence, since timorous merchants (who historically seem not to be daunted by much, given the example of the Polos) do not visit there.

Lacking trade, John's empire is still "very good and very rich, but not so rich as that of the Great Chan" (Higgins, *Book* 160; Deluz 433). Yet, the *Travels* describes such a superfluity of gems, gold, crystal, precious stones, exotic birds and animals (even parrots that speak); amazing shrubs that grow and shrink in the course of a day; and marvelous races in John's empire, and such a diversity of ecoscapes, with great mountains and plains, rivers, and sandy deserts, that we are left not with an impression of the empire's lack, but with an impression of its plenitude and infinite variety. This empire even has a wondrous Sandy Sea with savory fish in it, and a river that issues from paradise, made up "entirely of precious stones without water," that flows through the desert (Higgins, *Book* 161–2; Deluz 435).

Moreover, John's empire is *massive*. The *Travels* hints that John's empire is at least equivalent to the Mongol empire in size, albeit shaped differently, and very likely much more extensive. It takes more than seven years to traverse the Mongol empire (Higgins, *Book* 144; Deluz 399). But Prester John's land "extends in breadth for four months' travel and in length without measure: namely, [to] all the islands under [the] earth that we call under" (Higgins, *Book* 164; Deluz 440). Is the Mandeville author suggesting here that Prester John's land stretches in length, "without measure," to encompass *all* of the southern hemisphere, everywhere "that we call under"?

Richly multifarious and encompassing a diversity of subject populations ("many diverse peoples"), from the monstrous races of Plinian tradition, to the inhabitants of the false paradise of Gathalonabez, to the "large part" of the population that is Christian, John's empire has an administrative infrastructure as complex as Cathay's. The Mongol empire has 12 provinces, 2,000 cities, and countless towns, but Prester John's empire has "seventy-two provinces, and in each province there is a king, and these kings have under them still other kings and all of them have to pay him [John] tribute" (Higgins, *Book* 144, 161; Deluz 399, 435). The Mongol empire has two imperial capitals, Khanbalik and Shang-du, and John's empire has two imperial seats – "Nyse," in the province or "island" of "Pentoxoire," and Susa, where the emperor "generally dwells" in his "chief palace . . . which is so rich and so noble that its value cannot be calculated" (Higgins, *Book* 160, 163; Deluz 433, 438):

This Emperor Prester John possesses much land and many good cities and good towns in his kingdom and many diverse islands, large and wide, for this country of India is all divided by islands because of the large rivers that come from Paradise that divide all the land into many regions. And also in the sea there are many islands. The best city of the island of Pentoxoire has the name Nyse, which is the royal city, very noble and very rich.

(Higgins, *Book* 160; Deluz 433)

Possibly as large as Mongol Cathay – and perhaps infinitely larger, stretching "in length without measure" – John's empire of "India" is crisscrossed by rivers from Paradise: Is this a hint that Prester John's wondrous realm, unreachable by merchants and travelers because it is so far but vouched for by John Mandeville, knight, neighbors the Earthly Paradise itself? A country such as this would be a blessed land indeed, and much more worthy to be claimed for Christianity than even the magnificent, pagan Mongol empire of the fourteenth century.

With a touch of verisimilitude, the *Travels* admits that Prester John, the puissant and otherwise unexceptionable potentate of this extraordinary empire, is not quite a Latin Christian. This priest-king of the Orient does not have "all the articles of the faith such as we have" (Higgins, *Book* 161; Deluz 435).[176] Still, unlike the Great Khan of Mongol Cathay, Prester John *is* Christian, and, equally important, is piously devout. Having combed through the *Letter of Prester John* thoroughly for depictions of a fabulous, utopian Christian empire, the *Travels* also repeats nearly verbatim the *Letter*'s depiction of John's processional ritual in warfare and peacetime, a spectacle that attests John's Christian humility in tandem with his imperial supremacy and power:

This Emperor Prester John, when he goes into battle against some other lord, has no banners carried but rather has thirteen crosses made of fine gold borne ahead of him, large and tall, full of precious stones; and each of these crosses is set in a cart, and to guard each there are ten thousand men-at-arms and more than one hundred thousand foot soldiers in the manner that the standard is guarded in these regions when one goes to war ... When he is not at war and when he rides in private company, he has only a simple unpainted wooden cross borne ahead of him, without gold and precious stones, in remembrance that Jesus Christ suffered death on a cross. And he also has a gold plate full of earth borne ahead of him, to remind him that his nobility, his power, and his flesh will become earth and return to it; and another vessel made of silver with noble gold jewels and precious stones is carried along as a sign of his lordship and his nobility and his power.

(Higgins, *Book* 163; Deluz 437–8)[177]

Rather than dwell on the imperfect facsimile of Latin Christianity that John's faith, realm, and people represent ("they do not have all the articles of the faith such as we have"), the *Travels* prefers to emphasize instead this puissant Christian king's *piety* and *devotion* – the Christian humility of his plain wooden cross; the plate of earth to remind him that he is dust, even when symbols of his kingship and power are on display – and chooses to embrace a vision of Christian universalism over the dogmatic sectarianism of fourteenth-century Latin Christendom.

To the *Travels*, therefore, the varieties of Christianity in the Near East and elsewhere that are found by Sir John Mandeville are not to be damned as heresies and schisms any more than its hallowed priest-king, Prester John, is to be damned for his imperfect, inexact

Christianity. The *Travels* duly records the diverse Christianities of the Near East and Africa with equanimity, sans judgment. At the Holy Sepulcher, there is a chapel wherein

> Indian [i.e., Ethiopian] priests sing, not according to our law but according to theirs, and nevertheless they make the sacrament of the altar out of bread, saying *Pater Noster*, and little else with it, and the words with which the sacrament is consecrated, for they know nothing of the additions that several popes have made. But they sing very devoutly.
>
> (Higgins, *Book* 48; Deluz 192)[178]

We saw in Chapter 4 that the Ethiopian priests who had long served at the Holy Sepulcher were widely admired by medieval pilgrims for their piety. The *Travels* takes note of the priests' sacramental differences in "law" and liturgy as a kind of time-lag inadequacy, but admires their devotion. Indeed, Sir John Mandeville's traversal of the Near East brings recognition of a whole host of thriving alternative Christianities considered heretical by the Latin West:

> Know that here and there amongst these Saracens dwell many Christians of various kinds and different names, and all are baptized and have different laws and different customs, but all believe in God the Father and the Son and the Holy Spirit. But they always lack some articles of our faith.
>
> (Higgins, *Book* 73; Deluz 247)

Jacobites, Greeks, Syriacs, Georgians, Nestorians, Arians, Nubians, and "Indians who are from the land of Prester John" are all duly identified, listed, and noted, sometimes sparingly described and sometimes – as in the case of the Jacobites – described in great detail, with the narrative displaying some interest and curiosity in their differences from Roman Catholicism (Higgins, *Book* 73–4; Deluz 247–9).

The vituperation so much on display in the records of Franciscan missionaries who, unlike the fictitious Sir John Mandeville, actually put boots on the ground, so to speak (to apply a metaphor ironically), is conspicuously absent. Finally, the *Travels* tires of specifying the variety of differences: "They all have many articles of our faith, and they vary in others, and it would take too long to recount the variety so I will stop and say no more" (Higgins, *Book* 75; Deluz 250).

A sharp-eyed reader might attribute the *Travels'* tolerance for the many heretical and schismatic Christianities it finds in the world to the Mandeville author's great need to rescue the faith of the all-important Prester John, the *Travels'* high exemplar of ideal Christian rulership, from the taint of heresy. For comparison, we should keep in mind the views of the fourteenth-century Franciscan missionaries who, unlike the fictitious Mandeville, actually encountered face-to-face alternative Christianities around the world – especially Nestorianism – and had to negotiate relations with flesh-and-blood Nestorians.

John of Monte Corvino's second letter from China which relates his successful conversion of King George, the son-in-law of the Great Khan (and whom John thought to be Prester John's descendant), inveighs vociferously against the Franciscans' competitors-in-Christ – Nestorians, "who call themselves Christians, but behave in a very unchristian manner," bearing false witness against the archbishop and visiting "most grievous persecutions" upon him for five years, so that he was "often brought to judgment, and in danger of a shameful death" (Dawson 224–5; Wyngaert I: 346–7).

If John of Monte Corvino is to be heeded, the Nestorians of China were aggressive rivals who successfully reconverted King George's family and people back to the Church of the

East in the wake of the archbishop's strenuous efforts. Peregrine, the Bishop of Zayton, confirms the Franciscan rivalry with the Nestorians in China who "follow a schismatic and erroneous rite" (Dawson 232; Wyngaert 366). Peregrine is in no doubt as to what is at stake in that rivalry, and laments the grievous harm accomplished by the Nestorians' undoing of the archbishop's conversionary work:

> For as to that King George, it is certain that he [John of Monte Corvino] converted him [King George] completely and worthily to the true faith, though previously he [King George] had mingled with the Nestorians. And the king himself in one day converted several thousands of his people. And had he lived, we should indeed have subdued his whole people and kingdom to Christ, and a change might even have been wrought with the Great Chan.
>
> (Dawson 232; Wyngaert 365)

Even the phlegmatic Odoric, who reserves his greatest censure for the Saracens of the Delhi Sultanate, condemns Nestorians as "schismatics and heretics," and does not celebrate the presence of fifteen Nestorian houses in the city of Tana, although the Franciscan friars who suffered martyrdom in Tana had been given shelter in one of the Nestorian houses (Chiesa 80). We also saw how William of Rubruck virulently classed Nestorians and other heretical Christians, like the Armenian coreligionist with whom William lived, as virtually a separate species of people, a virtual race set apart by their blasphemies and sacrilegious travesties.

One might reasonably say, therefore, that the Mandeville author – unlike the Franciscan missionaries who traveled to proselytize and convert – had greater freedom to imagine a more heterogeneous global Christianity, because he did *not* travel, and likely did not have to transact with real-time Nestorians or other "heretics" in a competition for converts. Writing a travel romance promulgating a vision of Christian universalism, the Mandeville author can minimize variations in Christianity rather than dwell on them, unlike William of Rubruck or the Franciscans at the frontlines, battling for the faith. *Mandeville's Travels* is really a visionary text concerned with Christian *potential* and *possibility* in the world at large; its worldview is not the quotidian reality of missionary friars struggling to expand the toehold of Catholicism in Cathay and elsewhere.

Journey to the West: Rabban Sauma, a Nestorian Heretic, in Latin Christendom

But even in the Latin West, among dogmatic representatives of the faith, conditions could be found under which heretical Nestorians might not be condemned. In 1286 the Ilkhan Arghun sent Rabban Sauma, a Uighur or Ongut Nestorian monk from Khanbalik and a close friend of the recently elected Nestorian patriarch, Mar Yaballaha III, to the leaders of the West as Arghun's emissary. Reaching the Vatican in 1287 when Nicholas IV was elected pope, Sauma is closely interrogated by the Roman Curia on how Nestorian belief in the nature of the Trinity deviates from Roman Catholic dogma. The exchange proceeds hot and fast, reaching no satisfactory conclusion because "they [the College of Cardinals] terminated his discourse with many arguments" (Montgomery 58). Still, we are told by the Syriac text that survives to record the event, "they honored him for his discourse" (Montgomery 58).[179]

It would have been unwise, of course, to prosecute for heresy the envoy of Arghun Khan and the Nestorian Patriarch of the Mongols, and Sauma is unfailingly polite, modest, and careful to stress his ambassadorial status and lack of interest in pursuing doctrinal differences:

> Then he said to them: "I have come from far lands not to dispute nor to expound the themes of the Faith; but to receive a benediction from the Reverend Pope and to visit the shrines of the saints have I come, and to declare the business of the King and the Catholicus. If it be agreeable to you that we leave the discussion and you make arrangement and appoint some one who will show me the churches here and the shrines of the saints, you will confer a great favor on your servant and disciple."
>
> (Montgomery 59)

Thereafter Sauma is treated with forbearance, and, upon his return to the Vatican after visiting the dignitaries of Europe, is even permitted by Nicholas IV to say mass so that the Pope and the West "too may see our custom" (Montgomery 68):

> And on that day a great congregation assembled to see how the ambassador of the Mongols consecrates. And when they saw, they rejoiced and said: "The language is different, but the rite is one." ... And when he had solemnized the Mysteries, he went in to the Reverend Pope and greeted him. And he [the pope] said to Sauma: "May God receive thy offering and bless thee and pardon thy faults and sins."
>
> (Montgomery 68)

Rabban Sauma receives communion at the hands of the Pope, who "absolved him from his faults and sins and those of his ancestors," and the Nestorian monk rejoices with tears and weeping, "acknowledging the grace of God and thinking upon the mercy poured out upon him" (Montgomery 69). On Sauma's final departure from Rome, Nicholas IV gives him "small relics" from the garment of Christ, from the bonnet of the Virgin Mary, and of the saints, together with gifts for Arghun, 1,500 pounds of red gold for expenses, and special gifts for the Nestorian Patriarch Mar Yaballaha:

> a crown of pure gold for his head, adorned with very precious stones, and clothing for the vestments of his function, red and embroidered with gold, and shoes sewn with small pearls, and boots, and also a ring from his own finger; and letters patent which contained authorization of his Patriarchate over all the Orientals. And to Rabban Sauma he gave letters patent as Visitator over all Christians.
>
> (Montgomery 72)[180]

Such amity toward the Nestorian emissary from Asia was not confined to the Vatican. In Gascony in 1288, Edward I of England had received Sauma and his men with delight, accepting the dispatches from Arghun, and commanding Sauma to celebrate mass. At this mass of the eastern Syrian rite, the English king received the sacred host from Sauma's hands and instructed Sauma to tell Arghun: "in the lands of the Franks there are not two creeds, but only one, that which confesses Jesus Christ, and they are all Christians" (Montgomery 66).

We see that the Nestorian ambassador of a powerful Mongol Khan reputed for his friendliness to Christianity, and with whom the West hoped for an alliance against the Mamluks of Egypt, could be received without undue hostility, and with a consideration appropriate to his rank – especially a monk as unfailingly polite, deferential, and humble as Rabban Sauma. Deflecting too-inquisitorial aggressiveness with the insistence that he was only in the West at the behest of his Khan and his Patriarch, and because he wished so fervently to visit the Christian shrines and relics he revered, and receive benediction from the Pope, Sauma elicits from his Latin Christian hosts their best behavior.

For the Vatican, too, there is the felicitous diplomatic opportunity to confirm Mar Yaballaha III's Patriarchate by "letters patent," and Pope Nicholas IV's bestowal of a papal ring, a jeweled crown, vestments, and shoes for the Patriarch, ceremonially if not so subtly ushers the Patriarchate of the East under the aegis and authority of Rome. Even Edward I of England is driven to declare that there is no division in the Latin West, "not two creeds, but only one": a diplomatic proclamation of Christian universalism that either disingenuously disavows the existence of heresy in Europe or, more ominously, disavows the presence of Jews in the homeland (Edward, of course, would expel Jews from English soil two years later).[181]

Nonetheless, even if the politics of church and state conditioned the behavior of the representatives of the West, the Mandeville author might still have reason to rejoice at Rabban Sauma's diplomatic embassy to Europe generations earlier, under the umbra of potential political alliance between Eastern and Western rulers against the Mamluks of Egypt and Syria. Whatever its circumstances, the Nestorian monk's reception in Europe offered up a vision of possible Christian universalism *within the European homeland itself.* Differences in creed and liturgy, though noted, did not prevent a crusader king of England from receiving at the hands of a heretical Nestorian monk a host consecrated by that schismatic Nestorian – who himself received a consecrated host and absolution from the Roman pontiff, the supreme leader of the Latin church. In the European homeland of the thirteenth century, this was a vision worth having, under whatever circumstances.

Moreover, to someone like the Mandeville author, Sauma's success might also point to another reason for rejoicing. The Syriac text that records Sauma's journey repeatedly emphasizes the Nestorian monk's piety and saintliness. Sauma's conception and birth are couched in Biblically portentous terms, and as a youth, to the distress of his parents, Sauma had divested himself of all worldly goods and took to anchoritic solitude for seven years, living with utmost austerity and acquiring a reputation for holiness (Montgomery 28–30).

Indeed, during Sauma's first abortive pilgrimage to visit the shrines and relics in the West with Markos, his companion monk who later becomes the Nestorian Patriarch Mar Yaballaha III (Arghun's embassy is Sauma's second journey), both Sauma and Markos humbly refuse gold, silver, garments, and equipment for their pilgrimage from two Khans who wish to sustain them, because, they say, they need nothing – "For what can we do with possessions, and how can we burden ourselves with this great load?" (Montgomery 34).

Therefore, despite the fact that Sauma too did not have "all the articles of the faith such as we have," and despite the fact that the Nestorian monk came out of the heretical community in Khanbalik vilified by John of Monte Corvino and his Franciscan missionary brethren, Rabban Sauma's piety and holiness might well have affirmed and reinforced the *Travels'* optimistic vision of a global fraternity of Christians against the narrow, monolithic vision of the Latin Christian church of its time.

But what *is* "its time" – the "time" on display in the *Travels*? Critical of the fourteenth century, when Christians of the West had not launched a crusade for many years for lack of leadership and are sinful, lax, and negligent Christians, the *Travels* is enamored of the past – which it represents as a time when Christianity was global – and looks forward to a future when Christianity will be global again.

The *Travels'* narration of stories and events sometimes has a tendency to unfold time as if the past predicates the future: Christians once held the Holy Land, and Islamic prophecy promises that Christians will hold the Holy Land again. The *Travels* visits the past as a romance country in which a righteous spiritual and ethical ethos once obtained: a time when evil was defeated (the false paradise of Milstorak was destroyed), when Christianity prevailed internationally (faraway khans such as Mongke and Kublai were Christians), and great and powerful rulers like Prester John of India chose Christianity of their own free will and even became priests.

In the final image of Prester John that it leaves with us, the *Travels* conjures up a remarkable backstory for the Prester John legend from a time when Christianity was – the *Travels* insists – global, and wise rulers chose Christianity freely, without persuasion or war, and even became priests:

> I believe that you indeed know and have heard it said why this emperor is called Prester John, but yet for those who do not know I will briefly set down the reason. There was once an emperor who was a very brave prince and had Christian knights in his company like those that he has now, and he desired to see the manner of the service in the church of the Christians. At that time Christendom extended beyond the sea: all Turkey, Syria, Tartary, Jerusalem, Palestine, Arabia, Aleppo, and all the land of Egypt. This emperor came with a Christian knight into a church of Egypt, and it was a Saturday after Pentecost when the bishop performed the ordinations; and he watched and heard the service and asked what people they might be that the prelate had in front of him where he had so many great rites to perform. The knight answered him that they were priests; and he [the emperor] said that he would no longer be called king or emperor, but priest, and he wished to have the name of the first priest who came out [of the church], the one who had the name of John. Ever since he has been called Prester John.
>
> (Higgins, *Book* 177; Deluz 462–3)

We learn from this extraordinary story that the legendary Prester John was a convert to Christianity, and that he is either as old as Methuselah, living from this unspecified romance time onward, or else that "Prester John," like "the Great Khan," is a title held up in successive generations. The latter would support the *Travel*'s earlier claim that "This Emperor Prester John *always* takes the Great Chan's daughter as his wife, and the Great Chan [takes] Prester John's daughter as well" – a statement that suggests the repeated joining of two imperial houses over generations (Higgins, *Book* 161; Deluz 435, emphasis added).

Nostalgically, the *Travels'* invented story of how a nameless emperor becomes the celebrated priest-king Prester John as a result of seeing Christian ordination rites offers us a vision of a united, international Christian world that encompasses all of the Near East, Africa ("Egypt"), and Eurasia ("Tartary") – joining, in effect, the Greek/Byzantine empire and the Mongol empire – and, presumably, Europe, in an imagined heyday of pan-Christianity that is a mashup of different historical eras in convergence with fantasy. We recall the *Travels'* insistence that two Great Khans – Mongke and Marco Polo's Kublai – had both been Christian.

The nostalgia on display in this remarkable story is for an imagined world that never existed, a world issuing from desire and offered as historical fact. By contrast, the world through which Sir John Mandeville travels is now no longer as Christian as it had been in that ideal, romance past, but the *Travels* is certain the future can resemble the past again if its words are heeded. The key to joining future and past is the transformation of the present – which specifically requires transformation of the Christians of Europe:

> all Christians ought to be more devout towards Our Lord than they are, for without a doubt if there were no wickedness and sin among Christians, they would be lords of all the world. For the banner of Jesus Christ is always unfurled and ready to help his good servants. One true worthy man could put to flight one thousand wicked men ... if we would be good, no enemy could last against us.
>
> (Higgins, *Book* 155; Deluz 421–2)

We might be forgiven for being taken aback here by the *Travels'* casual assumption that military means would be required to achieve the return of global Christianity. The echo here of the Exordium's exhortation to wage war soberly reminds us that global Christendom in the Middle Ages is meant to be realized not only through reformed Christian behavior at home and missionary activity abroad, but also by transnational crusade. With the Exordium positioned at the beginning of the *Travels'* narrative, and this reminder here positioned near its close, we are afforded a sober view of what a panglobal Christianity might mean and would require, and remember that even a Franciscan missionary like William of Rubruck had imagined an army of the church subjugating countries and conquering the whole world (Jackson and Morgan 278; Dawson 220; Wyngaert I: 331).

Still, to give the Mandeville author due credit, recourse to military violence is not the *Travels'* only method of imagining how the world might again become more pleasing to God. Like its oscillating portrayal of Mongols – who are sometimes the savage barbarians of the thirteenth century and sometimes the urbane civilization of the fourteenth century – the text wavers between two poles of response to the non-Christian-ness of its contemporary world. Unfurling the banner of Jesus Christ against the enemy who cannot last against good Christian men is one pole of the *Travels'* response. Thankfully, the Mandeville author's faith in the vital importance of true devotion and human virtue also allows for a more charitable response to the non-Christian peoples of the world who are virtuous and devout.

In its most generous manifestation, the *Travels'* belief that sheer human virtue surpasses narrow subscriptions to dogma will embrace even people in the world who are palpably not Christian, like the famed Brahmans of India, those legendarily philosophic, gentle interlocutors of Alexander whose reputation was secured in Europe for centuries by the Greek, Latin, and vernacular Alexander romances:

> although they are not Christians and do not have perfect law, nevertheless through natural law they are full of virtues and they flee all vices and all wickedness and all sins. For they are not proud, nor greedy, nor slothful, nor envious, nor angry, nor gluttonous, nor lustful, and they do unto others only what they want done unto them, and in this custom they fulfill the Ten Commandments. They are not concerned with goods or wealth, and they do not lie at all, and they do not swear oaths for any reason ... This land is called the island of Bragmey, and others call it the Land of Faith.
>
> (Higgins, *Book* 172–3; Deluz 456–7)[182]

Where Christianity has not yet reached a good people, such as the Brahmans, "natural law" – the law that inheres in "God's created world," as Higgins puts it – becomes for the

Travels a surrogate for the Christian God of "perfect law" (*Book* 172 n.548; Deluz 456). Obedience to God's natural law – when God's "perfect law" is unavailable – produces virtuous behavior that is still pleasing to God, and rewarded by God:

> Because they are so trustworthy and so just and full of such good qualities, there have never been storms or lightning, nor hail, nor any plague, nor war, nor famine, nor other tribulation such as we have many times had over here for our sins. This is why it appears that God loves them and favorably accepts their belief and their good works. They indeed believe in God who created and made all things and they worship him, and value as nothing all earthly goods, and they are all just, and live so reasonably and so moderately in eating and drinking that they live very long.
>
> (Higgins, *Book* 173; Deluz 457)

The ascetics known as the Brahmans become, for the *Travels*, a gauge and a symbol of non-Christian human goodness that can be embraced because such goodness and virtue follows God's natural law. Sans doctrinal instruction, the Brahmans live so virtuously that they *naturally* abide by the Ten Commandments, and God's favor toward them is seen in His protecting them from climatic catastrophe, plague, war, famine, and tribulations visited on the less virtuous, if more doctrinal, Latin West.

The Mandeville author even finds a precedent in the Bible for the hypothesis that God recognizes and loves those who serve him humbly out of virtue and goodness – even if, technically, they are not Christians – and fastens on the Biblical Job as his illustration:

> Although this people do not have the articles of the faith such as we have, nevertheless for their natural good faith and for their goodwill I believe it to be certain that God loves them and that God favorably receives their service just as he did from Job, who was pagan; all the same He accepted him [Job] as his loyal servant. Therefore although there are many diverse laws [religions] throughout the world, I believe that God always loves those who love him and serve humbly in virtue and loyalty and who do not value the vainglory of this world, just as these people do, and as Job likewise did ... Also, Our Lord says in the Gospel: "Alias oves habeo qe non sunt ex hoc ovili." [I have other sheep that are not of this fold; John 10–16] That is to say that He had other servants than [those] under Christian law.
>
> (Higgins, *Book* 175; Deluz 459–60)

Charitably, the *Travels* arrives at a decision: "one ought not to despise any earthly people for their diverse laws, nor any one person. For we do not know whom God loves and whom he hates" (Higgins, *Book* 175; Deluz 460). Such commendable charity, Iain Higgins points out,

> partly contradicts the Fourth Lateran Council (1215) whose first canon declared: "there is one universal church, outside of which there is no salvation." As the Latin Christian sense of the world expanded, some writers (e.g., William Langland, likely author of *Piers Plowman*, Julian of Norwich, and Margery Kempe) wondered at the possible injustice of so many damned souls.
>
> (Higgins, *Book* 176 n.559)

Perhaps aware of its own audacity, the *Travels* concludes this disquisition on how readers can think about the non-Christian virtuous peoples of the world by finding a way to suggest that the Brahmans of the Alexander legend are still, in some fashion, intermingled with Christianity and, like the Saracens, believe in Christianity's core tenets. Nimbly, the *Travels* falls back again on its large inventive powers and attaches these virtuous pagans firmly to the Christian story:[183]

> Therefore I say of this people that they are so faithful that God loves them, for there are amongst them many prophets and there always have been; and on these islands they prophesied the Incarnation of Our Lord Jesus Christ, how he would be born of a virgin three thousand or more years before Our Lord was born of the Virgin Mary. They believe perfectly well in the Incarnation, but they do not well know the way in which He suffered passion and death for us.
>
> (Higgins, *Book* 176; Deluz 461)

For *Mandeville's Travels*, all roads lead back to Christianity. Muslims believe in the Incarnation, and so do Hindus and their prophets. And beyond the Brahmans of India, the diverse peoples of the world who lack the "perfect law" of Christian doctrine, when they are virtuous, can still follow God's *natural law* and God's surrogate, Nature, and find their way to the central tenets of Christianity, through reason and "*natural* understanding" (Higgins, *Book* 184; Deluz 477, emphasis added):

> Know that in all these countries about which I have spoken . . . and among all these diverse peoples that I have described to you, and the diverse laws and the diverse beliefs they have, there is no people – because they have reason and understanding – who do not have some articles of our faith and some good points of our belief, and who do not believe in God who made the world, whom they call God of Nature, according to the prophet, who said: "*Et metuent eum omnes fines terre.*" [And all the ends of the earth shall fear Him; Ps. 96 (95): 9] And elsewhere: "*Omnes gentes servient ei.*" [All nations shall serve Him; Ps. 72 (71): 11]
>
> But they do not know how to speak perfectly, for they have no one to explain it to them, except insofar as they understand it with their natural understanding. They do not know how to speak about the Son, nor about the Holy Spirit. But they all know how to speak about the Bible, especially about Genesis, the sayings of the prophets, and the books of Moses.
>
> (Higgins, *Book* 184; Deluz 477)[184]

Nevertheless, for all the *Travels'* charity toward the as yet unconverted and ignorant, but somehow *naturally* Christian, peoples of the world, there is one group of fellow humans that does not meet with charitable consideration: the Jews.

Race, Religion, and the Return of the Jews

The *Travels* may admonish readers that "one ought not to despise any earthly people for their diverse laws, nor any one person. For we do not know whom God loves and whom he hates," but the text also unhesitatingly judges, despises, and condemns the Jews. Disappointingly, in virtually every mention of medieval Jews, the *Travels* hews to the most conventional, reflexive, and vituperative characterization of the group, offering nearly every cliché found in medieval European anti-Semitism.

At the very beginning of the narrative, in the Exordium, we are reminded that the Savior was "harmed by the cruel Jews" and suffered passion and death (Higgins, *Book* 3; Deluz 90). An account of the destruction of the Temple of Jerusalem then offers an opportunity to reiterate that the Jews, not the Romans, "had put Our Lord to death" and "had sold Jesus Christ for thirty pennies" (Higgins, *Book* 50–1; Deluz 200). The wondrous Holy Land, where every rock bears the imprint of the Savior's body and memories of His life, presents yet another occasion to remember "the cruel Jews" and their perfidy:

> for the Jews led Him to a high rock to throw Him into the valley to kill Him, but Jesus passed through them and leapt onto another rock, and the footprints are still visible in the said rock.
>
> (Higgins, *Book* 69; Deluz 241)

Even the Quran is conscripted into service, and made to condemn the Jews: "This book also speaks about the Jews, who it says are wicked because they will not believe that Jesus was sent by God" (Higgins, *Book* 84; Deluz 275).[185] Mount Sion brings to mind a favorite medieval anti-Semitic libel, that Jews tried repeatedly to desecrate the body of the Blessed Virgin: "And there is the place where the Jews wanted to cast the body of Our Lady when the Apostles brought it for burial in the valley of Josaphat" (Higgins, *Book* 56; Deluz 209).

Even when Sir John Mandeville has left the Holy Land behind, and is ranging in faraway archipelago Southeast Asia (probably in Borneo, "east of Sumatra and north of Java," Higgins hazards [*Book* 117 n.400]), we are not released from the rehearsal of anti-Semitic libels. An apparition of Jews suddenly materializes in the midst of a description of trees (in Borneo?) that bear honey, wine, and poison:

> The Jews in recent years sent [someone] in search of this toxin to poison all Christendom, as I have heard them say in their confession at death. But thank God, they failed in their aim, but they nevertheless caused much death.
>
> (Higgins, *Book* 118; Deluz 345–6)

This medieval calumny – that the Black Death of the fourteenth century was caused by Jews who poisoned the wells of Europe – startlingly surfaces as we are serenely contemplating the ecoscape of maritime Southeast Asia.

Jews seem to be eternally present not just in the near and far corners of the world, but *in every period of time*: in the time of the New Testament, where they are tormenting the Savior and seeking to desecrate his mother's body; in the contemporary present when they travel to faraway lands for poison to destroy Christians; and in an apocalyptic future, when the Ten Lost Tribes of Israel will emerge from their enclosure behind the wall erected by Alexander the Great, to war on Christendom.[186] The *Travels* reserves this most horrific anti-Semitic portrayal of projective catastrophe for a detailed disquisition in which it shows how its vision of a pan-Christian future is imperiled because of the Jews.

"Jews do not have their own land [anywhere] in the world," the *Travels* tells readers, except in the Caspian ("Caspie") mountains, where "the Jews of the Ten Tribes, who are called Goth and Magoth [Gog and Magog] are enclosed, and "cannot get out by any route" (Higgins, *Book* 157–8; Deluz 428). Between these mountains, twenty-two kings, with all their people, were shut in and held captive by Alexander, with the help of the "God of Nature" (since Alexander lived before the time of Christ). The captive Jews of the Ten Tribes and their twenty-two kings pay tribute to the Queen of the Amazons ("the Queen of Amazonia"), "who keeps a very careful eye on them so that they do not come out towards her side of the land, for her land borders on these mountains" (Higgins, *Book* 158; Deluz 429).

We are to understand thus that warrior *women* are guarding these Jews in these Caspian mountains, preventing Jews from escaping their captivity via Amazonian lands and harassing the Latin West. Women on one side and Jews on the other, gender against race: The *Travels* has succeeded in making women and Jews into antagonists, positioned in opposing camps. Here is a medieval version of a divisive tactic we see in postmedieval race-making maneuvers – the pitting of one minority, or disenfranchised group, against another. However, in the long run, the Jews will win out over the women:

> Nevertheless, it is said that they will come out in Antichrist's time and that they will slaughter a great many Christians. Therefore all the Jews that dwell throughout all lands always learn to speak Hebrew, in this hope that, when those of the mountains of Caspie come out, the other Jews know how to speak to them and lead them into Christendom to destroy Christians. For the other Jews say that they know well enough through their prophecies that those of Caspie will come out and spread throughout the world, and that furthermore, Christians will be subject to them for as long as and longer than they have been subject to Christians.
>
> (Higgins, *Book* 159; Deluz 430)

The use of a *language* here to characterize a people is an inspired move in the delineation and marking of a race, a precise action in race-making. Hebrew, Kathleen Biddick points out, is used by the *Travels* to set off Jews, the companions of Antichrist, from the rest of the world. Because the confined Jews only know a single language, even if occasional strays slip past the eyes of watchful Amazons and escape from captivity before the advent of Antichrist, the *Travels* says, "they know no language but Hebrew and do not know how to speak to [other] people" (Higgins, *Book* 159; Deluz 430).

"The *Travels* ... insists ... that the Jews have persisted in this seemingly counterproductive monolingualism," Biddick drily remarks, "in order to be able to recognize each other as fellow conspirators in the last days" (*Typological Imaginary* 32). Biddick reasonably concludes that Hebrew is transformed by the *Travels* – a text fascinated with languages, and that presents several "alphabets" for its readers to contemplate – into "a language of conspiracy, a technology of Antichrist" (*Typological Imaginary* 32). Higgins draws out the implications: "as the universal Jewish language ... [Hebrew] can be read as marking the Jews as permanent outsiders and eternal enemies" (*Book* 268).

Permanent outsiders and eternal enemies: Enmity with Jews will last eternally, longer than enmity with Saracens, and Jews will be outsiders forever, longer than the pagans of the outside world. What is the logic of such exclusion, and how does such exclusion serve narrative reasoning in this immensely popular, influential, and widely circulating text?

In the *Travels'* expansive vision of a future global Christianity, narrative openness toward the diverse pagan peoples of the world issues in large part from an optimism that virtuous peoples who follow natural law can, with instruction (at present "they have no one to explain it to them"), come to follow the "perfect law" of Christianity. Muslims, the *Travels* believes, do not pose an epistemological challenge to Christian dominion, merely a (temporary) logistical obstacle that even their own prophetic beliefs say will evanesce. Moreover, the *Travels* asserts that Muslims and Hindus believe in the Incarnation, the central principle of Christianity. Not so the Jews, who pose the most serious, indeed incommensurable, kind of epistemological challenge, by their rejection of the Messiah as the Incarnation of God in Man.

Jews are thus decisively shut out of the *Travels'* expansive vision of a Christian future in which even Muslims and pagans who already have "some articles of our faith" or are guided by natural understanding and natural law ("the God of Nature") will be able to come to Christendom's perfect law. Worst of all, Jewish prophecies, the *Travels* says, present a countervailing vision of the future – one in which it is *Jews*, not Christians, who will prevail worldwide. This horrific apocalyptic vision that the *Travels* presents (which is not, of course, a Jewish vision but another medieval calumny, though attributed here to the Jews) is a rival, nightmarish alternative to the *Travels'* hopeful Christian vision.[187]

Instead of pan-Christianity peaceably – or militaristically – spreading across the world, Jews will swoop down from the mountains, joined by their coreligionists in Europe's heartlands who are waiting landless in the diaspora, to wage war on Christendom and destroy Christians. Rather than the world being Christianity's oyster, then, "Christians will be subject to them [the Jews] for as long as and longer than they have been subject to Christians." If the nightmarish vision the *Travels* ascribes to the Jews comes to pass, the global pan-Christianity dreamed of by the *Travels* is extinguished, and will never come to pass.[188]

The charity of the *Travels* toward other religions is thus relative, contingent on how the text assesses the recuperability of races and religions for Christianity.

The *Travels* may find anthropologically interesting such peculiar religious beliefs as the transmigration of souls or augury by birds, but its concern is with the Christian faith, and is driven by a wistful optimism and vision that the world can be more like home, and home can be a better place, with better Christians. For the *Travels*, after all, Jerusalem is the center of the world; the pyramids of Egypt are Joseph's barns; only Christians can cultivate balm; the Great Khan prefers Christian physicians and medics to Saracen practitioners; the Quran accepts the Incarnation and the central tenets of the Gospels; Islamic prophecies favor Christian victory; Hindu prophets prophesied the Incarnation, and Hindus believe in the Incarnation; and the diverse peoples of the world "all know how to speak about the Bible, especially about Genesis, the sayings of the prophets, and the books of Moses" (Higgins, *Book* 184).[189]

In a world where differences of religion-and-race are there to function, ultimately, in the service of the same – in the service of Christianity and Christians – the Jews, the original people of scripture who above all races know how to speak about Genesis, the sayings of the prophets, and Moses, cannot be reconciled to the *Travels'* Christian vision.

What happens to Jewish difference in the *Book of Sir John Mandeville*, an extraordinary fantasy of travel and a remarkable romance of the world, which taught Europe for centuries what the world and its peoples were like? In the end we see that Jews, an example of *real difference* – not differences that are recuperable back into the same – are excluded by that mechanism of sorting in premodern Europe which conceptualized absolute and fundamental divisions between peoples: religion functioning as race.

Notes

1 The original Latin passages of the epigraphs are as follows: John of Plano Carpini, "*Cibi eorum sunt omnia que mandi possunt. Comedunt enim canes, lupos, vulpes, et equos, et ... carnes humanas manducant ... Alluviones que egrediuntur a iumentis cum pullis manducant ... eos etiam vidimus pediculos manducare*" (Wyngaert 47–8); William of Rubruck, "*Quando ergo ingressi sumus inter istos barbaros, visum fuit michi, ut dixi superius, quod ingrederer aliud seculum*" and "*cum circumdarent nos*

homines et respicerent nos tamquam monstra" (Wyngaert 187, 245); Andrew of Perguia, "*De divitiis, magnificentia et gloria huius magni Imperatoris, de vastitate Imperii, multitudine populorum, numerositate civitatum, et magnitudine earumdem, et de ordinatione imperii, in quo nemo adversus alium ausus est levare gladium, transeo, quia longum foret scribere, et audientibus incredibilia viderentur. Nam ego ipse qui presens sum, talia audio, que vix ipse credere possum etc*" (Wyngaert 374).

2 Jackson and Morgan suggest that *Tartar*, the name by which Mongols were commonly called in the Latin West, derives both from a corruption of *Tatar* and from a pun, likely intended, on *Tartarus*, attributed to several personages, including Louis IX, Frederick II, and Innocent IV (16). Connell believes *Tartar* not to be a corruption of *Tatar*, but rather a deliberate derogation that "carried all the terrible connotations of the danger to the West" that stemmed from the word's evocation of Tartarus, the Greek hell (118). Matthew Paris specifically attributes the pun to Louis IX, who supposedly responded to his mother's anxiety at the Mongol invasions by quipping: "either we shall push them back to their home Tartarus, whence they came, or they will carry all of us up to heaven" (Luard, *Mathaei Parisiensis . . . Chronica majora* IV: 3 [Matthew Paris . . . Greater Chronicle]). Documents of encounter and contact show that Franciscan missionaries who journeyed to the steppe in fact became aware of the ethnoracial diversity of the Turco-Mongolian-Altaic peoples they encountered and had a more complex sense of who Tartars were. William of Rubruck identifies several ethnoracial groups by name (see the section entitled "Prayers as Currency"), and John of Plano Carpini indicates he knows well that Tartars are actually Mongols, but are called Tartars by Latin Christians out of convention (Dawson 60, 72; Wyngaert I: 115, 130).

3 Four main Mongol khanates were established: the Khanate of the Golden Horde in Eurasia and Russia; the Chagatay Khanate in Central Asia; the Khanate of Cathay or Yuan Dynasty Khanate in China; and the Ilkhanate of Persia and Mesopotamia in West Asia.

4 Earlier in the century, in 1262, Hulegu, who established the Mongol Ilkhanate of Persia, took the initiative of suggesting to Louis IX a joint action against the Mamluks of Egypt, in which the French king was to attack by sea and the Mongols by land. "This proved to be the first of a series of negotiations between the Mongols of Persia and the Latin West, directed against the Mamluks and lasting till around 1307" (Jackson and Morgan 39). Hulegu's initiative, however, was not without precedent, as we shall see: It was not the first time a Mongol commander had approached Louis IX with a suggestion of joint action. But the English Edward I's approach to Abaga suggests something novel in the Latin West, despite the discouragement of a midcentury mission to the Mongol empire by the Franciscan William of Rubruck: a level of trust and willingness that leads a European king, rather than a Mongol commander, to initiate a proposal of joint military action. Reuven Amitai's critical assessment of the politico-military efforts of Edward and Abaga to forge an alliance against the Mamluks of Egypt presents a detailed account of these seemingly improbable geopolitical relations.

5 Mongol names are transliterated and spelled variously, so that "Genghis Khan," for example, can be rendered as "Chinggis Qan." I strive for consistency in spelling, so that, for example, I use "y" when sources variously use "i" and "y" interchangeably in transliteration, and "k" when sources variously use "q," "c," and "k" interchangeably. I omit diacritical marks, which are distracting to nonspecialists and unneeded by specialists familiar with Mongol names. As far as possible, I also strive for ease of reading in transliterating names – e.g., *Ugedey*, rather Ögödei – and use English titles where possible: e.g., Great Khan, instead of *khaghan* or *qaghan*; however, I use Mongol titles where unavoidable, e.g., *khan* and *khatun*.

6 It is impossible adequately to treat the vast literature on the Mongol invasions of Europe and the world, and the empire that culminated, but for points of entry see Allsen (*Culture and Conquest, Commodity and Exchange; Mongol Imperialism*), Atwood (*Encyclopedia*), Halperin (*Mongols and the West*) Jackson (*Studies*), Lane (*Mongols*), Morgan (*Medieval Persia*), Rossabi (*Khubilai Khan*), and Vernadsky.

7 John of Plano Carpini's *Ystoria Mongalorum* (History of the Mongols) circulated widely, existing in several manuscripts, and was incorporated into Vincent de Beauvais' popular and encyclopedic

Speculum Historiale (Mirror of History). There are two redactions: a comprehensive version and a shorter version that, John tells us near the end of his narrative, exists because people he encountered on his journey in Poland, Bohemia, Germany, Liège, and Champagne copied his account before it was complete (Dawson 71–2; Wyngaert 130). I cite the translation in Dawson, and Wyngaert's edition of the *Ystoria Mongalorum* based on Corpus Christi, Cambridge, MS. 181, which is held to be the best manuscript of the comprehensive version.

8 See my *Empire of Magic*, chapter 1, for a discussion of the meaning and significance of historical and imagined cannibalism, including crusader cannibalism of Turkish cadavers during the First Crusade.

9 Sophia Menache ("Tartars, Jews"), Gregory Guzman, and Peter Jackson ("Medieval Christendom's") note Matthew Paris's equation of Mongols with the Ten Lost Tribes of Israel, "dismissing the inconvenient circumstances that their language is not Hebrew and . . . they know nothing of the Mosaic law" (Jackson, "Medieval Christendom's" 354). Menache scrutinizes the "nonevent" of the so-called "Jewish-Mongol 'plot' of 1241" detected by Matthew as typical of Matthew's dangerous fictions ("Tartars, Jews" 319, 320). In Germany, there were even "pogroms against the Jews in 1241 on the grounds that they were ready to welcome the Mongols as deliverers and were trying to ship arms to these their co-religionists, in order to exact revenge for Christian persecution" (Jackson, "Medieval Christendom's" 354). Guzman observes that medieval Jews furnished a ready template for how the other monstrous races of the world should be understood. Connell adds that Mongols were also linked to the Antichrist, with Ivo of Narbonne referring to them as "satellites of Antichrist" (124); and Jackson points out that "two of the letters reproduced by Matthew Paris have Chinggis Khan branding captured children with his mark, a clear allusion to the activity of Antichrist as found in the Book of Revelation (XIII: 16)" ("Medieval Christendom's" 354). Frey and Gow each offers excellent studies on Jews as the servants of Antichrist in Christian eschatology.

10 *The Secret History*, an official Mongol biography of the life of Genghis Khan and his Golden Family until the time of Genghis' death and the accession of Ugedey as Great Khan, is not always flattering to Genghis. The narrative unflinchingly details fratricide committed by the young Temujin as he rids himself of a future rival in his half-brother, and Genghis' betrayal of sworn companions such as Jamuka and sometime allies such as the Ong Khan of the Kereits. Genghis' chief men are admiringly allegorized in the *Secret History* as fierce and rapacious beasts of prey, yet no mention of historical cannibalism is recorded in this text – a text that in its manuscript history, transcription, and descent suggests intervention on the part of the Chinese, who had no love of their Mongol conquerors and might well have been pleased to mention Mongol cannibalism.

I cite from Igor de Rachewiltz' magisterial two-volume translation of the *Secret History*. For a discussion of manuscript history and transmission see de Rachewiltz (*Secret History* I: xxv–cxiii). Allsen cautions that Mongol historiography came to inherit Chinese traditions, including "the committee approach to official history" that "favored shared/divided responsibility and a collegial system of decision making" in the creation of narratives (*Culture and Conquest* 101, 98). But whether primarily single-authored, as de Rachewiltz suggests, or multiply authored, the *Secret History* does not detect any Mongol cannibalism at all, let alone any committed by order of Genghis Khan.

11 Citing Isidore of Seville and "Russian clerics" ("*Ruthenis clericis*") as his authorities, John describes a race of people who, like apple-sniffers, live only on the smell of meat cooking in a pot. He also describes cynocephali, cyclopedes, and wild men who have no joints in their legs and do not speak (Dawson 30–1, 20, 58; Wyngaert I: 73–5, 54–5, 111). See Chapter 1 for a discussion of the location of the Plinian monstrous races on medieval world maps of the thirteenth century.

12 The account of Benedict the Pole, John's companion, is a brief summary, a mere stub compared to John's (which Benedict's account corroborates), while that of Simon of St. Quentin, another

emissary, has not survived (though a portion is incorporated into Vincent de Beauvais' *Speculum Historiale*). Dominican envoys sent by Innocent IV, the pope who dispatched John – Ascelin of Lombardia and Simon of St. Quentin – did not reach the *orda* of Guyuk Khan, but stopped at the camp of Bayju Noyon, a subsidiary who was extending Mongol rule in Persia, before the advent of Hulegu's establishment of the Ilkhanate. In contrast to the Franciscans, the Dominicans appear to have antagonized their hosts.

13 John's description of the women's exaggerated headdresses is succinct compared to William of Rubruck's in his *Itinerarium*, which presents a lengthy, detailed description of the towering headgear of the matrons (Jackson and Morgan 88–9, Dawson 102; Wyngaert I: 182–3). John invokes the modesty topos and merely says he is unable to describe the women's headgear in a way that his Western audience would understand (Dawson 8; Wyngaert I: 35). William, as he does with almost every cultural item on which his eye alights, offers a prolix, minutely detailed rendition of the headgear.

14 Of the 1245 missions to the Mongols sent by Innocent IV, nothing is known of Laurence of Portugal's, which may have been aborted. De Rachewiltz believes Benedict the Pole to have been a replacement for one of John's original companions, Stephen of Bohemia (de Rachewiltz, *Papal Envoys* 90–1). Benedict met and joined up with John of Plano Carpini at Breslau, and the two friars traveled together (de Rachewiltz, *Papal Envoys* 91). Besides the Franciscan missions of John, Benedict, and Laurence, Innocent also sent Dominicans – Andrew of Longjumeau (who knew Persian and was dispatched again in 1248, this time by Louis IX), Ascelin of Lombardia, and Simon of St. Quentin, with companions.

John's embassy, with Benedict, traveled through Bohemia, Poland, and Russia to Central Asia. Andrew and Ascelin each took the Levantine route. When Andrew approached Tabriz, he encountered a Mongol army detachment, handed over Innocent's two letters for the Great Khan to the officer-in-charge, and made for Antioch. Nothing is known of whether the letters ever reached Guyuk Khan (de Rachewiltz, *Papal Envoys* 113, 115). Ascelin reached the camp of Bayju Noyon in Armenia, where Ascelin handed over the papal letters and massively antagonized Bayju, who considered having the Dominicans flayed and executed. However, after intercession by intermediaries and the arrival of a high Mongol official from Karakorum – Aljigiday, who was familiar with John of Plano Carpini's mission – Bayju decided to reply to Innocent's two bulls, his letter much in the same vein as the Great Khan's. Bayju and Aljigiday also sent two envoys, a Turk and a Nestorian Syrian, to accompany Ascelin, Simon, and their companions back to the Pope for Innocent's reply (de Rachewiltz, *Papal Envoys* 117).

"Ascelin's mission was overshadowed by that of Carpini, for two reasons. Firstly, it arrived back later; but . . . more importantly, Carpini's embassy was the only one to have travelled all the way to the court of the *qaghan*, a fact which clearly made some impression on contemporaries" (Jackson and Morgan 31).

15 *Dei patris immensa* ("God the father's boundless [benevolence]"), the more pastoral letter, furnishes a condensed catechism of the Latin Christian faith and exhorts the Mongol "king" to accept Christianity, while *Cum non solum* ("Since not only [men]") a more political letter, expresses outrage at Mongol hostilities and demands their cessation, especially against Christians, and insists on receiving an explanation and knowledge of the Mongols' future intentions (Dawson 73–6; Rodenberg 73–4, 75). In a muted threat that reflects his double status as pastoral and political leader, in *Cum non solum*, Innocent IV urges the Mongols to conciliate by a fitting penance the wrath of Divine Majesty lest He may no longer put off the punishment of their wickedness *in this life*, as well as taking greater vengeance *in the world to come* (Dawson 76, emphasis added; Rodenberg 75).

16 Jackson and Morgan add that John "appears to have told his fellow Franciscan, the chronicler Salimbene, that the Mongols intended to occupy Italy" (18). A dark vision of incipient Mongol

reinvasion of Eastern and Western Europe thus seems to inhabit the *Ystoria*'s anxious imaginary. But in fact, John was wrong: The plans being put in place focused on the invasion of Islamdom, not Christendom (see section of this chapter entitled "As if We Were Monsters").

17 The ecoscape of the steppe, and the socioeconomic practices the steppe supports, are in fact diverse and varied, as Jackson and Morgan, as well as other scholars, remind us (6–7). For instance, unlike the pastoral nomads who practiced transhumance, forest tribes might fish; some mining existed in small settlements; and around some oases agriculture might be practiced, especially in the famed oasis regions of the Tarim basin (Jackson and Morgan 8). My discussion focuses however on the *shock* experienced by John of Plano Carpini and William of Rubruck, who register stark extremes of environment, terrain, climate, economy, and sociocultural practices that make a profound impression on them. John's and William's accounts emphasize differences from Europe, rather than the variety of steppe environments and socioeconomic cultures emphasized today by scholars.

For example, approaching the country of the Naimans, John acknowledges the existence of woods and rivers, but declares that the rivers are not large and the woods do not stretch far in depth (Dawson 60; Wyngaert I: 115). William also emphasizes stark extremes. On his journey to Sartak, William encounters a vast wilderness – thirty days' journey wide in some places – with no forest, mountain, or stone, just grass; and his party comes across no water except in holes dug in hollows and two little streams (Jackson and Morgan 105; Dawson 112; Wyngaert I: 194). The Franciscans also see the climate of the steppe as extreme, contrary, and inexplicable. John, we've seen, is struck by the extreme cold that takes place in *summer* (Dawson 6; Wyngaert I: 36).

18 John tells his audience that the Mongols did not keep pigs or other farm animals, underscoring the point that they were pastoralist herders, not farmers practicing domestic animal husbandry (Dawson 8; Wyngaert I: 36).

19 William of Rubruck, in his turn, affirms that Mongols eat all dead animals indiscriminately, but does not exhibit the extreme revulsion of John or mention Mongol ingestion of lice and placentas (Jackson and Morgan 79; Dawson 97; Wyngaert I: 176).

20 William's *Itinerarium* (Itinerary – an account of a journey) reiterates that Mongols never wash their clothes or their dishes; they rinse dishes in meat broth and return the broth to the cauldron (Jackson and Morgan 90–1; Dawson 103–4; Wyngaert I: 184).

21 William's *Itinerarium* nonetheless describes an economical method of using and reusing a very little water that enables Mongols to wash their mouth, hands, and head with the same tiny amount of water (Jackson and Morgan 91; Dawson 103–4; Wyngaert I: 184).

22 William observes this also of Cumans on the steppe, and relates the burial of even a *baptized* Cuman that involved the skins of sixteen horses, four facing each of the cardinal directions, and hung up between tall poles (Jackson and Morgan 95–6; Dawson 105; Wyngaert I: 187).

23 The letter Mongke Khan sends through William of Rubruck to Louis IX, a policy statement that has the entire world and its populations as its ultimate addressee, is intended to go "wherever ears can hear, and wherever a horse can go" ("*ubicumque possunt aures audire, quocumque potest equus ambulare*": [Jackson and Morgan 248; Dawson 202; Wyngaert I: 307]). On his journey to Mongke's *orda*, William crosses a plain where there had once been large towns – but the Mongols destroyed the towns, he says, so as to return the land to pasturage for their horses and herds (Jackson and Morgan 147; Dawson 136; Wyngaert I: 226).

24 William's *Itinerarium* adds that Batu Khan takes feudal rent in the form of milk from 3,000 mares. Just as peasants in Syria tender a third of their produce, the *Itinerarium* tells us, Mongols bring to the *orda* of their lords the mare's milk of every third day (Jackson and Morgan 82; Dawson 99; Wyngaert I: 179).

25 If the *Ystoria* seems to have an outsized conception of the role of Mongol women – the *Ystoria* seems to suggest that women do virtually every kind of economic, social, and domestic labor in the Mongol world (Dawson 18; Wyngaert I: 50–1) – William's *Itinerarium* has a more nuanced account

of the division of labor between the genders (Jackson and Morgan 90–1; Dawson 103; Wyngaert I: 183–4).

26 This moving assemblage of a human, a horse, and a bow, multiplied tens of thousands of times over, formed the feared war machine of the Mongol empire. Rossabi, in "All the Khan's Horses," calls Mongol horses the ballistic missiles of the thirteenth century.

27 Twenty-first-century popular culture would reimagine the kind of hive-mind in warfare that Mongol armies seemed to John to display, as well as Mongol assimilationist tendencies. The Borg, a race of beings in the sci-fi world of *Star Trek*, formed a war machine in which each individual existed as a piece of the composite organism that functioned like a distributed but unified, single entity, and inexorably assimilated conquered enemies into their own ranks, like the Mongols.

28 Historians have variously estimated the range of the recurved composite Mongol bow of bamboo, horn, and sinew at between 350 and 500 yards (compare this with the English longbow's range of 250–400 yards): www.atarn.org/mongolian/mongol_1.htm

29 In this feat of reconnaissance, John's intelligence proved not to be quite accurate. At the kuriltay, Guyuk did indeed discuss plans for an invasion of the West; however, the intended targets were not European lands but the Abbasid Caliphate, with its capital at Baghdad, and the seemingly impregnable fortresses of the Nizari Ismailis. Though Guyuk did not live to accomplish these goals, Genghis' grandson Hulegu conquered Alamut in northern Persia in 1256 and Baghdad in 1258, and thus founded the Mongol Ikhanate of Persia. The relentless Mongol advance into Islamdom was finally halted in 1260 by Baybars, leading the Mamluks of Cairo at the Battle of Ain Jalut, as we saw in Chapter 3.

30 An observant and canny agent for the West, John adds however that such reinforcements of Mongol armies by newly subjected peoples also meant a potential Fifth Column in Mongol armies, which could be exploited by invaders from the West (Dawson 49; Wyngaert I: 101).

31 John is helped and sustained by a Russian goldsmith named Cosmas, whom he meets at the court of Guyuk Khan – a skilled craftsman who is much favored by the Great Khan, and who made the Khan's golden throne and imperial seal (Dawson 66; Wyngaert I: 122). In his turn, William of Rubruck encounters a Parisian goldsmith at Karakorum, William Boucher, who fashions a fantastic silver fountain issuing different beverages at the feast of the Great Khan Mongke (Jackson and Morgan 209–10; Dawson 175–6; Wyngaert I: 276–7). Several studies exist by art historians who track worldwide crossfertilizations of motifs, patterns, and cultural forms that resulted from Mongol translocations of artisans far from their countries of origin.

32 Guyuk's response to Innocent IV articulates Mongol political theology pithily: For the Mongol khans, "God, in distributing favours ... made his favour known through granting political, military, and economic success" (Atwood, "Validation by Holiness" 253). "The purpose of religion was the securing of blessings," and "true religion" could know that it received "heavenly validation" when the religion came to possess "sovereign power" like that of the Mongols (Atwood, "Validation by Holiness" 253, 255).

33 Jean de Joinville never seems to realize, however, that the great king of the Tartars that he describes was actually a woman – Guyuk's widow and regent (Shaw 287). William of Rubruck reports that Oghul Gamish ("Chamus") is later vilified by Mongke Khan as a wicked sorceress who was viler than a dog (Jackson and Morgan 249; Dawson 203; Wyngaert I: 308). She, her husband Guyuk, and Guyuk's father Ugedey all belonged to a rival branch of the Golden Family of Genghis Khan that was extirpated when Mongke, the son of Toluy, Genghis' youngest, ascended to power with the help of Batu, the son of Jochy, another of Genghis' four sons.

34 John is particularly troubled by his encounter with *Corenza*, an official whom he views as little more than a brigand-extortionist out to maximize profit. This Corenza not only demands gifts up front (every Mongol official seems to do this), but he is also dissatisfied with the quality and

quantity of what he receives, so that the papal envoy is further obliged to empty his stores (Dawson 54; Wyngaert I: 106–7).

35 John describes tribute and gifts to Guyuk that were marvelous to behold: silk, samite, velvet, brocade, girdles of gold-threaded silk, an umbrella or sunshade ornamented with precious gems, forty or fifty camels decked with brocade, horses and mules covered with trappings or armor, and more than 500 carts filled with gold, silver, and silken garments, all of which were shared out among the Great Khan and his chieftains. A wonderful tent of red velvet, given by the northern Chinese, was already in use (Dawson 64; Wyngaert I: 120).

36 Benedict the Pole's narrative thrice corroborates John's account of the gift system. Though not as impassioned in his indignation as the papal envoy, Benedict reports that Batu's servants demanded forty beaver skins and eighty badger skins from the Franciscans (Dawson 79–80; Wyngaert I: 135–7).

37 For a selection of studies on the international relations, embassies, ethnographic accounts, field reports, papal and missionary letters, diplomatic missions, and explorations of this period, see Dawson; de Rachewiltz (*Papal Envoys*); Fernández-Armesto; Moule; Muldoon (*Popes*); and Setton. "As early as 1235 the master-general [of the Dominican friars], writing from Milan to all the order, called for men 'prepared to learn Arabic, Hebrew, Greek, or some other outlandish language'" for programs of conversion (Burns 1402). "As early as 1259, the Dominicans established *studia Arabicum* in Barcelona and Tunis, and soon after in Murcia, Valencia, and other locations, in order to train missionaries to preach and dispute in the Muslims' own language" (Catlos 333). "In the 1260s Roger Bacon hungrily eyed the multitudes of Muslims, Mongols, Buddhists, and pagans ripe for conversion" (Burns 1391), and by the end of the thirteenth century, as Muldoon's survey of Vatican registers suggests, there was "a general process of reducing the world to two classes of people, those within the Church and those outside of it" (Muldoon, *Popes* 52).

   In the early fourteenth century, a polemical tract by Pierre Dubois even envisages training *women* in foreign languages, theology, and medicine for missionary work: "Pierre Dubois accorded girls an equal place with boys in the schools which he proposed should be founded for the education of a generation which should convert the East ... Like the boys the girls were to be highly educated in the languages which they would need ... trained in medical skills ... especially in those skills needed to deal with women's ills, so that they might then proceed to their conversion ... the girls were also to be trained in theology, since they would need to be able to instruct the women in the tenets of the Christian faith" (Purcell 61). "Conversion," however, Catlos suggests, "was essentially seen as an effort to expand the sovereignty of Christendom rather than save individual souls" (334).

38 Indeed, when soft power was unsuccessful, crusading warfare was resorted to: "Ramon Llull, committed at one time to peaceful conversion, became an advocate of armed Crusade late in life in the face of the failure of the application of reason to bring an end to Islam ... [and] the fall of Acre in 1291 precipitated a flurry of polemical tracts and essays aimed at recovering the Holy Land from the Muslims (and eradicating the Greeks, who were seen as their collaborators)" (Catlos 334).

39 See Chapter 4 for Wolfram's elaboration of this backstory.

40 These cultural manifestations of the belief that Christianity had a foothold in the far regions of the world were not without historical basis. Ethiopia's conversion to Christianity in the fourth century and Nubia's in the sixth meant that devout sub-Saharan Africans made pilgrimages to the Holy Land, and Ethiopian monks were found in Jerusalem – that most visited of international pilgrimage destinations – from the fourth century, and admired for their "moral standard" and "purity of life" (Selassie 112). See Chapter 4 for a discussion. I discuss early Nestorian missionizing in India, China, and Eurasia in various places throughout this chapter.

41 The Mongol envoys accompanied Ascelin and Simon back to Europe ostensibly for the purpose of conveying Bayju's letter to Innocent IV. The Eurasian studies scholar Igor de Rachewiltz assumes the envoys, like John of Plano Carpini, were intended to conduct reconnaissance and espionage (*Papal Envoys* 117).

42 "Although Eljigidei addressed Louis as 'son' and thereby still implied some degree of superiority on the part of the *qaghan*, the letter contained none of the habitual statements about the world-empire or demands for submission. The general wished Louis well in his operations against the Muslims; announced that his own task was to see to the exemptions of all Christians from labour services and taxation and to the restoration of their churches; and concluded with a request that the French king avoid discriminating between Latin and non-Latin Christians, since under Mongol rule all sects were held to be equal" (Jackson and Morgan 33–4).

43 De Rachewiltz adds that the Dominican was "presumably also entrusted by Louis with an oral message for Eljigidei concerning his intention of collaborating with the Mongols against the Moslems" (*Papal Envoys* 122). Andrew's second mission to the Mongols – this time to the heart of the empire and the Great Khan himself – was relatively large, a seven-man embassy that included his brother William (also a Dominican), a third friar, and clerks and guards, along with Aljigiday's two envoys (de Rachewiltz, *Papal Envoys* 122).

44 "It is impossible to say whether these stories were fabricated by the envoys eager to ensure the success of their mission, or whether they had been instructed to relate them by the cunning Eljigidei" (de Rachewiltz, *Papal Envoys* 121).

45 John's *Ystoria* retails a story that suggests Guyuk Khan's mother, Toreghana Khatun, may have assassinated Yaroslav I ("Jerozlaus"), Grand Duke of Vladimir, by giving him poisoned food and drink – hardly a friendly act to a fellow Christian, if she had been the daughter of Prester John (Dawson 65).

46 The struggle between the families of two of Genghis' sons – Ugedey and Toluy – for control of the empire, was headed by powerful Mongol women: Guyuk's widow, Oghul Gamish, and John of Plano Carpini's "Sorocan," or Sorghaghtani Bekhi, the wife of Toluy, and mother of Mongke, Kublai, Hulegu, and Arik-Boke. Innocent IV's envoy, who considered "Sorocan" the most powerful and renowned person in the Mongol empire next to Batu, was correct in his conclusion: Sorghaghtani Bekhi, with the support of the powerful Batu, succeeded in having her son Mongke succeed Guyuk as Great Khan. The papal envoy's astuteness can be seen in this.

47 William's account has been preserved in five copies, derived from four manuscripts: three at Corpus Christi College, Cambridge, and one in the British Museum. Corpus Christi College, Cambridge, MS 181, pp. 321–98, the oldest manuscript, dates from the last quarter of the thirteenth century, and also contains the *Ystoria Mongalorum*. Corpus Christi College, Cambridge, MS 66A, ff. 67r–110r, the most attractive manuscript, with illustrations, dates from the first third of the fourteenth century. Corpus Christi College, Cambridge, MS 407, ff. 37r–66r, incomplete, dates from the beginning of the fifteenth century; and British Library, MS Royal 14 C. XIII, ff. 225r–236r, incomplete, from the fifteenth century. The title given in each manuscript varies; William's account is cited here as the *Itinerarium*. For full descriptions of the MSS, see Beazley.

The only known contemporary reference to the *Itinerarium* is by Roger Bacon, who was interested in its geographical material, which he quotes at length in his *Opus Maius* (Greater Work). After centuries of oblivion, the *Itinerarium* was discovered and published by Richard Hakluyt in 1598 with a partial English translation based on British Library, MS Royal 14 C. XIII; Samuel Purchas completed and reissued the translation in 1625–6. Apart from a fourteenth-century Leiden manuscript derived from Corpus Christi College, Cambridge, MS 181, all other versions derive from Hakluyt's printed text. References and quotations in English are from Peter Jackson's translation in Jackson and Morgan, supplemented by Dawson; original Latin is from Anastasius van den Wyngaert's edition in *Sinica Franciscana*, based on Corpus Christi College, Cambridge, MS 181.

48 John of Plano Carpini has already told us that Mongols take punitive vengeance on those who harm Mongol envoys, and Guyuk Khan's reply to Innocent IV makes the execution of Mongol envoys the *raison d'être* for the invasion of Europe. The same *casus belli*, Jackson and Morgan

observe, had functioned in 1218 to justify the invasion of the Khwarezmian empire (26). Indeed, Innocent's envoys, the Dominicans Ascelin and Simon, were protected from those who would execute them at Bayju's camp because of their status as envoys. William of Rubruck describes the trouble Mongke took over a cleric from Acre named Theodulus, who started out as a member of Andrew of Longjumeau's embassy, but parted from Andrew in Persia, and later claimed to be the envoy of a bishop to whom God had sent a letter written in gold letters predicting Mongke's dominion over the earth. After Mongke made elaborate arrangements that included sending back with Theodulus a Mongol envoy who bore Mongke's imperial *paiza* – the Great Khan's gold seal of authority – and extraordinary silver arrows bearing a symbolic political message for Louis IX, the so-called embassy of Theodulus came to naught (Jackson and Morgan 184–6; Dawson 159–60; Wyngaert I: 255–6).

Imposters like Theodulus, William says, roam the world, and the Mongols put them to death when they catch them (Jackson and Morgan 187; Dawson 160; Wyngaert I: 256). Given that Mongke must apportion time and effort to distinguish the charlatans from the authentic ambassadors who come his way, we see why Mongols might execute false ambassadors who waste their time.

49 William had already presented to Sartak the modest gifts he had brought: a flagon of muscatel wine, fruit, and a basket of biscuits. Having been asked by the Mongols to show them his mass equipment, books, and vestments, William's display of these in one cart, alongside another cart with the food and beverage gifts, perhaps renders the status of the books and equipment ambiguous, and blurs the distinction between gifts for presentation and objects only for show-and-tell (Jackson and Morgan 116; Dawson 118; Wyngaert I: 201–2).

50 William tells Louis he succeeded in retaining certain vestments (those he had worn at the audience with Sartak the day before), the Bible Louis gave him, and some of his favorite books (Jackson and Morgan 119–20; Dawson 120; Wyngaert I: 204). He mentions again with regret toward the end of his narrative that the Queen's psalter was irretrievable: an unsurprising outcome, given Mongol fondness for gilded deluxe art and artifacts and luxury goods.

51 It is possible, of course, that Sartak's men were acting on Sartak's orders in confiscating these beautiful goods. But since William has already shown himself to be rhetorically resourceful, with a silver tongue, in his earlier audience with Sartak, William may have thought he could have induced a reversal of the orders, or at least their mitigation, had he been allowed access to Sartak.

52 "It should be remembered that the middle of the thirteenth century was a period of great evangelical fervour, caused principally by the Council of Lyons' emphatic affirmation of the need to undertake missionary work on a world-wide scale, and that reports like [the conversion of Sartak to Christianity] had a profound effect on the clergy" (de Rachewiltz, *Papal Envoys* 126).

53 William's little group had five members: two Franciscan friars, Bartholomew of Cremona and William himself; Gosset, a French secretary from Louis who kept their accounts; a dragoman, "*Omodeo*" (*Homo Dei* = Abdullah), who acted as translator; and a slave boy, Nicholas, purchased by William in Constantinople with money from Louis (Jackson and Morgan 69; Dawson 92; Wyngaert I: 170).

54 Jackson and Morgan have a less colorful translation: "with bare feet, wearing our habits but with our heads uncovered, and presented quite a spectacle for them" (132).

55 The episode is useful for how William registers the distinction between John of Plano Carpini's status and his own. Dressed in their habits, barefoot and bareheaded, William and Bartholomew are a spectacle for the Mongols' eyes, but not John: Since John was the ambassador of the lord Pope, William says, he had changed out of his habit so as not to incur contempt (Jackson and Morgan 132; Dawson 127; Wyngaert I: 213–14). John's ambassadorial attire thus signaled his official status to the Mongols, a people keenly attuned to attire, livery, and dress. By William's report, John would have had little reason to imagine how he might look in the eyes of the other. How did

William know that his predecessor, unlike him, had changed into robes appropriate for his ambassadorial rank? According to Salimbene, after John's return to Innocent IV, the pope sent John on an embassy to Louis, where he "presumably furnished ... a detailed account of his experiences" (Jackson and Morgan 29).

56 "His report is one of the most important contributions to the physical geography of Central Asia until the nineteenth century. He discovered, among other things, the true character of the Caspian Sea, and was the first writer to give the correct course of the Don and the Volga" (de Rachewiltz, *Papal Envoys* 129). De Rachewiltz adds that "William's description of Buddhist ritual, including the use of the famous formula *Om mani padme hum*, is the first of its kind in Western literature," and William's observation that the Nestorians continued to use Sogdian in their writing and liturgy, when throughout Asia the liturgical language of the Nestorian Church was Syriac, is invaluable for showing that Sogdian – an Iranian language that was once the lingua franca of Central Asia – was still in use in the middle of the thirteenth century (*Papal Envoys* 130–1).

57 See, for instance, the *Itinerarium's* description of a yurt: "The dwelling in which they sleep is based on a hoop of interlaced branches, and its supports are made of branches, converging at the top around a smaller hoop, from which projects a neck like a chimney. They cover it with white felt: quite often they also smear the felt with chalk or white clay and ground bones to make it gleam whiter, or sometimes they blacken it. And they decorate the felt around the neck at the top with various fine designs. Similarly, they hang up in front of the entrance felt patchwork in various patterns ["*filtrum opera polimitario variatumi*"]: they sew onto one piece others of different colors to make vines, trees, birds and animals. These dwellings are constructed of such a size as to be on occasion thirty feet across: I myself once measured a breadth of twenty feet between the wheel-tracks of a wagon, and when the dwelling was on the wagon it protruded beyond the wheels by at least five feet on either side. I have counted twenty-two oxen to one wagon, hauling along a dwelling, eleven in a row, corresponding to the width of the wagon, and another eleven in front of them. The wagon's axle was as large as a ship's mast, and one man stood at the entrance to the dwelling on top of the wagon, driving the oxen" (Jackson and Morgan 72–3; Dawson 94; Wyngaert I: 172–3).

58 "*Respexit ergo nos diligenter et nos eum*" (Wyngaert I: 214; Jackson and Morgan 132: "He regarded us with a keen gaze, as we did him").

59 Later the *Itinerarium* says that Sartak's Nestorian priests also kept the Franciscans' chrism, so that William is unable to anoint a dying Nestorian priest with his own holy oil but must use the oil of the Nestorians at Mongke's *orda, which they said was holy*, William adds ("*quod ipsi dicebant sanctum*" [Jackson and Morgan 219; Dawson 183; Wyngaert I: 284]). On his return journey, William, exercising utmost diplomacy, is able to retrieve some of their belongings, but not all. The Franciscans lose three albs, an amice embroidered in silk, a stole, a girdle, an altar-cloth adorned with gold embroidery, a surplice, their thurible, their phial containing the chrism, a Bible in verse, a book in Arabic worth thirty bezants, the French queen's beautiful illuminated psalter, and several other things (Jackson and Morgan 258; Dawson 209, 210; Wyngaert I: 316).

60 At Mongke's *orda*, William finally gains news of the Germans but recognizes the impossibility of reaching them to minister to them, given the fact that he could not deviate from his route. The Germans had been taken to a village called Bolad to act as miners for gold and to manufacture arms (Jackson and Morgan 145–6; Dawson 136; Wyngaert I: 224–5). When he is eventually told he needs to leave Mongke's orda (the Great Khan authorizes a stay of two months for the Franciscans so that Bartholomew of Cremona may rest and heal from the ordeals of steppe travel, but William and Bartholomew stay for more than six months), William petitions for permission to return to minister to the Germans, but receives no positive answer from Mongke (Jackson and Morgan 238–9; Dawson 196–7; Wyngaert I: 299–300).

61 David Morgan, who remarks that "religious belief as such seems to have sat rather lightly on the Mongols," links the Mongol lack of zealotry to their famed pragmatism (37). Significantly,

Mongol emissaries to the West driven by faith as well as diplomacy, such as Rabban Sauma (see discussion of Sauma in the section entitled "Mandeville and Fantasies of Race-and-Religion"), were Nestorian or Eastern Christians, not shaman priests. Atwood ("Validation by Holiness") offers us the limits of the Mongols' famed religious tolerance, showing tolerance to be firmly wedded to military and political pragmatism: e.g., Mongke bans the Nizari Ismaili branch of Islam and puts to death anyone refusing to "abjure his faith," because the Nizaris constituted "a defiant rival state that had on occasion assassinated Mongol commanders and protected fugitives from Mongol taxation" (251). Atwood suggests that Kublai Khan, so lauded for tolerance by Marco Polo, may have been the least tolerant of all: "Late in his reign, he showed a strong streak of intolerance. In 1280, he decreed the death penalty for anyone who slaughtered animals by slitting their throats in the Islamic or Jewish fashion or performed circumcision" ("Validation by Holiness" 251). The malfeasance of the Muslim high official Ahmad the Bailo may well have played a role in Kublai's decree (see discussion in the section "Race-as-Religion Returns").

62 The *Itinerarium* reports that Mongke's letter to Louis offers a clear option of peace or war: If Louis wishes to make peace with the Mongols, and offer obedience, he should send envoys to them (Jackson and Morgan 250; Dawson 203; Wyngaert I: 309). Jackson and Morgan recognize that the letter to Louis follows a common template: "Voegelin demonstrated the specific formulae common to [Mongol letters] and their noticeably consistent structure. The recipients were notified that their dominions were part of the world-empire of the Mongols. They were ordered to submit, to pay tribute, and to place their own forces at the *qaghan*'s disposal. And the letters concluded with a suggestion – no less sinister for being couched in vague terms – of the consequences of disobedience" (25).

63 Jackson and Morgan emphasize Mongol disbelief in visitations for nonpolitical reasons (25). Moreover, the *Itinerarium*'s account of how Mongke treats the false ambassador Theodolus – sending back with Theodolus their own envoy bearing the imperial seal, a sheaf of magnificent arrows, and a message for Louis IX that offered to leave the French king's territories unmolested and not to extend Mongol conquest beyond the lands of Islamdom if Louis wished to make "peace" with the Mongols – suggests that Mongke had an interest in establishing an entente with Louis (Jackson and Morgan 185–6; Dawson 159; Wyngaert I: 255).

64 The tips of William's toes froze the next morning after he had gone barefoot again to meet the envoys of the Byzantine emperor (Jackson and Morgan 175; Dawson 152; Wyngaert I: 247). The cold in those parts was so severe, William adds, that ice never thawed in winter, and even mornings in May had frozen ice. At Easter, the cold was so bad countless animals perished, and such a heavy snowfall filled and blocked the streets of Karakorum that snow had to be hauled away in cartloads (Jackson and Morgan 176; Dawson 152; Wyngaert I: 247).

65 William frankly confesses he is terrified when he suspects the intent of Sartak's men to steal the books and vestments of the Franciscans (Jackson and Morgan 116; Dawson 118; Wyngaert I: 202). His terror continues as he journeys between Sartak and his father, and he is overcome with fear again at the immensity of Batu's camp (Jackson and Morgan 127, 131; Dawson 124, 126; Wyngaert I: 210, 212–13). The emotions of the Franciscan group's members can be imagined from their tears when they are forced by Batu to separate (Jackson and Morgan 134; Dawson 129; Wyngaert I: 216). Their ordeal in the journey to Mongke may be guessed at from Bartholomew's refusal to accompany William on the return journey home, after a rest of over six months with Mongke. Pleading that he could not survive the trials of the journey back, Bartholomew insisted he needed more rest before being sufficiently well to attempt return to Europe (Jackson and Morgan 250–1; Dawson 204–5; Wyngaert I: 309–10).

66 Nor do the Mongols hesitate to remind William of his powerlessness. When he attempts to argue during his first major ordeal – the confiscation of the Franciscans' valuables – William is darkly told that it would behoove him to be patient and humble (Dawson 120; Jackson and Morgan 119; Wyngaert

I: 204). William learns well the lesson that a foreigner who is not an envoy or ambassador is vulnerable on the steppe. Later, on his return journey to Louis, when he encounters a group of five Dominicans sent by the pope with letters to Sartak, Mongke, and Buri requesting permission for them to stay in the Mongol empire and preach, William discourages the friars, telling them of the hardships they would meet and adding that if they were not official envoys but only there to preach, they would be held of little account (Jackson and Morgan 270–1; Dawson 216; Wyngaert I: 326).

67 John tells us that he and his embassy feared they might be killed by the Tartars, imprisoned for life, or afflicted with hunger, thirst, cold, heat, injuries, and exceedingly great trials almost beyond their powers of endurance, and that in fact all this fell to their lot, with the exception of death and imprisonment, to a much greater degree than they had imagined beforehand (Dawson 3; Wyngaert I: 27–8).

68 Perhaps a germ of this idea is implanted even earlier, when William first meets Sartak and the Mongol khan asks the friars to pronounce a blessing on him, which William says they did (Jackson and Morgan 115; Dawson 117; Wyngaert I: 201). William then represents his modest gifts of muscatel wine, biscuits, and fruit to Sartak not as a gift, but *as a blessing* (*pro benediction* [Jackson and Morgan 116; Dawson 118; Wyngaert I: 202]). As the Franciscans enter Sartak's *ger*, they are also asked to sing some blessing for him, and they enter singing the "*Salve Regina*" (Jackson and Morgan 117; Dawson 118–19; Wyngaert I: 202).

69 William admits to Louis that his request to stay was in fact prompted by Bartholomew, who was too weak to travel further after the ordeal of the journey to Mongke. It is Bartholomew, William says, who entreated William to ask for special grace to remain at Mongke's *orda* (Jackson and Morgan 180; Dawson 155; Wyngaert I: 250).

70 There is a pecking order in how the Christian religious issue prayers for the Great Khan. First the Nestorian priests say their prayers, then the Armenian monk Sergius says his, and then finally the Franciscans say theirs (Jackson and Morgan 212–13; Dawson 178; Wyngaert I: 279). The *Itinerarium* says, of all the religious: "they all follow [Mongke's] court as flies do honey, and he makes them all gifts and all of them believe they are on intimate terms with him and forecast his good fortune" (Jackson and Morgan 187; Dawson 160; Wyngaert I: 256).

71 William takes pride in detailing for Louis their many refusals of compensation and gifts. They are given a length of *nasij* (brocade) by Mongke's chief wife, which they refuse: Their incorrigible interpreter takes it, and, though it is ruined on their return journey, sells it for eighty Cyprian bezants, which imparts some idea of the value of such gifts even when ruined (Jackson and Morgan 191; Dawson 163; Wyngaert I: 259). They are also given ten marks of silver (a *iascot*) when they visit the sick *khatun*, but William refuses it, and the Armenian monk Sergius seizes it instead (Jackson and Morgan 198; Dawson 168; Wyngaert I: 266). They are given padded grey silk clothes, tunics and trousers, which are light and warm, and which William accepts only for the ailing Bartholomew – whose fur cloak is too heavy – but not for himself (Jackson and Morgan 204–5; Dawson 172; Wyngaert I: 272). Finally, William agrees to accept compensation in the form of three tunics, so as not to offend the Mongols any further with his refusals and leave disgracefully emptyhanded (Jackson and Morgan 251; Dawson 205; Wyngaert I: 310).

72 Usefully, William's entry into the gift-and-service economy of the Mongols also results in improved access to Mongke when William begins to collaborate, gingerly, with the Nestorian priests who are ubiquitous at Mongke's *orda* and with the Armenian monk Sergius, all of whom have access to the Great Khan for purposes of ritual, prayer, blessing, and so on. The status of the Franciscans also improves when they are allowed to leave their tiny hut and move in with Sergius, but together with the other Christian clerics, they are still housed furthest away from the Great Khan among the various religious men.

73 The teasing question of how to name William's and Bartholomew's roles however continues to the end. Mongke's letter to Louis IX, carried back by William in lieu of the Mongol envoys that

William, like John, prudently refuses to escort to Europe, initially calls the Franciscans Louis's "envoys" (*nuncios*). Finally, corrected by William, the final version of the letter refers to the Franciscans as Louis's "monks or priests" (*monachos* [Jackson and Morgan 250; Dawson 203–4; Wyngaert I: 309]).

74 A more satisfying drink *to a hungry man*, William adds – and William is perennially hungry (Jackson and Morgan 264; Dawson 212; Wyngaert I: 321). When he is first given *koumiss* to drink, William tells Louis that he sweated all over from fright and the novelty of it, for he had never drunk it before. But even then, he says, *koumiss* struck him as very tasty – an impression that only grows in the course of his journey (Jackson and Morgan 99; Dawson 108; Wyngaert I: 189).

75 Moreover, William also notices the alcoholic beverages of non-nomads, such as the Chinese. Since William repeats himself, however, it is likely that some of the beverages he mentions by slightly different names and descriptions overlap, or are the same concoctions.

76 William Boucher, who is the slave of Mongke's brother Arik-Boke, earns 1,000 marks from Mongke for this work of art (Jackson and Morgan 224; Dawson 185; Wyngaert I: 287–8).

77 John of Plano Carpini also mentions musical accompaniment to drinking, but it is an observation in passing. John notices the *koumiss* positioned by the door of a yurt, but fails to mention any musical instrument or musician alongside the *koumiss*, and in general does not remark on art and artistry on the steppe except insofar as it relates to power or wealth, like Guyuk Khan's ornate yurt and throne (Dawson 57, 64; Wyngaert I: 110, 120).

78 William mentions repeatedly on his journey to Sartak that nothing was for sale for gold or silver, only for fabric (Jackson and Morgan 103, 108, 110; Dawson 110, 113, 115; Wyngaert I: 192, 196, 198). The Franciscans' possession of cotton or other fabrics would have enabled them to make purchases among the Alans (Jackson and Morgan 103; Dawson 110; Wyngaert I: 192). The *Ystoria Mongalorum* also mentions the tributary gift of a splendid tent all of red velvet from the Chinese at Guyuk Khan's *kuriltay* (Dawson 64; Wyngaert I: 120). This is not to say, of course, that Mongols did not possess gold or silver – we see silver frequently being distributed to the religious men of Mongke's *orda* – or that tribute did not take the form of precious metals. William tells Louis, for instance, that the Chinese tender tribute variously in the form of silver, silk, and foodstuffs (Jackson and Morgan 162; Dawson 144; Wyngaert I: 236–7).

79 John of Plano Carpini observed that Guyuk Khan's *ger* was also covered in gold brocade on the inside (Dawson 63; Wyngaert I: 119).

80 The *Ystoria Mongalorum* also notices display with livery in the form of color and luxury fabric, so that on the first day of Guyuk Khan's *kuriltay*, his chieftains were all dressed in white velvet; on the second day, in red velvet; on the third day, in blue velvet; and on the fourth day, in the finest brocade (Dawson 61; Wyngaert I: 117). The *Secret History of the Mongols* shows us that white, red, and blue are particularly esteemed colors in Mongol society. The *Itinerarium* shows Mongke Khan invoking the same kind of display at one of his feasts in Karakorum: On each of the four days of feasting, Mongke's men wore clothes of a single color from shoes to headgear, changing color with each day (Jackson and Morgan 246; Dawson 201; Wyngaert I: 306). See Allsen (*Commodity and Exchange*) on Mongols and textiles.

81 John of Plano Carpini mentions some of these groups, but only in a long list of *countries* conquered by the Mongols that includes Armenians, Circassians, "Saracens," Jews, Ethiopians, Hungarians, etc., rather than as constituent populations commonly classed under the name of "Tartars" (Dawson 41; Wyngaert I: 88–9). By contrast, as early as Sartak's *orda*, William begins to learn the process of internal differentiation, when he is told that Mongols wish to be differentiated from Tartars and are proud to be called Mongols (Jackson and Morgan 120; Dawson 121; Wyngaert I: 205). Though there was a significant Nestorian Christian presence among the Onguts, oddly enough William seems not to notice the presence of Onguts (nor of Oirats) among the populations classed under the name of "Tartars."

82 If William is unwilling to accept supernatural marvels, he is willing to accept material ones, and relates on good authority, he tells Louis, that in China there is a town with walls of silver and ramparts of gold (Jackson and Morgan 161; Dawson 144; Wyngaert I: 236). Elsewhere, he also muses over an odd "fact": the area around Karakorum, where Mongke traveled, only seems to slope uphill, never downhill – a feature William confirms by citing Baldwin of Hainault, whom William had met at Constantinople, and who had noticed the same odd "fact." William even cites priests from China who attested to this same factoid (Jackson and Morgan 200; Dawson 170; Wyngaert I: 268). It seems that, while impervious to the tradition of the Plinian races and travel-romance marvels, William can be credulous about geography.

83 William's prosaic version of the Prester John legend may be contrasted with John of Plano Carpini's, which retains the fiction that Prester John is the ruler of India, and moreover "defeated Chingis Khan's army with a stratagem involving metal dummies and Greek fire. The story is reminiscent of the legendary account of Alexander's defeat of the Indian king Porus, whose elephants were routed by the Macedonian's soldiers using red-hot bronze statues filled with burning embers and placed on iron carts. However, John's account also reflects current stories about the Mongols' well-known use of manikins and incendiaries in their campaigns, and the defeat of one of their generals by the Khorezmians in 1221" (de Rachewiltz, *Papal Envoys* 107). The Ong Khan and his brother were Onguts and not Naimans, as William believes.

84 The *Itinerarium* calls Basil, who was born in Hungary, the son of an Englishman (Jackson and Morgan 212; Dawson 177; Wyngaert I: 278).

85 This Armenian "monk," Sergius, with whom William and Bartholomew reside, turns out to be neither a monk nor a priest (as he claims) but an illiterate cloth-weaver, according to the *Itinerarium* (Jackson and Morgan 198; Dawson 168; Wyngaert I: 266). Sergius, whose antics William righteously documents, appears to be one of the great trickster figures of literature: a man of grandiose self-importance who believes he has been sent by God to the Mongols, and who claims to be about to baptize the Great Khan Mongke (Jackson and Morgan 174, 187; Dawson 151, 160; Wyngaert I: 246, 256). Indeed, the Armenian has promised Mongke that were the Khan to convert to Christianity, the whole world would come under his dominion, and the French and the Pope would be subject to him; and Sergius advises William, when they first meet, to repeat the same message to Mongke (Jackson and Morgan 174; Dawson 151; Wyngaert I: 246).

The Armenian even promises Mongke that he would go to the Pope and bring all the nations of the West ("*omnes nationes occidentis*") under Mongke's dominion (Jackson and Morgan 205; Dawson 173; Wyngaert I: 273). Sergius politicks freely and readily among the religious men at Monkge's court, and creates trouble by threatening some Muslims, so that he is out of favor for a time until he manages to appease Mongke by shrewd diplomacy (Jackson and Morgan 225, 251–2; Dawson 186, 205; Wyngaert I: 288, 310–11). William even intimates that the Armenian, in his powermongering, likely sped the death of Jonas, the Nestorian archdeacon the Armenian saw as a competitor, by giving Jonas rhubarb and potions to drink: Sergius tells William afterward he killed Jonas through his prayers so that they might be rid of a rival at court and in order for them to have more control over Mongke (Jackson and Morgan 217, 219; Dawson 181, 183; Wyngaert I: 282, 285). William's testiness toward Sergius is colored by disdain and contempt comingled with a sense of dependency: Unlike the Franciscans, Sergius speaks Mongolian; and Sergius has been willing to share his quarters with the Franciscans. To William's horror, however, their housemate articulates Manichean heresy, and dabbles in divination with the help of a shaman and a Russian (Jackson and Morgan 206, 219; Dawson 173–4, 182–3; Wyngaert I: 274, 284–5). The *Itinerarim* treats Louis to a detailed account of Sergius' petty, vainglorious habits – the Armenian ornaments his fingernails with unguents, has a faldstool made for himself like a bishop, and has gloves and a cap made of peacock feathers with a little gold cross on top – and shows how Sergius cheats, pretending to fast during Lent while secretly eating high-energy snacks such as almonds, raisins, and prunes that he has stashed away (Jackson and Morgan 199, 207; Dawson 169, 174; Wyngaert I: 268, 275). Bristling with vigorous indignation, William's resentment of Sergius in fact produces a characterization of the Armenian as an extraordinary individual: This fraudulent "monk" is a colorful, larger-than-life medieval pretender and Rasputin-like trickster who does not amount to the kind of systemic threat and competition that the Nestorian priests collectively pose for William and the Franciscans.

86 A gulf separated "these eastern Christians, with their own tradition of eight centuries' standing, and Friar William, who represented the newly founded intellectual and evangelistic shock-troops of the Latin West" (Jackson and Morgan 47). Indeed, William describes Nestorian rites as if he were a reluctant tourist in Nestorian-Christian-land, with an air of holding his nose, as it were (Jackson and Morgan 213–14; Dawson 179; Wyngaert I: 280–1). Jackson and Morgan remark tartly: "Rubruck's strictures on [the Nestorian] church are in fact redolent of the criticisms levelled at the Roman church prior to the Gregorian Reform in the eleventh [century]. It is worth noting, in any case, that Friar William never met a Nestorian cleric of higher rank than archdeacon, and that he only mentions one Nestorian monk, apparently 'a man of sense', who arrived at court shortly before his own departure, so that it is unlikely they actually met (XXXVI, 17). A rather different view of the eastern church is to be derived from the report of the Nestorian monk Rabbân Sawma, who visited the West three decades later" (50).

87 Christian and Muslim medieval authors alike conflated Taoist priests and Buddhist monks, generically calling both *tuins* or *toyins* (Atwood, "Validation by Holiness" 242).

88 After the expulsion of the Greek patriarch's followers from Edessa in 489, the Nestorians moved to Persia along the trade routes, and thence to South Asia, Eurasia, and East Asia. Rumors of successful Nestorian missionizing intermittently filtered back to Europe through East–West commercial routes, Constantinople, and Syria. The famous Nestorian Stele declares that "A-lo-pen" brought the "shining religion" to China in 635. "The Christian chronicler Bar Hebraeus (d. 1286) ... learned that the majority of the Kereyit tribe had accepted baptism in 1007–8 ... According to Juwayni, the western neighbors of the Kereyit, the Naiman, were mostly Christian ... There was also a significant Christian element among other peoples in the region, notably the Merkit and the Öngüt" (Jackson and Morgan 23).

Kereits, Naimans, and Onguts, Atwood adds, all practiced Christianity as their "state religion" ("Validation by Holiness" 244). In India, the apocryphal account of St. Thomas' preaching, de Rachewiltz notes, "is almost certainly related to the work of the Nestorian missionaries in southern India, which eventually led to the establishment of the Syro-Malabar church still active today" (*Prester John* 2). The assignation of Prester John's legend to India is thus another beneficiary of Nestorian Christianizing, which made available in the Latin West knowledge of Christian Oriental communities that existed far to the east of Persia and Armenia – knowledge the West urgently needed to fuel its hopes for military aid at an exigent moment in the twelfth century, when the legend arose – so that the Prester John legend "must be regarded as being fathered by the Nestorians and mothered by the Christian nations of the West" (de Rachewiltz, *Prester John* 8).

89 "Kirakos tells us that Sartaq was reared by a Christian nurse and was then baptized by 'Syrians' (i.e. Nestorians) as an adult; his death was allegedly 'a great blow' to all Christians. According to the Armenian Vardan, Sartaq was 'a true Christian' who won over many to his faith. Bar Hebraeus even claims the prince was a deacon, though this may have derived from the Nestorian practice of ordaining all male children in the course of extremely infrequent visitations by the bishop" (Jackson, *Studies* IV: 24). Bar Hebraeus also says that Guyuk "'was a true Christian' and that in his time 'the position of many followers of Christ was exalted'" (Jackson, *Studies* IV: 25). But it was not only Nestorians and Armenians who promulgated the belief that Guyuk Khan was a Christian. According to the Persian historian and Mongol apologist Ata Malik Juvaini, one of Guyuk Khan's ministers, Kadak (John of Plano Carpini's "Kadac," the "procurator of the whole

empire," "*procuratorem totius imperii*" [Dawson 66; Wyngaert I: 123]), was a Nestorian who raised Guyuk in the Christian faith, and was responsible for the Great Khan's substantial favoring of Christians (Boyle, *Genghis Khan* 259).

90 Ryan's "Christian Wives of Mongol Khans" details the influence of several prominent imperial women – mothers, wives, daughters, nieces, etc. – who were Christian, including in the Ilkhanate of Persia, where Dokuz Khatun – Hulegu's chief wife, who was lauded as a veritable St. Helena – played an important role. Ryan remarks that under Dokuz Khatun's influence, new churches were built everywhere, and Hulegu supported and promoted Christians. A chapel was always set up near her tent, and bells were rung. After her death, a Christian niece continued her practices (416). Hulegu's son, the Ilkhan Abaga, also had Nestorian Christian wives, as did the Ilkhan Arghun, Abaga's son. Pope Nicholas IV wrote to his most beloved daughters in the royal family of the Ilkhanate, addressing a letter to Nukdan, the queen-mother (one of Abaga's Christian wives), which praised her as "a shining example" of the faith and urged her to help convert others; the Pope also addressed another "pastoral exhortation for assistance in the task of spreading the faith" to "Elegag," yet another Christian queen and one of Arghun's wives or daughters (Ryan 417, 417 n.41).

91 Juvaini suggests that the authority and influence of Chingay and Kadac were immense, and directly responsible for the favoring of Christians during Guyuk's reign: "because of the attendance of Qadaq and Chinqai he [Guyuk] naturally was prone to denounce the faith of Mohammed . . . the emperor . . . entrusted the binding and loosening, the tying and untying of affairs to Qadaq and Chinqai and made them responsible for good and evil, weal and woe. Consequently the cause of the Christians flourished during [Guyuk Khan's] reign, and no Moslem dared to raise his voice to them" (Boyle, *Genghis Khan* 259).

92 Jackson says that Abaga was baptized "immediately prior to his marriage to a Byzantine princess [i.e., Maria Palaiologina], and attended Easter service in a Christian church in Hamadan in 1282, shortly before his death" (*Studies* IV: 27).

93 De Rachewiltz, who considers "William's failure [to be] largely due to his own uncompromising attitude," suggests that the Nestorians were "very friendly at first, [but] later came to regard him as a trouble-maker," so that "rumors about him began circulating and the value of his teaching was questioned. Mönke too seems to have found him too zealous and overbearing" (*Papal Envoys* 137). De Rachewiltz relates an anecdote by Hethum I of Cilician Armenia, to help explain William's lack of success: "King Hethum I of Lesser Armenia (1226–69), who visited Karakorum shortly after . . . was told there how Friar William had tried to convert the Great Khan by threatening him with hellfire. To this Möngke is said to have replied, not without wisdom: 'The nurse at first lets some drops of milk into the infant's mouth, so that by tasting its sweetness he may be enticed to suck; only then does she offer him her breast. In the same way you should persuade Us, who seem to be totally unacquainted with this doctrine, in a simple and rational manner. Instead you immediately threaten Us with external punishments.'" (*Papal Envoys* 137). William does not relate this episode, so unflattering to himself, in the *Itinerarium*.

94 Though John's first church – said to have been established at Khanbalik/Beijing – has been sought in China, Donald Lach, citing N. Egann's article "Olon-Sume et la découverte de l'église catholique romaine de Jean de Montecorvino," says that the remains of this first Roman Catholic church have in fact been found at a site "between Inner and Outer Mongolia" (I [book I] 39n.125). De Rachewiltz laments that "Only the ruins of the Roman church at Olon Süme, discovered by Japanese archaeologists before World War II, still bear testimony to Montecorvino's work" (*Papal Envoys* 168). But hints of potential discoveries – traces of as yet unverified residues – of Franciscan activity in China continue to elicit interpretation: "Some years ago (1935) . . . the Danish architect Johannes Prip-Møller pointed out how astonishingly like an Avignon basilica was the ruined Ling ku ssu, situated to the east of Nanking, built about the years 1324–27, with its beamless brick wall, its bell tower on the west and not the east side, its lack of a drum tower, and its measurements of

150 pieds du roy by 102 pieds, etc . . . [J]ust last year John Foster has published in the *Journal of the Royal Asiatic Society* (London) many fresh indications of Franciscan residence in the great Yüan city of Ch'üan-chou" (Goodrich 2).

95 Dawson adds in a note: "John of Monte Corvino in no way exaggerates the importance of this conversion. The princes of the Ongut, who were Nestorian Christians and lived on the frontiers of China by the northern loop of the Yellow River, held an exceptionally influential position in the Mongol Empire owing to their intermarriages with the descendants of Chingis Khan" (225 n.1). Prince George was a son-in-law of the Great Khan, and had "the unique distinction in the East of being both a ruler and a Christian, a characteristic traditionally ascribed to Prester John," so perhaps the archbishop may be forgiven for believing George indeed to have been the descendant of the legendary, nonexistent, Prester John (de Rachewiltz, *Papal Envoys* 166).

96 Andrew of Perugia similarly extols the bounty of the Yuan Mongol emperor on whose generosity he lives, and from whom he received about a hundred gold florins, according to the estimate of Genoese merchants (Dawson 236; Wyngaert I: 376). We saw in Chapter 3 that Genoese merchants were among medieval Europe's greatest experts on revenue and income, so the estimate is likely accurate. Andrew, who becomes Archbishop of Khanbalik after John of Monte Corvino and Peregrine, like William of Rubruck, attests to a tenaciously syncretist Christianity in East Asia, even among those he baptizes to the Catholic faith: "when they are baptized they do not adhere strictly to Christian ways" (Dawson 237; Wyngaert I: 376). It would take the advent of the Jesuits in the early modern period for Roman Catholic missionaries to China to be comfortable with syncretizing local coloration and customs to advance the faith.

97 Jackson and Morgan emphasize the strategic basis underlying Mongol religious tolerance. From a Mongol point of view, "any religion might be true: the best course was to secure the goodwill of the 'religious class' within each group or sect and thereby seek to guarantee Heaven's favour toward the dynasty by every means possible. With this in mind, Christian priests and monks, Buddhist lamas, and Islamic lawyers, judges and religious foundations were exempted from forced labour and from payment of taxes. But it was nevertheless important that the Mongol ruling establishment should not become more closely identified with any one religious group . . . Whatever the religious sympathies of any individual Mongol prince or general, his prime commitment was to the maintenance and extension of the Mongol empire" (24). Nederman agrees: "the religious convictions of the Mongols are almost indistinguishable from their military pretensions . . . To the Mongols . . . strict adherence to any confession would probably appear extraneous to, if not incompatible with, their aspirations for global hegemony" (57).

98 Jackson tells us that interreligious disputation was not an uncommon phenomenon under Mongol rule: "Like earlier steppe rulers, the Mongol qa'ans presided over public debates between representatives of different faiths" (*Studies* IV: 9). While the motives of these khans are unclear – "It has been proposed that a debate took place at the point when the sovereign meditated a change of religious allegiance" – Jackson urges that "we cannot discount the possibility that one purpose was entertainment – that the public religious disputation, in other words, was the intellectual counterpart of the bloody gladiatorial conflicts which the Mongols staged between captured enemy soldiers" (*Studies* IV: 9).

99 De Rachewiltz, who calls the disputation both "historic" and "somewhat incongruous," notes that it was the first of many, which suggests a keen interest in comparative religion on the part of the Khans: "The debate in which Friar William participated was the first of several religious disputes that took place at the Mongol court in the following decade. The representatives of Tibetan Buddhism eventually emerged as the real victors, a fact that accounts largely for the favour accorded to Lamaism by Möngke's successors" (*Papal Envoys* 138).

100 "On all these counts . . . Friar William's mission was a failure. He never made contact with the Germans, whose master Büri had been executed in 1251/2 for his opposition to Mönke. They [the

German slaves] had then been appropriated by the *qaghan* [Mongke] and transferred from Talas to Bolad, several hundred miles to the east. On his way to Möngke's court, where he first discovered their whereabouts, Friar William passed within a short distance of Bolad (XXIII, 3); but on his return journey he was taken by a different route (XXXVII, 1 and n.2). Hardly more success attended his efforts to spread the gospel ... There is a certain pathos in his statement that when he finally set out from Qaraqorum he had baptized in all six souls" (Jackson and Morgan 44–5).

101 Compounding the obstacles William faced in his attempts at converting the Mongols – including the difficulty of gaining frequent audiences with Mongol commanders, since William did not have an ambassador's privileges of access and lacked a consistently reliable translator, notwithstanding the skills of William Boucher's adopted son – may have been William's own personality. An anecdote retailed by Giacomo d'Iseo suggests that William may have pressed his case with the Great Khan (or with Batu Khan, as Jackson and Morgan believe) without sufficient tact: "When he [William] ... appeared before the great king of the Tartars, he began to press on him the Christian faith, saying that the Tartar – and every infidel – would perish eternally and be condemned to everlasting fire. He [the Khan] replied as one surprised at the stance he had taken in seeking to attract him to the Christian faith." Giacomo then relates Mongke's story of how a nurse should treat an infant to sweet drops of milk first, as an inducement to suckle, a story we have already noted. "The word came through the king of Armenia that the religious who had gone about it differently found favour with the king of the Tartars" (Jackson and Morgan 282).

102 On his return journey, when William is given an armed Mongol escort to protect him from possible attack by Alans and Muslims who were still resisting the Mongols, William is delighted because it gives him an opportunity to inspect Mongol weapons closely. He had not before managed to scrutinize Mongol weapons, he tells Louis, although most anxious to do so (Jackson and Morgan 259; Dawson 210; Wyngaert I: 317). The reader thus becomes aware that the *Itinerarium*'s lack of description of war materiel has issued not from a lack of interest on William's part, but rather from a lack of access, despite William's six-month stay.

103 Among other things, William receives *koumiss*, wine, mead, a ram, a sheep, millet and grain, flour, oil, monkey skin cloaks, and tunics from Mongke; sheepskin cloaks and trousers from Batu; and padded silk tunics and trousers from Mongke's chief wife, as well as various gifts of silver, brocade, and other items, which he refuses (Jackson and Morgan 176, 188, 204–5, 207, 251, 253; Dawson 152, 161, 172, 174, 205, 206; Wyngaert I: 247, 257, 271–2, 275, 310, 312). As he departs, his group receives 1,000 marks (ten *iascot*) of silver for the expenses of their journey, and a sheep for food (Jackson and Morgan 252–3; Dawson 206; Wyngaert I: 311–12).

Bartholomew, who remains behind after William's departure, continues to live on the hospitality and charity of Mongke. On his return journey, William is also given two tunics at Sartak's *orda*, one for him and the other for Louis IX; he accepts both for Louis, neither for himself (Jackson and Morgan 256; Dawson 208; Wyngaert I: 314). William peevishly complains to Louis, however, that from the time they left Persia they had not been given a sufficient supply of necessities (Jackson and Morgan 252; Dawson 206; Wyngaert I: 311). John of Plano Carpini, we remember, had been astounded by how little food Mongols lived on, and how little they needed for sustenance: only one meal a day, and even then a very spartan meal – which is not, apparently, sufficient for a Minorite friar like William, despite his order's commitment to asceticism.

104 William also mentions his anger when he is asked, at Mongke's court, for details about France, such as whether there are many sheep, oxen, and horses there (the Mongols being people who are especially interested in animals, and who calculated wealth by the possession of animals). William bristles at the inquiry, which he takes as a prelude to the intention of the Mongols to march in at once and take everything in France (Jackson and Morgan 180; Dawson 155–6; Wyngaert I: 251).

105 Matthew Paris reports that, asked what the English should do about Mongols and Muslims, Peter des Roches, the Bishop of Winchester, suggests that England should leave the dogs to

devour one another, so that they may all be consumed and perish, and when [Christians] proceed against those who remain, they shall slaughter the enemies of Christ and cleanse the face of the earth, so that the whole world may be subject to one catholic church (Luard, *Mathaei Parisiensis ... Chronica majora* III: 489). William relays yet another vision of world domination when he recounts to Louis a prophecy told William by an Armenian bishop. The prophecy retails how the Franks (i.e., crusaders) will issue from Jerusalem, the center of the world, and attack the Mongols with the help of the Armenians, with the result that all the races of unbelievers will be converted to the faith of Christ (Jackson and Morgan 266–7; Dawson 214; Wyngaert I: 322–3). William, who had heard the prophecy before, tells Louis he decided to pay it more attention this time (Jackson and Morgan 267; Dawson 214; Wyngaert I: 323).

106 Foremost among naysayers who find *Le Devisement* far-fetched as the descriptive account of a journey, Frances Wood has suggested that Marco Polo probably went no further than Persia, but picked up stories from traders who traveled farther east. Among the objections are that *Le Devisement* curiously never mentions the Great Wall, Chinese footbinding, tea, or tea-houses. In response, *Le Devisement*'s defenders, who are many, have been been quick to point out that "much of [the Great Wall] had fallen down by the thirteenth century" and that neither Odoric of Pordenone nor John of Marignolli mentions the wall in the fourteenth century either, since "Almost everything the tourist is normally shown today was built in the sixteenth century" (Larner, *Marco Polo* 59).

John Larner also correctly points out that footbinding – a Chinese, not a Mongol, practice – "was at this period limited to upperclass ladies who were confined to their houses, and would rarely be observed by anyone outside their family," let alone subjected to the rude gaze of male foreigners (*Marco Polo* 59). "Tea-culture," Larner adds, "at that time had not reached North and Central China, where Marco mostly resided" (*Marco Polo* 59). Ingeniously, Larner sees the absence of authenticating details that critics might want as a plus, pointing out that "it is because Marco so often merely grazes the surface of his materials that he can take on the whole of Asia" ("Plucking Hairs" 136).

A more serious wrinkle, however, is that Chinese sources do not mention Marco Polo at all. But it is possible – and perhaps likely – that Marco may have aggrandized his role as a factotum of the Mongol empire. If Marco's role was more minor than he suggests (if, for example, we read *Le Devisement*'s account of how the Polos were responsible for Kublai Khan's triumph in the siege of Xiangyang – which I discuss below – as one example of self-aggrandizement, and suspect there are others), there is scant reason for Chinese records to take note of him.

A *Po-Lo* does appear in Chinese records, but has been identified as *Bolad*, a Mongol of the Oirat tribe who was "a major political player in both China and Iran, a shaper of events, while [Marco] Polo, at best, was ... [a] low-level official on the periphery of events ... [Bolad] was a pivotal figure in the flow of science, technology, and culture between China and the Islamic world" (Allsen, *Culture and Conquest* 61). Allsen offers a fascinating thick description of the Po-lo who was *not* Marco – offering us a window into a human life in the cosmopolitan thirteenth century of intermeshing multilingual, multireligious, and multiethnic environments, lived by a man of adaptability and resourcefulness (see chapters 9–11 of *Culture and Conquest*). Igor de Rachewiltz' "Marco Polo Went to China," John Larner's *Marco Polo and the Discovery of the World*, Stephen Haw's *Marco Polo's China*, and Hans Ulrich Vogel's *Marco Polo Was in China* represent scholarship that has tilted scholarly opinion in the direction of conviction that the Polos indeed were in China. My conversations with Tom Allsen and Chris Atwood suggest that Mongol studies scholars themselves do not doubt the veracity of Polo's journeying to the Far East.

107 The manuscript history of *Le Devisement* is complex and continues to pose challenges to editors and literary scholars, who do not always agree on the most important rescensions, manuscripts,

and texts. Moule and Pelliot offer an early discussion of the manuscript stemma (1938), following Luigi Foscolo Benedetto's 1928 analysis of the manuscript tradition, and their edition/translation attempts the massive task of interleaving all the major manuscripts within a single continuous narrative. Each editor and translator of *Le Devisement* rehearses the stemmata at length or in abbreviated form; more recently, Gaunt offers a succinct summary of textual and transmissional traditions in his literary discussion of *Le Devisement* (11–28). For a thorough study of the manuscripts, see Dutschke.

108 Marco's own belongings, inventoried after his death, "include bedding of Tartar workmanship, sendal from Cathay, and a *paiza*, a gold tablet 'di comandamento' from the Great Khan" (Larner, *Marco Polo* 45). Marco released his Mongol slave, Peter, from slavery, and "died aged sixty-nine, on Sunday 8 January 1324, between sunset and midnight, and was buried, as his father had been, in San Lorenzo. Moule and Pelliot, tallying up Marco's relatively modest worldly fortunes at his death, cast doubt on Ramusio's story that "the nickname ["Milione"] was given to him because of the exaggerated numbers with which his often repeated stories of the wealth of the East were filled" (I: 35). "Milion or Milione, nevertheless, he and his book were called in his lifetime," though "It seems to be the case that the real meaning of the name was not certainly known even in the fourteenth century, and . . . we must be content to remain uncertain ourselves" (Moule and Pelliot I: 31, 33).

109 Scholarship on *Le Devisement* is vast. For economy, I cite only scholarship most pertinent to my analysis, with deep apologies to the many literary critics who have published fine interpretive readings of the text. For an example of literary readings of *Le Devisement*, see the anthology of essays by Akbari and Iannucci.

110 Gaunt, for example, quarrels with Philippe Ménard's recent multivolume critical edition (which I cite in Chapter 3). Ménard, "an insistent advocate for the quality (and authority) of the French redaction in recent years" (Gaunt 22), has suggested that the French manuscripts should take priority over the Franco-Italian because "from Ménard's point of view . . . [the Franco-Italian manuscript's] French is simply not good enough because it is too tainted by Italian" (Gaunt 26).

111 Gaunt is persuasive on why an extended discussion of *Le Devisement* should be based on the Franco-Italian text: "BNF f.fr.1116 is the only surviving manuscript that preserves the language of the original (or some approximation of this), as well as being the most complete manuscript" and "deserves pride of place" (13). Moreover, "the language and length of the *Devisement* in BNF f. fr.1116 remain . . . decisive arguments in favour . . . of continuing to give it the 'posto d'onore' . . . as a version approximating the source from which other redactions derive" (Gaunt 13–14). BNF f. fr.1116, moreover, is a very early text dated to 1310, a scant twelve years after the date of the original composition – though Gaunt cautions that "it is worth bearing in mind that one manuscript of the [six-manuscript] Tuscan redaction, Florence, Biblioteca Nazionale II.IV.88" is currently dated to 1309 (13 n.47).

112 I use the name "Polo" here, as in Chapter 3, for both the subject who narrates and the character in the narration – an established convention of critical practice – rather than the names of the authorial pair, while not forgetting that *Le Devisement* is a collaborative work with Rustichello da Pisa. I avoid speculating on when it is Marco or Rustichello who speaks, and whether use of the second-person plural indicates both speaking at once; the reader is free, however, to come to her own conclusions. I cite from Ronchi's standard edition; translations from the Franco-Italian are from Moule and Pelliot. Kinoshita (*Marco Polo*) has recently produced a fine new paperback translation of the Franco-Italian intended for classroom use (according to the backmatter) that should replace the frequently used Penguin Classics translation (which is something of a mashup of manuscripts).

Though I cite Moule and Pelliot's translation, which follows the original syntax closely, Kinoshita is wonderful on meaning and readability for contemporary readers. An example: "*jeo,*

Marc Pol, que plusor foies oi fai[r]e le conte de la rende de tous cestes couses senç le saf" (Ronchi 520–1) appears as "I, Marc Pol, who several times heard the count of the revenue from all these things, without the salt" in Moule and Pelliot (I: 342) and as "I, Marco Polo, who on several occasions heard tell that each year, the income from all these things (minus the salt)" in Kinoshita (*Marco Polo* 137). Varying dates are supplied in the diverse manuscript tradition; the dates I cite are from the Franco-Italian manuscript.

113 A thoughtful and thought-provoking recent contribution to informed scholarly speculation on Polo's languages is Alexander Wolfe's "Marco Polo, Factotum, Auditor."

114 It's well known that the Mongol empire employed servitors of various races for diplomacy and administration, as well as for trade, crafts, construction, religion, engineering, etc. – a practice, Rossabi suggests, that began with Genghis Khan: "One of his more enduring legacies was the use of foreigners as scribes, interpreters, tutors, advisers, merchants, and even soldiers – a policy pursued by his successors, and particularly by Khubilai Khan" (*Khubilai* 8). John of Plano Carpini and William of Rubruck found European craftsmen and translators working for the Mongols, either as free or as unfree men, and the *Itinerarium* tells us that Karakorum had a specialized division into two districts, one housing Muslim merchants and the other Chinese craftsmen (Jackson and Morgan 221; Dawson 184; Wyngaert 285–6). Larner, who sees Marco as "a Mongolian civil servant" ("Plucking Hairs" 136), suspects that "the use of foreigners, whether Muslims, Khitans, Uighurs or Europeans, particularly in tax-collection, was aimed to provide a non-Mongol focus for Chinese resentment against Mongol government" (*Marco Polo* 41).

115 Khanbalik, or Da-Du, was built slightly to the northeast of the site of the old Beijing, while Shang-Du, Kublai's summer residence, "the Ciandu of Marco Polo and the Xanadu of Coleridge, some 225 miles northwest" of Beijing (de Rachewiltz, *Papal Envoys* 163–4). The orthography of the names of cities and persons varies considerably across redactions, manuscripts, and editions. For convenience, I supply Moule and Pelliot's orthography.

116 Kublai's summer residence, Shang-Du (originally named K'ai-p'ing, but subsequently renamed by him in 1263 when it was elevated to the rank of a capital), appears to have been similarly magnificently apportioned, with an outer city in the shape of a square of 4,500 feet on each side, surrounded by a wall twelve to eighteen feet high, and an inner city, where the Khan and his retinue lived, in the shape of a nearly square rectangle. The imperial palace, 500 feet by 150 feet, was erected on a raised earthen platform; palaces and government offices were scattered throughout the inner city. Japanese archeologists explored the site in the 1930s, and "innumerable tiles and glazed roof tile decorations have been found on the site" (Rossabi, *Khubilai* 31–3). A hunting preserve formed the third section of the city, an innovation to the footprint of a Chinese capital – a "magnificent man-made park," with meadows, woods, streams, and buildings, enclosed by an earthen wall, moats, and gates (Rossabi, *Khubilai* 33).

117 Hangzhou was the most populous city in the world at the time. Rossabi suggests that a conservative estimate of its population size was 1.5 million inhabitants. "By contrast, Venice, one of the commercial centers of Europe, had 100,000 inhabitants" (Rossabi, *Khubilai* 43).

118 We might like to contrast this blanket encomium of Kublai's sons with the actual performance of Kublai's son Nomukhan (who, like Kublai's presumptive heir, Zhenjin, had Chabi for a mother), sent by Kublai to deal with the rebellious Kaidu in 1266. The ineffectual Nomukhan suffered factionalism among the princes of his army and was finally made a prisoner by his own men, who delivered him to Kaidu, who in turn kept Nomukhan a prisoner for nearly a decade (Rossabi, *Khubilai* 107–9).

119 Though *Le Devisement* suggests that the Chinese were astounded by the devilish new technology introduced by the Europeans, Rossabi points out that "flaming arrows, rockets, flame-throwers, and ... bombs cast by catapults," as well as "fragmentation bombs," were all technological innovations of Song inventors, who were by no means backward in military technology (*Khubilai*

79). The Polos (who, in any event, did not arrive at Kublai's court until two years after the siege of Xiangyang) also need not have introduced Mongol forces to catapults. Bayan, Kublai's chosen general for the defeat of the cities of the Southern Song, had been with the Ilkhan Hulegu, Kublai's brother, on campaigns in Persia and the Near East, and deployed at Xiangyang the tactics he had honed there. "Throughout late 1274 and early 1275," Bayan would attack resistant towns and fortifications with "catapults and flame-throwers" till they submitted (Rossabi, *Khubilai* 87–8).

120 Victory over the Song in Xiangyang required naval and siege warfare, and was not the quick success depicted in *Le Devisement*, but took nearly five years to accomplish. "Hsiang-yang [Xiangyang] and the adjacent town of Fan-ch'ang ... protected the paths ... to the western regions of the Southern Sung" and needed to be captured en route to the Song capital of Hangzhou (Rossabi, *Khubilai* 82). "The inhabitants of Hsiang-yang had stored vast quantities of provisions, and a few ships on occasion slipped through the Mongol [naval] blockade to supply essentials to ... the Chinese population" (Rossabi, *Khubilai* 83). The siege was not continuous. Ultimately, Mongol victory was indeed abetted by catapult technology, but did not owe anything to the labor of the Latin West. For a detailed account of the final conquest of the cities and ports of the Southern Song, see Rossabi, *Khubilai* 82–90.

121 "As an official envoy John [of Monte Corvino] not only drew a generous stipend from the Mongol government, but he also enjoyed the privilege denied to the ordinary citizen of travelling freely on the state post-relay system" (de Rachewiltz, *Papal Envoys* 166–7). Nevertheless, unlike Marco, the Franciscans are never seduced into identifying with Mongol interests, the Great Khan, or the empire.

122 Even beasts bow down before this vision of wealth and imperial splendor. A great lion is brought before Kublai at his white feast, and the lion throws himself down before the Khan, making signs of great humility and appearing to acknowledge the Khan as lord. The lion is not chained or constrained in any way, so it is a marvel to see, the narrator tells us (Moule and Pelliot I: 226; Ronchi 429).

123 Kublai had four main wives, in addition to subsidiary wives and concubines. Rossabi points out that Korea, a Mongol vassal, had to send tribute that included women for the Great Khan's harem, but *Le Devisement* stresses a certain ethnic purity here in showing that Kublai limits his sexual tastes to Mongol women (*Khubilai* 98).

124 In a study of Chinese documentary sources on tax revenues in Hangzhou (where *Le Devisement* presents such precise figures), salt production and trade, and the circulation of currencies (paper, cowries, salt), Hans Ulrich Vogel persuasively argues that the figures in *Le Devisement* are accurate, checked against Chinese records. See especially his chapter 6, "Tax Revenues of Hangzhou and Its Territory." Interestingly, Herbert Franke shows that *Le Devisement*'s reviled Ahmad the Bailo, one of Kublai's foremost officials and a Muslim, was responsible for increasing the empire's immense revenues from agricultural and mineral production and from tariffs and taxes over the decades, to finance Kublai's military commitments and produce the figures at which Marco is agog. Ahmad is found in Ramusio's redaction of *Le Devisement*, not the Franco-Italian manuscript.

125 Wan-Chuan Kao adds an important reminder that the Mongol postal system isn't brand new as such in the thirteenth century, but was inherited by the Mongols from the Chinese, who extended and organized the communications network during the Tang dynasty (44). Kao shrewdly adds that the postal system would also function, of course, as a convenient surveillance and military system for China's rulers.

126 Marco's accountant's eye is such that in his admiration for this system, he even points out how the Khan *profits* – by 3 percent! – when old paper money is exchanged for new paper money at Khanbalik's mint (Moule and Pelliot I: 240; Ronchi 441). Similarly, when discussing the

marvelous system of posts, Marco points out how, in cities that are located near the post-stations, the Khan manages to have some horses cared for at the expense of the locals (Moule and Pelliot I: 246; Ronchi 445). At such moments, one hardly knows whether to cheer the Khan's fiscal sagacity or Marco's keen eye for accounting.

127 Kublai Khan, Sharon Kinoshita decides, is thus the greatest wonder in the East ("Marco Polo's *Le Devisement dou monde* and the Tributary East").

128 Rossabi confirms that the record of Kublai's early years registers significant efforts at relief for Chinese subjects in northern China. "In 1261, he waived taxes on Huai-meng in Honan and other regions because of reports that they were experiencing economic difficulties. In April of 1262, he did the same for the area around modern Peking, Kuang-ning, and other localities that had suffered as a result of the warfare in the north. He also reduced the tax levies on peasants whose mulberry trees and silk worms had been damaged during these battles. In the same year, he granted paper money to peasants in Ho-hsi whose lands had been devastated by natural disasters. He repeatedly provided grain to widows and orphans without other means of support" (*Khubilai* 117–18).

Nor did Kublai neglect his subjects in Mongolia: He had grain transported "to the poverty-stricken, remitting taxes," and in times of crisis "caused by natural disasters, he sent emergency rations of grain to the afflicted areas" (Rossabi, *Khubilai* 113). Rossabi also describes the granaries Kublai established to store surplus grain as insurance against shortages of food among his people: "Khubilai's capital would eventually have fifty-eight such granaries, which stored 145,000 *shih* (each *shih* being equivalent to about 133 pounds) of grain" (*Khubilai* 119–20).

129 Marco, in his awe, fails to tell us that this intimidating machinery of household surveillance, if it existed all over the empire (and not just in Hangzhou and other metropolises) in the form *Le Devisement* specifies, was more a product of Kublai's later reign, rather than in place throughout Kublai's tenure as Great Khan: "It seems that an annual census was taken, but that only the number of households and not the individuals per household were counted, since all census figures from Qubilai's reign prior to 1290 record the former only" (Franke 544).

130 Kublai "delegated more power to the Censorate than had any earlier dynasty in Chinese history" and even put his own officials and administrators under surveillance: "the Censorate was divided up into branches that oversaw the local officials. Censors periodically toured the country to ferret out financial and political abuses by the court, the military, or the local governments," so that "the [Mongol] censorial system was ... far more pervasive than any preceding one, and its degree of tightly knit centralization was never exceeded in Chinese censorial history. The Mongols' surveillance apparatus can be reckoned as one of the institutional marvels of Chinese history" (Rossabi, *Khubilai* 74).

131 Rossabi offers yet another example of the Mongol state's modernity, in a new institution to be established among the peasantry: the *she*, a state-sponsored rural organization that would simultaneously set up schools for village boys to teach the rudiments of literacy and efficient methods of farming, and function "as an aid in surveillance and in conducting periodic censuses." Each *she*, "composed of about fifty households under the direction of a village leader," would be required to establish "charity granaries" to "assist unfortunates during bad harvests or droughts and to provide grain for orphans, widows, and the elderly," thereby extending the resources of the Mongol welfare system (*Khubilai* 120–1). In Mongol institutional practices, charity, social welfare, education, skills training, and surveillance thus seemed to converge.

132 Jack Weatherford sums up the problems posed by Khutulun's infamous independence: "Leading such a colorful and unusual life without a husband, she became the object of constant interest in her actions and speculations about her motives. Numerous reports maintain that she considered marrying Il-khan Ghazan, one of her cousins, who ruled Persia and Mesopotamia, and that they had an exchange of correspondence and envoys. But she showed no inclination to leave the steppe

and live the life of a proper Muslim lady. Because of her reluctance to marry, her detractors alleged that she had entered into an incestuous relationship with her father and thus would take no other man while he lived.

In the wake of the salacious accusations against her and her father, she married Abtakul of the Choros clan. He was described as 'a lively, tall, good-looking man,' and the chronicles state clearly: 'She chose him herself for her husband'" (122). Rashid al-Din, never friendly to this formidable Amazon, has an alternative version: Kaidu, "out of excess shame and the reproaches of the people, gave her in marriage to a Khitayan" (Boyle, *Successors* 26–7). Boyle cites Tashkent and Istanbul manuscripts of Rashid al-Din's chronicle that say Khutulun had two sons by Abtakul and "lived modestly" in the region of Shongkorlog, in the high mountains between the Ili and the Chu rivers where her father Kaidu was buried, "guarding her father's secret burial place" (27 n.74). Weatherford also retails accounts of Kaidu's desire for Khutulun to become Khan after his death, and her refusal because of her desire to continue to head the military, supporting her brother Orus to take her father's place instead (124). In a reminder that the hecklers who hooted "iron my shirts!" during Hillary Clinton's 2008 bid for the American presidency had centuries of predecessors, Rashid al-Din hoots that insults were hurled at the suggestion that Khutulun become the next Khan: "Thou shouldst be working with scissors and needle. What concern hast thou with the kingdom and the *ulus*?" (Boyle, *Successors* 27). Khutulun nonetheless continued as she always had: "in 1306 she followed [Kaidu] into death. Some reports claim that she died fighting in battle, others that she was assassinated. These speculations only heighten the mystery of this unusual woman" (Weatherford 124).

Warrior women, Weatherford urges, were always part of Mongol armies (121). Letters from a Dominican friar and an archbishop between 1234 and 1238 reported that a Mongol princess led an army into the Russian cities, according to terrified refugees; and Thomas of Spalato, describing the Mongol invasion of Dalmatia and the siege of Split in 1242, tells us that "many women fought in the Mongol army and were braver and wilder than the men" (Weatherford 121). Adrienne Mayor's book *The Amazons*, based on archeological data, also features Khutulun and other steppe warrior women.

133 See Rossabi on the care Kublai took not to be overdependent on any single ethnoracial/religious group among the administrators and officials who served his empire. Although he relied on Chinese administrators early in his reign, their intrigues and politicking led Kublai to consult Nestorian Christians, Tibetan Buddhists, and Central Asian Muslims as well (*Khubilai* 14–15). He relied on Uighur Turkish officials as military advisers, interpreters, and translators, had a Nestorian Christian as a senior secretary, and retained about forty Central Asian Muslim advisers (Rossabi, *Khubilai* 16). Rossabi, who details the infighting among the Confucian, Taoist, and Buddhist officials and administrators, reports that Kublai's administration ended up with a large and diverse coterie of Chinese Confucian scholars, Tibetan lamas, Central Asian Muslims, and Uighur Turks (*Khubilai* 17). Twenty-one Uighur Turks were resident commissioners; several served as tutors to the imperial princes; a few were translators; and Kublai also employed "men of other Turkic groups (Khanglis, Kipchaks, etc.) in similar government positions" (Rossabi, *Khubilai* 119). Perhaps Marco Polo's 100 Latin Christian men of learning, had they materialized, might also have served Kublai well. Already by the early 1260s, "Kublai had an international staff working for him" (Rossabi, *Khubilai* 119).

134 This story is fantastical and antihistorical in more ways than one. By 1275, of course, no Caliph of Baghdad existed – Baghdad having been conquered, and its last Caliph executed, by Hulegu Khan in 1258.

135 Pope Nicholas IV, as we've seen above, wrote not only to Arghun – urging the Ilkhan to undertake baptism – but also to the Christian royal women at Arghun's court, including Nukdan, who had been one of Abaga's wives, and "Elegag," either one of Arghun's wives or his daughter by

Arghun's Christian wife Uruk Khatun (Ryan 417, 417 n.41). The history of the Mongol Ilkhanate's rapprochements with the Latin West weaves through several decades. Hulegu sent an embassy to Europe in 1263–4 to propose a joint Mongol–Latin campaign against the Mamluks, and his son Abaga sent a large entourage to the Second Council of Lyons from Persia in 1274, where, dramatically, some of the Mongol envoys were baptized as a sign of Abaga's good faith (Ryan 413–14). For Abaga's overtures to the crusader monarch Edward I of England, see Amitai. Abaga's son Arghun also "proposed specific military cooperation to the king of France: Philip IV (1285–1314) was to rely on Arghun to provide twenty to thirty thousand horses, as a gift if necessary, plus cattle and grain to feed the French host. He also promised to be baptized in Jerusalem, after its liberation from the Mamluks" (Ryan 414).

136 I leave readers to decide if the Arthurian romancer Rustichello da Pisa is responsible for these narrative conventions of pitched battle and its aftermath.

137 Franke, who points out Ahmad's "exclusive concern with government income," details Ahmad's efforts in increasing revenues from the government's salt monopoly, his abolition of tax exemptions and intensification of taxations (in Hangzhou "It is said that he doubled the people's burden"), and his determination to increase grain production and extraction of ores from mines, including newly discovered asbestos from the mountains of Central Asia: "Ahmad strove to mobilize even the smallest potential sources of additional state revenue" (543, 548, 542). Song paper money was taken out of circulation by being exchanged for Yuan paper money at a rate that was "almost confiscatory; fifty notes of Sung money were declared equivalent to one note of Yüan money of the same denomination" (Franke 545–6). From a spectrum of fiscal measures and appropriations, "Ahmad was able to provide the government with the financial resources needed for the many costly campaigns ordered by Qubilai. At the same time he was successful in supplying the wherewithal to keep up the splendor of the imperial court" (Franke 555).

138 *Le Devisement* says Ahmad governed Khanbalk/Beijing, but Franke tells us that Ahmad in fact had his son, Husain, appointed as the general administrator of Khanbalik, and concurrently as metropolitan prefect (544–5). Furthermore, though *Le Devisement* insists Ahmad's moral depravity brought about his downfall, Franke's meticulously detailed study shows that opposition to Ahmad occurred early, even before the accusations of sensational abuse, patronage, and corruption were laid at his door. Franke concludes that Ahmad's downfall, which took two decades and encompassed many enemies, issued from his having consistently operated in culturally marked ways alien to China: "Ahmad's whole career shows that his ideas of government were those of a politician brought up in the neareastern tradition of statecraft, where an omnipotent vizier served an equally omnipotent ruler or despot. Chinese government with its carefully balanced and departmentalized institutions remained basically alien to a man like Ahmad: he belonged to a type of politician that differed radically from those Chinese advisors of Qubilai who had opposed him throughout his career" (556).

139 "Two Muslim engineers," Ismail and Ala al-Din, were sent by the Ilkhan Abaga, Kublai's nephew, at Kublai's request. The engineers built "a mangonel and a catapult capable of hurling huge rocks over a considerable distance ... Battered by a barrage of rocks and projectiles ... Fan-ch'eng fell within a few days" (Rossabi, *Khubilai* 86). For the attack on Xiangyang, the "Muslim engineers ... 'inspected the strength of the position and set up an engine at the southeast corner of the city. The missile weighed 150 catties. When the machinery went off the noise shook heaven and earth; everything that [the missile] hit was broken and destroyed'.... acknowledging the superior firepower ... [Xiangyang] finally surrendered" (Rossabi, *Khubilai* 86).

140 Iain Higgins' recent translation of Insular, the Anglo-Norman version of *Mandeville's Travels*, summarizes the text's manuscript history, including scholarly disagreement on whether the *Travels* originated in England or in France – a disagreement that may not ever be satisfactorily resolved (*Book* xv–xvi, 187–218). See also *Empire of Magic* 423–4 n.2 and Chapter 3 for summary

discussions. The Mandeville author's offer of an English knight as his narrator, and his lively interest in authenticating England as the narrator's provenance, is supported in the text by the mention of English calculations of distance, English letters of the alphabet like the yogh and thorn, and the pretext that St. Helena was the daughter of King Coel, all of which somewhat suggest that at least the strategic *pretext* of English provenance mattered to the Mandeville author (Higgins, *Book* 89; Deluz 283). While the discussion of the *Travels* in Chapter 3 is based on Egerton, which substantially agrees with Insular in the areas I discuss, I use Insular in Chapter 6. The Anglo-Norman is from Deluz' edition; the English translation is Higgins' (*Book*). I also continue to defer to the convention of calling this work of fiction *Mandeville's Travels*, though "Mandeville" did not travel, or, likely, exist.

141 "From its initial publication in the late 1350s until about 1600 [*The Book of John Mandeville*] was one of the most widely circulated medieval books. Including fragments and excerpts, it survives in some three hundred manuscripts (some expensively made and lavishly illustrated) and in more than ten languages: the original French as well as Czech, Danish, Dutch, English, German, Irish, Italian, Latin, Spanish, and Welsh, plus an unfinished, text-free pictorial version. Marco Polo's *Description of the World*, by contrast, survives in about half as many copies and several fewer languages" (Higgins, *Book* xii–xiii).

142 In *Empire of Magic*, I suggested the usefulness of a travel narrative like "Mandeville's": "One of the reasons travel narratives are enjoyable . . . involves the displacement of the world from outside to inside, as an external reality – large and amorphous, disorderly, chaotic, in motion – is brought home and managed by being rendered internal, and possessed internally, first within the manuscript environment of a purported travelogue, and then within the mind of a listening, reading audience . . . The outside world [is] transformed into an archive of thrilling, virtually real particulars in manuscript and mind, [and] that virtual world, reproduced within, registers as contained and knowable – under control – in ways that the outside world is not. In effect, the virtual world created by a vast travel account like "Mandeville's" transforms the world outside Europe – processing it through narrative – into a collection of facts, artifacts, and details, much like the collections in anthropological and natural history museums today, even as it allows an audience to become keepers and users of the collection" (247–8). The sense of control afforded by miniaturizing the world into a narrative is also useful for the story of a triumphal Christianity that the Mandeville author tells, as we see below.

143 Where Jesus has a white rock with red stains from his blood, the Virgin Mary has a red stone with white stains from her breast milk. At a Church of Saint Nicholas, "Our Lady rested after having given birth; and because she had too much milk in her breasts and because they were sore, she squirted some [milk] there on the red marble stones such that the white spots are still there on the stones" (Higgins, *Book* 43; Deluz 180).

144 The imprint of a sacred, divine body distributed ex post facto around the Holy Land attests, Bynum suggests, to a medieval concept of the body that assumes "some kind of material continuity between Christ's body in the *triduum* and in heaven" (*Resurrection* 319). Each bodily part, Bynum argues, recalls and reproduces a bodily totality: "Fourteenth century images imply the part . . . to be the whole . . . finger or toe was also sometimes self," and "stories that circulated in the Middle Ages implied that the body was in some sense alive after death" (Bynum, *Resurrection* 319, 326). Beckwith also urges "a late medieval identification with Christ" that understood "Christ's body . . . as both image *and physical presence*" (60–1, emphasis added).

145 These stories (some of which follow the *Travels'* source, William of Boldensele, but with subtle differences) make the Holy Land resemble "a marvelous reliquary," Higgins says (*Writing East* 105). Howard suggests that the entire "Holy Land is presented as a relic of sorts" (9). For medieval Latin Christians, of course, relics carried the intimate presence of the body and kept alive contact with the original body even across the passage of time.

146 The pull exerted by the topography of the Holy Land did not end with the Middle Ages, as pilgrims today can attest. James Carroll, a former priest, the author of *Constantine's Sword* – a searing indictment of Christendom's persecution of Jews – and a fierce critic of papal fundamentalism, is among those who attest the enduring charisma of sacred geography. In Carroll's journey to Jerusalem, he "was disgusted by the commercialism and grubbiness of many of the holy places. But then 'a skeptical old Frenchman' took him to an excavation site where he pointed out a large stone slab. 'This was the threshold stone of the city gate at the time of Jesus,' he said. 'It was buried in the rubble of the Roman destruction and is only now being uncovered. It is certain – the Frenchman had used this expression of nothing else he had shown me – that Jesus of Nazareth would have stepped on this stone as he left the city for Golgotha.' Carroll kneels and kisses the stone. It is a deeply Catholic moment – its physicality, its sacramental simplicity, its faith that . . . the living Jesus can still be found and felt and loved" (Sullivan 6).

147 Bennett's chapter, "The English Mandevilles," discusses a number of historical candidates in the fourteenth century who went by the name of "John Mandeville." Intriguingly, prominent English knights were among the *Travels'* readers: e.g., among the possessions of Sir Thomas Urswyck, Recorder of London and Chief Baron of the Exchequer in 1479, were the *Travels*, Chaucer, Froissart, and law books (Salter 39).

148 Describing an idol in the church of Saint Thomas in Mylapur ("Mabaron") on the Coromandel coast of southeastern India before which devotees stab themselves and spill their blood, kill and sacrifice their children, and even knife themselves to death to reverence the idol, the *Travels* is less interested in the horrific form these devotions take than in pointing out how the fervor of the idol's devotees contrasts with the pallid devotion of Latin Christians: "no Christian would scarcely dare undertake to do a tenth as much for love of his Christ" (Higgins, *Book* 109; Deluz 328).

149 In *Empire of Magic*, I defined romance as a desiring mode of narration in which fantasy and history are made to jostle together and collide, each vanishing into the other, without explanation or apology, at precisely the junctures where both may be mined to best advantage. Cultural fantasy in the form of romance, I suggested, often effloresces as a mode of rescue for historical trauma or profoundly vexatious historical conundrums, and surfaces into discussion what would be otherwise taboo or impermissible, and, in the process, furnishes a vocabulary of discussion in which pleasure, not horror, pain, or danger, is paramount.

In chapter 5 of *Empire of Magic*, I argued that the fourteenth-century world inhabited by the *Travels* was beset by looming losses and unassuageable fears – the failure of repeated crusades to recapture Jerusalem, raising the specter of the unlikelihood of recapture; the precariousness of Constantinople, a city that had been the bulwark of Christianity in the East for a thousand years (Constantinople would fall to the Ottoman Turks in 1453); and recognition of the immense power of the Islamicate world vested in the Mamluks and the Ottomans. By the fourteenth century, hopes of joint military actions with the Mongol Ilkhanate of Persia against the Muslims were a thing of the past, after the conversion to Islam of the Ilkhan Ghazan and his brother and successor Oljeitu (erstwhile "Nicholas," as we saw above) at the end of the thirteenth century.

150 Higgins tells us that the *Tractatus de statu Sarracenorum* [Treatise on the State of the Saracens] attributed to William of Tripoli is the *Travels'* principal source on Islam (the *Travels'* depiction of the Assassins' paradise, however, is from Odoric of Pordenone's *Relatio* [Account]). It is the *Tractatus*, compiled after 1273, that "emphasizes Islam's closeness to Christianity, the consequent likelihood of Muslims being peacefully converted, and the supposed Muslim prophecies of Islam's demise. The work was twice translated into French. The *Mandeville* author drew heavily on the *Tractatus* in Chapter 15, freely rearranging it" (Higgins, *Book* 235). The *Travels'* account of Islam and its Prophet is a mashup of accurate and made-up or garbled details: e.g., it tenders a more or less accurate description of what a caliph is, but then misplaces the Andalusian caliphate

in Morocco (Higgins, *Book* 27–8; Deluz 142–5). The text also has the Prophet buried under a mosque in Mecca, rather than under the house of his favorite wife, Aisha, in Medina (Higgins, *Book* 27; Deluz 142).

151 The *Travels* renders the *shahada* as baptismal words of a sort, spoken not by the entrant into Islam but by the Islamic cleric who receives the entrant, uttering: "'*La illec ella sila Machomet Roses Alla hec.*' That is to say in English: 'There is no God but one alone and Machomet [is] his prophet'" (Higgins, *Book* 89; Deluz 283). Compare with the *shahada*: *La illaha illa Allah, wa Muhammad rasul Allah* ("There is no god but God, and Muhammad is the messenger of God"). The *Tractatus* has a rendition closer to the Arabic: "*La eleh ella Alla, Mahomad rosol Alla*" (Higgins, *Book* 239).

152 The *Travels* repeats this explanation elsewhere as well: "when it pleases God, just as this land has been lost because of the sins of the Christians, so will it be won again because of their bravery with God's help" (Higgins, *Book* 48; Deluz 191). By contrast, the *Tractatus* – with details pieced together from Al-Kindi – retails a murky prophecy of Islam's end, after the death of certain sultans and caliphs, and does not specify conditions under which a time can be identified ("God knows when" [Higgins, *Book* 239]). The *Travels* however ties eventual Christian victory not to the death of Muslim leaders but to Latin Christians once again serving their Lord and Savior well.

153 Rather than going to Europe himself, however, like the romance Saladin, the *Travels'* Sultan of Egypt sends intermediaries (multitasking spies?) "in the guise of merchants" to scout out the land, the courts, and the people of Europe: "he knew the whole state of the courts of the Christian princes and the state of the commons by means of the people whom he sends through all countries in the guise of merchants of precious stones and other things, to know the behavior of each country" (Higgins, *Book* 87; Deluz 279). The Sultan then sends for four lords, who proceed to deliver to Mandeville the state of each country in Latin Christendom "as well as if they were from the country [itself], and they spoke French very well, and so did the Sultan, at which I marveled greatly" (Higgins, *Book* 87; Deluz 280).

154 "'For', [he said,] 'your priests are not concerned to serve God. They ought to set an example for lay folk to do well, and they set an example of doing ill. Therefore the common people, on holy days when they should go to church to serve their God, go then to the taverns to be in gluttony all day and all night, and they eat and drink like animals that do not know when they have had enough. And all the Christians also seek in every way they can to make trouble and to deceive one another. On top of this, they are so proud that they do not know how to dress, [wearing clothes that are] now long, now short, now narrow, now wide, now embroidered, now cut close, and in all kinds of shapes and dress and other things. They ought to be simple and humble and true and charitable as was Jesus in whom they believe. But they are just the opposite and completely inclined to do wrong. And they are so greedy that for a little silver they sell their daughters, their sisters, their own wives into debauchery, and they seduce one another's wives, and they do not keep their word to one another. But they break their entire law that Jesus has given them and set out for their salvation'" (Higgins, *Book* 86–7; Deluz 278–9).

155 The *Gesta Francorum* has an invented episode in which the mother of Karbuqa, the atabeg of Mosul who has besieged the Franks of the First Crusade at Antioch, warns her "sweetest son" ("*dulcissime fili*") of imminent loss and disaster because "their god fights for them everyday" ("*deus eorum pro ipsis cotidie pugnat*"), quoting a so-called prophecy that the Christians – her son's enemies, and her own – will be victorious (Hill 53). "Beloved," Karbuqa's mother loftily pronounces, "those Christians are called 'sons of Christ' and, by the mouth of the prophets, 'sons of adoption and promise' and the apostle says that they are 'heirs of Christ,' to whom Christ has even now given the promised inheritance, saying by the prophets, 'From the rising of the sun to the going down thereof shall be your bounds, and no man shall stand against you'" (Hill 54). From Karbuqa's mother to the Sultan of Egypt two and a half centuries later, it seems that Muslim enemies are still extolling the efficacy of the Christian God and Christianity and vouching for

projective Christian victory by citing prophecy of one kind or another. The genius of the Mandeville author resides in how old matter is reconfigured, rather than new matter invented.

156 Dorothee Metlitzki suggests that *Gathalonabez* may derive from the Arabic "*qatil an-nafs*" (meaning "murderer") or a transposition of "*abu l-qatilin*" into "*qatilin abu'l*," meaning "father of those who kill" (Metlitzki 298 n.35). Odoric of Pordenone's *Relatio*, the *Travels'* source for this episode, does not give the Old Man of the Mountain a name, but calls the mountain fastness in Persia *Millestorte* (Chiesa 155).

157 The close resemblance between the Assassin paradise and the Islamic paradise in the *Travels* makes the Assassins of Alamut seem more part of Islamdom than this breakaway group of Nizari Ismaili Shiites historically was, as we have seen. See Chapter 3 for a full discussion of the Nizaris/Assassins, a minority faction considered heretical by the Sunni Muslims who formed their principal targets of assassination. But the *Travels* manages in subtle ways to have its cake and eat it too: The logic of Gathalonabez' fake paradise dramatizes a warning that an Islamic paradise is not what it promises to be, yet even as Gathalonabez is introducing his youthful dupes to his illusionary replica, he ventriloquizes the God of the Hebrews saying, "*Dabo vobis terram fluentem lacte et melle*" ("I will give to you a land flowing with milk and honey") – a partial quotation from Exodus 33:3 and Leviticus 20:24, as Higgins points out (*Book* 165 n.530). That is to say, even in this extreme context, the *Travels* manages to have Gathalonabez subtly remind readers that Islam is an Abrahamic faith that shares some "articles of our faith" – or, more accurately here, the faith of the Hebrews.

158 Odoric of Pordenone's *Relatio*, despite its "simple literary quality," is a work with a complicated textual history and a "vast quantity of manuscripts" that have yet to receive adequate study (Chiesa 52–3). I cite in this section Paolo Chiesa's reissue of Henry Yule's much-loved translation based on several manuscripts. The Latin edition of the *Relatio* most commonly cited, but that no one seems to find adequate, is Wyngaert's, in *Sinica Franciscana* Vol. I, 413–95. Higgins (*Book*) supplies full bibliographic information for all the sources of the *Travels* that he meticulously traces, including Vincent de Beauvais' *Speculum Historiale* and Hayton's *Flor des estoires de la terre d'Orient*.

159 The pronounced difference between how a mercantile mind like Marco's and how religious men like Odoric of Pordenone and (presumably) the Mandeville author understand paper money is striking. The *Travels'* description of paper money hews closely to Polo's in *Le Devisement*, but the Mandeville author, like Odoric, does not seem to grasp the principle that paper money has to be backed by gold; he merely assumes that the Khan "can spend as much as he likes, an incalculable amount," since it's all just signs "printed on bark or paper" (Higgins, *Book* 143; Deluz 396). Odoric mentions paper money only cursorily (Chiesa 148), and also doesn't understand it is real money. Lacking much curiosity about paper currency, there is no mention in the *Relatio* of how old bank notes can be exchanged for new, which the *Travels*, like *Le Devisement*, duly narrates. In like fashion, the *Relatio's* tendency for pared-down description has the Khan's barons arrayed in robes of green, red, and yellow silk, but doesn't mention the elaborate magnificence of jewels, pearls, and gold embroidery that so impresses the *Travels* and *Le Devisement* (Chiesa 146). "Philosophers" are mentioned by Odoric, but unlike their counterparts in the *Travels*, they are not paraded as proto-scientists, with instruments and technologies (Chiesa 146–7).

160 With one eye trained on thirteenth-century Mongol descriptions and the other on later accounts of sumptuous Mongol Cathay and its Great Khan, the *Travels* sometimes hilariously oscillates between two poles in characterizing Mongols. On the one hand, "neither Prester John who is emperor of high India, nor the Sultan of Babylon, nor the emperor of Persia, compares to [the Great Khan] in power, in nobility, or in wealth, for in all this he surpasses all the earthly princes" (Higgins, *Book* 146; Deluz 402). On the other hand, Mongols "live very wretchedly and eat only once a day," and are still Matthew Paris's cannibals, who cut off human body parts for delicacies – here, the ears of enemies – "and put them in vinegar to steep and with them they make food for the great lords" (Higgins, *Book* 149; Deluz 409).

161 The *Travels* is willing to concede, however, that the Mongol *people*, if not Mongke and Kublai, are pagan deists who worship idols: They "believe in a god that created and made everything, and nevertheless they have idols of gold and silver and felt and cloth; and to these idols they always offer their first milk from their animals and also some of their meat and some of their drinks before they consume them, and they often offer horses and animals. They also call God of Nature *Yroga*" (Higgins, *Book* 147; Deluz 406). Moreover, Mongols "greatly revere the moon and the sun and often kneel to them" (Higgins, *Book* 148; Deluz 406).

162 Higgins remarks that the *Travels'* claim that Mongke was Christian is aided and abetted by Hayton's chronicle, which makes a similar claim (Higgins, *Book* 138 n.464). No source has yet been found for why the *Travels* believes Kublai also to have been Christian.

163 Marchesino claims to have heard Odoric tell of an incident where Odoric and other Franciscan friars opportunistically enact a kind of teaching moment with the Great Khan: "once upon a time, when the Great Khan was on his journey from Sandu [Shang-Du] to Cambalech [Khanbalik], he (Friar Odoric), with four other Minor friars, was sitting under the shade of a tree by the side of the road along which the Khan was about to pass. And one of the brethren was a bishop. So when the Khan began to draw near, the bishop put on his episcopal robes and took a cross and fastened it to the end of a staff, so as to raise it aloft; and then those four began to chant with loud voices the hymn, *Veni Creator Spiritus*! And then the Great Khan, hearing the sound thereof, asked what it meant. And those four barons who go beside him replied that it was four of the Frank Rabbans (i.e. of the Christian monks). So the Khan called them to him, and the bishop thereupon taking the cross from the staff presented it to the Khan to kiss. Now at the time he was lying down, but as soon as he saw the cross he sat up, and doffing the cap that he wore, kissed the cross in the most reverent and humble manner" (Chiesa 162).

By contrast, the *Travels'* vignette, we notice, makes the Khan appear much more conversant with Christianity's rituals than the episode involving Odoric. The *Travels'* Khan does not have to be tutored, but actively seeks out the monks when he hears their chant, and obeisance to the cross is at the Khan's initiative, not arranged by opportunistic Franciscan friars. The *Travels* also uses the occasion to emphasize, yet again, the Khan's great wealth as seen in his magnificently bejeweled headwear. Chiesa's introduction to Yule's translation of the *Relatio* adds a brief account of the ambiguous provenance of this anecdote about the Khan: "the important story that tells of the Great Khan paying homage to the cross (chapter 51) was added ... According to some manuscripts ... we owe the recollection of this episode to Brother Marchesino of Bassano, who lived in the Franciscan monastery of Padua. In Henry of Glarus' edition, the report of the Khan's reverence to the cross is given in an appendix separate from the text. The most widespread version of the *Relatio*, however, bears the signature of another Paduan monk, William of Sologna. In this edition, the story of the Khan and the cross is incorporated into the narration and Marchesino's name is not cited" (51).

164 Jackson points out that the Latin West, in its desire to evangelize, had in fact failed to grasp the deep historical meaning of Mongol friendliness toward symbols of the Christian faith in Eurasia: "A case in point is what the friars took to be reverence for the Cross ... what these Western observers did not realize was that the use of the Cross, *inter alia* as a magical device to secure protection against spirits in this life, even by the Nestorian communities, already had a long history in Central Asia. In these circumstances, it was quite possible for an individual prince to make some gesture that implied the acceptance of, say, Christianity while continuing to sanction and observe the 'shamanistic' practices of his forebears or favouring another religious group altogether" (*Mongols and the West* 270–1).

165 In the medieval period, *India* is a name that stretched to signify, at different times, locations in Asia (the Indian subcontinent, or even Yunnan or southern China), Africa (Ethiopia or the Horn), and the Near East (Edessa). "The three Indias were Nearer or Lesser India, Further or

Greater India, and Middle India. Nearer or Lesser India meant, approximately, the north of the subcontinent, Further or Greater India meant the south, Malabar and Coromandel ... [F]or some European peoples at certain times the south of India was more interesting, more important, and more accessible than the north. The monsoon winds made it easy to reach from the Arabian and East African ports; its pepper and other exports and re-exports were far more worth obtaining than the products of Gujerat and Kathiawar. Its fertility, its wealth, the presence of a Christian community, however small and politically uninfluential it may have been, above all its role in the oceanic trade of Asia justify the preference given to it over the north. In comparison Nearer India seemed forbidding and unproductive. What Europeans knew about it, or supposed they knew, was commonly ascribed to Alexander the Great. Middle India was, of course, Ethiopia" (Beckingham, "Achievements" 15).

Beckingham adds that two Indias, "India Major and India Minor[,] occur as early as the fourth century ... [but] three Indias appear for the first time in 1118 in a manuscript of Guido Paisano" (17). Syrian Edessa, moreover, was also sometimes synonymous with India: Citing the fifteenth-century *Pilgerfahrt* of Arnold von Harff, Beckingham points out that, for Arnold, Lesser India is not northern India but Malabar in southern India, while "Greater India is Prester John's domain, with its capital at Edessa, to which [John] had removed the head of St. Thomas after forcing the King of Moabar [Malabar] to pay tribute ... It is its association with St. Thomas that has brought Edessa into India" (Beckingham, "Achievements" 19). To indicate the range of geographical associations, Lach correctly points out that Marco Polo also called southern China "'Upper India,' a term that was still current as late as the seventeenth century" (40). Conceding that the confusion of India and Ethiopia, in particular, "dates back to at least the time of Homer" (225 n.38), Kaplan sums up the fluid geographical placement of *India* neatly: "The medieval placement of the many Indias – first, second, third, major, minor, upper, lower, near, middle, furthest – is extremely variable" (*Rise* 64). From the fourteenth century on, especially, "the third India was often associated with East African regions" (Kaplan, *Rise* 64): Perhaps because of Indian Ocean trade relations between East Africa and India, "Ethiopia was regarded in the Middle Ages as one of the Three Indias" (Ross 178).

166 One strain of scholarship on Prester John suggests that the legend remembers, in veiled fashion, the existence of Christian kings in Africa: "The African hypothesis comes from Constantine Marinescu ... who announced it in 1923 ... Prester John ... was the monarch of Ethiopia, a land whose conversion to Christianity began in the fourth century and which later was cut off from communication with Europe by the Arab conquest of Egypt and the Sudan. In spite of this Ethiopian isolation, persistent rumors floated westward of a Christian ruler beyond the outer fringe of Islam. Subjects of his occasionally visited Jerusalem and other holy places, where now and then they met and conversed with Europeans. An exaggerated notion of Ethiopia, lacking any geographical orientation, gradually took shape in the occidental mind, until finally, says Marinescu, it emerged in concrete, if imaginary, form in the Prester John letter" (Nowell, "Prester John" 437). Nowell adds, "Ethiopia alone had priest kings in the Middle Ages ... [and] in Gez and Amharic, the religious and aristocratic languages of the country, the word for 'king' or 'majesty' is one that can be written *Zan* ... and pronounced somewhat like the French 'Jean' or the Italian 'Gian,' both of which stand for John" ("Prester John" 438; see also Ross).

Most scholars who discuss Prester John in Ethiopia tend to focus on the legend's African location in the fourteenth century and after (see, e.g., Beckingham, "Ethiopian Embassy," "West Africa," and also Ross). Kaplan (*Rise*) assigns the Africanization of the Prester John legend to the fourteenth and fifteenth centuries: Giovanni da Carignano, a Genoese cleric and cartographer, reports an Ethiopian embassy in 1306, and in this report "Prester John is clearly Emperor of Ethiopia" (52). "In 1402, for the first time in nearly a hundred years, Ethiopian emissaries are known to have arrived in Europe. These ambassadors ... led by a Florentine, one Antonio

Bartoli, are described in Venetian documents as representatives of 'Lord Prester John, lord of the regions of India,' but all scholars agree that the embassy was from Ethiopia. With this renewal of actual contact between Ethiopia and Western Europe, the introductory phase of the Africanization of Prester John comes to an end. In the fifteenth century the black [African] version of Prester John is the norm, and it would be tedious to cite every example of his appearance in European culture" (Kaplan, *Rise* 57).

167 For an important psychoanalytic reading of the Prester John legend and utopia, see Michael Uebel's *Ecstatic Transformation*. Christopher Taylor's work (which includes an online digital mapping project and transhistorical database on Prester John) is the latest addition to the corpus of scholarship on the legend: http://scalar.usc.edu/works/prester-john/index

168 See note 149 for a definition of romance and a brief discussion of the cultural work performed by romance.

169 Nonetheless, Prester John was "forced to abandon his campaign and go home because of an impassable river" (Beckingham, "Achievements" 5). Thus, "despite a notable victory, Prester John had ... been unable to come anywhere near the Holy Land, even though he had spent some years, *aliquot annos*, trying to do so and had lost many of his soldiers, *multos de excercitu*, in the attempt" (Beckingham, "Achievements" 5).

170 Goodrich questions the authenticity of the Nestorian princeling George's conversion to Latin Christianity, because of George's cultural syncretism and his devotion to Confucianism: "Was Prince George really a Christian? Professor Ch'en Yüan doubts it, and shows how Chinese records – the tablets of Yen Fu (1236–1312) and Liu Min-Chung (1243–1318), the biography in the *Yüan Shi* [History of the Yuan dynasty] and the local history of Chi-an (Kiangsi) – dwell on his adherence to the Chinese culture around him. Prince George, we learn from these records, was a brave man, well versed in military matters, and especially devoted to Confucian ideals. He built a library housing ten thousand volumes in his palace; also temples and schools. Every day he was wont to discuss with scholars the Confucian canon, histories, ethical principles and the masculine and feminine principles of divination. With one literatus in particular, Wu Tsou of Chi-an, he took up the study of the *I* (*The Changes*) and was responsible for making the woodblocks of Wu's book the *Chou I chu*, or Annotations of the *I*, in ten *chüan*, at P'ing-yang, the chief printing center of those times" (7–8).

By contrast, de Rachewiltz sees no contradiction in the behavior of Prince George, who was the son-in-law of the Great Khan: "The sincerity of Prince George's conversion is evidenced by his acceptance of the minor orders of the Roman Church, and by his naming his son John in honour of Montecorvino ... recent research has shown that Prince George was also a keen Confucian. This is not surprising since many Nestorians living in China had by then become sinicized in language as well as in customs. Clearly Prince George, like the Jesuits at the Peking court in the seventeenth century, did not regard these two doctrines as mutually exclusive" (*Papal Envoys* 167). We might note that Confucianism, unlike Christianity, is not a "religion" in the sense of organizing a metaphysic centered on a god, but is a moral philosophy prescriptive of human conduct and centering on personal, moral, social, and political relations, not relationship to a deity. It may have been possible for Prince George, therefore, to have been devoted both to Confucian and Christian ideals without contradiction, as de Rachewiltz says, though a certain cultural syncretism is suggested by his interest in the *I Ching* (the Book of Changes) and divination.

171 Interestingly, Prince George, the Nestorian princeling converted to Latin Christianity by John of Monte Corvino and believed by him to be a descendent of the original Prester John, was son-inlaw to the Great Khan of his time – a historical nugget buttressing the claim that "Prester John" (a personal honorific that devolved over the generations into a title) and the Great Khan repeatedly exchanged daughters or other imperial women in marriage (de Rachewiltz, *Papal Envoys* 166).

172 The *Travels'* insistence that the Mongol empire only eats once a day pertains to all classes of Mongol society: Mongol "princes and others eat only once a day and less" and "all the common people" also "eat only once a day" (Higgins, *Book* 80, 133; Deluz 266, 375).

173 The *Travels* derives the detail of once-a-day dining by 30,000 people in John's court from the Latin *Letter of Prester John*, which contains a number of features pertinent to the Byzantine Empire – a place where, according to the English historian William of Malmsbury (2: 483), the custom of dining once a day is attested (Uebel, *Ecstatic Transformation* 158, Zarncke 86). Describing Kublai's lavishly extravagant feasts, Marco Polo had not mentioned a court custom of dining only once a day, although *Le Devisement* does mention that 30,000 dined at court on the Great Khan's charity daily (Moule and Pelliot I: 251, Ronchi 450).

174 In the *Letter* John claims that in his realm, "There is not a liar among us, nor is anyone able to lie. And if someone there should begin to lie, he immediately dies, that is, he would be considered just as [a] dead man among us, nor would any mention of him be made among us, that is, he would receive no further honor among us. We all follow truth and we love one another. There is no adulterer among us. No vice rules among us" (Uebel 157, Zarncke 84). While John of Plano Carpini had inveighed against Mongol deceit, avarice, cunning, and treachery, Marco Polo had extolled the lack of adultery among Mongols (Dawson 16; Wyngaert 47; Moule and Pelliot I: 169; Ronchi 387).

175 The Mandeville author's fascination with science serves here to proffer an explanation for why the merchants in his audience will not be able to verify the existence of John's empire through direct empirical experience. Moreover, merchants "are very much afraid of the long route, and thus they take to the island of Cathay [for the Mandeville author, much of the world is composed of "islands" – the author's term for a discrete region, whether bounded or not by water, as Higgins observes], which is closer; and it is not so close that it does not take eleven or twelve months to go by sea and by land from Genoa or Venice all the way to Cathay – and Prester John's Land is still many days' travel further" (Higgins, *Book* 161; Deluz 433–4).

176 Toward the end of the book, the *Travels* expatiates on the nature of the Christianity in John's land, which resembles the Greeks': "In his land there are many Christians of good faith and good law . . . and they all commonly have their chaplains who sing the mass and make the sacrament of the altar from bread as the Greeks do. But they do not say as many things at the mass as one does over here, for they say only what Our Lord's Apostles taught them, such as Saint Peter and Saint Thomas and the other Apostles sung the mass, saying *Pater Noster* and the words with which our Lord's body is consecrated. But we have many additions that the popes have since made about which they know nothing" (Higgins, *Book* 177; Deluz 463). These differences, notably, do not seem to turn John into an irredeemable heretic in the Mandeville author's eyes.

177 There were "statements in the documents circulating within the Fifth Crusade that the forty divisions of King David's army were each preceded by a cross" (Jackson, *Studies* IV: 4). King David was believed to have been the son, grandson, or nephew of Prester John, and the imminent arrival of John's, or David's, armies was anticipated by the Fifth Crusade at Damietta, as we saw in Chapter 3. The Christian practice of having a cross or crosses carried before the army was so well known on the Eurasian steppe that Mongols copied the practice at war to fool their Christian enemies. "The Georgian Constable Ivané . . . complained to Pope Honorius III that the Mongols had tricked his people by having a cross carried in front of their army . . . The people were thus deceived and made no preparations for defence, while one priest and his flock . . . even went to meet the invaders holding crosses aloft; they were massacred" (Jackson, *Studies* IV: 5). "'We did not take precautions against them,' the Georgian Queen Rusudan told the Pope, 'because we believed them to be Christians'" (Jackson, *Studies* IV: 6).

In this ironically tragic historical episode, we catch a glimpse of how the epistolary-literary legend of an Oriental Christian king who carried the cross before his armies, and who promised to avenge "the injuries inflicted on the Christians by the Muslims," was cannily manipulated by Mongols in their real-time wars against Christians. The *Travels*, of course, does not cite this kind of resemblance between the Mongols and Prester John.

178 See Chapter 4 for a discussion of medieval Ethiopian priests, who were praised for their "moral standard" and "purity of life" (Selassie 112). Ethiopian monks were even said to have custody of the flame that burnt continuously in the Church of the Holy Sepulcher in Jerusalem (Selassie 143).

179 The Syriac text we have is imperfect and highly problematic. Its anonymous author narrated a "History of Mar Yaballaha" (Rabban Markos, Sauma's companion, before he ascended to the Nestorian Patriarchate) based on a diary Rabban Sauma kept in Persian (Montgomery 25). A manuscript of the Syriac text was published in 1888, after which other manuscript copies came to light (the original, like so many medieval ur-texts, has been lost). The Syriac narrative says it abbreviates the account Sauma wrote in Persian (Montgomery 73). In 1895, a second edition was published, with a "brief apparatus in Syriac of dates and biographical and geographical identifications" (Montgomery 1). A French translation ensued, with notes, chronological and dynastic tables, and several appendices (Montgomery 2). Montgomery's English translation offers only the part of the narrative concerning Rabban Sauma and the travels of the two Nestorian monks (the first half of the biography – 99 out of 205 printed pages), terminating with the death of Yaballaha in 1317 (Montgomery 24). Events and dates are crossconfirmed by other texts, including a biography of Yaballaha in the fourteenth-century Arabic *Chronicle of the Patriarchs* by Amr ibn Matta and entries in the *Ecclesiastical Chronicle* of Bar Hebraeus (Montgomery 20, 18). I quote from Montgomery's translation in English. Wallis Budge has a slightly longer English translation similar to Montgomery's.

180 Nicholas IV's words explain why Sauma only receives the "small" relics the Nestorian mentions. "If it were our custom to give everyone these relics," the Pope says, "although they were mountains high, they would soon be finished off by the myriads. But since thou hast come from a far country, we will give thee a few" (Montgomery 72).

181 We should remember that Edward's declaration is uttered in the context of a diplomatic message to the Ilkhan Arghun that Sauma is intended to convey, and may well be tactical and strategic. Moreover, as we have seen, it was well known that Arghun had a Nestorian Christian wife famed for her piety, and who may have rejoiced at a message like this. Dokuz Khatun was influential at court, and on Sauma's return, she had the church at court built that Sauma mentions with satisfaction (Montgomery 73, 76).

182 Higgins sums up the well-known accounts of the "Brahmans" in the Alexander legends: "In the Punjab in 326 BCE Alexander the Great encountered 'naked philosophers,' gymnosophists. In the Alexander legends they became a people, also called Brahmans (the Hindu priestly caste) . . . The *Mandeville* author. . .follows a common tradition in recording *two* encounters between Alexander and Indian ascetics. In them the author offers his interpretation of a well-known imaginary correspondence between Alexander and Dindimus (Dandamis), king of the Brahmans, in which ascetic and worldly values are debated" (*Book* 174 n.551).

183 See Frank Grady on the important cultural, intellectual, and structural work performed by "righteous heathens" and "virtuous pagans" – key figures who lived before the time of Christ, and to whom salvation was thus unavailable, but who were nonetheless recuperated by authors in Christendom for a variety of purposes in cultural and devotional texts. The Mandeville author's virtuous pagans are actually not located in a time before the life of Jesus, but are located in non-Christian or, more optimistically, pre-Christian spatial vectors of the world – space here, therefore, functions somewhat like time.

184 The *Travels* even rescues idol worshipers, by making a careful distinction between *idols* and *simulacra* – a shrewd distinction that also serves to vindicate Latin Christian reverence toward statues of sacred figures. Higgins suggests that the Mandeville author's "defense ultimately comes

from Pope Gregory the Great's remarks in two letters written around 600 to Seremus, Bishop of Marseilles. In the later 1300s in England there was vigorous debate over religious images; the *Mandeville* author's interest perhaps supports his claim to be English by birth" (*Book* 184 n.585).

185 "Jewish wickedness and waywardness . . . now according to the Koran" is "a theme dear to the *Mandeville*-author's heart" – here, it is also "a move that makes Christians and Saracens potential allies" (Higgins, *Writing East* 114). The *Travels'* use of the Quran is of course selective, since "the Koran has a few remarks on Christian misbeliefs as well, but these are rebutted flat out: 'and in this their faith errs'" (Higgins, *Writing East* 114).

186 Like many medieval texts, the *Travels* makes a distinction between the Hebrews of the Old Testament – who lived before, and foreshadowed, the appearance of the Savior and are thus treated with reverence – and medieval Jews, seen as having rejected the Savior, and whose forebears were guilty of deicide. Kathy Biddick's theorization of a "cut" in genealogical Christian thinking about Hebrews and Jews is widely influential ("Cut of Genealogy").

187 "The Jews have no land . . . but want the world, whereas the Christians have much, but not the crucial center. Jewish fidelity to one another is conspiratorial, whereas that of other peoples is a virtue reflecting on Christian selfishness. Jews who travel remain eternal outsiders, whereas Christians (like Sir John) enter into mutually illuminating contact with other peoples. Jewish prophecies announce their own ultimate triumph, whereas those of others either look ahead to their demise (as with the Tartars) or to the re-expansion of a reformed Christianity (as with the Saracens)" (Higgins, *Writing East* 184).

188 As we saw in Chapter 2, medievalists have pointed out how after the Expulsion, in the absence of Jews-of-the-flesh in England, there is a remarkable explosion of virtual Jews in literature and art, where Jews-of-the-imagination are conjured up in anti-Semitic outbursts that served the ends of Christian communal identity and the imagined medieval Christian nation of England. Though likely originally written in French, *Mandeville's Travels* foregrounds *England* as the supposed provenance of its narrator – an *English* knight, not a French one – and at junctures takes care to mark itself as emanating from England, e.g., with the mention, as we have noted, of English letters of the alphabet and English measures of distance, and the identification of St. Helena as British (as the daughter of King Coel).

189 Linda Lomperis describes the *Travels* as "a kind of Christian, colonialist fantasy . . . all the world is quite literally a stage for Christianity, insofar as everyone in this text seemingly has the potential to pass as a Christian," and adds: "the text of Mandeville's *Travels* . . . with the sense that it conveys of a world entirely filled with Christians and others wishing to be Christian, can be understood as a significant testament to the power and longevity of this fantasy within the imagination of Latin Christendom" (161–2).

7

World III

"Gypsies": A Global Race in Diaspora, A Slave Race for the Centuries

The enslavement of Gypsies came to an end [just] over a century ago ... well over half of the entire Romani population in Europe at the time of its institution in the fourteenth century were thus subjugated and, during the following five hundred years, were the mainstay of the economy which oppressed them.

Ian Hancock, *The Pariah Syndrome: An Account of Gypsy Slavery and Persecution* (1)

OUR EFFORTS in this book to understand how Europe viewed the races and peoples of the world end by considering a persecuted but resilient people whose history in the medieval period has been pieced together by records and laws in the countries through which they passed – an accretion of the written record that, over the centuries, has defined who these people are and attached to them characteristics that enduringly decided their group identity and personality, judging them collectively as a race.

This endeavor to consider how Europe saw the "Gypsies," who were called by many names in the countries where they were found – *Atsinganoi* or *Atzinganoi* in Greek, *Zigeuner* in German, *Tsiganes* in French, *Zingari* in Italian, *Cigányok* in Hungarian, *Gitano* in Spanish, among others – will serve as a conclusion in our long foray into medieval race, and, I hope, also as an invitation and a prompt to future work on the Romani of the premodern period – a people whose lives and histories, unlike those of premodern Jews and Muslims, are as yet under-researched in medievalist scholarship.[1]

It is a tragedy in our knowledge of the medieval period that scholars have yet to be able reliably to recover the lives, cultures, and histories of medieval Romani from within the Romani communities themselves. Instead, thus far we have only the word of others – medieval contemporaries who were as often as not hostile and contemptuous – for an understanding of who and what the Romani were, and for glimmers of motivations and meanings that even the most radically sympathetic today can only guess at.

The earliest glimpses of the medieval peoples we call the Romani might be found in tenth- and eleventh-century romance-like stories of origin that tie a group of diasporic peoples from India to an occupation, and to character attributes, that would come to define the Romani themselves for a millennium. The Arab historian Hamza of Isfahan (*c.* 950) assigns a key story to the fifth-century Persian monarch Bahrum Gur, who, deciding that "his subjects should work for only half the day and spend the rest of their time eating and drinking together to the sound of music," encountered subjects who did not have musicians or music and persuaded the King of India to send him 12,000 musicians; Bahram Gur then distributed the musicians throughout Persia, where they multiplied. "'Their descendants,' remarked Hamza, 'are still there, although in small numbers; they are the Zott'" (Fraser 33).

Another version of this romance origin appears in Firdawsi's eleventh-century Persian epic, the *Shahnameh*. Again, Bahram Gur seeks musicians for his people – this time for the poor, who, unlike the wealthy, must drink their wine without musical accompaniment. The Persian Shah writes to his father-in-law Shangal, the King of India:

> "You must help me out now: choose ten thousand of those Luris, men and women both, who know how to play the lute. Send them to Persia so that they can entertain the poor here." Shangal read the letter, chose the Luris, and sent them to the king, just as he had asked. When the Luris arrived at court, the king admitted them and gave an ox and a donkey to each of them, hoping to make farmers of them. He also donated a thousand ass-loads of wheat, so that they could use the animals to plough the land, sow the wheat, and so bring it to harvest. They were also to be musicians for the poor, so that commoners would be like the nobility. Off the Luris went, but they ate the oxen and the wheat, and by the end of the year, their faces were pale with hunger. The king said to them, "You weren't supposed to waste the seed like this, and forget about seed time and harvest! Well, you still have the donkeys; load up your goods and put silk strings on your lutes!" And now, because of his words, the Luris wander the world trying to make a living, traveling and stealing by day and night.
>
> (Dick Davis 677)

Angus Fraser remarks that the names used for these musician-migrants – *Zott*, by Hamza, and *Luris*, by Firdawsi – are still in current use:

> *Zotti* (plural *Zott*) and *Luli* or *Luri* are still Persian names for "Gypsy"; in Syria, Palestine and Egypt, *Luri* is found in a variant from *Nuri* (plural *Nawar*). *Zott* is an Arabicized version of the Indian tribal name *Jat*. Whether the original Gypsies were identical with the Jats of India (a people strongly represented in the Punjab) is a matter which has been debated for a hundred years or more.
>
> (35)

It's uncertain if the *Zott* and *Luri* are an early Romani community – the attribution of their appearance outside India to the fifth century leads the renowned Romani scholar Ian Hancock to believe these were the *Dom* or *Domari* people of northwest India, a precursor migration group (*We* 5–7) – but the recognition or miscognition here of a people who were a gift from an Indian potentate nonetheless outlines an ominous trajectory.[2]

The Persian king who asks for them is presented by Firdawsi's story as admirably demotic in his lofty concern for the poor in his country, but the skilled performers who arrive in Persia in answer to his request are not praised for their music or their gifts of artistry to the Persian people. Generously afforded resources by the ruler of an ancient sedentary civilization, the new immigrants instead exhibit fecklessness and an ungrateful irresponsibility. Contrary to the Shah's hopes, they do not commit to working hard for the long-term future through tilling and cultivation – labor that is the backbone of preindustrial sedentary civilizations – but elect for short-term gratification and consumption instead, and are punished by the Shah with enforced nomadism and the necessity to survive through their musical skills.

Travelers of this kind, who make a living as they travel – the story assumes – are also, naturally, thieves.[3] This is the kind of story that a sedentary civilization tells about diasporic peoples who possess neither wealth nor military might, are without political influence and economic power, and must live on the portability of their skills and by their wits.

From India to Europe: A People Emerge, Adapt, and Are Received

Linguistic analysis and, more recently, DNA evidence attest that Romani came out of northwest India in the Middle Ages through migrations beginning around the eleventh century, by reason, scholars suspect, of the displacements attending war. Hancock suggests that Rajput groups may have been brought westward to Iran by the Persian Ghaznavids, as fighters or as camp followers after the Ghaznavid invasion and subjugation of northern India. On Ghaznavid defeat by the Seljuk Turks, the groups were then transposed to the Seljuks, who helped to disperse the groups to Armenia and Byzantium as Seljuk conquests proceeded through Anatolia (Hancock, *We* 8–13, Soulis 144, Gresham et al., Kalaydjieva et al.):

> In those days, armies were accompanied by large numbers of camp followers . . . These were men and women whose jobs included clearing the battlefields, erecting tents, cooking for the soldiers and entertaining them, mending broken weapons and attending to the wounded. These people did not belong to the Kshatriya (warrior caste), but together with the Rajputs, whether as prisoners of war or with victors routing the enemy, they left India through the Hindu Kush. Women were well represented among the camp followers, though they were not part of the military, and it is to this that the female Indian genome in the modern genetic makeup of the Romani population may be traced.
>
> (Hancock, *We* 11)[4]

From India into Persia, then Armenia, then Byzantium – where there may be documentation of their presence from the second half of the eleventh, and more clearly from the twelfth, century – segments of the Romani population spread thereafter to the Balkans and to Western Europe, and as far west as the British Isles by the early modern period:[5]

> As the migration moved toward the northwest and on towards Europe, new words from other languages were picked up and added to the vocabulary and these help to provide a map of the route that was taken. The presence of many words adopted from Persian . . . and some from Kurdish . . . show that the migration must have passed through Iran; Armenian and Greek words . . . show passage through what is now Turkey; Slavic and Romanian words . . . indicate a presence in the Balkans.
>
> (Hancock, *We* 9)

the Romanies' move out of India and through the Middle East would seem to have taken place comparatively rapidly, in fifty years or less. If they had left as a defeated people . . . then going back into India and the territories now occupied by Mahmud [of Ghazni]'s armies would have been an unattractive option – and no option at all if they were prisoners of war. But if it took so little time to reach Anatolia, it was another two and a half centuries before the Romanies moved on into Europe. There are more than 250 Greek words in the European Romani dialects taken together, second only in number to the Indian vocabulary. There is also some fundamental grammar of Greek origin; it was probably in the Byzantine Empire that Romani crystallized into the language we recognise today. This, and other cultural characteristics point to a long and close contact with the Byzantines.

(Hancock, *We* 15)

Not only did their departure from India and their long sojourn in Greek Byzantium create a likely matrix for the emergence of the Romani language among the diasporic peoples we are considering, but that matrix also conduced to the emergence of the Romani *as a race*. With their arrival and sojourn in countries west of India, attributes of a sociocultural and somatic kind, along with distinctive occupations, begin to be attached to them in the documentary record, and register the responses in the Byzantine Empire and Europe to these diasporic peoples. The cumulative attributions, we will see, would stick, and would come to define the Romani.

As early as 1068, a Georgian hagiographical text composed at the Monastery of Iviron on Mount Athos in northern Greece, the *Life of Saint George the Athonite*, tells of a people "named Adsincani, who were renowned sorcerers and villains," and who were employed by the Emperor Constantine Monomachus (1042–55) in the year 1050 "to exterminate the wild animals that had invaded the imperial park of Philopation in Constantinople and were devouring the game which the Emperor kept there for hunting purposes" (Soulis 145). "These Adsincani," the *Life* relates, "succeeded in destroying many of the ferocious beasts simply by leaving in places frequented by them pieces of meat endowed with magical properties, which, when eaten, killed them instantly" (Soulis 145):

> The name Adsincani used in this text is the Georgian form of the Greek *Atsínganoi* or *Atzínganoi*, the term by which the Byzantines commonly referred to Gypsies. The German *Zigeuner*, French *Tsiganes*, Italian *Zingari*, Hungarian *Cigányok* and similar forms in several other languages all derived from this Byzantine name. The origin of *Atsínganos* has been much debated ... The most widely accepted view is that it was a corrupt form of the name of the heretical sect of the *Athínganoi*, applied to the Gypsies because both groups enjoyed a similar reputation for fortunetelling and sorcery. The original, heretical, Athinganoi were severely reduced in numbers, perhaps even wiped out, by persecutions in the ninth century.
>
> (Fraser 46; see also Soulis 146–7)

The early attribution of sorcery, magic, and occult arts as an identifying characteristic is quickly joined by identifying occupations such as snake-charming, and animal-keeping, in a twelfth-century reference:

> The Canonist Theodore Balsamon (d. *ca.* 1204), commenting on Canon LXI of the Council in Trulo (692) ... wrote: ... Athinganoi ... would have snakes wound around them, and they would tell one person that he was born under an evil star, and the other under a lucky star; and they would also prophesy about forthcoming good and ill fortunes.
>
> (Soulis 146)

Balsamon's commentary on Canon LXV also names the Athinganoi among the false prophets and wizards who are "inspired satanically and pretend to predict the unknown" (Soulis 146–7).

From the eleventh to the fifteenth centuries we thus see the documentary record yoke fortune-telling, snake-charming, magic, and animal-keeping to the Romani peoples until "references to Gypsies . . . had begun to be used as a contemptuous insult" (Fraser 48):

> in a circular letter the Patriarch of Constantinople Athanasius I (1289–93, 1301–9) wrote to all the clergy to admonish their flocks not to associate with fortunetellers, bearkeepers, and snake charmers, and "especially not to allow the Gypsies [*Adingánous*] to enter their homes, because they teach devilish things." Some decades later the learned Joseph Bryennius (*ca.* 1340-*ca.* 1431) . . . lamented the fact that the people daily associated "with magicians, soothsayers, Gypsies [*Athingánous*] and charmers." Similarly, we read the following passage in a fifteenth-century Byzantine nomocanon: "Those who consult the Gypsy women [*Aiguptíssas*] for fortunetelling . . . when they are ill or suffer from some other cause . . . should be forbidden to partake of Holy Communion for five years according to canon XXIV of the Council of Ancyra."
>
> (Soulis 147; see also Fraser 47)

Fraser points out that "*Aiguptíssas* designates the Gypsy women engaged in fortune-telling, and not Egyptians . . . proved by the Slavic version of the canon, where the word is translated as *ciganki*," and observes that the legend of the Romani peoples' Egyptian origin was current in fifteenth-century Byzantium – aided, he adds, "no doubt by Egypt's arcane association with occultism and divination" – and that the "modern Greek name for Gypsies – *Gúpthoi* – [goes] back to this usage" (47, 48).[6]

In these early and late strictures against occupational practices that were associated with the Romani, we thus have remarkable glimpses of a spectacular failure in cultural translation. "Fortune telling," Ian Hancock drily remarks, "is a highly regarded profession in India" (59) – a land in which Hinduism folds prophecy and investigation of the future into the normal faith practices of everyday life, and where soothsayers are routinely consulted for anything ranging from the birth of children, to illness, to decisions on marriage, business ventures, travel, education, and indeed anything projective, so that all of life itself becomes ritually punctuated by such consultations.

Transposed to the Christian West, however, the time-honored practices of one civilization's culture become the demonized abhorrences of another society's religion, and those who continue to practice their originating culture become themselves abhorred. Like palmistry and fortune-telling, snake-charming too becomes transformed into a bizarre phenomenon.[7]

Anonymous Greek poems possibly datable to the fourteenth century demonstrate how the Romani were enriching Greek culture's vocabulary of insults. A poetic satire, "A Jocular Tale about the Quadrupeds," depicts a hare lambasting a fox for being "a liar, a thief, and a Gypsy," while in the same poem a wolf scorns a bear for being "an amusement of the foolish Gypsies" (Soulis 151). Yet another anonymous poem, the "Book of the Birds," depicts a goose who calls a seagull "all sorts of insulting names, among them Gypsy" – all of which unfortunately suggests, Soulis is forced to conclude, "the contemptuous attitude of the Byzantines toward the Gypsies" (151). Byzantine attitudes of this kind, Fraser reminds us, are "a one-sided picture; we shall never know what view the Gypsies took of Byzantine society or what kind of treatment they received from it" (48).

Ominously, the documentary record also attests to a scrutinizing gaze that rested on Romani darkness of skin, for among the medieval Romani, Ian Hancock reminds us, "[d]ark skin was much more a factor 700 years ago than today" (*We* 57). An anonymous Byzantine poem also possibly from the fourteenth century finds fault with "the 'dark Gypsy'" (Soulis 150), and descriptions by German travelers to the Venetian colony of Modon, where there was a notable Romani settlement, batten on the distinctive skin color of Romani peoples.

Soulis and Fraser both note that "Bernhardt von Breydenbach (1483) mentions in his itinerary . . . certain poor folk like the Ethiopians, black and ungainly" at Modon, while Arnold von Harff of Cologne (1497) points to "many poor black naked people . . . [who] are called Gypsies" there (Fraser 53–4, Soulis 155). Slurs about their skin color would dog the Romani who wind their way deep into the Latin West, and would become a motif of their identification; and darkness of skin, as we saw in Chapter 4, was not innocent of meaning in the eye of the beholder in the Latin West, especially after the thirteenth century.[8]

The long Romani sojourn in Byzantine lands is particularly intriguing and instructive, because it opposes any easy assumption by us moderns – who are casting an eye backward from later eras – that the Romani were, and always had been, a nomadic people, ineluctably peripatetic, and therefore likely to have come from India's itinerant populations. Puzzling over the Romani language, Ian Hancock cites scholars who argue that "the presence of native Indian words in Romani for such concepts as 'king,' 'house,' 'door,' 'sheep,' 'pig,' 'chicken,' 'landowner' . . . and so on point to *settled*, rather than nomadic, peoples" (*We* 14, emphasis added).

By contrast, Hancock adds, vocabulary that depicts movement, such as "the words for 'tent,' 'wagon,' 'buffalo,' 'set up camp,' 'strike camp,' and even 'road' are not of Indian origin" (*We* 14). If Hancock and the scholars he cites are correct, such linguistic cues might indicate that nomadism became, or had to become, a Romani way of life *after* the departure from India, rather than a priori being the original way of life of those who left India.

Provocatively, Romani *settlements* in Greek territories are found in the archival record of the thirteenth through fifteenth centuries. Hancock locates a document from Constantinople "dated 1283 referring to taxes collected from 'the so-called Egyptians and Tsigani'" (*We* 15). Soulis considers a description in a Greek literary epistle, the "Sojourn of Mazaris in Hades," dated September 21, 1415, in which "Egyptians" are described as one of the seven "nations" residing in the Peloponnese, and distinguishable by ear because of their spoken language:

> Mazaris' Egyptians are undoubtedly the Gypsies, because . . . other contemporary sources testify to the presence of Gypsies in the Peloponnese at that time. On the basis of Mazaris' account that the Gypsies were one of the principal nations living in the Peloponnese at that time and that they still spoke their own language, one may conclude that their number in the peninsula was considerable.
>
> (152)

Soulis discusses a Venetian document dated August 12, 1444, that reveals the Romani also to be "well established in the area of the Venetian town of Nauplion" (152). The Venetian document orders the reinstatement of "John the Gypsy (*Johannes cinganus*)," who had been improperly removed from his office as "*drungarius acinganorum*" (roughly translatable as "military commander of the Romani") by Matteo Barbaro, the Venetian governor of Nauplion, whose act the document condemns (Soulis 153). Interestingly, this official record also refers to "privileges granted to the *predecessors and progenitors* of the said John by our government and by the nobleman Ottaviano Bono," suggesting that the Romani settlement at Nauplion survived across generations (Soulis 153, emphasis added):

> From a careful examination of this document one may conclude that the Gypsies of the Nauplion region were, at least, from the end of the fourteenth century, an organized group under a military leader, who at the time of the above document bore the Christian name of John and the purely Byzantine title of *drungarius* . . . this is, as far as I know, the first record of any privileges having been granted to Gypsies . . . the Venetians may have granted certain rights to the Gypsies with the expectation of receiving, in return, military assistance from the *drungarius acinganorum* and his men, in the event of enemy [i.e., Turkish] attack. Furthermore, the Venetians may have decided, too, that such a step would induce . . . Gypsies to undertake the cultivation of the land in the Nauplion area, which was depopulated as a result of the frequent Turkish inroads . . . an exactly parallel program had been carried out with the Albanians who had been installed in the Nauplion-Argos area at the end of the fourteenth century.
>
> (Soulis 153)

If this glimpse of the medieval Romani as a settled people in Venetian-controlled Nauplion – with privileges being granted to their military commander, who bears a Byzantine title and rank, as well as to his predecessors – disrupts the stereotype of Romani nomadism, scholarship also suggests that Soulis' speculation that the Venetians' hope for the Romani to cultivate the land was not extravagant. In a 1909 article on the production of "Romeney" wine in regions where there were known Romani settlements, such as in Nauplion and Modon, Eric Otto Winstedt recalls that "the Gypsies of Corfu early became agriculturists" (62). Indeed,

> There exist extensive accounts of a Gypsy settlement on Corfu, starting in the second half of the fourteenth century before the island fell into Venetian hands in 1386. By the time we hear of these Corfiote Gypsies, their annual dues have become sufficient to form an independent fief, the *feudum acinganorum* (which survived right down to the nineteenth century), and their arrival in Corfu must have been considerably earlier. Their numbers were probably swelled by the presence of Gypsies in the steady stream of poverty-stricken migrants (*homines vageniti*), who were, in the late fourteenth and early fifteenth centuries, pouring across the sea into Corfu from the mainland of Epirus, where Gypsies lived at that time in considerable numbers.
>
> (Fraser 50–1)

The Romani fief in Corfu, Fraser tells us, was highly lucrative for the feudal baron on whom the fief was conferred. In 1470 a Venetian decree conferred the fief upon a Michael de Hugot, who was given jurisdiction not only over the Romani settlement in Corfu but also over Romani living in Venetian possessions on the Epirus coast (Fraser 51):

> his serfs had to make many payments, both in money and in kind, to their feudal lord, who had the right to bring to trial and punish any of them in all matters of civil or criminal law, with the sole exception of homicide: these were privileges denied to other feudal barons. Moreover, every foreign Gypsy (*Cinganus forensic*) was obliged to pay a fee on entering or leaving the territory under the jurisdiction of the Venetian governor of Corfu, as well as having to pay the annual dues while resident.
>
> (Fraser 51)[9]

Despite Romani agriculture in Corfu, however, Winstedt decides that the Romani presence "in the special wine-growing districts can only be regarded as a coincidence," because Romani were "carrion-crows" who were "not over energetic," and too lazy and parasitic for the hard work entailed by vineyard cultivation and wine production (62–3).

Winstedt, however, notices that "Romeney" wine (the name of which, he decides, has nothing to do with the Romani) was also produced in Crete, as witnessed by Peter Fassbender while on pilgrimage in 1492, and Crete was an island, where – by another coincidence – Romani also dwelt (62).[10] Fraser, too, relates that the Franciscan friar Symon Simeonis, who visited Candia (Iraklion) on the island of Crete in 1323, found "a race" that was "identifiable as Gypsies" (50). Defying their legendary stereotype, some Romani communities seemed to have been agricultural. Were there vintners among these agriculturalists?

Most intriguing of all, perhaps, was the Romani settlement in Venetian-controlled Modon in the Peloponnese, which has been described in some detail by travelers of the fourteenth and fifteenth centuries. In the fourteenth century, "Lionardo di Niccolò Frescobaldi, who visited Modon in 1384, reports that he saw a number of *Romniti* outside the walls of the city" (Soulis 154). A century later, Bernhard von Breydenbach offers a more precise account; and his travel companion, the artist Eberhard Reüwich, even made a drawing of Modon that accompanies Breydenbach's text, which depicts the Romani settlement clustered outside the city walls, below a hill (Soulis 154).[11]

Breydenbach in 1483 and Konrad Grünemberg in 1486 counted about 300 Romani houses at Modon – "hovels," Breydenbach calls them, whose inhabitants were "black and unshapely" (Soulis 154, Winstedt 60). By 1495, however, "Alexander Pflazgraf bei Rhein . . . speaks of only 200 houses, while Arnold von Harff (1497) reduces them to one hundred, and about twenty years later Ludwig Tschudi (1519) found only thirty Gypsy huts there" (Soulis 154).

It would seem from these estimates that the Modon settlement did not thrive over the thirty-six years of the late fifteenth century in which it was observed by travelers. Soulis attributes the decline in population to a "gradual but steady departure undertaken because of Turkish advances, which culminated in the capture of Modon itself in 1500" – advances by the Ottomans that diminished pilgrim traffic through Modon, decreased commercial activity, and eroded the safety and security earlier provided by the Venetians (154). Modon was a seaport conveniently located midway between Venice and Jaffa, and had been a stopping-place for pilgrims journeying by the most popular route to the Holy Land.[12] Before the Ottoman incursions, the Romani at Modon may well have prospered.

Unsurprisingly, Romani occupations observed there in the fifteenth century were service trades. Arnold von Harff of Cologne (1497) documented occupations such as shoemaking, cobbling, and smithing; Peter Fassbender (1492) and Dietrich von Schachten (1491) called the Romani mainly smiths; and Dietrich graciously, if a touch condescendingly, allows that the smiths of Modon made "a great number of nails and very well" (Soulis 155; Fraser 53; Winstedt 65). The observers, who remarked on the poverty of the settlement by the end of the fifteenth century, also furnish detailed descriptions of Romani smith craft and methods that looked bizarre to the eyes of these Western Europeans (Soulis 154–5; Fraser 54; Winstedt 65).

Usefully for us, Modon's important location midway along a popular pilgrim route to the Holy Land may make it possible to elicit some understanding of an important development that occurred when the Romani finally arrived in Western Europe in the late fourteenth or early fifteenth century. Fraser's comprehensive account of Romani travels in the Latin West is struck by how, after brief appearances in the documentary record in Hungary in the 1370s and possibly Lower Saxony in 1407 and Switzerland in 1414 (60–2), suddenly, from 1417 onwards, "Gypsies appear as organized pilgrim groups, claiming, and obtaining, subsidies" (61).[13]

With slight variations, these pilgrim groups seem to have presented to the inhabitants of Western Europe an extraordinary, coherent narrative that offered penitence as the reason for their travels, and for requests of support and alms. Sebastian Münster's *Cosmographia universalis* of 1550 summed up the phenomenon:

> it was told how their ancestors in Lesser Egypt [*in minori Aegypto*] had formerly abandoned for some years the Christian religion and turned to the error of the pagans and that, for as many years, some members of their families should wander about the world and expiate in exile the guilt of their sin.
>
> (Fraser 65)

Fraser recalls how medieval attitudes toward pilgrims and penitence-driven peregrination made a narrative of this kind a stroke of genius:

> For Gypsies the important point was that . . . it was still considered a duty to entertain the pilgrim and help him on his journey. Thus charitable persons could share in the blessings that descended upon the pilgrim, and pilgrims were instruments for winning grace. Rulers might encourage them by granting letters of recommendation. Charlemagne had in his time imposed it as a legal obligation that pilgrims should be given roof, hearth and fire wherever they traveled. By claiming to be penitents and pilgrims, the Gypsies could ensure that they were received with a warmer welcome than they had enjoyed hitherto.
>
> (62–3)

Dubbing the story of repentance and wandering "the great trick" of the Romani peoples in Europe, Fraser retails the story's efficacy:

> Suddenly, we find Gypsies behaving in an unprecedented manner. They are no longer unobtrusive, but almost court attention. They are no uncoordinated rabble, but move in an apparently purposeful way under leaders with impressive titles. And at first they are not hounded or harried, but treated with a measure of consideration. It was as if some unsung genius . . . had realized the potential advantages to be drawn from the religious environment of the time and had devised a strategy for exploiting it and enhancing the prospects of survival.
>
> (62)

For Fraser, the Romani narrative of their repentance and redemption is no more than a "great trick" – an expression coined in Spain for "a certain method of relieving some gullible dupe of a large sum of money" (62). Fraser hazards that the "trick" was somehow learnt in Greece, where the Romani acquired familiarity with the Christian world:

> On the roads and in the ports, they had encountered travellers from all over Europe. They may have learned additional languages. They would certainly have heard of the Holy Land; they had seen that pilgrims were privileged travellers. All this knowledge would be profitable to them . . . when they decided to pursue their migrations into the world of western Christianity.
>
> (56)

Modern literature, of course, has long taught us to admire trickster figures who can weave a brilliant tale to their advantage, and it is not difficult to admire the creative ingenuity of a displaced, powerless peoples who must try to harness whatever mechanisms might be at hand for their and their children's survival. But this story of penitence might also serve to open a window that enables us to catch a glimpse of an extraordinary process, this time, of *successful* cultural translation by the Romani.

The request for alms, Hancock reminds us, is not seen as shameful in India, or, indeed, in many Asian and Middle Eastern cultures, "where giving alms to beggars is a religious obligation" (*We* 59). More than a religious obligation, the giving of alms to those who ask – and those who ask would include religious men and women bound by ascetic vows of poverty, and devotees such as the Jains, who expressly disavow earthly possessions and must beg for their daily bread – is a blessed act that brings honor and grace upon the giver who is so fortunate as to be asked.

In the outlines of the narrative offered by the Romani in Europe, we may perhaps detect a brilliant translation of the Eastern understanding of charity, obligation, and blessedness into terms that are comprehensible to Western societies – a translation of religious vocabulary that takes cognizance of Christianity, a faith that also specifies the importance of charity and alms giving, especially under certain conditions such as penitence and pilgrimage, which the Romani may have come to understand.[14]

In effect, the Romani had devised for themselves an original sin that required expiation through a period of exile: a narrative that Christian Europeans who were still expiating the original sin of Adam and Eve could sympathize with and well understand. A people who were not recognized as possessing a history that could legitimize them had found a way to create for themselves a legitimating history, in a vocabulary that was recognized in the lands where they traveled.[15]

Arriving in groups ranging in size from a mere thirty (for example in Ratisbon, Bavaria, 1423) to 200 and 300 (for example in Metz, France, 1494), the Romani who appeared in Western Europe also seemed to have leaders who were variously identified as "duke" and "count" and, later, "captain," "knight," and "master" – another indication, perhaps, of increasing Romani competencies in cultural translation, and their acquisition of the Latin West's concepts and vocabulary that denoted stratifications and rank (Fraser 67, 74, 92, 93, 96, 98, 104, passim).[16]

Bearing letters of protection and safe conduct issued by the princes of Europe, including Sigismund (1368–1437), King of Hungary and Holy Roman Emperor, and later apparently also Pope Martin V, the Romani groups were by and large not initially treated with outright hostility, but were watched with inquisitive wariness ("suspicion" is Fraser's preferred term) or even welcomed in the European countries which they visited, and where they were initially afforded varying degrees of hospitality (Fraser 64–5, 74).[17]

At the little town of Châtillon-en-Dombes in 1419, a group of Romani was given bread and wine, and five weeks later, at Sisteron in Provence, food was sent to sojourners who had been refused admittance but were encamped in a field (Fraser 69). In Brussels, civic accounts show that in 1420, the burghers supplied a group led by a Duke of Little Egypt named Andries with beer, wine, bread, a cow, four sheep, and twenty-five gold coins (Fraser 70).[18] The accounts of Deventer in the same year indicate that 100 men, women, and children led by Lord Andreas, Duke of Little Egypt, received twenty-five florins in cash, together with bread, beer, herrings, and straw for their forty horses: "the town also bore the cost of cleaning out the barn in which they slept, and of conducting them eastwards to Goor" (Fraser 70).

In 1421 the aldermen of Tournai presented "Sir Miquiel, prince of Latingham in Egypt" with twelve gold coins, bread, and a barrel of beer, "out of pity and compassion, for the sustaining of him and several other men and women of his company who were driven out of their country by the Saracens because they had turned to the Christian faith" (70). This slight variation at Tournai in the narrative of journeying, we notice, depicts the Romani as Christians who were refugees from Ottoman territorial incursions.

In 1429, Tournai again gave an unnamed Count of Egypt, and a company of about sixty, wine, wheat, beer, herrings and firewood, and "notices were put up by the aldermen to warn the townspeople to do them no harm and to encourage alms-giving" (Fraser 77–8). Nevers gave alms to Count Thomas of Little Egypt and thirty followers in 1436; the chapter of St. Andrew at Grenoble gave two florins to Count Philippe and a company of forty in 1442; and Arles gave a duke of Little Egypt ten florins in 1438, and two other leaders – John and George – six, then four florins some years later (Fraser 92). The diminishing sums of alms received at Arles as the years passed indicate, perhaps, the beginnings of compassion fatigue.

Fraser is acutely conscious of the cost borne by the towns that showed hospitality to the Romani:

> Their visits also led to incidental costs. In May 1428 Hildesheim had to pay for the cleaning of a house where the Gypsies had lodged. There were similar expenses in Flanders about this time when Gypsies were put up in the Woolhouse at Bruges; in Deventer in 1429, when the town also bore the cost of escorting them northwards to their next stopping-place; and in 1429/30 in Rotterdam "for cleaning the school-house, after the duke and his retinue had lain in it."
>
> (78)

Yet for a decade or two in Europe, the Romani creation of a self-legitimating history that allowed the Latin West to put its best self forward and demonstrate its capacity for Christian charity meant that the travelers could count on occasional hospitality, exercised unevenly by the cities and towns through which they passed (towns in Germany, Fraser shows, were by and large less kindly than those in France).

Christians, and Yet Not Christian: Epidermal Race, Custom, and Spectacle in the Gaze of the West

Nevertheless, in a number of places the Romani visited, the gaze of Western European societies that was trained upon these sojourners saw dark-skinned, alien-looking foreigners. Hermann Cornerus' *Chronica novella*, completed *c.* 1435, relates the passage of the Romani in 1417 through the northern German territories of Holstein, Mecklenburg, and Pomerania:

> They numbered about 300 men and women, not including the children and infants, and were very ugly in appearance and black as Tartars; they called themselves *Secani*. They also had chieftains among them, that is a Duke [*Ducem*] and a Count [*Comitem*], who

administered justice over them and whose orders they obeyed . . . They also carried letters of recommendation from princes and especially from Sigismund, King of the Romans, according to which they were to be admitted and kindly treated by states, princes, fortified places, towns, bishops and prelates to whom they turned. Certain among them were on horseback, while others went on foot. The reason for their wandering and travelling in foreign lands was said to have been their abandoning of the faith and their apostasy after conversion to paganism. They were committed to continue these wanderings in foreign lands for seven years as a penance laid upon them by their bishops.

(Fraser 67)

"The Germans," Fraser observes, "found them very ugly, evidently because of the colour of their skin; and they also had the reputation of being light-fingered" (67). Romani groups began to accrue a spectrum of names. Notwithstanding their narrative of Christian penitence, they were called *Heiden* (heathens or pagans), Saracens, and Tartars, as well as Egyptians, Bohemians, and variations on their original Greek name, *Atzinganoi.* One contemporary chronicler, Conrad Justinger, refers to the arrival of more than 200 *baptized* heathens (*Heiden*) in Switzerland, at Berne, in 1419 – as if baptized Romani were still pagans, unlike everyone else in Europe, and could not be called Christians (Fraser 68).

The Swiss chronicler's naming of Christian Romani as *Heiden* is an active act of exclusion, not an act of ignorance. Fraser points out that Swiss chroniclers often recognized the Romani as, in fact, Christian:

Zürich, Basle, Solothurn and Berne are all credited with visits. The chroniclers represent the Gypsies as an outlandish and very dark people; they had their dukes and counts, and said they came from Little Egypt . . . They related that they had been driven out by the Turks and that they were condemned to do penance in poverty for seven years. They followed the Christian customs as regards baptism and burial. Their clothing was poor but they had a great deal of gold and silver, ate well and drank well and paid well.

(68)

Elsewhere, the historical record also recognizes Romani as Christians. At Colmar in 1450, the authorities "granted Count Philip a safe-conduct certifying that he and his company had comported themselves in a worthy and Christian manner" (Fraser 93). The journal of Jean Aubrion records the baptism at Metz in 1494 of a baby girl, born to the Romani duke who led a visiting group of 300, in the church of Saint Julian, "with three godfathers and two godmothers drawn from the principal families of Metz" (Fraser 93).

Fraser unkindly scents an ulterior motive in the selection of godparents for this christening at Metz: "The Gypsies had obviously become aware of the advantages – in terms of protection and of gifts – that could accrue from having *gadžé* godparents for their children, and there would be plenty of other occasions when they followed the same practice" (93). Fraser's remark seems to imply that by contrast, when medieval Christian Europeans chose powerful or wealthy godparents as patrons for *their* infants at baptism (a thoroughly common practice), *they* can be presumed innocent of such ambitions. Calculation and canny cultivation of the powerful thus seem to the otherwise reasonably good-willed Fraser to be *racial* behavior, rather than survival strategies exercised by Romani and Europeans alike.

Ominously, the gaze of Europe on the Romani searches out the darkness and blackness of their skin again and again. Hair and physique are critically scrutinized, while the

European gaze is agog at cultural markers such as alien clothing, headgear, and ornaments. At Colmar in Alsace, in 1418, when thirty, then one hundred *Heiden* appear, the "darkness of their skin is . . . emphasized; new observations are the silver ear-rings and the palmistry of the women, who were dressed in rags which looked like blankets" (Fraser 68). At St. Laurent, near Mâcon, where Andrew, Duke of Little Egypt arrived in 1419 with 120 or more followers, the followers are described as "men of terrible stature in person, in hair, as well as otherwise" (Fraser 69). In Burgundian Arras in 1421, the thirty "foreigners from the land of Egypt" and their count bearing letters from the emperor are eyed closely in the aldermen's accounts:

> The men were very dark-skinned, long-haired and heavily bearded, while the women had cloths wound around their heads like turbans, and wore low-cut chemises covered by a coarse sheet fastened at the shoulder; women and children had rings in their ears.
>
> (Fraser 71)

Sometimes the Romani courted attention, with mixed results: At Meiningen, they performed acrobatics in the marketplace, and "seemed outlandish to the citizens because of the darkness of their skins; in the end the priest had them driven away" (Fraser 78). A benign reception saw the travelers transformed into an exotic spectacle for the vulgar: The journal of the *Bourgeois* of Paris tells us that Romani arrivals at La Chapelle in 1427, "[w]ith their dark skins and silver earrings," attracted crowds of curious onlookers (Fraser 77).

More commonly, we glimpse communal observation of the Romani that is tinged at best with ambivalence, and at worst with contempt. A Bologna chronicle records that in 1422 a band of about a hundred arrived, led by a Duke Andrea whose wife was astonishingly skilled in revealing the future and hidden knowledge, and was consulted by numerous people because "In many cases she told truly" (Fraser 72). The chronicle adds:

> Note that they were the ugliest brood ever seen in those parts. They were thin and black and ate like pigs. Their women went about in shifts and wore a coarse outer garment across the shoulder, rings in their ears, and a long veil on their head. One of them gave birth to a child in the market-place and, at the end of three days, she went on with the other women.
>
> (Fraser 72–3)

Dropping an infant in the marketplace then traipsing along with the other women shortly after, this nameless Romani woman who caught the eye of the Bologna chronicle seems scarcely human – more a pregnant beast that whelps in public, then has to move on with her pack.

Within a short time of their arrival in the Latin West, therefore, a full-fledged "Gypsy" physiotype had congealed in the eyes of their Western observers and would endure for several centuries to come, snaking its way through folklore, literature, song, the visual arts, and the cultural imagination. A "Gypsy" was dark-skinned; the men had long hair and heavy beards, while women were turbaned or had a veil over their hair and wore a low-cut chemise covered by an outer garment fastened at the shoulder; women and children wore rings in their ears. They behaved like the animals they bred and kept.

But what were the lives of these Romani really like as they traveled in Europe? With their communities viewed only from the outside under the critical, often contemptuous scrutiny of chroniclers and the like in the countries through which they passed, it seems impossible to know. The sudden glimpse, in an unsympathetic account, of a woman who had to give birth in the marketplace of Bologna and then move on three days later is startling and poignant. Duke Andrea's talented wife, whose skills of foreknowledge and insight were admired and acknowledged by the townspeople, also points to a story that needs to be told.

Fraser sees the Romani in Germany as a single, relatively organized, moving mass: "They appear frequently to have split up into smaller groups, but they all came under the same chief; they marched in concert, and followed each other closely" (67). Indeed, for Fraser, the Romani of Europe fell into

> fairly cohesive bands which travelled widely and in detachments, and in many cases under some form of control by a few leaders. There was in effect a degree of unity of action and close connection with each other. They appear to have told the same tales and shown similar supporting documents, first from the Emperor and other potentates and afterwards from the Pope.
>
> (79)

The medieval record is silent on what language or languages these travelers spoke, and there are few windows into how they lived while on the road:

> It is ... surprising that nothing is said, until well into the sixteenth century, about the Gypsies having their own language; nor do we hear of any difficulty in their communicating with the inhabitants of countries they were visiting for the first time ... we have only sparse details of vehicles and shelters. Tents are mentioned but rarely. The original migrants appear to have had few conveyances and to have bivouacked in the open or under makeshift shelters when they could not persuade townspeople to give them lodging. Most obscure of all are the social and political organization and the communication network underlying these forays.
>
> (Fraser 79)[19]

The collective record that Fraser reads seems to disclose varying degrees of well-being and poverty. In Switzerland, the Romani were seen to have "a great deal of gold and silver," and were reported to have eaten, drunk, and *paid* well – payment, presumably, for food, beverage, goods, and/or services they required (Fraser 68). At the Spanish frontier post of Canfranc, at the foot of the Somport Pass, in 1435, the Romani "Count Tomas" had to declare his personal effects, among which were "5 horses each worth 20 florins," "5 robes which were of silk," and "4 silver goblets each weighing one mark (c. 8 oz) more or less" (Fraser 77).

The accounts of Deventer record that the 100 men, women, and children led by the Duke of Little Egypt, Andries, who arrived in 1420 possessed about forty horses (Fraser 70). Romani leaders, moreover – the historical record amasses some two dozen names of dukes and counts – were by and large "finely dressed and well mounted" (Fraser 79). But the poverty of some of these peripatetic groups is also mentioned, and Fraser aptly registers differences in how class-conscious medieval Europeans assessed and treated Romani leaders and commoners:

> the records of their visits from 1417 onwards often make a marked distinction between the treatment given to the duke or count, who was lodged like a man of some quality, and that meted out to his followers who were quartered in meaner surroundings.
>
> (80)

Slightly more information exists on the work undertaken by the Romani in Western Europe. From prohibitions issued by church and state, records of payment, and other documentary entries, we see the kind of services these peripatetic peoples performed as they traversed countries, towns, and villages. In the diocese of Troyes in 1456–7, "there were several instances when ecclesiastical penalties . . . were imposed on those who had had their hands read or resorted to the healing crafts of the Gypsies" (Fraser 93). Despite church prohibitions, however, local peoples seemed to have an irrepressible desire to know their futures, and continued to resort to Romani talents. In 1509, "the citizens of Rouen, *including a priest*, were flocking to have their fortunes told by Gypsies, at the peril of their souls" (Fraser 95, emphasis added).

In one of the earliest associations of Romani in Europe with music, an account book of the Duke of Ferrara in the Duchy of Modena records a 1469 payment to "a *Cingano* for playing a citole" (Fraser 106). In Hungary, too, the Romani acquired a reputation as musicians, with royal payments being recorded in 1489 and 1525; Romani musicians are mentioned again in letters in 1532 and 1543 (Fraser 109).

Healing, palmistry, music, horse dealing, and entertainments such as acrobatics were thus observed as Romani skills (Fraser 71, 81, 97, 125). Women are singled out for mention in the cultural record: An impressive palmist appears in England in 1514, described in *A Dialogue of Sir Thomas More, Knight*, as an "Egypcyan" woman "who could tell marvellous things simply by looking into a person's hand" (Fraser 112). In a sixteenth-century collection of sketches in Arras in northern France, there is a portrait of a striking, long-haired woman in a wrapped turban and medieval Romani-style clothing, with an extraordinary caption testifying to who she is: "The Egyptian woman who by medical art restored health to the King of Scotland, given up by the physicians" (Fraser 120).[20] Who were these remarkable women who so impressed with their skills – one of them healing the King of Scotland after his professional physicians had failed – that the cultural record is forced to take notice of them?

Inevitably, Romani women were also eyed with lascivious scrutiny:

> Not a few members of the Spanish nobility would . . . remain protectors of the Gypsies and give them valuable succour even in the hardest of times. Their complicity would be given a variety of explanations by those who denounced it later, with a good deal of malicious stress on the seductive qualities of the Gypsy women and on the talents of the men in procuring fine horses for the stables of their friends.
>
> (Fraser 97)[21]

Fraser attempts to account for the "malicious stress" that would cast innuendo on an ability to procure fine horses as somehow immoral or suspect: "Settled people, on the whole, do not trust nomads" (127).

The work undertaken by the Romani as they traveled in Western Europe highlighted portable skills that transfer readily with continual human movement. But Romani agriculture in Corfu and perhaps Nauplion and elsewhere, and their metalworking, shoemaking, and other trades in Greek lands, in addition to the linguistic evidence cited by Hancock and other scholars, all suggest that we need not assume the Romani to have *perennially* been an itinerant people, even in India before their diaspora, and somehow therefore *naturally* predisposed to nomadism rather than varieties of sedentary labor.

Nicolae Gheorghe holds that the Romani in Western Europe were forced to move from place to place because the settled societies of the Latin West had little need for the kinds of trades at which Romani excelled: Cities and towns in France, Germany, the Low Countries, and elsewhere already had plenty of smiths, cobblers, and the like, and agriculture was well advanced (25). Fraser points out that the well-established economic infrastructure of Western Europe did not leave room to incorporate Romani readily into extant trades and agricultural work:

> the guilds regulated crafts and trades, commerce was also tightly controlled, and peasants were not in the habit of employing casual labour, so that what was left for Gypsies as a livelihood was limited to small services and minor trading and entertainment.
>
> (81)

Like medieval Jews who could not own land but needed to forge an economic niche of their own (Jews in a specialization, unfortunately, that proved to be highly dangerous in the end for Jewish survival), Romani traveled, taking their skills where they could, and hoped for hospitality in the Christian West. Despite the initial success of the Romani explanation for their peregrinations, however, compassion fatigue set in rapidly. Accusations of theft dogged the travelers, with women again bearing the brunt of symbolic attention. Hermann Cornerus complains that "They were great thieves . . . especially their women, and several of them in various places were seized and put to death" (Fraser 67). The Bologna chronicle indignantly insists that

> The women of the band wandered about the town, six or eight together; they entered the houses of the citizens and told idle tales, during which some of them laid hold of whatever could be taken. In the same way they visited the shops under the pretext of buying something, but one of them would steal. Many thefts were committed in this way in Bologna.
>
> (Fraser 72)

The accusations of light-fingeredness sound curiously reflexive, and are easy to levy, perhaps, on those who are passing through when items go missing. Despite the negative stereotype, however, the *Bourgeois* of Paris is forced to admit: "I must say I went there three or four times to talk to them and could never see that I lost a penny" (Fraser 77). In their way, clichés of this kind, attached to a vilified group, remind us of the accusations of witchcraft that were levied against the vulnerable and those without the ability to state their case for the historical record. We remember that another minority group in the Latin West – medieval Jews – also faced ubiquitous, clichéd condemnations, and accusations of a more violent kind: of ritual murder, bloodletting and vampirism, host desecration, and a slew of other libels in the European countries where they were to be found.

Interestingly, the one-sidedness of the accusations against the Romani is sporadically punctuated by (inadvertent?) asides that mention crimes committed by *townspeople* against the Romani: The inhabitants of Alagón, near Saragossa, for instance, stole from the visiting Romani count a greyhound and a mastiff, and were ordered by Alfonso V of Aragon to return the animals (Fraser 76). The Bologna chronicle also confesses that the townspeople of Bologna stole Romani horses – "several men slipped one night into a stable where some of their horses were shut up, and took the finest of them" – but represents this criminal act as revenge for Romani theft (Fraser 72). Fraser, putting it mildly, reminds us: "the prejudices and economic structure of the countries they passed through meant that people who were not sedentary were seldom assured of a continuing welcome" (81).

R. A. Scott Macfie expresses best the distorted perspective the documentary record affords for any attempt to reconstruct the lives of Romani in medieval Western Europe from the documents of officialdom alone:

> Records ... give a grotesquely false picture of Gypsy life, for they notice only Gypsies who by spectacular or criminal behaviour have made themselves conspicuous ... So it should not be forgotten that for every Gypsy who is pilloried in the records ... for his crimes there were a thousand living a more or less honest, or at all events unobtrusive, life. From chronicles no account of the normal Gypsy way of life can be extracted: in fact their value is that they show what Gypsies ordinarily did NOT do. To write a history of the Gypsies from such records, therefore, is as foolish as it would be to base a history of England on the Newgate Calendar.
>
> ("Gypsy Persecutions" 78)

Surveillance, Punishment, and Expulsion in Western Europe: The Beginning of the End

Western Europe's capacity for Christian charity and magnanimity proved not to be enduring. In Germany, the Romani were accused of espionage: of spying for the Turks – from whose incursions, ironically, the Romani had likely fled in the first place, as their diminishing numbers in places such as Modon attest. During the reign of Emperor Maximilian I, the Imperial Diet issued edicts of expulsion for espionage in 1497, 1498, and 1500, which "set the tone for decrees promulgated by princes, dukes, and other potentates of the empire" (Fraser 85). Fraser points out the unjustness of accusing as spies those who must, as a matter of course, gather information on places and peoples as they travel.

> The suspicion of espionage ... was primarily a German preoccupation. Gypsies were especially vulnerable to it since they were obliged to acquire, for their own use, intimate knowledge of a country and information about its inhabitants.
>
> (85)

Accusing the itinerant Romani of being spies is somewhat like accusing Jewish financiers of coin clipping because their livelihood required them to handle metal coinage.[22] In both, necessity became the fertile ground of calumny. But, even worse, there is yet another way in which the response to Romani in Germany resembled the response to medieval Jews. Somehow, a tale had been circulated – adapted, perhaps, from the original narrative of Romani penitence and redemption – that the Romani were in exile because their forefathers in Egypt had turned away the Holy Family when the latter had sought refuge there from Herod. The German chronicler, Aventinus (Johann Thurmaier), writing in 1522, recounts this alternate story under the year 1439 in his *Bavarian Chronicle*:

> At this time, that thieving race of men, the dregs and bilge-water of various peoples, who live on the borders of the Turkish empire and of Hungary (we call them *Zigeni*), began to wander through our provinces under their king Zindelo, and by dint of theft, robbery and fortune-telling they seek their sustenance with impunity. They relate falsely that they are

from Egypt and are constrained by the gods [or "by their rulers," *a superis*] to exile, and they shamelessly feign to be expiating, by a seven year banishment, the sins of their forefathers who turned away the Blessed Virgin with the child Jesus.

(Fraser 84–5)[23]

Fraser wonders if the Romani themselves had invented and circulated this "imprudent" adaptation of the original narrative of penance and travel (we might also ask if this is a garbled account produced by the imprecision or ill-will of certain chroniclers) because of the great danger of presenting medieval Christian Europeans with a story of ill-treating the Lord:

> it offered European populations the same kind of righteous pretext for intolerance as that which fostered the anti-Semitism fed by allegations of Jewish complicity in the Crucifixion and of sacrifice of Christian children at Passover.

(85–6)

There were indeed uncanny homologies in how medieval Jews and medieval Romani were treated in Europe. A charge of turning away the fugitive infant Jesus and a charge of betraying the adult Savior to the Romans made up bookend accusations in the central Christian story of Jesus' life that linked hapless Romani and Jews through the putative culpability of the two groups' forebears. Hancock points to several analogies in how Jews and Romani were imagined, and how calumnies against them subtly intertwined:

> Like Asahuerus, the Jew doomed to wander throughout eternity because he refused to allow Jesus to rest in his doorway while on his way to Calvary, Romanies were accused of forging the nails with which Christ was crucified. And while Jews were accused of drinking the blood of Christian babies in hidden rites to which no outsider was allowed access, Romanies were likewise charged with stealing and even eating those babies. Paralleling even more closely the Asahuerus myth is the belief that the original sin of the Romanies was their refusal to give Mary and the baby Jesus shelter during their flight from King Herod into Egypt.

(*We* 57–8)

Romani skills in smithing – we remember Dietrich von Schachten (1491) admiring the well-made nails of the smiths of Modon – were twisted into a horrifying tale of how Romani ancestors once forged the nails of the Crucifixion: a weirdly ahistorical libel, like the tale of turning away the Holy Family in Egypt, since the Romani would not yet leave India for another thousand years after the first century CE. But like Jewish financiers who handled coin and were accused of coin clipping, Romani smiths were damned through the very tools and skills of their profession.

Also like the Jews, the Romani peoples of Western Europe became subject to periodic expulsions. Fraser tracks the banishments and expulsions that ensued in rapid succession in the late fifteenth century and in the sixteenth:

> In 1471 the Tagsatzung (Diet) at Lucerne enacted that Gypsies were not to be housed or sheltered within the Swiss Confederation; and the city-state of Geneva, outside the Confederation, expelled a number of "Saracens" in 1477. In 1510, again at Lucerne, after complaints that they stole and were dangerous, *Zegynen* were banished from the Confederation, under a penalty of hanging if they returned.

(90)

In Milan in 1493, under the rule of Ludovico il Moro, an edict ordered the Romani to leave at once, and in 1506 two edicts declared them a public menace and again banned them; statutes specifying banishments and penalties continued (including the *tratto di corda*, "which involved hoisting the victim by his hands, tied behind his back, so that the entire weight of the body hung from his wrists") until finally, in 1534, Francesco Sforza "proscribed 'all *Egiptii* commonly called *Cingali*' on pain of hanging" (Fraser 106–7).

In France, Macfie finds that some Romani were executed as witches in 1467, and in 1560 "they were ordered to depart within two months, after which they were to be shaved and the men sent to the galleys for three years" ("Gypsy Persecutions" 68).

> In July 1504, a missive from Louis XII ordered the bailiff of Rouen to seek out and expel Egyptian vagabonds, notwithstanding any safe-conduct they might produce; and in 1510 the Grand Council, in the course of imposing a sentence of exile on seven Gypsies who had appeared in court, extended the banishment to all other Gypsies in the kingdom of France.
>
> (Fraser 94–5)

Spain, where the Romani had initially been well received and protected, followed suit:

> On 4 March 1499, seven years after their expulsion of the Jews, and three years before the forced conversion of the Muslims, a decree of the Catholic Kings [Ferdinand and Isabella] ... stated the Gypsies' options bluntly: either they became sedentary and sought masters, or after 60 days they would be banished. King Charles I ... renewed these provisions several times and added some refinements of his own: those caught wandering for the third time could be seized and enslaved forever; and those who did not settle or depart within 60 days were to be sent to the galleys for six years if between the ages of 20 and 50. This last provision reflected the government's difficulties in manning the galley squadrons as they grew in response to the constant warfare between Spain and the Islamic empire in the Mediterranean ... The oarsmen spent much of their sentence chained to the galley bench.
>
> (Fraser 98–9)

By this time, Fraser observes, the Romani "took the precaution of traveling in smaller bands so as not to attract attention," and "when the archives do take notice of them now, they are no longer accorded the status of pilgrims and their leaders are stripped of noble titles" (105).

The late fifteenth-century and the sixteenth-century Romani expulsions and banishments queerly mimic the country-by-country Jewish expulsions that took place from the late thirteenth century onward in Europe. But for all the homologies we have of how these two minority peoples were imagined and treated, there were crucial ways in which Jews and Romani, and their fates in Europe, also significantly diverged. Fraser highlights some internal differences of class and culture in the two groups that especially underscore the vulnerability of the Romani people:

> The Gypsies' diaspora has sometimes been compared with that of the Jews: however, theirs was a diaspora of a people with no priestly caste, no recognized standard for their language, no texts enshrining a corpus of beliefs and code of morality, no appointed custodians of ethnic traditions.
>
> (44)

We should also consider a development of great import, with consequences that would endure for centuries afterward: the fact that the Romani were enslaved as a race during their centuries-long sojourn in parts of southeastern Europe – in Wallachia and Moldavia, two territorial polities that later joined to become Romania in 1859 (with Transylvania added at a later date).[24]

There, the Romani peoples did not have to shunt from pillar to post, hoping for hospitality and charity, the way they did in Western Europe. Romani skills in metalworking and other trades were highly prized and much needed in the Wallachian and Moldavian economies. Ironically, however, the very necessity of Romani labor in these economies proved eventually to be the downfall of a people who became an indispensable labor force. From being a free people, large sections of the Romani population became enslaved by the monasteries and the boyars, and suffered in slavery (*robie*) until their modern-day emancipation in 1855 and 1856.[25]

Hancock estimates that perhaps half of the Romani populations who moved out of Byzantine (and, increasingly, Ottoman) territories in the thirteenth and fourteenth centuries entered the Balkans and southeastern Europe, while the rest moved onward to Western Europe ("Gypsy Stereotype" 181). Gheorghe finds "Roma people ... early recorded in all three provinces" of the Romanian territories, though undisputed dating is relatively late: "1385 in Wallachia, 1402 in Moldavia, and 1417 in Transylvania" (13). Gheorghe holds that the "early presence of Roma [i]n the Romanian territory, beginning with the end of [the] XIII century" meant that there were "great numbers" of Romani in such places, with groups initially enacting "their migration voluntarily within the boundaries of the Rumanian Principalities," though later forced migrations also occurred (14):

> during their numerous wars in the South-Danubian territories, the Rumanian Princes frequently took great numbers of Roma from the Balkans bringing them back to Rumanian Principalities, in Wallachia and then in Moldavia. A document tells us that in September 1445 the Wallachian Prince, Vlad the Devil, took by force from Bulgaria to Wallachia 11,000–12,000 persons, without luggage and animals, who looked like Egyptians; it is presumed that these people were Gypsies ... It is recorded also that the Moldavian Prince, Stephan the Great, after a victorious war with his Wallachian neighbors (1471) transported into Moldavia over 17,000 *Tsigani* (Gypsies) in order to use their labour force.
>
> (16)

The Romanian principalities were important transshipment centers in the region, and were well positioned for the transit trade between Europe and the East, with thriving, prosperous East–West commerce that began early and lasted until the late fifteenth and the sixteenth centuries:

> This era of wealth and prosperity began just after the Crusades and lasted until the Rumanian ports on the Danube and the Black Sea fell under the domination of the Turks (1484–1540). It endured, therefore, for [almost] 300 years, and it was just at this date, about the beginning of the fourteenth century, that the Tziganes arrived in these two countries [i.e., Wallachia and Moldavia] ... trade was then brisk and it was easy to earn a living. Business and wealth were so abundant in Walachia and Moldavia that the Tziganes,

with all their natural endowments, allowed themselves to be attracted by the profit they believed they would make from their varied trades.

(Panaitescu 64)

P. N. Panaitescu points out that although the Romanian territories had skilled local tradesmen, the number and type of trades to be found in the territories was limited: e.g., "there were no blacksmiths among the peasants, and it is certain that this trade was one much sought after on the big estates in an era of great prosperity" (63). Tools and equipment were essential to the agricultural estates in Romania, and military equipment was essential for the armies. And Romani were skilled in various kinds of craft:

they worked for everyone, each of them being capable of engaging in one or several occupations at the same time, and, if necessary, they could learn other trades with the utmost rapidity. Town-dwellers as well as country-folk benefited by their work, for these Gypsy artisans were needed on the properties of the monasteries as well as on the big estates of the Boyards. The Tziganes were useful for making the implements needed by the armies ... They came to Walachia and Moldavia because they found much work there, and because they were well paid.

(Panaitescu 65)

In addition to metalworking and carpentry, Gheorghe indicates that Romani immigrants carried on a lively trade in animals (19). Panaitescu suggests that the Romani even took on new kinds of manual labor, such as bricklaying and the manufacture of bricks – and that they may have been induced to do this – because Romanians themselves "disliked mason's work" and this was essential labor in a growth economy (65). It transpired that the Romani were relied on to such an extent that they became indispensable over the generations, till "it was well-nigh impossible to find blacksmiths, locksmiths, farriers, tinsmiths, etc. except among the Tziganes" (Panaitescu 67; see also Marushiakova and Popov, "Gypsy Slavery" 105).

Gheorghe carefully disaggregates the Romani workforce in the Romanian Principalities so as to have us understand the differential statuses of Romani labor in these territories as time passed. Romani who reached the Romanian lands in the late thirteenth century and the beginning of the fourteenth in voluntary migrations, he tells us, arrived as "free people and remained free during a significant period before falling into slavery" (16). In addition, despite the large-scale descent into slavery later, there remained in the "medieval history of the Rumanian Principalities ... a small but constant number of free Roma," a segment of the labor force that escaped enslavement (16).[26] Scrupulously, Gheorghe qualifies for us what the status of being "free" meant for Romani immigrants to these lands, because Romani, once they arrived in the Romanian polities, had to become the dependents of the Prince in a fundamental sense:

To be "native" (*pamintean*) in Rumanian principalities meant literally to be the owner of a piece of land (*pamint*). The new-comers to the Rumanian territories were prevented to have access to the right over the land, so that as "stranger" they became *de jure* dependent persons of the local Prince, a relation expressed by the payment of some specific taxes to the Prince ... The Prince was considered as the nominal owner of the whole territory of the Rumanian Principalities. Similarly the same Prince was considered as the nominal "owner" of the foreigners settled in their country, who were treated as part of the Prince's property.

(Gheorghe 17–18)

The dependency on the Prince in the manner Gheorghe describes appears, in some ways, to be again curiously homologous to the condition of medieval Jews, who were themselves dependents of the European monarchs in whose countries they lived, and who were bound by law and custom to each monarch who "owned" them and oversaw their protection and rights in exchange for taxes and tallages, in a kind of "royal serfdom" that was a peculiarly medieval institution, as we saw in Chapter 2. To our modern eyes this state of relative dependency might seem grievous – a contradiction to the concept of being a free people – but Gheorghe emphasizes there are important distinctions to be made:

> The Roma groups enjoyed a significant degree of freedom according to the norms and standards of the time. They were free to maintain their occupations and to move throughout the country to practise them. They maintained their customs, their community life and their leaders. It was like a "contract" between the Rumanian Princes and Roma's chiefs, a contract beneficial to both sides.
>
> (19)

These so-called "Princely Gypsies" or "Roma belonging to the Prince," according to Gheorghe, "maintained their rights and privileges" throughout the centuries in which the rest of the Romani population were abjected as slaves of the monasteries and boyars of Wallachia and Moldavia, until the abolition of Romani slavery in the nineteenth century (19).

Nevertheless, technically being the "property" of the Prince had certain unfortunate implications:

> As part of the Prince's "properties" (as they were foreigners in Rumanian Principalities), Roma families and groups . . . were also given to the monasteries and the boyars, as servants to assure the skills and the labour needed by the agricultural economy of the time . . . But what was donated by the Princes to the monasteries and boyars was . . . not the right of *property* over their persons, but the right . . . of the specific monasteries and/or boyars to collect the taxes (in work, money or goods) that the Roma were obliged to pay to the Princes. What was transferred from the Princes to the private owners was the relation of dependency which was limited and which included elements of freedom and rights.
>
> (Gheorghe 20–1)

Communities of medieval Jews, we saw in Chapter 2, were sometimes loaned out or temporarily mortgaged by monarchs to family members or to favorites, so that a son or a brother could profit from the taxes and moneys tendered by such "royal" Jews. Gheorghe's account of Romani dependency, and their transfers to new incumbents through donations and gifts, explains why "the first records on Roma in Rumanian Principalities tell us that at that time (the XIV century) Roma were in a position of *dependency* (something quite 'normal' in the social organization of those times), but not necessarily in a position of *slavery*" (Gheorghe 21).[27]

The earliest extant mention of princely donation to the monasteries dates from 1385: "In a deed issued that year, Dan I, the prince of Wallachia, amongst other things awards to the Tismana monastery . . . forty families of Gypsies [*atsigani*]" (Achim 13). These Romani are mentioned in all subsequent confirmations of the possessions of the monastery, "in 1387, 1391–92, circa 1392, 1439" (Achim 14). Gifts and donations were the principal means by which the Romanian monasteries acquired their Romani labor force (Achim 32; Marushiakova and Popov, "Gypsy Slavery" 94).

> In 1388, the Wallachian prince Mircea the Old donated to the Cozia monastery, the monastery that he founded, 300 dwellings of Gypsies. In general, in the fifteenth century, all the most important monasteries and boyars owned Gypsies as slaves ... In Moldavia, the Gypsies are mentioned for the first time in 1428 when prince Alexander the Good awards to the Bistrita monastery thirty-one families of Gypsies [*tsigani*].
>
> (Achim 14)

> In the course of the fifteenth century Gypsies were also mentioned as slaves at the monasteries of Visnevati (1429), Poiana and Moldovita (1434), Pobrat (4,000 [families] of Gypsies donated to the monastery by the Moldavian Prince Petru Voievode in 1444), Putna (11 [family groups] of Gypsies donated to the monastery by Prince Stefan cel Mare (Stephen the Great) in 1490), as well as in other monasteries.
>
> (Marushiakova and Popov, "Gypsy Slavery" 91)

Viorel Achim believes that the first princely donation of Romani families would actually have taken place earlier than 1385, in a deed of gift which has not been preserved, arguably "between 1371 and 1377" because the 1385 donation by Dan I to the monastery of the Holy Virgin in Tismana was in fact a *transfer* of possessions from the defunct Vodita monastery to Tismana (13).

Gheorghe estimates that the Romani "kept their state of freedom or at most a state of limited dependency some 150–200 years" after their arrival in the Romanian Principalities before falling into slavery (23). Gheorghe's maintenance of a careful distinction between the stages of relative freedom and unfreedom is prudent, since Achim indicates that the terms "slave" (*rob*) and "slavery" (*robie*) in fact "appear as such only at a relatively late stage," *slavery* being mentioned for the first time in a deed by the Moldavian prince Stephen II dated to September 30, 1445, and *slave* being attested for the first time in 1470 in a document issued by Stephen the Great (Achim 35; confirmed by Marushiakova and Popov, "Gypsy Slavery" 96).

All the careful calibration of rights and statuses, however, changed drastically with the deterioration of the Romanian economy after the capture and occupation of Romanian ports on the Danube and the Black Sea by the Ottoman Turks in 1484 and 1540. Toward the end of the fifteenth century and after, Panaitescu tells us, the flourishing transshipment trade of Romania "stopped almost completely," and the economy of the Principalities foundered. After the fall of Constantinople to the Ottomans in 1453, Wallachia and Moldavia, now transformed into "the Sultan's food treasury," also had to supply provisions to Istanbul, a city that "produced nothing" but commandeered "enormous quantities of food ... to nourish the population" (Panaitescu 66).[28]

There were numerous consequences to the tanking economies, including the impoverishment of most peasant landholders, and their subsequent descent into servitude and bondage, or what has been called a "second serfdom" (Panaitescu 66, Gheorghe 25):[29]

> there existed at this time two classes of big landowners – in the first place the monasteries, which for some considerable time had already owned numerous estates, all of which had come into their possession as holy gifts; and secondly the Boyards, the new owners of the

latifundia, acquired at the expense of the wretched peasants. And, in their treatment of the Gypsies, the Boyards followed in the footsteps of the Church.

(Panaitescu 67)

Falling into Slavery: The Romani in Southeastern Europe

From our vantage point in time, we might find the monastic enslavement of a race of people so shocking as to think this historical development bizarre and improbable. But Romani studies scholars assure us that the monasteries' need of slave labor was greater than that of the boyars, who were more readily able to coerce peasant agriculturalists to work land that the poor souls had formerly owned – land now commandeered by the boyars – with the peasants laboring as serfs, unfree bondsmen to their boyar masters.[30]

By contrast, the monasteries required manpower for a greater range of labor, including agricultural work, and had greater need of field slaves as well as house slaves and craftsmen. Gheorghe outlines the process by which the Romani labor force fell into slavery:

> The monasteries and the boyars obtained from the Prince the right to exempt Roma groups donated to them from the payment of the taxes which all Roma were obliged to pay as a guarantee of their freedom, be it a limited freedom. The monasteries and the boyars paid the taxes for the Roma settled on their domains, but with the price of extracting from them more and more non-paid work and services. In time, the initial limited and contractual dependency of Roma was transformed into an unlimited and hereditary dependency on the feudal private owners who managed also to subordinate ... the initially free communal villages of the native peasants. As the Roma were given to these owners together with such economic goods as land, animals, etc., Roma individuals began to be considered as economic goods also, juridically treated as "things," rather than as persons ... the owners ... felt entitled to use and abuse Roma, to extort a complete power and control over the persons and goods of Roma, except the formal right to kill them (although there were records of such cases). Treated as mere objects Roma were bought and sold, transmitted as inheritance and dowry. There were Roma who were exchanged for other goods, animate or not, like horses and cows, houses and gardens, domestic animals, etc.
>
> (21–2)

The distinction between a slave and the kind of "royal serf" that Gheorghe allows for, who is dependent on the monarch but possessed of certain freedoms and rights, is a juridical one: Unlike the crown dependents, slaves "had no status as legal persons" (Achim 35). In the eyes of the law, "Gypsy slaves were not defined as persons" (Marushiakova and Popov, "Gypsy Slavery" 96). "The slave was wholly the property of his master, figuring among his personal property" (Achim 35):

> The possessions of the slave (consisting mainly of cattle) were also at the discretion of the master. Masters were constantly abusing their rights, as slaves could at any time be punished with a beating or with prison without the need for the intervention of the state authorities.
>
> (Achim 35)

Slavery was an economic solution to which the monasteries and other large landowners resorted because it seemed a ready answer to workforce needs. Romani labor was already at hand, and the degeneration of the Romani labor force into slave status was merely a process of the erosion of rights:

> This process took place at a time when the technological level of the domestic agricultural economy was low and the supply of man-power was permanently in danger because of demographical fluctuations resulting from both the numerous wars of the Rumanian Principalities and also escaping from the service of the landlords. In such a context, Roma groups and people offered to the emerging feudal owners the perspective of a safe, cheap and qualified man-power. Roma were also numerous and among the few and most talented metal or wood-workers in the villages and in the feudal domains.
>
> (Gheorghe 21)

"Then began the hunt for the Gypsies and the holding of them down to the land," Panaitescu laments; "to prevent their escape from Walachia and Moldavia, they were made slaves by the Boyards as they had previously been by the monasteries" (68). Hancock provides a detailed list of the various categories of Romani slaves that devolved, as well as the type of labor extracted from them, noting that the primary division in practical terms was between *field* slaves and *house* slaves (*Pariah Syndrome* 16).[31] In general, field slaves had the worst fates:

> the Gypsies of the monasteries were worsely treated and exploited more than the Gypsies of boyars, as the monasteries had fewer native peasant[s] to work their fields. Among the Gypsies of the boyars, those who worked in agriculture (the "field Gypsies") had a harder life than the "servant Gypsies" of the boyars ... Among the latter category there were many craftsmen who were better treated.
>
> (Gheorghe 22)

We see that the economic model accounting for Romani slavery emphasizes rationality and functionalism, and usefully recognizes temporal intervals in the progressive erosion of rights:

> Roma's falling under slavery was a gradual process of slow transformation from the Roma's initial limited fiscal dependency on the Rumanian Princes into an unlimited personal dependency on the big landlords of the country, the monasteries and the boyars. Formally speaking, the whole process of Roma's enslavement was an *abuse* committed by the feudal landlords, without any legalistic base and legitimation; initially an individual and local abuse gradually became a generalised "de facto" situation, part of a vaguely defined "obiceiul pamintului" (the land's custom). Much later, at the end of the XVIII century to the beginning of the XIX century, this was recorded into a sort of "slave's code," the interpretation of which depends on the owner's interests.
>
> (Gheorghe 23)

Importantly, Sam Beck argues that the economic role played by Romani slavery in the Romanian polities was not epiphenomenal, but constitutive and formative – first for the feudal economy in the medieval period, and later for Romanian nationalism and statism in the modern period. "Gypsies (Tigani) were central to the creation of the Romanian feudal economy," Beck maintains, and the monasteries played a key role in the development of slavery by generating the dynamic through which the feudal economy of Romania operated (60–1).

Up to now, we have seen how the operations of religious discourse and political theology time and again conduced to the emergence of a people as a race in the medieval period. Here, we see how the *economic structure* of monastic holdings in Eastern Europe powered the creation of a race of worker slaves.

As owners of large estates, the monasteries of the Romanian principalities extracted slave labor from a race of landless immigrants and "held them down to the land," as Panaitescu expressively puts it. Without this pitiless labor, Panaitescu concludes, "the great wealth which was enjoyed" by the monasteries and their complicitous fellow landowners "would never have existed" (69). Questions of morality and ethics, right and wrong, fairness, justice, religious principles, and spiritual ideals appear not to have been obstacles to the Romanian monasteries' enslavement of the Romani people.

Monasteries also found creative ways to enlarge their slave population organically:

> Gypsy slaves in monasteries were originally donated by rulers and boyars, which was a widespread practice. Thus, monasteries in Wallachia and Moldavia became large slave owners. Another way of acquiring slaves by monasteries was that of allowing for their marriages with free people. As a result previously free spouses of Gypsy slaves became slaves themselves, and the status was passed onto their children.
> (Marushiakova and Popov, "Gypsy Slavery" 94)

Not surprisingly, we have few particulars of what the lives of Romani slaves were like in the medieval and early modern period. But most "Princely Gypsies" appear to have been able to move freely, practicing a variety of crafts: "As for the princely slaves, with the exception of the few slaves who worked at the princely court, almost all of them wandered the country in search of means of making a living" (Achim 52). This traveling workforce possessing unhindered mobility may well have been numerous (Gheorghe 19, Achim 52). How these "princely slaves" should be distinguished from the "free" Romani who were also itinerent and practicing their trades, and paying taxes to or performing acts of labor for the state, is still an unanswered question.

But Gheorghe, whose scholarship has been considered authoritative and foundational in Romani studies, reiterates that the "Roma groups belonging to the Princes" experienced largely "a sort of administrative and fiscal dependency with few, if any, of the personal and humiliating dependency usually denoted by the term 'slavery'" (20). Marushiakov and Popov concur, citing the evidence of recorded behavior: "numerous Gypsies presented by the prince to monasteries and boyars escaped from their new owners and joined the ... Gypsies of the prince" (103). Such shunning of slave-masters and flight to the prince speaks for itself. "The Roma who experienced real slavery," Gheorghe concludes, "were those who belonged to the private feudal owners: the monasteries and the boyars" (20).

Among the private feudal owners, the type of labor to which a slave was deployed crucially determined the conditions of life. A small category of slaves, known as *Laiesi*, were allowed to become seasonal itinerant craftsmen like the majority of the "princely slaves," traveling and practicing their crafts and returning to work on their masters' estates in the winter (Marushiakova and Popov, "Gypsy Slavery" 94, 103). "On the whole," the taxation imposed on these itinerant slaves of the prince and the private estates "was lighter than that of the rest of the population" (Marushiakova and Popov, "Gypsy Slavery" 103).[32]

But Marushiakova and Popov conclude that "Rather few [monastic slaves] were nomads"; "the majority toiled on the monasteries' fields" ("Gypsy Slavery" 94).[33] The conditions of life experienced by a Romani slave in the principalities were thus determined by *who* owned the slave, and to what *type of work* the slave was put.[34]

Among the "princely slaves" whom Gheorghe and others find to have been more fortunate than those of the monasteries and boyars, there was an exceptional individual who sought a way out of bondage and forged a remarkable life, as Achim relates (41):

> One of the princes of Moldova, Stefan Razvan, was himself of Gypsy origin. In a text originating from Michael the Brave, we learn that Razvan was the son of a princely slave woman from Wallachia. He managed to become a boyar, was sent in delegation to Constantinople, became hetman in the Cossack and Polish armies and finally occupied the throne of Moldavia for a short period of time (April to August 1595).

Marushiakova and Popov offer a thick description of the ambiguous circumstances and complex negotiations that produced this extraordinary Romani individual's fate:

> One story says that [Stefan Razvan] was a son of a Romanian serf mother, while his father was a Gypsy slave of Prince Mihai Vitezul of Wallachia. Another story claims that he was a son of a Gypsy slave mother owned by the Prince of Wallachia, but fathered by an unknown person, probably a high-ranking court official. As a child, Stefan was a slave of Anastasi, the Metropolitan of Moldavia in 1572–1578, who gave him a good education. Subsequently, in his will, the metropolitan freed him. Stefan Razvan's life was turbulent. He became a boyar (in the Orthodox world, nobility was not a closed category), and as a government official he was sent on a diplomatic mission to Istanbul. Then he established himself in Zaporozhia, where Cossacks lived. Stefan Razvan reached the position of Hetman, or commander in chief of the Cossack forces. Next he served in the Polish-Lithuanian army under King Sigismund III Bathori . . . and became a colonel and a noble. Stefan Razvan returned to Moldavia, where he became the commander of the personal guards of Prince Aron Tiranul. In the internal strife of Wallachia and Moldavia in 1595, Stefan Razvan succeeded in overthrowing the prince and ascended to the throne for five months (from April to August 1595), thanks to Poland-Lithuania's support. While he successfully fought against the Ottoman armies in Wallachia, capturing Bucharest, Giurgiu, Braila, and besieging Tirgoviste and Izmail; boyar Ieremia Movila . . . was proclaimed Prince of Moldavia, also with Polish-Lithuanian support. Stefan Razvan returned to Moldavia, but 14 December 1595 he was defeated in the battle of Areni by the united armies of King Sigismund III and Prince Iremia Movila, which led to his subsequent execution on 6 March 1596.
>
> ("Gypsy Slavery" 98)

Marushiakova and Popov point out that Stefan Razvan's life was spectacularly atypical ("Gypsy Slavery" 98). More often, what little information that exists conveys less than felicitous outcomes, and sometimes made its way into the historical record because of its sensational nature. Hancock recounts the savage cruelty of the infamous Vlad Tepes III, "better remembered as Vlad the Impaler, who [returned] to the Wallachian throne in 1476. He disposed of some *scindromes*, or Gypsy slaves, presumably for sport, thus":

> He invited them to a festival, made them all drunk, and threw them into the fire. Another amusement of his was the construction of an enormous cauldron, into which he thrust his

victims. Then, filling it with water, he made it boil, and took pleasure in the anguish of the sufferers. When the people whom he impaled writhed in agony, he had their hands and feet nailed to the posts. Some ... were compelled to eat [a] man roasted.

(Hancock, Pariah Syndrome 22)

Renowned for his exorbitant, promiscuous cruelty, Vlad the Impaler may have been a uniquely heinous master, so Hancock offers more quotidian examples. For instance, among the house slaves kept by nobles, "there was a category called the skopici, Gypsy males who had been castrated as boys and whose job it was to drive the coaches of the women of the aristocracy without their being in fear of molestation" (Hancock, Pariah Syndrome 22). Hancock also points out that the presence of later generations of light-skinned, fair-haired Romani house slaves very likely testified to the sexual abuse of Romani women slaves by their European owners (Pariah Syndrome 21–2).

With few exceptions, accounts of the lives of Romani slaves issue from later periods, where there is more testimonial literature. If we like, we can try to imagine from these later accounts – which are compiled in more modern, and thus presumptively more progressive times – what the lives of Romani slaves in earlier eras might have been like. Hancock has a description of punishment:

> The boyars had a special penal code for Gypsies; beating on the soles of the feet until the flesh hung in shreds ... when a runaway was caught, his neck was placed in an iron band lined with sharp points so that he could neither move his head nor lie down to rest. The boyars had no right to kill their slaves, but there was nothing said about slowly torturing them to death. No law forbade the boyar to take the most beautiful girls as his mistresses, or to separate wives from husbands, and children from parents.

(Pariah Syndrome 20)

Presented at greater length is an account recorded in the diary of a French journalist, Félix Colson, describing a visit to the home of a boyar in 1839, where Romani house slaves served:

> When our traveler arrives, he is led to a couch, whereupon six young women appear. Discreetly, and with care, they wash his hands, while others serve him with refreshments. Their skins are hardly brown; some of them are blonde and beautiful. Handsome too are the boys who, in groups of three, will light his pipe. No, the domestics do not work themselves to death; it's not unusual some times to find a hundred or more working in the same household ... could this kind of life be Heaven on Earth for them?

(Hancock, Pariah Syndrome 20)

Despite Colson's patronizing smugness and insufferable facetiousness, Hancock points out that the journalist observed a less happy scene at the dinner table, where he admits: "Misery is so clearly painted on the faces of these slaves that, if you'd happened to glance at one, you'd lose your appetite" (Hancock, Pariah Syndrome 21). There is more to come:

> The Gypsy slaves are addressed by Christian names. Basil seems to be the most common, but they are also given house-names, such as Pharoah, Bronze, Dusky, Dopey or Toad, or for the women, Witch, Camel, Dishrag or Whore ... Never does a group revolt. In the evening, the master makes his choice among the beautiful girls – maybe he will offer some of them to the guest – whence these light-skinned, blonde-haired Gypsies ... The next morning at dawn, the [visitor] is awakened by piercing shrieks: it is punishment time. The current

penalty is a hundred lashes for a broken plate or a badly-curled lock of hair . . . it is at this time that the abominable *falague* is finally outlawed: this was when the slaves were hung up in the air and the soles of their feet were shredded with whips made of bull sinews.

(Hancock, *Pariah Syndrome* 20–1)[35]

If it makes us ill to read this modern, post-Enlightenment account, perhaps we are better served by *not* having descriptions of Romani slaves' lives from the medieval and early modern period. Custom, or customary law ("the tradition of the land"), was equally draconian: "Gypsy slaves could not marry without permission. Members of the same family were sold separately, and children often taken away" (Hancock, *Pariah Syndrome* 24). A slew of evolving laws more clearly disciplined marriages contracted between Romanian persons and Romani slaves in later periods. A proclamation of 1776 inveighing against such marriages indicated that the children of these mixed unions would be slaves and that "any priest who has had the audacity to perform such marriages, which is a great and everlasting wicked act . . . will be removed from his post and severely punished," while a law of 1785 prohibited the unions altogether because they were "causing individuals with Rumanian blood to become slaves" (Hancock, *Pariah Syndrome* 25).

Hancock lists a selection of statutes governing Romani slavery in the Wallachian and Moldavian penal codes of the nineteenth century. In the Wallachian Penal Code of 1818, "Gypsies are born slaves," and anyone "born of a mother who is a slave, is also a slave." Any owner "has the right to sell or give away his slaves," and, in a reminder of medieval dispensations, a statute specifies: Any "Gypsy without an owner is the property of the Prince" (Hancock, *Pariah Syndrome* 28). The Moldavian Penal Code of 1833 stipulates that "Legal unions cannot take place between free persons and slaves" and marriage "between slaves cannot take place without their owner's consent." The price of a slave, by this time, is regulated: It "must be fixed by the Tribunal, according to his age, condition and profession" (Hancock, *Pariah Syndrome* 29).[36]

Sam Beck stresses that "anti-Gypsy prejudice in Romania" over time became "central to the formation of the Romanian state" (54). "Gypsies came to be seen as universally marginal sub-humans," enabling Romanians increasingly to "identify themselves in contradistinction to their low-class status, a process that helped shape the Romanian national states and Romanian ethnic identity" (Beck 54, 61). If Beck is correct, the emergence of the Romani people in Romania as a slave race conduced both to the development of the feudal economy and to the development of Romanian nationalism and statism. Provocatively, Beck poses a class-related, economic question to solicit future work:

Unique to Romania is the ethnic quality of slavery, an aspect of the Romanian social formation that by the 17th and 18th centuries appeared as an accepted condition of Gypsies, paralleling the ideas of "natural" inferiority of certain races that dominated capitalist development in western Europe . . . Is it possible that the acceptance of this kind of segmentation of labor, a cultural division of labor based on color and ethnicity and the idea of a "natural" slavery, was an element in the experience of capitalist penetration and exploitation of Central, Eastern, and Balkan Europe?

(57)

Manumission would follow, in multistep processes during the 1840s and 1850s, for the Romani slaves. In the 1840s, estimates of the number of Romani slaves in Romania ranged from 250,000 to 262,000 (Marushiakova and Popov, "Gypsy Slavery" 109–10). Not surprisingly, perhaps, the Romanian church participated unevenly in the public discourse on manumission:

> The Orthodox hierarchy also contributed to the abolitionist movement. For instance, Eufrasin Poteka, who as early as 1827, in an Easter sermon publicly appealed to Prince Grigore Gika to abolish slavery by quoting appropriate passages from the Bible ... Nevertheless the position of the Church was not always consistent. After all the monasteries were the largest slave owners.
>
> (Marushiakova and Popov, "Gypsy Slavery" 113)

Moldavia began to free its slaves in 1844 and conclusively freed all slaves by 1855; Wallachia freed its slaves in legislative stages from 1843 to 1856 (Achim 108–112, Marushiakova and Popov, "Gypsy Slavery" 114–116). By 1856, all categories of slaves in the Principalities would be freed; at the time of their manumission, Achim holds, "the Gypsies represented 7 per cent of the population of the principalities" (2).[37]

Panaitescu suggests that, like their descent into slavery, the eventual "liberation of the Gypsies" was also primarily "due to economic causes," mischievously adding: "perhaps their maintenance was beginning to cost too much" (70, 71). Others, like Gheorghe, more commonly prefer to emphasize political pressures and social movements, and the changing of the times: "the emancipation of Roma *robie* (slaves) in the XIX Rumanian Principalities appears as part of the broader international abolitionist movement of that time" (26). Marushiakova and Popov appraise the international pressures that helped to bring internal change in Romania, deepening a national sense of shame and a vision of Romania's backwardness, relative to the nations of the West:

> The European abolitionist movement fighting for ending slavery in the colonies, and the abolitionists in the United States also exerted an influence on the public opinion. It was not by chance that the first American book translated into Romanian was *Uncle Tom's Cabin* ... Numerous speeches and publications in Europe about Gypsy slavery brought about a strong social reaction. For example, the Swiss Emil de Guggsberg, in his book published in Iasi in 1841, directly posed the question: 'Will anyone ever dare think of your nation as civilized, [when] one can read an advertisement in some of your papers, announcing "For sale, Young Gypsy"?'
>
> ("Gypsy Slavery" 114)

David Crowe offers more graphic particulars:

> One 1834 scene described the horror that stimulated some Romanians to begin to reconsider the institution. Barbu Stirbei, a wealthy landowner, needed funds to redo his palace and thus auctioned 3,000 Gypsy slaves in Bucharest to pay for the renovations. At the auction, "passers-by quicken[ed] their steps and lower[ed] their eyes so that they [didn't] have to look at the men and women tearing at their rags in anguish. Dishevelled, dark-skinned, these are Gypsies. You can't escape the entreaties of the mothers whose children are being torn from them, nor their sobs and screams of fear, nor their curses; you can't escape the cracking of the whips breaking down their stubborn resistance to the separations inevitably to come."
>
> (114)

Stirbei, it turned out, "was so disturbed by public reaction to the sale of his *robi* that he 'hurriedly suggested abolition as a means of regaining face – but this was at once overridden by the boyars'" (Crowe 114). Resistance to abolition, however, bucked the rising tides of national shame and sense of ignominy:

> Gypsy slavery had come to symbolize the backwardness of Moldavia and Wallachia, while efforts to eradicate it indicated broader changes in the provinces' political, social, and economic landscapes. In 1837, Mihail Kogalniceanu, the liberal writer, social critic, and later one of the architects of Romanian nationhood, described his childhood memories of *robi*: "I saw human beings wearing chains on their arms and legs, others with iron clamps around their foreheads, and still others with metal collars about their necks. Cruel beatings, and other punishments such as starvation, being hung over smoking fires, solitary imprisonment and being thrown naked into the snow or the frozen rivers, such was the fate of the wretched Gypsy."
>
> (Crowe 115)

Scholars of Romanian slavery still disagree on a number of central issues, but they agree that the Romani of Wallachia and Moldavia were abjected in a sociopolitical and economic culture in which *their very name and ethnoracial identity became synonymous with "slave"* (Gheorghe 24; Beck 54; Achim 29).[38] *To be a Romani was to be a slave.* An act abolishing serfdom in Moldavia in 1749 even announced, "*only Gypsies* are slaves" (Marushiakova and Popov, "Gypsy Slavery" 108, emphasis added). And slavery produced identity erasure of a fundamental kind: Less even than a serf, a slave was not a human subject under the law, recognized by law as possessing the status and rights of a person. Romani in the polities of Wallachia and Moldavia were *a race of slaves*, humans invisible to the law of the land and indispensable to the work of the land: non-persons living under erasure.

Free to Embrace the Ethnoracial: The Romani, and Our Endings and Beginnings

In spite of Romani abjection, an extraordinary outcome was the tough resilience of these indomitable peoples:

> What is outstanding in the case of Roma's history in the Rumanian Principalities is the fact that in spite of their hard conditions of life, they managed to upkeep, to reproduce and to enrich their cultural heritage and distinct identity. That is why many of the present-day Roma in Rumania, the descendants of the former slaves, display distinct cultural traits and communal life, as well as a strong identification as Roma.
>
> (Gheorghe 23)

Our sojourn into medieval race has made a practice of emphasizing how operations of race-making proceeded from the outside: how differences among humans were selectively essentialized in absolute and fundamental terms, and attached to a human group to characterize it definitively, positioning the group within a hierarchy of power relations.

Like the Jews, Muslims, Africans, Native Americans, Mongols, and others we have considered, the Romani of Western and Eastern Europe were indeed identified, defined, and positioned in this way, whether as unwelcome itinerants chased from town to town or as indispensable slaves held down to the land, with labor forcibly extracted from them.[39]

But the Romani iconize the tenacity of race and racial constructions not just from the oppressor's point of view. Implicitly embracing a racialism of their own, the Romani seem to have clung to their own version of racial identity: an identity that shifted and remade itself, as groups of Romani spread through the Near East and the countries of the West, telling and retelling stories about themselves, adjusting to hostile environments, and securing what means of life were available.[40] That adherence to an ethnoracial identity of protean and shifting particulars has seemed baffling and paradoxical to some, such as Angus Fraser.

Lacking a "promised land as a focus of their dreams" and without a "priestly caste" to act as cultural and religious leaders," Fraser intones, with no "appointed custodians of ethnic traditions" and "no texts enshrining a corpus of beliefs and code of morality," or even a "recognized standard for their language," the Romani nonetheless persisted as a distinctive group, surviving across the centuries and continuing to identify as an ethnoracial community in diaspora, against the odds and against their own heterogeneity.

Fraser, of course, is alert to the dynamics of persecution as a force for consolidating group identity through a circling of the wagons – arguably a prime reason why Romani felt themselves apart from all other peoples – but is still driven to admiration:

> In being uprooted from India and maintaining a mobile existence, a changing identity had become inevitable. Their ethnicity was to be refashioned and remoulded by a multitude of influences, internal and external. They would assimilate innumerable elements which had nothing to do with India, and they would eventually cease to be, in any meaningful way, Indians; their identity, their culture would, however – regardless of all the transformations – remain sharply distinct from that of the *gadzé* who surrounded them and on whom their economic existence depended.
>
> (44)

Yes, the presence and actions of *gadzé* served, and no doubt still serve, to prod the Romani into identifying themselves as *not-gadzé* (and scholars have also noted the assimilation of some Romani into the populations in which they lived and their ethnoracial disappearance upon assimilation).[41] Fraser also appositely points out how mutable and fluid Romani identity has been – *has had to be* – after the migrations from India.

For us, such necessary refashionings, adaptations, and transformations in Romani identity eloquently thematize the fluidity of *all* human identities, individual and group, which are always, inevitably, in process – undergoing transition and change. The racial history of the Romani thus expressively dramatizes the fluidity of human ethnoracial identity while also vividly attesting its persistence, and the desire of a community *to belong to a race*, to be part of an ethnoracial group, however dispersed or mutable.

With the Romani, therefore, *we have seen a race being made* in the course of a people's migration and diaspora – a race-making issued not only by those who persecuted and exploited them, but also at the insistence of the Romani themselves. We thus arrive, at the end of our long journey, to marvel at a population of humans who decided to exercise *their will* as power, even in the face of historic conditions of extreme powerlessness. *Race as self-identification* – not race that is intrinsic in biology, DNA, or the somatic envelope, or forged by colonization, economic conditions, war, religion, law, theology, mythology, tradition, medicine, or science – might seem to us a peculiarly modern, nonmedieval phenomenon: race embedded in an act of will, a modality of group performance, or even a product, say, of census data collection today.

But the medieval Romani would prove us wrong. With the example of the Romani before us, we see that race can be made from the outside, *against* a people, or from the inside, *by* a people whose identity in the end could not, despite custom and law and the abjection of slavery, be erased and destroyed.[42]

At the end of our long journey we see that the story of race does not end, but re-begins again and again, finding its way through strange corridors, and always with surprises.

Notes

1 Ian Hancock, one of the foremost Romani scholars today, suggests that "Romani" would be the preferred name for the peoples who are also sometimes referred to as "Roma" – Roma being, he indicates, "actually only a plural masculine noun" (*We* xx). Hancock gives the plural of "Romani" as "Romanies."

2 If the fifth-century attribution of this migration from India is to be trusted, linguistic evidence in the form of grammatical genders, Hancock argues, would identify these early migrants as Dom or Domari, and not Romani (*We* 7). These are not trivial disagreements, since the Dom or Domari "may well have been of Dravidian" and not of Indo-Aryan origin (Fraser 26). Moreover, the name *Dom* preserves a caste/class status: "There are references to Doms as musicians as far back as the sixth century. In Sanskrit the word took on the sense of 'man of low caste living by singing and music.' In modern Indian tongues the corresponding words have a variety of similar meanings: e.g., 'caste of wandering musicians' (Sindhi); 'menial' (Lahnda); 'strolling musician' (Punjabi); 'low-caste black-skinned fellow' (West Pahari)" (Fraser 25). As supporting evidence, Fraser points to the occupations of Domari in India today ("vagrant tribes, with a variety of trades and activities – basket-maker, scavenger, bard, musician, smith and metal-worker") that resemble the occupations of medieval Romani, and suggests: "The name could preserve for us the original caste and status of the ancestors of the Asiatic and European Gypsies" (25). Fraser thus assumes Romani to have been low-caste and itinerant in India before moving westward (43).

 By contrast, Hancock cites scholars who argue that "the presence of native Indian words in Romani for such concepts as 'king,' 'house,' 'door,' 'sheep,' 'pig,' 'chicken,' 'landowner' . . . point to settled, rather than nomadic, peoples" (*We* 14). Hancock also points out that "Indian scholars have observed that many aspects of Romani culture closely parallel high-caste behaviour rather than low-caste, a further argument against the *dom* or low-caste origins hypothesis" (*We* 14). Finally, although Fraser prefers room for "dispute as to exactly who, in terms of caste, occupation and ethnic origin, left the Indian subcontinent a thousand years or more ago" (28), the scientific analysis of blood types, Hancock argues, concludes that the Romani of today "are genetically most like the Rajput populations in India and least like the present-day Dom" (*We* 14, 13).

3 The translation of the *Shanameh* that Fraser quotes is even more dismissive and contemptuous of these musician-migrants from India: The Luri have to "sing for the amusement of the high and the low," and "wander the world, seeking employment, associating with dogs and wolves, and thieving on the road by day and by night" (Fraser 35).

4 Hancock cites geneticists studying Romani and Indian blood types, and also adduces contemporary anthropological evidence: Among ethnic groups in modern India who claim descent from the Rajputs, the Banjara say that "numbers of their ancestors left India forever at the time of Ghaznavid invasions . . . spreading out to the four points of the compass," and Banjara today

"recognise a relationship with Romanies," sometimes attending Romani functions in Europe, and inviting the Romani to their own meetings in India (*We* 13).

5 Fraser issues a reminder that we should keep in mind, however, that the movements of human populations across a continent are untidy, irregular, and not fully knowable processes that do not resemble the necessarily neat tracings heuristically deployed by scholars in analyzing the past: "The danger is that the talk of successive 'splits' in language and separations into different 'bands' [of Romani peoples] risks creating an unconscious image of the Gypsy migration as consisting of hordes of people trooping out of India and, at certain points along their route, neatly breaking into two subdivisions each of which proceeds on its divergent but generally westward way. Such a frame of mind is encouraged by the maps which have sometimes been produced, with arrows showing the probable lines of advance of the early Gypsy migrations. It cannot have been quite like that in practice" (42).

6 An accusation by fifteenth-century German travelers who visited Modon in the Peloponnese calls the Romani liars who *claim* to have come from Egypt. Travelers to Modon such as Bernhard von Breydenbach (1483) and Alexander Pfalzgraf bei Rhein (1495) intimated that a hill behind the town called Mount Gyppe, and not Egypt, was the genuine provenance of the Romani: "Near Modon lies a hill called Gype . . . Some people call this hill and its appurtenances Little Egypt" (Winstedt 61). Might the name "Gypsy," with its etymology supposedly denoting Egypt but really attributable to a hill called Gype near Modon, be somewhat analogous to "Saracens": a name, as we saw in Chapter 3, that characterizes a people as liars while in the act of lying – fabricating a story – about them?

7 Soulis also points to a group of "Egyptian" acrobats, described by Nicephorus Gregoras, who "appeared in Constantinople during the reign of Andronicus II (1282–1328)," as likely to have been Romani. This group, a veritable Cirque du Soleil, gave spectacular performances that were "stupendous and full of wonder," that featured tightrope walking, trick riding on well-trained horses, complicated dances, and astounding acrobatics that must have involved considerable skill and practice. Despite the dangers of the acts, children were also performers. Nicephoras Gregoras concludes: "Having collected much money from the spectators, they wandered all over the world, both for profit and to display their own art. Moving from Byzantium, they travelled through Thrace and Macedonia and went as far as Gadeira [i.e. Gades in Spain], and they made almost the whole world a theater for their art" (148–9).

8 As late as the eighteenth century, a writer "described Romanies as 'black horrid men . . . the dark brown or olive coloured skin of the Gipseys, with their white teeth appearing between their red lips, may be a disgusting sight to an European, unaccustomed to such objects'" (Hancock, *We* 56). Hancock sums up part of our discussion in Chapter 4 succinctly: "The Church also viewed negatively the appearance of the first Romanies, because mediaeval Christian doctrine associated light with purity and darkness with sin. The earliest church records documenting the arrival of Romanies alluded to the swarthiness of their complexion and the inherent evil which that supposedly demonstrated" (*We* 56–7).

9 Soulis itemizes the baron's jurisdiction over Romani who were resident in Parga, La Bastia, Butrinto, Sopoto, and Chimara (158). His powers were considerable: He could "send any of his Gypsy serfs into exile, confine them in prison, make them galley slaves, or use them for corvée work" (158). Romani attachment to the land also brought many fiscal burdens (see Soulis 158).

10 Winstedt speculates that the Romani or *Romiti*, as a fifteenth-century manuscript calls them (59), may have derived their name from "Romania," "a name which once embraced the whole Byzantine Empire, but had come to be confined roughly to modern Greece," but refuses to connect the Romani to Romany wine or the "wyne of Romeney," though "it is very tempting to connect the two" (62). That temptation to connect, he acknowledges, is because certain places, such as Modon, were famous *both* for their Romani population *and* their Romany wine (59). But Winstedt, in a

spectacular demonstration of racial politics masquerading as scholarly opinion, decides that the Romani "presence in the special wine-growing districts can only be regarded as a coincidence. Perhaps, indeed, the existence of the wine drew them thither ... They are thirsty souls that dwell in tents, and not over energetic. Had they had a hand in its making, there would probably have been little to export" (63).

11 Winstedt issues the cautionary reminder that "such pictures are of course always suspicious, as the artist may have drawn them from memory," but deems the artist in this instance reliable, based on another of the artist's illustrations – "a five-foot picture of Venice," which Winstedt pronounces accurate (60). Fraser and Winstedt have plates of the illustration, Fraser on page 52 (plate 5) and Winstedt between pages 60 and 61.

12 We may recall the Mandeville author's recommendation of Jaffa as the "closest port to the city of Jerusalem," from which the holy city is only a day and a half away (Higgins, *Book* 20; Deluz 125). Modon is thus ideally positioned on one of the chief routes to the Holy Land, a route recommended by the Mandeville author to his multitudes of readers for centuries.

13 Hancock's chronology of Romani arrival in Western Europe lists their first appearance only in Hildesheim, Germany, in 1407, after which they possibly appear in Hesse in 1414. In 1416, he observes, the first "anti-Gypsy law [was] issued in Germany. Forty-eight such laws are passed between this date and 1774" ("Gypsy History" 11).

14 Fraser arrives at this conclusion, but – perhaps because he does not recognize Indic pieties? – frames the whole thing as an exploitative ruse, rather than an act of cultural translation: "Perhaps it was the Gypsies' acquaintance with pilgrims at places such as Modon that led them later to adopt that guise when they needed a cover-story to facilitate their arrival in western Europe" (53).

15 Due to obvious restrictions of length, I cannot in this chapter offer an account of how the Romani fared in every country of Europe, but Fraser has a comprehensive country-by-country account covering the fifteenth and sixteenth centuries.

16 There is also a "prince" of Latingham in Egypt, and a "king" of Little Egypt (Fraser 70, 103, 104). Fraser finally totals up "some two dozen different names of Gypsy leaders" (80). It is possible, of course, that some of the time, the documents that record Romani arrivals are themselves making the cultural translations. Fraser, however, shows a practice of self-naming when the Romani arrive that is widespread and ubiquitously repeated all over Europe, suggesting Romani, rather European, practices in identifying Romani leaders.

17 Macfie ("Gypsy Visit") scrutinizes the evidence of passports carried by the Romani, said to be issued by Pope Martin V, which guaranteed safe conduct and ordered "every bishop and mitred abbot to give them one payment of ten 'livres tournois'" (112). The surviving papal registers of Martin V contain no record of letters granted by the pope, but Macfie cites a Vatican official who cautions that the papal archives "have suffered many losses, so that it does not follow that a given document which is not to be found there to-day never existed there" ("Gypsy Visit" 114).

18 As we have seen, Winstedt attempted to shed some light on the curious repeated mention in the historical record that the Romani issued from "Egypt" (and thus were "Egyptians" – a name subsequently abbreviated to "Gypsies") by proposing that a hill near Greek Modon, called "Gype" or "Gyppe," was the "Little Egypt" from which the Romani issued. He cites fifteenth-century travelers to Modon such as Grünemberg (1486) who attest that "all Gypsies had 'their origin thence, and their home there'" (61). Winstedt seems to accept that their putative Egyptian provenance was thus a lie cultivated by the Romani themselves, rather than a tale assigned to them by outsiders, since the Romani, it seems, really came from the "Little Egypt" of Mount "Gyppe," so called, if we believe the stories told by the European travelers he cites.

19 In one of the few glimpses of their portable lodgings, the journal of Jean Aubrion tells us that at Metz in 1494, 200 "Egyptians" pitched their tents on the banks of the Moselle in September, joined two days later by another 300 (Fraser 93).

20 Fraser speculates that James IV or V seems to be the most promising candidate for this dramatic cure by the unnamed Romani healer: "James V, when he married his first wife, the eldest daughter of François I, was absent for eight and a half months from Scotland in France (1536–7). Some such incident would help to explain the royal favour shown to Gypsies in Scotland at a time when most other monarchs were becoming decidedly less tolerant of them" (120).

21 See Hancock's "The 'Gypsy' Stereotype" on the so-called "seductive qualities" of Romani women and the sexualization of them, especially in the postmedieval period.

22 Romani and Jew are spectacularly conflated in a 1517 burlesque epic, *Baldus*, by the Benedictine monk Teofilo Folengo in the Marquisate of Mantua, in which a Romani character "by the name of Cingar, a cheat, an assassin, a street brigand, a thief" is also "a scoundrel who mints fake coins and subtly files down real ones" (Fraser 107).

23 The priest-chronicler Andreas of Ratisborn, in his journal entry for 1424, has an earlier version of this story that does not specify Romani guilt, but instead likens Romani exile in Europe to the exile of the Lord when fleeing from Herod: "they said that they had been exiled as a sign or remembrance of the flight of Our Lord into Egypt when he was fleeing from Herod, who sought to slay him. But the common people said they were spies in the country" (Fraser 75). In Andreas' account we may be glimpsing a transitional stage of the story – and also, ominously, an accusation of espionage already appearing early in Germany.

24 Though the composite name "Romania" only came into use in the nineteenth century, I follow scholarly conventions that use the name in discussing the Romani in these lands in premodernity.

25 There is some disagreement over how the Romani became enslaved in the Danubian principalities. I adhere in this chapter to the arguments of Gheorghe, Panaitescu, and Hancock, who are treated by Romani studies scholars as authoritative and are frequently cited. I also cite recent scholarship by Marushiakova and Popov – who offer an even-handed, carefully considered analysis of the evidence – and Achim for occasional support.

26 Marushiakova and Popov modify this claim: They believe that by the second half of the fifteenth century "there were no free Gypsies in Wallachia and Moldavia" ("Gypsy Slavery" 93).

27 Not all Romani studies scholars make this calibrated distinction between *dependency*, with its modulated freedoms and rights, and outright slavery, as Gheorghe does. Hancock, for instance, considers the legal documentation of this period as attesting already to Romani slavery: "The earliest legal documentation referring to Gypsies as slaves date back to the reigns of Rudolph IV and Stephan Dusan (Uros IV), 1331–1355, who made one fifth of their number the property of the monasteries and landowners ... They are referred to variously as *sclavi, scindromi* or *robie* in the documents, Rumanian and Slavic terms meaning 'slave'" (*Pariah Syndrome* 16). Achim, too, does not distinguish between the early state of dependency that Gheorghe describes and the later state of full slavery, but believes the Romani to have fallen into slavery immediately upon their arrival in these lands. "From the first attestations of their presence in Wallachia and Moldavia," Achim declares, "the Gypsies were slaves" (27).

This is a position that makes it harder to explain the attraction of immigration by Romani to the Romanian polities, and Panaitescu's economic argument seems to offer a more efficient rationale. Achim, however, does allow that in Transylvania, the majority of Romani "were a kind of 'royal serfs,' directly dependent on the king" – with the only obligations imposed on them being the requirement "to pay taxes and to provide certain services for the State" (43). This condition of "royal serfdom," we might notice, seems very similar to the status of the "Princely Gypsies" in Wallachia and Moldavia described by Gheorghe.

28 The vassal status of Wallachia and Moldavia under the Ottomans "meant the payment of an annual tribute to the empire and the approval ... of the candidates for the princely thrones" (Marushiakova and Popov, "Gypsy Slavery" 89). Marushiakova and Popov cite a 1480 record of Romani being used for agriculture, and follow Achim in deducing that large-scale use of Romani

as field hands proceeded largely in the sixteenth century, which "coincided with the founding of the large estates specialized in the production of wheat for the Ottoman Empire" ("Gypsy Slavery" 107–8).

29 "The stopping of the transport trade had very serious consequences in all the countries which had benefited by this traffic. Poland rapidly fell into decay in the second half of the sixteenth century; Hungary collapsed after the battle of Mohacz (1562), after which she became a Turkish protectorate; while its cessation in Walachia and Moldavia decided the unhappy fate of the majority of peasants and affected the fate of the Gypsies who had arrived more than 200 years before" (Panaitescu 66–67).

30 Like Panaitescu, Marushiakova and Popov concur that the monasteries largely used their Romani slaves as field slaves, but unlike Panaitescu, they believe that "Gypsies living on boyars' estates worked mainly as servants. Only a smaller number of them worked the land" ("Gypsy Slavery" 94). In the modern period, however, they agree that the boyars resorted to using the Romani more extensively for agricultural labor and objected to Romani manumission and emancipation in the nineteenth century because their estates needed the Romani field slaves' labor. Church responses to calls for emancipation were also mixed: "After all the monasteries were the largest slave owners" (Marushiakova and Popov, "Gypsy Slavery" 113).

31 Other scholars taxonomize categories of slaves by slave-owners – with divisions into "princely slaves," slaves of the monasteries, and slaves of the boyars – or by the many types of labor Romani slaves performed. Marushiakova and Popov usefully add another division: "nomadic" slaves – mostly princely slaves, but with a small category of monastic slaves and the slaves of boyars – who were allowed to be seasonally itinerant, returning to live on their masters' estates for winter work, and "sedentary" slaves who remained permanently on their masters' estates, performing field labor or craft labor such as smithing and carpentry, or acting as household servants for their masters. Among these "sedentary slaves," Marushiakova and Popov believe that agricultural labor was the primary work of slaves in monastic estates.

32 "*Laiesi* (itinerant Gypsies) were usually blacksmiths or ironmongers, who also made bone combs and leather sieves . . . They led a nomadic way of life and were free to roam at will (even outside the borders of the Danubian Principalities, as attested by numerous accounts). Their only obligation to the state was the payment of the . . . annual tax" (Marushiakova and Popov, "Gypsy Slavery" 95). Marushiakova and Popov add: "The way of life of monastery and boyar *Laiesi* slaves did not differ from that of the *Laiesi* owned by the prince. All of them paid an annual tax and roamed freely throughout the country ("Gypsy Slavery" 95). If these itinerant slaves were "free to roam at will" even outside Wallachia and Moldavia, the fact that they returned to pay their annual tax to the state suggests that they found it worthwhile to return to their lives in the principalities, buttressing Gheorghe's reasoning that the kind of unfreedom or slavery experienced by the "Roma belonging to the prince" – most of whom were *Laiesi* – was qualitatively different from the slavery experienced by the Romani slaves who belonged to the monasteries (most of whom were field slaves) and boyars.

33 "The ratio of sedentary Gypsies to nomads varied in different historical periods," Marushiakova and Popov indicate ("Gypsy Slavery" 118). By the mid-nineteenth century, data show, "the ratio of nomadic Gypsies to sedentary ones was one to three" (Marushiakova and Popov, "Gypsy Slavery" 118). In addition to working in the fields, from "the 15th to the mid-19th centuries, Gypsy slaves belonging to the monasteries in Cozia and Govora worked in Wallachia's biggest salt mine. These monasteries were paid for the labor of their Gypsies" (Marushiakova and Popov, "Gypsy Slavery" 107).

34 Among the features of autonomy for the *Laiesi* in Wallachia and Moldavia "was the post of Gypsy leader (*jude/juge*), to which a male was elected by his nomadic Gypsy extended family . . . He represented the family before the authorities. He was referred to as a *voivode* in Transylvania. The

leader's basic prerogative was to dispense justice among the Gypsies in his [extended family], not in line with state law, but with Gypsy custom law" (Marushiakova and Popov, "Gypsy Slavery" 100–1). By contrast, the sedentary Romani slaves living on the large feudal estates "were regularly under the control of their owners, and not only paid the highest taxes . . . but were also subjected to severe exploitation and cruel treatment, as evidenced by numerous documents in Wallachia and Moldavia" (Marushiakova and Popov, "Gypsy Slavery" 104).

35 Marushiakova and Popov offer another description – by a Russian traveler in the nineteenth century – who says of the Romani slaves he has seen: "boyars do not treat them as humans; it is shameful, disgusting and sad to see these ragged, dirty, half-naked Gypsies, both men and women, working for no pay in the richly decorated palaces of the landowners" ("Gypsy Slavery" 105).

36 In 1785, when Alexander Mavrocordat "presented a Gypsy slave family to an impoverished boyar, a good slave cost 4,500 aspri or about 37 gold ducats, which was a substantial sum at that time" (Marushiakova and Popov, "Gypsy Slavery" 100).

37 Marushiakova and Popov offer more precise figures for Wallachia: "In 1857 statisticians recorded 33,267 Gypsy families in Wallachia, out of whom 6,241 were state slaves and 12,081 were monastery ones. The remaining 14,945 families belonged to landowners" ("Gypsy Slavery" 116).

38 Summarizing two opposing views in Romani studies, Marushiakova and Popov point out that Hancock, "one of the founders and leading exponents of the Roma (Gypsy) national historical school," affords attention mainly to *sedentary* Romani slaves on the feudal estates, who unquestionably were "cruelly exploited, sold at the market, and subjected to cruel punishment," whereas Achim emphasizes the relative freedom and autonomy of the *itinerant* Romani slaves, the *Laiesi* – especially those belonging to the prince and the state, who Achim claims to be the majority of the total Romani slave population – and marginalizes the sedentary slaves, especially the most abjected of all, the field slaves ("Gypsy Slavery" 117–18).

39 In the Ottoman Empire too, "Gypsies were classified on the basis of their ethnicity, an anomaly for the Ottoman Empire, with no clear distinction between Muslim and Christian Gypsies as regards tax and social status" (Marushiakova and Popov, "Historical and Ethnographic Background" 42).

40 The tenacity of Romani ethnoracial identity may be better appreciated when we see the efforts made by certain ruling powers to erase that identity. In the Austro-Hungarian Empire of the eighteenth century, Romani were "no longer allowed to speak their language, were obliged to dress like peasants and were even issued with replacement, non-Gypsy names" (Marushiakova and Popov, "Historical and Ethnographic Background" 42). Special taxes were demanded from the Romani, and "Gypsy children were separated from their parents at the age of four, forbidden contact with them and brought up in peasant families. Meanwhile, state and religious education were made compulsory for Gypsy children . . . The ultimate aim of this comprehensive series of measures was the annihilation of a distinct Gypsy community as such and the complete assimilation of all Gypsies" (Marushiakova and Popov, "Historical and Ethnographic Background" 42).

41 Marushiakova and Popov remind us that, like all ethnoracial groups, the Romani too are not exempt from "attempts at 'passing' by individuals of non-Roma appearance as members of the majority community" ("Historical and Ethnographic Background" 53 n.10).

42 This is not to suggest, of course, that ethnoracial identification *by* the Romani *as* Romani elides or minimizes heterogeneity in Romani identity, or to deny the identity transformations that scholars have registered. Marushiakova and Popov point to how the "Gypsy community is divided into a widespread archipelago of separate groupings, split in various ways into metagroups, groups and subgroups, each with their own ethnic and cultural features," so that even within "a specific group or subgroup," individuals may pursue "contrasting strategies" in "ethnic identification" ("Historical and Ethnographic Background" 33, 53 n.10). Additionally, they note, Central and Eastern European Romani have a powerful sense of national belonging that is layered over ethnoracial

identity, and class differences – including the emergence of international, highly educated elites – and also obviously shapes identity configurations ("Historical and Ethnographic Background" 41, 49). The puzzle of Romani identity today seems both to bedevil and to delight. With a touch of satisfaction, Marushiakova and Popov call Romani "an intergroup ethnic community" which "has no parallel among other European nations" ("Historical and Ethnographic Background" 33). An anthropological study by Judith Durst sums up, in its very title, the conundrums of an ethnoracial consolidation of identity via repeated acts of will and self-identification: "'What Makes Us Gypsies, Who Knows. . .?!': Ethnicity and Reproduction."

Bibliography

Abou El Fadl, Khaled. *And God Knows the Soldiers: The Authoritative and Authoritarian in Islamic Discourses.* Lanham, MD: University Press of America, 2001.

Abrahams, B. L. *The Expulsion of the Jews from England in 1290.* Oxford: Blackwell, 1895.

Abulafia, Anna Sapir. "Jewish Carnality in Twelfth-Century Renaissance Thought." *Christianity and Judaism.* Ed. Diana Wood. Oxford: Blackwell, 1992. 59–75.

——"Bodies in the Jewish-Christian Debate." *Framing Medieval Bodies.* Ed. Sarah Kay and Miri Rubin. Manchester: Manchester University Press, 1994. 123–37.

——"Twelfth-Century Renaissance Theology and the Jews." *From Witness to Witchcraft: Jews and Judaism in Medieval Christian Thought.* Ed. Jeremy Cohen. Wiesbaden: Harrassowitz, 1997. 125–39.

Abulafia, David. *Frederick II: A Medieval Emperor.* New York: Oxford University Press, 1988.

——"Monarchs and Minorities in the Christian Western Mediterranean around 1300: Lucera and Its Analogues." *Christendom and Its Discontents: Exclusion, Persecution, and Rebellion, 1000–1500.* Ed. Scott L. Waugh and Peter D. Diehl. Cambridge: Cambridge University Press, 1996. 234–63.

Abu-Lughod, Janet L. *Before European Hegemony: The World System A.D. 1250–1350.* New York: Oxford University Press, 1989.

Achim, Viorel. *The Roma in Romanian History.* Budapest: Central European University Press, 2004.

Adler, Marcus N. *The Itinerary of Benjamin of Tudela: Critical Text, Translation, and Commentary.* London: H. Frowde, 1907.

Adler, Michael. *Jews of Medieval England.* London: Jewish Historical Society of England, 1939.

Akbari, Suzanne Conklin. *Idols in the East: European Representations of Islam and the Orient, 1100–1450.* Ithaca: Cornell University Press, 2009.

Akbari, Suzanne Conklin, and Amilcare A. Iannucci, eds. *Marco Polo and the Encounter of East and West.* Toronto: University of Toronto Press, 2008.

Allsen, Thomas T. *Mongol Imperialism: The Policies of the Grand Qan Möngke in China, Russia, and the Islamic Lands, 1251–1259.* Berkeley: University of California Press, 1979.

——*Commodity and Exchange in the Mongol Empire: A Cultural History of Islamic Textiles.* Cambridge: Cambridge University Press, 1997.

——*Culture and Conquest in Mongol Eurasia.* Cambridge: Cambridge University Press, 2001.

Almqvist, Bo. "'My Name is Guðríðr': An Enigmatic Episode in *Grœnlendinga saga.*" *Approaches to Vínland.* Ed. Andrew Wawn and Þórunn Sigurdardóttir. Reykjavik: Sigurður Nordal Institute, 2001. 15–30.

Amer, Sahar. *Crossing Borders: Love between Women in Medieval French and Arabic Literature.* Philadelphia: University of Pennsylvania Press, 2008.

Amitai, Reuven. "Edward of England and Abagha Ilkhan: A Reexamination of a Failed Attempt at Mongol-Frankish Cooperation." *Tolerance and Intolerance: Social Conflict in the Age of the Crusades.* Ed. Michael Gervers and James M. Powell. Syracuse: Syracuse University Press, 2001. 75–82.

Anidjar, Gil. *Blood: A Critique of Christianity.* New York: Columbia University Press, 2014.

Appiah, Kwame Anthony. "Race." *Critical Terms for Literary Study.* Ed. Frank Lentricchia and Thomas McLaughlin. Chicago: University of Chicago Press, 1990. 274–87.

——"Racisms." *Anatomy of Racism*. Ed. David Theo Goldberg. Minneapolis: University of Minnesota Press, 1990. 3–17.

Arnold of Lübeck. *Arnoldi Chronica Slavorum*. Ed. G. H. Pertz and J. M. Lappenberg. Hanover: Hahn, 1868.

Asad, Talal. *Formations of the Secular: Christianity, Islam, Modernity*. Stanford: Stanford University Press, 2003.

Ashtor, Eliyahu. *A Social and Economic History of the Near East in the Middle Ages*. Berkeley: University of California Press, 1976.

——"Levantine Sugar Industry in the Late Middle Ages: A Case of Technological Decline." *The Islamic Middle East: 700–1900*. Ed. A. L. Udovitch. Princeton: Darwin, 1981. 91–132.

——*Levant Trade in the Later Middle Ages*. Princeton: Princeton University Press, 1983.

——"The Economic Decline of the Middle East during the Later Middle Ages: An Outline." *Technology, Industry and Trade: The Levant versus Europe, 1250–1500*. Ed. B. Z. Kedar. Brookfield, VT: Variorium, 1992. 253–86.

Atiya, Aziz Suryal. *The Crusade of Nicopolis*. London: Methuen, 1934.

——*The Crusade in the Later Middle Ages*. London: Methuen, 1938.

Atwood, Christopher Pratt. *Encyclopedia of Mongolia and the Mongol Empire*. New York: Facts on File, 2004.

——"Validation by Holiness or Sovereignty: Religious Toleration as Political Ideology in the Mongol World Empire of the Thirteenth Century." *The International History Review* 26(2) (2004): 237–56.

Ayalon, David. "The Muslim City and the Mamluk Military Aristocracy." Princeton Near East Paper No. 20, Princeton University Program in Near Eastern Studies, 1967.

——"The Impact of Firearms on the Muslim World." Princeton Near East Paper No. 20, Princeton University Program in Near Eastern Studies, 1975.

——*Studies on the Mamluks of Egypt (1250–1517)*. London: Variorum, 1977.

——*The Mamluk Military Society: Collected Studies*. London: Variorum, 1979.

——*Outsiders in the Lands of Islam: Mamluks, Mongols and Eunuchs*. London: Variorum, 1988.

——*Eunuchs, Caliphs, and Sultans: A Study in Power Relationships*. Jerusalem: Magnes Press, Hebrew University, 1999.

Babbington, Churchill, and Joseph Rawson Lumby, eds. *Polychronicon Ranulphi Higden Monachi Cestrensis*. 9 vols. London: Longman, 1865–86.

Bale, Anthony Paul. *The Jew in the Medieval Book: English Antisemitisms 1350–1500*. Cambridge: Cambridge University Press, 2006.

——*Feeling Persecuted: Christians, Jews and Images of Violence in the Middle Ages*. London: Reaktion, 2012.

Balibar, Étienne. "Racism and Nationalism." *Race, Nation, Class: Ambiguous Identities*. Étienne Balibar and Immanuel Wallerstein. London: Verso, 1992.

——"Election/Selection." Keynote address at the University of California Humanities Research Institute (UCHRI) conference, "tRaces: Race, Deconstruction, Critical Theory." Unpublished paper. 2003.

Barber, Malcolm. *The Trial of the Templars*. Cambridge: Cambridge University Press, 1978.

——*The New Knighthood: A History of the Order of the Temple*. Cambridge: Cambridge University Press, 1994.

Bartlett, Robert. *Gerald of Wales: 1146–1223*. Oxford: Clarendon, 1982.

——*The Making of Europe: Conquest, Colonization and Cultural Change 950–1350*. Princeton: Princeton University Press, 1993.

——"Medieval and Modern Concepts of Race and Ethnicity." *Journal of Medieval and Early Modern Studies* 31 (2001): 38–56.

——"Illustrating Ethnicity in the Middle Ages." *The Origins of Racism in the West*. Ed. Miriam Eliav-Feldon, Benjamin Isaac, and Joseph Ziegler. Cambridge: Cambridge University Press, 2009. 132–56.

Barton, Simon. "Marriage across Frontiers: Sexual Mixing, Power and Identity in Medieval Iberia." *Journal of Medieval Iberian Studies* 3(1) (2011): 1–25.

——*Conquerors, Brides, and Concubines: Interfaith Relations and Social Power in Medieval Iberia.* Philadelphia: University of Pennsylvania Press, 2015.

Beazley, C. Raymond. *The Texts and Versions of John de Plano Carpini and William de Rubruquis.* London: Hakluyt Society, 1903.

Beck, Sam. "The Origins of Gypsy Slavery in Romania." *Dialectical Anthropology* 14(1) (1989): 53–61.

Beckingham, Charles F. "The Achievements of Prester John." *Prester John, the Mongols, and the Ten Lost Tribes.* Ed. Charles F. Beckingham and Bernard Hamilton. Aldershot: Variorum, 1996. 197–206.

Beckwith, Sarah. *Christ's Body: Identity, Culture, and Society in Late Medieval Writings.* New York: Routledge, 1993.

Begg, Ean. *The Cult of the Black Virgin.* London: Penguin, 1996.

Bennett, Josephine Waters. *The Rediscovery of Sir John Mandeville.* New York: Modern Language Association of America, 1954.

Benson, Larry D., Robert Pratt, and F. N. Robinson, ed. *The Riverside Chaucer.* Boston: Houghton Mifflin, 1987.

Bernal, Martin. *Black Athena: The AfroAsiatic Roots of Classical Civilization.* 2 vols. New Brunswick: Rutgers University Press, 1987.

——*Black Athena Writes Back.* Durham: Duke University Press, 2001.

Berry, Henry F., ed. *Statutes and Ordinances, and Acts of the Parliament of Ireland: King John to Henry V.* Dublin: Alexander Thom, 1907.

Besamusca, Bart. "The Influence of the *Lancelot en prose* on the Middle Dutch *Moriaen*." *Arturus Rex: Volumen II: Acta Conventus Lovaniensis.* Ed. Willy Van Hoecke, Gilbert Tournoy, and Werner Verbeke. Vol. II. Leuven: Leuven University Press, 1991. 352–60.

Bhabha, Homi. *The Location of Culture.* London: Routledge, 1994.

Biagioli, Mario. "The Scientific Revolution Is Undead." *Configurations* 6(2) (1998): 141–48.

Biddick, Kathleen. "The Cut of Genealogy: Pedagogy in the Blood." *Journal of Medieval and Early Modern Studies* 30(3) (2000): 449–62.

——*The Typological Imaginary: Circumcision, Technology, History.* Philadelphia: University of Pennsylvania Press, 2003.

——"Dead Neighbor Archives: Jews, Muslims, and the Enemies' Two Bodies." *Points of Departure: Political Theology on the Scenes of Early Modernity.* Ed. Julia Reinhart Lupton and Graham Hammill. Chicago: University of Chicago Press, 2011. 124–142.

Biller, Peter. "Views of Jews from Paris around 1300: Christian or 'Scientific'?" *Christianity and Judaism.* Ed. Diana Wood. Oxford: Blackwell, 1992. 187–207.

——"A 'Scientific' View of Jews from Paris around 1300." *Micrologus* 9 (2001): 137–68.

——"Black Women in Medieval Scientific Thought." *Micrologus* 13 (2005): 477–92.

——"Proto-Racial Thought in Medieval Science." *The Origins of Racism in the West.* Ed. Miriam Eliav-Feldon, Benjamin Isaac, and Joseph Ziegler. Cambridge: Cambridge University Press, 2009. 157–80.

Bindman, David, Henry Louis Gates Jr., Karen C. C. Dalton, eds. *Image of the Black in Western Art: From the "Age of Discovery" to the Age of Abolition.* Vol. 3 Pt. 1: Artists of the Renaissance and Baroque (Sixteenth and Seventeenth Centuries). Cambridge: Belknap Press of Harvard University Press; Houston: Menil Collection, 2010.

Bjørn, Claus, Alexander Grant, and Keith J. Stringer, eds. *Nations, Nationalism, and Patriotism in the European Past.* Copenhagen: Academic, 1994.

Bonfil, Robert. "The Devil and the Jews in the Christian Consciousness of the Middle Ages." *Antisemitism through the Ages.* Ed. Shmuel Almog. Trans. Nathan H. Reisner. Oxford: Pergamon, 1988. 91–125.

Boswell, John. *Christianity, Social Tolerance, and Homosexuality: Gay People in Western Europe from the Beginning of the Christian Era to the Fourteenth Century.* Chicago: University of Chicago Press, 1980.

Boyarin, Adrienne. *Miracles of the Virgin in Medieval England: Law and Jewishness in Marian Legends.* Cambridge: D. S. Brewer, 2010.

Boyarin, Jonathan. *The Unconverted Self: Jews, Indians, and the Identity of Christian Europe.* Chicago: University of Chicago Press, 2009.

Boyd, Beverly. *The Middle English Miracles of the Virgin.* San Marino, CA: Huntington Library, 1964.

———ed. *The Prioress's Tale. A Variorum Edition of the Works of Geoffrey Chaucer, Vol. 2: The Canterbury Tales, Part 20.* Norman: University of Oklahoma Press, 1983.

Boyle, John Andrew, trans. *The Successors of Genghis Khan: Translated from the Persian of Rashid al-Din.* New York: Columbia University Press, 1971.

———trans. *Genghis Khan: The History of the World Conqueror by Ata-Malik Juvaini.* Manchester: Manchester University Press, 1977.

Bracton, Henry de. *De legibus et consuetudinibus Angliae* (On the Laws and Customs of England). Trans. Samuel E. Thorne. Cambridge: Belknap Press of Harvard University Press, 1968.

Brand, Paul. "The Jewish Community of England in the Records of English Royal Government." *The Jews in Medieval Britain: Historical, Literary, and Archaeological Perspectives.* Ed. Patricia Skinner. Woodbridge: Boydell, 2003.

Braude, Benjamin. "The Sons of Noah and the Construction of Ethnic and Geographical Identities in the Medieval and Early Modern Periods." *William and Mary Quarterly* 54 (1997): 103–42.

Brennan, Timothy. "The National Longing for Form." *Nation and Narration,* Ed. Homi K. Bhabha. New York: Routledge, 1990. 44–70.

Brewer, J. S., ed. *Giraldi Cambrensis Opera.* Rolls series. 8 vols. London: Longman, 1861–91.

Brown, Carleton. *A Study of the Miracle of Our Lady Told by Chaucer's Prioress.* London: Chaucer Society Publications, 1910.

———"The Prioress's Tale." *Sources and Analogues of Chaucer's Canterbury Tales.* Ed. W. F. Bryan and Germaine Dempster. New York: Humanities Press, 1958. 447–485.

Brown, Nancy Marie. *The Far Traveler: Voyagers of a Viking Woman.* Orlando: Harcourt, 2007.

Budge, E. A. Wallis, trans. *The Monks of Kublai Khan Emperor of China.* London: The Religious Tract Society, 1928.

Buell, Denise K. *Why This New Race: Ethnic Reasoning in Early Christianity.* New York: Columbia University Press, 2005.

———"Early Christian Universalism and Modern Racism." *The Origins of Racism in the West.* Ed. Miriam Eliav-Feldon, Benjamin Isaac, and Joseph Ziegler. Cambridge: Cambridge University Press, 2009. 109–31.

Bugner, Ladislas. "Foreword." *Mauritius: Der Heilige Mohr.* Gude Suckale-Redlefsen. Zurich: Verlag Schnell & Steiner, 1987. 8–13.

Bulliet, Richard. *Conversion to Islam in the Medieval Period: An Essay in Quantitative History.* Cambridge: Harvard University Press, 1979.

Burman, Thomas E. *Reading the Qu'ran in Latin Christendom, 1140–1560.* Philadelphia: University of Pennsylvania Press, 2007.

Burns, Robert I., S.J. "Christian-Islamic Confrontation in the West: The Thirteenth-Century Dream of Conversion." *American Historical Review* 76 (1971): 1386–1434.

Bynum, Caroline Walker. *The Resurrection of the Body in Western Christianity, 200–1336.* New York: Columbia University Press, 1995.

Byron, Gay L. *Symbolic Blackness and Ethnic Difference in Early Christian Literature.* London: Routledge, 2002.

Calabrese, Michael. "Performing the Prioress: 'Conscience' and Responsibility in Studies of Chaucer's *Prioress's Tale." Texas Studies in Literature and Language* 44(1) (2002): 66–91.

Carpenter, David. "The Fine of the Month: January 2010" and "The Fine of the Month: February 2010." In "Henry III Fine Roll Project." www.finerollshenry3.org.uk/content/month/fm-01-2010.html and www.finerollshenry3.org.uk/content/month/fm-02-2010.html

Cassagnes-Brouquet, Sophie. *Vierges Noires.* Rodez: Éditions du Rouergue, 2000.

Catlos, Brian A. *Muslims of Medieval Latin Christendom c. 1050–1614.* Cambridge: Cambridge University Press, 2014.

Caviness, Madeline. "From the Self-Invention of the Whiteman in the Thirteenth Century to *The Good, the Bad, and the Ugly." Different Visions: A Journal of New Perspectives on Medieval Art* 1 (2008): 1–33.

Chakrabarty, Dipesh. *Provincializing Europe: Postcolonial Thought and Historical Difference.* Princeton: Princeton University Press, 2000.

Chaliand, Gérard, and Arnaud Blin. *The History of Terrorism: from Antiquity to Al Qaeda.* Trans. Edward Schneider, Kathryn Pulver, and Jesse Browner. Berkeley: University of California Press, 2007.

Chambers, Frank M. "The Troubadours and the Assassins." *Modern Language Notes* 64(4) (1949): 245–51.

Chan, J. Clara. "Medievalists, Recoiling from White Supremacy, Try to Diversify the Field." *The Chronicle of Higher Education*, July 16, 2017. www.chronicle.com/article/Medievalists-Recoiling-From/240666.

Chase, Kenneth Warren. *Firearms: A Global History to 1700.* Cambridge: Cambridge University Press, 2003.

Chazan, Robert. "Twelfth-Century Perceptions of the Jews: A Case Study of Bernard of Clairvaux and Peter the Venerable." *From Witness to Witchcraft: Jews and Judaism in Medieval Christian Thought.* Ed. Jeremy Cohen. Wiesbaden: Harrassowitz, 1997. 187–201.

Chiesa, Paolo, ed. *The Travels of Friar Odoric: A 14th-Century Journal of the Blessed Odoric of Pordenone.* Italian Texts and Studies on Religion and Society. Trans. Sir Henry Yule. Grand Rapids: William B. Eerdmans, 2002.

Claassens, Geert H. M., and David F. Johnson, eds. *King Arthur in the Medieval Low Countries.* Leuven: Leuven University Press, 2000.

Classen, Albrecht. "Medieval Europe and Its Encounter with the Foreign World: Late-Medieval German Witnesses." *Medieval Cultures in Contact.* Ed. Richard F. Gyug. New York: Fordham University Press, 2003. 85–103.

Cohen, Jeffrey Jerome. "Hybrids, Monsters, Borderlands: The Bodies of Gerald of Wales." *The Postcolonial Middle Ages.* Ed. Jeffrey Jerome Cohen. New York: St. Martins, 2000. 85–104.

——"On Saracen Enjoyment: Some Fantasies of Race in Late Medieval France and England." *Journal of Medieval and Early Modern Studies* 31(1) (2001): 113–46.

——"The Flow of Blood in Medieval Norwich." *Speculum* 79(1) (2004): 26–65.

Cohen, Jeremy. *The Friars and the Jews: The Evolution of Medieval Anti-Judaism.* Ithaca: Cornell University Press, 1982.

——"The Muslim Connection: On the Changing Role of the Jew in High Medieval Theology." *From Witness to Witchcraft: Jews and Judaism in Medieval Christian Thought.* Ed. Jeremy Cohen. Wiesbaden: Harrassowitz, 1997. 141–62.

——*From Witness to Witchcraft: Jews and Judaism in Medieval Christian Thought.* Wiesbaden: Harrassowitz, 1997.

——*Living Letters of the Law: Ideas of the Jew in Medieval Christianity.* Berkeley: University of California Press, 1999.

——"*Synagoga conversa*: Honorius Augustodunensis, the Song of Songs, and Christianity's 'Eschatological Jew'." *Speculum* 79(2) (2004): 309–40.

Colbert, Edward P. *The Martyrs of Córdoba (850–859): A Study of the Sources.* Washington, DC: Catholic University of America Press, 1962.

Colvin, Howard M. "Royal Gardens in Medieval England." *Medieval Gardens.* Ed. Elisabeth B. McDougall. Dumbarton Oaks Colloquium on the History of Landscape Architecture 9. Washington, DC: Dumbarton Oaks, 1986. 9–22.

Comnena, Anna. *The Alexiad of Anna Comnena.* Trans. E. R. A. Sewter. London: Penguin, 1969.

Connell, C. W. "Western Views of the Origin of the 'Tartars': An Example of the Influence of Myth in the Second Half of the Thirteenth Century." *Journal of Medieval and Renaissance Studies* 3(1) (1973): 115–37.

Constable, Olivia Remie. "Muslim Spain and Mediterranean Slavery: The Medieval Slave Trade as an Aspect of Muslim-Christian Relations." *Christendom and Its Discontents: Exclusion, Persecution, and Rebellion, 1000–1500.* Ed. Scott L. Waugh and Peter D. Diehl. Cambridge: Cambridge University Press, 1996. 264–84.

Coope, Jessica A. "Religious and Cultural Conversion to Islam in Ninth-Century Umayyad Córdoba." *Journal of World History* 4(1) (1994): 47–68.

——*The Martyrs of Córdoba: Community and Family Conflict in an Age of Mass Conversion.* Lincoln: University of Nebraska Press, 1995.

Couch, Julie Nelson. "'The Child Slain by Jews' and 'The Jewish Boy'." *Medieval Literature for Children.* Ed. Daniel T. Kline. New York: Routledge, 2003. 204–26.

Crosby, Alfred W., Jr. *The Columbian Exchange: Biological and Cultural Consequences of 1492.* Westport, CT: Praeger, 2003.

——*Ecological Imperialism: The Biological Expansion of Europe, 900–1900.* Cambridge: Cambridge University Press, 2009.

Crowe, David M. *A History of the Gypsies of Eastern Europe and Russia.* New York: Palgrave Macmillan, 2007.

Cutler, Allan Harris, and Helen Elmquist Cutler. *The Jew as Ally of the Muslim: Medieval Roots of Anti-Semitism.* Notre Dame: University of Notre Dame Press, 1986.

Daftary, Farhad. *Ismailis in Medieval Muslim Societies.* London: I. B. Tauris, 2005.

——*The Assassin Legends: Myths of the Isma'ilis.* London: I. B. Tauris, 2006.

Dahan, Gilbert. *Les intellectuels chrétiens and les Juifs au Moyen Age.* Paris: Éditions du Cerf, 1990.

——"Juifs et judaîsme dans la littérature quodlibétique." *From Witness to Witchcraft: Jews and Judaism in Medieval Christian Thought.* Ed. Jeremy Cohen. Wiesbaden: Harrassowitz, 1997. 221–45.

Dahood, Roger. "English Historical Narratives of Jewish Child-Murder, Chaucer's *Prioress's Tale*, and the Date of Chaucer's Unknown Source." *Studies in the Age of Chaucer* 31 (2009): 125–40.

——"Anglo-Norman "Hugo de Lincolnia': A Critical Edition and Translation from the Unique Text in Paris, Bibliothèque Nationale de France MS fr. 902." *The Chaucer Review* 49(1) (2014): 1–38.

Daniel, Norman. *The Arabs and Mediaeval Europe.* London: Longman, 1975.

——*Heroes and Saracens: An Interpretation of the Chansons de Geste.* Edinburgh: Edinburgh University Press, 1984.

——*Islam and the West: The Making of an Image.* Oxford: Oneworld, 1993.

Davies, R. R. *The First English Empire: Power and Identities in the British Isles 1093–1343.* Oxford: Oxford University Press, 2000.

Davis, Dick, trans. *Shahnameh: The Persian Book of Kings.* London: Penguin, 2006.

Davis, Kathleen. *Periodization and Sovereignty: How Ideas of Feudalism and Secularization Govern the Politics of Time.* Philadelphia: University of Pennsylvania Press, 2008.

Dawson, Christopher, ed. *Mission to Asia.* Toronto: University of Toronto Press, 1980.

DeBoer, Warren R. "Colors for a North American Past." *World Archaeology* 37(1) (2005): 66–91.

de Clari, Robert. *La Conquête de Constantinople.* Ed. Philippe Lauer. Paris: Champion, 1956.

Dee, James. "Black Odysseus, White Caesar: When did 'White People' Become 'White'?" *The Classical Journal* 99(2) (2003/4): 157–67.

Delano-Smith, Catherine and Roger J. P. Kain. *English Maps: A History.* London: British Library, 1999.

Deluz, Christiane, ed. *Le Livre de Merveilles du Monde,* Jean de Mandeville. Paris: CNRS Éditions, 2000.

De Miramon, Charles. "Noble Dogs, Noble Blood: The Invention of the Concept of Race in the Late Middle Ages." *The Origins of Racism in the West.* Ed. Miriam Eliav-Feldon, Benjamin Isaac, and Joseph Ziegler. Cambridge: Cambridge University Press, 2009. 200–16.

Demurger, Alain. *Vie et Mort de l'Ordre du Temple: 1118–1314.* Paris: Éditions du Seuil, 1985.

——*Les Templiers: Une Chevalerie Chrétienne au Moyen Age.* Paris: Éditions du Seuil, 2008.

de Rachewiltz, Igor. *Papal Envoys to the Great Khan.* Stanford: Stanford University Press, 1971.

——*Prester John and Europe's Discovery of East Asia.* Canberra: Australian National University Press, 1972.

——"Marco Polo Went to China." *Zentraleasiatische Studien* 27 (1997): 34–92.

——ed. and trans. *The Secret History of the Mongols: A Mongolian Epic Chronicle of the Thirteenth Century*. 2 vols. Leiden: Brill, 2004.

de Solla Price, Derek J. "Automata and the Origins of Mechanism and Mechanistic Philosophy." *Technology and Culture* 5(1) (1964): 9–23.

Despres, Denise L. "Cultic Anti-Judaism and Chaucer's Litel Clergeon." *Modern Philology* 91(4) (1994): 413–27.

——"Mary of the Eucharist: Cultic Anti-Judaism in Some Fourteenth-Century English Devotional Manuscripts." *From Witness to Witchcraft: Jews and Judaism in Medieval Christian Thought*. Ed. Jeremy Cohen. Wiesbaden: Harrassowitz, 1997. 375–401.

——"Immaculate Flesh and the Social Body: Mary and the Jews." *Jewish History* 12(1) (1998): 47–69.

——"The Protean Jew in the Vernon Manuscript." *Chaucer and the Jews: Sources, Contexts, Meanings*. Ed. Sheila Delany. New York: Routledge, 2002. 145–64.

Devisse, Jean. *The Image of the Black in Western Art: From the Early Christian Era to the "Age of Discovery."* Trans. William G. Ryan. Vol. 2 Pt. 1: From the Demonic Threat to the Incarnation of Sainthood. New York: William Morrow, 1979.

Devisse, Jean and Michel Mollat. *The Image of the Black in Western Art: From the Early Christian Era to the "Age of Discovery."* Trans. William G. Ryan. Vol. 2 Pt. 2: Africans in the Christian Ordinance of the World (Fourteenth to the Sixteenth Century). New York: William Morrow, 1979.

de Weever, Jacqueline. *Sheba's Daughters: Whitening and Demonizing the Saracen Woman in Medieval French Epic*. New York: Garland, 1998.

Dimock, Wai Chee. *Through Other Continents: American Literature across Deep Time*. Princeton: Princeton University Press, 2006.

Dinshaw, Carolyn. *Getting Medieval: Sexualities and Communities, Pre- and Postmodern*. Durham: Duke University Press, 1999.

Dobson, R. B. *The Jews of Medieval York and the Massacre of March 1190*. York: St Anthony's, 1974.

——"The Role of Jewish Women in Medieval England." *Christianity and Judaism*. Ed. Diana Wood. Oxford: Blackwell, 1992. 145–68.

Dols, Michael. "The General Mortality of the Black Death in the Mamluk Empire." *The Islamic Middle East: 700–1900*. Ed. A. L. Udovitch. Princeton: Darwin, 1981. 397–428.

Doyle, Laura. "Inter-imperiality and Literary Studies in the Longer Durée. *PMLA* 130(2) (2015): 336–47.

Du Bois, W. E. B. *Black Folk Then and Now: An Essay in the History and Sociology of the Negro Race*. New York: Octagon, 1970.

Duparc-Quioc, Suzanne, ed. *Chanson d'Antioche. La Chanson d'Antioche*. 2 vols. Paris: Paul Geuthner, 1976–82.

Durst, Judith. "'What Makes Us Gypsies, Who Knows...?!': Ethnicity and Reproduction." *Multi-Disciplinary Approaches to Romany Studies*. Ed. Michael Stewart and Márton Rövid. Budapest: Central European University Press, 2011. 13–34.

Dutschke, Consuelo W. "Francesco Pipino and the Manuscripts of Marco Polo's *Travels*." 3 vols. PhD dissertation, UCLA, 1993.

Ebenesersdóttir, Sigríður Sunna, Ásgeir Sigurðsson, Frederico Sánchez-Quinto, Carles Lalueza-Fox, Kári Stefánsson, and Agnar Helgason. "A New Subclade of mtDNA Haplogroup C1 Found in Icelanders: Evidence of Pre-Columbian Contact?" *American Journal of Physical Anthropology* 144 (2011): 92–9.

Edson, Evelyn. *Mapping Time and Space: How Medieval Mapmakers Viewed Their World*. London: British Library, 1997.

Edwards, Cyril, trans. *Wolfram von Eschenbach: Parzival*. Oxford: Oxford University Press, 2006.

Edwards, John. "The Church and the Jews in Medieval England." *The Jews in Medieval Britain: Historical, Literary and Archaeological Perspectives*. Ed. Patricia Skinner. Woodbridge: Boydell, 2003. 85–95.

Edwards, Paul. "The Early African Presence in the British Isles." *Essays on the History of Blacks in Britain: From Roman Times to the Mid-Twentieth Century.* Ed. Jagdish S. Gundara and Ian Duffield. Aldershot: Avebury, 1992. 9–29.

Ehrenkreutz, Andrew. "Strategic Implications of the Slave Trade between Genoa and Mamluk Egypt in the Second Half of the Thirteenth Century." *The Islamic Middle East: 700–1900.* Ed. A. L. Udovitch. Princeton: Darwin, 1981. 335–45.

Eidelberg, Shlomo, ed. and trans. *The Jews and the Crusaders: The Hebrew Chronicles of the First and Second Crusades.* Madison: University of Wisconsin Press, 1977.

El-Hajji, Abdurrahman. "Intermarriage between Andalusia and Nothern Spain in the Umayyad Period." *Islamic Quarterly* 11(1/2) (1967): 3–7.

Eliav-Feldon Miriam, Benjamin Isaac, and Joseph Ziegler, eds. *The Origins of Racism in the West.* Cambridge: Cambridge University Press, 2009.

Elukin, Jonathan M. "From Jew to Christian? Conversion and Immutability in Medieval Europe." *Varieties of Religious Conversion in the Middle Ages.* Ed. James Muldoon. Gainesville: University of Florida Press, 1997. 171–89.

——"The Discovery of the Self: Jews and Conversion in the Twelfth Century." *Jews and Christians in Twelfth Century Europe.* Ed. Michael A. Signer and John Van Engen. Notre Dame: University of Notre Dame Press, 2001. 63–76.

Encyclopaedia Judaica. 17 vols. Jerusalem: Encyclopaedia Judaica, 1972(?)–1982.

Epstein, Steven A. *Genoa and the Genoese, 958–1528.* Chapel Hill: University of North Carolina Press, 1996.

——*Speaking of Slavery: Color, Ethnicity, and Human Bondage in Italy.* Ithaca: Cornell University Press, 2001.

——*Purity Lost: Transgressing Boundaries in the Eastern Mediterranean, 1000–1400.* Baltimore: Johns Hopkins University Press, 2006.

"Eurocentrism, Sinocentrism and World History: A Symposium." *Science and Society* 67(2) (2003): 173–217.

Fernández-Armesto, Felipe. *Before Columbus: Exploration and Colonisation from the Mediterranean to the Atlantic 1229–1492.* Houndmills: Macmillan, 1987.

Fleischman, R. A. "Human Piebald Trait Resulting from a Dominant Negative Mutant Allele of the C-Kit Membrane Receptor Gene." *The Journal of Clinical Investigation* 89(6) (1992): 1713–1717.

Fogle, Lauren. "Between Christianity and Judaism: The Identity of Converted Jews in Medieval London." *Essays in Medieval Studies* 22 (2005): 107–16.

——"The *Domus Conversorum*: The Personal Interest of Henry III." *Jewish Historical Studies* 41 (2007): 1–7.

Forde, Simon, Lesley Johnson, and Alan V. Murray, eds. *Concepts of National Identity in the Middle Ages.* Leeds: University of Leeds Press, 1995.

Foucault, Michel. *"Society Must Be Defended": Lectures at the Collège De France 1975–1976.* Ed. Mauro Bertani and Alessandro Fontana. Trans. David Macey. New York: Picador, 2003.

——*The Birth of Biopolitics: Lectures at the Collège De France 1978–1979.* Ed. Michel Senellart. Trans. Graham Burchell. New York: Picador, 2010.

Fowden, Gareth. *Empire to Commonwealth: Consequences of Monotheism in Late Antiquity.* Princeton: Princeton University Press, 1993.

Fradenburg, Louise Olga. "Criticism, Anti-Semitism, and the *Prioress's Tale.*" *Exemplaria* 1(1) (1989): 69–115.

——*City, Marriage, Tournament: Arts of Rule in Late Medieval Scotland.* Madison: University of Wisconsin Press, 1991.

Frakes, Jerold C. *Vernacular and Latin Literary Discourses of the Muslim Other in Medieval Germany.* New York: Palgrave Macmillan, 2011.

Frank, Robert W., Jr. "Miracles of the Virgin, Medieval Anti-Semitism, and 'The Prioress's Tale'." *The Wisdom of Poetry: Essays in Early English Literature in Honor of Morton*

W. Bloomfield. Ed. Larry D. Benson and Siegfried Wenzel. Kalamazoo: Medieval Institute, 1983. 176–88.

Franke, Herbert. "Ahmad (?–1282)." *In the Service of the Khan: Eminent Personalities of the Early Mongol-Yüan Period.* Wiesbaden: Harrassowitz, 1993. 539–57.

Fraser, Angus. *The Gypsies.* Oxford: Blackwell, 1995.

Fredrickson, George M. *Racism: A Short History.* Princeton: Princeton University Press, 2002.

Frey, Winfried. "Gottesmörder und Menschenfeinde: Zum Judenbild in der deutschen Literatur des Mittelalters." *Die Juden in ihrer mittelalterlichen Umwelt.* Ed. Alfred Ebenbauer and Klaus Zatloukal. Vienna: Böhlau, 1991. 35–51.

Fulcher of Chartres. *Historia Hierosolymitana (1095–1127).* Ed. Heinrich Hagenmeyer. Heidelberg: Carl Winters, 1913.

——*A History of the Expedition to Jerusalem, 1095–1127.* Ed. Harold S. Fink. Trans. Frances Rita Ryan. Knoxville: University of Tennessee Press, 1969.

Gabrieli, Francisco, trans. *Arab Historians of the Crusades.* London: Routledge, 1957.

Galison, Peter, and David J. Stump, eds. *The Disunity of Science: Boundaries, Contexts, and Power.* Stanford: Stanford University Press, 1996.

Gaunt, Simon. *Marco Polo's Le Devisement du Monde.* Cambridge: D. S. Brewer, 2013.

Gerald of Wales. *Giraldi Cambrensis Opera.* Ed. J. S. Brewer. Rolls series. 8 vols. London: Longman, 1861–91.

——*The History and Topography of Ireland.* Trans. John J. O'Meara. Harmondsworth: Penguin, 1982.

Gheorghe, Nicolae. "Origins of Roma's Slavery in the Rumanian Principalities." *Roma* 7 (1983): 12–27.

Ghosh, Amitav, and Dipesh Chakrabarty. "A Correspondence on *Provincializing Europe.*" *Radical History Review* 83 (2002): 146–72.

Gibb, H. A. R., trans. *The Damascus Chronicle of the Crusades: Extracted and Translated from the Chronicle of Ibn Al-Qalanisi.* London: Luzac, 1932.

Gibbs, Marion E. "Ideals of Flesh and Blood: Women Characters in *Parzival.*" *A Companion to Wolfram's Parzival.* Ed. Will Hasty. Columbia, SC: Camden, 1999. 12–36.

Goitein, S. D., and Mordechai Akiva Friedman, eds. and trans. *India Traders of the Middle Ages: Documents from the Cairo Geniza ('India Book').* Leiden: Brill, 2008.

Golb, Norman. *The Jews in Medieval Normandy: A Social and Economic History.* Cambridge: Cambridge University Press, 1998.

Goldberg, David Theo. *Racist Culture: Philosophy and the Politics of Meaning.* Oxford: Blackwell, 1993.

——*The Racial State.* Oxford: Blackwell, 2002.

Goldenberg, David M. *The Curse of Ham: Race and Slavery in Early Judaism, Christianity, and Islam.* Princeton: Princeton University Press, 2003.

——"Racism, Color Symbolism, and Color Prejudice." *The Origins of Racism in the West.* Ed. Miriam Eliav-Feldon, Benjamin Isaac, and Joseph Ziegler. Cambridge: Cambridge University Press, 2009. 88–108.

Goldstein, R. James. *The Matter of Scotland: Historical Narrative in Medieval Scotland.* Lincoln: University of Nebraska Press, 1993.

Goldstone, Jack A. "Efflorescences and Economic Growth in World History: Rethinking the 'Rise of the West' and the Industrial Revolution." *Journal of World History* 13(2) (2002): 323–89.

Goodich, Michael. "Foreigner, Foe, and Neighbor: The Religious Cult as a Forum for Political Reconciliation." *Meeting the Foreign in the Middle Ages.* Ed. Albrecht Classen. New York: Routledge, 2002. 11–26.

Goodrich, L. Carrington. "Westerners and Central Asians in Yuan China." *Oriente Poliano.* Rome: Istituto italiano per il Medio ed Estremo Oriente, 1957. 1–21.

Gottheil, Richard, and Joseph Jacobs. "Archa." *Jewish Encyclopedia.com.*

Gow, Andrew Colin. *The Red Jews: Antisemitism in an Apocalyptic Age 1200–1600*. Leiden: Brill, 1995.

Grady, Frank. *Representing Righteous Heathens in Late Medieval England*. New York: Palgrave Macmillan, 2005.

Grayzel, Solomon. *The Church and the Jews in the XIIIth Century*. New York: Hermon, 1966.

Gresham, David, Bharti Morar, Peter A. Underhill, Giuseppe Passarino, Alice A. Lin, Cheryl Wise, Dora Angelicheva, Francesc Calafell, Peter J. Oefner, Peidong Shen, Ivailo Tournev, Rosario de Pablo, Vaidutis Kucinskas, Anna Perez-Lezaun, Elena Marushiakova, Vesselin Popov, and Luba Kalaydjieva. "Origins and Divergence of the Roma (Gypsies)." *American Journal of Human Genetics* 69(6) (2001): 1314–1331. www.ncbi.nlm.nih.gov/pmc/articles/PMC1235543/

Groebner, Valentin. "The Carnal Knowing of a Colored Body: Sleeping with Arabs and Blacks in the European Imagination, 1300–1550." *The Origins of Racism in the West*. Ed. Miriam Eliav-Feldon, Benjamin Isaac, and Joseph Ziegler. Cambridge: Cambridge University Press, 2009. 217–31.

Gross, Charles. *The Exchequer of the Jews of England in the Middle Ages*. London: Office of the Jewish Chronicle, 1887.

Guzman, Gregory. "Reports of Mongol Cannibalism in the Thirteenth Century." *Discovering New Worlds: Essays on Medieval Exploration and Imagination*. Ed. Scott D. Westrem. New York: Garland, 1991. 31–68.

Hagenmeyer, Heinrich, ed. *Die Kreuzzugsbriefe aus den Jahren 1088–1100*. Innsbruck: Verlag der Wagnerschen Universitäts-Buchhandlung, 1901.

Hahn, Thomas, ed. Special Issue on Race and Ethnicity in the Middle Ages. *Journal of Medieval and Early Modern Studies* 31(1) (2001).

——"The Difference the Middle Ages Makes: Color and Race before the Modern World." *Journal of Medieval and Early Modern Studies* 31(1) (2001): 1–37.

Hall, Jonathan M. *Hellenicity: Between Ethnicity and Culture*. Chicago: University of Chicago Press, 2002.

Hall, Kim F. *Things of Darkness: Economies of Race and Gender in Early Modern England*. Ithaca: Cornell University Press, 1995.

Halperin, Charles. *Russia and the Golden Horde: The Mongol Impact on Medieval Russian History*. Bloomington: Indiana University Press, 1985.

Hambis, Louis. "Le Voyage de Marco Polo en Haute Asie." *Oriente Poliano*. Rome: Istituto italiano per il Medio ed Estremo Oriente, 1957. 173–91.

Hamelius, P., ed. *Mandeville's Travels...Edited from MS. Cotton Titus c. XVI, in the British Museum*. 2 vols. EETS Original Series Vol. 153. London: Kegan Paul, 1919.

Hamilton, Bernard. "Continental Drift: Prester John's Progress through the Indies." *Prester John, the Mongols, and the Ten Lost Tribes*. Ed. Charles F. Beckingham and Bernard Hamilton. Aldershot: Variorum, 1996. 237–69.

Hammond, James. "The Darkness of Memory: 'Post-Race' in Premodernity." Honors thesis, University of Texas, 2010.

Hancock, Ian. *The Pariah Syndrome: An Account of Gypsy Slavery and Persecution*. Ann Arbor: Karoma, 1987.

——"Gypsy History in Germany and Neighboring Lands: A Chronology Leading to the Holocaust and Beyond." *The Gypsies of Eastern Europe*. Ed. David Crowe and John Kolsti. Armonk, NY: M. E. Sharpe, 1991. 11–30.

——*We Are the Romani People*. Hatfield: University of Hertfordshire Press, 2002.

——"The 'Gypsy' Stereotype and the Sexualization of Romani Women." *Gypsies in European Literature and Culture*. Ed. Valentina Glajar and Domnica Radulescu. New York: Palgrave Macmillan, 2008. 181–91.

Hardy, Thomas Duffus, ed. *Rotuli chartarum in Turri Londinensis asservati*. London: G. Eyre and A. Spottiswoode, 1837.

Harris, Stephen J. *Race and Ethnicity in Anglo-Saxon Literature*. New York: Routledge, 2003.

Hart, Roger. "The Great Explanandum." *The American Historical Review* 105(2) (2000): 486–93.

——*The Chinese Roots of Linear Algebra*. Baltimore: Johns Hopkins University Press, 2010.

——*Imagining Civilizations: China, the West, and Their First Encounter.* Baltimore: Johns Hopkins University Press, 2011.

Hartwell, Robert. "A Revolution in the Chinese Iron and Coal Industries during the Northern Sung, 960-1126 A.D." *Journal of Asian Studies* 21(2) (1962): 153–62.

——"A Cycle of Economic Change in Imperial China: Coal and Iron in Northeast China, 750–1350." *Journal of the Social and Economic History of the Orient* 10 (1967): 102–59.

Harvey, John Hooper. *Mediaeval Gardens.* London: B. T. Batsford, 1981.

Harvey, Paul D. A. *Mappa Mundi: The Hereford World Map.* Toronto: University of Toronto, 1996.

Haskins, Charles Homer. *The Renaissance of the Twelfth Century.* Cambridge: Harvard University Press, 1927.

Haw, Stephen G. *Marco Polo's China: A Venetian in the Realm of Khubilai Khan.* London: Routledge, 2006.

Hawkins, Daniel. "'Chimeras that Degrade Humanity': The *Cagots* and Discrimination." September 2014. www.academia.edu/15057536/Chimeras_that_degrade_humanity_the_cagots_and_discrimination

Heck, Gene W. *Charlemagne, Muhammad, and the Arab Roots of Capitalism.* Berlin: De Gruyter, 2006.

Heng, Geraldine. *Empire of Magic: Medieval Romance and the Politics of Cultural Fantasy.* New York: Columbia University Press, 2003.

——"Jews, Saracens, 'Black men,' Tartars: England in a World of Racial Difference." *A Companion to Medieval English Literature, c.1350–c.1500.* Ed. Peter Brown. Oxford: Blackwell, 2007. 247–69.

——"Holy War Redux: The Crusades, Futures of the Past, and Strategic Logic in the 'Clash' of Religions." *PMLA* 126(2) (2011): 422–31.

——"The Invention of Race in the European Middle Ages 1: Race Studies, Modernity, and the Middle Ages." *Literature Compass* 8(5) (2011): 258–74.

——"The Invention of Race in the European Middle Ages 2: Locations of Medieval Race." *Literature Compass* 8(5) (2011): 275–93.

——"Sex, Lies, and Paradise: The Assassins, Prester John, and the Fabulation of Civilizational Identities." *differences* 15(1) (2012): 1–31.

——"An African Saint in Medieval Europe: The Black Saint Maurice and the Enigma of Racial Sanctity." *Sainthood and Race: Marked Flesh, Holy Flesh.* Ed. Molly H. Bassett and Vincent W. Lloyd. London: Routledge, 2014. 18–44.

——"Early Globalities and Its Questions, Objectives, and Methods: An Inquiry into the State of Theory and Critique." *Exemplaria* 26(2–3) (2014): 234–53.

——"Reinventing Race, Colonization, and Globalisms across Deep Time: Lessons from the *Longue Durée*." *PMLA* 130(2) (2015): 358–66.

Henze, Paul B. *Layers of Time: A History of Ethiopia.* New York: Palgrave Macmillan, 2000.

Hermannsson, Halldór, ed. *The Vinland Sagas.* Ithaca: Cornell University Press, 1944.

Higgins, Iain Macleod. *Writing East: The "Travels" of Sir John Mandeville.* Philadelphia: University of Pennsylvania Press, 1997.

——ed. and trans. *The Book of John Mandeville with Related Texts.* Indianapolis: Hackett, 2011.

Hill, John Hugh, and Laurita L. Hill, eds. *Le "Liber" de Raymond d'Aguiliers. Historia Francorum qui ceperunt Iherusalem.* Paris: Paul Geuthner, 1969.

Hill, Rosalind, ed. and trans. *The Deeds of the Franks and the Other Pilgrims to Jerusalem.* [*Gesta Francorum et aliorum Hierosolymitana*] Oxford: Clarendon, 1962.

Hillaby, Joe. "The Ritual-Child-Murder Accusation: Its Dissemination and Harold of Gloucester." *Jewish Historical Studies* 34 (1994–6): 69–199.

——"Testimony from the Margin: the Gloucester Jewry and Its Neighbors, c. 1159–1290." *Jewish Historical Studies* 37 (2002): 41–112.

Hodgson, Marshall G. S. *The Secret Order of the Assassins: The Struggle of the Early Nizârî Ismâ'ilis against the Islamic World.* Philadelphia: University of Pennsylvania Press, 1955.

Hoffmann, Richard C. "Outsiders by Birth and Blood: Racist Ideologies and Realities around the Periphery of Medieval European Culture." *Studies in Medieval and Renaissance History* New Series 6 (1983): 1–24, 28–36.

Holsinger, Bruce W. *Neomedievalism, Neoconservatism, and the War on Terror*. Chicago: Prickly Paradigm, 2007.

Holt, P. M. *The Age of the Crusades: The Near East from the Eleventh Century to 1517*. London: Longman, 1986.

Holt, Thomas C. *The Problem of Race in the Twenty-First Century*. Cambridge: Harvard University Press, 2000.

Hornstein, Lillian H. "The Historical Background of the *King of Tars*." *Speculum* 16(4) (1941): 404–14.

Howard, Donald. "The World of Mandeville's Travels." *The Yearbook of English Studies* 1 (1997): 1–17.

Hughes, Malcolm K. "Was There a 'Medieval Warm Period,' and If So, Where and When?" *Climatic Change* 26 (1994): 109–42.

Husain, Ali Akbar. *Scent in the Islamic Garden*. Oxford: Oxford University Press, 2000.

Ibn Khaldun. *The Muqaddimah*. Trans. Franz Rosenthal. Bollingen series. Princeton: Princeton University Press, 2005.

Ibn Shaddad, Beha ed-Din. *Saladin or, What Befell Sultan Yusuf (Salah ed-Din 1137–1193 A.D.)*. Trans. C. W. Wilson. London: Committee of the Palestine Exploration Fund, 1897. Rpt. Lahore: Islamic Book Service, 1976.

Ingham, Patricia Clare. *Sovereign Fantasies: Arthurian Romance and the Making of Britain*. Philadelphia: University of Pennsylvania Press, 2001.

Isaac, Benjamin. *The Invention of Racism in Classical Antiquity*. Princeton: Princeton University Press, 2004.

——"Racism: A Rationalization of Prejudice in Greece and Rome." *The Origins of Racism in the West*. Ed. Miriam Eliav-Feldon, Benjamin Isaac, and Joseph Ziegler. Cambridge: Cambridge University Press, 2009. 32–56.

Jackson, Peter. "Medieval Christendom's Encounter with the Alien." *Historical Research* 74(186) (2001): 347–69.

——*The Mongols and the West, 1221–1410*. Harlow: Pearson Longman, 2005.

——*Studies on the Mongol Empire and Early Muslim India*. Farnham: Ashgate, 2009.

Jackson, Peter, and David Morgan, eds. *The Mission of Friar William of Rubruck: His Journey to the Court of the Great Khan Möngke 1253–1255*. Trans. Peter Jackson. Hakluyt Society publications, 1990. Repr. Indianapolis: Hackett, 2009.

Jacobs, Joseph. *Jewish Ideals and Other Essays*. New York: Macmillan, 1896.

Jakobsson, Sverrir. "'Black Men and Malignant-Looking': The Place of the Indigenous Peoples of North America in the Icelandic World View." *Approaches to Vínland*. Ed. Andrew Wawn and Þórunn Sigurdardóttir. Reykjavik: Sigurður Nordal Institute, 2001. 88–104.

Jansson, Sven B. F., ed. *Sagorna om Vinland: Handscrifterna till Erik den rödes saga*. Vol. 1. Lund: Hakan Ohlssons Boktryckeri, 1944.

Jauss, Hans Robert. "The Alterity and Modernity of Medieval Literature." *New Literary History* 10 (1979). 409–16.

Jenkinson, Hilary. "The Records of the Exchequer Receipts from the English Jewry." *Transactions of the Jewish Historical Society of England* 8, 1915–1917. 19–54.

Jessop, Augustus and Montague Rhodes James, eds. *The Life and Miracles of St. William of Norwich by Thomas of Monmouth*. Cambridge: Cambridge University Press, 1896.

Johnson, Willis. "The Myth of Jewish Male Menses." *Journal of Medieval History* 24(3) (1998): 273–95.

Jones, Gwyn, trans. *Eirik the Red, and Other Icelandic Sagas*. Oxford: Oxford University Press, 1961.

——*The Norse Atlantic Saga*. Oxford: Oxford University Press, 1986.

Jordan, Mark D. *The Invention of Sodomy in Christian Theology*. Chicago: University of Chicago Press, 1997.

Jordan, William C. *The French Monarchy and the Jews: From Philip Augustus to the Last Capetians*. Philadelphia: University of Pennsylvania Press, 1989.

——"Why Race?" *Journal of Medieval and Early Modern Studies* 31(1) (2001): 165–73.

Juvaini, Ata Malik. *Genghis Khan: The History of the World-Conqueror*. Ed. and trans. J. A. Boyle. Introduction by David O. Morgan. Manchester: Manchester University Press, 1997.

Kagay, Donald J. "The Essential Enemy: The Image of the Muslim as Adversary and Vassal in the Law and Literature of the Medieval Crown of Aragon." *Western Views of Islam in Medieval and Early Modern Europe: Perception of Other*. Ed. David R. Blanks and Michael Frassetto. New York: St. Martins, 1999. 119–36.

Kalaydjieva, Luba, David Gresham, and Francesc Calafell. "Genetic Studies of the Roma (Gypsies): A Review." BMC Medical Genetics 2.5 (2001): no pagination. www.biomedcentral.com/1471-2350/2/5

Kantorowicz, Ernst. *Frederick the Second 1194–1250*. Trans. E. O. Lorimer. New York: Frederick Ungar, [1931] 1957.

Kao, Wan-Chuan. "Hotel Tartary: Marco Polo, *Yams*, and the Biopolitics of Population." *Mediaevalia* 32 (2011): 43–68.

Kaplan, Paul H. D. *The Rise of the Black Magus in Western Art*. Ann Arbor: UMI Research Press, 1985.

——"Black Africans in Hohenstaufen Iconography." *Gesta* 26(1) (1987): 29–36.

——"Introduction." *The Image of the Black in Western Art: From the Early Christian Era to the "Age of Discovery."* Trans. William G. Ryan. Ed. David Bindman and Henry Louis Gates, Jr. Vol. 2 Pt. 1: From the Demonic Threat to the Incarnation of Sainthood. 2nd edition. Cambridge: Belknap Press of Harvard University Press; Houston: Menil Collection, 2010. 1–30.

Karkov, Catherine E. "Tales of the Ancients: Colonial Werewolves and the Mapping of Postcolonial Ireland." *Postcolonial Moves: Medieval Through Modern*. Ed. Patricia Clare Ingham and Michelle R. Warren. New York: Palgrave, 2003. 93–109.

Kaufmann, Virginia Roehrig. "The Magdeburg Rider: An Aspect of the Reception of Frederick II's Roman Revival North of the Alps." *Intellectual Life at the Court of Frederick II Hohenstaufen*. Ed. William Tronzo. Washington, DC: National Gallery of Art, 1994. 62–88.

Kedar, Benjamin Z. *Merchants in Crisis: Genoese and Venetian Men of Affairs in the Fourteenth-Century Depression*. New Haven: Yale University Press, 1976.

Kelly, Kathleen Ann. "'Blue' Indians, Ethiopians, and Saracens in Middle English Narrative Texts." *Parergon* n.s. 11(1) (1963): 35–52.

Khanmohamadi, Shirin A. *In Light of Another's Word: European Ethnography in the Middle Ages*. Philadelphia: University of Pennsylvania Press, 2014.

Kinoshita, Sharon. "The Politics of Courtly Love: *La Prise d'Orange* and the Conversion of the Saracen Queen." *Romanic Review* 86(2) (1995): 265–87.

——"'Pagans are wrong and Christians are right': Alterity, Gender, and Nation in the *Chanson de Roland*." *Journal of Medieval and Early Modern Studies* 31(1) (2001): 78–112.

——*Medieval Boundaries: Rethinking Difference in Old French Literature*. Philadelphia: University of Pennsylvania Press, 2006.

——"Marco Polo's *Le Devisement dou monde* and the Tributary East." *Marco Polo and the Encounter of East and West*. Ed. Suzanne Conklin Akbari and Amilcare Iannucci. Toronto: University of Toronto Press, 2008. 60–86.

——trans. *Marco Polo: The Description of the World* (trans). Indianapolis: Hackett, 2016.

Knight, Rhonda. "Procreative Sodomy: Textuality and the Construction of Ethnicities in Gerald of Wales's *Descriptio Kambriae*." *Exemplaria* 14 (2002): 47–77.

Krey, A. C., ed. and trans. *The First Crusade: The Accounts of Eye-Witnesses and Participants*. Princeton: Princeton University Press, 1921.

Kritzeck, James. *Peter the Venerable and Islam*. Princeton: Princeton University Press, 1964.

Kruger, Steven F. "The Bodies of Jews in the Late Middle Ages." *The Idea of Medieval Literature: New Essays on Chaucer and Medieval Culture in Honor of Donald R. Howard*. Ed. James M. Dean and Christian K. Zacher. Newark: University of Delaware Press, 1992. 301–23.

——"Conversion and Medieval Sexual, Religious, and Racial Categories." *Constructing Medieval Sexuality*. Ed. Karma Lochrie, Peggy McCracken, and James A. Schultz. Minneapolis: University of Minnesota Press, 1997. 158–79.

——*The Spectral Jew: Conversion and Embodiment in Medieval Europe*. Minneapolis: University of Minnesota Press, 2006.

Krummel, Miriamne Ara. *Crafting Jewishness in Medieval England: Legally Absent, Virtually Present*. New York: Palgrave Macmillan, 2011.

Kunz, Keneva, trans. "The Vinland Sagas." *The Sagas of Icelanders: A Selection*. New York: Penguin, 2001. 626–74.

Lach, Donald F. *Asia in the Making of Europe*. Vol. 1 Book 1: The Century of Discovery. Chicago: University of Chicago Press, 1965.

Lachmann, Karl, ed. *Wolfram von Eschenbach: Parzival*. 2 vols. Rev. Eberhard Nellmann. Trans. Dieter Kühn. Frankfurt am Main: Deutscher Klassiker, 1994.

Lacy, Norris J. "Narration and Textual Grammar in the Moriaen." *King Arthur in the Medieval Low Countries*. Ed. Geert H. M. Claassens and David F. Johnson. Leuven: Leuven University Press, 2000. 125–34.

Lampert, Lisa. *Gender and Jewish Difference from Paul to Shakespeare*. Philadelphia: University of Pennsylvania Press, 2004.

——"Race, Periodicity, and the (Neo-) Middle Ages." *Modern Language Quarterly* 65 (2004): 392–421.

Lane, George. *Early Mongol Rule in Thirteenth-Century Iran: A Persian Renaissance*. New York: Routledge, 2003.

Langmuir, Gavin I. "The Knight's Tale of Young Hugh of Lincoln." *Speculum* 47(3) (1972): 459–82.

——"Thomas of Monmouth: Detector of Ritual Murder." *Speculum* 59(4) (1984): 820–46.

——*Toward a Definition of Antisemitism*. Berkeley: University of California Press, 1990.

Larner, John. *Marco Polo and the Discovery of the World*. New Haven: Yale University Press, 1999.

——"Plucking Hairs from the Great Cham's Beard: Marco Polo, Jan de Langhe, and Sir John Mandeville." *Marco Polo and the Encounter of East and West*. Ed. Suzanne Conklin Akbari and Amilcare Iannucci. Toronto: University of Toronto Press, 2008. 133–55.

Lasater, Alice. *Spain to England: A Comparative Study of Arabic, European, and English Literature of the Middle Ages*. Jackson: University Press of Mississippi, 1974.

Lavezzo, Kathy, ed. *Imagining a Medieval English Nation*. Minneapolis: University of Minnesota Press, 2004.

——"The Minster and the Privy: Rereading the *Prioress's Tale*." *PMLA* 126(2) (2011): 363–82.

——*The Accommodated Jew: English Antisemitism from Bede to Milton*. Ithaca: Cornell University Press, 2016.

Lefkowitz, Mary, and Guy Maclean Rogers, eds. *Black Athena Revisited*. Chapel Hill: University of North Carolina Press, 1996.

Letts, Malcolm, ed. *Mandeville's Travels: Texts and Translations*. London: Hakluyt Society, 1953.

Levtzion, Nehemia, ed. *Conversion to Islam*. New York: Holmes and Meier, 1979.

Lewis, Bernard. *The Assassins: A Radical Sect in Islam*. New York: Basic Books, 1967.

——*Race and Color in Islam*. New York: Harper and Row, 1971.

——"The Other and the Enemy: Perceptions of Identity and Difference in Islam." *Religionsgespräche im Mittelalter*. Ed. Bernard Lewis and Friedrich Niewöhner. Wolfenbütteler Mittelalter Studien Vol. 4. Wiesbaden: Harrassowitz, 1992. 371–82.

——*Race and Slavery in the Middle East: An Historical Enquiry*. New York: Oxford University Press, 1992.

Lilley, Keith D. "Imagined Geographies of the 'Celtic Fringe' and the Cultural Construction of the 'Other' in Medieval Wales and Ireland." *Celtic Geographies: Old Culture, New Times*. Ed. Rhys Jones, Neil McInroy, and Christine Mulligan. London: Routledge, 2002. 21–36.

Lipman, V. D. *The Jews of Medieval Norwich*. London: Jewish Historical Society of England, 1967.

Little, Lester K. *Religious Poverty and the Profit Economy in Medieval Europe*. Ithaca: Cornell University Press, 1978.

Lloyd, Vincent, and Molly Bassett, eds. *Sainthood and Race: Marked Flesh, Holy Flesh*. New York: Routledge, 2015.

Lomperis, Linda. "Medieval Travel Writing and the Question of Race." *Journal of Medieval and Early Modern Studies* 31(1) (2001): 147–64.

Lotter, Friedrich. "The Position of the Jews in Early Cistercian Exegesis and Preaching." *From Witness to Witchcraft: Jews and Judaism in Medieval Christian Thought.* Ed. Jeremy Cohen. Wiesbaden: Harrassowitz, 1997. 163–85.

Lowe, Kate. "'Representing' Africa: Ambassadors and Princes from Christian Africa to Renaissance Italy and Portugal, 1402–1608." *Transactions of the Royal Historical Society* 17 (2007): 101–28.

Luard, Henry Richards, ed. *Annales monastici.* 5 vols. Rolls series. London: Longman, 1864–1869.

——*Mathaei Parisiensis, monachi Sancti Albani, Chronica majora.* 7 vols. Rolls series. London: Longman, 1872–1883.

Lupack, Alan, ed. "Introduction: The Sultan of Babylon." *Three Middle English Charlemagne Romances: The Sultan of Babylon, the Siege of Milan, and The Tale of Ralph the Collier.* Kalamazoo: TEAMS, Medieval Institute, 1990. 1–6.

Lydon, James F. *The Lordship of Ireland in the Middle Ages.* Dublin: Gill, 1972.

——"Nation and Race in Medieval Ireland." *Concepts of National Identity in the Middle Ages.* Ed. Simon Forde, Lesley Johnson, and Alan V. Murray. Leeds: University of Leeds Press, 1995. 103–24.

Lyons, M. C. *The Arabian Epic.* 3 vols. Cambridge: Cambridge University Press, 1995.

Macfie, R. A. Scott. "The Gypsy Visit to Rome in 1422." *Journal of the Gypsy Lore Society* Third Series. 11 (1932): 111–15.

——"Gypsy Persecutions: A Survey of a Black Chapter in European History." *Journal of the Gypsy Lore Society* Third Series. 22(3–4) (1943): 65–78.

Magnusson, Magnus and Hermann Pálsson, trans. *The Vinland Sagas: the Norse Discovery of America.* Harmondsworth: Penguin, 1965.

Maitland, Frederic William. *Roman Canon Law in the Church of England: Six Essays.* New York: Burt Franklin, 1968.

Mann, Charles C. "1491." *The Atlantic.* March 2002. www.theatlantic.com/magazine/archive/2002/03/1491/302445/

Marcus, Ivan G. "Jews and Christians Imagining the Other in Medieval Europe." *Prooftexts* 15 (1995): 209–26.

——"Images of the Jews in the *Exempla* of Caesarius of Heisterbach." *From Witness to Witchcraft: Jews and Judaism in Medieval Christian Thought.* Ed. Jeremy Cohen. Wiesbaden: Harrassowitz, 1997. 247–56.

Mariscal, George. "The Role of Spain in Contemporary Race Theory." *Arizona Journal of Hispanic Cultural Studies* 2 (1998): 7–22.

Mark, Peter. *Africans in European Eyes: The Portrayal of Black Africans in Fourteenth and Fifteenth Century Europe.* Syracuse: Maxwell School of Citizenship and Public Affairs, 1974.

Marushiakova, Elena and Vesselin Popov. "Historical and Ethnographic Background: Gypsies, Roma, Sinti." *Between Past and Future: The Roma of Central and Eastern Europe.* Ed. Will Guy. Hertfordshire: University of Hertfordshire Press, 2001. 33–53.

——"Gypsy Slavery in Wallachia and Moldavia." *Nationalisms Today* (2009): 89–124.

Mastnak, Tomaz. *Crusading Peace: Christendom, the Muslim World, and Western Political Order.* Berkeley: University of California Press, 2002.

——"Europe and the Muslims: The Permanent Crusade?" *The New Crusades: Constructing the Muslim Enemy.* Ed. Emran Qureshi and Michael A. Sells. New York: Columbia University Press, 2003. 205–48.

——"Holy War and the Question of Humanity: The Crusades as Political Theology." Unpublished typescript, presented to the seminar "In the Name of Humanity: Humanitarianism and its Antecedents," Center for International History, Columbia University, November 30, 2007.

——"The Muslims as Enemy of Faith: The Crusades as Political Theology." *Quaderni Fiorentini* 38 (2009): 143–200.

Mayor, Adrienne. *The Amazons: Lives and Legends of Warrior Women across the Ancient World.* Princeton: Princeton University Press, 2014.

McAleese, Kevin. "*Skrælingar* Abroad – *Skrælingar* at Home?" *Vinland Revisited: The Norse World at the Turn of the First Millennium.* Ed. Shannon Lewis-Simpson. St. Johns: Historic Sites Association of Newfoundland and Labrador, 2000. 353–64.

McCulloh, John M. "Jewish Ritual Murder: William of Norwich, Thomas of Monmouth, and the Early Dissemination of the Myth." *Speculum* 72 (1997): 698–740.

McGhee, Robert. "Contact between Native North Americans and the Medieval Norse: A Review of the Evidence." *American Antiquity* 49(1) (1984): 4–26.

——"The *Skraellings* of Vinland." *Viking Voyages to North America.* Roskilde: The Viking Ship Museum, 1993. 43–53.

——"Disease and the Development of Inuit Culture [and Comments and Reply]." *Current Anthropology* 35(5) (1994): 565–94.

Meale, Carol M. "The Miracles of Our Lady: Context and Interpretation." *Studies in the Vernon Manuscript.* Ed. Derek Pearsall. Cambridge: D. S. Brewer, 1990. 115–36.

Mehta, Uday. "Liberal Strategies of Exclusion." *Politics and Society* 18 (1990): 427–54.

Mellinkoff, Ruth. *Outcasts: Signs of Otherness in Northern European Art of the Late Middle Ages.* 2 vols. Berkeley: University of California Press, 1993.

Menache, Sophia. "Faith, Myth, and Politics: The Stereotype of the Jews and their Expulsion from England and France." *The Jewish Quarterly Review* 75 (1985): 351–74.

——"Tartars, Jews, Saracens and the "Jewish-Mongol 'Plot' of 1241." *History* 81 (1996): 334–8.

Ménard, Philippe, ed. *Le Devisement du Monde.* 6 vols. Geneva: Droz, 2001.

Menocal, María Rosa. "The Myth of Westernness in Medieval Literary Historiography." *The New Crusades: Constructing the Muslim Enemy.* Ed. Emran Qureshi and Michael A. Sells. New York: Columbia University Press, 2003. 249–87.

Metcalfe, Alex. *The Muslims of Medieval Italy.* Edinburgh: Edinburgh University Press, 2009.

Metlitzki, Dorothee. *The Matter of Araby in Medieval England.* New Haven: Yale University Press, 1977.

Michel, Francisque, ed. *Hugues de Lincoln.* Paris: Silvestre, 1834.

Migne, J.-P., ed. *Patrologiae Latinae Cursus Completus.* 221 vols. Paris: Garnier, 1844–64.

Moll, Richard J. "'Off quhat nacioun art thow?' National Identity in Blind Hary's *Wallace.*" *History, Literature, and Music in Scotland, 700–1560.* Ed. R. Andrew McDonald. Toronto: Toronto University Press, 2002. 120–43.

Montgomery, James A. *The History of Yaballaha III Nestorian Patriarch and of his Vicar Bar Sauma Mongol Ambassador to the Frankish Courts at the End of the Thirteenth Century.* New York: Columbia University Press, 1927.

Moore, R. I. *The Formation of a Persecuting Society: Power and Deviance in Western Europe, 950–1250.* Oxford: Blackwell, 1987.

——"Anti-Semitism and the Birth of Europe." *Christianity and Judaism.* Ed. Diana Wood. Oxford: Blackwell, 1992. 33–57.

Moorehead, Warren K. "The Red-Paint People of Maine." *American Anthropologist* New Series 15(1) (1913): 33–47.

Morgan, David. *Medieval Persia, 1040–1797.* London: Longman, 1988.

——*The Mongols.* Malden, MA: Blackwell, 2007.

Morris, Richard, ed. *Cursor Mundi.* London: R. Trübner, 1879–93.

Morrison, Karl F. *Understanding Conversion.* Charlottesville: University of Virginia Press, 1992.

Moseley, C. W. R. D., trans. *The Travels of Sir John Mandeville.* London: Penguin, 2005.

Moule, A. C. *Christians in China before the Year 1550.* New York: Macmillan, 1930.

Moule, A. C., and Paul Pelliot, ed. and trans. *Marco Polo: The Description of the World.* 2 vols. London: Routledge, 1938.

Muldoon, James. *Popes, Lawyers, and Infidels: The Church and the Non-Christian World 1250–1550.* Philadelphia: University of Pennsylvania, 1979.

——*Identity on the Medieval Irish Frontier: Degenerate Englishmen, Wild Irishmen, Middle Nations.* Gainesville: University of Florida Press, 2003.

Mundill, Robin R. *England's Jewish Solution: Experiment and Expulsion, 1262–1290.* Cambridge: Cambridge University Press, 1998.

Murray, Gordon. *Slavery in the Arab World.* New York: New Amsterdam, 1989.

Nederman, Cary J. *Worlds of Difference: European Discourses of Toleration, c. 1100–c. 1550.* University Park: Pennsylvania State University Press, 2000.

Nirenberg, David. "Conversion, Sex, and Segregation: Jews and Christians in Medieval Spain." *The American Historical Review* 107 (2002): 1065–93.

——"Mass Conversion and Genealogical Mentalities: Jews and Christians in Fifteenth-Century Spain." *Past and Present* 174 (2002): 3–41.

——"Race and the Middle Ages: The Case of Spain and Its Jews." *Rereading the Black Legend: The Discourses of Religious and Racial Difference in the Renaissance Empires.* Ed. Margaret R. Greer, Walter D. Mignolo, and Maureen Quilligan. Chicago: University of Chicago Press, 2007. 71–87.

——"Was There Race Before Modernity? The Example of 'Jewish' Blood in Late Medieval Spain." *The Origins of Racism in the West.* Ed. Miriam Eliav-Feldon, Benjamin Isaac, and Joseph Ziegler. Cambridge: Cambridge University Press, 2009. 232–64.

——*Anti-Judaism: The Western Tradition.* New York: Norton, 2013.

Norris, H. T. *The Adventures of Antar.* Approaches to Arabic Literature Vol. 3. Warminster: Aris and Phillips, 1980.

Nowell, Charles E. "The Old Man of the Mountain." *Speculum* 22 (1947): 497–519.

——"Historical Prester John." *Speculum* 28 (1953): 435–45.

Odess, Daniel, Stephen Loring, and William W. Fitzhugh. "*Skraeling*: First Peoples of Helluland, Markland, and Vinland." *Vikings: The North Atlantic Saga.* Ed. William W. Fitzhugh and Elisabeth I. Ward. Washington: Smithsonian Institution Press, 2000. 189–207.

Ogilvie, A. E. J., L. K. Barlow, and A. E. Jennings. "North Atlantic Climate c. A.D. 1000: Millennial Reflections on the Viking Discoveries of Iceland, Greenland, and North America." *Approaches to Vínland.* Ed. Andrew Wawn and Þórunn Sigurdardóttir. Reykjavik: Sigurður Nordal Institute, 2001. 173–88.

Ogilvie, A. E. J., and T. Jónsson. "'Little Ice Age' Research: A Perspective from Iceland." *Climatic Change* 48 (2001): 9–52.

Ogilvie, Astrid E. J., and Thomas H. McGovern. "Sagas and Science: Climate and Human Impacts in the North Atlantic." *Vikings: The North Atlantic Saga.* Ed. William W. Fitzhugh and Elisabeth I. Ward. Washington: Smithsonian Institution Press, 2000. 385–93.

Oleszkiewicz-Perabala, Malgorzata. *The Black Madonna in Latin America and Europe.* Albuquerque: University of New Mexico Press, 2007.

Olschki, Leonardo. *Marco Polo's Asia.* Trans. John A. Scott. Berkeley: University of California Press, 1960.

O'Meara, John J., trans. *Gerald of Wales: The History and Topography of Ireland.* Harmondsworth: Penguin, 1982.

Omi, Michael, and Howard Winant. *Racial Formation in the United States: From the 1960s to the 1980s.* New York: Routledge, 1986.

Panaitescu, P. N. "The Gypsies in Walachia and Moldavia: A Chapter of Economic History." *Journal of the Gypsy Lore Society* Third Series. 20 (1941): 58–72.

Pape, Robert. *Dying to Win: The Strategic Logic of Suicide Terrorism.* New York: Random House, 2005.

Paris, Matthew. *Chronica Majora.* Ed. Henry Richards Luard. 7 vols. London: Longman, 1872–1883.

Patterson, Lee. "'The Living Witnesses of Our Redemption': Martyrdom and Imitation in Chaucer's *Prioress's Tale*." *Journal of Medieval and Early Modern Studies* 31(3) (2001): 507–60.

Pearsall, Derek, ed. *Studies in the Vernon Manuscript.* Cambridge: D. S. Brewer, 1990.

Perryman, Judith, ed. *The King of Tars.* Heidelberg: Carl Winter, 1980.

Peters, Edward, ed. *Christian Society and the Crusades 1198–1229*. Philadelphia: University of Pennsylvania Press, 1971.

——*The First Crusade: The Chronicle of Fulcher of Chartres and Other Source Materials*. Philadelphia: University of Pennsylvania Press, 1971.

Phillips, William D. Jr. *Slavery from Roman Times to the Early Transatlantic Trade*. Minneapolis: University of Pennsylvania Press, 1985.

——"Sugar Production and Trade in the Mediterranean at the Time of the Crusades." *The Meeting of Two Worlds: Cultural Exchange between East and West during the Period of the Crusades*. Ed. Vladimir P. Goss and Christine Verzár Bornstein. Studies in Medieval Culture vol. 21. Kalamazoo: Medieval Institute, 1986. 393–406.

——*Slavery in Medieval and Early Modern Iberia*. Philadelphia: University of Pennsylvania Press, 2014.

Piponnier, Françoise and Perrine Mane. *Dress in the Middle Ages*. Trans. Caroline Beamish. New Haven: Yale University Press, 1997.

Pohl, Walter and Gantner, Clemens, eds. *Visions of Community in the Post-Roman World: The West, Byzantium, and the Islamic World, 300–1100*. New York: Routledge, 2016.

Pollock, Sir Frederick, and Frederic William Maitland. *The History of English Law Before the Time of Edward I*. Cambridge: Cambridge University Press, [1895] 1911.

Powicke, F. M. *Medieval England, 1066–1485*. London: Oxford University Press, 1958.

Prawer, Joshua. *The Crusaders' Kingdom: European Colonialism in the Middle Ages*. New York: Praeger, 1972.

Pringle, Heather. "Evidence of Viking Outpost Found in Canada." *National Geographic*. October 19, 2012. http://news.nationalgeographic.com/news/2012/10/121019-viking-outpost-second-new-canada-science-sutherland/

Purcell, Maureen. "Women Crusaders: A Temporary Canonical Aberration?" *Principalities, Powers, and Estates: Studies in Medieval and Early Modern Government and Society*. Ed. L. O. Frappell. Adelaide: Adelaide University Union Press, 1979. 57–65.

Radice, Betty, trans. *The Letters of Abelard to Heloise*. London: Penguin, 1974.

Ramey, Lynn T. *Black Legacies: Race and the European Middle Ages*. Gainesville: University Press of Florida, 2014.

Raymond d'Aguiliers. *Historia Francorum Qui Ceperunt Iherusalem*. Trans. John Hugh Hill and Laurita L. Hill. Philadelphia: American Philosophical Society, 1968.

——*Le "Liber" de Raymond d'Aguiliers. Historia Francorum qui ceperunt Iherusalem*. Ed. John Hugh Hill and Laurita L. Hill. Paris: Paul Geuthner, 1969.

Recueil des Historiens des Croisades. Paris: Académie des Inscriptions et Belles-Lettres. Series Historiens Occidentaux. 5 vols. 1844–95.

Recueil des Historiens des Croisades. Paris: Académie des Inscriptions et Belles-Lettres. Series Historiens Orientaux. 5 vols. 1872–1906.

Richard of Devizes. *Cronicon Richardi Divisensis De Tempore Regis Richardi Primi*. Ed. John T. Appleby. London: Thomas Nelson, 1963.

Richard, Jean. "The *Relatio de Davide* as a Source for Mongol History and the Legend of Prester John." *Prester John, the Mongols, and the Ten Lost Tribes*. Ed. Charles F. Beckingham and Bernard Hamilton. Aldershot: Variorium, 1996. 139–58.

Richardson, Henry Gerald. *The English Jewry under Angevin Kings*. London: Methuen, 1960.

Richmond, Colin. "Englishness and Medieval Anglo-Jewry." *Chaucer and the Jews: Sources, Contexts, Meanings*. Ed. Sheila Delany. New York: Routledge, 2002. 213–27.

Rigg, J. M. *Select Pleas, Starrs, and Other Records from the Rolls of the Exechequer of the Jews, A.D. 1220–1284*. London: B. Quaritch, 1902.

Robbert, Louise Buenger. "Venice and the Crusades." *A History of the Crusades, Vol. 5: The Impact of the Crusades on the Near East*. Ed. Norman P. Zacour and Harry W. Hazard. Madison: University of Wisconsin Press, 1985. 379–451.

Rodenberg, Carl, ed. "102: *Dei patris inmensa*" and "105: *Cum non solum*." *Monumenta Germaniae Historica 4: Epistolae Saeculi XIII e regestis Pontificorum Romanorum selectae, t. ii. Vol. 3: Epistolae*. Berlin: Weidmann, 1888. 73–4 and 74–5.

Roger of Howden. *Chronica Magistri Rogeri De Houedene*. Ed. William Stubbs. 4 vols. London: Longman, 1868–71.

Roger of Wendover. *Rogeri De Wendover Liber Qui Dicitur Flores Historiarum Ab Anno Domini MCLIV Annoque Henrici Anglorum Regis Secundi Primo*. Ed. Henry G. Hewlett. 3 vols. London: Longman, 1886–9.

Rokéah, Zefira Entin. "Money and the Hangman in Late-13th-century England: Jews, Christians and Coinage Offences Alleged and Real (Part I)." *Jewish Historical Studies* 31 (1988–90): 83–109.

——"Money and the Hangman in Late-13th-century England: Jews, Christians and Coinage Offences Alleged and Real (Part II)." *Jewish Historical Studies* 32 (1990–2): 159–218.

Ronchi, Gabriella, ed. *Milione: Le devisement dou monde. Il milione nelle redazioni Toscana e franco-italiana*. Milan: Mondadori, 1982.

Ross, Sir E. Denison. "Prester John and the Empire of Ethiopia." *Travel and Travellers of the Middle Ages*. Ed. Arthur Percival Newton. New York: Knopf, 1926. 174–94.

Rossabi, Morris. *Khubilai Khan: His Life and Times*. Berkeley: University of California Press, 1988.

——"All the Khan's Horses." *Natural History* 103 (1994). Asian Topics in World History: http://afe.easia.columbia.edu/mongols/conquests/khans_horses.pdf

Roth, Cecil. *A History of the Jews in England*. Oxford: Clarendon, 1941.

——*The Jews of Medieval Oxford*. Oxford: Clarendon, 1951.

Rotman, Youval. *Byzantine Slavery and the Mediterranean World*. Trans. Jane Marie Todd. Cambridge: Harvard University Press, 2009.

Rubenstein, Jay. "Cannibals and Crusaders." *French Historical Studies* 31 (2008): 525–52.

Rubin, Miri. "Desecration of the Host: the Birth of an Accusation." *Christianity and Judaism*. Ed. Diana Wood. Oxford: Blackwell, 1992. 169–85.

——"The Eucharist and the Construction of Late Medieval Identities." *Culture and History 1350–1600: Essays on English Communities, Identities, and Writing*. Ed. David Aers. New York: Harvester Wheatsheaf, 1992. 43–63.

——*Gentile Tales: The Narrative Assault on Late Medieval Jews*. New Haven: Yale University Press, 1999.

Ruggles, D. Fairchild. "The Gardens of the Alhambra and the Concept of the Garden in Islamic Spain." *Al-Andalus: The Art of Islamic Spain*. Ed. Jerrilynn D. Dodds. New York: The Metropolitan Museum of Art, 1992. 163–71.

——*Gardens, Landscape, and Vision in the Palaces of Islamic Spain*, University Park: Pennsylvania State University Press, 1999.

——"Mothers of a Hybrid Dynasty: Race, Genealogy, and Acculturation in al-Andalus." *Journal of Medieval and Early Modern Studies* 34(1) (2004): 65–94.

——*Islamic Gardens and Landscapes*. Philadelphia: University of Pennsylvania Press, 2008.

Runciman, Steven. *A History of the Crusades*. 3 vols. Cambridge: Cambridge University Press, [1951] 1995.

Russell, Josiah. "Demographic Factors of the Crusades." *The Meeting of Two Worlds: Cultural Exchange between East and West during the Period of the Crusades*. Ed. Vladimir P. Goss and Christine Verzár Bornstein. Studies in Medieval Culture Vol. 21. Kalamazoo: Medieval Institute, 1986. 53–8.

Ryan, James D. "Christian Wives of Mongol Khans: Tartar Queens and Missionary Expectations in Asia." *Journal of the Royal Asiatic Society of Great Britain and Ireland* 8(3) (1998): 411–21.

Rymer, Thomas, Robert Sanderson, and George Holmes, eds. *Foedera*. 20 vols. London: A. and J. Churchill, 1704–35.

The Sagas of Icelanders: A Selection. Preface by Jane Smiley. Introduction by Robert Kellogg. Various translators. New York: Penguin 2001.

Sager, Alexander. "Hungarians as *vremde* in Medieval Germany." *Meeting the Foreign in the Middle Ages*. Ed. Albrecht Classen. New York: Routledge, 2002. 27–44.

Salter, Elizabeth. *Fourteenth-Century English Poetry: Contexts and Readings*. Oxford: Clarendon, 1983.

Scheer, Monique. "From Majesty to Mystery: Change in the Meaning of Black Madonnas from the Sixteenth to Nineteenth Centuries." *The American Historical Review* 107(5) (2002): 1412–40.

Scheil, Andrew. *The Footsteps of Israel: Understanding Jews in Anglo-Saxon England*. Ann Arbor: University of Michigan Press, 2004.

Schroeder, Henry Joseph. *Disciplinary Decrees of the General Councils: Text, Translation and Commentary*. London: B. Herder, 1937.

Seaver, Kirsten A. "Unanswered Questions." *Vikings: The North Atlantic Saga*. Ed. William W. Fitzhugh and Elisabeth I. Ward. Washington: Smithsonian Institution Press, 2000. 268–79.

Segol, Marla. "Medieval Cosmopolitanism and the Saracen-Christian Ethos." *CLCWeb: Comparative Literature and Culture* 6(2) (2004): Article 4. http://docs.lib.purdue.edu/clcweb/vol6/iss2/

Sellassie, Sergew Hable. *Ancient and Medieval Ethiopian History to 1270*. Addis Ababa: United Printers, 1972.

Setton, Kenneth M. *The Papacy and the Levant (1204–1571)*. Philadelphia: American Philosophical Society, 1976.

Seymour, M. C. and Gabriel M. Liegey, eds. *On the Properties of Things: John Trevisa's Translation of Bartholomaeus Anglicus De Proprietatibus Rerum*. 3 vols. Oxford: Clarendon, 1975–88.

Shaw, M. R. B., trans. *Joinville and Villehardouin: Chronicles of the Crusades*. Harmondsworth: Penguin, 1963.

Sherwood, Merriam. "Magic and Mechanics in Medieval Fiction." *Studies in Philology* 44(4) (1947): 567–92.

Shiloah, Amnon. *Music in the World of Islam: A Socio-Cultural Study*. Detroit: Wayne State University Press, 1995.

Sinanoglu, Leah. "The Christ Child as Sacrifice: A Medieval Tradition and Corpus Christi Plays." *Speculum* 58(3) (1973): 491–509.

Skinner, Patricia. *The Jews in Medieval Britain: Historical, Literary and Archaeological Perspectives*. Woodbridge: Boydell, 2003.

Slessarev, Vsevolod. *Prester John: The Letter and the Legend*. Minneapolis: University of Minnesota Press, 1959.

Snowden, Frank M. *Before Color Prejudice: The Ancient View of Blacks*. Cambridge: Harvard University Press, 1983.

So, Billy K. L. *Prosperity, Regions, and Institutions in Maritime China: The South Fukien Pattern, 947–1368*. Cambridge: Harvard University Press, 2000.

Soulis, George C. "The Gypsies in the Byzantine Empire and the Balkans in the Late Middle Ages." *Dumbarton Oaks Papers* 15 (1961): 141–65.

Southern, R. W. *Western Views of Islam in the Middle Ages*. Cambridge: Harvard University Press, 1962.

Spenser, Edmund. *The Works of Edmund Spenser: A Variorum Edition*. Cambridge: Chadwyck-Healey, 1992.

Stacey, Robert C. "Royal Taxation and the Social Structure of Medieval Anglo-Jewry: The Tallages of 1239–1242." *Hebrew Union College Annual* 56 (1985): 175–249.

——"1240–60: A Watershed in Anglo-Jewish Relations?" *Historical Research* 61(145) (1988): 135–50.

——"The Conversion of Jews to Christianity in Thirteenth-Century England." *Speculum* 67(2) (1992): 263–82.

——"Jewish Lending and the Medieval English Economy." *A Commercialising Economy: England 1086 to c. 1300*. Ed. Richard H. Britnell and Bruce M. S. Campbell. Manchester: Manchester University Press, 1994. 78–101.

——"Parliamentary Negotiation and the Expulsion of the Jews from England." *Thirteenth Century England VI: Proceedings of the Durham Conference 1995*. Ed. Michael Prestwich, R. H. Britnell, and Robin Frame. Woodbridge: Boydell, 1997. 77–101.

——"From Ritual Crucifixion to Host Desecration: Jews and the Body of Christ." *Jewish History* 12(1) (1998): 11–28.

——"Crusades, Martyrdoms, and the Jews of Norman England, 1096–1190." *Juden und Christen zur Zeit der Kreuzzüge.* Ed. Alfred Haverkamp. Sigmaringen: Jan Thorbecke Verlag, 1999. 233–51.

——"Anti-Semitism and the Medieval English State." *The Medieval State: Essays Presented to James Campbell.* Ed. J. R. Madicott and D. M. Palliser. London: Hambledon, 2000. 163–77.

——"Jews and Christians in Twelfth Century England: Some Dynamics of a Changing Relationship." *Jews and Christians in Twelfth-Century Europe.* Ed. Michael A. Signer and John Van Engen. Notre Dame: University of Notre Dame Press, 2001. 340–54.

——"The Massacres of 1189–90 and the Origins of the Jewish Exchequer, 1186–1226." *Christians and Jews in Angevin England: The York Massacre of 1190, Narratives and Contexts.* Ed. Sarah Rees Jones and Sethina Watson. York: York Medieval Press, 2016. 106–24.

Statutes of the Realm. London: Eyre and Strahan, 1810–28. 11 vols.

Stock, Lorraine. "Froissart's *Chroniques* and Its Illustrators: Historicity and Ficticity in the Verbal and Visual Imaging of Charles VI's *Bal des Ardents.*" *Studies in Iconography* 21 (2000): 123–80.

Stocker, David. "The Shrine of Little St Hugh." *Medieval Art and Architecture at Lincoln Cathedral.* Ed. T. A. Heslop and V. A. Sekules. Leeds: British Archaeological Association, 1986. 109–17.

Stoler, Ann Laura. *Race and the Education of Desire: Foucault's History of Sexuality and the Colonial Order of Things.* Durham: Duke University Press, 1995.

——"Racial Histories and Their Regimes of Truth." *Political Power and Social Theory* 11 (1997): 183–206.

Stow, Kenneth R. *Alienated Minority: The Jews of Medieval Latin Europe.* Cambridge: Harvard University Press, 1992.

Strickland, Debra Higgs. *Saracens, Demons, and Jews: Making Monsters in Medieval Art.* Princeton: Princeton University Press, 2003.

Stroll, Mary. *The Jewish Pope: Ideology and Politics in the Papal Schism of 1130.* Leiden: Brill, 1987.

Suckale-Redlefsen, Gude. *Mauritius: Der Heilige Mohr.* Zurich: Verlag Schnell & Steiner, 1987.

Sullivan, Andrew. "Christianity's Original Sin." *New York Times Book Review* January 14, 2001: 5–6.

Summit, Jennifer, and David Wallace. "Rethinking Periodization." *Journal of Medieval and Early Modern Studies.* 37 (3) (2007): 447–51.

Sutherland, Patricia D. "The Norse and Native North Americans." *Vikings: The North Atlantic Saga.* Ed. William W. Fitzhugh and Elisabeth I. Ward. Washington: Smithsonian Institution Press, 2000. 238–47.

Sveinsson, Einar, and Matthías Þórðarson, eds. "Grœnlendinga saga." *Íslenzk Fornrit* Vol. 4. Reykjavik: Íslenzka Fornritafélag, 1935. 239–69.

Sweetenham, Carol, trans. *Robert the Monk's History of the First Crusade: Historia Iherosolimitana.* Aldershot: Ashgate, 2005.

Szigorich, Thomas. "Sanctified Violence: Militancy as the Tie That Bound Christian Rome and Islam." *Journal of the American Academy of Religion* 77(4) (2009): 895–921.

Tambling, Jeremy. *Confession: Sexuality, Sin, the Subject.* Manchester: Manchester University Press, 1990.

Taylor, Christopher. "Prester John, Christian Enclosure, and the Spatial Transmission of Islamic Alterity." *Contextualizing the Muslim Other in Medieval Christian Discourse.* Ed. Jerold Frakes. New York: Palgrave, 2011. 39–64.

——"Global Circulation as Christian Enclosure: Legend, Empire, and the Nomadic Prester John." *Literature Compass* 11(7) (2014): 389–485.

——"The Peregrinations of Prester John: How a Global Story is Created across 600 Years." The Global Middle Ages Project: www.globalmiddleages.org

Taylor, Julie Anne. *Muslims in Medieval Italy: The Colony at Lucera*. Oxford: Rowman and Littlefield. 2003.

Tentler, Thomas N. "The *Summa* for Confessors as an Instrument of Social Control. *The Pursuit of Holiness in Late Medieval and Renaissance Religion*. Ed. Charles Trinkaus and Heiko Oberman. Leiden: Brill, 1974. 103–37.

Terrall, Mary. "Heroic Narratives of Quest and Discovery." *Configurations* 6(2) (1998): 223–42.

Terzioglu, Arslan. "The First Attempts of Flight, Automatic Machines, Submarines and Rocket Technology in Turkish History," an online publication from the Foundation for Science, Technology, and Civilization, Publication ID 634 (January 2007). 1–15. http://www.muslim heritage.com/uploads/Rocket_Technology_in_Turkish_history1.pdf

Thomas, David, et al. *Christian-Muslim Relations: A Bibliographical History*. Leiden: Brill, 2009–13.

Thorpe, Lewis, trans. *Einhard and Notker the Stammerer: Two Lives of Charlemagne*. Harmondsworth: Penguin, 1984.

Thrupp, Sylvia. *The Merchant Class of Medieval London, 1300–1500*. Chicago: University of Chicago Press, 1948.

Tinsley, David. "Mapping the Muslims: Images of Islam in Middle High German Literature of the Thirteenth Century." *Contextualizing the Muslim Other in Medieval Christian Discourse*. Ed. Jerold C. Frakes. New York: Palgrave Macmillan, 2011. 60–101.

Tolan, John V. *Saracens: Islam in the Medieval European Imagination*. New York: Columbia University Press, 2002.

——*Sons of Ishmael: Muslims through European Eyes in the Middle Ages*. Gainesville: University Press of Florida, 2008.

——"Of Milk and Blood: Innocent III and the Jews, Revisited." *Jews and Christians in Thirteenth-Century France*. Ed. Elisheva Baumgarten and Judah Galinsky. New York: Palgrave Macmillan, 2015. 139–49.

——"'A wild man, whose hand will be against all': Saracens and Ishmaelites in Latin Ethnographical Traditions, from Jerome to Bede." Ed. Walter Pohl and Clemens Gantner. *Visions of Community in the Post-Roman World: The West, Byzantium, and the Islamic World, 300–1100*. New York: Routledge, 2016. 513–30.

Tolan, John Victor, Gilles Veinstein, and Henry Laurens. *Europe and the Islamic World: A History*. Trans. Jane Marie Todd. Princeton: Princeton University Press, 2013.

Tomasch, Sylvia. "Postcolonial Chaucer and the Virtual Jew." *The Postcolonial Middle Ages*. Ed. Jeffrey Jerome Cohen. New York: St. Martins, 2000. 243–60.

Tovey, D'Blossiers. *Anglia Judaica*. Oxford: The Theatre, 1738.

Trachtenberg, Joshua. *The Devil and the Jews: The Medieval Conception of the Jew and Its Relation to Modern Antisemitism*. New Haven: Yale University Press, 1943.

Trapp, Frank Anderson. "The Emperor's Nightingale: Some Aspects of Mimesis." *Critical Inquiry* 4(1) (1977): 85–103.

Truitt, E. R. "'Trei poëte, sages dotors, qui mout sorent di nigromance': Knowledge and Automata in Twelfth-Century French Literature." *Configurations* 12 (2004): 167–93.

Turville-Petre, Thorlac. *England the Nation: Language, Literature, and National Identity, 1290–1340*. Oxford: Clarendon, 1996.

Twiss, Sir Travers. *Henrici de Bracton: De legibus et consuetudinibus Angliæ*. 6 vols. London: Longman, 1878–83.

Udovitch, Abraham L. *At the Origins of the Western Commenda: Islam, Israel, Byzantium?* and *Credit as a Means of Investment in Medieval Islamic Trade*. Princeton: Princeton Near East Papers Numbers 9 and 10, 1969.

Uebel, Michael. *Ecstatic Transformation: On the Uses of Alterity in the Middle Ages*. New York: Palgrave, 2001.

——"Imperial Fetishism: Prester John among the Natives." *The Postcolonial Middle Ages*. Ed. Jeffrey Jerome Cohen. New York: Palgrave, 2001. 264–91.

Van Buren, Anne Hagiopian. "Reality and Literary Romance in the Park of Hesdin." *Medieval Gardens*. Ed. Elisabeth B. McDougall. Dumbarton Oaks Colloquium on the History of Landscape Architecture 9. Washington, DC: Dumbarton Oaks, 1986. 117–34.

Van Millingen, Alexander. *Byzantine Churches in Constantinople*. London: Variorum, 1974.

Verkerk, Dorothy Hoogland. "Black Servant, Black Demon: Color Ideology in the Ashburnham Pentateuch." *Journal of Medieval and Early Modern Studies* 31(1) (2001): 57–77.

Verlinden, Charles. *L'esclavage dans l'Europe médiévale I: Péninsule ibérique - France*. Bruges: De Temple, 1955. Rijksuniversiteit te Gent; Werken, uitgegeven door de Faculteit van de Letteren en Wijsbegeerte Vol. 119.

——*L'esclavage dans l'Europe médiévale II: Italie - Colonies italiennes du Levant - Levant latin, Empire byzantine*. Bruges: De Temple, 1977. Rijksuniversiteit te Gent; Werken, uitgegeven door de Faculteit van de Letteren en Wijsbegeerte Vol. 162.

Vernadsky, George. *The Mongols and Russia*. History of Russia Vol. 3. New Haven: Yale University Press, 1953.

Vincent, Nicholas. "Two Papal Letters on the Wearing of the Jewish Badge." *Jewish Historical Studies* 34: 1994–6. 209–24.

Viswanathan, Gauri. *Outside the Fold: Conversion, Modernity and Belief*. Princeton: Princeton University Press, 1998.

Vogel, Hans Ulrich. *Marco Polo Was in China: New Evidence from Currencies, Salts and Revenues*. Leiden: Brill, 2013.

Von Hammer, Joseph, and Oswald C. Wood. *The History of the Assassins*. London: Smith and Elder, 1835.

Wade, Geoff. "The Zheng He Voyages: A Reassessment." *Asia Research Institute Working Paper Series* No. 31, October 2004.

Walker, David. *Medieval Wales*. Cambridge: Cambridge University Press, 1990.

Wallace, Birgitta Linderoth. "L'Anse aux Meadows: Gateway to Vinland." *The Norse of the North Atlantic*. Ed. Gerald F. Bigelow. Copenhagen: *Acta Archaeologica* 61, 1991. 166–97.

——"An Archeologist's Interpretation of the *Vinland Sagas*." *Vikings: The North Atlantic Saga*. Ed. William W. Fitzhugh and Elisabeth I. Ward. Washington: Smithsonian Institution Press, 2000. 228–31.

——"Vinland and the Death of Þorvaldr." *Vinland Revisited: the Norse World at the Turn of the First Millennium*. Ed. Shannon Lewis-Simpson. St. Johns: Historic Sites Association of Newfoundland and Labrador, 2000. 377–90.

——"L'Anse aux Meadows and Vinland: An Abandoned Experiment." *Contact, Continuity, and Collapse: The Norse Colonization of the North Atlantic*. Ed. James H. Barrett. Turnhout: Brepols, 2003. 207–48.

Wallace, David. "Surinam: The Long History of Black and White." University of Texas, Austin. October 18, 2002. Lecture.

Waltz, James. "The Significance of the Voluntary Martyrs of Ninth-Century Córdoba." *Muslim World* 60 (1970): 226–36.

Warner, George F., ed. *The Buke of John Maundeuill*. London: Roxburghe Club, 1889.

Warren, F. M. "The Enamoured Moslem Princess in Orderic Vital and the French Epic." *PMLA* 29 (1914): 341–58.

Warren, Michelle R. *History on the Edge: Excalibur and the Borders of Britain 1100–1300*. Minneapolis: University of Minnesota Press, 2000.

Watson, Andrew M. "A Medieval Green Revolution: New Crops and Farming Techniques in the Early Islamic World." *The Islamic Middle East: 700–1900*. Ed. A. L. Udovitch. Princeton: Darwin, 1981. 29–58.

Watt, J. A. "The Jews, the Law, and the Church: The Concept of Jewish Serfdom in Thirteenth-Century England." *The Church and Sovereignty c. 590–1918*. Ed. Diana Wood. Oxford: Blackwell, 1991. 153–72.

Watt, W. Montgomery. *The Influence of Islam on Medieval Europe*. Edinburgh: Edinburgh University Press, 1972.

——*A History of Islamic Spain*. Edinburgh: Edinburgh University Press, 1996.

Wawn, Andrew and Þórunn Sigurdardóttir, eds. *Approaches to Vínland*. Reykjavik: Sigurður Nordal Institute, 2001.

Weatherford, Jack. *The Secret History of the Mongol Queens*. New York: Broadway, 2010.

Weiss, Judith. "The Wooing Woman in Anglo-Norman Romance." *Romance in Medieval England*. Ed. Maldwyn Mills, Jennifer Fellows, and Carol M. Meale. Cambridge: D. S. Brewer, 1991. 140–61.

Wells, D. A. "The Middle Dutch *Moriaen*, Wolfram von Eschenbach's *Parzival*, and Medieval Tradition." *Studia Neerlandica* 2 (1971): 243–81.

——"Source and Tradition in the *Moriaen*." *European Context: Studies in the History and Literature of the Netherlands Presented to Theodoor Weevers*. Ed. P. K. King and P. F. Vincent. Cambridge: Modern Humanities Research Association, 1971. 30–51.

Westrem, Scott D. "Against Gog and Magog." *Text and Territory: Geographical Imagination in the European Middle Ages*. Ed. Sylvia Tomasch and Sealy Gilles. Philadelphia: University of Pennsylvania Press, 1998. 54–75.

——*The Hereford Map: A Transcription and Translation of the Legends with Commentary*. Turnhout: Brepols, 2001.

Whitaker, Cord, ed. Special issue on Making Race Matter in the Middle Ages, *postmedieval* 6(1) (2015).

Willey, Peter. *The Castles of the Assassins*. Fresno: Linden, 2001.

——*The Eagle's Nest: Ismaili Castles in Iran and Syria*. London: I. B. Tauris, 2005.

William of Malmsbury. *De Gestis Regum Anglorum*. Ed. William Stubbs. 2 vols. London: Rolls, 1887–9.

William of Newburgh. *Historia Rerum Anglicarum. Chronicles of the Reigns of Stephen, Henry II, and Richard I*. Ed. Richard Howlett. Rolls Series, 82(1). London: Longman, [1884] 1964.

Winstedt, Eric Otto. "The Gypsies of Modon and the 'Wyne of Romeney'." *Journal of the Gypsy Lore Society* Third Series. 3 (1909–10): 57–69.

Wolf, Kenneth Baxter. *Christian Martyrs in Muslim Spain*. Cambridge: Cambridge University Press, 1988.

Wolfe, Alexander. "Marco Polo, Factotum, Auditor: Language and Political Culture in the Mongol World Empire." *Literature Compass* 11(7) (2014): 409–22.

Wolfram von Eschenbach. *Parzival*. Ed. Karl Lachmann. Rev. Eberhard Nellmann. Trans. Dieter Kühn. 2 vols. Frankfurt am Main: Deutscher Klassiker, 1994.

——*Willehalm*. Trans. Marion E. Gibbs and Sidney M. Johnson. Harmondsworth: Penguin, 1984.

Wood, Frances. *Did Marco Polo Go to China?* London: Secker and Warburg, 1995.

Wyngaert, Anastasius van den. *Sinica Franciscana, Vol. 1: Itinera et Relationes Fratrum Minorum saec. XIII et XIV*. Quaracchi: Franciscan Press, 1929.

Yeager, Suzanne M. *Jerusalem in Medieval Narrative*. Cambridge: Cambridge University Press, [2008] 2011.

Yule, Sir Henry, ed. and trans.; Cordier, Henri, rev. *Cathay and the Way Thither: Being a Collection of Medieval Notices of China*. 4 vols. Vol. 2: Odoric of Pordenone. London: Hakluyt Society, 1913–16.

Zacher, Samantha, ed. *Imagining the Jew in Anglo-Saxon Literature and Culture*. Toronto: Toronto University Press, 2016.

Zarncke, F. "Prester John's Letter to the Byzantine Emperor Emanuel, with a Note by B. Hamilton on Additional Latin Manuscripts of the Letter." *Prester John, the Mongols, and the Ten Lost Tribes*. Ed. Charles F. Beckingham and Bernard Hamilton. Aldershot: Variorum, 1996. 39–102.

Ziada, Mustafa M. "The Mamluk Sultans to 1293." *A History of the Crusades Vol. 2: The Later Crusades, 1189–1311*. Ed. Robert Lee Wolff and Harry W. Hazard. Madison: University of Wisconsin Press, 1969. 735–58.

——"The Mamluk Sultans, 1291–1517." *A History of the Crusades* Vol. 3: The Fourteenth and Fifteenth Centuries. Ed. Harry W. Hazard. Madison: University of Wisconsin Press, 1975. 486–512.

Ziegler, Joseph. "Physiognomy, Science, and Proto-Racism 1200–1500." *The Origins of Racism in the West*. Ed. Miriam Eliav-Feldon, Benjamin Isaac, and Joseph Ziegler. Cambridge: Cambridge University Press, 2009. 181–99.

Index